Physical Education

and the Study of Sport

Third Edition

Dr Bob Davis
Honorary Research Fellow, Worcester College of Higher Education;
Former Principal Lecturer in Physical Education, Madeley College of Higher Education;
Lecturer (p/t) in Sport, Health and Exercise, Staffordshire University;
Chief Examiner, Reviser and Practical Moderator, A-Level Physical Education (AEB; 1986–95);
Senior Adviser and Reviser, A-Level Physical Education (OCEAC; 1995–present)

Ros Bull BEd (Hons) MSc
Principal Lecturer in Physical Education, Liverpool John Moores University;
Former Chief Moderator, A-Level Physical Education and Sports Studies (AEB; 1988–93)

Jan Roscoe BEd (Hons) MSc
Former Teacher of A-Level Physical Education and Human Biology, Widnes Sixth Form College;
Anatomy and Physiology Consultant for A-Level Physical Education (AEB; 1989–97)

Dr Dennis Roscoe
Former Head of School of Maths and Sciences, Knowsley Community College;
Biomechanics Consultant (1989–97) and Assistant Examiner and Team Leader for A-Level Physical Education (1989–93)

Mosby
London · Philadelphia
St Louis · Sydney · Tokyo

Publisher
Geoff Greenwood

Development Editor
Simon Pritchard

Project Manager
Linda Horrell

Index
Anne McCarthy

Production
Siobhan Egan

Design
Greg Smith

Layout
Marie McNestry

Cover Design
Paul Phillips

Illustration Management
Lynda Payne

Illustrators
Mike Saiz
Rob Curran
Rob Dean

ISBN 0 7234 2642 2

First published in 1991 by Wolfe Publishing Ltd, ISBN 0 7234 1571 4; reprinted 1992.

Second Edition published in 1994 by Mosby, an imprint of Times Mirror International Publishers Ltd, ISBN 0 7234 1972 8; reprinted 1995, 1996.

Third Edition published in 1997 by Mosby, an imprint of Times Mirror International Publishers Ltd (a division of Times Mirror International Publishers Ltd), Lynton House, 7–12 Tavistock Square, London WC1H 9LB, UK.
Reprinted in 1998 by Mosby International Ltd.

Printed in Barcelona, Spain, by Grafos S.A. Arte sobre papel, 1997.

Teachers' guides for Parts One and Two are available from Jan Roscoe Publications, 'Holyrood', 23 Stockswell Road, Widnes, Cheshire WA8 4PJ, UK. Teachers' guides for Part Three are available from Bob Davis, 223 Longton Road, Trentham, Stoke-on-Trent ST4 8DQ, UK.

Cataloguing in Publication Data
Catalogue records for this book are available from the British Library and the US Library of Congress.

Contents

Contents

Preface

The first edition of *Physical Education and the Study of Sport* was designed as a necessary text for new A-level candidates in Physical Education and Sport Studies. Written by a team of teachers engaged in producing and teaching the syllabuses, the book set out to give teachers and candidates the necessary knowledge and understanding for this level of study while adopting a user-friendly style and a practical approach. The expansion and refinement of these syllabuses soon led to the need for a revised second edition. In addition to increasing the quality of presentation, the second edition addressed the lessons learnt after more than three years of scrutiny from teachers and students alike.

The third edition of *Physical Education and the Study of Sport* has been written to address current and future changes in the subject area. Our examination programme is now taught at well over a thousand centres and is administered by two examination boards. Annually, more than 1500 candidates find the A-level a valuable entry qualification into higher education.

The recent Dearing Report, which is being acted upon by the SCAA, requires us to re-submit syllabuses that take modularization and the AS-level into account. The main objectives and areas of study remain the same, as does the overall structure of this textbook. Nevertheless, necessary updates have been made to the text, and there is a remodelling of pro-active teaching styles in the presentation and an increased diversity of review and examination-style questions, which will help individual candidates test their knowledge and understanding of our subject. These revisions include the recognition of the advances in sports science, the introduction of Australian material, and reference to British 'initiatives' arising from the publication of the Government document 'Raising the Game' and the development of a National Sports Academy.

Although expanded to some 600 pages, a single textbook can never provide enough content for ambitious teachers and candidates, and so every effort has been made to include up-to-date references and further reading. In addition, the authors are producing new teachers' guides which provide detailed analysis of specific areas of the book, supported by slides and acetates.

Physical Education and the Study of Sport has also proved to be a valuable text for the early years of higher education. The radical plans to expand coaching in this country mean that an increasing number of people need a general theoretical text to act as a foundation for their coaching development. In our A-level teachers, we have a superb group of knowledgeable enthusiasts who are the potential bed-rock of future coaching in this country; in our candidates, the National Coaching Foundation are already aware that they have a wealth of potential coaches for the future; and in *Physical Education and the Study of Sport,* you have an ideal foundation text for all those committed to making British Sport 'great' again.

Bob Davis
March 1997

Acknowledgements

We would like to thank Pamela Baxby, Derek Benning, Janet Chapman, Derek Cocup, John Honeybourne, David Kellett, Peter Morris, Gary Pullan, Jean Sivori, Kevin Sykes, Carol Taylor, Peter Walder, Mark Wazenczuk and Australians Janet and Frank Pyke and Ian Maddison for their invaluable comments on the draft manuscripts for this and previous editions.

Shirley Doolan, John Helms, Peter Cullen and Rosemary Watts supplied many of the illustrations and cartoons for the book; we are also grateful to Ken Travis for the photographs that appear in Part Two. Further acknowledgement is due to the Macmillan Company of Australia Pty Ltd for their permission to use material from *Physical Education: Theory and Practice* by Davis *et al.*, also in Part Two.

Acknowledgement is also due to the Associated Examining Board and to the Oxford and Cambridge Assessment and Examinations Council for taking the initiative in creating two worthwhile A-level courses in physical education.

Part One

The Performer in Action

If we are to understand the **performer in action** we need to know how the body is put together, how it functions, how it moves, and how it applies forces to itself and other bodies with which it comes into contact.

Two main sections have been combined within Part One. These are the application of **human anatomy** and **physiology** (Chapters 1–5), and **biomechanics** (Chapters 6–8) to the study of physical education and sport.

The aim of 'The Performer in Action' is to develop, very simply, and by no means completely, some of the concepts in these areas of study in the mind of the student, in as relevant and as practical a manner as possible. It will therefore be essential for the student to look at other texts on intermediate level Human Anatomy, Physiology, Biomechanics and Physics to search out more detail than is provided here, or to progress the concepts further as interest takes him or her.

The results tables included in this text are available for students to copy and use.

A short bibliography of texts, the reading of which would extend understanding and knowledge of relevant concepts is to be found, where appropriate, at the end of each chapter and at the end of both sections.

For the teacher, 'The Performer in Action' provides a series of practical activities that should help the non-scientific student to understand the essentials of anatomical, physiological and biomechanical concepts without the need for a detailed programme of specialist lessons.

Chapter 1

The Anatomy of Physical Performance

Athletic activity in all its forms of movement is made possible by the arrangement and functioning of bodily systems. The aim of this section is to discover how we move.

1.1 The Human Skeleton in Action

Keywords & concepts

appendicular skeleton	epiphyseal plate	osteoblast
articular	epiphysis	osteoclast
axial skeleton	flat bone	osteocyte
bony features	Haversian system	protrusions
cancellous bone	hyaline or articular	short bone
cartilage	cartilage	skeleton
compact bone	intramembranous	white fibrocartilage
depressions	ossification	yellow elastic cartilage
diaphysis	irregular bone	
endochondral ossification	long bone	

The human skeleton consists of 206 bones (Figure 1.1), many of which move or hinge at joints and which, in combination with over 600 skeletal muscles, enable the human body to achieve a variety of

APPENDICULAR SKELETON

pectoral girdle

pelvic girdle

limbs

AXIAL SKELETON

skull
sternum
ribs
vertebral column

Figure 1.1 The 206 bones are divided into the appendicular and axial skeleton.

actions, such as running, throwing, striking, jumping, pulling and pushing.

Joints are covered with compressible **articular** (articular is a word that describes surfaces which move or hinge), or **hyaline cartilage**, which serves to cushion the impact of large forces on bone ends. Joint movements are varied and complex. For example, the **shoulder joint** is constructed to permit swinging, throwing, striking and supporting movements. The **foot** is designed to support the body weight, to act as a shock absorber and to provide great flexibility of movement. All these skeletal bones and joints enable the body to carry out a vast range of complex movements demanded by a variety of differing physical and sporting situations. This section will help you to identify skeletal bones, skeletal connective tissues and their functions, and to understand bone development in relation to a variety of physical activities and the influence of exercise on the developing skeleton.

The **human skeleton** has been created by evolution to perform the following functions:

1. To provide a lever system against which muscles can pull.

2. To provide a large surface area for the attachment of muscles.

3. To protect delicate organs (for example, the cranium protects the brain).

4. To give shape to the body.

5. To give support to the body (for example, the firm construction of the thorax, which permits breathing).

6. To manufacture red blood cells and to store fat, calcium and phosphate.

Investigation

1.1. Types of skeleton

Using the information in this section, work out the functions specific to the **appendicular** and **axial** skeletons.

Types of bones

The shape and size of bones are designed according to their specific functions. They can be **long**, **short**, **flat** or **irregular** (see Figure 1.2).

A long bone

A long bone consists of a hollow cylindrical shaft formed of compact bone with cancellous bone located at the knobbly ends of the shaft (see Figure 1.9). The **tibia** is an example of a long bone.

A short bone

A short bone consists of entirely cancellous bone surrounded by a thin layer of compact bone. The **carpals** in the wrist are examples of short bones.

Flat and irregular bones

Flat and irregular bones consist of two outer layers of compact bone with cancellous bone between them. The **cranium** is an example of a flat bone. Examples of irregular bones include the **vertebrae, the patella** or **sesamoid** bone (sited in the patella knee tendon) and wormian bones, which are small irregular bones sometimes formed in cranial sutures.

Irregular bones have no definite shape. The **vertebral column**, which is part of the axial skeleton, is composed of 24 unfused vertebrae—five fused sacral vertebrae attached to four fused coccygeal vertebrae—making a total of 26 bones.

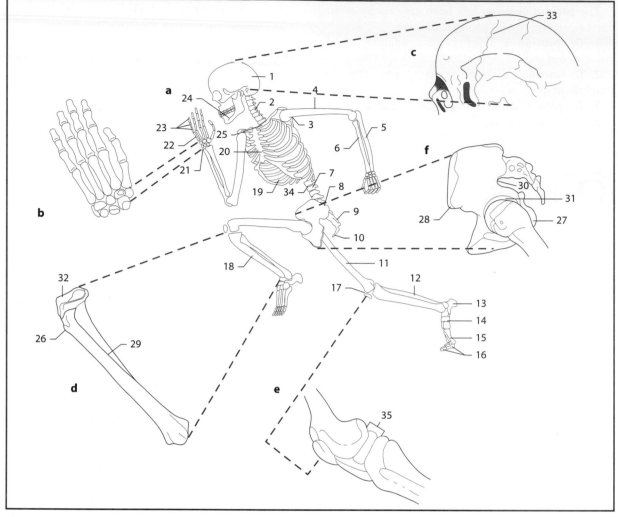

Figure 1.2 The human skeleton in action.

a. The human skeleton

Examples and types of bone

b. Short

c. Flat

d. Long

e. Irregular

f. Flat (drawn from the non-viewing aspect)

Some examples of bony features

26. Tuberosity
27. Tubercle
28. Spine
29. Ridge
30. Notch
31. Fossa
32. Condyle

Types of joint

33. Fibrous joint—suture
34. Cartilaginous joint—intervertebral disc
35. Synovial joint—knee

 ## Investigation

1.2: Identification of skeletal bones

Materials: skeleton. Figure 1.2, posters.

Task One

Refer to the skeleton drawing (Figure 1.2a) and identify the bones numbered 1–25.

Task Two

Define the axial and appendicular skeletons. Using a skeletal model and Figures 1.1 and 1.2a, identify the major bones that make up the axial and appendicular skeletons.

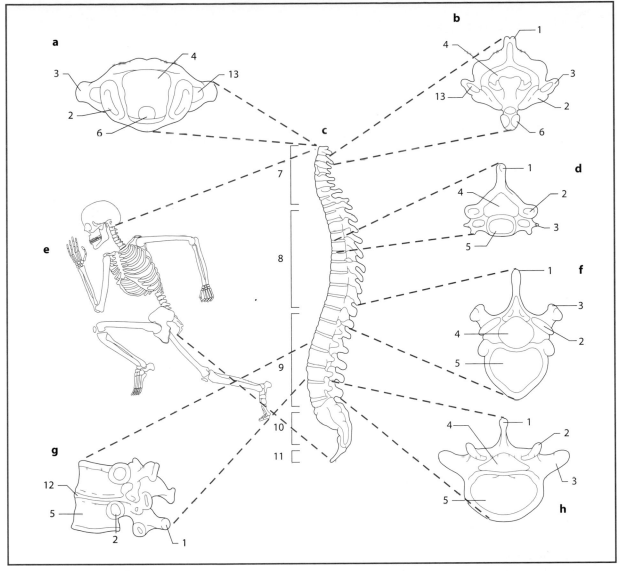

Figure 1.3 Vertebral column.

a. Atlas, superior view
b. Axis, superior view
c. Vertebral column, lateral view
d. Cervical vertebra, superior view
e. Human skeleton
f. Thoracic vertebra, superior view
g. Two lumbar vertebrae
h. Lumbar vertebra, superior view

1. Spinal process for attachment of back muscles
2. Articulating surface connection for ribs and other vertebrae
3. Transverse processes provide attachment for muscles and ligaments
4. Spinal canal through which spinal cord runs
5. Centrum or body of the vertebra, which bears the body weight

6. Odontoid process of axis
7. Cervical vertebrae (seven)
8. Thoracic vertebrae (twelve)
9. Lumbar vertebrae (five)
10. Sacrum (fused)
11. Coccyx
12. Intervertebral disc (cartilaginous joint)
13. Foramen for vertebral artery

Investigation

1.3: Identification of skeletal bones

Task One (use the information in Figure 1.3)
1. Identify those structural features common to all unfused vertebrae.
2. Identify the five main regions of the vertebral column, numbered 7–11.
3. How is the basic plan of vertebrae modified in different regions of the vertebral column to perform different skeletal functions?
4. Identify the **axis** and **atlas** vertebrae. State the principal function for both vertebrae.
5. Which part of the nervous system does the vertebral column protect?

Task Two
Using the information in Figure 1.2, identify the labelled sesamoid bone. What is its function in relation to physical activity?

Task Three
Complete the following exercise in which you are asked to match the bone type to example in the body and specific function. That is, join the linked types, examples and functions as shown for the femur.

Bone type	Example in the body	Specific function
flat	femur	gives strength
long bone	tarsal	protective
short	axis	acts as a lever
irregular	sternum	large surface area for muscle attachment

Task Four
Using a skeletal model and Figure 1.2, classify other examples for each of these four types of bones.

Task Five
Bend down and touch your toes. Explain what joints and bones are involved and what movement is brought about.

Investigation

1.4: The identification of bony features
Materials: Figure 1.2, and skeletal bones.
Your task is to identify various bony features from the collection of bones supplied for this investigation and from diagrams of the skeletal bones in this text or elsewhere.

Task One
Run your fingers along different types of long, short, flat and irregular bones. Feel for bumps and dents on the surface of these bones. These bony features are called **protrusions** and **depressions**, respectively.
Identify the following types of **depression**:
1. A **fossa**, which is a rounded depression—e.g. the **acetabular fossa**.
2. A **groove**—e.g. the deep **bicipital groove** near to the head of the humerus, which is occupied by one of the tendons of the biceps muscle.
3. A **notch**—e.g. the **sciatic notch**.

Protrusions are classified into the following types:
1. A **tuberosity**, which is a broad, rough, uneven bump—e.g. the **tibial tuberosity**.
2. A **tubercle** is a smaller version of a tuberosity—e.g. the **tubercle** of the iliac crest.
3. A **spine**, which is a sharp pointed feature—e.g. the **iliac spine**.
4. A **ridge**, crest or line runs along the shaft of a bone—e.g. along the **tibial crest**.
Protrusions that form part of a joint are called **condyles** and **epicondyles**. For example, the rounded condyles and the adjacent epicondyles of the femur that form part of the knee joint.

Task Two
Identify other examples of protrusions and depressions on a skeleton.

Task Three
What do you think are the functions of the protrusions and depressions you have found?

Investigation

1.5: A comparison of bone measurements
Materials: tape measures, skeleton poster.

Task One
Using a tape measure, on a partner or yourself, measure the circumference of bones at the wrist, elbow, ankle and knee.
1. Make a results table in which it is possible to compare measurements between males and females in the class or group.
2. Is the circumference (which is directly related to thickness) of bone an indication of maturity and strength of bones?

Task Two
Bones of males are more dense than those of females and the bones of an Afro-Caribbean skeleton are denser than those of the Caucasian skeleton. What effect would this information have when planning physical activity programmes?

Task Three
1. Identify the positions of the bones of the elbow joint (**humerus, radius, ulna**) and shoulder joint (**scapula, humerus**) on a partner and relate the positioning of these bones to a skeletal chart and/or Figure 1.2a.
2. Discuss and list the joint types and ranges of movement of the elbow and shoulder joints (see Table 1.1 for details on joint types and movement patterns).

Task Four
1. Identify the **acromion** process of the scapula, **olecranon** process at the elbow end of the ulna and **styloid** process at the wrist end of the ulna.
2. Using a tape measure, measure the distance from the:
a. acromion process to the styloid process;
b. acromion process to olecranon process;
c. olecranon process to the styloid process.
3. Identify the **head** of the **femur, femoral condyle** of the knee joint and **lateral malleolus** of the fibula.
4. Measure the distance from the:
a. head of femur to the femoral condyle;
b. femoral condyle to the lateral malleolus.
5. Record the results in a table for each individual—include gender, skeletal height, bone measurement data from above and major sporting activity.

6. Collect data from males and females and record on bar charts the distribution of measurements from all individuals for each category of measurement.
7. Discuss and comment on the distribution of results obtained from different sporting groups, and from males as opposed to females.

Task Five
Eight new events (handball, basketball and six rowing events) were introduced for women in the Olympic Games at Montreal in 1976. The data on heights of 186 medallists from these newly introduced events are shown (Figure 1.4) superimposed on the height distribution of women aged 18–24 in the United States, who were used as a reference population. (Volleyball statistics have been included to give a complete set of women's team games in these Olympic Games. Reference source data adapted from Khosla, 1983.)
   Note from Figure 1.4 that the mean for the general population is 162 cm, and for the medallists 174 cm.
1. Using the information in Figure 1.4, discuss the proposition that there is an overwhelming bias in favour of the very tall in many team contests.
2. From the graph, work out the approximate proportion of the general population with height above 174 cm. What are the implications of this for selection of National Squads from groups of ordinary sportspeople?
3. Give other examples from sports where tallness, specific limb dimensions and shortness would be beneficial to performance.

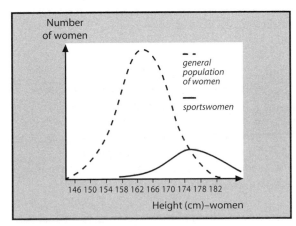

Figure 1.4 Height distributions of female Olympic medallists compared with those of women aged 18–24 in the United States. (*Adapted from Khosla, 1983.*)

Types of skeletal connective tissue

There are two types of **skeletal connective tissue**: namely, **cartilage** and **bone**.

Cartilage

Cartilage is a soft, slightly elastic tissue, which consists of a matrix of **chondrin** (a gelatinous protein) that is secreted by specialized cells called **chondrocytes**. These cells position themselves in tiny cavities called **lacunae**, and are nourished by nutrients that diffuse across from the capillary network outside the cartilaginous tissue. There are three types of cartilage found in the human body:

a) **Yellow elastic cartilage** (Figure 1.5), which consists of yellow elastic fibres running through a solid matrix, with cells lying between the fibres. The pinna or ear lobe and epiglottis are examples of this tissue.

b) **Hyaline**, or **articular cartilage** (Figure 1.6), which appears as a smooth bluish-white matrix tissue. The matrix is solid, smooth, firm and yet resilient and the cells appear in groups forming a cell nest. This type of cartilage is located on the surfaces of bones that form joints; it forms the costal cartilages, which attach the ribs to the sternum; it is also found in the larynx, trachea and bronchi.

c) **White fibrocartilage** (Figure 1.7), which consists of a dense mass of white fibres in a solid matrix, with the cells spread thinly among the fibres. It is a tough, slightly flexible tissue that is found between the bodies of the vertebrae (called intervertebral discs, refer to Figure 1.3g, item 12), in semi-lunar cartilages in the knee joint and it surrounds the rim of the bony sockets of the hip and shoulder joints.

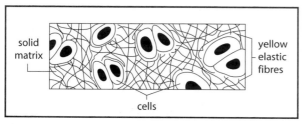

Figure 1.5 Yellow elastic cartilage.

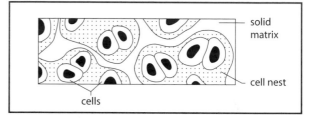

Figure 1.6 Hyaline or articular cartilage.

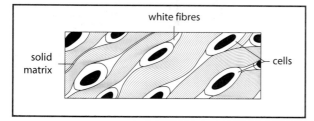

Figure 1.7 White fibrocartilage.

 Investigation

1.6: To examine cartilaginous tissue
Materials: projector slides and/or diagrams of cartilaginous tissue.

1. Examine the slides and/or diagrams of types of cartilage. For each type of cartilage, give a brief description of its specific function.

2. Why do you think cartilaginous tissue contains no blood vessels?

3. Explain the importance of cartilaginous tissue during physical activity.

Bone

Bone is classified as either **hard** (or **compact**) **bone** or **spongy** (or **cancellous**) **bone**. It is the hardest connective tissue in the human body and is composed of water, organic material (mainly **collagen**, a structural fibrous protein that supports many body tissues) and inorganic salts, namely calcium phosphate, calcium carbonate and fluoride salts.

Compact bone

Compact bone consists of thousands of collagen-based structures called **Haversian systems** (0.5 mm in diameter), which consist of a central canal surrounded by concentric ring-shaped calcium-based plates called lamellae. Figure 1.8 shows the microscopic detail of a Haversian system.

Spongy or cancellous bone (see Figures 1.9 and 1.10)

Spongy or **cancellous** bone has a honeycomb appearance and consists of a thin criss-cross matrix of bone tissue called **trabeculae** (a general term describing connective tissue that supports other tissues), with red bone marrow filling the tiny spaces.

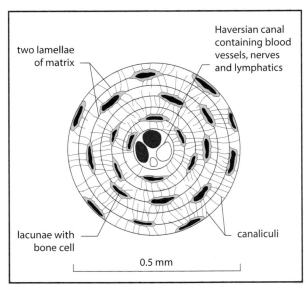

Figure 1.8 A microscopic Haversian system.

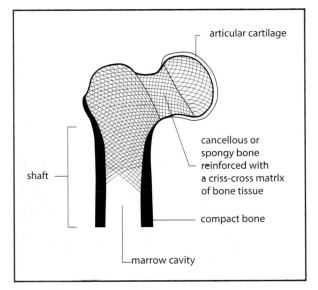

Figure 1.9 The head of the femur.

Investigation

1.7: To examine the structure of bone

Task One

Consider the labelled structures in Figure 1.8 and/or projector slides (if available) and relate these structures to the following description:

*The bone cells are located in spaces called **lacunae** (which contain lymph) and they are arranged concentrically around a canal containing blood vessels, nerves and lymphatics (the Haversian canal). These bone cells run into a system of fine channels or **canaliculi**. It is the lymph in these channels that is responsible for carrying food and oxygen to the bone and for removing waste products.*

Compact bone is surrounded by a tough, vascular tissue (tissue that contains vessels containing blood) called the **periosteum.**

Task Two

If you cut a long bone in half down the middle, you would be able to observe the structures shown in Figure 1.10.

Using the information in Figures 1.9 and 1.10 and from specialist Human Biology texts, answer the following questions:

1. Where in a long bone is spongy bone located?
2. Why do you think red bone marrow is present in spongy bone?
3. Suggest reasons why long bones are hollow.
4. What is the function of the **yellow bone marrow** located in the **diaphysis**?
5. The surface of bones, except for articular surfaces, is covered by the **periosteum,** which attaches itself to the bone via tiny roots. What do you think are the principal functions of the **periosteum**?
6. Why is it important for the ends of bones to be reinforced with a criss-cross matrix of bone tissue, as shown in Figure 1.9?
7. Observe and comment on the positioning of the compact bone in Figure 1.9.
8. Observe and comment on the positioning of the articular cartilage.

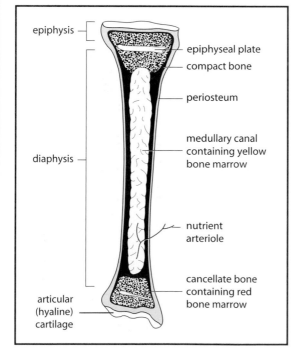

Figure 1.10 Longitudinal section of a long bone.

The development of bones

Ossification is the process of bone formation or the conversion of fibrous tissue or cartilage into bone.

Within the developing foetus the short and long bones are formed as a result of **indirect ossification**, since the foetal cartilage is replaced by bone. This process is called **endochondral ossification**.

Figure 1.11a–d Endochondral ossification in a long bone.

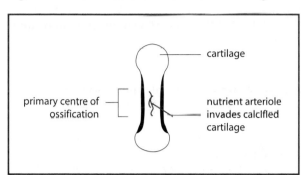

a Bone-forming cells called **osteoblasts** (*os* means bone and *blast* means immature cell) first appear in the centre of the **diaphysis** (the primary centre of ossification), and surround themselves with calcium and phosphate ions supplied by the blood. Blood vessels invade the calcified cartilage and a cavity begins to form once the cartilage is replaced by bone. When the **osteoblast** becomes embedded in the lacuna of the bone matrix, it becomes an **osteocyte**.

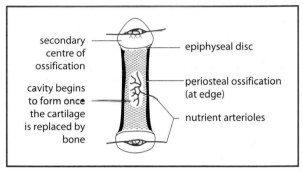

b At birth most of the **diaphysis** consists of bone, and bone has started to appear in the **epiphysis** (the secondary centre of ossification). On the exterior, **periosteal ossification** continues.

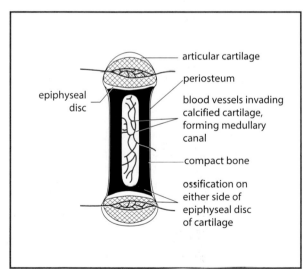

c A disc of cartilage separates the bone at the **diaphysis** from the bone at the **epiphysis**. This disc is called the **epiphyseal disc** or growth disc because it is the only place where an increase in the length of the bone can take place. As the young child grows, increase in length of the long bone can occur only at the **epiphyseal discs**. On the exterior, **periosteal ossification** continues.

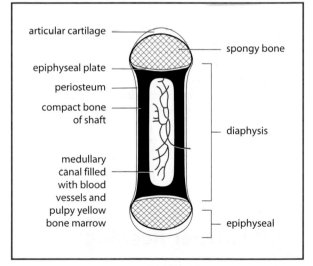

d When the growth ceases, the bony **diaphysis** is united with the **epiphysis** and the line of fusion is marked by a dense layer of bone called the epiphyseal plate. The age at which this fusion occurs varies, but long bones normally cease growing in late adolescence.

Throughout the development of the long bone, parts of the bone are reabsorbed so that unnecessary calcium phosphate is removed and structures such as the **medullary canal** are created. Specialized cells called **osteoclasts** carry out this job. Remodelling is the ongoing replacement of old bone tissue by new bone tissue and redistribution of bone tissue along lines of mechanical stress.

In addition, the bone becomes wider as a result of the **osteoblasts** laying down new layers of bone tissue in the deeper layers of the **periosteum**.

The process of **ossification** in a short bone takes place from the centre of the bone and radiates outwards.

Flat and irregular bones are developed in one stage directly from connective tissue. This process is called **intramembranous ossification**. At ossification centres, within the membrane, osteoblasts produce bone tissue along the membrane fibres to form cancellous bone. Beneath the periosteum, osteoblasts lay down compact bone to form the outer surface of the bone. The sutures of the skull gradually ossify during the development of a young child into adulthood, as do the clavicle, scapula and pelvis.

As a result of **ossification**, the two types of bone tissue described earlier are formed, namely **cancellous** and **compact bone**. It is only at the joint sites that cartilage remains to form the edges where bones meet.

 ## Review Questions

1. Draw a diagram to represent a longitudinal section of a long bone. Label your diagram to show the main structural features and the progress of ossification.
2. Distinguish between spongy and compact bone in terms of microscopic appearance, location and function.
3. Make a list of the activities that you are involved in which may help to promote bone development. Explain your answer.
4. What considerations, with respect to skeletal development, must a coach make in the planning of a training programme for a growing adolescent?
5. What beneficial effects does exercise have on the skeletal system?

 ## Summary

1. You should be able to classify and identify skeletal bones in the axial and appendicular skeletons.
2. You should be able to classify and recognize the specific functions of bones according to their shape.
3. You should be able to recognize bony features and understand their functioning within the human body.
4. You should be able to appreciate variations of bone thickness, density and length in relation to sporting activities.
5. You should be able to identify the two types of skeletal tissue and be able to write briefly about their structure and function within the human body.
6. You should be able to describe the process of ossification in the different types of bones.
7. You should be able to understand the influence of exercise on the developing skeleton.

 ## Further Reading

Bastian G.F. *An Illustrated Review of Anatomy & Physiology: The Skeletal & Muscular Systems*, HarperCollins, 1993.

Khosla T. Sport for tall. *British Medical Journal*, 1983; 287: 736–738.

McMinn R.M.H. *et al. The Human Skeleton*, Wolfe, 1987.

Seeley R.R., Stephens T.D., Tate P. *Anatomy and Physiology* 2e, Mosby–Year Book, 1992.

Wirhed R. *Athletic Ability and the Anatomy of Motion* 2e, Mosby, 1997.

1.2 Joints in Action

Keywords & concepts

Joint feature:
bursae
capsule
cartilaginous joint
fibrous joint
ligaments
menisci
pads of fat
synovial fluid
synovial joint
synovial membrane

Movement patterns:
abduction
adduction
circumduction
depression
dorsiflexion
elevation
extension
external rotation
flexion
internal rotation
plantar flexion
pronation
supination

Synovial joints:
ball and socket
condyloid
gliding
hinge
pivot
saddle

Cardinal planes:
frontal
sagittal
transverse

So far our investigation into how we move has been concerned with an understanding and identification of the main bones and bony tissues in the human body. This next section will help you to understand how bones are connected to each other in order to achieve movement.

A **joint** is a site in the body where two or more bones come together, and joints are classified according to the amount of movement there is between the articulating surfaces.

Types of joint

Fibrous or fixed joint

A fibrous or a fixed joint has no movement at all. Tough fibrous tissue lies between the ends of the bone, which are dovetailed together. Examples in the human body are the sutures in the skull, as illustrated in Figure 1.12 (also refer to Figure 1.2c).

Cartilaginous joint

A cartilaginous joint allows some slight movement. The ends of bones, which are covered in articular or hyaline cartilage, are separated by pads of white fibrocartilage and slight movement is made possible only because the pads of cartilage compress. In addition, the pads of cartilage act as shock absorbers. The intervertebral discs are examples of this type of joint, as illustrated in Figures 1.13 and 1.3g.

Synovial joint

A synovial joint (Figure 1.14) is a freely moving joint, and is characterized by the presence of a joint capsule and cavity. This type of joint is subdivided according to movement possibilities, which are dictated as a result of the bony surfaces that actually form the joint (the knee joint is an example of this type of joint, which is illustrated in Figure 1.15).

Figure 1.12 Fibrous joint.

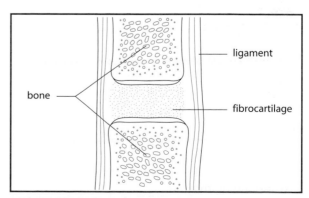

Figure 1.13 Cartilaginous joint.

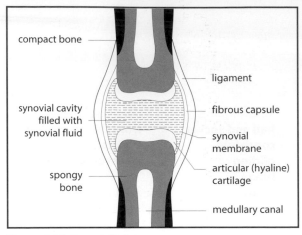

Figure 1.14 Synovial joint.

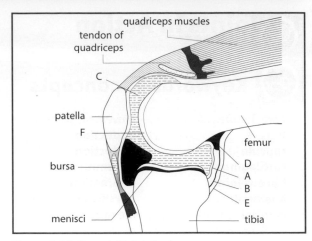

Figure 1.15 Synovial joint: the knee.

Investigation

1.8: To consider the structure and function of the main types of joint
Materials: Human skeleton, skeleton and/or joint posters.

Task One
Identify the three types of joint classified so far. Locate the positioning of examples for each of these three types of joint on your own body.

Task Two
a. Jump off a box.
b. Run and bound.
c. Rotate your upper trunk against your lower body.
Explain the role of cartilaginous joints in these movements.

Investigation

1.9: To examine the structures of a synovial joint

Task One
Using the synovial joint illustrated in Figure 1.15, match each letter to one of the structures listed below and explain the function of each structure by using appropriate reference books.
For example:
Structure:
1. Articular or hyaline cartilage—a smooth, shiny cartilage that covers the ends of bones and absorbs synovial fluid.
Answer: F.
Function: to prevent friction between bones; it is thought that when the joint is exercised, synovial fluid is squeezed out of the articular cartilage at the point of contact (McCutchen's Weeping Lubrication Theory).
2. Joint capsule—a sleeve of fibrous tissue surrounding the joint.

3. Ligament—a sleeve of tough, fibrous connective tissue, which is an extension of the joint capsule.
4. Synovial membrane—a sheet of epithelial cells inside the joint capsule.
5. Synovial fluid—the fluid enclosed in a joint, some of which is absorbed by hyaline cartilage during exercise.
6. Pad of fat—pads of fat that occupy the gaps in and around the joint.

Task Two
Two other features, **bursae** and **menisci**, appear in synovial joints. **Bursae** are little sacs of synovial fluid, and **menisci** are extra layers of fibrocartilage located at the articulating surfaces of joints. Suggest the functions of these special joint features and give examples from the human body.

Task Three
Identify the intracapsular ligaments.

Investigation

1.9 continued

Task Four
Sketch a diagram of a named **ball** and **socket** type of joint, labelling all the structures that provide joint strength and mobility.

Task Five
The effect of long-term training on hyaline cartilage is to cause a permanent cartilaginous thickening as a result of the laying down of additional cartilaginous cells. Suggest reasons why you think an increase in hyaline cartilage thickness would be beneficial to an athlete.

Types of synovial joints and their movement range

As the title suggests, all synovial joints are characterized by the presence of synovial fluid.

The possible ranges of movements within a synovial joint vary according to the shape of the articulating surfaces and therefore according to the joint type (this information is contained in Table 1.1). In addition, specific movement patterns are briefly described in the following summary:

1. **Flexion**, or bending.
2. **Extension**, or straightening.
3. **Plantar flexion**, or pointing the toes.
4. **Dorsiflexion**, or bringing the toes towards the tibia.
5. **Adduction**, or movement towards the midline of the body.
6. **Abduction**, or movement away from the midline of the body.
7. **Circumduction**, or a combination of flexion, extension, abduction and adduction.
8. **Rotation**, or movement around the long axis of a bone (this may be **internal**—rotation inwards towards the body axis, or **external**—rotation away from the body axis).
9. **Pronation**, or turning the palm downwards.
10. **Supination**, or turning the palm upwards.
11. **Inversion**, or turning the sole of the foot inwards.
12. **Eversion**, or turning the sole of the foot outwards.
13. **Elevation**, or an upward movement of a part of the body.
14. **Depression**, or a downward movement of a part of the body.

A full-page illustration of these different types of synovial joint and the type of movement allowed by them can be found on pp. 7–8, Figures 1.14–1.19, of Wirhed (1997).

Table 1.1 : Types of synovial joint

Joint type	Shape of joint	Movement range	e.g. in the body
ball and socket	ball-shaped bone fits into a cup-shaped socket	3 axes— flexion and extension, abduction and adduction, rotation, circumduction	hip
hinge	convex and concave surfaces fitting together	1 axis— flexion and extension	distal joints of phalanges
pivot	ring-shaped, surrounding a cone	1 axis— rotation	radioulnar joint below elbow
condyloid	a modified ball and socket	2 axes— flexion and extension, abduction and adduction, giving circumduction	metacarpophalangeal joints of the fingers
saddle	shaped like a saddle	2 axes— flexion and extension, abduction and adduction, giving circumduction	carpometacarpal joint of the thumb
gliding	2 flat gliding surfaces	a little movement in all directions	joint between the clavicle and sternum

Movement in relation to major body planes and their axes

Body planes are points of reference used to assist in the understanding of movement of body segments with respect to one another. Within each plane an axis can be identified in association with a particular joint about which the movement takes place. Body planes are related to the standard anatomical standing position, as illustrated in Figure 1.16. There are three imaginary planes of reference (known collectively as the **Cardinal Planes**), which pass through the centre of gravity of the body, located below the umbilicus.

1. **Frontal**, which divides the body into front (anterior) and back (posterior) sections.

2. **Sagittal** divides the body into right and left sections. Within the sagittal plane the midline is a vertical line passing through the centre of the body. Within the body, medial points are said to be close to this midline and lateral points away to one side (left or right) of the midline.

3. **Transverse**, which divides the body into upper and lower sections. Within the transverse plane superior means towards the top of the body and inferior means towards the bottom of the body.

Figure 1.16 gives a diagrammatic representation of the primary cardinal reference planes.

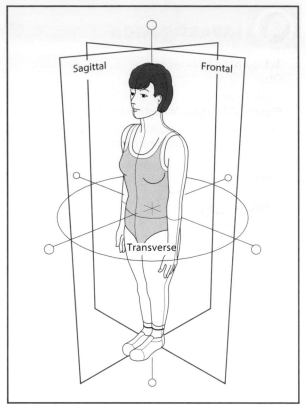

Figure 1.16 Major body axes and planes.

 Investigation

1.10: To associate movement patterns with types of synovial joint and the primary cardinal reference planes

Task One
Identify other examples of synovial joints located in the human body.

Task Two
Using the specific terms that are given to describe the basic movement categories, identify the possible movement patterns at your selected joints.

Task Three
Classify movement patterns listed above according to the three major body planes and axes.

Investigation

1.11: Joints in action
Observe the action pictures in Figure 1.17.

Figure 1.17a and b Swimming and basketball actions.

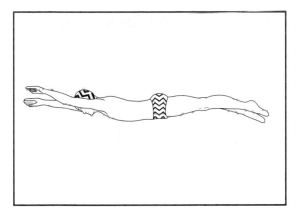

a Swimming

b Basketball

Task One
Name the types of synovial joint located at the knee and hip of the swimmer and basketball player. Analyse the movement patterns happening at these joints.
You may wish to select your own action pictures and answer the same questions.

Task Two
Choose a selection of flexibility exercises that are part of your normal warm-up (refer to p. 153 onwards for ideas). In groups compare the ranges of flexibility at selected joint sites. You may wish to use the idea of the mobility assessment test described in Chapter 4.

Task Three
During most physical activity, the knee joint plays a vital role in movement.
1. Describe how the anatomical structures of the knee joint protect and stabilize the joint.
2. Describe how the anatomical structures of the knee joint make movement possible.
3. In many sports, the knee joint is often injured as a result of impacts (with other sportspeople or objects), or excessive forces (as in weightlifting, throwing or jumping) or overuse. Make a list of the common injuries that occur in the knee joint. (You may wish to extend this line of investigation to other joint sites.)
4. Describe some of the ways you could prevent such injuries from occurring.

Review Questions

1. Define articulation. What factors determine the degree of movement at joints?
2. List the bones that articulate in the following joints:
a. knee,
b. elbow,
c. shoulder,
d. thoracic vertebrae,
e. hip.
3. Explain how the articulating bones in a synovial joint are held together.
4. What differences in their joints produce the differences in mobility between the hip joint and the elbow joint?

5. Identify and categorize four joints which are involved in the arm action of the tennis serve.
6. Identify the movement patterns performed at the joint sites listed for the following physical activities:
a. Pushing hockey ball: knees, elbows, wrists.
b. Sit and reach test (Task 5 described in Investigation 4.1): trunk, hip.
c. Step up onto a bench (Task 3 described in Investigation 4.1): knees, hip.
d. Basketball shooting: wrists, elbow, shoulders.
e. Vertical jump [Task 1(2) described in Investigation 4.1]: ankles, knees, hip.

 Exam-Style Questions

1. Figure 1.18 shows a gymnast in the crucifix position of the rings
a. Identify the **three** planes and the **three** axes of motion indicated in the diagram. (3 marks)
b. In which plane does each of the following movements take place:
i. cartwheel,
ii. forwards somersault,
iii. ice skating spin with legs together and arms overhead? (3 marks)
c. Identify the main axis of rotation for each of the sports movements shown in Figures 1.19a–1.19c. (3 marks)

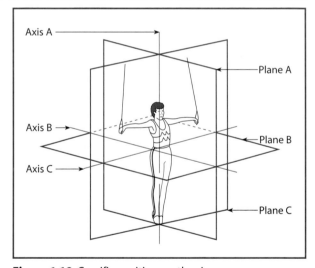

Figure 1.18 Crucifix position on the rings.

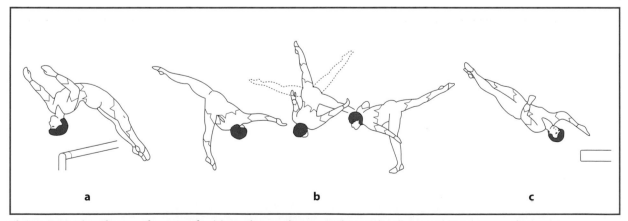

Figure 1.19 Identify axes of rotation for (a) rear layout dismount, (b) aerial walkover and (c) twisting dismount.

Summary

1. You should be able to classify joints into fibrous, cartilaginous and synovial.
2. You should to be able to identify and describe the features of the different types of synovial joint.
3. You should be able to appreciate how joint structure allows for a variety of different skeletal movements.

4. You should be able to classify movement in relation to the major body planes and axes.
5. You should be able to describe briefly some of the common joint injuries and methods of prevention.

Further Reading

Bastian G.F. *An Illustrated Review of the Skeletal and Muscular Systems*, HarperCollins, 1993.

Clegg C. *Exercise Physiology*, Feltham Press, 1995.

Hay G.H. and Reid J.G. *Anatomy Mechanics and Human Motion* 2e, Prentice Hall, 1988.

Tortora G. *Principles of Anatomy and Physiology* 8e, HarperCollins, 1996.

1.3 Muscles in Action

 Keywords & concepts

agonist	*fibre types*:	fusiform	pennate
antagonist	type I	insertion	periosteum
antagonistic	IIa (FOG)	ligaments	skeletal muscle
aponeuroses	IIb (FTG)	muscle group	synergist
fascia	fixator	origin	tendon

One of the important functions of the human skeleton is to enable movement. Physical activity is achieved as a result of the action of over 600 muscles that contract or shorten, thereby facilitating the movement of the skeleton across its joints.

Muscles are the converters of energy, since they change chemical energy into mechanical energy. This is achieved as a result of the contraction of hundreds of muscle fibres within the connective tissue of each muscle.

During muscular contraction a muscle tightens to produce a state of tension that is adequate to meet the demands of the activity. The effect of regular physical activity is to develop and sustain local muscle strength and endurance. Some skeletal muscles, for example, the soleus muscle, are very fatigue resistant (this is because they consist of a high proportion of **slow twitch** fibres), while other muscles, for example the biceps and gastrocnemius muscles, fatigue more quickly because they are essentially **fast twitch** (the details of slow and fast twitch muscle fibres are described later in this section). The effects of training in adapting muscle tissue to stress demands are discussed in Chapter 4. However, all muscles will contract *only* when stimulated by nerve impulses.

This section helps you to identify muscles, and to understand muscle structure and tension, how muscles are arranged in groups, how they are attached to bones so that movement can be produced and how muscle action can be analysed by performing simple motor tasks.

Shapes of muscles (Figures 1.21b–1.21e)

Skeletal muscles vary in shape and function. Each muscle shape, its origins, insertions and positioning, has evolved specifically to deal with its unique functioning.

Fusiform

Fusiform means **spindle-shaped**, since the muscle fibres run the length of the muscle belly to converge at each end. This strap-like, round shape enables the muscle to perform a large range of movement fluidity.

Pennate

Pennate means **featherlike**. A pennate muscle is a flat muscle in which fibres are arranged around a central tendon, like barbs of a feather.

The major types of pennate muscles are grouped according to the way in which the fibres are arranged around the central tendon (Figure 1.21).

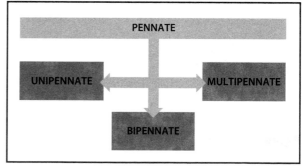

Figure 1.20 Pennate muscle types.

Pennate muscles have a very limited range of movement, but are very strong and powerful.

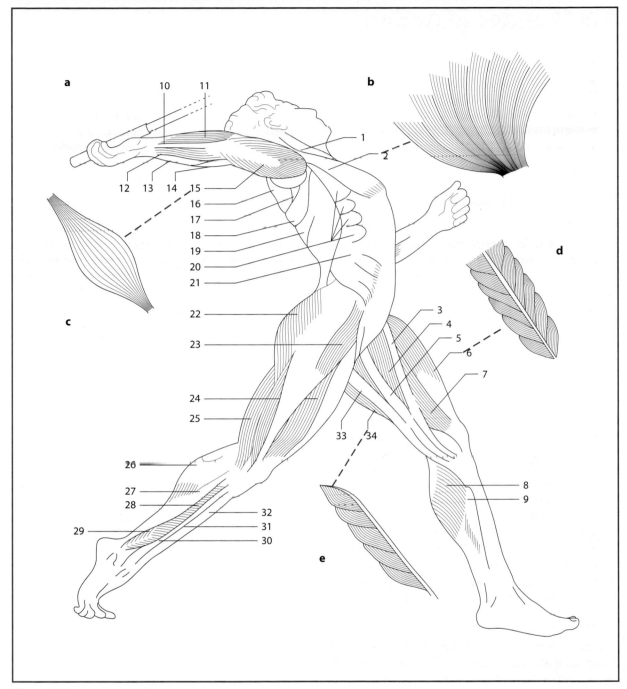

Figure 1.21 Muscles in action.

a. Superficial muscles of the human body (1–34)
Muscle shapes:
b. Multipennate
c. Fusiform
d. Bipennate
e. Unipennate

Investigation

1.12: Identification of muscle shapes and the relationship of muscle shape to its functioning

1. Give an example for each type of fusiform and pennate muscle shape illustrated in Figure 1.21.

2. Describe how the three types of **pennate** muscle shape are designed for efficient functioning within the human body.

Investigation

1.13: Identification of muscles and their movement patterns

Materials: Figure 1.21 and muscle chart and/or slides.

Task One

Identify and label the muscles numbered 1–34 in Figure 1.21.

Task Two

Using the labelled muscles from Figure 1.21 and other reference material, identify the groups of muscles of the upper leg, their origins and insertions, and classify them into functional categories: that is, flexors, extensors, adductors, abductors and rotators (for example, see Table 1.2).

Table 1.2 : Flexors—bending of the knee

Muscle	Origin	Insertion
Group		
HAMSTRINGS Biceps femoris	**Long head**—ischial tuberosity **Short head**—linea aspera of femur	Head of fibula & lateral condyle of tibia
Semimembranosus	Ischial tuberosity	Medial condyle of tibia
Semitendinosus	Ischial tuberosity	Below medial condyle of tibia

Task Three

Identify the groups of muscles of the shoulder and upper arm according to functional categories.

Task Four

Identify the groups of muscles of the trunk according to functional categories.

You may wish to extend this investigation by identifying the origins and insertions of other major muscles on skeletal bones.

Investigation

1.14: To identify muscles in relation to simple motor tasks and to relate muscle size to performance

Materials: tape measures, muscle chart.

Figure 1.22 A standing long jump.

Task One

Perform a standing long jump (Figure 1.22) and measure the distance covered from the start line to the nearest point of landing. Record the best of three trials.

Task Two

By appropriate use of the muscle chart and by palpation, identify the muscles on the front of the thigh:
1. What is this group of muscles commonly called?
2. Name each main muscle located within this group.

Task Three

Stand normally, feet slightly apart. Using the tape, your partner measures (in cm) the circumference of your contracted thigh at its maximum girth or mid-distance from the hip to the knee joint, for both left and right legs. Record these measurements in Table 1.3.

Table 1.3 : Results table—the relationship of muscle size to performance

		Performance and measurements of class members			
	self	1	2	3	4
Standing long jump distance in metres					
Thigh girths left thigh in cm right thigh in cm					

Task Four

1. Compare within small groups the relationship between standing long jump and maximum thigh girths. Plot a graph of performances from the standing long jump (*x*-axis) against the maximum thigh girths (*y*-axis) of as many of your colleagues as possible. What does your graph show?

2. Are there differences in left and right thigh girths? Give possible reasons for any differences.
3. Identify any errors that may have affected your results.

You may wish to extend this investigation by using other muscle groups such as those of the trunk and shoulder regions of the body.

Types of muscle fibre

Muscle tissue is composed of muscle fibres that contain **two main fibre types**, which contract at different speeds; namely, **fast twitch fibres** (or **type II**) and **slow twitch fibres** (or **type I**).

Within an individual there are different proportions of these fibre types to be found in different muscles, and evidence supports the view that fibre type distribution is inherited.

All muscle contains a mixture of **slow** and **fast twitch fibres**. The major differences between the two types are related to:

1. **Speed of contraction**—slow twitch muscle fibres contract at a rate of about 20% when compared with fast twitch muscle fibres.

2. **Muscle fibre force**—fast twitch fibres are bigger in size than slow twitch fibres, have larger motor neurones and therefore can generate high force rapidly.

3. **Muscle endurance**—slow twitch fibres are capable of resisting fatigue whereas fast twitch fibres are easily fatigued.

More recently, it has been discovered that type II fibres are subdivided into type IIa and type IIb. Type IIa fibres, otherwise known as **FOG** (**Fast** twitch high **Oxidative Glycolytic**), have a greater resistance to fatigue compared with type IIb (**Fast Twitch Glycolytic—FTG**). The fatigue resistant nature of type IIa is entirely due to muscle adaptation in response to endurance training.

A summary of comparisons of these three types of muscle fibres is listed in Table 1.4.

Table 1.4 : Characteristics of fibre types

Characteristic	Slow twitch	Fast twitch	
	type I	**FOG** **type II**	**FTG** **type IIb**
Size	midway	small	large
Colour	red	midway	white
Aerobic			
Myoglobin content	high	high	low
Capillary density	high	midway/high	low
Oxidative enzymes	high	midway/high	low
Mitochondrial density	high	midway	small
Activity during low intensity exercise	high	midway	low
Anaerobic			
Myosin ATPase activity	low	high	high
Glycogen stores	low	high	high
Phosphocreatine content	low	midway	high
Fatigue level	low	midway	high
Contractile time	slow	midway	fast
Relaxation time	slow	midway	fast
Activity during high intensity exercise	low	high	high

(Some of the terms used to describe the characteristics of fibre types may be unfamiliar, but you should be able to understand them once you have referred to relevant sections within this text.)

Investigation

1.15: To consider some of the characteristics of fibre types

Task One
1. It can be deduced from the information summarized in Table 1.4 that slow twitch fibres are best suited to **aerobic** (performed with a full and adequate supply of oxygen) types of exercise, whereas fast twitch are specifically adapted for high intensity and mainly **anaerobic** (performed without sufficient oxygen to cope with the energy demand) types of exercise. Describe some of the characteristics that support this deduction.

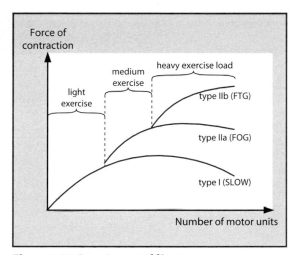

Figure 1.23 Recruitment of fibre types.

2. The effects of specialized training can alter the metabolic functioning of fast twitch type IIb fibres so that they take on some of the characteristics of type I fibres and become type IIa fibres. Describe the ways in which metabolic functioning of type IIa fibres change as a result of specialist aerobic training.
3. In which sporting activities would the adaptation of fast twitch (type IIb) fibres to type IIa fibres be relevant to a sportsperson?
4. What types of training would cause the adaptation of fast twitch fibres to type IIa fibres?
5. Give examples of types of training that would stress slow twitch fibres and fast twitch glycolytic fibres.

Task Two
Using the information in Figure 1.23, describe the order in which fibre types are recruited as the number of motor units increases.

Task Three
Another interesting study is the relationship between distribution of fibre type and different sporting activities.

Two diagrams illustrating this concept are found in *Sports Physiology* by Bowers and Fox (third edition), pages 128 and 129, Figures 6–17a and b (see Further Reading). Basically, the more explosive and intense the demands of a sport, the more likely it is that successful sportspeople will have a higher proportion of fast twitch muscle fibres in their muscles.
1. Using the information from this reference, comment on the distribution of fibre type (for males and females) with respect to different sporting activities.

2. Discuss the role of genetics in determining the proportions of muscle fibre types and the potential for success in selected activities.
3. What is the pattern of muscle fibre recruitment during:
a. high jumping,
b. running a 5 km race,
c. running a 400 m race.
4. Using the information contained within Table 1.4 give two pieces of evidence that:
a. suggest that fast twitch fibres may easily build up an oxygen debt;
b. might account for the difference in speed of contraction of the two types of fibre;
c. suggest why muscles concerned with maintaining the posture of the body might be expected to have a large proportion of slow twitch fibres.

How skeletal muscle works

Muscles and bones have specialized skeletal structures, such as **tendons** and the **periosteum** (peri—around, oste—bone) of a bone, which generally transmit muscular forces to bones or, in the case of **ligaments**, attach bone to bone (**ligaments** limit the range of movement of joints). These structures are commonly known as **musculo-skeletal attachments**.

Tendons

Muscles are attached to bones by **tendons**, which pass over joints. Tendons are strong and inelastic, and vary in length and structure from one to another. Small tendons, such as those to the muscles that control eye movement, have no nerve and blood supply; whereas large tendons, such as the Achilles tendon, are connected to the **central nervous system** and the **circulatory system**, and therefore have nerves and a blood supply both of which are substantially less prolific and effective than in the actual muscles. In some cases the tendinous attachment to bone is a more flattened or ribbon-shaped connection, called an **aponeurosis**. This type of tendon is without nerves. An example is the aponeurosis of the internal oblique muscles (which tilt and rotate the trunk relative to the hip girdle).

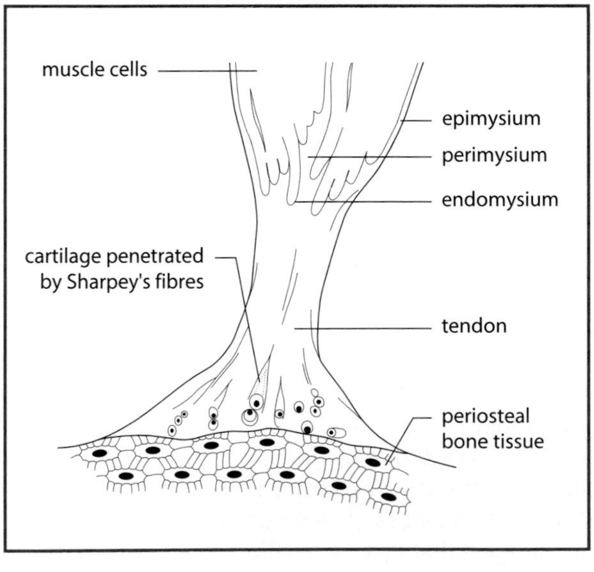

Tendons are rigidly cemented to the **periosteum**, as illustrated in Figure 1.24.

Where the tendon fastens on to the periosteum, structures called **Sharpey's fibres** firmly attach tendon tissue on to periosteal tissue.

The **periosteum** is tough connective tissue whose function is to attach muscle tendons to bone, and to assist bone growth.

Other connective tissue

Fascia is a general form of connective tissue that overlays or underlines many body structures. A specialist example of this is the **epimysium**, which is the name for the sheath or membrane that envelopes muscle systems (shown in Figure 1.24, and discussed in more detail later in this chapter).

Superficial fascia underlies the skin and forms the connective link between the skin and **deep fascia** of muscle.

The origin and insertion of muscles

The tendon at the static end of the muscle is called the **origin**, and the tendon at the end of the muscle closest to the joint that moves is called the **insertion** of that muscle.

Figure 1.24 How a tendon connects muscle to bone.
(*After Solomon and Davies, 1983.*)

The arrangement of muscles

Muscles that cause joints to bend are called **flexors**, while those muscle that straighten a joint are called **extensors**.

Skeletal muscles are normally arranged in pairs so that as one muscle is contracting the other is relaxing, thus producing co-ordinated movement.

The muscle that actually shortens to move the joint is called the **prime mover** or **agonist**, whereas the muscle that relaxes in opposition to the agonist is called the **antagonist**. Muscles that are prime movers for one movement act as antagonists for the opposite movement. For example, the **biceps** (agonist) contracts while the **triceps** (antagonist) relaxes (Figure 1.25a). This combined action causes the elbow to flex. When the elbow straightens the reverse occurs: the **triceps** (agonist) contracts while the **biceps** (antagonist) relaxes (Figure 1.25b). The action of muscles working in pairs is called **antagonistic muscle action**. Antagonistic muscle action limits and controls movements, especially when there are groups of muscles acting together.

In addition, there are muscles that stabilize the origin to the prime mover so that only the bone into which it is inserted will move. These are called **fixators** and **synergists**. **Fixator** muscles hold joints in position and are sited so that the origin and insertion are on opposite sides of a stabilized joint. **Synergists** are muscles that hold body position to enable the agonist to operate (*syn*—together, *ergon*—work). Note that the terms 'fixator' and 'synergist' could be applied to the same muscle.

Figure 1.25a and b

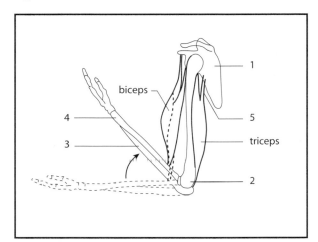

a Flexion of the elbow.

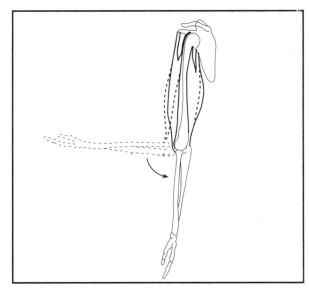

b Extension of the elbow.

Figure 1.26a and b Performing a curl with a light bar.

a

b

Investigation

1.16: An analysis of limb movement
Materials: bar with secured discs, Figures 1.25 and 1.26.

Task One
1. Perform a curl with a light bar (see Figure 1.26: make sure that your teacher shows you the correct technique).
2. Identify the bones numbered 1–4 in Figure 1.25a.
3. Identify the structure numbered 5 in Figure 1.25a.
4. Using an example from one of the muscles shown in Figure 1.25a, explain what is meant by 'origin' and 'insertion'.
5. Identify and classify the muscles that are used in the action of curling a bar into the functional categories of **agonist** (or prime mover) and **antagonist**.
6. Using your own musculature and Figure 1.21, identify those muscles that act as **fixators** and **synergists** in the action of curling a bar.

Task Two
List the main agonists active in:
a. The legs while cycling.
b. The leg action of a swimmer during breast stroke.
c. The shoulder, arm and forearm while performing a push up.
d. Work out the muscles that are relaxing in opposition to the agonist muscles in a, b and c.

 Review Questions

1. What is the function of tendons?
2. What is the function of ligaments?
3. What are the functions of periosteal layers?
4. Identify the agonists that are active in:
a. Elevating the shoulders.
b. Hyper-extending the back.
c. Abducting the hip.
d. Dorsiflexing the ankle.
e. Flexing the knee.
5. Work out the muscles which are relaxing in opposition to the agonist muscles of 4a–e.
6. Identify the agonist muscles that are active in:
a. A pull up.
b. Hitting a stationary hockey ball.
c. A sit up.
d. A vertical jump.
e. Shooting in basketball.

 Exam-Style Questions

1. A backward roll, as illustrated in Figure 1.27, involves a series of co-ordinated muscle actions.
a. Describe the movements at the hip and knee joints during the whole of the backward roll. (4 marks)
b. Identify the agonist muscles acting on the shoulder joint during the push-off phase from the mat. (2 marks)

Figure 1.27 Backward roll.

Table 1.5 : Percentage composition of slow twitch fibres in male leg muscles

Event	Mean % slow twitch fibres	Range of % slow twitch fibres
Marathon runners	85	50–95
800 m runners	55	50–80
100/200 m sprinters	35	20–55

2. Table 1.5 shows the percentage composition of slow twitch fibres found in the leg muscles of male athletes specializing at different distances of athletic event.
a. Briefly discuss the relationship between the percentage of slow twitch fibres and race

Exam-Style Questions

continued

distance, as suggested by the data in Table 1.5. (3 marks)

b. Which group of athletes is the most specialized in terms of slow twitch muscle fibre composition? Explain your choice by reference to Table 1.5. (2 marks)

c. Arrange the group of runners in rank order according to how closely their slow twitch

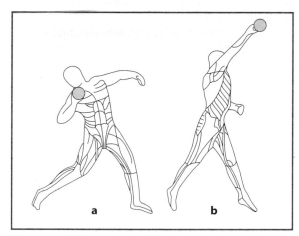

Figure 1.28 Shot putter action.

muscle fibre composition matches the 'ideal' for their distance. (6 marks)

d. List **three** features of slow twitch fibres that contribute to their greater aerobic capacity. (3 marks)

e. In terms of muscle fibre types, explain why it is sometimes said that 'endurance kills speed'. (3 marks)

f. Why is it more accurate to refer to slow twitch motor units rather than slow twitch muscle fibres? (3 marks)

3. Figures 1.28a and 1.28b show a shot putter during the delivery phase of the technique.

a. List the bones that articulate in the shoulder and knee joints. (4 marks)

b. Briefly explain the movement sequence of the right arm during the delivery phase of the shot put. (3 marks)

c. With reference to Figures 1.28a and 1.28b, name the main contracting muscles involved in the extension of the right elbow, knee and hip joints. (6 marks)

d. Using an example from either Figure 1.28a or 1.28b, explain what is meant by a **fixator** muscle. (2 marks)

Summary

1. You should be able to classify and identify skeletal muscle according to its shape and group.

2. You should be able to locate, name and appreciate the movement patterns of major muscles.

3. You should be able to discuss the relationship between muscle size and performance.

4. You should be able to understand the role of fibre types with respect to sporting situations.

5. You should understand the role of musculo-skeletal attachments in limb movement and analyse movements in terms of muscle action.

6. You should understand what is meant by origin and insertion and antagonistic muscle action.

Further Reading

Bastian G.F. *An Illustrated Review of Anatomy & Physiology: The Skeletal & Muscular Systems*, HarperCollins, 1993.

Bowers R.W. and Fox E.L. *Sports Physiology* 3e, Wm C. Brown, 1992.

Clegg C. *Exercise Physiology*, Feltham Press, 1995.

Kingston B. *Understanding Muscles—A practical guide to muscle function*, Chapman & Hall, 1996.

Thompson C.W. *Manual of Structural Kinesiology* 2e, Mosby–Year Book, 1994.

Wirhed R. *Athletic Ability and the Anatomy of Motion* 2e, Mosby, 1997.

1.4 Types of Muscular Contraction

 ## Keywords & concepts

ballistic	isokinetic mc	muscular contraction
concentric	isometric muscle	plyometrics
dynamic	contraction (mc)	static
eccentric	isotonic mc	

In Investigation 1.16 you flexed or contracted the biceps muscle in your upper arm. This action was brought about by a changing state of contraction within the muscle tissue.

Muscular contractions can vary in speed, force and duration. For example, in cycling the action is cyclical and rhythmical, involving the interplay of agonist and antagonist, whereas the action of a boxer throwing a punch is ballistic in nature, since the arm is moved fluidly by a short, fast contraction of the agonist, and the movement is stopped as a result of the antagonist brake action.

During muscular contraction, a muscle may shorten, lengthen or stay the same. Where a muscle changes length the contraction is classified as **dynamic**. When a muscle remains the same length, a **static** contraction occurs.

Static contractions—isometric muscle contraction

Another name for a static muscular contraction is an isometric contraction. (*Iso* means same and *metric* means length, hence same length.) This concept can be expressed as in Figure 1.29, or as:

$$\frac{\text{FORCE OF MUSCLE}}{\text{CONTRACTION}} = \frac{\text{FORCE EXPRESSED BY}}{\text{RESISTANCE}}$$

The result is that the muscle length and tension in the arm wrestling contest remain static. It is found that pushing or pulling **without moving** can produce a strength gain in the muscles used. In a training situation this is done by exerting the maximum possible force in a fixed position for sets of 10 seconds, with a 60 second recovery interval. Its advantage is that a large amount of strength training can be done in a short time. Another advantage of **isometric training** is that it needs no special place or equipment and it can be done at any time throughout the day. However, isometric training does little for cardiovascular fitness.

Concentric contractions—isotonic and isokinetic muscle contraction

The sort of exercise in which muscles are used in a normal **dynamic** way and in which muscles contract at a speed controlled by the sportsperson in whatever activity is being done is called **isotonic**. In this case, the work is labelled **concentric** or positive because the resulting tension causes the muscle to create movement by shortening its length. The advantage of this type of exercise is that it stimulates **real** sporting use of the musculature. One of the adaptations produced by this type of training or exercise is to increase the capillarization of both skeletal and cardiac muscle and to enable these muscles to become more resistant to the onset of fatigue. Therefore, it is most likely to lead to improvement in sporting performance.

In **isokinetic** exercise the point at which force acts moves at constant speed. For example, in a squat the shoulders move upwards at a constant speed regardless of the effort put into the exercise. Special machines are needed for isokinetics (the nearest usually available is a hydraulic exercise machine). Isokinetic exercises (concentric and eccentric) are used in special strength-training programmes and human movement research.

Figure 1.29

The advantage of isokinetic training is that it removes from the exercise the differences between forces exerted at different angles of limbs at a joint (refer to Investigation 7.5, Task Seven, p. 218, for a discussion on the effect of joint angle on forces applied by muscle systems). Like isotonic exercise, isokinetic training improves muscle strength and endurance, as well as cardiovascular fitness.

Eccentric contractions—plyometrics

It is found that if maximum effort is put into an exercise **while a muscle group is lengthening**, then the muscle exerts a bigger force than in any of the other types of exercise mentioned above. In this case the work is labelled **eccentric** or negative, as, for example, in the controlled lowering of a weight.

This is the effect of the stimulus trying to prevent muscle lengthening, and it produces the biggest overload possible in a muscle, thereby enhancing its development as far as strength is concerned. Eccentric contractions can be produced isotonically and isokinetically.

The chief practical use of eccentric contractions is in **plyometric work**, in which the sportsperson jumps down from a box and immediately jumps back over a bar or hurdle (Figure 1.30), or in fact performs any jumping exercise in which a landing followed by a jump occurs. You may wish to try some of these examples! (For a detailed discussion on the adaptations produced by training refer to Chapter 4.)

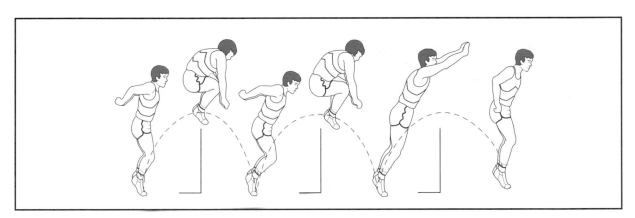

Figure 1.30 Examples of plyometric exercises.

Investigation

1.17: Types of muscular contraction in relation to physical activity
Materials: chinning bar.

Task One
1. Hang from a bar, as shown in Figure 1.31a, holding a 90° angle in the elbow joint.
2. From the bent arm position pull yourself up, as shown in Figure 1.31b.
3. When you have completed the chin-up, lower yourself slowly down to an arms extended position, as shown in Figure 1.31c.

Task Two
With the aid of the diagrams, work out the agonist muscles used for each exercise, their origins and insertions, and the type of muscular contraction being used. Write your answers in Table 1.6.

Figure 1.31a–c Chinning bar.

  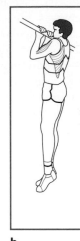

a   b   c

Table 1.6 : Results

	Agonist muscles	Origin	Insertion	Type of contraction
a.				
b.				
c.				

Task Three
1. In which part of the movement sequence is eccentric work being done?
2. Identify the muscle that is exerting force while lengthening.

Task Four
Figure 1.32 shows four different actions from different sports.

Figure 1.32a–d

b Sprinting.

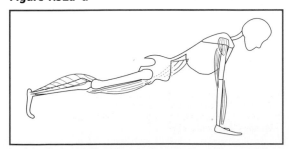

a The push-up position.

(See next page for Figure 1.32c–d)

Investigation

1.17 contlnued

Figure 1.32a–d (*continued*)

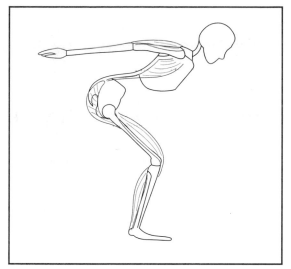

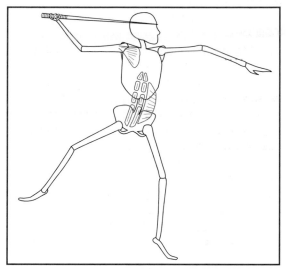

c Starting position for swimming.

d Throwing the javelin.

The muscles indicated in the figures are the active ones used in the position or movements.

Make a table similar to Table 1.6 and complete the task of identifying the active muscles, their origins and insertions, and the types of muscle contraction. (*Adapted from* Basic Sport Science *by Klaus Klausen.*)

 Review Questions

1. Differentiate and give examples of concentric, static and eccentric work.
2. Discuss the advantages and disadvantages of isometric, isokinetic and isotonic muscle contraction.

 Summary

1. You should understand the concepts and the advantages and disadvantages of dynamic (isotonic and isokinetic) and static (isometric) contraction.
2. You should understand the concepts of concentric and eccentric contractions.
3. You should the able to identify types of muscle contraction in relation to practical situations, co-jointly with agonist muscle identification.

 Further Reading

Bowers R.W. and Fox E.L. *Sports Physiology* 3e, Wm C. Brown, 1992.
Chu D.A. *Jumping into Plyometrics*, Human Kinetics, 1992.
Clegg C. *Exercise Physiology*, Feltham Press, 1995.
Kingston B. *Understanding Muscles—A practical guide to muscle function*, Chapman & Hall, 1996.

Klausen K., Hemmingsen I., Rasmussen B. *Basic Sport Science*, McNaughton and Gunn, 1982.
Thompson C.W. *Manual of Structural Kinesiology* 2e, Mosby–Year Book, 1994.

1.5 A Typical Muscle and Its Structure from Gross to Molecular Detail

 Keywords & concepts

cross bridges	myofibril	sarcomere
endomysium	myoglobin	sarcoplasm
epimysium	nervous impulse	striated muscle
filaments—actin and myosin	perimysium	triad vesicles
Huxley's theory of muscle contraction	ratchet mechanism	troponin
	red muscle	tropomyosin
muscle fibre	sarcolemma	white muscle

To understand how a muscle converts chemical energy into mechanical energy, we need to understand the structural detail of voluntary muscle and what makes it contract.

Voluntary muscle is often referred to as **skeletal** muscle because it normally moves bones. Other descriptions include **striped** or **striated**, which derive their names as a result of the striped microscopic appearance of the muscle cells.

A typical muscle is the **gastrocnemius** or calf muscle, which has its origin on the lateral and medial condyles of the femur and its insertion through the Achilles tendon on the calcaneum, or heel hone.

Figure 1.33c shows that the entire muscle is surrounded by a layer of connective tissue called the **epimysium**, which consists mainly of collagen fibres. The function of the epimysium is to provide a smooth surface against which other muscles can glide, and to give the muscle its form. The epimysium is the total envelope surrounding the muscle and connecting it to the outer **fascia**.

Within the muscle are large bundles of muscle fibres or **fasciculi**, which are surrounded by the **perimysium** (middle layer) consisting of collagen and elastic fibres. This information is illustrated in Figures 1.33c and d.

Within each bundle or fasciculus are **muscle cells** or **fibres**, each individually wrapped by a very thin layer of connective tissue or **endomysium** (*endo*—final, *mysium*—muscle; refer to Figure 1.33d).

All three connective tissue layers (epimysium, perimysium and endomysium) are connected to each other so that when the muscle fibres contract, they are ultimately linked to the tendons, which are attached to bones across joints, thus creating voluntary movement [refer back to section on how skeletal muscle works (p. 26)].

The muscle cell (see Figure 1.33e)

Each cell consists of a multinucleate (multinucleate means containing many nuclei) fibre and is highly specialized for contraction. Although the diameter of the muscle cell is very small (l0–l00 μm—microns), its length can be extremely long (up to 0.5 m), depending on the length of the whole muscle. Therefore, it is important that the muscle cell can transmit its nerve impulses throughout the entire length of the fibre. As a consequence, skeletal muscle is a good conductor of electricity. The cell membrane or **sarcolemma** is very thin, which is important to allow efficient diffusion of oxygen and glucose into the cell, and carbon dioxide out of the cell. Positioned just inside the sarcolemma are numerous nuclei, hence the term 'multinucleate'. (The **nucleus** is the control centre of a cell.)

The **sarcoplasm** inside the cell is a specialized cytoplasm containing **sarcoplasmic reticulum**, '**T' (triad) vesicles**, **enzymes** and **mitochondria**.

The **sarcoplasmic reticulum** is a network of internal membranes that run throughout the sarcoplasm and is responsible for the transportation of materials within the cell. A '**T' vesicle** is a sac that contains cellular secretions, such as calcium ions needed to initiate muscle contraction. **Enzymes** are the organic catalysts in that they regulate all chemical reactions within the cell [for example, ATPase is needed to activate adenosine triphosphate (ATP), which provides the energy needed for muscular contraction].

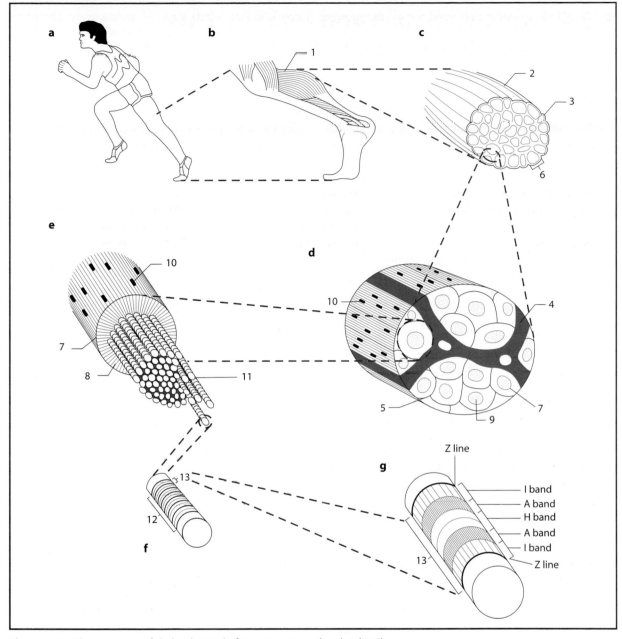

Figure 1.33 The structure of skeletal muscle from gross to molecular detail.

a. Sprinter in action
b. Lower part of leg showing positioning of the gastrocnemius muscle
c. Cross-section through the gastrocnemius muscle
c, d. Sections of the fasciculi
e. Muscle cell
f, g. Myofibril

1. gastrocnemius muscle
2. belly of muscle
3. epimysium
4. perimysium
5. endomysium
6. muscle bundle or fasciculus
7. sarcolemma
8. sarcoplasm
9. muscle cell

10. nucleus
11. myofibril
12. banding pattern of myofibril
13. sarcomere with labelled banding pattern

Mitochondria are often referred to as the **power plants** of the cell, because most of the reactions of cellular respiration and hence energy release take place within them.

Figure 1.34 shows the distribution of mitochondria within slow twitch, type I muscle fibres. Those mitochondria positioned beneath the sarcolemma provide energy for the transport of ions and metabolites across the sarcolemma. Those mitochondria positioned deep within the muscle fibres provide energy for muscle contraction via ATP regeneration (refer to p. 97 for additional information on the role of mitochondria within skeletal muscle tissue).

Some muscle fibres contain more sarcoplasm than others; these appear darker due to the presence of **myoglobin** (a form of haemoglobin that occurs in muscle cells). This type of muscle is called **red muscle** and is best suited for long-term powerful contractions, as in the postural extensor muscles (such as the rectus abdominus or erector spinae muscles, which tend to hold the body upright). **White muscle** contains less sarcoplasm and myoglobin, but more ATPase (the enzyme needed to assist release of energy from ATP—see Chapter 3.2 for a discussion on energy generation and ATP). Therefore white muscle is best suited for speed. Flexor muscles, such as vastus medialis or biceps muscles, which can move limbs quickly, are examples of white muscle. Red and white muscles are also described as

slow and fast twitch muscles, respectively. The properties of these different types of muscle cells or fibres are discussed in detail in the section on types of muscle fibre (p. 24).

Muscle myoglobin

Muscle myoglobin (a similar molecule to haemoglobin) has a temporary, but **greater**, affinity for oxygen than does haemoglobin. Therefore, muscle myoglobin captures oxygen from saturated haemoglobin, thereby transferring oxygen **into** the muscle cell structure. Since myoglobin is present throughout the cell, oxygen is transferred from myoglobin molecule to myoglobin molecule **until** it reaches the mitochondria (where it is needed for energy-producing reactions). This process is **in addition** to the **diffusion** of oxygen between capillaries (from the haemoglobin of red blood cells) and muscle cells, caused by the larger concentration (or partial pressure) of oxygen in haemoglobin than in the muscle cells. (See Chapter 2, pp. 77–80, for a discussion about gas diffusion into muscle cells.)

Muscle cell structure (see Figure 1.33g)

Running longitudinally within the sarcoplasm are long, slender, light and dark structures called **myofibrils** (3 μm in diameter), which therefore create a striated appearance. Each myofibril consists of numerous units called **sarcomeres**.

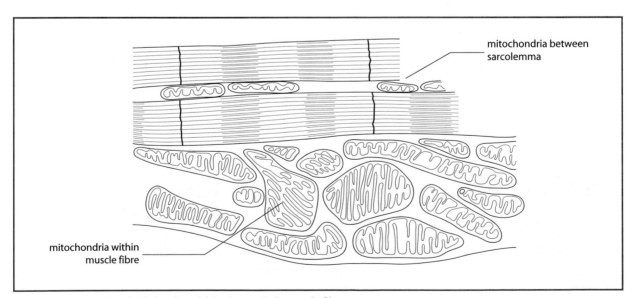

Figure 1.34 Mitochondrial density within slow twitch muscle fibres.

The sarcomere (see Figures 1.33g and 1.35)

Each sarcomere is the functional basic unit of a myofibril and thousands of sarcomeres form a long chain within each myofibril. The **Z** membrane indicates the boundary from one sarcomere to the next.

The reason for this light and dark striated banding pattern (hence the name '**striped muscle**') is that it is composed of two types of longitudinal protein filaments:

- **Thick filaments of myosin**—confined to the dark **A** band and **H** zone in the middle, which has only thick myosin filaments.
- **Thin filaments of actin**—which are found in the light **I** band and between myosin at the ends of the dark **A** band. An actin filament is composed of molecules of **actin**, **tropomyosin** and **troponin**.

The **A** bands are positioned in the centre section of the sarcomere and consist of thick and thin filaments separated by an **H** zone that has only thick filaments. The **I** band is positioned at both ends of the sarcomere and consists exclusively of thin filaments.

The thin filaments connect the **Z** membrane and the inner edge of the nearer **A** band at each end of the sarcomere. The thick filaments join the outer edges of both **A** bands and therefore overlap the thin filaments in the **A** band. This arrangement is illustrated in Figure 1.35a.

What happens when the muscle contracts?

The theory of muscle contraction is based on **Huxley's sliding filament theory of muscle contraction**.

In the relaxed muscle all the bands are visible, whereas in the contracted muscle the light **I** band narrows then disappears, since the thin actin filaments are being drawn further in between the thick myosin filaments (refer to Figure 1.35 to observe these differences between relaxed and contracted muscle).

Figure 1.35a–d Diagrammatic detail of sarcomere. (*After Huxley.*)

a and **c.** Relaxed muscle.

b and **d.** Contracted muscle. During muscle contraction the light I band narrows, then disappears, as actin filaments are drawn further and further between filaments of myosin.

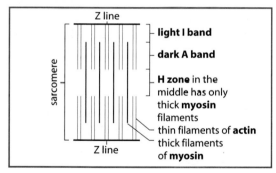

a

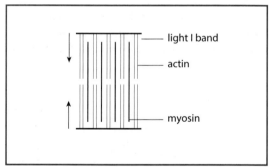

b

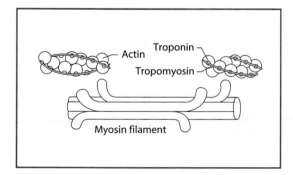

c

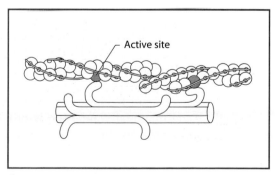

d

How do the two sets of filaments move between each other?

The key to the process of muscle contraction lies in the **overlapping** of the thick myosin and thin actin filaments, as seen in Figure 1.35. The thin actin filaments are made up of two chains of globular proteins, called tropomyosin and troponin, which are involved in the process of muscular contraction. Tropomyosin strands are wound about the thin actin filaments and troponin is attached to the tropomyosin at regular intervals. At rest troponin holds the tropomyosin in position to block the myosin-binding sites on actin filaments (Figure 1.35c).

When the nervous impulse reaches the muscle cell it initiates the release of calcium ions (Ca^{++}) from special storage 'T' vesicles in the sarcoplasmic reticulum. Troponin has a high affinity for calcium ions and, as the Ca^{++} bind to the troponin, the shape of the troponin–tropomyosin complex changes to expose the active sites on the actin filaments. The calcium ions stimulate the contraction of the muscle by exposing the active sites on the actin filaments.

At the same time the heads of the myosin filaments become activated by ATP which, when broken down into ADP and free phosphate (P_i), releases large amounts of energy. The myosin heads attach themselves to selected sites on nearby actin filaments to form **actin–myosin** bonds, usually called **cross bridges**. This process is illustrated in Figures 1.35d and 1.36. This is immediately followed by the detachment of the cross bridges and the reattachment of the myosin heads to the next actin sites and so on. The whole effect is to pull the actin filaments past the myosin filaments so that they form a bigger overlap (than in the resting state) and therefore shorten the sarcomere. The attachment, detachment and reattachment of cross bridges is called the **ratchet mechanism**.

With many thousands of thin filaments pulling past thick filaments in a single cell, and many thousands of muscle cells contracting in this way in the gastrocnemius and other voluntary muscles, skeletal muscle can quickly respond to the demands of ballistic activity, such as in a flat-out 100 m swim or sprint.

The strength of the muscular contraction is proportional to the number of cross bridges in harness, with the result that a muscle in a full state of contraction has a greater region within each cell of actin–myosin overlap, and hence a greater number of cross bridges in harness. There is no slippage within the cross bridges because of the non-aligned or offset attachments of the actin–myosin bonds (refer to Figure 1.36). When the calcium is reabsorbed and the nervous stimulation withdrawn, the troponin–tropomyosin system resumes the blocking of the cross-bridge connections—contraction stops and the muscle relaxes (refer to Figures 1.35a and 1.35c).

Types of muscular contraction

When the muscle fibre is held at a certain point of stretching simultaneous with the actin–myosin bonding occurring, the result will be an isometric contraction (although what happens in this sort of contraction is that different fibres alternate in contraction). When the muscle fibre is stretched outwards at the same time as the actin–myosin bonding, an eccentric contraction will occur. The contraction becomes concentric when the actin filaments slide in between the myosin filaments.

Energy used for muscular contraction is derived from glucose and free fatty acids, which are converted in the mitochondria into ATP that is then delivered to the contractile filaments.

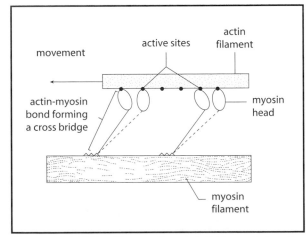

Figure 1.36 Sliding filament theory: actin–myosin bonds.

Review Questions

1. An understanding of the functional structure of muscle cells is an important basis for an understanding of physical activity. Discuss this statement.

2. List the proteins involved in muscular contraction and describe the role of each one.

3. Comment on the number and distribution of mitochondria with respect to muscle fibre types.

Summary

1. You should be able to describe the gross and microscopic structural detail of striated muscle cells.

2. You should be able to understand the mechanisms involved in striated muscle contraction.

3. You should be able to relate tension to types of exercise and muscular contraction.

Further Reading

Bastian G.F. *An Illustrated Review of Anatomy & Physiology: The Skeletal & Muscular Systems*, HarperCollins, 1993.

Bowers R.W. and Fox E.L. *Sports Physiology* 3e, Wm C. Brown, 1992.

Clegg C. *Exercise Physiology*, Feltham Press, 1995.

Prentice W. *Fitness for College and Life* 4e, Mosby–Year Book, 1994.

Seeley R.R., Stephens T.D., Tate P. *Anatomy and Physiology* 2e, Mosby–Year Book, 1992.

Wilmore J.H. *Physiology of Sport and Exercise*, Human Kinetics, 1994.

1.6 How Co-ordinated Movement is Produced

 ## Keywords & concepts

action potential	motor end-plate	repolarization
all-or-none law	motor neurone	saltatory conduction
central nervous system	motor neurone pool	sensory neurone
cerebellum	muscle spindle apparatus	spatial summation
depolarization	muscle twitch	synapse
Golgi tendon apparatus	peripheral nervous system	tetanic contraction
gradation of contraction	potassium/sodium pump	voluntary movement
hyperpolarization	reflexive movement	wave summation

Muscle can contract only when a nerve ending is stimulated by outgoing impulses from the **central nervous system** (CNS), which consists of the brain and spinal cord. The contractile system for muscles is organized into a number of distinct parts, each of which is controlled by a single **motor neurone** (Figure 1.37b), and each motor neurone controls a large number of muscle fibres. A group of fibres and its neurone is called a **motor unit** (Figure 1.37a).

A motor neurone (Figure 1.37b) begins as a cell body within the grey matter and its axon passes out of the ventral root of the spinal cord to innervate muscle cells. It consists of three major parts including a **cell body** containing the nucleus, mitochondria and other organelles, cellular extensions called **dendrites** and an **axon**. Dendrites are highly branched extensions

of the cytoplasm that project from the cell body within the grey matter of the spinal cord. Following sensory stimulation a relay neurone transmits neural impulses to the dendrites of the motor neurone; they are specialized to receive electrical impulses and conduct these towards the cell body. The **axon** arises from the thickened area of the cell body and emerges out of the ventral root of the spinal cord. Its function is to transmit neural impulses away from the cell body towards muscle tissue or a gland. The surrounding myelin sheath acts as an insulator to speed up the transmission of the impulse. A typical motor neurone divides into several branches as it reaches the muscle bed. These branches connect the motor neurone to the muscle fibres by specialized structures known as **motor end-plates** (Figure 1.37). Control by the brain is possible because of the ascending and descending fibres to the motor cortex.

The transmission of neural messages along a neurone is an electrochemical process. When a neurone is not conducting an impulse it has a **resting potential**

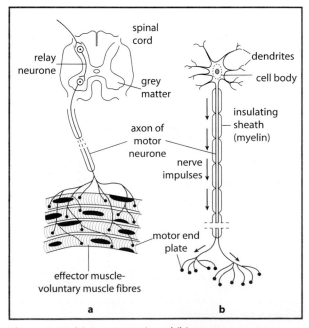

Figure 1.37 (a) A motor unit and (b) a motor neurone.

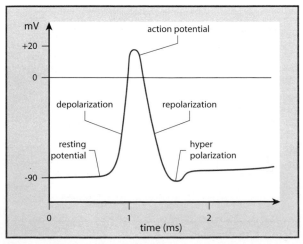

Figure 1.38 An action potential.

brought about by the outward diffusion of potassium ions (K^+) along a concentration gradient and a negatively charged inside cell membrane when compared with the outside of the cell membrane.

An **action potential** (Figure 1.38) occurs at the point along the axon where the neural impulse is being propagated. It is initiated when sufficient numbers of sodium ions (Na^+) are allowed to diffuse into the neurone. This **depolarizes** the axon to a critical threshold level. Action potentials occur in an **all-or-none** fashion. If an action potential occurs at all it is of the same magnitude and duration no matter how strong the stimulus.

Repolarization is the return of the membrane potential towards the resting membrane potential because of K^+ movement out of the cell and because Na^+ movement into the cell slows to resting levels. The after potential is a short period of **hyperpolarization**. The resting potential is restored by the sodium/potassium pump, which establishes ion concentrations to their resting values.

An action potential initiated in one part of the cell membrane stimulates action potentials in adjacent parts of the membrane and so on (Figure 1.39). The speed of propagation along neurones varies greatly from cell to cell. Neurones that have large diameter myelinated axons conduct action potentials faster than small diameter unmyelinated axons. A myelin sheath (see Figure 1.39) offers increased conduction velocity as a result of the action potential jumping from node to node. This process is called **saltatory conduction** and is less costly in terms of ion 'run down' since ion exchange occurs only at the Nodes of Ranvier.

Transmission of an impulse between sensory and relay, and relay and motor neurones occurs at specialized junctions called **synapses** (Figure 1.40). (Note that the motor end-plate described earlier works in a similar way to a synapse.) The wave of depolarization is unable to jump across the synaptic cleft; however, the problem is solved by the release of transmitter substances, such as acetylcholine, from the synaptic knobs. The transmitter substance diffuses across the synaptic cleft to bind with postsynaptic receptors. The sodium gates in the membrane open, allowing sodium to enter the axon and initiate the action potential. The electrical impulse can now pass directly from one cell to another. Once the action potential is completed, the enzyme cholinesterase breaks down the acetylcholine, thus clearing the gap in readiness for the arrival of the next impulse.

The electrical impulse travels down the spinal cord and motor neurone to the **effector muscle** (the active muscle) in the way described above. The function of the **motor end-plates** is to transfer the impulses from the small, branching motor neurones to large muscle fibres (in all directions). This is achieved when the nerve action potential is followed by a muscle action potential. There is a delay of 0.5 milliseconds (ms) due to the time needed for the release of acetylcholine from the synaptic knobs. An area of depolarization travels down the muscle cell, passing the entrances to the 'T' vesicles, which secrete Ca^{++} needed to initiate muscle contraction (see p. 38 for the subsequent reactions within the muscle cell). Each different fibre type is innervated by a different kind of motor neurone. When an electrical impulse reaches the muscle fibres of a **single motor unit**, the muscle cells contract simultaneously since they receive the same impulse from a single cell body of a motor neurone.

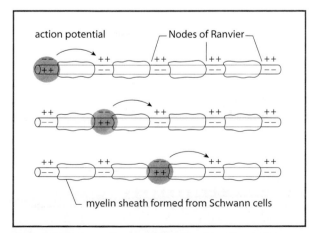

Figure 1.39 A myelin sheath. Conduction of an action potential.

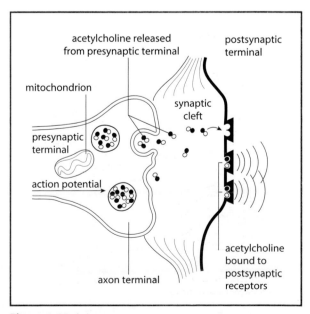

Figure 1.40 A synapse.

Each whole muscle consists of a large number of motor units. In muscles such as those in a leg or arm, there are about a thousand muscle fibres serviced by one motor unit; whereas, on smaller more sensitive muscles such as those in fingers, there are fewer fibres per motor unit. The nerve cell bodies of all motor units are, for a given muscle, bound together at an appropriate level in the spinal cord to give the nearest access point to that specific muscle, and leave as a concentrated bundle from the ventral root of the spinal cord. These concentrated bundles or patches are called **motor neurone pools**, and there is a motor neurone pool for each muscle in the body.

The nature of the stimuli received at the muscle bed will determine the type of muscular response.

Motor-neural firing patterns

A muscle twitch (see Figure 1.41)

Stimuli received by the motor neurone pools are transmitted to the different motor units, which do not necessarily work in unison. The strength of the stimulus must be sufficient to activate at least one motor unit to produce any contraction at all. Once activated, **all** the muscle fibres in that motor unit will contract maximally by giving a **muscle twitch** that lasts a fraction of a second. This is known as the ALL-OR-NONE LAW.

The contractile time of fast twitch fibres is much quicker than that in slow twitch fibres. Therefore, fast twitch fibres produce greater contractile forces sooner.

Region A of Figure 1.41 shows the approximate time scale for a single motor unit muscle twitch.

Wave summation

The strength of a muscle can be increased in another way. If a second impulse is received at the motor neurone pool very quickly after the first, there will not have been time for relaxation to be completed before the next contraction begins. Therefore, the total contraction is increased. This adding on of contractions to produce a stronger effect due to an increase in the rate of stimulation is known as **wave summation**. This is shown in region B of Figure 1.41: a stimulus (marked S on the graph) arrives **before** the motor unit has fully relaxed after the previous contraction.

Tetanic contraction

When impulses fire off so fast that there is no time for any relaxation at all, a state of absolute contraction is produced called **tetanic contraction**. Region C of Figure 1.41 shows this effect.

Gradation of contraction

Muscles can of course be contracted for longer than a fraction of a second. This is performed by a stronger stimulus activating many motor neurones in succession (different motor units will be involved, not necessarily the same ones in succession). This enables a muscle to exert forces of **graded** strengths, whose efforts range from fine, delicate, precision-controlled movements to strong, dynamic, powerful movements. This is called **gradation of contraction**.

Spatial summation (see Figure 1.42)

The term **spatial summation** refers to the fact that any given stimulus will cause motor units to be

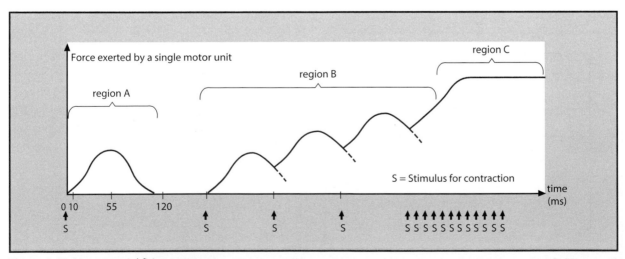

Figure 1.41 Motor-neural firing patterns.

successively activated **over the volume** of muscle, i.e. different motor units are involved throughout the muscle. The advantage of **different** muscle fibres being activated throughout a muscle is that ATP consumption (the energy-producing reaction) is shared throughout the muscle instead of being confined to single motor units, and therefore fatigue is spread throughout the muscle instead of being confined to small groups of fibres.

Spatial summation is shown in Figure 1.42 in which the effects of five **different** motor units add up to produce a **resultant** whole muscle contraction.

This slight **out of step** action of motor units is a very important factor in maintaining **sustained** contraction at any strength. If some motor units are contracting while others are relaxing, and if this is **staggered** throughout the muscle, quite long periods of sustained contraction can be achieved, depending on the load being moved, or, in the case of **isometric contraction**, the tension being produced. All muscular action has to develop sufficient isometric tension in order to apply sufficient force to begin movement.

All the above ways of varying the strength of contraction depend on the size of stimulus, and normally they are used together to produce co-ordinated movement patterns that may vary from finely graded strengths to maximal contractions.

In addition to the action of motor units, co-ordinated movements are adjusted by **sensory feedback**. Within physical performance, the sportsperson is aware of pressure, pain, joint angles, muscle tension and speed of actions as a result of specialized proprioceptors such as **Golgi tendons** and **muscle spindles**. The Golgi tendon apparatus provides proprioceptive information associated with tendon movement. The muscle spindle apparatus detects and monitors muscle activity (Figure 1.43). When muscle fibres contract, ends of the muscle spindle come closer together, stimulating the sensory or afferent nerves, which relay electrical impulses to the spindle cord. Motor or efferent nerves then relay electrical impulses to the muscle bed, followed by an adjustment in the state of muscle tension required for the execution of the physical task. This involuntary stretch reflex provides information such as state of muscle tension, length, position and rate of change of muscle length. Muscle spindles are important in the control and tone of postural muscles. Information from such proprioceptors is used as a basis for **decision making**. This sensory aspect of physical activity is included in the area 'The Performer as a Person', and provides the initial source of information that enables the muscle system to operate **stretch reflexes**.

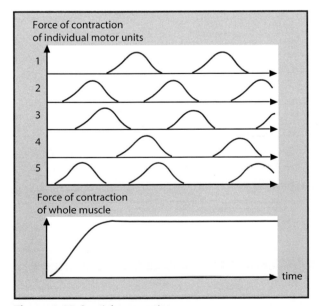

Figure 1.42 Spatial summation.

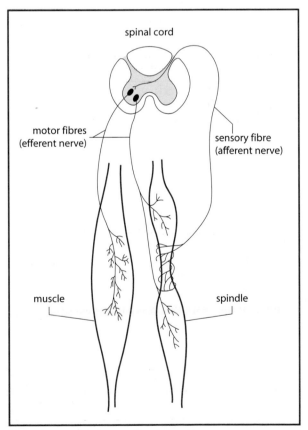

Figure 1.43 Muscle spindle apparatus.

The role of reflexes in co-ordinated movement

Reflexes play an important role in all forms of movement. The two types of reflex that originate from the CNS are:

a. **Voluntary reflexes**: where impulses originate in the voluntary motor cortex.

b. **Involuntary reflexes**: which originate from the stimulation of sense organs, which produce electrical impulses in sensory neurones.

The **reflex arc** is the pathway along which unlearned and automatic learned responses travel.

How reflexes work

Figure 1.44 shows the unlearned reflex of the knee jerk reflex.

The hammer strikes the knee, and the impulse travels up the sensory neurone into the spinal cord to the motor neurone, which transmits the impulse to motor units of quadriceps femoris, stimulating it to contract, thus causing the lower leg to jerk outwards. This is a monosynaptic reflex because a chain of only two neurones (one synapse) is necessary.

Modification of movements

The self regulation of rhythmical movements between one muscle group and its antagonist is called **reciprocal innervation**. This concept explains how the flow of sensory information (from the muscle to the spinal cord) is linked by a relay neurone (within the grey matter of the spinal cord) to the motor neurone of the antagonistic muscle, to provide the necessary feedback for the continual adjustments of tension between muscle groups.

Modification of all muscular actions is under the control of the **cerebellum** of the brain. The cerebellum is rather like a final sorting section of a computer being fed continuously with information from all the sense organs, giving position of limbs, state of muscles (whether contracting or relaxing) and so on. It helps to create fine co-ordination and ensures that physical activity is carried out smoothly.

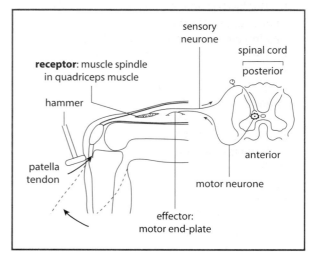

Figure 1.44 Mechanism of knee jerk reflex.

 # Investigation

1.18: The reflex arc

Task One

Work in pairs. One of you sits with legs crossed in a relaxed position. Your partner firmly taps your patella tendon using a patella hammer or ruler (the patella tendon is positioned just below the knee cap). Describe and record the response of the knee to the tap. How can you tell that this response was a reflex action?

Task Two

Give an example of a skill you have learned that has become an automatic response to a stimulus.

Task Three

Distinguish between automatic (reflex response) and fast reactions. Use examples from sporting situations to illustrate your answer.

Exam-Style Questions

1. Name the different regions of a motor neurone. (3 marks)

2. Figure 1.45 has been created from a slide of skeletal tissue as seen with a light microscope at a magnification of 800 times. It shows part of two motor units.

a. Use evidence from the drawing to suggest:

i. a meaning of the term 'motor unit', (2 marks)

ii. why all the muscle fibres shown will not necessarily contract at the same time. (3 marks)

b. Briefly describe the sequence of events at the muscle end-plate that leads to an action potential passing along the muscle fibre. (4 marks)

c. Describe some of the factors which determine muscle speed and tension characteristics. (4 marks)

d. Explain the role of motor units in controlling the strength of muscular contractions in sports movements. (10 marks)

3. Figure 1.46 shows the pathways of transmission of impulses through the central nervous system during the knee jerk reflex.

a. Give the names of the **five** structures lettered P–T on Figure 1.46. (3 marks)

b. With reference to the diagram, briefly describe the sequence of events in a knee jerk reflex. (3 marks)

c. Describe briefly the structure and function of a synapse. (3 marks)

d. Explain the difference between this reflex action and a similar movement carried out under voluntary control. (4 marks)

e. A sports commentator might say a games player, when referring to a good interception made by him or her, has **lightning reflexes**. Discuss whether or not **reflex** is the correct term for such an interception. (7 marks)

4. The trace in Figure 1.47 shows an intracellular recording of the potential within a nerve cell and the changes resulting from its excitation by other nerves which synapse with it.

a. Explain the following terms:

i. resting membrane potential, (2 marks)

ii. action potential. (2 marks)

b. Explain why, individually, the excitatory impulses did not generate an action potential, but collectively they did. (3 marks)

c. Explain briefly how the myelin sheath influences the speed of contraction of a nerve impulse. (3 marks)

d. Explain why the release of a transmitter substance, such as acetylcholine, into a neuromuscular junction does not stimulate the muscle to go into prolonged contraction. (3 marks)

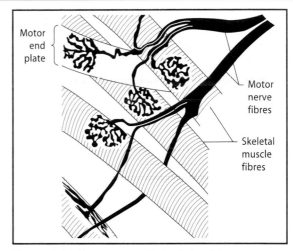

Figure 1.45 Two motor units in skeletal tissue.

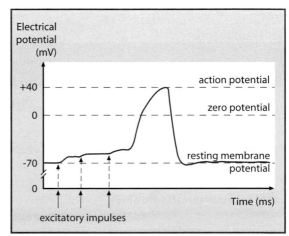

Figure 1.46 Knee jerk reflex.

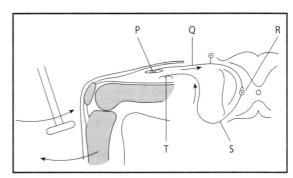

Figure 1.47 Electrical potential across the membrane of a motor neurone during the propagation of a nerve impulse.

or **serous membrane** containing a thin film of fluid, the pericardial fluid (serum is a watery liquid, which consists of plasma minus fibrinogen—a blood protein used in the clotting mechanism). The function of the pericardium is to reduce friction (with the other contents of the thoracic cavity and the cavity wall itself) and maintain heart shape.

b) The **myocardium** (Figure 2.1) or **cardiac striped muscle tissue** forms the largest part of the heart wall. Cardiac muscle contracts in the same way as skeletal muscle. Each cell, with one nucleus positioned towards the cell centre, branches to unite with other cells. It is separated from adjacent cells by an **intercalated disc**, which offers very little resistance to the neural impulse. Therefore, the cardiac impulse

is transmitted throughout the myocardium. The whole effect is to create a united sheet of muscle.

The heart has a **pacemaker** (see Figure 2.2), which sends impulses throughout the myocardium and which is independent of the **central nervous system** (CNS) (since the heart generates its own impulses it is said to be **myogenic**). Because of its united structure, all cells forming the entire myocardium muscle sheet contract together, producing a heartbeat. This is an application of the ALL-OR-NONE LAW.

c) The **endocardium** is a smooth, glistening **inner serous membrane** consisting of flattened epithelium that lines the heart cavities. Its function is to prevent friction between the heart muscle and flowing blood.

 # Investigation

2.1: To examine the structure of the heart
Materials: Heart model, heart and circulatory posters, fresh hearts (pig or sheep), dissection materials.

The following tasks assume the availability of animal hearts for dissection. If none are available, then these can be substituted by the appropriate use of models and charts.

Task One—external features
1. Work out the ventral (the front surface) and dorsal (the rear surface) sides of the heart.
2. Identify the external features of the heart that are labelled in Figure 2.1b.
3. Observe and identify the narrow vessels branching over the surface of the ventricles. These blood vessels supply the heart with food and oxygen, and transport carbon dioxide and other waste products away from the heart.
4. What happens if one of the main arteries to the myocardium becomes blocked with fatty lesions or a blood clot?

Task Two—heart valves (Figure 2.1c and 2.1d)
1. Cut a small opening in the right atrium and look down into the atrioventricular opening (this opening is between the top and bottom chambers of the heart). Pour a small amount of water into the atrium and observe the action of the valve as the bottom chamber fills. Write down your observations.

2. Now squeeze the bottom chamber containing the water. Observe and identify the vessel from which the water emerges.
3. Repeat this task on the left side of the heart.
4. Identify the valves located between the top and bottom chambers on both sides of the heart.
5. How are these valves supported?
6. Identify the heart valves sited in the vessels leaving the bottom chambers.
7. What is the function of heart valves?

Task Three—heart muscle (Figure 2.1c–2.1f)
1. Cut off a small part of the apex of the heart. Observe the myocardial tissue and small openings to the ventricles. Observe the very thick section of the myocardial tissue and place a seeker into this small opening. The seeker should emerge out of the aorta. Now repeat this process on the right side of the heart. Which vessel does the seeker emerge from on this side?
2. Cut the heart open longitudinally into two equal halves. Observe that the heart is divided into a four-chambered muscular bag.
3. Identify and name the structure that separates the left and right sides.
4. Name the top and bottom chambers.
5. Describe how the top chambers differ in their shape and thickness when compared with the bottom chambers. Suggest reasons for the functional significance of these differences.
6. Observe the walls of both bottom chambers. What type of tissue are these walls made of?

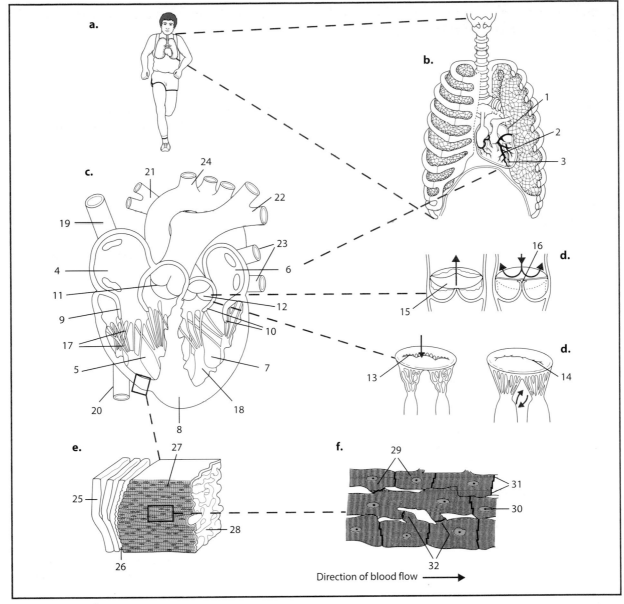

Figure 2.1 Cardiac anatomy.

a. Position of the heart within the body
b. Position of the heart within the thorax
c. Longitudinal section of the heart
d. Heart valves
e. Heart wall
f. Microscopic detail of myocardium

Atrioventricular valves:
9. Tricuspid valve
10. Mitral valve

Semi-lunar valves:
11. Pulmonary valve
12. Aortic valve
13. Mitral valve open
14. Mitral valve closed
15. Semi-lunar valve open
16. Semi-lunar valve closed by cusps
17. Chordae tendinae
18. Papillary muscle
19. Superior vena cava

1. Pericardium
2. Coronary artery
3. Coronary vein
4. Right atrium
5. Right ventricle
6. Left atrium
7. Left ventricle
8. Septum

20. Inferior vena cava
21. Right pulmonary artery
22. Left pulmonary artery
23. Left pulmonary veins
24. Aortic arch
25. Parietal pericardium
26. Visceral pericardium
27. Myocardium
28. Endocardium
29. Striations made up of myofibrils
30. Nucleus
31. Step-like intercalated discs
32. Connecting branches

Cardiac output ($\dot{Q}$) is defined as the volume of blood pumped by each ventricle in one minute. At rest this is approximately 5 litres per minute. During vigorous exercise cardiac output may increase up to 30 litres per minute.

The following formula links cardiac output to stroke volume and heart rate:

cardiac output = stroke volume × heart rate
or $\dot{Q}$ = SV × HR

For example, if a person has a stroke volume of 75 cm^3 and a heart rate of 70 beats per minute (bpm), the cardiac output would be:

$$\dot{Q} = 75 \times 70$$
$$= 5250 \text{ cm}^3$$
$$= 5.25 \text{ litres per minute.}$$

Starling's Law of the Heart

Cardiac output is dependent on the amount of venous blood returning to the right-hand side of the heart, otherwise known as **venous return**. During exercise, venous return increases and therefore cardiac output increases. This is caused by the myocardium being stretched, resulting in the myocardium contracting with greater force. Therefore, the stimulus that causes the greater force of contraction is the stretching of the muscle fibres themselves. This relationship is known as **Starling's Law of the Heart**. **Intrinsic factors** such as Starling's Law of the Heart, changes in electrolyte balance (sodium and potassium) in the heart muscle and increased myocardial temperature, result in changes in heart rate.

The pulse

The **pulse** is a peristaltic wave produced in an artery. It is due to the contraction of the left ventricle forcing out 70–90 cm^3 of blood (stroke volume) into an already full aorta. The frequency of waves represents the number of heartbeats per minute.

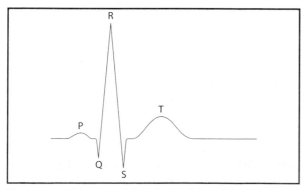

Figure 2.4 ECG trace of electrical activity of the heart.

Electrical activity of the heart

Heart rate can be measured by **palpation**, **heart rate telemetry**—or by using an **electrocardiogram (ECG)**. As the cardiac impulse travels across the atria and ventricular walls its electrical activity produces a recorded trace (ECG), as in Figure 2.4, which shows the three components of an ECG:

1. The **P** wave,
2. The **QRS** complex,
3. The **T** wave.

The **P** wave represents the excitation of both atria, known as atrial depolarization (this concept is explained on p. 40). It occurs when the electrical impulse travels from the SA node across the atrial walls to the AV node. The **QRS** complex of waves represents excitation of both ventricles, known as ventricular depolarization. It occurs when the electrical impulse travels from the AV node via the bundle of His to the Purkinje fibres (refer to Figure 2.2). The **T** wave indicates the repolarization of both ventricles as they relax. You can see from this diagram that the heart spends more time in its resting state than in the working phase. For further information, refer to a specialist physiology text, such as McKenna and Callender.

Heart rate taken during or immediately after exercise can be used to indicate cardio-respiratory or **aerobic fitness**.

Regulation of heart rate

The continual adjustment of heart rate is controlled by the **sympathetic** and **parasympathetic nervous systems**, as illustrated in Figure 2.5.

These two nervous systems originate in the **cardiac centre** in the **medulla oblongata** and they work antagonistically. The effect of exercise is to speed up heart rate, which is achieved by the sympathetic nerves transmitting impulses to the SA node and the release of **noradrenaline**, a transmitter substance produced by the adrenal medulla (glands situated at the top of each kidney) and released by the sympathetic neurones.

On the other hand, circulatory messages initiated by **baroreceptors** located in the aorta and carotid arteries, which respond to high blood pressure, are received by the cardiac centre, which responds by sending out impulses via the **vagus nerve** (parasympathetic nerves) to the SA node, and heart rate slows down. This is an example of **negative feedback control**, important in maintaining **homeostasis** within the body (a term described in Chapter 4 in the section looking at control of body temperature).

Other factors, such as elevated temperature, and hormones, such as adrenaline, increase heart rate. For example, just prior to a competitive situation, the hormone **adrenaline** (fright, fight and flight) is released,

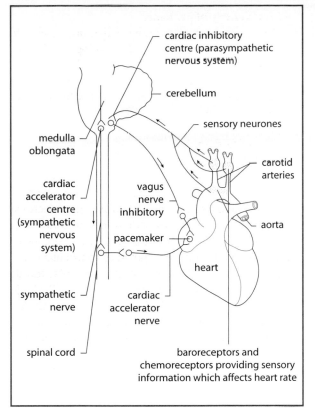

Figure 2.5 Nervous control of the heartbeat.

which prepares the body for action. Adrenaline is released by the adrenal medulla (sited above the kidneys) in response to stimulation by the sympathetic nervous system. This hormone targets itself on the heart, blood vessels, liver and fat cells. The release of adrenaline stimulates glycogenolysis (the process of breaking down glycogen to liberate glucose), intracellular metabolism of glucose in skeletal muscle cells and the breakdown of fats and proteins to form glucose.

The release of adrenaline results in a reduced blood flow and cellular activity to organs, such as the gut, skin and kidneys, that are not essential for physical activity and increases blood flow to those organs, such as skeletal muscle, lungs and cardiac muscle, that participate in physical activity (see Figure 2.21, p. 66). The effect of adrenaline lasts but a few minutes because it is rapidly metabolized, excreted or taken up by other tissues.

On the other hand, excessive potassium intake can slow down heart rate. In addition, gender and age also influence heart rate. It is found that females tend to have slightly higher heart rates than males and that heart rate generally slows down with age.

Ultimately, heart rate is dependent on a fine balance between the sympathetic and parasympathetic nerves, which continually adjust to changing conditions.

 # Investigation

2.2: Measuring heart rate
Materials: stop-watch or stop-clocks, heart and circulatory chart.
It is suggested that you work in mixed groups of five or six people.

Task One
1. Monitor your resting heart rate by palpation at the **carotid artery** and **radial artery** (the pulse can be located by pressing softly at the carotid artery, alongside the trachea in the neck, and across the wrist—the radial artery, when the arm is in a supine position). Count for 6 seconds, remembering that the count starts at zero. Then calculate your resting heart rate in beats per minute.
2. Repeat at each site using 10-second and 15-second counting periods. Do these counts in three positions:
a. sitting,
b. lying down,
c. standing.

Task Two
Collate your group results using a table like Table 2.1.

Task Three
1. Are there any differences between heart rate taken at the radial and carotid arteries? Suggest reasons for your answer.
2. Many factors affect resting heart rate. Consider the differences in heart rate within your group and give reasons for these differences.
3. How does body position affect resting heart rate? Suggest reasons for variation of resting heart rate in the sitting, lying and standing positions.
4. What is being measured when you measure heart rate?

[Allow two minutes' adjustment time (for each of these positions) prior to counting heart rate.]

Investigation

2.2 continued

	Table 2.1 : Results table—sitting					
	Heartbeats/min, Radial Artery			Heartbeats/min, Carotid Artery		
NAME	6	10	15	6	10	15
self						

Investigation

2.3: To listen to heart rate using a stethoscope
Materials: stethoscope.
1. Place the stethoscope upon the chest wall in the centre of the chest at the 5th intercostal space, as illustrated in Figure 2.6.
2. Describe what you can hear and which parts and actions of the heart are causing these sounds.

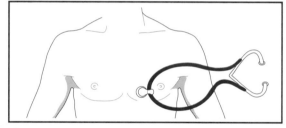

Figure 2.6 Listening to heart sounds using a stethoscope.

Investigation

2.4: To measure heart rate response to varying intensities of workload
Materials: select EITHER the step test OR cycle ergometer test described below for this investigation. Stop-watch or stop-clock. (Work in a mixed group so that you can compare your results.)

Task One
This investigation is best achieved with a heart rate monitor. If one is not available, work in pairs and get the passive partner to take and record heart rate values. Convert all 10 second counts to beats per minute (bpm).
1. Note your heart rate at the beginning of the lesson for a 10 second count.
2. Record your heart rate immediately before the exercise commences for a 10 second count.
3. Commence exercising by either riding the bike or stepping on and off a bench at a low intensity (HR 120–130 bpm) work rate, for a period of 3 minutes (for the cycle ergometer test this could be achieved without resistance, and in the case of the step test with the aid of a metronome, which establishes a low fixed rate of stepping).

Figure 2.7

Investigation

2.4 continued

4. Take heart rate values for a 10 second pulse count:
a. One minute after the start of the exercise.
b. Two minutes after the start of the exercise.
c. At the end of the 3 minutes of exercise.
d. Repeat the pulse count measurements every minute during the recovery phase until your heart rate has returned to its resting value prior to exercise.
5. Once your heart rate has returned to its resting value, repeat the same investigation but increase the workload (aim to achieve a heart rate of between 150 and 160 bpm). This can be achieved by increasing the frequency or resistance. (A weighted rucksack would be one way of increasing the resistance for the step test or, alternatively, one could increase the rate of stepping, which equates to an increase in the frequency of muscle contraction. Resistance or frequency could also be increased for the cycle ergometer investigation.)
6. Repeat this investigation once more at a workload just under maximal effort (in excess of 180 bpm), again by increasing the workload or frequency of exercise.

Task Two
1. Collate your results in table form (Table 2.2).
2. Convert heart rate values into beats per minute. Draw a graph of your own results, with time in minutes on the *x*-axis (from heart rate prior to exercise to full recovery period) and heart rate in beats per minute on the *y*-axis, for the three different workloads.

Table 2.2 : Results table—heart rate						
Intensity of workload	HR at start of class (bpm)	HR prior to exercise (bpm)	HR 1 min after start of exercise (bpm)	HR 2 min after start of exercise (bpm)	HR at end of exercise (3 min) (bpm)	HR during recovery (min) 1 2 3 4 etc. (bpm)
low						
medium						
high						

Task Three
1. Account for any differences between your heart rate counts at the start of the lesson and just prior to exercise.
2. Using your own results, describe the relationship between heart rate and low, medium and high intensity workloads.
3. Suggest physiological reasons for increased heart rate values as workload intensifies.
4. Suggest physiological reasons for the differing patterns of recovery from the stress of the exercise.
5. A low heart rate during exercise and a small increase in heart rate as the intensity of the work increases generally reflect a high level of cardiovascular fitness. Compare your own results with those of your group members.

Discuss your results in relation to gender, size, weight and levels of fitness.
6. Heart rate is increased and decreased as a result of the **sympathetic** and **parasympathetic nervous systems**, respectively. Using the information in the text, describe some of the factors that can influence heart rate.

Task Four
1. How reliable are the results of your investigation?
2. Does your investigation test what you set out to test?
3. Does your investigation produce a consistent pattern of results?
    The answers to these questions will outline the concepts of **reliability** and **validity** in scientific investigations.

Review Questions

1. Describe the relationship between stroke volume and submaximal and maximal exercise illustrated in Figure 2.8. Suggest reasons why maximal values for stroke volume are reached very early on in submaximal exercise.

2. Compare and suggest reasons for the trends shown in Figure 2.9, between cardiac output (bottom), stroke volume (top) and heart rate (middle) during rest, exercise and recovery.

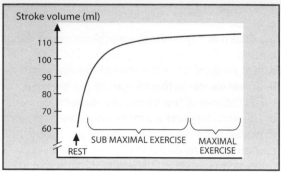

Figure 2.8 Stroke volume and exercise.

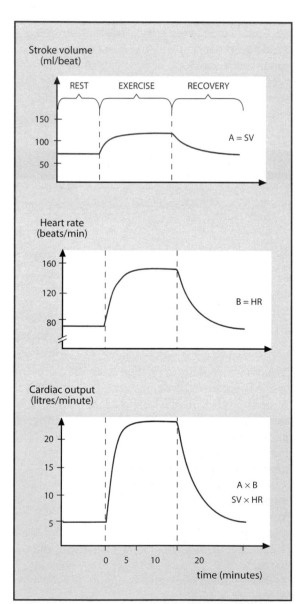

Figure 2.9 Stroke volume, heart rate and cardiac output during rest, exercise and recovery.

3. When you are running, contraction of skeletal muscles in the legs helps return of blood to the heart more rapidly. Would this effect increase or decrease stroke volume? Explain your answer.

4. Trained athletes often have resting heart rates of less than 60 bpm. This condition is known as '**bradycardia**' (*brady* meaning slow). Using the information in Figure 2.10, compare and contrast the hearts of a trained athlete and an untrained person.

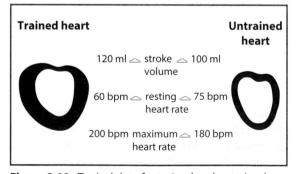

Figure 2.10. Typical data for trained and untrained hearts.

Exam-Style Questions

1. One cardiac cycle includes all the events that occur between two consecutive heartbeats, as illustrated in Figure 2.11:

a. i. Identify the **P** wave, **QRS** complex and **T** wave. (3 marks)

ii. What events in the cardiac cycle do each of the P, QRS and T represent? (3 marks)

b. Identify the cardiac phases labelled **a** and **b**. (2 marks)

c. Using the information in this diagram describe the relationship of an ECG to the cardiac cycle. (4 marks)

d. Indicate on Figure 2.11 the timing of the heart sounds 'lub-dub' in relation to the cardiac cycle. (2 marks)

2. Figure 2.12 shows a normal resting ECG (a) and an exercising ECG (b). Calculate the heart rates for both ECGs. (2 marks)

3. What events take place that allow the heart to contract and how is heart rate controlled? (8 marks)

4. Training induced changes of the heart may be considered as structural and functional. Discuss. (10 marks)

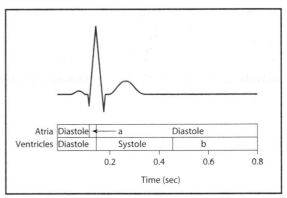

Figure 2.11 The relationship of the ECG to the cardiac cycle.

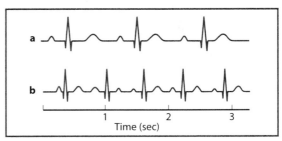

Figure 2.12 (a) Resting ECG and (b) excercise ECG.

Summary

1. You should be familiar with the functions of the coronary arteries and veins.

2. You should be able to identify and understand the structure of heart tissue in relation to its functioning.

3. You should understand the concepts of cardiac impulse, cardiac cycle, cardiac output, Starling's Law of the Heart and pulse, and be able to describe the events of the cardiac cycle.

4. You should understand that the heart is myogenic since it initiates its own electrical impulse.

5. You should be able to interpret an ECG trace of electrical activity of heart muscle.

6. You should understand that the changing rate of heartbeat is controlled by two sets of nerves: the sympathetic and parasympathetic nerves, and that factors such as hormones, temperature, venous return and electrolyte balance affect heart rate.

7. By using investigational methods, you should be able to describe the effects of changing the body position on resting heart rate.

8. You should be able to identify the factors that affect stroke volume, and understand heart rate response to varying workloads.

9. You should be able to interpret data on cardiac dynamics.

Further Reading

Bastian G.F. *An Illustrated Review—The Cardiovascular System*, HarperCollins, 1993.

Bowers R.W. and Fox E.L. *Sports Physiology* 3e, Wm C. Brown, 1992.

McKenna B.R. and Callender R. *Illustrated Physiology* 6e, Churchill Livingstone, 1996.

McArdle W.D., Katch F.I., Katch V.L. *Essentials of Exercise Physiology*, Lea & Febiger, 1994.

Seeley R.R., Stephens T.D., Tate P. *Anatomy and Physiology* 2e, Mosby—Year Book, 1992.

2.2 The Vascular System

Keywords & concepts

arteriole
artery
circulatory system
constituents of blood
corpuscles
plasma
platelets

pocket valves
precapillary sphincter
pulmonary circulatory system
red blood cells
smooth muscle
systemic circulatory system
vasomotor control

vein
venomotor tone
venule
white blood cells

The key role of the **vascular system**, which comprises **blood** and **circulatory vessels**, is **transportation**. The effect of athletic activity is to increase the demand from body cells for both nutrients from the digestive system and oxygen from the lungs, and to produce additional waste, which needs to be carried from body cells to the lungs and kidneys.

Blood is the specialized fluid tissue that carries out these functions within a closed system of vessels.

Blood

Blood is made up of 55% **plasma** and 45% **corpuscles**. In addition to the functions described above, it is involved in clotting, helps regulate body temperature and transports hormones such as adrenaline around the body.

Plasma is a straw-coloured fluid that contains approximately 90% water, 8% blood proteins, 1% salts, 0.5% food substances, 0.04% waste products, gases such as oxygen and carbon dioxide, enzymes, hormones, antibodies and antitoxins.

(You may wish to find out more about each of these constituents of blood. For example, the plasma and red blood cell proportions can be determined using a technique for measurement called a haematocrit; see Green, *An Introduction to Human Physiology*, p. 5.)

Investigation

2.5: To examine blood cells
Materials: slides of blood cells, microscopes.

Task One—structure and function of red blood cells
1. Using Figure 2.13, identify, draw and label a red blood cell.
2. What is unusual about the structure of a red blood cell? How does the structure affect its life span?
3. Name the red pigment in red blood cells. What is its function? Explain how this function is carried out.
4. Where are red cells formed and how many occur per mm³ of blood?
5. What effect does exercise have on the manufacture and destruction of red blood cells?

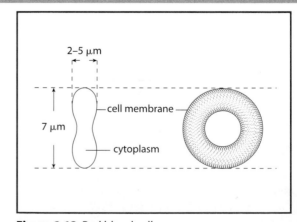

Figure 2.13 Red blood cell.

Investigation

2.5 continued

Task Two—structure and function of white blood cells

1. Using Figure 2.14, identify, draw and label two types of white blood cell—one granulocyte and one non-granulocyte—giving the percentage of each found in blood.

2. What are the functions of these two types of cells?

3. Where are white cells formed and how many occur per mm^3 of blood?

4. Of what relevance are white blood cells to the active sportsperson?

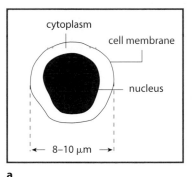

a

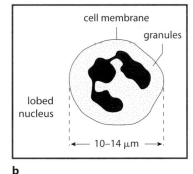

b

Figure 2.14a and b White blood cells.

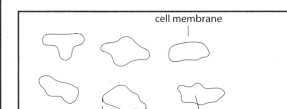

Task Three—structure and function of platelets

1. Using Figure 2.15, identify and draw a platelet.

2. Where are platelets formed?

3. What is their function, and how many occur per mm^3 of blood?

Figure 2.15 Platelets.

Blood circulation (see Figure 2.16)

As a result of the dual pumping action of the heart, there are about 5.5 litres (5.5 dm^3) of blood continually circulating throughout the body.

The closed system of vessels containing circulating blood flows within two major circulatory systems:

1. **Pulmonary circulatory system.**
2. **Systemic circulatory system.**

These two systems are illustrated on the diagrammatic plan of Figure 2.16b.

Investigation

2.6: To consider the two circulatory systems and the principal types of blood vessels

Materials: transverse section (TS) of blood vessels, microscopes, poster of the circulatory system.

Task One—blood circulation

1. Using Figure 2.16b, describe in your own words the course of blood from the time it enters the right atrium (then passes through the heart and the two circulatory systems) until it eventually returns to the right atrium again. Describe the changes in the composition of blood during this double circulation and name the heart chambers, organs and vessels the blood flows through.

2. The effect of exercise is to speed up heart rate. What effect will an increased heart rate have on blood circulation?

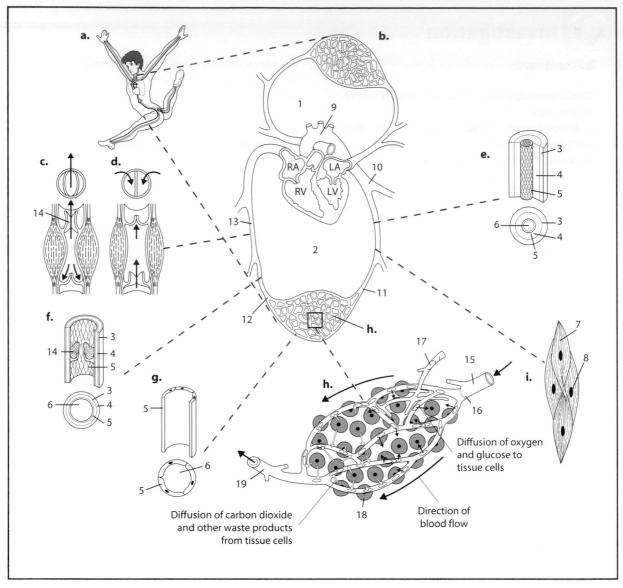

Figure 2.16 Blood circulation.

a. The human circulatory system
b. Diagrammatic plan of circulatory system
c. Skeletal muscle contracts: upper valve opened, lower valve closed
d. Skeletal muscle relaxes: upper valve closed, lower valve opened

e–g. Longitudinal and transverse section through:

e. artery
f. vein
g. capillary
h. Capillary bed for gaseous exchange
i. Involuntary or smooth muscle in walls of blood vessels

1. Pulmonary circulatory system
2. Systemic circulatory system
3. Tunica externa (fibrous collagen layer)
4. Tunica media (smooth muscle and elastic fibrous layer)
5. Tunica intima (endothelial layer)
6. Lumen
7. Smooth muscle (spindle-shaped)
8. Centrally positioned nucleus
9. Aortic arch (leading to aorta)
10. Artery

11. Arteriole
12. Venule
13. Vein
14. Pocket valve
15. Arteriole end of capillary bed (high pressure—oxygenated blood)
16. Precapillary sphincter
17. Lymph vessel
18. Tissue cell
19. Venule end of capillary bed (low pressure—deoxygenated blood)

Investigation

2.6 continued

Task Two—blood vessels
Blood vessels vary in thickness and structural composition of their walls, diameter and overall length, according to their specific function.
1. Using the information in Figure 2.16e–2.16g and prepared slides of blood vessels, identify an artery, a vein and a capillary network.

2. Observe the three layers of tissue that make up the walls of an artery and vein.
3. With the aid of diagrams, describe the structure of an artery, a vein and a capillary.
4. How is the structure of each of these three types of blood vessel suited to its specific function?

Arteries and veins

The walls of arteries and veins consist of smooth or involuntary muscle. Figure 2.16i illustrates the spindle-shaped muscle fibre structures, with each muscle fibre containing one centrally positioned nucleus. Unlike skeletal and cardiac muscles, smooth muscle fibres lack striations, hence the name 'smooth'. The function of smooth muscle in arteries and arterioles (see below) is to vary the diameter of these vessels, thereby controlling blood supply to a region in the body.

Arteries subdivide into arterioles

Arterioles have the same structure as arteries, but they are much narrower. In the **tunica media** region of the arteriole there is less elastic tissue, but there is a comparatively thick muscular coat. The function of arterioles is to control the inflow of blood to the **capillary bed**. This is achieved as a result of **vasomotor control** (described on p. 63) and the action of the precapillary sphincter, which is located at a point where the arteriole meets the capillary bed, as illustrated in Figure 2.16h.

Capillaries

Arterioles subdivide into **capillaries**, which are the smallest blood vessels in the body and which pass near to most muscle and other tissue cells.

The term **capillary bed** describes the total capillary structure within a muscle or other body organ. A capillary bed may contain thousands of **capillaries** for a given muscle; the number of capillaries passing

through a muscle can be increased by exercise, with the result that oxygen and other nutrients can be more efficiently carried to individual muscle cells.

Also, note that the large number of capillaries that eventually open out from the original artery have a much larger **total** cross-sectional area than the artery as a whole (see Figure 2.18). This means that blood slows down dramatically as it enters the capillary system and speeds up again as it leaves. This affects, and is affected by, the blood pressure in the venous and arterial systems, as explained below.

Capillary walls consist of a single layer of endothelium tissue (a simple tissue that lines all blood vessels), shown in Figure 2.16g. Their function is to be an exchange tissue, whereby dissolved materials diffuse in and out of the surrounding cells.

As blood passes through a muscle (or other) capillary system, it gradually gives up oxygen and nutrients and collects carbon dioxide and other waste products such as urea (as illustrated in Figure 2.16h). On leaving the capillary bed (the venous end of the capillary bed) the blood enters **venules** (refer to Figure 2.16b), which transport blood to the larger veins.

Veins

Veins have muscular coats that receive electrical stimulation. Alterations in the **venomotor tone** (explained on p. 64) produce changes in the capacity of circulation without affecting the veins' resistance to blood flow, since they are large diameter vessels.

With the exception of the **venae cavae**, all veins contain valves.

Investigation

2.7: Blood vessels

Task One—arterioles
Dilate means to widen and constrict means to narrow. Why is it physiologically important for an arteriole to dilate and constrict, and therefore allow blood to flow or prevent blood from flowing?

Task Two—capillaries
Using the information in Figure 2.16h, explain how capillaries act as exchange beds.

Task Three—veins
1. How do pocket valves operate? (Refer to Figures 2.16c and 2.16d.)
2. Why are veins situated between muscles?

Review Questions

1. Figure 2.17 shows a diagrammatic representation of blood flow for both pulmonary and systemic circulation. Copy this diagram and:
a. Label the pulmonary and systemic circulation.
b. Label the blood vessels leaving and entering the heart.
c. Use arrows to indicate the direction of blood flow within both systems.
d. Colour in the appropriate sections of each circulatory loop using blue for deoxygenated blood and red for oxygenated blood.
e. Suggest a reason why the human body needs a double circulatory system.
2. Describe two important mechanisms for returning blood back to the heart, while exercising in an upright position.
3. Construct a table that lists the different types of blood vessels and their structural and functional details.
4. In some ways heart muscle is similar to skeletal and smooth muscle. In other ways

these three types of tissue are different. Make a list of the similarities and differences between these three types of muscle tissue.

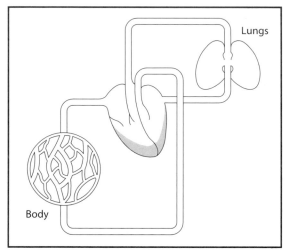

Figure 2.17 Blood flow.

Summary

1. You should be able to describe the characteristics of blood, and identify blood cells and their functions.
2. You should be able to identify the two major circulatory systems and the main blood vessels within them, and be able to trace the pathway of a blood cell through the heart and

the two circulatory systems.
3. You should to be able to compare and contrast the structure and function of arteries, veins, capillaries and venules.
4. You should to be able to compare and contrast the structure and function of cardiac, smooth and skeletal muscle.

Further Reading

Bastian G.F. *An Illustrated Review: The Cardiovascular System*, HarperCollins, 1993.
Green J.H. An Introduction to Human Physiology, Oxford Press, 1986.
McArdle W.D., Katch F.I., Katch V.L. *Essentials of Exercise Physiology*, Lea & Febiger, 1994.

McKenna B.R. and Callender B. *Illustrated Physiology* 6e, Churchill Livingstone, 1996.
Seeley R.R., Stephens T.D., Tate P. *Anatomy and Physiology* 2e, Mosby–Year Book, 1992.

2.3 Blood Flow in Muscles

Keywords & concepts

baroreceptors	peripheral resistance	vasoconstriction
blood flow	resistance	vasodilation
blood pressure	respiratory pump	vasomotor control
diastolic blood pressure	sphygmomanometer	venomotor control
lymph	systolic blood pressure	venous return mechanism
muscle pump	tissue fluid	

The rate at which blood circulates around the body depends on the needs of the body. During physical activity, working muscles may increase their oxygen consumption 20 fold when compared with the body's needs at rest. This section will help you to understand how and why the rate of blood flow changes as a result of physical activity.

The rate of blood flow depends on cardiac output and circulation ($\dot{Q} = SV \times HR$). Furthermore, any changes in cardiac output will result in changes in blood pressure.

BLOOD PRESSURE = BLOOD FLOW × RESISTANCE

The **resistance** to blood flow is produced by blood vessels **vasodilating** (or widening) and **vasoconstricting** (or narrowing) between working muscles. This is known as **peripheral resistance** caused by both **blood viscosity** (viscosity is a term that describes the resistance to flow of any fluid, in this case a steady flow of blood through the vessels) and the changing shape of arterioles. Arteries are elastic vessels with a narrower diameter **lumen** (or central space) than veins, where pressures remain high. However, it is in the arterioles that pressure can change by the dilation and constriction of their muscular walls and precapillary sphincters (the tiny rings of muscle

between arteriole and capillary vessels). This action is under the control of the **vasomotor** and **venomotor centres**.

Vasomotor and venomotor control

Both control centres are located in the medulla oblongata (in the brain) and are regulated by the sympathetic and parasympathetic nervous systems (refer to Figure 2.5).

Vasomotor control

At rest a fall in blood pressure reduces stimulation of the **baroreceptors** (Figure 2.5) in the aortic arch and carotid arteries. This reduction in stimulation is received in the vasomotor centre, which then acts by sending out nerve impulses (via the sympathetic nervous system) to the arterioles, causing them to vasoconstrict and hence increase the blood pressure and speed up the heart rate. Exercise increases blood pressure, which increases the stimulation of the baroreceptors. This increase in stimulation is received by the vasomotor centre, which then acts by reducing the sympathetic impulses along the vasomotor fibres that normally cause vasoconstriction. The net result is vasodilation of arterioles which lowers systemic vascular resistance and hence arterial blood pressure.

Venomotor control

Veins have a limited capacity to change their shape. This is the result of venomotor tone, whereby the vein's muscular coat receives stimulation from the sympathetic nervous system. The effect of limited vasoconstriction of veins causes a small increase in blood velocity and hence venous return.

Investigation

2.8: To consider blood pressure

Using the information in Figure 2.18 answer the following questions:

Task One

1. Suggest reasons why systolic and diastolic blood pressure drops as the blood travels away from the left ventricle.
2. How does peripheral resistance vary from the aorta to the venae cavae?
3. As blood flows through the capillaries, there is a negligible effect of the pulse on the blood flow. Compare the pressures in the arteries, capillaries and veins. Why is the pressure in veins so low?
4. The total cross-sectional area of the aorta is smaller than that of the arteries which branch from it; the cross-sectional area of the arterioles is greater than that of the arteries; the total cross-sectional area of the capillaries is greater than that of the arterioles.
   a. What will be the effect on blood flow as it travels from the aorta to arteries to arterioles to capillaries?
   b. Describe the changes in cross-sectional area from the capillaries to the venae cavae and the effect of these changes on blood flow.
5. What would be the effect of exercise on:
   a. rate of flow of blood within the systemic circulatory system?
   b. blood pressure?

Task Two

Blood pressure rises and falls in relation to the cardiac cycle. Sketch a graph of the relationship of blood pressure (*y*-axis) to points of time on the cardiac cycle (*x*-axis).

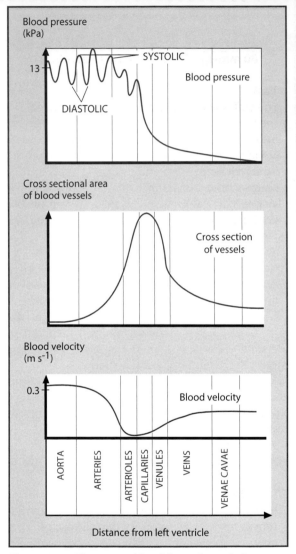

Figure 2.18 Changes as blood flows through the systemic system.

Investigation

2.9: To record blood pressure at rest

Materials: blood pressure meter (**sphygmomanometer**). (Blood pressure meters supplied by companies such as Griffin and George give digitalized values.)

A **sphygmomanometer** is used to record blood pressure. The recording is written as:

$$\frac{120 \text{ mmHg}}{80 \text{ mmHg}} \quad \text{or} \quad \frac{15.8 \text{ kPa}}{10.5 \text{ kPa}} \quad \begin{array}{l}\text{(systolic BP)} \\ \text{(diastolic BP)}\end{array}$$

Figure 2.19 Blood pressure cut off on arm.

Task One

The cuff is wrapped around the arm to cover the brachial artery (upper arm). Air is pumped into the cuff to **no more** than 180 mmHg (24 kPa), by which pressure the cuff will feel tight around the arm and will compress the brachial artery so that no pulse is recorded. The air pressure inside the cuff is gradually released until the blood is felt spurting into the artery. The pressure (systolic) is now read, and more air is released until the artery is completely open when the pressure is read again (diastolic). Both these values will be displayed on your monitor, in addition to pulse count.

The top line recorded represents the **systolic blood pressure**, which is the maximum pressure produced by the left ventricle during systole. The bottom line is the **diastolic blood pressure** or pressure in the artery at the end of diastole.

- *It is important that you follow your teacher's instructions carefully when using the blood pressure meter.*

Task Two

1. Measure and record your own blood pressure.
2. Compare and account for differing blood pressures within your class members.

Investigation

2.10: The effects of exercise on blood pressure, heart rate and blood flow

Materials: equipment for selected activity, blood pressure and pulse meter, graph paper, strip thermometer (a liquid crystal thermometer).

Task One

1. Work in mixed groups and select a demanding physical activity that all your group can manage. You may wish to choose a static and/or dynamic type of exercise. Make sure that you warm up prior to exercising.

2. Record your heart rate (HR), blood pressure (BP) and skin temperature (ST) prior to exercise.

3. Exercise flat out for a one minute period, then retake your blood pressure, heart rate and skin temperature immediately after completion of the exercise.

Figure 2.20

Investigation

2.10 continued

Task Two
Record your results in Table 2.3.

Table 2.3 : Results table	
SELECTED EXERCISE _____	
Prior to exercise	**At the end of exercise**
HR	
BP	
ST	

Task Four
The chart in Figure 2.21 shows how the percentage distribution of blood flow between different body systems changes when exercise is taken. Note that in the example the **total** blood flow is increased by **five times** during exercise compared to blood flow when a sportsperson is resting. This means that the heart muscle, for example, takes 5% of 5 litres per minute at rest (i.e. 0.25 litres per minute), whereas it takes 4% of 25 litres per minute during exercise (i.e. 1 litre per minute), an increase of four times the actual blood flow to the heart. **Total** blood flow will depend on the intensity of exercise; it is possible to increase blood flow by up to ten times the resting value. (The estimated blood flow to fatty tissue, up to 10% at rest and about 1% during exercise, is not included in the graph.)
1. Using the information in Figure 2.21, describe the proportion of total blood flow going to different organs or body systems during rest and during exercise.
2. Suggest physiological reasons that explain how blood flow is redistributed.

Task Five
The effect of exercise on the heart muscle is to increase blood flow to the myocardium by up to five times the resting value. Explain possible reasons for this increase.

Task Three—analysis of results
1. Plot your results on graph paper using the same x-axis for direct comparison.
Graph A: Arterial BP (mmHg) (y-axis) against time (min) (x-axis).
Graph B: Heart rate (bpm) (y-axis) against time (min) (x-axis).
Graph C: Skin temperature (°C) (y-axis) against time (min) (x-axis).
2. Compare the relationships between blood pressure, heart rate and skin temperature.
3. What is the effect of dynamic and/or static exercise on systolic and diastolic blood pressure?
4. A small increase in skin temperature indicates that there has been a shift of blood flow to the skin. Where has the blood come from and why does this happen?
5. Which part of the brain is responsible for detecting blood temperature?

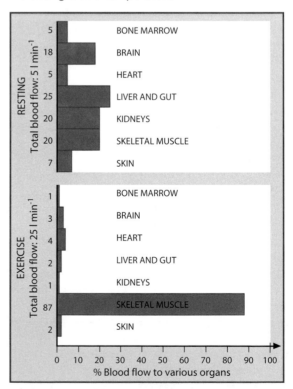

Figure 2.21 Change in percentage distribution of blood flow to various organs when exercise is taken.

Investigation

2.10 continued

Task Six
1. During exercise the heat generated by active muscles must be dissipated. Describe the method by which the body loses heat.
2. Describe how the body may gain heat.
3. What is meant by the term heat balance?
4. How does the body minimize excessive heat loss during cold exposure?
5. What factors should be considered to provide maximum protection when exercising in the cold?
6. The body's ability to lose heat generated during exercise depends on the formation and evaporation of sweat. Water loss is accelerated during exercise. Total water loss from the body at rest in a cool environment has been estimated at approximately 95.9 ml h^{-1}, whereas during prolonged exercise it has been shown to increase to values around 1325 ml h^{-1}. Identify the ways in which the body loses water and describe how most of the water loss is excreted.
7. What factors will affect the amount of sweat produced?
8. What effect does dehydration have on exercise heart rate and body temperature? How else does dehydration affect performance?
9. Electrolyte loss (such as sodium and chloride) during exercise occurs primarily along with water loss from sweating. How would you regulate salt and water replacement as a consequence of exercising in the heat? Identify some of the obvious benefits.
10. List the 'drinking guidelines' for athletes.

The venous return mechanism

The volume of blood leaving the heart depends directly upon the pumping action of the heart. This also results in an increase in blood flow in the veins (see Figure 2.16c and 2.16d), known **as the venous return mechanism**.

At any one time veins contain three-fifths of circulating blood. This volume is significant, since venous return must be in excess of the rest of the circulating blood. Veins offer little **resistance** to blood flow and they can alter their shape as a result of venomotor control. Venoconstriction increases venous return by reducing the volume capacity of veins to store blood. This means that more blood is moved back towards the heart.

During exercise, skeletal muscle contracts and relaxes, thus squeezing sections of veins and thereby increasing venous return (see Figure 2.16c and 2.16d). This phenomenon is called the **muscle pump**. During inhalation the pressure in the thoracic cavity is reduced, whilst the abdominal cavity pressure and pressure in other parts of the body is higher than the thoracic cavity pressure. Hence blood flowing towards the thoracic cavity will experience a force in the general direction of the heart. This phenomenon is called the **respiratory pump**. Stroke volume increases until it levels off prior to maximal effort being achieved.

Blood pressure and blood flow in the pulmonary circulatory system

Venous blood leaves the right ventricle and enters the pulmonary artery at a rate of about 5 litres per minute. The pulmonary blood vessels offer little resistance to blood flow (since they contain much less smooth muscle than systemic arteries, there is less energy stored in them during systole). The whole effect is to reduce peripheral resistance to blood flow.

Once the blood reaches the vast surface area of the pulmonary capillaries, it picks up oxygen by **gaseous exchange** from the alveoli. Then venules and veins stretch to accommodate the oxygenated blood and decreased blood flow as it travels to the left atrium of the heart.

Tissue fluid formation and drainage during exercise

At the arteriole end of the capillary bed, high blood pressure forces fluid (containing oxygen and glucose) through the capillary wall (Figure 2.22). This fluid permeates the spaces between the cells of all living tissues to become tissue fluid. Tissue cells extract the oxygen and glucose needed for tissue respiration; they excrete waste material, such as carbon dioxide and urea, at the venous end of the capillary bed, where blood pressure is low and where most of the tissue fluid returns into the capillary vessels.

Excess tissue fluid enters the surrounding lymph vessels and eventually returns to the blood via the lymphatic system. From this account it is clear that the lymphatic system plays a crucial role in maintaining the appropriate fluid levels in tissues, as well as maintaining blood volume itself.

One of the effects of exercise is to increase systolic blood pressure and hence to increase the formation of tissue fluid so that more nutrients are made available for tissue cell respiration. During exercise, lymph is returned to the blood more quickly due to the combined action of the muscle and respiratory pumps. These pumps contract and compress more forcibly on lymph vessels, thereby speeding up lymph flow.

Lymph nodes

The lymphatic system is not a major area of concern in the study of exercise physiology. However, while being a small part of the lymphatic structure as a whole, the tissues known as lymph nodes are relevant to our work. As lymph is transported, it passes through clusters of cells called lymph nodes (spread in groups throughout the lymphatic system), which contain cells that filter out and destroy debris such as damaged cells. Lymph nodes also contain lymphocytes that are part of the body's defence system. (You may wish to extend this area of study by referring to a specialist human biology text, such as Seeley *et al.*, *Anatomy and Physiology*.)

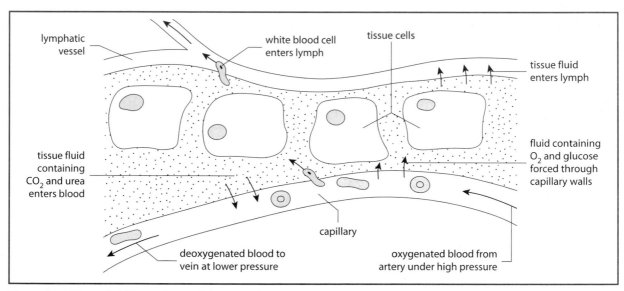

Figure 2.22 Tissue fluid formation and drainage during exercise.

 # Exam-Style Questions

1. What is the specialized structure in veins that prevents excessive distension and backflow of blood? (1 mark)

2. What effect will an increase in stroke volume have on venous return? (2 marks)

3. Why is it important that pressure and flow are low in the pulmonary circulatory system when compared with the systemic circulatory system? (4 marks)

4. Explain how arterioles affect blood pressure. (3 marks)

5. **a.** How does venous blood manage to return to the heart, despite the fact that it is travelling against gravity? (3 marks)

b. Describe two factors that affect flow of blood through the veins and back to the heart. (4 marks)

6. Explain which is more important in determining arterial blood pressure during rhythmical exercise: changes in vascular resistance or changes in cardiac output? (3 marks)

Exam-Style Questions

continued

7. What factors are involved in the maintenance of blood pressure? Explain what they do. (6 marks)

8. Figure 2.23 shows the variations in pressure and velocity of blood as it passes through the circulatory system while the body is at rest.

a. What types of blood vessels are represented by **A**, **B**, **C**, **D** and **E**? (3 marks)

b. Explain the variations in velocity and pressure in vessel type **A**. (5 marks)

c. Why is the velocity of the blood low in vessel type **C**? (2 marks)

d. What is the physiological significance of this? (5 marks)

e. What changes in Figure 2.23 would you expect during some form of rhythmic exercise? Explain your answer. (5 marks)

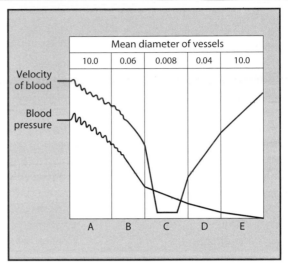

Figure 2.23 Variations in pressure and velocity of blood in the circulatory system. (*After Best and Taylor, 1964.*)

 Summary

1. You should be able to define blood pressure and describe the relationship between blood flow and peripheral resistance.

2. You should understand what is meant by vasomotor and venomotor control.

3. You should be able to compare blood pressure in different blood vessels and describe the effects of exercise on blood pressure and blood flow.

4. You should understand what is meant by the venous return mechanism, and the phenomena 'muscle pump' and 'respiratory pump'.

5. You should be able to explain the significance of a lower blood pressure in the pulmonary circulatory system when compared with the blood pressure in the systemic circulatory system.

6. You should be able to describe how tissue fluid is formed and drained away and explain the changes in flow that occur during exercise.

7. You should be able to explain how body temperature, water and electrolyte balance are regulated during exercise.

8. You should have a basic understanding of the importance of lymph glands in the defence of the body against infection.

 Further Reading

Bastian G.F. *An Illustrated Review: The Cardiovascular System*, HarperCollins, 1993.

Fox E.L., Bowers R.W., Foss M.L. *The Physiological Basis for Exercise and Sport* 6e, Wm C. Brown, 1997.

McArdle W.D., Katch F.I., Katch V.L. *Essentials of Exercise Physiology*, Lea & Febiger, 1994.

Seeley R.R., Stephens T.D., Tate P. *Anatomy and Physiology* 2e, Mosby–Year Book, 1992.

2.4 Respiratory Factors in Physical Performance

 Keywords & concepts

alveolar ducts	glottis	pleural cavity
alveoli	Hering–Breuer reflex	pleural fluid
baroreceptors	inspiration	pneumotaxic centre
blood acidity	intercostal nerves	proprioceptors
breathing	larynx	pulmonary pleura
bronchi	medulla oblongata	pulmonary ventilation
bronchioles	muscles used in expiration	respiratory bronchioles
carotid arteries	muscles used in inspiration	respiratory centre
chemoreceptors	nasal cavity	tissue respiration
epiglottis	parietal membrane	trachea
expiration	pharynx	vasomotor centre
gaseous exchange	phrenic nerves	visceral membrane

Running fast and breathing rapidly go hand in hand. As with the increase in heart rate, there is a corresponding increase in rate and depth of breathing. This is brought about by the actions of the **breathing system**, which is the mechanism whereby the gases, oxygen and carbon dioxide are exchanged between the atmosphere and the blood vessels in the lungs during **gaseous exchange**.

This section will help you to understand the structure of the breathing system, the mechanics involved and the ventilatory responses to exercise.

Tissue respiration is the process by which cells use oxygen in order to release energy.

Pulmonary ventilation is the process of supplying fresh air to the **alveoli**, which make up the lung tissue.

The structure of the lungs

Figure 2.24b illustrates the anatomy of the breathing system. Each lung is covered by serous membranes called **pulmonary pleura**. They are arranged like a double skin bag in which the outer membrane, called the **parietal membrane**, lines the chest cavity and the inner membrane, called the **visceral membrane**, lines each lung. In between the two membranes is the **pleural cavity**, which contains **pleural fluid**. The function of this lubricating fluid is to reduce friction between the two membranes during the dynamics of **breathing**. The pressure of this fluid is lower than the atmospheric pressure of air in the lungs. Atmospheric air pressure forces the pleural membranes against the inside of the thoracic cavity when it expands during inspiration

(breathing in), thus causing the lungs to move with the chest during the breathing action.

The route by which air reaches our lungs

Air enters the breathing system through the nose (consisting of two nostrils and a nasal cavity) and mouth. The nose is lined with a dense blood-capillary network and a ciliated mucous membrane. The air is warmed, filtered and moistened by this lining.

Incoming air proceeds into the **pharynx** (which is involved in both respiratory and digestive systems). The incoming air is warmed and moistened as it passes through the pharynx.

Next, the air passes through the **larynx** (the voice box situated at the top of the trachea), where it is further warmed, filtered and moistened. The larynx contains a semi-cartilaginous flap called the **epiglottis** which, when closed over the **glottis**, prevents food from entering the **trachea** (breathing stops when food is swallowed). The trachea is a single airway that extends from the larynx to the two dividing bronchi.

Air then passes down the trachea which, approximately level with the fifth thoracic vertebra, divides into two short branching **bronchi** (one bronchus going to each lung). The bronchi further subdivide into smaller branches called **bronchioles**. The **epithelium** (a general term used to describe the type of tissue lining inner body cavities), which lines the trachea, bronchi and bronchioles, contains goblet mucus cells and cilia (Figure 2.24c). Cilia carry the mucus, with trapped dust and pathogens, to the back of the throat where it is swallowed.

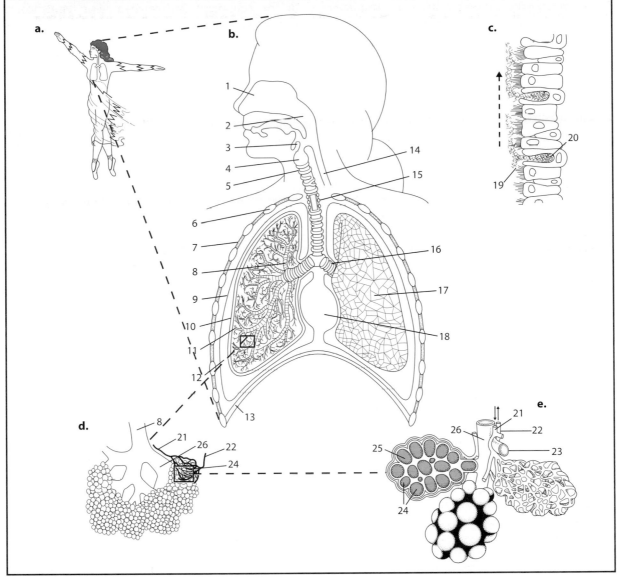

Figure 2.24 The anatomy of the breathing system.

a. The human breathing system
b. Section of head and thorax: left lung, surface view; right lung, section
c. Epithelial lining of cilia and goblet cells (found in structures 1, 2, 4, 8, 15 and 16)
d. Respiratory bronchioles leading to alveoli
e. Alveoli

- - - - - - - - - - - - - ▶
Flow of mucus and trapped pathogens and dust

━━━━━━━━━━━▶
Direction of blood flow

1. Nasal cavity
2. Pharynx
3. Epiglottis
4. Larynx
5. Incomplete ring of cartilage
6. Rib
7. Intercostal muscle
8. Bronchiole
9. Parietal membrane
10. Visceral membrane
11. Right lung
12. Pleural cavity containing pleural fluid
13. Diaphragm
14. Oesophagus

15. Trachea, section
16. Bronchus
17. Left lung
18. Position of heart
19. Cilia
20. Globlet mucus cell
21. Branch of pulmonary artery (poor in O_2)
22. Branch of pulmonary vein (rich in O_2)
23. Alveolar duct
24. Alveoli surrounded by capillary network
25. Alveolus , section
26. Respiratory bronchiole

The bronchioles further subdivide into **respiratory bronchioles**, which lead to **alveolar ducts**. Finally, the incoming air reaches millions of thin-walled air sacs, or **alveoli**, inside the lungs. **Gaseous exchange** takes place between the surface of the alveoli and the pulmonary capillaries, which are separated only by the single walls of both systems. The surface area of the delicate alveoli membrane is estimated at over 50 m^2

or the equivalent surface area of a tennis court (Figure 2.24d and e).

The alveoli contain **macrophage cells**, which are involved in the lung's defence mechanism. These cells engulf pathogens and transport them to the bronchioles. The pathogens are subsequently dealt with by the cleaning mechanism of the lungs, as described above.

Investigation

2.11: To understand the structure and functioning of the respiratory organs

Task One—to examine the structure of the trachea
Materials: transverse section (TS) slide of a trachea.
1. The trachea has walls supported by curved hoops (incomplete rings of cartilage). Feel the cartilaginous rings through the skin of your own neck just below the larynx. What is the function of these rings of cartilage?
2. Why are these rings of cartilage incomplete?
3. Make a drawing that shows the TS of the trachea. Indicate on it where you think the oesophagus is positioned.

Task Two—to examine the structure of animal lungs
Materials: lung model, fresh animal lungs, rubber tubing and disinfectant, suitable charts and diagrams.
(The following task assumes the availability of fresh animal lungs—if they are not available, charts or models should be substituted.)
1. How many lobes has each lung?
2. Press the lung tissue with your fingers. Describe what it feels like.
3. Identify the larynx, trachea and bronchi.
4. Using a piece of tubing, fill the lungs with

water from the tap. Alternatively, use an electrical air pump. Describe what happens to the lungs and explain your observations.
5. Empty out the water, then cut through a small section of lung tissue below one of the bronchi. Identify the smaller branching bronchioles, arterioles and venules.

Task Three—to examine the structure of alveoli
Materials: TS slide of lung tissue, microscope.
1. Examine the prepared slide of a section of lung tissue.
2. Describe the structure of an alveolus. Figure 2.24e may assist you to observe some of the structures.
3. Why does the connective tissue below the epithelium lining the alveolus contain elastic tissue?
4. There are approximately three million alveoli in a pair of human lungs, varying in diameter between 70 and 300 microns (μm—a millionth of a metre or 10^{-6} m). Why is it important to have such a vast surface area of alveoli?
5. The alveoli are surrounded by an extensive vascular (blood) capillary network (shown in Figure 2.24e). Why is this necessary?
6. What effect does physical activity have upon size, structure and functioning of the alveoli?

Review Questions

1. Beginning with atmospheric air entering the nasal cavities, trace the pathway of an oxygen molecule until it reaches an alveolar duct, and identify all the respiratory structures it passes on the way.

2. Using the information in Figure 2.24 and the text above, work through the pathway of outgoing air.
3. How would breathing cold air affect the capability to perform exercise?

The mechanics of breathing

The actual mechanism of breathing is brought about as a result of the changes in air pressure (intrapulmonary pressure) in the lungs, relative to atmospheric air pressure. The latter changes are in turn brought about by the muscular action of the **intercostal** muscles and **diaphragm**.

The respiratory muscles

The intercostal muscles (Figure 2.25)

The 11 pairs of intercostal muscles (which are arranged in two layers) occupy the spaces between the 12 pairs of ribs. The layers nearest to the lungs are called the **internal intercostal muscle fibres**. These fibres extend in a downwards and backwards direction from the lower margin of the rib above to the upper margin of the rib below, with the upper attachment being nearer to the sternum. The **external intercostal muscle fibres** lie on top of the internal intercostal muscles and extend in a downwards and forwards direction, with the lower attachment nearer to the sternum, in opposition to the internal intercostal muscles.

The first rib is a fixed rib and so when the **external** intercostal muscles contract, the other ribs are pulled towards this fixed rib, which results in an upwards and outwards movement of the thoracic cage during the process of **breathing in**. During quiet breathing the internal intercostal muscles remain passive.

The intercostal nerves, which originate from the **medulla oblongata**, located in the brain, stimulate the intercostal muscles.

The diaphragm (Figure 2.26)

The diaphragm is a dome-shaped sheet of muscle forming the floor of the thoracic cavity. It is attached to the vertebral column, lower ribs and sternum and radiates from a central tendon. It separates the thoracic cavity from the abdominal cavity, and it is innovated by the phrenic nerves, whose nerve impulses originate from the medulla oblongata.

When the diaphragm contracts, its muscle fibres shorten and the central tendon is pulled downwards. The effect is to increase the depth of the thoracic cavity (and therefore assist in the intake of air).

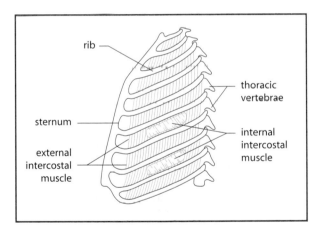

Figure 2.25 Lateral view of rib cage to show intercostal muscles.

The breathing mechanism at rest
During inspiration
The external intercostal muscles contract, while the internal intercostal muscles relax. This action causes the ribs and sternum to move upwards and outwards, thereby increasing the chest width from side to side and from back to back. In the meantime, pressure between the pleural membranes is reduced from –2 mmHg (–0.26 kPa) to –6 mmHg (–0.79 kPa). This negative pressure relative to the gas pressure in the lungs allows the pressure of air in the lungs to stretch the elastic pulmonary tissue, which therefore expands in contact with the chest cavity. At the same time the diaphragm contracts, which causes this dome-shaped sheet of muscle to descend by approximately 1.5 cm (the effect is to increase the depth of the thoracic cavity). Stimulation of the phrenic and intercostal nerves causes the contraction of these breathing muscles.

The combined effect of the contraction of the external intercostal muscles and of the diaphragm is to increase the volume occupied by the lungs. Therefore, the air pressure inside the lungs reduces. This results in atmospheric air being forced into the lungs via the nasal passages, trachea, bronchi and bronchioles, until air reaches the alveoli and air pressure inside the lungs is equal to the atmospheric pressure.

During expiration
The diaphragm and external intercostal muscles relax and return to their original positions. The ribs and diaphragm press on the pleural fluid. The relative pressure between the pleural surfaces increases from –6 mmHg (or –0.79 kPa) to –2 mmHg (or –0.26 kPa). The effect is to reduce the lung volume, thereby increasing air pressure inside the lungs so that it is above atmospheric pressure, and so air is forced out via the respiratory passages. This is aided by the elastic recoil of alveolar tissue (from the stretched state of full lung expansion) until the lungs deflate to their original volume.

Figure 2.26a and b The breathing mechanism.

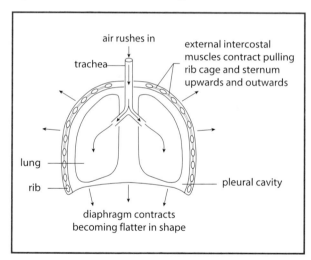

a Breathing in.

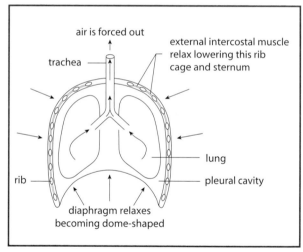

b Breathing out.

The breathing mechanism during exercise
During inspiration
A much larger volume of inspired air is achieved by the contraction of accessory inspiratory muscles.

In addition to the external intercostal muscles and diaphragm muscles contracting, **scaleni** and **sternocleidomastoids** contract. The effect is to raise the first and second ribs and sternum, respectively. During maximum efforts, the **trapezius** and **back** and **neck extensors** also contract and increase the size of the thorax even more.

During expiration
The combined contraction of the **internal intercostal** and **abdominal** muscles forces air out of the lungs (when the internal intercostal muscles shorten, the rib cage is actively moved downwards and the abdominal muscles force the diaphragm upwards).

Nervous and chemical regulators of the breathing mechanism

The rate of breathing is controlled subconsciously by the **medulla oblongata**, which regulates inspiration, and by the **pneumotaxic centre** in the **pons varolii**, which regulates expiration. Both these control centres are located in the **respiratory centre** in the brain stem.

During exercise

Increases in respiratory rates are brought about as a direct result of increases of carbon dioxide and increases in blood acidity levels. Blood acidity increases as a result of dissolved carbon dioxide forming carbonic acid (H_2CO_3) and the presence of lactic acid, resulting from anaerobic energy processes in working muscles.

In addition, the walls of the arch of the **aorta** and **carotid arteries** contain groups of sensitive cells called **chemoreceptors**, which respond to chemical changes in the blood (their main action is that of increasing respiration rates when the oxygen content in arterial blood drops), and **baroreceptors**, which respond to changes in blood pressure, by sending messages to the vasomotor centre in the medulla (refer to Figure 2.5).

Both the respiratory centre and chemoreceptors are stimulated by an increase in the partial pressure of carbon dioxide concentration, which raises the concentration of hydrogen ions in the blood via the reaction:

$$H_2CO_3 \rightarrow H^+ + HCO_3^-$$

thereby lowering blood pH. This causes an increase in both depth and rate of breathing.

Proprioceptors (sensors which feed information to the brain about joint angles, muscle stretch and body balance—see p. 43) in joints and muscles and psychological factors such as anxiety and alertness are also responsible for increased ventilation rates. Stretch receptors located in the bronchi and bronchioles are stimulated by overstretching, experienced in hyperventilation. Impulses travel via the vagus nerve to the respiratory centre where inspiration is inhibited and expiration is stimulated. This mechanism is called the **Hering–Breuer reflex**.

The effects of exercise stress on the breathing system are to increase depth and rate of breathing, which are regulated by the muscular, neural and chemical mechanisms summarized in Figure 2.27.

During recovery

The rate of breathing is controlled by the medulla and pons varolii as a direct result of the change in carbon dioxide concentration and factors listed above. During the recovery phase, the carbon dioxide concentration falls and consequently there is a reduction in the stimulation of the phrenic and intercostal nerves. Therefore ventilation rates decrease. This reduction is rapid at first and then tails off until the breathing rate returns to normal.

The effect of exercise stress and recovery is that of a **continual** balance between **excitatory** (positive) and **inhibitory** (negative) factors, some of which are shown in Figure 2.27.

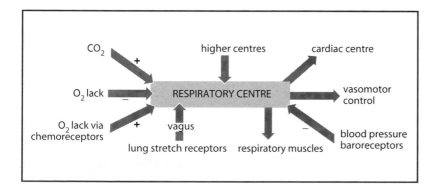

Figure 2.27 Factors affecting the activity of the respiratory centre. (*After Green, 1986.*)

Review Questions

1. Complete Table 2.4, which investigates the muscles that are involved in breathing at rest and during exercise.

2. Describe the mechanism of inspiration during physical activity.

3. a. Identify the chemical stimuli that control the rate and depth of breathing.

b. How do these stimuli control respiration during exercise?

c. What other stimuli control ventilation during exercise?

4. What do you think will be the long-term effects of an aerobic training programme on the respiratory system?

5. During exercise, ventilation rates may increase ten-fold. How is this achieved?

Table 2.4 : Muscles involved in breathing

Respiratory phase	Muscle acting	Action
e.g. Inspiration **at rest** **during exercise**	diaphragm	flattens
Expiration **at rest** **during exercise**		

 # Summary

1. You should be able to describe the structure and function of the nasal cavity, pharynx, trachea, bronchi, bronchioles, terminal respiratory units and alveoli in the role of transportation of atmospheric air in and out of the lungs.

2. You should understand the process by which air moves in and out of the lungs (pulmonary ventilation), and how this process is achieved by the action of muscles at rest and during exercise.

3. You should have an understanding of the nervous and chemical regulators of breathing and how they affect ventilation rates.

4. You should have an understanding of the effects of training on improving pulmonary function.

 # Further Reading

Bastian G.F. *An Illustrated Review: The Respiratory System*, HarperCollins, 1993.

Clegg C. *Exercise Physiology*, Feltham Press, 1995.

McArdle W.D., Katch F.I., Katch V.L. *Essentials of Exercise Physiology*, Lea & Febiger, 1994.

Tortora G. *Principles of Anatomy and Physiology* 8e, HarperCollins, 1996.

2.5 Gas Exchange in the Lungs

Keywords & concepts

a-$\bar{v}O_2$ diff
carbaminohaemoglobin
carbonic acid
diffusion capacity
diffusion gradient
driving pressure

exhaled air
gaseous exchange
haemoglobin
haemoglobinic acid
hyperventilation
inhaled air

myoglobin
oxygen dissociation curve
oxyhaemoglobin
quiet breathing
respiratory frequency
tissue respiration
ventilation rate

One of the main functions of the breathing system is to operate in conjunction with the vascular system in the process of **gaseous exchange**.

This section will help you to understand how it is possible for two-way traffic to exist, whereby **oxygen** is transported in one direction from lung alveoli to tissue cell sites, for the intracellular use of oxygen in the **mitochondria** (during **tissue respiration**), while **carbon dioxide** travels at the same time and in the same place in the opposite direction.

How gaseous exchange is achieved

During inspiration, alveolar pressure is lower than atmospheric pressure; therefore, air rushes in via the respiratory tract until the gas pressures are equalized. During expiration, the opposite occurs.

Also, despite a dense pulmonary capillary network, some alveoli have a poor or even non-existent blood supply. How do the lungs overcome this problem? At rest, inspired air goes to those alveoli with a good capillary network. The effect of regular exercise is to improve the capillary bed surrounding the alveoli and therefore increase the surface area available for gaseous exchange.

The movement of gases in and out of the circulatory system occurs by the process of **diffusion** (gas molecules moving from a region of high concentration to a region of low concentration) across the **epithelium** (membrane) that separates alveoli from lung circulatory capillaries. This is due to differences in **partial pressures** of carbon dioxide and oxygen in the pulmonary systems.

Partial pressures

The **partial pressure (p)** of a gas refers to its actual pressure as it exists within a mixture of gases. The **partial pressure** of oxygen (pO_2) in the atmosphere is about 20 kPa, which therefore means that oxygen contributes about 20% of the gas pressure in atmospheric air, the total pressure of which is 100 kPa. An oxygen partial pressure of 20 kPa represents a **concentration** of gas molecules equivalent to its normal atmosphere concentration. The partial pressure of oxygen in **alveolar air** is about 13 kPa, and from Figure 2.28 you can see that this oxygen pressure will force about 98% of haemoglobin in blood passing through the alveolar capillary bed, to become oxygenated.

Figure 2.28 Haemoglobin–oxygen dissociation curve.

Standard conditions: 37°C, CO_2 = 5.26 kPa, pH = 7.4.

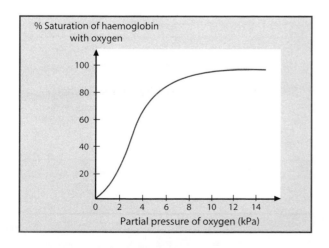

Oxygenation of haemoglobin (Figure 2.29a)

As blood is pumped through the pulmonary capillaries by blood pressure created by the heart, the red corpuscles are squeezed out of shape. This is the effect of the pressure of blood trying to force tiny corpuscles through tiny capillaries. This has the effect of forcing greater surface contact of the corpuscles with the capillary walls, which means that the oxygen diffusing across from the alveoli can more readily reach the haemoglobin in the red corpuscles.

Exercise increases the rate of expiration of air (VE, the volume of expired air per minute, is increased) tenfold, which means that up to ten times the resting amount of oxygen is exchanged. This is done by the heart increasing **pulmonary blood pressure** (the **driving pressure of blood** in the lung–alveoli transport system) by a small amount which is, however, sufficient to cause a much greater distortion of the red corpuscles in the pulmonary capillaries, and thus a much more rapid take-up by the haemoglobin in the corpuscles.

Oxygen attaches to haemoglobin in red corpuscles in the following manner:

$$\text{Hb} + \text{O}_2 \rightarrow \text{HbO}_2$$
$$\textbf{haemoglobin} \quad \textbf{oxygen} \quad \textbf{oxyhaemoglobin}$$

Blood then carries oxyhaemoglobin to the tissue sites where the oxygen is released:

$$\text{HbO}_2 \rightarrow \text{Hb} + \text{O}_2$$

and used in the process known as tissue respiration.

Tissue respiration

Oxygen

When oxyhaemoglobin reaches tissue cells where the oxygen is required for energy release, the process of **diffusion** of **oxygen** across the tissue capillary walls **into** the tissue cells occurs (as illustrated in Figures 2.16h and 2.29b).

The diffusion process is helped by a low oxygen molecular concentration in the tissue cells (because energy creation uses up oxygen stored in the cells) and a relatively high molecular concentration in the haemoglobin in the capillary.

Muscle cells contain a substance called **myoglobin** (a molecule similar to haemoglobin but which has a greater affinity for oxygen), which is depleted of oxygen by energy-creating processes in the cells. Oxygen therefore diffuses via the myoglobin across muscle cells to the cell **mitochondria**, where it is used to produce the adenosine triphosphate (ATP) needed for muscle contraction (see Chapter 3.2 for a description of this aerobic process).

The absorption and utilization of oxygen from the blood leads to a difference in the oxygen content of arterial and venous blood. At rest the blood's oxygen content varies from 20 ml of oxygen per 100 ml of arterial blood to 15 ml of oxygen per 100 ml of venous blood. The difference between these two values, (20 ml – 15 ml) = 5 ml, is referred to as the **arterio-venous difference** (a-$\bar{\text{v}}$O$_2$ **diff**). This value represents the extent to which oxygen has been removed from the blood as it passes through the body. With increasing rates of exercise, the a-$\bar{\text{v}}$O$_2$ diff increases up to values of 15–16 ml per 100 ml of blood. These two models are illustrated in Figure

Figure 2.29a and b

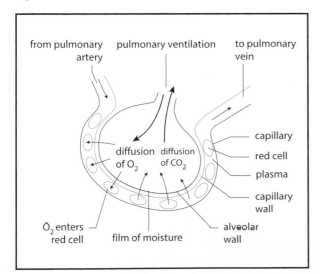

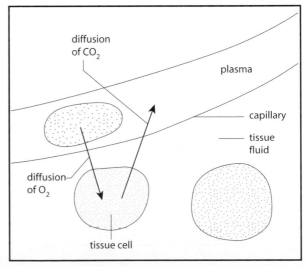

a Oxygenation of haemoglobin.

b Tissue respiration.

2.30. This increase reflects an increased extraction of oxygen, since more oxygen is required by active muscles, resulting in a reduction in pO_2 in muscle tissue when compared with the pO_2 in arterial blood. However, less oxygen is extracted from blood from inactive areas and so, as blood is mixed from active and inactive areas, the a-$\overline{v}O_2$ diff remains essentially unchanged. Cardiac output indicates how much blood leaves the heart in one minute, whereas the a-$\overline{v}O_2$ diff indicates how much oxygen has been extracted from the blood by the tissues. The product of these two values gives the rate of oxygen consumption.

$$\dot{V}O_2 = SV \times HR \times a\text{-}\overline{v}O_2 \text{ diff}$$

The arterio-venous difference increases with training, reflecting greater oxygen extraction at the tissue level and a more effective distribution of total blood volume (i.e. more blood going to active sites). This in turn can account for increases in $\dot{V}O_{2\,max}$.

Carbon dioxide

As energy is released in muscle cells, **carbon dioxide** is produced with the result that the concentration of carbon dioxide in the muscle cells is higher than that in the blood flowing through adjacent capillaries. Therefore, carbon dioxide **diffuses** across cell and capillary walls **into** the blood (see Figures 2.16h and 2.29b). Blood carbon dioxide loading increases as the blood reaches the venous end of the capillary bed.

There are three ways in which carbon dioxide can be carried by the blood—dissolved in plasma, as bicarbonate ion and as carbaminohaemoglobin.

Carbon dioxide dissolved in plasma

About 7% is carried as dissolved carbon dioxide in blood plasma.

Bicarbonate ion

About 70% carbon dioxide produced is carried in the form of a **bicarbonate ion**. Carbon dioxide and water molecules combine to form carbonic acid (H_2CO_3) within the red blood cell (RBC), assisted by the enzyme carbonic anhydrase, which acts as a catalyst. This acid is very unstable and so quickly dissociates, freeing the hydrogen ion (H^+) and forming a bicarbonate ion (HCO_3^-) (see Step 1 below), thereby lowering the pH of venous return. The H^+ reacts with oxygenated haemoglobin to form haemoglobinic acid, which triggers the release of oxygen for tissue cell respiration (see Step 2 below).

Step 1:
$$H_2O + CO_2 \rightarrow H_2CO_3 \rightarrow H^+ + HCO_3^-$$
$$\text{(carbonic} \qquad \text{(leaves}$$
$$\text{anhydrase catalyst)} \qquad \text{RBC)}$$

Step 2:
$$H^+ + HbO_2 \rightarrow HHb + O_2$$
$$\text{(remains} \qquad \text{(haemoglobinic} \quad \text{(for tissue}$$
$$\text{in RBC)} \qquad \text{acid)} \qquad \text{respiration)}$$

This is one of the mechanisms by which increased carbon dioxide in the blood causes the release of oxygen from haemoglobin. The binding of H^+ to haemoglobin triggers the Bohr effect, which shifts the oxygen–haemoglobin dissociation curve to the

Figure 2.30a and b The arterio-venous oxygen difference (a-$\overline{v}O_2$ diff).

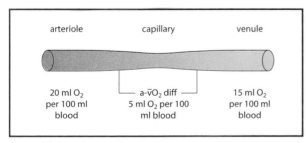

a At rest.

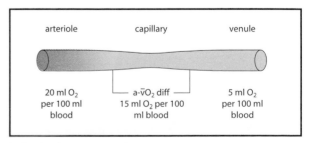

b During intense exercise.

right. A further drop in pH caused by lactic acid accumulation during intense exercise will additionally stimulate oxygen release by the same process.

Carbaminohaemoglobin
About 23% of carbon dioxide produced chemically combines with haemoglobin, once the haemoglobin has released its oxygen at the tissue site.

$$CO_2 \;+\; HbO_2 \;\rightarrow\; HbCO_2 \;+\; O_2$$
(carbamino-haemoglobin)

The carbon dioxide is **not** absorbed at the same molecular site as oxygen, but still stimulates the release of oxygen for further tissue respiration.

These processes are in effect reversible when conditions of carbon dioxide and oxygen partial pressures are changed. For example, when venous blood carrying carbon dioxide reaches pulmonary capillaries in contact with oxygenated alveoli, pulmonary blood carbon dioxide partial pressure is higher than that in the alveoli. Carbon dioxide dissolved in plasma comes out of solution, the H+ and bicarbonate ions combine to form carbonic acid, which then splits into carbon dioxide and water, and carbon dioxide is released from haemoglobin. Carbon dioxide diffuses from the blood into the alveoli and is expired out of the lungs (Figure 2.29a).

Efficiency of gas process
Steep diffusion gradients of oxygen and carbon dioxide are maintained by:
a. good lung ventilation.
b. the vast surface area of alveoli.
c. the very short distance between alveolar lining and blood (only 0.5 µm in thickness).
d. constant blood flow.
e. the large amount of red corpuscles and muscle myoglobin.
f. moist lining.

At rest, approximately 250 ml of oxygen diffuse per minute. The effects of exercise can increase this to around 2–2.5 litres per minute. One of the effects of training is to increase this rate by increasing the surface area of alveoli available for diffusion; another is to strengthen the musculature involved in breathing so that lung capacity becomes larger and the rates of breathing become higher.

Investigation

2.12: Differences between inhaled and exhaled air

Task One
Consider the information in Table 2.5. What conclusions can you draw from the figures given in this table?

Table 2.5 : Proportion of O_2 and CO_2 breathed during exercise, compared to at rest			
	Inhaled air	Exhaled air during quiet breathing	Exhaled air during exercise
% O_2	21	17	15
% CO_2	0.03	3	6

Task Two—The oxygen dissociation curve (data in Table 2.6)
Exercise displaces the oxygen dissociation curve to the right as blood pH falls due to increased carbon dioxide pressure (concentration), and temperature increases.

1. Plot both sets of data in the same way as the oxygen dissociation curve. On the *y*-axis plot % saturation of haemoglobin with oxygen, and oxygen partial pressure on the *x*-axis.
2. Draw a vertical line at a spot on the *x*-axis

Investigation

2.12 continued

Table 2.6 : Oxygen dissociation data

Partial pressure of O_2 (kPa)	% saturation of haemoglobin with oxygen for	
	$pCO_2 = 5.3$ kPa	$pCO_2 = 9.3$ kPa
1.3	7	4
2.6	27	15
3.9	53	35
5.3	70	58
6.6	79	71
7.9	85	82
9.3	90	88
10.5	95	94
11.8	98	98
13.0	100	100

where the oxygen partial pressure is at 5 kPa and follow the line up through the curves. What do you notice about the saturation of haemoglobin with oxygen for the two curves?

3. What effect does the increased pCO_2 in venous blood, as it passes through muscle tissue, have on the release of oxygen from haemoglobin into muscle cell tissue? (Note that pO_2 is about 5 kPa in venous haemoglobin.)

4. On leaving the lungs, blood again has an oxygen partial pressure of 13 kPa. Trace the passage of the blood from this point through the circulatory system (see Table 2.7), highlighting:
a. Oxygen partial pressure,
b. Carbon dioxide partial pressure,
c. Haemoglobin oxygen saturation until the blood returns through the complete circuit.

Table 2.7 : Partial pressures in the circulatory system

Location of blood	pO_2 (kPa)	pCO_2 (kPa)	% HbO_2 saturation
leaving lungs	13	5.3	100
entering muscle tissue	13	5.3	100
leaving muscle tissue—venous	5	9.3	35
venous blood arriving at lungs	5	9.3	35

Review Questions

1. The lungs have no skeletal tissue, so how do they increase in size on breathing in?
2. Describe how alveolar ventilation changes during exercise.
3. What three factors affect oxygen dissociation during exercise, and how?
4. Describe the relationships between haemoglobin, pO_2, acidity, pCO_2 and temperature.
5. Explain how CO_2 is picked up by the tissue capillary blood and then released into the alveoli.

6. **a.** Distinguish between cardiac output and arterio-venous difference.
b. Briefly describe and account for the changes that occur in cardiac output and arterio-venous difference from rest to maximal exercise.
7. Identify the major vascular substance that determines the amount of oxygen that can be delivered to body tissues and explain how it functions.

 Exam-Style Questions

1. Figure 2.31 shows the relative partial pressure (amount) of oxygen (pO_2) and carbon dioxide (pCO_2) in the atmosphere, in the alveoli of the lungs and in the blood vessels of the pulmonary circulation. Use the information given in Figure 2.31 to answer the questions which follow.

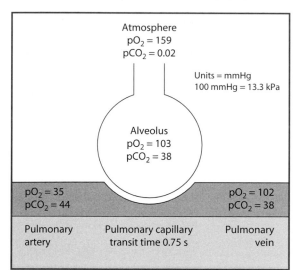

Figure 2.31

a. Explain, in terms of diffusion, how the changes in pO_2 and pCO_2 between the pulmonary artery and the pulmonary vein are brought about. (4 marks)
b. What are the barriers to diffusion between the air in the alveoli and the haemoglobin in the blood, through which the oxygen must pass? (5 marks)
c. How could you deduce from the data that gas exchange occurring in the alveoli is at an optimum? (3 marks)
d. i. Explain briefly the purpose of a sports performer breathing pure oxygen immediately before competing. (2 marks)
ii. Comment on the value of this procedure at sea level and at altitude. (3 marks)
e. With reference to the information in the diagram, what changes in blood composition will occur during strenuous exercise? (3 marks)

 Summary

1. You should be able to understand the function of the breathing system in respect of gaseous exchange with the blood.
2. You should be able to describe how the breathing system adapts as a result of physical activity.
3. You should be able to summarize the concept of the partial pressures of gases and how the partial pressures of oxygen and carbon dioxide

affect the oxygen-carrying capacity of haemoglobin.
4. You should be able to appreciate how changes in carbon dioxide partial pressure in blood enables delivery of oxygen from haemoglobin to tissue sites.
5. You should be able to understand the concept arterio-venous difference.

Further Reading

Bastian G.F. *An Illustrated Review: The Respiratory System*, HarperCollins, 1993.

Clegg C. *Exercise Physiology*, Feltham Press, 1995.

McArdle W.D., Katch F.I., Katch V.L. *Essentials of Exercise Physiology*, Lea & Febiger, 1994.

Seeley R.R., Stephens T.D., Tate P. *Anatomy and Physiology* 2e, Mosby–Year Book, 1992.

Wilmore J.H. *Physiology of Sport and Exercise*, Human Kinetics, 1994.

2.6 Lung Volumes and Physical Activity

Keywords & concepts

expiratory reserve volume, or expiratory capacity

inspiratory reserve volume or inspiratory

minute ventilation: $\dot{V}E$ and $\dot{V}I$

pulmonary ventilation

quiet breathing

residual volume or functional residual capacity

spirometer

tidal volume

total lung volume

vital capacity

During quiet breathing, we exchange about 0.5 litres (0.5 dm³) of air per breath (the **tidal volume** or TV), of which 350 ml is alveolar ventilation and 150 ml is **dead space** air (dead space represents the volume of the trachea, bronchi and other structures that do not take part in gas exchange). The **tidal volume** is the volume of air inspired or expired per breath.

Minute ventilation, or minute volume, is the amount of air inspired or expired in one minute. Minute ventilation is expressed as:

$$\dot{V}E = \text{volume of air expired in a minute}$$
or
$$\dot{V}I = \text{volume of air inspired in a minute}$$

The **inspiratory reserve volume** (IRV) is the volume of air that can be forcibly inspired after a normal quiet breath. Similarly, the **expiratory reserve volume** (ERV) is that volume of air that can be forcibly expired over and above resting tidal volume. **Residual volume** (RV) is the volume of air remaining in the lungs after maximum expiration. These lung volumes are illustrated in Figure 2.32.

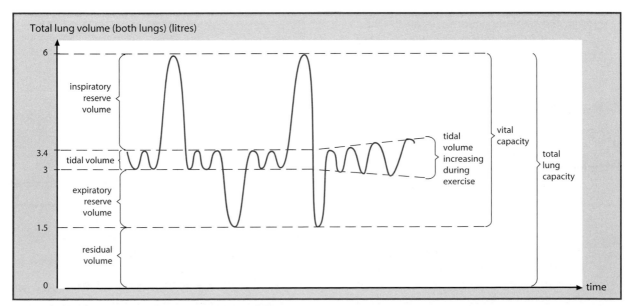

Figure 2.32 Diagram of lung volumes and capacities.

Vital capacity (VC) is the maximal volume of air that can forcefully be expired after maximal inspiration in one breath. **Total lung capacity** (TLC) is the volume of air in the lungs after maximal inspiration and can be between 4 and 8 litres in healthy adults. **Inspiratory capacity** (IC) is the tidal volume plus inspiratory reserve volume, **expiratory capacity** (EC) is the tidal volume plus expiratory reserve volume and the **functional residual capacity** (FRC) is a combination of the expiratory reserve volume and the residual volume.

Lung volumes and capacities can be measured by using a spirometer (Figure 2.33a), which produces a trace as illustrated in Figure 2.33b. Note in Figure 2.32 how tidal volume increases during exercise.

Investigation

2.13: To determine lung volumes using a spirometer

Materials: spirometer with graph paper attached, wide-bore flexible tube, mouthpiece and noseclip, scales and tape-measure, disinfectant.

Figure 2.33a and b

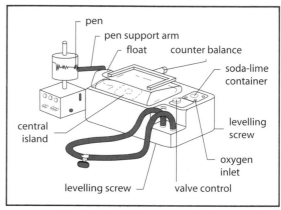

a Spirometer.

Task One
1. Weigh yourself and measure your height.
2. Sitting down, clip on the noseclip and insert a freshly disinfected mouthpiece. Breathe normally and set the cylinder in motion so that you are inspiring and expiring into the spirometer.
3. Now take a maximal breath in and out. Repeat three normal breaths followed again by maximal inspiration and expiration.
(The rotating cylinder records the different lung volumes described earlier; however, unless the rotating cylinder is suitably calibrated, the printout is only qualitative.)
4. Remove the graph paper and, using the descriptions on lung volumes, mark on the graph your TV, IRV, ERV and VC. Figure 2.33b should assist you with this.

Task Two
1. Assuming that your tidal volume in quiet breathing is 0.5 litres, work out your IRV and ERV.
2. Calculate your VC using the following equation:
VC = TV (at rest) + IRV + ERV

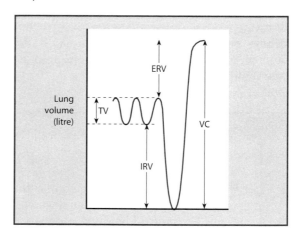

b Spirometer trace.

Investigation

2.13 continued

Task Three—collation of results
1. Record your results in Table 2.8.

2. Collate the results of other students in your class.

Table 2.8 : Results table

NAME OF SUBJECT	Height (metres)	Weight (kg)	TV (litres)	IRV (litres)	ERV (litres)	VC (litres)
self						

Task Four—analysis of results
1. Comment on the differing vital capacities. Discuss the relationship between vital capacity and height, weight and gender.

2. Describe two experimental errors that could have affected the results.
3. What volume of gas remains in the lungs at the end of maximal expiration?

Investigation

2.14: The measurement of lung volumes
Materials: a 5 litre calibrated plastic bottle, rubber tubing, disinfectant.
A simple method of determining **vital capacity** and **tidal volume** is to use a calibrated plastic bottle, illustrated in Figure 2.34.

Task One
1. Calibrate a large plastic bottle up to 5 litres by filling it with water, 1 litre at a time, marking the levels.
2. Fill a sink with water and invert the bottle (full of water up to the 5 litre mark) into the sink.
3. Insert one end of the rubber tube into the neck of the bottle.
4. Take a deep breath and then exhale as hard as you can through the disinfected tubing so that the exhaled air displaces the water in the bottle.
5. The level of the water left in the bottle will give you your **vital capacity**.

Task Two
1. Push the rubber tubing half way up inside the bottle, making sure that it is clear of the waterline.
2. Breath in and out normally through the rubber tubing. The rise and fall in the water line with each breath accounts for the volume of air that is exchanged during quiet breathing. This volume is known as **tidal volume**.

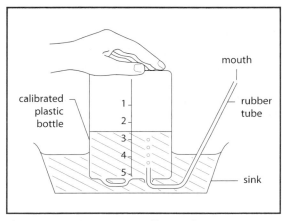

Figure 2.34 Measurement of lung volumes.

Exam-Style Questions

1. What are the important respiratory volume indices and how do they change during exercise? (4 marks)

2. Figure 2.36 shows a diagram of lung volumes of an 18-year-old student.
a. Identify the four lung volumes A, B, C, D and indicate their approximate values and units. (4 marks)
b. What happens to the volumes C and D during sub-maximal exercise? (2 marks)

3. Figure 2.37 shows the responses of respiration and heart rate to exercise that might occur when running in a 3000 m track race.
a. Using the information in Figure 2.37, explain why both heart rate and ventilation follow similar trends. (6 marks)
b. Discuss how the **sympathetic** and **parasympathetic** nervous systems affect heart and ventilation rates. (4 marks)

4. Describe and account for some of the long term effects of regular exercise on the respiratory volumes. (6 marks)

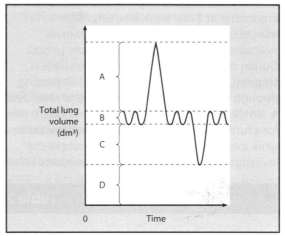

Figure 2.36 Lung volumes of an 18-year-old student at rest.

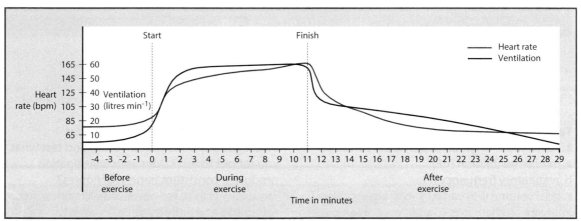

Figure 2.37 Respiration and heart rate responses when running a 3000 m track race. (*After Solomon and Davis, 1983.*)

 Summary

1. You should be familiar with the concepts of, and be able to measure, lung volumes and capacities.
2. You should understand the concepts of minute ventilation, tidal volume and ventilation rates during quiet breathing and during exercise.
3. You should be able to account for the differences in lung volumes and capacities between untrained and trained sportspersons.

 Further Reading

Clegg C. *Exercise Physiology*, Feltham Press, 1995.
Fox E., Bowers R., Foss M. *The Physiological Basis for Exercise and Sport* 6e, Brown & Benchmark, 1997.
McArdle W.D., Katch F.I., Katch V.L. *Essentials of Exercise Physiology*, Lea & Febiger, 1994.
McKenna B.R. and Callender R. *Illustrated Physiology* 6e, Churchill Livingstone, 1996.

Chapter 3

Energy for Exercise

3.1 Energy and Work

In scientific terms, energy and work mean the same thing and are interchangeable as concepts, energy being the capacity or ability of a system to do work.

The definition of **work** is:

work = force × distance moved (by the system acted upon by the force) in the direction of the force.

The unit of **work** and therefore of **energy** is the **joule** (J), which is defined as the work done (or energy used) when a force of **one newton** (N) acts through a distance of **one metre** (m).

This formula can be used to measure human energy output or work done—this will be illustrated by one of the following two investigations.

Investigation

3.1: Energy output of a person running upstairs

This investigation uses the **weight** of the athlete as the **force** used, and the **vertical height** moved as the **distance** through which the force is applied. Here the energy output by the body equals the work done in climbing the stairs and is an approximate value, not taking into account the motion of the student's body.

Task One—the experiment

1. The student should find his/her **weight** in **newtons** using bathroom scales.
To convert from kilograms, multiply by 10 to obtain the weight in newtons. (This is because the Earth pulls down with a force of 10 N for every kilogram mass—the force of gravity is called the **weight**. Refer to p. 193 for a further discussion about weight and mass.)

2. Measure the **height** of the stairs to be climbed in **metres**.

3. The student should run up the stairs as fast as possible—the **time in seconds** recorded for this activity.

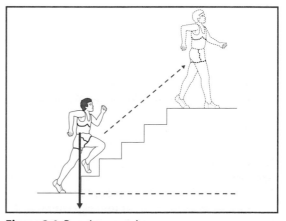

Figure 3.1 Running upstairs.

Investigation

3.1 continued

Task Two—analysis of results
Calculate the energy output of the student using:

$$\begin{aligned} \text{energy} &= \textbf{force} \times \textbf{distance} \\ &= \textbf{weight} \times \textbf{height} \\ &= \textbf{m}g \times \textbf{h} \end{aligned}$$
(The answer will be in **joules**.)

Task Three—calculation of power output
1. **Power** is defined as:

Energy (or **work**) used per **second**

2. The values from Task Two are therefore placed in the equation:

$$\textbf{power} = \frac{\textbf{energy (joules)}}{\textbf{time (seconds)}}$$

The answer will be in **watts**, where **one watt** is defined as the power produced when **one joule** of energy is used per **second**.

 Investigation

3.2: Energy output of a person operating a bicycle ergometer

Task One—the activity
1. The **force** setting on the bike (load on bike wheel—marked L in Figure 3.2) is noted and the distance (on the milometer) set to zero.
If the force setting is in kilograms, this needs converting into **newtons** using the information that the weight of one kilogram mass is 10 N.
2. The student then pedals as fast as possible for 30 seconds, and the **distance** travelled in metres (as recorded on the milometer) is noted.

Figure 3.2 A bicycle ergometer.

If the machine has no milometer, the distance travelled by the outer rim of the bike wheel as it turns past the friction belt is measured. This can

be calculated by multiplying the circumference of the wheel by the number of revolutions done by the wheel in the time of the experiment.
(Remember the answer to this should be in metres.)

Task Two—analysis of results
Energy output is now calculated using the formula:

$$\textbf{energy} = \textbf{force} \times \textbf{distance}$$
(The answer will be in **joules**.)

Task Three—calculation of power output
Using the definition of **power** in the investigation of energy output of a person running upstairs, this can be calculated using the formula:

$$\textbf{power} = \frac{\textbf{energy (joules)}}{\textbf{time taken (seconds)}}$$
(Answer in **watts**.)

Extension of investigation
With more sophisticated apparatus, the speed of the bike wheel can be monitored by a computer sensor, and a full profile of power output with time obtained. Alternatively, power measurements can be made over 10 seconds, 20 seconds and 30 seconds by using the bicycle ergometer method above. It is then possible to observe maximal power output, and how the power output changes as the athlete becomes more fatigued. This can be related to anaerobic power as discussed on p. 109.

Chemical energy

The question of where this energy comes from now arises, and it is fairly obvious that the original source of the energy is the food eaten by the person doing the exercise.

In fact, the energy is produced by a complex series of **chemical reactions** (to be discussed in detail below) and is then made available for contraction of muscles and other body functions.

This type of energy is called **chemical energy** since the energy is produced by chemical reactions, and is converted into **work** by the contraction of muscle.

If we were able to calculate the full energy value of all food eaten by a person and compare this with measured energy output (as in the investigations above), we would find that only a small proportion of this energy is converted into useful work.

The power needs of sporting activity

From the definition of power in the investigations above, we have:

$$\text{power} = \frac{\text{energy}}{\text{time}} = \frac{\text{force} \times \text{distance}}{\text{time}}$$

But $\frac{\text{distance}}{\text{time}}$ is a definition of speed; therefore

$$\text{power} = \text{force} \times \frac{\text{distance}}{\text{time}} = \text{force} \times \text{speed}$$

or, if the direction of the speed is fully taken into consideration:

$$\text{power} = \text{force} \times \text{velocity}$$

So it can be seen that power is a measure of force being applied at speed, and therefore is the appropriate concept in the bulk of sports requiring fast dynamic movements, such as jumping, throwing, sprinting, weightlifting and most games.

It is suggested that another convenient activity (highly correlated with the two activities discussed in Investigations 3.1 and 3.2) that could be used to assess athletic power would be a timed 30 m sprint. Each of the three activities would assess a slightly different athletic **capability**, but would be a measure of the individual's **power**.

Measurement of chemical energy stored in food as fuel

There are two ways of measuring the amounts of chemical energy stored in food (which would then be available for conversion into useful forms of energy—such as mechanical energy—by the person who eats the food). The chemical process that releases the stored energy amounts to the combination of food with oxygen—a process identical to the burning of food fuel in air.

The first method (called the **direct** method, since it directly measures energy produced by combination of the food with oxygen) therefore involves the burning of the food in a controlled way, and measuring the heat energy produced. This heat energy is measured by observing the rise in temperature of a quantity of water heated by the burning food. An alternative direct method that can measure energy usage during exercise is to measure the body's heat production in a calorimeter chamber. Such a unit is illustrated in Figure 3.3. The heat energy that is created by the subject radiates to the walls and warms the water. The temperatures of the incoming and outgoing water and air are recorded and used to calculate basal metabolic rate and total energy expenditure. This method is rarely used today since the apparatus is very costly, takes up considerable space and is slow in generating results.

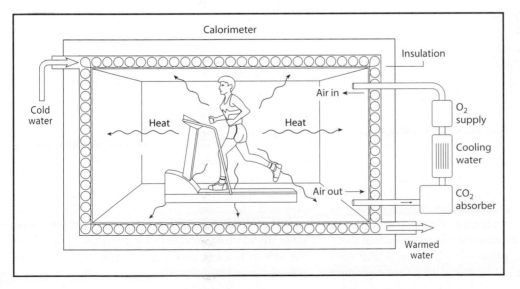

Figure 3.3 Human calorimeter used to measure heat production.

The second method is called the **indirect** method, since it uses the fact that every atom of carbon in food combines with a molecule of oxygen during the chemical reaction to produce one molecule of carbon dioxide and release a definite and constant amount of energy. Similarly, two hydrogen atoms in food combine with one atom of oxygen to produce one molecule of water and release a different but also constant amount of energy. The method involves the measurement of the **amount of oxygen** consumed—which can therefore be related to the amount of energy released by food.

For example, 134.4 litres of oxygen will oxidize 180 g of glycogen to release 2867 kJ of heat energy (1 kJ = 1 kilojoule = 1000 joules). Therefore, for all food fuels, one litre of oxygen produces 22 kJ of heat energy.

Figure 3.4 gives an idea of the equipment used to measure carbon dioxide production and oxygen consumption by calculating the respiratory exchange ratio (RER) (for further details of this method refer to specialist texts such as McArdle *et al.*, *Essentials of Exercise Physiology*, or Wilmore and Costill, *Physiology of Sport and Exercise*). (For a detailed discussion on **oxygen consumption**, see Section 3.4.)

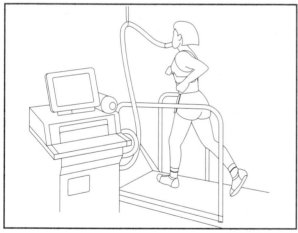

Figure 3.4 The indirect method of measuring energy usage, using open circuit indirect calorimetry.

The respiratory exchange ratio

The energy released for a given volume of oxygen depends on whether carbohydrates, fats or proteins are being oxidized. This is because there are inherent chemical differences in the composition of carbohydrates, fats and proteins and therefore different amounts of oxygen are required to oxidize completely the carbon and hydrogen to carbon dioxide and water. In general the amount of oxygen needed to completely oxidize a molecule of carbohydrate or fat is proportional to the amount of carbon in that fuel.

It is possible to estimate which particular substrate is being oxidized by calculating the **respiratory**

exchange ratio (RER) or the relationship of carbon dioxide (CO_2) produced to oxygen (O_2) consumed. This concept is also known as the **respiratory quotient** (RQ).

Thus, if carbohydrates are completely oxidized to CO_2 and water (H_2O) the relationship can be described as:

$$6O_2 + C_6H_{12}O_6 \longrightarrow 6CO_2 + 6H_2O + 38ATP$$

(ATP = adenosine triphosphate) and it follows that:

$$RER = \frac{\text{volume of carbon dioxide given off}}{\text{volume of oxygen consumed}} = \frac{6CO_2}{6O_2} = 1$$

If fat is used as a source of energy the ratio is different. For example a typical fat, such as palmitic acid, being oxidized into carbon dioxide and water can be summarized by the following equation:

$$C_{16}H_{32}O_2 + 23O_2 \longrightarrow 16CO_2 + 16H_2O + 129ATP$$

$$RER = \frac{16}{23} = 0.70$$

The RER for protein metabolism is estimated as approximately 0.80. However, protein plays a very small part in energy metabolism and therefore is not important to the present discussion. A value between 0.70 and 1.0 indicates a mixture of fat and carbohydrate being burnt. A value over 1.0 indicates anaerobic respiration due to more CO_2 being produced than O_2 being consumed.

The efficiency of the human machine

The human body is a machine performing work, but all machines use more fuel energy than they need for the task. The **mechanical efficiency** of any machine, including the human body, can be defined as:

$$\% \text{ efficiency} = \frac{\text{useful work done} \times 100}{\text{energy used doing that work}}$$

Energy expenditure refers to the amount of energy required to perform an activity measured by oxygen consumption in the way outlined above.

The difference between the total oxygen consumed during the exercise (and subsequent recovery) and the resting oxygen consumption for the period of time involved (of exercise plus recovery) gives the **net oxygen cost** of the exercise—and hence the energy used to perform the exercise at 22 kJ per litre of oxygen consumed.

With respect to the investigations above, in which amounts of **useful work done** are measured for students running up stairs or cycling on a bicycle ergometer, if the net oxygen cost is measured it would be possible to compute the efficiency of the exercise process.

The percentage efficiency is usually within the range of 12–25% for the human body. This means that for every movement made, only 25% of the energy consumed is used doing the actual movement (above that which is needed for the basal metabolic rate) and the other 75% is converted into heat energy. Part of this heat energy is used to keep the body temperature above that of the surroundings (and stable at about 37°C) and the rest is lost to the surroundings. This means that whenever exercise is taken a lot of heat energy is produced, which can be used to raise body temperature (refer to your answers to p. 67, Task Six). This is why shivering occurs (muscles contract involuntarily as a response to low temperatures) and why people clap their hands and stamp their feet when cold.

In activities such as walking or running the efficiency level is around 20–25%. In swimming it is around 2%.

A study of stair climbing has shown that the maximum efficiency (lowest energy costs) occurs at a speed of 50 steps per minute. As soon as this rate increases, efficiency is reduced. One can say that running even a fraction faster up the stairs means large increases in energy expenditure and rapid exhaustion. Conversely, tiny increases in efficiency, as a result of changes in technique or improved skill, will bring large reductions in energy expenditure. Therefore, improving skill levels is a much more profitable approach to improving performance than a simple increase in muscle strength.

Review Questions

1. Describe the main features of a cycle ergometer and how it can be used to calculate power output as a fitness measurement.

2. What is the respiratory exchange ratio (RER)?
3. Explain how you would determine the oxidation of carbohydrate and fat.

Summary

1. You should be familiar with the concepts of work and energy, and particularly the definition:

work = force × distance
= weight × height

and should be aware of the joule as the unit of measurement of work and energy. 1 kilojoule (kJ) = 1000 joules.

2. You should understand the concept of power as defined by:

$$\text{power} = \frac{\text{energy used or work done}}{\text{time taken}}$$

$$= \text{force} \times \text{velocity}$$

and that the watt is the unit of power.

3. You should be familiar with the concept of chemical energy in respect of the energy store in muscles, and its relationship to actual food consumption and oxygen consumption.

4. You should be familiar with the concept of respiratory exchange ratio as an indication of the energy being oxidized during cellular respiration.

5. You should be aware of the concept of efficiency defined by:

$$\% \text{ efficiency} = \frac{\text{useful work done} \times 100}{\text{energy used doing that work}}$$

6. You should appreciate that gains in skill development rather than strength development are more likely to improve efficiency of the human machine.

Further Reading

McArdle W.D., Katch F.I., Katch V.L. *Essentials of Exercise Physiology*, Lea & Febiger, 1994.

Wilmore J.M. and Costell D.L. *Physiology of Sport and Exercise*, Human Kinetics, 1994.

Since there is no oxygen present, **anaerobic metabolism** takes place. **Pyruvic acid**, formed during glycolysis, is converted by the enzyme lactate dehydrogenase (LDH) into **lactic acid**. As the lactic acid accumulates, muscle fatigue and pain occur. This is because the resultant low pH within the cell inhibits **enzyme** action in the cell **mitochondria**, which normally promotes the change of glycogen into energy. Hence the effect of lactic acid fatigue is to inhibit muscle action so that physical performance deteriorates. All anaerobic processes occur in the **sarcoplasm**, whereas aerobic

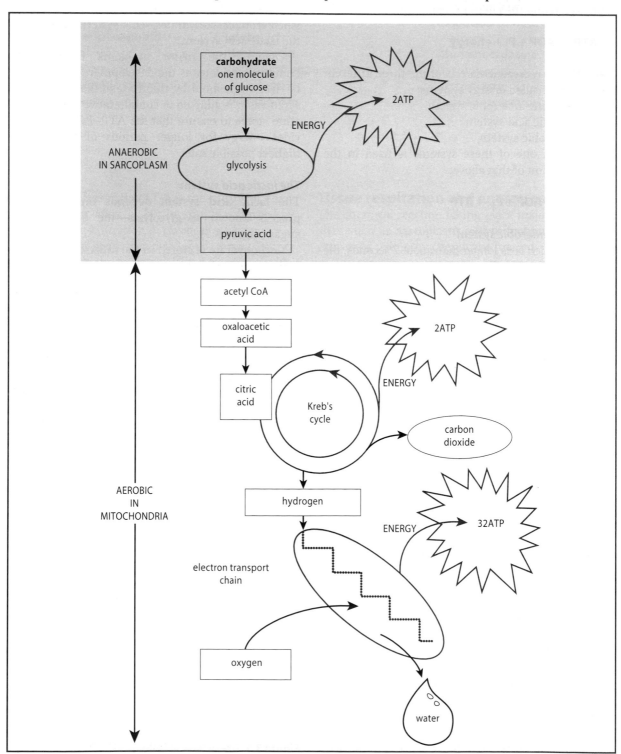

Figure 3.6 The aerobic system.

processes take place within the confines of the cell **mitochondria** (see Figure 3.6).

Events such as a 400 metre race rely heavily on the lactic acid system. After exercise has stopped extra oxygen is taken in to remove the lactic acid by changing it back into pyruvic acid. This is known as repaying the **oxygen debt** and is described in detail in Section 3.3.

The aerobic system

The aerobic system (Figure 3.6) relies on the presence of oxygen to break down completely carbohydrates and fats into carbon dioxide, water and energy. The energy yield is high—one molecule of glucose yields 36 molecules of ATP (in the lactic acid process the yield is two molecules of ATP!).

The first stage of the **aerobic** process is the same as that in the anaerobic lactic acid system: **glycolysis**, i.e. the conversion of glycogen into two molecules of pyruvic acid (see Figure 3.5), two ATP molecules and a number of **hydrogen atoms**. This process occurs via a series of ten chemical reactions in the cell **sarcoplasm**.

From this point on, all chemical reactions involved in the aerobic system take place within the muscle cell **mitochondria** (see p. 36). The mitochondrion is often referred to as the **power house** of the cell, as it is the site of most energy production. Figure 3.7 shows the microscopic detail of a mitochondrion. The structures labelled in Figure 3.7 are discussed below.

Krebs cycle, or the citric acid cycle

The two molecules of pyruvic acid are converted into a form of **acetyl coenzyme A (CoA)** (a 2-carbon compound), which enters the citric acid cycle by combining with **oxaloacetic acid** (a 6-carbon compound).

This process takes place in the inner fluid-filled matrix of the mitochondrion, which contains the enzymes of the citric acid cycle. Within this cycle there are a large number of reactions in which the two molecules go through a series of changes until they are degraded into pairs of hydrogen atoms and carbon dioxide. Fatty acids are taken up by the cycle at this point. (The total release of energy from acetyl CoA, as a result of fat metabolism, is 34 ATP.)

The electron transport chain

Oxygen is given off from the muscle myoglobin or made available from blood haemoglobin and is taken in by the **mitochondria** to be used to oxidize hydrogen atoms:

$$H \rightarrow H^+ + e^-$$
(hydrogen atom) (hydrogen ion) (electron)

The hydrogen ions and electrons are charged with potential energy. The electron transport chain consists of a chain of hydrogen ion–electron pairs, linked to the folds of the inner membrane (cristae) of the cell mitochondria. Energy is released in a controlled step-by-step manner (each reaction is exothermic). For each pair of hydrogen atoms that enter this pathway, the net effect is the production of three molecules of ATP (endothermic) and one molecule of water. This is an **aerobic process**, with the final pair being accepted by molecular oxygen which combines with H^+ to produce water. Therefore the electron transport chain yields 32–34 molecules of ATP and several molecules of water.

The total possible yield produced by the aerobic metabolism is 36 or 38 molecules of ATP—the total energy yield is dependent on the biochemical pathway taken by the food fuel. This is the maximum possible from the complete oxidation of one molecule of glucose. The overall equation that expresses **aerobic respiration** is:

$$C_6H_{12}O_6 + 36ADP + 36P_i + 6O_2 \rightarrow 6CO_2 + 36ATP + 6H_2O$$

The aerobic route is 18 or 19 times more efficient than the anaerobic route, depending on the food fuel biochemical pathway.

Provided there is an adequate supply of oxygen to the working muscles, glucose and free fatty acids can be metabolized to produce ATP. The major advantage of fat fuels is that there is a much larger supply available to sustain steady state endurance activities, such as marathon running.

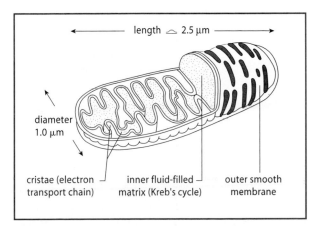

Figure 3.7 The mitochondrion—the organelle of respiration.

Investigation

3.3: To determine the energy sources for practical activities

(The material for this investigation was devised by Kevin Sykes, Principal Lecturer at Chester College of Higher Education, as part of an AEB 'A' level course.)

Materials: tape-measure and stop-watch.

Task One—a standing long jump

Crouch down low with flexed knees and prepare to take off from both feet. Spring forwards as far as possible and measure the distance achieved. The distance is measured between the front of the toes at take off and the rear of the heels on landing. Record the maximum distance from three attempts.

Task Two

Identify the two baselines of a badminton court in your gym or sportshall. Start at one end and on the command 'GO' sprint as fast as you can to the far baseline and back three times altogether, making a total of six shuttle sprints. Use a partner to record your time.

Task Three—shuttle runs

Using the same baselines, perform a 30 length shuttle run at a steady pace. Use a partner to record your split times at 5, 10, 15, 20, 25 and 30 lengths. Record your split times in Table 3.1.

Task Four

1. Comment on the split times in your run.
2. How did you feel at various stages of the run and at the finish?
3. Roughly how long did it take you to recover?
4. Which of the energy systems is dominant in each of the three tasks?

Figure 3.8 A standing long jump.

Figure 3.9 A shuttle sprint.

Task Five—collation of results

Collate your own results and those of five other students in your class in Table 3.1 provided.

Task Six—analysis of results

1. Discuss your group results in relation to gender, height, weight and sporting interests.
2. Discuss the meaningfulness of these results and the limitations of such measurements.
3. How would these results differ as you become fitter'? Explain your answer.

Table 3.1 : Results table

Name	Standing broad jump (meters)	Shuttle sprint (seconds)	Shuttle runs (split times min/sec) 5 10 15 20 25 30
self			

Review Questions

1. Write an equation which summarizes:
a. aerobic respiration,
b. anaerobic respiration.
2 a.What do the initials ATP stand for?
b. What role does ATP play in energy release?
3. Describe the relationship between phosphocreatine (PC) and muscle ATP during a 100 metre sprint.
4. Describe the special role mitochondria play in energy release.
5. During any event of low or high intensity, all three energy systems are used. However, the physical demands of the event will determine the relative proportions of the energy system(s) being used. Complete the gaps in Table 3.2, identifying the major energy systems and examples in sporting activities in relation to performance time.

Table 3.2 : Performance, energy systems and activity

Area	Performance time	Major energy system(s)(seconds)	Examples of type of activity
1	less than 10 sec	ATP–PC	100 metres sprint gymnastics vault
2	10–30 seconds		
3	30 sec–1.5 minutes		
4	1.5–3 minutes		
5	greater than 3 minutes		

Exam-Style Questions

1. Describe the **predominant** energy system being used in the following activities (remember this will be related to the time of the activity and the effort involved):
shot-put, marathon, 200 metres breaststroke, a game of hockey, 100 metres hurdles race, gymnastics vault, modern pentathlon, a brisk walk. (7 marks)
2. Figure 3.10 represents the energy systems used during the following athletic events:
100 metres, 400 metres, 1500 metres and marathon, but not necessarily in that order.
a. Identify each event with an energy block and comment briefly on the reasons for your choice. (4 marks)
b. Using the same key, complete a block to show the approximate proportions of aerobic and/or anaerobic work during a basketball game. (2 marks)
3. The energy sources for a 1500 metre race are very specific. During the first 10 seconds the ATP–PC system is used, followed by a transition to the lactic acid system during the next minute. The pace settles into a short aerobic phase,

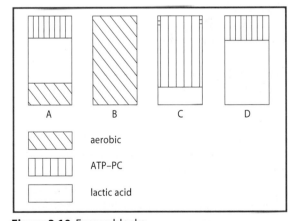

Figure 3.10 Energy blocks.

followed by a return to the lactic acid system during the final sprint for the line.
    Using the same format, analyse the energy sources used in a game of hockey. (12 marks)
4. Select a sport with which you are familiar and briefly describe the energy systems used in your selected sport. How can a knowledge of the three energy systems assist you in devising a training programme for your selected sport? (9 marks)

99

Summary

1. You should be able to understand how energy is stored as chemical energy in ATP within muscle.
2. You should be able to understand how energy is released and ATP is used for muscle contraction.
3. You should be able to understand that glycolysis is common to both anaerobic and aerobic energy release.

4. You should be able to understand that energy is released to recreate ATP via three sets of mechanisms—alactic anaerobic, lactic acid anaerobic and aerobic systems, and how each system works.
5. You should be able to apply the concept of energy systems to practical situations.

Further Reading

Fox E.L., Bowers R.W., Foss M.C. *The Physiological Basis for Exercise and Sport* 5e, Wm C. Brown, 1992.

McArdle W.D., Katch F.I., Katch V.L. *Essentials of Exercise Physiology*, Lea & Febiger, 1994.

Tortora G. *Principles of Anatomy and Physiology* 8e, HarperCollins, 1996.

Wilmore J.H. and Costill D.L. *Physiology of Sport and Exercise*, Human Kinetics, 1994.

3.3 The Recovery Process after Exercise

Keywords & concepts

alactacid oxygen debt component	**lactacid oxygen debt component**	**onset of blood lactate accumulation (OBLA)**
excess post-exercise oxygen consumption (EPOC) or oxygen debt	**muscle fatigue**	**oxygenated myoglobin**
	muscle glycogen stores	**oxygen deficit**
gluconeogenesis	**muscle soreness**	**phosphagen restoration**

Normally, provided the effort or duration of exercise has not been too large, breathing and pulse rates rise as the need for oxygen rises to levels that enable ATP to be regenerated in muscles at the same rate as it is consumed. This is a continuous process, which varies according to the work or energy performed by muscles during a sportsperson's day.

Initially, as exercise begins, ATP is consumed directly, then replaced via the ATP–PC anaerobic energy system, **as well as** glycolysis and aerobic conversion of carbohydrates to provide energy for ATP manufacture. The important point to note is that **all three mechanisms** of ATP manufacture occur continuously, but the **proportion** produced by the mechanisms changes as the exercise continues.

If exercise is intense enough, the cells rapidly run out of PC (so replacement of ATP by the ATP–PC

mechanism stops: the alactic–lactic threshold); not enough ATP is produced by aerobic processes, so **glycolysis** takes over as the predominant method of ATP supply, with its production of lactic acid and rapid depletion of muscle glycogen (and oxygenated myoglobin, which is another way in which oxygen is supplied to muscle cells to generate energy aerobically).

Eventually, both ATP and glycogen will be used up, and exercise must stop, or the sportsperson will collapse! During the exercise period an **oxygen deficit** is incurred (refer to Figure 3.11). This is because the oxygen needs and oxygen supply differ. The oxygen deficit is calculated as the difference between oxygen required for a given work rate and the oxygen actually consumed.

Again, the important issue to stress is that **all mechanisms for manufacture of ATP are continuous**, and of course will continue when exercise stops—the evolutionary aim of the mechanisms being then to replace ATP and glycogen as quickly as possible—so that further exercise is possible.

Oxygen consumption during recovery

After every strenuous exercise, therefore, there are four tasks that need to be completed before the exhausted muscle can operate at full efficiency again:

    a. replacement of ATP,
    b. removal of lactic acid,
    c. replenishment of myoglobin with oxygen,
    d. replacement of glycogen.

The first three of these require oxygen in substantial quantities—hence the need for rapid breathing and high pulse rate to carry oxygen to the muscle cells. This need for oxygen to rapidly replace ATP and remove lactic acid is known as the **oxygen debt**—a more common term today is **excess post-exercise oxygen consumption (EPOC)**.

Item (d) (replacement of glycogen) is a long-term process which can take 24–48 hours depending on the fitness level, diet of the sportsperson and the intensity and duration of the exercise.

There are many other processes involved in oxygen recovery. For example, restoration of cardiac and/or pulmonary functioning to resting values, reversal of the high phosphate breakdown and return of body temperature to normal. All these processes need additional oxygen (although substantially less than that used during the alactacid and lactacid components illustrated in Figure 3.11) and therefore adds time to paying back the oxygen deficit to reach the pre-exercise level.

Figure 3.11 shows how the need for oxygen falls following cessation of exercise. Obviously, the more rapidly this process is completed, the quicker the sportsperson can resume exercise.

The two major traditional components of oxygen recovery are:

    1. **Alactacid oxygen debt** (or fast component),
    2. **Lactacid oxygen debt** (or slow component).

The contribution made by each to the overall process of oxygen recovery is marked on Figure 3.11, but note that both processes will occur initially, even though the alactic process is more rapid and is completed more quickly.

Alactacid oxygen debt component

Alactacid oxygen debt recovery is a rapid process involving the conversion of ADP back into PC and ATP, both of which will have been almost completely exhausted in the muscle cell sarcoplasm during intense exercise. This is achieved mainly by using the aerobic energy system, during which ATP and PC stores are replenished. This process is commonly known as **the restoration of muscle phosphagen stores** and its main function is to restore ATP and provide normal levels of PC in the muscle (which is used in the coupled reaction that restores ATP via the ATP–PC mechanism). Three mechanisms contributing to this are described below:

    a. Energy from aerobic conversion of carbohydrate into carbon dioxide and water is used to manufacture ATP from ADP and P_i (the products of ATP consumption).

    b. Some of this ATP is immediately utilized to create PC using the coupled reactions:

$$ATP \rightarrow ADP + P_i + energy$$
$$energy + P_i + C \rightarrow PC$$

    c. A very small percentage of ATP is remanufactured via glycolysis to produce small quantities of lactic acid.

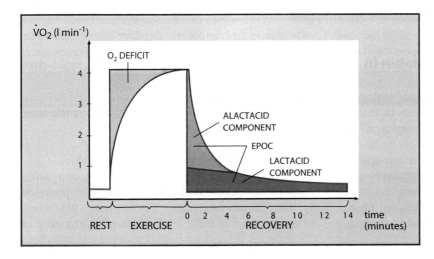

Figure 3.11 The relationship between oxygen deficit, oxygen consumption and the time before, during and after maximal exercise.

Muscle fatigue

Many bodily systems contribute towards fatigue levels; however, in this section we restrict our interest to muscle fatigue. Muscle fatigue can be defined as a reduction in muscular performance or a failure to maintain expected power output.

Within Sections 1.5 and 1.6 of this textbook, there is a full description of how nerve impulses are transmitted across the motor end plate to activate the sarcoplasmic reticulum and release calcium, which binds with troponin to initiate muscle contraction. It is thought that the interruption of these neuromuscular events could contribute towards muscle fatigue. Fatigue could occur at the motor end plate (refer to p. 41) since a delay in the release and synthesis of acetylcholine could reduce the conduction of the action potential and in turn could decrease the release of Ca^{++} available for muscle contraction. The muscle fibre membrane might develop a higher threshold level and the central nervous system might perceive fatigue prior to physiological fatigue and therefore act as a protective mechanism.

Other proposed theories of muscle fatigue are that it is due to depletion of energy substrates, such as the high energy phosphates (PC) (which are depleted very rapidly during maximal intensity exercise) and glycogen stores, and to the accumulation of metabolites, such as lactate and carbon dioxide. There is considerable evidence that supports the importance of accumulation of H^+ (released from lactic acid and carbonic acid) as a limiting factor in performance.

Experimental work has shown that fast twitch fibres are capable of generating large forces, but **local muscular fatigue** occurs more rapidly and is confined to the contractile mechanism. This is probably due to their low aerobic capacity and energy creation via anaerobic glycolysis, which leads to lactic acid accumulation.

Fatigue resulting from endurance-based exercise is probably due to depletion of muscle glycogen stores in both fast twitch and slow twitch fibres. **Total body fatigue** (that is often visible in marathon events) includes local muscular fatigue, plus additional factors such as low blood glucose levels, liver glycogen depletion and electrolyte loss in sweat (e.g. sodium chloride and potassium are filtered out of blood plasma). Fluid loss decreases plasma volume and therefore blood pressure, which in turn reduces blood flow to the skin and muscles. To overcome a reduction in plasma volume the heart has to work harder and, because blood flow to the skin is reduced, the body retains more heat. The optimal muscle temperature is somewhere between 27 and 30°C. Fatigue occurs at a much greater rate either above or below these values.

Restoration of muscle glycogen stores

There are about 350 grams of glycogen in the body, some stored as muscle glycogen, the remainder in the liver. During strenuous exercise, blood glucose increases as the liver metabolizes its glycogen stores and the amount of glycogen (stored within muscles) will be metabolized to glucose within the muscle tissue. Depletion of muscle glycogen stores appears to be a significant factor in muscular fatigue.

For short-distance, high intensity exercise, such as an 800 metre race, muscle glycogen stores are replenished within about 2 hours.

In long-distance endurance activities, such as marathon racing, a **glycogen-loaded diet** prior to the competition increases muscle and liver glycogen levels. However, during prolonged exercise, muscle and liver glycogen levels fall until a state of exhaustion is reached (refer to Fox *et al.*, p. 32, Fig. 2.17).

Complete restoration of muscle and liver glycogen stores is accelerated by a high carbohydrate diet. A detailed account of carbohydrate loading and its effect on performance is described on p. 115. It has been found that replenishment of muscle glycogen stores is most rapid during the first few hours and then can take several days to complete.

Another factor that may account for the speed of recovery of muscle glycogen stores during high intensity exercise, as compared with low intensity exercise, is that restoration of muscle glycogen is quicker in fast twitch fibres than in slow twitch fibres.

The factors discussed so far in relation to the replenishment of muscle glycogen are important to sportspersons and coaches alike. They must understand the need to plan their training sessions and competitions or games so that recovery has occurred in time for the next bout of high-intensity exercise.

Table 3.5 : Blood lactate and rate of working

Blood lactate (mmol l^{-1})	Rate of working (watts)
1	100
1.2	200
1.5	400
2.2	600
4.5	800
6.5	900
8.5	1000

Review Questions

1. a. What is the physiological basis for muscle soreness?

b. How could the information on lactic acid removal be of use to an athlete and coach in the design of training sessions?

c. Explain the importance of cool-down in the assistance of lactacid oxygen recovery and in the avoidance of muscle soreness.

2. Using the information in the sections on energy systems and oxygen recovery, complete the spaces in Table 3.6 with the major characteristics of the three energy systems in relation to the speed of running (refer to Bowers and Fox, p. 30, Table 2.2).

Table 3.6 : Phosphagen, lactic acid and oxygen systems

ATP–PC (phosphagen) system	Lactic acid system	Oxygen system
	Anaerobic	Aerobic
Very rapid		
Chemical fuel: PC	Food fuel:	Food fuel:
	Limited ATP production	
Muscular stores limited	By-product, lactic acid causes muscular pain	
Used with sprint or any high-power, short-duration work up to 10 sec		Used with endurance or long-duration activities over 2–3 min duration

(After Bowers and Fox, 1992.)

Exam-Style Questions

1. a. A student performs a flat-out 50 metre freestyle swim in 50 seconds.

i. Describe how most of the ATP is regenerated during the swim. (6 marks)

ii. Sketch a graph that shows the use of the appropriate energy systems against time during the swim. (3 marks)

b. i. What is **muscle fatigue**? (2 marks)

ii. Explain the process of **lactate conversion** that takes place during recovery from a swim. (3 marks)

c. The data in Table 3.5 illustrate the relationship between the concentration of blood lactate and rate of working.

i. Using the data in Table 3.5, plot a graph to illustrate the relationship between blood lactate concentration and rate of working (watts). (3 marks)

ii. Using the data, explain how you would deduce that at around 200 watts most of the work is done aerobically, and at around 900 watts most of the work is done anaerobically. Identify the approximate point at which the lactate threshold or OBLA occurs on your graph. (3 marks)

iii. What processes are involved in excess post-exercise oxygen consumption? (4 marks)

d. i. Discuss the fate of lactate removal during recovery. (4 marks)

ii. What organs and tissues are involved in this process? (2 marks)

e. How does light exercise influence lactate removal. (3 marks)

2. Describe the possible causes of fatigue during:

i. maximal exercise lasting between 2 and 10 seconds, (3 marks)

ii. submaximal exercise lasting from between 2 and 4 hours. (3 marks)

Summary

1. You should understand what is meant by **oxygen deficit**.
2. You should understand what is meant by **EPOC** and **OLBA**.
3. You should understand the importance of cool-down in the removal of lactic acid and in the reduction of muscle soreness.
4. You should understand the role of oxygenated myoglobin during recovery from intensive exercise.
5. You should understand the significance of the time factor and the effects of diet on the restoration of muscle phosphagen and muscle and liver glycogen levels.
6. You should understand the application of energy concepts to sporting activities.

Further Reading

Bowers R.W. and Fox E.L. *Sports Physiology*, Wm C. Brown, 1992.
de Vries H.A. *Physiology of Exercise* 5e, Wm C. Brown, 1994.
Fox E.L., Bowers R.W., Foss M.C. *The Physiological Basis for Exercise and Sport* 5e, Wm C. Brown, 1993.
Karlsson J. Lactate and phosphagen concentrations in working muscles of man. *Acta Physiologica, Scandinavica*, 1971; 358.

McArdle W.D., Katch F.I., Katch V.L. *Essentials of Exercise Physiology*, Lea & Febiger, 1994.
Newsholme E. and Leech T. Fatigue stops play. *New Scientist*, 1988; 22 Sept.
Newsholme E., Leech T., Duester G. *Keep on Running*, Wiley, 1994.

3.4 Oxygen Uptake/Oxygen Consumption

Keywords & concepts

aerobic power
alactacid capacity
anaerobic power
fatigue index

Harvard step test
lactacid capacity
minimum anaerobic power
oxygen consumption

peak anaerobic power
$\dot{V}O_{2max}$
Wingate anaerobic power test

Oxygen uptake, or **oxygen consumption**, is defined as the amount of oxygen a person consumes per unit of time (usually one minute). This concept is expressed as $\dot{V}O_2$, where V is volume, O_2 is oxygen and the dot over the V means *per unit of time*.

The oxidation of fuel foods requires a definite amount of oxygen per unit mass of fuel (1 kg), which can be measured indirectly by collecting expired air and comparing it with the composition of inspired air (i.e. by measuring the amount of **oxygen** that has been removed from the atmosphere and the amount of **carbon dioxide** that has been produced by the body).

At rest, oxygen uptake varies between 0.2 and 0.3 litres per minute. However, once an individual starts to exercise, the total body oxygen uptake increases proportionally with the intensity of the exercise, until a maximal work rate is reached. The highest $\dot{V}O_2$ achieved is expressed as $\dot{V}O_{2max}$. This concept of **maximum oxygen uptake** ($\dot{V}O_{2max}$) is also known as **aerobic power**.

$\dot{V}O_{2max}$ can therefore be quantitatively represented as the maximum amount of oxygen that a person can consume per minute during a progressive exercise test to exhaustion. This highest value represents the individual's maximal physiological capacity to transport and use oxygen.

A mean value of $\dot{V}O_{2max}$ for male students is about 3.5 litres per minute and for females it is about 2.7 litres per minute. Endurance athletes, such as those who participate regularly in middle- and long-distance running, rowing and cross-country skiing, may reach 4–6 litres per minute. However, $\dot{V}O_{2max}$ depends on body mass as well as physical fitness, so it is sometimes expressed in millilitres per kilogram of body mass per minute (ml kg^{-1} min^{-1}).

Factors affecting maximum aerobic power

The availability of oxygen in the tissues is the limiting factor in any exercise. The physical limitations that restrict the rate at which energy can be released aerobically are dependent upon the chemical ability of the **muscular cellular tissue system** to use oxygen in breaking down fuels, and the combined ability of **cardiovascular** and **pulmonary systems** to transport oxygen to the muscular tissue system.

Simple aerobic tests

Aerobic tests that are used as indicators of aerobic fitness include the Physical Work Capacity Test (PWC 170), the Cooper Run Test, the NCF Multistage Shuttle Run, the Fitech Step Test and the Queen's College Step Test.

 Investigation

3.5: To measure maximum aerobic power
The Queen's College Step Test

This investigation is a very simple method of determining maximum aerobic power. The data used to predict $\dot{V}O_{2max}$ (ml kg^{-1} min^{-1}) were based on the results of male and female college students at Queen's College in New York, who had their $\dot{V}O_{2max}$ measured (using a treadmill test procedure) and then plotted in relation to the corresponding recovery heart rate scores obtained on the step test, to produce predicted maximal oxygen uptake scores as shown in Table 3.7.
Materials: stepping bench (41 cm high), stopwatch, metronome.

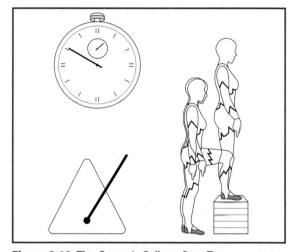

Figure 3.12 The Queen's College Step Test.

Table 3.7 : Queen's College Step Test

Percentile ranking	Recovery HR, female (bpm)	Predicted $\dot{V}O_{2max}$ (ml kg^{-1} min^{-1})	Recovery HR, male (bpm)	Predicted $\dot{V}O_{2max}$ (ml kg^{-1} min^{-1})
100	128	42.2	120	60.9
95	140	40.0	124	59.3
90	148	38.5	128	57.6
85	152	37.7	136	54.2
80	156	37.0	140	52.5
75	158	36.6	144	50.9
70	160	36.3	148	49.2
65	162	35.9	149	48.8
60	163	35.7	152	47.5
55	164	35.5	154	46.7
50	166	35.1	156	45.8
45	168	34.8	160	44.1
40	170	34.4	152	43.3
35	171	34.2	164	42.5
30	172	34.0	166	41.6
25	176	33.3	168	40.8
20	180	32.6	172	39.1
15	182	32.2	176	37.4
10	184	31.8	178	36.6
5	196	29.6	184	34.1

Investigation

3.5 continued

Task One

1. Establish the step cadence: for females set the metronome at 88 beats per minute, for males at 96 beats per minute. Practise the step rhythm to adjust to the cadence of the metronome. The sequence is left up/right up/left down/right down—each element to a single metronome beat.

2. Take a rest and when you are ready, begin to step for 3 minutes at the set step cadence.

3. At the end of the exercise period remain standing for 5 seconds. Then take your pulse count at the carotid artery for a 15 second count. Multiply by four to give the heart rate score in beats per minute (bpm).

4. Using the information in Table 3.7, work out your predicted $\dot{V}O_{2max}$ and percentile ranking, based on your recovery heart rate value.

Task Two—collation of results

1. Record in Table 3.8 your results and those of male and female students in your class.

2. Compare group results. Work out the percentage differences between male and female values. Are there any differences within your group? Account for these differences.

3. Work out your predicted $\dot{V}O_{2max/min}$ for your total body mass by multiplying $\dot{V}O_{2max}$ (ml kg^{-1} min^{-1}) by your body weight (kg). How does this value relate to the values given earlier in this unit?

Table 3.8 : Results table

Name	Percentile ranking	Recovery HR	Predicted $\dot{V}O_{2max}$ (ml kg^{-1} min^{-1})
self			

Task Three

1. Describe the two main factors that limit aerobic power.

2. Describe some of the ways in which aerobic capacity could be improved.

3. Which muscle fibre type is used predominantly in aerobic work?

4. Discuss the purpose of testing aerobic power with respect to endurance events.

5. Describe the energy systems used during the step test.

Task Four

Figure 3.13 shows how oxygen consumption changes as an athlete runs at a constant pace up a series of hills increasing in slope.

1. Describe and account for the pattern of oxygen consumption from the level ground until the end of the third hill.

2. Why does oxygen consumption begin to level off after the third hill?

3. The athlete is only just able to run up the final sixth hill where he/she achieves his/her $\dot{V}O_{2max}$. Explain what this concept means and why the athlete is unable to continue running at the set pace.

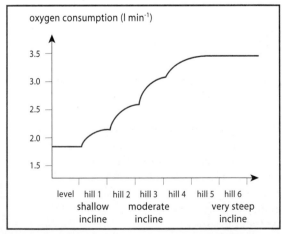

Figure 3.13 Change in oxygen consumption as an athlete runs, at a constant pace, up a series of hills increasing in slope.

Investigation

3.5 continued

4. How would this pattern of oxygen consumption change if the athlete trained regularly over this terrain? Suggest possible reasons in your answer.

Task Five
1. Sketch a graph that illustrates the amount of oxygen consumed in litres per minute (on the *y*-axis) against time (on the *x*-axis) for a jogger who at rest consumes 0.3 litres per minute, and who then starts to run at a steady pace for 20 minutes, having reached a 'steady state' of oxygen consumption at 1.75 litres per minute, 5 minutes into the run.
2. Label on your graph the part of the curve that is referred to as 'steady state' and explain what this concept means.

Task Six
$\dot{V}O_{2max}$ decreases by about 10% per decade with ageing, starting in the late teens for women and in the mid-20s for men. Account for the effects of age on $\dot{V}O_{2max}$ values.

Oxygen consumption as an indirect way of measuring energy costs—a hypothetical example

Consider the following calculation as an example of how to go about estimating energy costs indirectly.

First, work out the **net oxygen cost** (the oxygen consumed during exercise above that which is needed at rest) from the resting and exercise rates of consumption. In our example these values are 0.4 litres per minute and 2.15 litres per minute, respectively, thereby giving a net oxygen cost total of 1.75 litres per minute.

Next, let us assume that the person undertaking the exercise works for a 10 minute period at this rate. The net oxygen cost for the 10 minutes will be $10 \times 1.75 = 17.5$ litres. As 1 litre of oxygen produces 22 kJ of heat energy by combination with food fuel in the body, the energy cost of the exercise will be:

$$22 \times 17.5 = 385 \text{ kJ}$$

In practice the net oxygen cost will always be greater than that calculated for the duration of exercise, as the net oxygen cost continues after exercise stops until oxygen consumption reaches its resting value.

You may wish to work out your own hypothetical example.

Anaerobic capacity

In addition to the assessment of aerobic fitness, the measurement of **anaerobic capacity** (the ability to do physical work, which is dependent upon the anaerobic mechanisms of energy supply) may also be of interest to those who are interested in short, explosive physical activities.

Investigation

3.6: Measurement of alactacid anaerobic capacity and lactacid capacity

The **Wingate Anaerobic Cycling Test** was devised at the Wingate Institute in Israel (Figure 3.14). This test is a 30 second all-out cycling test, which is used to determine **maximal anaerobic power**. Anaerobic power **is the ability to produce energy by the ATP–PC system** (adenosine triphosphate–phosphocreatine system). (Refer to Inbar *The Wingate Anaerobic Test*.)

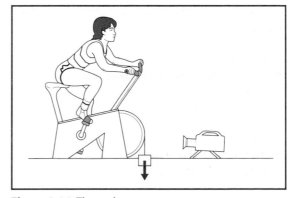

Figure 3.14 The cycle ergometer.

Exam-Style Questions

continued

e. Comment on the validity of $\dot{V}O_{2max}$ as a predictor of performance in sport. (2 marks)
f. How would cardiovascular endurance conditioning be important in anaerobic sports? (2 marks)
4. Briefly describe tests that can be used to

evaluate one's capacity when performing:
a. i. aerobic work, (3 marks)
ii. anaerobic work. (3 marks)
b. Show how your selected tests can be evaluated. (4 marks)
c. Comment on the advantages and disadvantages of the tests you have described. (4 marks)

 Summary

1. You should be able to understand which energy mechanisms predominate in practical activities.
2. You should understand what is meant by oxygen uptake, aerobic power, $\dot{V}O_{2max}$, anaerobic power and anaerobic capacity.
3. You should be able to describe the factors affecting aerobic power.
4. You should be able to discuss the purpose of testing aerobic power in relation to endurance activities.
5. You should be able to discuss the purpose of testing anaerobic power in relation to explosive exercise activities.

 Further Reading

Bowers R.W. and Fox E.L. *Sports Physiology* 3e, Wm C. Brown, 1992.
de Vries H.A. *Physiology of Exercise* 5e, Wm C. Brown, 1994.
Fox E.L., Bowers R.W., Foss M.L. *The Physiological Basis for Exercise and Sport* 6e, Wm C. Brown, 1997.
Inbar O., OrBar O., Skinner S.S. *The Wingate Anaerobic Test*, Human Kinetics, 1996.
McArdle W.D., Katch F.I., Katch V.L. *Essentials of Exercise Physiology*, Lea & Febiger, 1994.
Sharkey B.J. *New Dimensions in Aerobic Fitness*, Human Kinetics, 1991.
Wilmore J.H. *Physiology of Sport and Exercise*, Human Kinetics, 1994.

3.5 Nutrition for Exercise

 Keywords & concepts

carbo-loading	fatty acids and glycerol	lipids
carbohydrates	glucose	proteins
fats	glycogen	triglyceride

The food and drink a sportsperson consumes daily provide the energy, from carbohydrates and fats, to maintain bodily functions, in addition to providing all the energy needed for training and competition. Food also contains other nutrients, namely proteins, minerals, vitamins, water and roughage.

This section will help you to understand how these nutrients are vital to life processes and how carbohydrates and fats are the main energy providers for physical activity.

A **balanced diet** containing the correct proportions of carbohydrates, fats and proteins, together with minerals, vitamins, water and roughage, is important to an individual, whether active in sport or not, in order to maintain good health.

Proteins

Protein is present in most foods; it is present in large quantities in meat, eggs and milk. It is needed for growth and body building. For example, protein is used to increase the strength of muscle fibres, described in Chapter 1 (p. 25). Damaged tissues (resulting from fracture, dislocations, sprains, muscle strains and bruising, often incurred during physical activity) need proteins to repair injury sites. Proteins are also essential to make enzymes required for metabolic functioning, **but** they are used as an energy source only when the body is depleted of all carbohydrates and fat sources.

Minerals

Minerals are essential because they contain elements or small groups of elements needed to form part of the molecular structure of chemicals required by the body for life processes. For example, haemoglobin and muscle myoglobin contain an **iron** atom without which synthesis of haemoglobin would be impossible (lack of haemoglobin causes anaemia).

Vitamins

Vitamins perform a similar role except that complex organic **radicals** are provided which are needed for the synthesis of molecules that participate in life processes. Such radicals cannot be manufactured by the body, and therefore have to be ingested as part of the nutrition process (a radical is a stable group of atoms, which forms part of a complex molecule). For example, ascorbic acid, otherwise known as vitamin C, contains the radical **ascorbate**, which is needed as part of the physiological **process** that prevents scurvy.

(See a specialist text on nutrition for a full list of vitamins and their effects on human health, such as Katch and McArdle, 1993; or the *Nutritional Needs of Athletes* by Fred Browns, 1993.)

Water

Water accounts for two-thirds of body weight. It is an essential ingredient in a daily diet because it dissolves more substances than anything else. As a result nearly all chemical reactions essential to life take place in a watery medium. It also allows materials to move from one place of the body to another. For example, blood plasma consists of 90% water and transports a variety of substances, such as glucose, all around the body.

Water is very important as a heat regulator (heat is released as a result of tissue respiration). For example, blood plasma is able to take up heat and transport it to the body surface where it can be radiated away from the body. Another method of losing heat energy from the body surface involves water being excreted through the skin (sweating). As the water evaporates, the energy necessary to do this is extracted from the skin itself, thereby causing the skin to cool. Water is also lost as water vapour during expiration.

Roughage

Roughage or dietary fibre, found for example in cereals, provides bulk needed for the functioning of the large intestine.

Carbohydrates and fats—the energy givers

The bulk of chemical energy released by the chemical reactions involved in tissue respiration comes from carbohydrates and fats. Carbohydrates are the body's principal fuel, yielding 75% of our energy requirements; fats provide the remainder.

Figure 3.18 A balanced diet.

Carbohydrates

Carbohydrates include sugar, starch and cellulose. The sugars can be either **simple sugars** or **monosaccharides** (e.g. glucose and fructose, both having the chemical formula $C_6H_{12}O_6$), or **complex sugars** or **disaccharides** (e.g. sucrose, maltose and lactose, all having the chemical formula $C_{12}H_{22}O_{11}$). Starch, found in food sources such as rice and potatoes, and cellulose are **polysaccharides**, since their molecular structures are chain-like multiples of glucose, and have the formula $(C_6H_{10}O_5)_n$ where n represents the number of glucose units in the molecule. This number varies between 100 and 1000 depending on the biological origin of the starch. Most of the carbohydrates we ingest are in the form of starch and cellulose.

Cellulose does not provide energy, but is dietary fibre important for peristalsis in the large intestine. Peristalsis is a chain of muscular contractions that drives food along, thus preventing constipation.

Within the digestive tract, polysaccharides are hydrolysed to glucose and are stored as glycogen in both liver and muscle cells (the liver also has the function of converting glycogen into glucose when it is needed for tissue respiration).

One gram of carbohydrate provides 17 kJ of energy.

Fats

Fats are found in both animal and vegetable sources and should provide about 25% of energy requirements. Foods such as butter and bacon contain animal fats, with nuts and soya beans containing vegetable fats.

Within the digestive system, fats or **lipids** are converted by the enzyme **lipase** into **fatty acids** and **glycerol**.

Fats provide twice the energy yield of carbohydrates at 39 kJ g^{-1}.

In the bloodstream, glucose (derived from fats and carbohydrates) can be sent directly to muscles for energy release by direct involvement in the ADP to ATP conversion reaction or the PC coupled reaction for the creation of ATP. Otherwise surplus glucose, not needed by these reactions, is converted (by the actions of the hormone **insulin**) into glycogen. This is stored in the liver (as **liver glycogen**) or in the muscle cell sarcoplasm (as **muscle glycogen**). If the body does not need the glucose, it enters the **fat metabolic system**, where it is converted into fatty acids and glycerol and is stored in the body as **triglycerides** (body fat) in adipose tissue and skeletal muscle. When energy is required from fat fuels, the contents of each individual adipose cell or muscle triglyceride are broken down into glycerol and free fatty acids. These are then transported by the circulatory system to the liver, where conversion into glucose takes place.

Other hormones that take part in the conversion of fat into carbohydrate are **glucagon** and **adrenaline** (insulin and glucagon are secreted by the Islets of Langerhans in the pancreas, and adrenaline is secreted from the adrenal glands situated on the top of each kidney).

The layer of fat formed under the skin (adipose tissue) acts as a heat insulator and, in a sporting context such as long-distance swimming, can be formed as adaptation to cold conditions (and also by the eating of suitably large amounts of carbohydrates).

Energy metabolism

The total intake of food must be sufficient to supply enough energy to keep cells alive, their systems working and to meet the demands of any activity that the body undertakes. The **basal metabolic rate** is the body's basic cost of living and the **total metabolic rate** is the sum of the basal metabolic costs plus all the energy needed to carry out all daily activities. The energy requirements of an individual vary according to age, size, metabolic rate, gender, environment and life-style, and they are discussed in Chapter 5.

Fuel foods for action

Both carbohydrates and fats are used to supply **glycogen** necessary for all forms of physical activity. However, the utilization of carbohydrates and fats as nutrient fuels for muscle contraction during physical activity depends on the types of muscular activity; whether the work is intermittent, prolonged, light or heavy—in other words, the **exercise duration** and **exercise intensity**. Table 3.10 describes these relationships.

Training and fuel use

The influence of endurance training on metabolic mixture and rate of energy utilization is illustrated in Figure 3.19. This graph shows that untrained sportspersons who exercise at a low intensity will obtain the majority of their energy requirements from carbohydrates (column A). But if they continue to exercise long term at the same intensity, their metabolic systems will adapt by using more fat from the diet (and therefore less carbohydrate proportionately, column B). This means that more carbohydrate is available for the energy needed for increased effort during aerobic exercise (column C). Therefore, the total energy available to the adapted metabolism from both fats and carbohydrates increases, and the sportsperson becomes fitter and capable of more exercise.

Table 3.10 : Fuel and exercise

Exercise intensity	Exercise duration	Fuel used
maximal sprint	short	carbohydrate
low to moderate	moderate up to 2 hours, e.g. jogging	carbohydrate and fat equally
severe	prolonged, e.g. cycling	less carbohydrate more fat

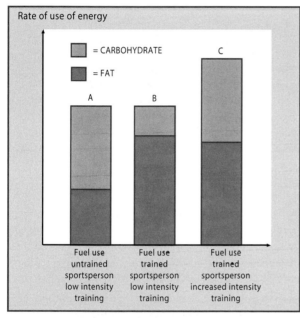

Figure 3.19 Endurance training and fuel use.

Carbo-loading and performance

The concept of a **glycogen-loaded diet** was first devised in the 1960s; such a diet super-charges glycogen stores in muscle fibres. This can be achieved by using an intensive training run that **depletes** muscle glycogen levels 7 days prior to a major event. At this point, and for the next 3 days, the athlete eats mainly fats and proteins to deprive the muscle of carbohydrates. This has the effect of **increasing** the activity of glycogen synthase (the enzyme responsible for glycogen synthesis). During this period, the training intensity is reduced to prevent total glycogen depletion and possible injury. The final 3–4 day period prior to the major event utilizes a carbohydrate-rich diet, restricted intake of fats and proteins and high fluid intake, along with low-intensity training. Because glycogen synthase activity has been boosted during the previous period, carbohydrate dietary intake now results in increased muscle glycogen storage. The overall effect is for performance times to improve significantly. However, there are **disadvantages** in using this dietary regime, since some athletes observe an increase in body weight (since more water is needed to store the increased glycogen stores), and during the depletion phase many athletes feel weak, depressed and irritable.

More recently, athletes have found alternative methods when preparing for major competitions. For example, following depletion of glycogen stores, athletes have reduced the period of low carbohydrate dietary intake to a single day or skipped it completely, and have followed this by a 3–4 day period during which a carbohydrate-rich diet is taken. Recent studies have shown that a gradual tapering off in training alongside increased carbohydrate intake offers similar ergogenic benefits to those observed in early studies (which utilized the full programme as outlined above).

The best time to eat on the competition day is 2–3 hours prior to the event, and meals should be of low volume and contain carbohydrates and plenty of fluids. This is because liver glycogen stores need topping up, even in a well-nourished glycogen-laden athlete.

It is possible to measure the rate of respiration using simple respirometers and calculate respiratory quotients for proteins, fats and carbohydrates, as described on p. 92.

115

Review Questions

1. What are the purposes of each of the three basic groups of food?
2. How can high-carbohydrate diets influence metabolism?
3. How do you think different types of exercise could alter food intake?
4. Select two physical activities, one of short duration and high intensity and one of long duration and low intensity.

a. Describe, with the aid of a bar chart, the relative contributions of carbohydrates and fats as fuel foods for your two chosen activities.
b. Account for the differences between fuel usage for your two chosen activities.
c. Sketch a graph to illustrate the relationship between short, high intensity exercise and prolonged low intensity exercise and food fuel usage (refer to Bowers and Fox, *Sports Physiology*, Fig. 4.1, p. 57).

 Exam-Style Questions

1. The digestion of fats results in the release of glycerol and fatty acids into the bloodstream.
a. With reference to both short-term and long-term provision of energy for muscle contraction, describe what can happen to these compounds once they are released into the bloodstream. (5 marks)
b. Very little fat is stored in muscle fibres, yet fat is a main source during aerobic exercise. Explain how the fat stores of the body become available to working muscles. (4 marks)
c. What are the disadvantages of fat as an energy source during exercise? (2 marks)
d. After prolonged, continuous exercise there can be a severe drop in available energy, even though the body still has considerable fat reserves. Explain why this is so. (5 marks)
e. Although fat reserves have value as a source of energy for exercise, in other ways they can be detrimental to sport performance. Explain why this is so. (4 marks)
2. a. Explain how marathon runners can overcome the following problems:
i. depletion of carbohydrate reserves, (3 marks)
ii. temperature regulation. (3 marks)
b. Describe and justify a preferred pre-competition meal prior to a marathon. (5 marks)
3. Give a brief outline and comment critically upon the effects of glycogen loading on the enhancement of sport performance. (12 marks)

 Summary

1. You should understand the functions of carbohydrates, fats, proteins, minerals, vitamins, roughage and water in the context of a balanced diet.
2. You should be able to appreciate the role of carbohydrates and fats in relation to intensity and duration of the exercise period.
3. You should be able to understand the effects of carbo-loading and performance.

 Further Reading

Bowers R.W. and Fox E.L. *Sports Physiology* 3e, Wm C. Brown, 1992.
Browns F. *Nutritional Needs of Athletes*, Wiley, 1993.
Katch F.I. and McArdle W.D. *Introduction to Nutrition, Exercise and Health* 4e, Lea & Febiger, 1993.
McArdle W.D., Katch F.I., Katch V.L. *Essentials of Exercise Physiology*, Lea & Febiger, 1994.
Paish W. *Nutrition for Sport*, Crowood Press, 1990.
Sharkey B.J. *Fitness and Health* 4e, Human Kinetics, 1997.

Chapter 4

Training for Physical Performance

4.1 Physical Fitness and Fitness Testing

 Keywords & concepts

agility	fitness	PWC-170 test
balance	flexibility	reaction time
body composition	motor fitness	speed
construct validation	physical fitness	
co-ordination	power	

Physical fitness is one of the basic requirements of life. Broadly speaking, it means the ability to carry out our daily tasks without undue fatigue. In the sporting context it is difficult to define since it can refer to psychological, physiological or anatomical states of the body. To most physical education teachers it is seen as a concept obtained by measuring and evaluating a person's state of fitness by using a battery of tests.

This section will help you to understand those aspects of **fitness** that are important to physical performance and good health.

Types of fitness test

1. **Motor fitness tests** aim to look at neuromuscular components of fitness and therefore consider skill-related exercises and the capacity of the individual to repeat a particular exercise.

2. **Physical fitness tests** aim to look at anatomical and physiological components that determine a person's physical performance capacity. These tests make direct measurements of physiological parameters such as heart rate, oxygen uptake and flexibility.

The ability of a person to perform successfully at a particular game may not be an indicator of physical fitness, but an assessment of the motor fitness of the individual to perform the specific skills relevant to the game. Motor fitness refers to the **efficiency** of movements and, although including the **power** component, is mostly about **balance**, **agility** and **co-ordination**.

Physical fitness

The concept of **physical fitness**, in general athletic terms, means the capability of the individual to meet the varied physical and physiological demands made by a sporting activity, without reducing the person to an excessively fatigued state. Such a state would be one in which he/she can no longer perform the skills of the activity accurately and successfully.

The components of physical fitness are defined in Figure 4.1.

Strength

Strength is defined as the force exerted by muscle groups during a single maximal muscle contraction. (Refer to Chapter 1, which describes different types of muscle contractions.)

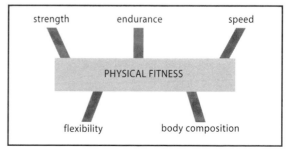

Figure 4.1 Components of physical fitness.

Investigation

4.1 continued

Task Six—self-evaluation of body composition
Skinfold measurements: to test skinfold measurements taken at three sites on the body.
Materials: skinfold calipers.
Take three skinfold measurements at the three locations indicated in Figure 4.10. Add together these three skinfold measurements and evaluate your body fatness in relation to the skinfold rating chart (Table 4.8).

Table 4.8 : Skinfold rating

| Sum of skinfold thickness (mm) | | Rating |
males	females	
< 22	< 25	excellent
34–22	42–25	good
73–35	65–43	average
90–74	82–66	fair
> 90	> 82	poor

(The information for this rating chart has been taken from Pollock, Schmidt and Jackson, 1980.)

Figure 4.10a–c Skinfold measurements.

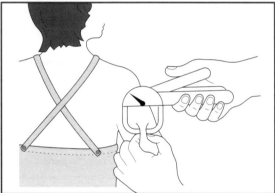

a Triceps.

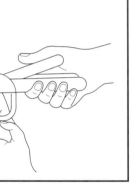

b Scapula.

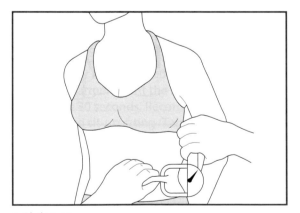

c Abdomen.

Investigation

4.1 continued

Task Seven—self-evaluation of agility
The Illinois Agility Run: to test speed and agility.
Materials: cones, tape-measure.
Mark out an area of 10 m in length and place four obstacles 3.3 m apart, as shown in Figure 4.11. Lie prone, head to start line, hands beside your shoulders. On the command '*go*' run the course as fast as possible. Have a member of your group issue the start command and time the run. Record your time and fitness rating (Table 4.9).

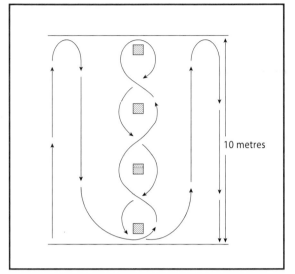

Figure 4.11 Agility run.

Table 4.9 : Agility run rating

Time in seconds		Rating
males	females	
< 15.2	< 17.0	excellent
16.1–15.2	17.9–17.0	good
18.1–16.2	21.7–18.0	average
18.3–18.2	23.0–21.8	fair
> 18.3	> 23.0	poor

Task Eight—self-evaluation of static balance
Balancing on a beam: to test a timed static balance.
Materials: gymnastics bench (Figure 4.12).
Time how long balance can be maintained on one foot, with eyes closed, on a balance beam or inverted bench. Within your class use everyone's results to devise a rating scale.

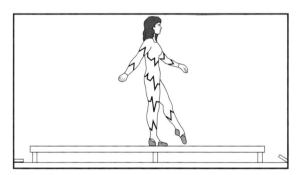

Figure 4.12 Balancing on a beam.

Figure 4.20 shows changes in ATP–PC to **lactic** thresholds between trained and untrained people. The unbroken line shows how power output at maximum effort changes with time for the untrained person. The point at which power rapidly falls is the point at which ATP–PC stores are used up, and is therefore the **ATP–PC** to **lactic** threshold (at 7 seconds in this example).

On the other hand, the trained athlete (dashed line) has a higher maximum power output and a delay in threshold (to about 10 seconds) due to larger ATP–PC stores.

Muscle and soft tissue effects
Muscle adaptation
It is found that the most noticeable effect of anaerobic training in muscle fibres (particularly fast twitch, which respond when large forces are applied to a given muscle) is **muscle hypertrophy**. This is due to an increase in muscle width because more actin and myosin are assimilated: this increases the strength of each fibre because more contractile protein allows for more cross-bridges to be formed (see p. 37), so the net effect is an increase in the strength of contraction. In addition, there is evidence that more fibres are generated, possibly by longitudinal splitting of existing fast twitch fibres. The effect, therefore, is to make muscle bigger and stronger.

In highly trained anaerobic athletes fast twitch muscle fibres occupy a greater cross-sectional area when compared with the slow twitch fibre content of a given muscle, whereas in highly trained aerobic athletes the reverse situation is found.

In trained sportspersons there is a noticeable increase in the recruitment of motor units (see p. 42) and improved co-ordination of the firing of motor units to allow increases in strength (see p. 43).

Capillarization and arterio-venous oxygen difference
It has been found that the blood supply to muscles undertaking aerobic exercise is enhanced by new capillaries being generated within the muscle bulk. An increase in capillary density results in a shorter diffusion distance between blood and muscle cells. This is in addition to increased myoglobin and mitochondrial density. The net effect is an increase in the arterio-venous oxygen difference (a-$\bar{v}O_2$ diff), since venous blood on returning from working muscles to the heart is almost completely depleted of oxygen. However, this blood then mixes with venous blood from less active parts of the body, and hence the arterio-venous oxygen difference shows little change in the overall venous return. The net effect is the development of a more efficient oxygen transport system.

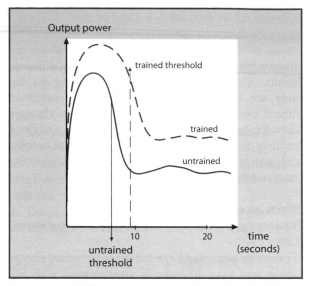

Figure 4.20 Difference in ATP–PC to lactic thresholds between trained and untrained people.

Bradycardia
One of the most obvious adaptations that occurs with endurance-based training is a decrease in resting heart rate. Endurance athletes often have resting heart rates in the low 40s (bpm). **Bradycardia** is a term that describes a reduction in heart rate to below 60 bpm; it is caused by the enlargement of the heart muscle in response to its increased rate of activity, in the same way that skeletal muscle hypertrophy occurs. An increase in the thickness and strength of the left ventricular wall causes an increase in the stroke volume and a lowering of resting pulse for a given cardiac output (see Figure 2.10, p. 56). This is the means by which greater blood volumes, and hence oxygen-carrying capacity, are available to the remaining musculature. Blood flow to the myocardium is slightly less during submaximal work rates since the heart is more efficient. Maximal cardiac output is increased to about the same extent as maximum stroke volume (see Figure 2.10, p. 56).

Effects on tendons and other connective tissue
Tendon thickness and ligament strength and thickness are enhanced by stress. This appears to be a process of gradual protein assimilation. Articular cartilage also becomes thicker and more compressible when large forces are repeatedly applied. This has the effect of providing more cushioning to the ends of long bones under impact.

Respiratory effects
In response to the demand for oxygen, more lung alveoli become utilized, the capillary network surrounding the alveoli increases and there is a slight increase in

Figure 4.21

lung volumes. Hence the lungs have a greater surface for gaseous exchange. The respiratory muscles become stronger, enabling gas in larger volumes per intake to be breathed and exhaled more rapidly. This has the effect of developing a more efficient breathing system.

Recovery enhancement

This is not a separate effect, but more the combination of heart and lung adaptations that enable more oxygen to become available more rapidly during and immediately after exercise. Also, an enhanced capillary system supplies nutrients and glucose more efficiently to the muscle sites where they are needed.

Sweating

Homeostasis is the maintenance of a constant internal bodily environment despite possible changes in external conditions. During exercise, the amount of heat energy produced is proportional to the intensity and duration of the exercise. The **thermoregulation centre**, which is situated in the **hypothalamus**, is sensitive to the temperature of the blood and sends out impulses to the skin, where appropriate action (for example, **sweating**) is taken. Another action is diversion of blood to the skin so that heat energy can be carried via blood from the musculature to the skin, where it is radiated away.

Sweating is therefore an evolutionary development that enables the human body to maintain approximately constant temperature, in spite of the inefficient transformation of energy from chemical energy to useful work energy in the musculature.

Sweating provides moisture, which evaporates from the skin surface. The energy required for this process is extracted from the skin, which therefore loses heat energy and cools down. This response is again subject to adaptation when the body generates

more heat as more exercise is done. Therefore, the capability of sweat production is enhanced by training. Similarly, if the individual moves to a warmer or more humid climate, bodily heat loss to the surroundings is reduced by external physical factors and the need to lose heat from the body surface is increased.

Regression

It has been found that all the effects of training mentioned above **regress** to their normal untrained state if training ceases. Interestingly, it is found that effects established by **longer** periods of training remain for **longer** after training stops. Figure 4.23 shows an example of this.

Time is measured from the point at which training stops, which is when peak performance is observed. What is found is that exercise regimes that begin a long time before this point (A on the graph) enable the body to **retain** the increased fitness for a long time after training stops. On the other hand, training begun a short while beforehand (B on the graph), even though it may achieve high levels of fitness, will not promote much biological adaptation. In this case, fitness levels fall quickly after training stops.

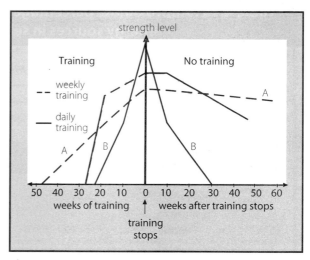

Figure 4.23 Regression after training is stopped. (*After Harre* et al., *1982.*)

Figure 4.24

Figure 4.22

Warm-up and cool-down

The final principles of training discussed here are preparation of the body for exercise, and what to do immediately after exercise to minimize the risk of injury and muscle soreness.

Warm-up

Although anaerobic work can be done without using the oxygen carrying and delivery capacity of the cardiovascular system, replenishment of ATP and muscle glycogen depends on an efficient blood capillary system. Therefore, recovery from the oxygen debt is improved if light aerobic exercise is undertaken before training. This dilates capillaries and raises the pulse rate, pumping blood around the body more quickly.

A further effect of warm-up is to raise the body temperature. It has been shown that ATP conversion, glycolytic enzyme action and muscle reaction response times are quicker at a slightly higher temperature.

Also, blood viscosity is slightly reduced at higher temperatures, so that the flow of blood (and its ability to pass through the capillary system) is improved. It is also found that light muscle stretching prepares the musculature for operation over its full range.

Cool-down

It seems important to do a small amount of aerobic work immediately after completion of a training session. This has the purpose of flushing the capillary system with oxygenated blood, thereby enabling oxygen debt in muscles to be fully purged, and lactic products of lactic anaerobic work to be converted and removed. This will hopefully limit muscle soreness and enhance recovery.

Altitude training

Since the beginning of the twentieth century the effects of altitude on physical performance have been catalogued by mountaineers. The decision to hold the 1968 Olympic Games in Mexico City at an altitude of 2242 m (7450 feet) resulted in intense physiological research into human acclimatization.

Human difficulties experienced at altitude

Sportspeople training or competing at high altitude suffer from acute drops in performance in sports that rely on aerobic capacity. This is due to lack of oxygen. Figure 4.31 illustrates the oxygen transport system at sea level and at altitude before and after acclimatization (Pugh, 1967).

The degree to which haemoglobin is saturated with oxygen depends on the partial pressure of the alveolar air. (See Chapter 2, p. 77, to review the concept of the oxygen–haemoglobin dissociation curve.) At sea level, the partial pressure of oxygen in inspired air is sufficient to ensure that the haemoglobin is fully saturated. At altitude, the partial pressure of oxygen in the atmosphere and pulmonary air is reduced. The result is that the haemoglobin is not fully saturated, therefore less oxygen is carried to muscle tissues and the aerobic working capacity of these tissues is reduced.

Physiological changes during acclimatization

Three major physiological changes occur in the body as a result of acclimatization, as outlined below.

Increase in blood haemoglobin concentrations

During acclimatization there is an increase in red blood cell count and therefore an increase in haemoglobin

Figure 4.31a–c The oxygen transport system at sea level and at altitude, both before and after acclimatization.

RBC, red blood cells; Hb, haemoglobin, pCO_2, partial pressure of carbon dioxide. (*After Pugh, 1967.*)

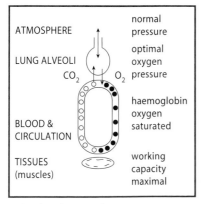

a Sea level, normal.

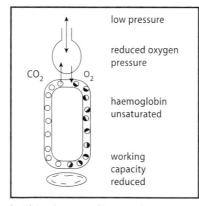

b Altitude, unacclimatized.

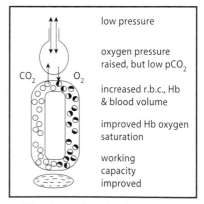

c Altitude, acclimatized.

concentration, but the haemoglobin remains unsaturated with oxygen. The increase in red blood cell count is brought about by an increase in the manufacture of red blood cells, which is a rapid response made by the body to altitude, and a reduction in the plasma volume, which is a slow long-term response to a result of acclimatization. It has been found that the haemoglobin concentrations of residents (who are presumably acclimatized) at altitude are inversely proportional to the prevailing barometric pressures (Pugh, 1964).

Increased rate of breathing
To compensate for a decrease in the partial pressure of oxygen in the alveoli, breathing rate increases. This response develops over several days (Pugh, 1967). Increased ventilation reduces the partial pressure of carbon dioxide, which makes the blood too alkaline.

This problem is corrected by the kidneys, with the urine secretion being more alkaline than normal.

Cellular changes
There is an increase in the myoglobin content of the muscles, and changes in characteristics and amounts of mitochondria (Tappen and Reynafarje, 1957).

Net effect
The net effect of human acclimatization to altitude is to improve the aerobic working capacity of muscles to compensate for the reduced partial pressure of atmospheric oxygen, and to improve the capacity of the oxygen transport system to purge the oxygen debt. Pugh (1967) showed that at least 4 weeks of acclimatization are required if sea-level athletes are to stabilize their performances at altitude.

 # Investigation

4.6: To consider the results of running events in the Mexico Olympic Games, 1968, and the benefits of altitude training camps to sea-level performances

Task One
Consider the information in Figure 4.32. Suggest reasons why world records were broken at 100, 200 and 400 metres.

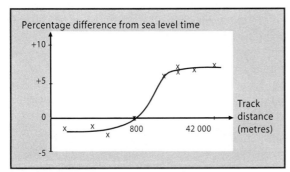

Figure 4.32 Results of running events in the 1968 Olympic Games.

Task Two
In the endurance events above 1500 metres, there was a uniform reduction in performance of about 6%. Suggest reasons for this observation.

Task Three
The data in Table 4.15 refer to Olympic Games held at the sites stated. Carefully explain why acclimatized athletes were relatively successful during the 10 000 metres race at the Mexico Olympic Games.

Table 4.15 : Results of the 10 000 m race	
Tokyo 1964 (200 m above sea level)	**Tokyo 1964 (2242 m above sea level)**
1. M. Mills, USA	1. N. Temu, Kenya••
2. M. Gammoudi, Tunisia••	2. M. Wolde, Ethiopia••
3. R. Clarke, Australia	3. M. Gammoudi, Tunisia••
4. M. Wolde, Ethiopia••	4. J. Martinez, Mexico••
5. L. Evanov, Russia	5. N. Sviridov, Russia•
6. K. Tsudurova, Japan	6. R. Clarke, Australia•
7. M. Halberg, New Zealand	7. R. Hilll, UK•
8. A. Cook, Australia	8. W. Masresha, Ethiopia•

•• had lived at high altitude for most of their life
• trained at high altitude for an extended period prior to the Games

Investigation

4.6 continued

Task Four

Haemoglobin reversal occurs between 3 and 8 days after return to sea level. Any respiratory changes are reversed immediately and cellular changes reverse within 1–2 weeks.
Since the Mexico Olympic Games it has been common for endurance athletes to spend a period of several weeks at high altitude training camps and then return to sea level to compete within about 3 days. How useful is the rationale of altitude camps to sea-level performances?

Task Five—aids to performance

Acclimatization is one way in which performance in sporting activities may be enhanced. What other methods are used by current sportsmen and women to aid performance?

Task Six—the ethics of aids to performance

Doping is defined as the administration or use of substances in any form alien to the body or of physiological substances in abnormal amounts and with abnormal methods by healthy persons with the exclusive aim of attaining an artificial and unfair increase in performance in competition. Furthermore, various psychological measures to increase performance in sports must be regarded as doping. (Statement by the International Olympic Committee.)

Using this definition of doping, and your answers to Task Five, decide whether you think there are any ethical objections to the use of such aids to enhance performance.

Exam-Style Questions

1. The data in Table 4.16 show the relationship between altitude and maximum oxygen uptake in suitably trained sports performers.
a. Plot a graph to show the relationship between altitude and maximum oxygen uptake. (4 marks)
b. The 1968 Olympic games were held in Mexico City at an altitude of 2300 m:
i. Using the graph estimate the percentage decrease in maximum oxygen uptake in Mexico City. (2 marks)
ii. With reference to Table 4.16, briefly state what implications arise from the data for race times of 5000 metres and longer. (2 marks)
iii. At a height of 5450 m the amount of oxygen in 1 dm^3 of air is 50% that at sea level. Using the graph, estimate the maximum oxygen uptake at 5450 m as a percentage of the maximum at sea level. With reference to physiological adaptations, account for the differences between the percentages. (8 marks)
iv. What advantage is there for an altitude-trained athlete returning to sea level? (2 marks)
v. What effect would altitude training have on the anaerobic processes of metabolism? (2 marks)

Table 4.16 : Altitude and oxygen uptake

Altitude in metres above sea level	Oxygen uptake as % of maximum at sea level
0	100
1000	98
2000	95
3000	90
4000	85
5000	75
6000	60
7000	40

Exam-Style Questions

continued

2. a. What is the meaning of the term ergogenic aid? (2 marks)

b. Under what circumstances might beta blockers be ergogenic aids? (3 marks)

3. Give a brief outline of, and comment critically upon, the following techniques which may be employed in the belief that they will enhance sport performance:

a. the use of anabolic steroids, (5 marks)

b. ingestion of drinks containing caffeine, (5 marks)

c. blood doping. (5 marks)

4. a. Certain sportspeople have been banned from sport for using illegal substances:

i. What advantages does the use of steroids give to the performer? (2 marks)

ii. What is a 'masking' agent and why is it significant? (3 marks)

b. Discuss why sportspeople might wish to use banned substances. In your answer identify the hazards of taking such substances. (5 marks)

(An excellent resource for these questions is Wilmore and Costill, *Physiology of Sport and Exercise*, Human Kinetics, pp. 320–345.)

Summary

1. You should be aware of the aims and objectives of training with respect to enhancement of performance at sport or improvement of health.

2. You should be familiar with the concepts of the principles of training:

- duration
- repetition
- overload
- regression
- warm-up and cool-down
- specificity
- variance

3. You should be aware of the physiological adaptations produced by training.

4. You should be aware of the neuromuscular adaptations produced by training.

5. You should understand that ceasing training allows the body to regress to fitness levels required by ongoing activities.

6. You should understand the effects on the body of a reduction in the partial pressure of oxygen in atmospheric air.

7. You should understand the changes brought about by acclimatization to altitude, and the beneficial effects to the athlete competing at altitude.

8. You should understand the benefits of altitude training camps on sea-level performances.

9. You should be able to discuss the issue of aids to performance.

Further Reading

Brotherhood J.R. Human acclimatization to altitude. *British Journal of Sports Medicine*, 1974; 8(1).

de Vries H.A. *Physiology of Exercise*, Brown & Benchmark, 1994.

Dick F.W. *Training Theory*, BAAB/AAA, 1991.

Fox E.L., Bowers R.W., Foss M.L. *The Physiological Basis for Exercise and Sport* 5e, Wm C. Brown, 1993.

Harre *et al. Principles of Training*, Sportverlag, 1982.

McArdle W.D., Katch F.I., Katch V.L. *Essentials of Exercise Physiology*, Lea & Febiger, 1994.

Pugh L.G.C.E. Man at high altitude. *The Scientific Basis of Medicine Annual Reviews*, British Postgraduate Medical Federation, Athlone Press, 1964, pp. 32–54.

Pugh L.G.C.E. Athletes at altitude. *Journal of Physiology*, 1967; 192: 619–646.

Tappen D.V. and Reynafarje B. Tissue pigment manifestations of adaptation to high altitudes. *American Journal of Physiology*, 1957; 190: 99–103.

Voy R. and Deeter K.D. *Drugs, Sport and Politics*, Human Kinetics, 1991.

Wilmore J.H. and Costill D.L. *Physiology of Sport and Exercise*, Human Kinetics, 1994.

4.3 Types of Training

 Keywords & concepts

active mobility	interval training	passive mobility
circuit training	isokinetic	period
concentric	isometric	plyometric
continuous training	isotonic	repetition
cycle	kinetic/ballistic mobility	set
eccentric	mesocycle	stage training
interval	microcycle	

The following two investigations attempt to bring out the essential differences between types of training.

 Investigation

4.7: Continuous training—jogging or swimming

1. Students should work in groups of at least two people, so that conversation can be held during the exercise. For the purposes of this investigation, the jogging should be done as quickly as is allowed by the holding of a conversation—hard breathing without breathlessness should be aimed at. A similar breathing regime should be adopted for swimming. This will stress your bodies' aerobic energy systems, and we expect some adaptations to occur that will enhance aerobic capacity.

2. Pulse rate (beats per minute) and respiration rate (breaths per minute) are recorded before starting. Pulse rate is then recorded for the first 15 seconds after finishing, and then for 15 seconds after a rest of 60 seconds. Results are recorded in Table 4.17.

3. The initial jog is one mile (1600 m) in 10 minutes (the distance is a guide; the time is what is required), or a swim (any stroke) of 10 minutes. This forms an initial assessment of pulse rates and recovery rate.

Table 4.17 : Results table

Pulse rate before activity	Repiration rate before activity	Approx. length of swim	Time to be taken	Approx. length of run	Pulse rate at finish	Pulse rate 60 sec after finish	Recovery rate
		metres	min	metres			
		250	10	1600			
		375	15	2400			
		500	20	3200			
		250	10	1600			

Task Two—the exercise

1. The same measures are taken for three further sessions (at the times or approximate distances that are shown in Table 4.17) spread over a minimum of 2 weeks. Results are recorded in Table 4.17.

2. Now work out the recovery rate for each session. Recovery rate can be expressed as:

recovery = pulse rate (per min) – pulse rate after rate   at end of run/swim   60 sec rest

Recovery rate results are recorded in Table 4.17.

Investigation

4.7 continued

Task Three—conclusions
1. What effects are observed after the last session?

2. Make a direct comparison between the first and last sessions. Are any improvements found in either recovery or ability of the cardiovascular system to cope with the exercise?

Continuous exercise

Exercise regimes lasting longer than 60 seconds, involving low forces and where breathing is comfortable, are essentially aerobic.

The following types of exercise fall into this category:

- jogging, variation by changing distance and speed (as illustrated in Investigation 4.7),
- swimming, variation by changing stroke, distance and speed (Investigation 4.7),
- aerobics (a means of total body exercise, aerobically),
- rowing,
- game or skill simulations without full effort,
- fartlek—speed play without full effort.

Investigation

4.8: Interval training

Task One—sprint and/or swim interval training
1. The following session is attempted four times in 2 weeks. At least two students are needed to monitor the timing of each other.
2. The session is:
Running sprints
a. Five **repetitions** of a 40 m sprint with a 30 second **interval** between repetitions. (This is written as 5 × 40 m sprint at 30 seconds, and is called a **set**.)
b. Followed by 5 minutes at rest.
c. Followed by a further **set** of 5 × 60 m sprints with 60 second intervals.
Swimming
a. Five **repetitions** of 50 m (flat-out, choice of stroke), with a 30 second interval between repetitions.
b. Followed by 5 minutes at rest.
c. Followed by a further **set** of five repetitions at 75 m, with 60 second intervals.

These sessions will stress the lactic anaerobic energy system for the muscle groups involved, and we will look for adaptations to thresholds and oxygen debt recovery.
3. Pulse rates are taken (for 15 seconds, and then multiplied by four to obtain pulse count/minute) before the session and immediately after completion of the exercise. A further count is taken after 60 seconds at rest, and counts are entered in Table 4.18.
4. Now work out the recovery rate for each session (refer to bottom of p. 142) and record results in Table 4.18.

Table 4.18 : Results table

Session	Pulse rate before exercise	Pulse rate at finish	Pulse rate 60 sec after finish	Recovery rate
1				
2				
3				
4				

Investigation

4.8 continued

Task Two—results analysis
1. Have recovery rates been enhanced by this training regime? Use evidence from Table 4.18 to support your answer.

2. Identify the changes that occur in muscle which might reduce fatigue levels during this high-intensity exercise.
3. Discuss the long-term physiological effects of anaerobic sprint training on the human body.
4. Are there any advantages of this training system over the continuous exercise method?

Interval training

As can be seen from Investigation 4.8, **interval training** is characterized by **repetitions** with an **interval** of time between; these are organized in **sets**, with a longer period of time between the sets. Figure 4.33 shows typical variations of a number of physiological indicators during interval training.

Figure 4.33 shows that this method can be more effective in establishing levels of fitness, and therefore biological changes, than the continuous exercise method. This is because of the repeated high-level stressing of anaerobic systems for energy production, and the forcing of repetitions before full recovery is achieved (i.e. applying stress upon stress).

The idea can be used for acquiring fitness, utilizing both anaerobic and aerobic energy mechanisms. The sorts of training incorporating the interval concept include:
• weight training,
• circuit training,
• stage training,
• sprint training,
• endurance training,
• training for a game utilizing game skills but composed of sets and repetitions.

Examples of endurance training for 5000 metre runners could be:
• 4 × 1500 m at 80% 5000 m pace with 5 min intervals
• 20 × 40 m in 65 sec with 20 sec intervals
• 3 × (8 × 200 m) with 30 sec rest relief and 5 min between sets.

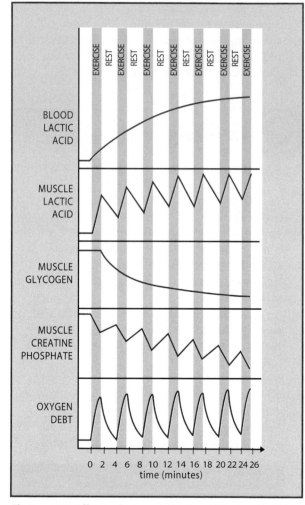

Figure 4.33 Effects of interval training. (*After Lamb, 1983, Chapter 4.*)

Measurement of intervals

We have already mentioned the idea of using time for measuring the interval between repetitions and sets. Another way is to assess the pulse rate of the sportsperson immediately after a repetition. The next repetition is then begun when the pulse rate falls to a predetermined percentage of its value at the end of the effort, or to a value set beforehand (say 120 bpm).

For example, if the sportsperson has a pulse rate of 180 bpm at the end of an effort, then the next repetition would begin when his/her pulse rate falls to 70% of this value, i.e. 126 bpm.

This means that pulse rate needs to be continually monitored by the sportsperson after each exercise effort. This has the advantage that the interval is individualized, and is related to the person's recovery rate. As training progresses and the sportsperson becomes fitter, recovery rates become faster and the intervals smaller. This obviously enhances fitness even further, since now the individual is doing the same amount of work in a shorter time.

Training activities—weight training

There are a range of activities under this heading, the basic features of which are:

- exercises with intervals arranged in repetitions and sets,
- **progressive resistance** exercises, in which the load can be increased by increasing either the forces applied or the number of repetitions.

Equipment that can be used includes:

- free weights with barbell, dumb-bells and discs (Figure 4.34),
- exercise machines of the multigym or Nautilus type in which slotted weights are moved by levers (Figures 4.35 and 4.36),
- hydraulic exercise machines in which a system of levers operates a hydraulic dash pot, which can be set for different forces,
- exercises using body weight as the load (see Figure 4.38).

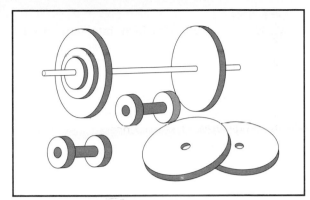

Figure 4.34 Barbell, dumb-bell and discs.

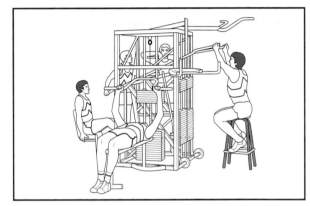

Figure 4.35 Exercise machine.

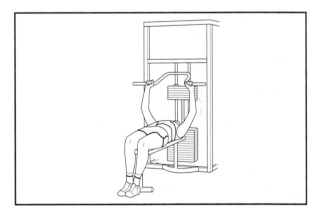

Figure 4.36 Exercise machine.

The exercises

Exercises are usually classified into four groups, from which a few examples are given in Figures 4.37–4.40.

If you need to know about more exercises than are shown here, refer to a specialist text on weight training.

Shoulders and arms

Figure 4.37a–f Shoulders and arms.

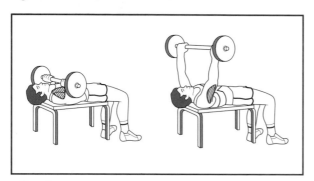

a Bench press.

b Curls.

c Pull downs.

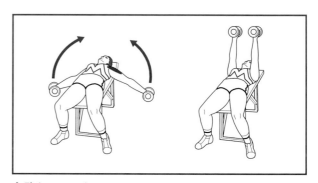

d Flying exercise.

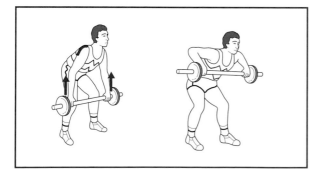

e Bent over row.

f Military press.

Trunk and back

Figure 4.38a–c Trunks and back.

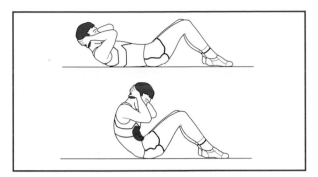

a Sit-ups.

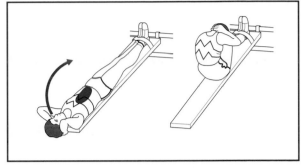

b Inclined sit-up with twist.

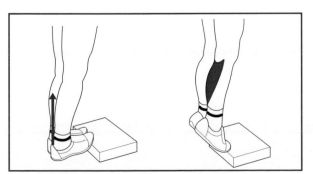

c Back hyperextensions.

Legs

Figure 4.39a–d Legs.

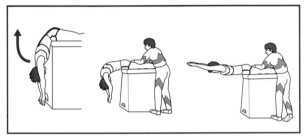

a Squat.

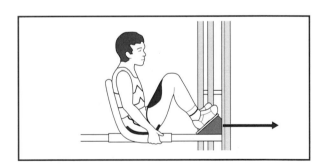

b Leg press.

c Calf raise.

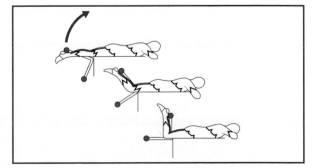

d Hamstring curl.

'All body' exercises
a. **Power clean** (Figure 4.40).

b. **Snatch:** the snatch is a variation of the same technique as the clean, except that the bar is lifted overhead to arms' length in a single movement.

c. **Dead lift:** the bar is again picked up in the same manner as the clean, but the bar is lifted to thigh level only, with arms held straight at all times.

Figure 4.40a–c Power clean.

a Stage 1.

b Stage 2.

c Stage 3.

Safety

First, it should be said that certain exercises can be dangerous if not performed correctly, particularly those in which the back is used (power clean, snatch, squat and dead lift). It is important for students to be aware that loadings at these exercises should be low until the skills of the activities are learnt.

Further injury can result from dropping the bars and discs on to the weight trainer. It is therefore essential for weight trainers to train in groups, and to evolve a safety 'catching' protocol, wherever this danger is a possibility (exercises for which this is particularly important are the bench press, snatch, squat and military press).

Some exercises can involve very large loadings, and can be dangerous if too large a weight is attempted (squat and bench press, for example).

Frequency and intensity

The beauty of weight training is that almost any combination of exercises can be chosen (specifically related to the sporting activity for which the training is being done), with any combination of load and repetitions.

If 100% represents the maximal force that can be exerted (see Investigation 4.3) for any given exercise, then the loadings and repetitions relevant to different requirements are suggested in the following. These suggestions are examples of how an exercise regime can be organized to develop a particular energy system; there are many other possibilities.

Alactic (ATP–PC) anaerobic energy system: fast twitch muscle fibres

a. • Three to five sets of up to six repetitions per set— between 80% and 100% load,
   • with full (1 minute) recovery intervals between sets,
   • two to three times per week.

b. • Three sets of very fast dynamic work at 10 to 15 repetitions per set,
   • 60% load,
   • full recovery intervals,
   • three to four times per week.

Lactic anaerobic energy system: fast twitch muscle fibres

a. • Five sets of six to ten repetitions per set,
   • 60–80% load,
   • restricted intervals (60 sec),
   • two to three times per week.

b. • Five sets of four to six repetitions per set,
   • 80% load,
   • 60 sec recovery,
   • three times per week.

c. • Three sets of 20 repetitions per set,
   • 50% load,
   • full recovery intervals,
   • three to five times per week.

Aerobic energy system: slow twitch muscle fibres

Any exercise done slowly at less than 50% load; most training programmes would have between 10 and 20 repetitions per set.

Choice of exercise

It is usual to choose exercises that:
• relate to the muscle groups used in the sport,
• exercise the antagonists to these muscle groups,
• give all-round body fitness.

Investigation

4.9: The effects of circuit training

This investigation attempts to introduce the concepts of **circuit training** and its offshoot **stage training** (see Figure 4.41), within a mini fitness programme.

Task One—the exercises

1. As its name implies, circuit training involves a **circuit** of exercises (which could be the same ones mentioned in the section on weight training). The circuit is organized so that the different exercises are done one after the other, instead of in multiple sets of the same exercise (see Figure 4.41a).

2. So, for our example we choose the body-weight exercises in Figure 4.42 for our circuit.

3. Sessions consist of a warm-up followed by one set each of press-ups, sit-ups, free squats, squat thrusts, pulls to bar and back hyperextensions—this would be one **circuit** of exercises.

4. Three circuits are then completed without rest between circuits.

Figure 4.41a and b Training regimes.

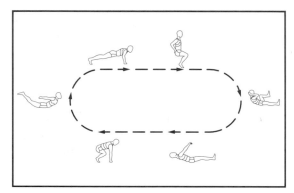

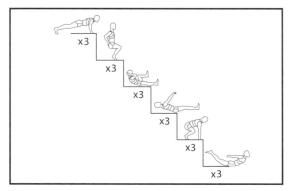

a Circuit training.

b Stage training.

Figure 4.42a–f Circuit training.

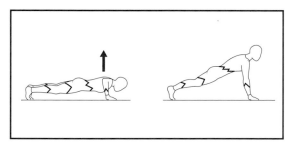

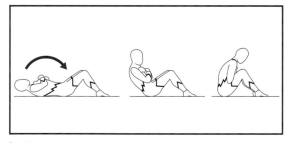

a Press-up.

b Sit-up.

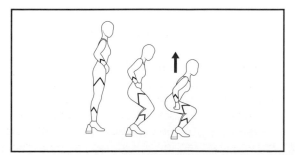

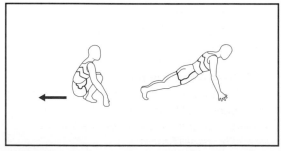

c Free squats.

d Squat thrusts.

(See next page for Figure 4.42e–f.)

Investigation

4.8 continued

Figure 4.42a–f (*continued*)

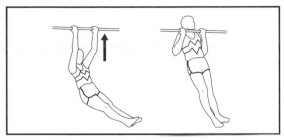

e Pulls to bar.

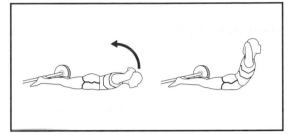

f Back hyperextensions.

Task Two—determination of repetitions
1. Students should work in pairs, one scoring and timing the exercises while the other does the training.
2. The first session is used to assess the number of repetitions possible in 30 seconds for each exercise. So, the exercises are done in turn for 30 seconds, with 3 minutes' rest between each exercise. The count is recorded in Table 4.19.

Task Three—the training
1. Two further sessions are now done, with three circuits per session (as explained above). Each session is done continuously at **half** the 30-second loading per exercise.
2. For example, if the student achieves 30 press-ups in his 30-second assessment, he will perform 15 press-ups on each circuit (and so on for the other exercises).
3. Times for the second and third sessions are recorded. The aim is to improve on times.

Table 4.19 : Results table

Session	Press-up	Sit-up	Free squat	Squat thrust	Pulls to bar	Back hyper.
1						
2						
3						
4						

Time for session 2 =   min   sec   Time for session 3 =   min   sec

Task Four—final assessment
1. Repeat Task Two, record reassessed 30-second counts for each exercise in the 'session 4' row of Table 4.19.
2. This should be done at least 3 days after the previous session.

Task Five—conclusion
1. What improvement has been made over the short period of this investigation?
2. What other measures could be taken to assess improved fitness?
3. Which energy system does this type of training develop?

4. What has been the effect on your body of this type of training?

Stage Training (see Figure 4.41b)
This investigation could be modified by organizing the exercises in sets with the same exercise (at one-third of the number of repetitions found in the initial 30-second test) done three times at 15-second intervals before moving to the next exercise. This is more lactic than straight circuit training. It should be possible to detect differences between two groups of students, one performing circuits, the other stages.

Other circuit training exercises

Circuits can be organized using any combination of exercises that give all-body fitness; other exercises not already mentioned include:
- Star jumps, bar jumping, straddle jumps to bench, full star jumps, bunny hops, shuttle runs, step-ups, box jumps, sergeant jumps.
- Bench dips, burpees, alternate dumb-bell press, chins, rope climbs, V sit-ups, hip thrusts, chinnies, alternate leg squat thrusts.

Categories of muscle use

The bulk of the discussion above has involved muscle **contractions**, in which the exercise is achieved by contracting the agonist (muscle that produces the desired body movement) more or less rapidly, depending on how vigorously the exercise is done and what the loading is.

It is, however, possible to exercise a muscle in several different ways, with different effects on strength gain (these aspects were discussed in detail in Chapter 1, p. 30 and Investigation 4.3, p. 128):
- **Static contractions—isometric exercise,**
- **Concentric contractions—isotonic and isokinetic exercise,**
- **Eccentric contractions—plyometric exercises.**

During **static** contractions, the type of effort predominantly affects the ATP–PC anaerobic system. The main advantage of this **isometric** work is that it causes muscles to enlarge **(hypertrophy)**. For further muscle development the training programme should include working the joint throughout a range of angles. However, despite the physiological benefits of increases in size and strength of muscles, the isometric training method does not enhance aerobic power and endurance, nor elevate heart rate values, to the same degree as does dynamic exercise. Whereas for **concentric** and **eccentric contractions**, the physiological benefits include increased capillarization of skeletal and cardiac muscle tissues, improved **pulmonary** functioning and many other cardiovascular **adaptations** mentioned herein.

Track intervals

As discussed above, any exercise organized in repetitions and sets with time intervals between them comes under the general heading of **interval training**. The proportions of interval training that develop the different energy systems are set out in Table 4.20, and linked to the athletic event for which they are most suitable.

Table 4.20 : Percentage aerobic/anaerobic work within different interval training regime

Activity	% Aerobic	% Anaerobic
Continuous running	90	10
Fartlek running	75	25
Long slow running	60	40
Short fast intervals	40	60
Repetition intervals	25	75
Sprint running	10	90

(*After* Athletics Weekly, *29 October 1988*.)

Mobility training

The purpose of mobility training is not to enhance energy production muscles, but to improve (or maintain) the range of movement over which muscles can act and joints can operate.

This works on the stress–overload principle in the same way as other types of training, only now the biological response is to make a muscle capable of operating more efficiently over a larger range of joint movement. This happens by inhibiting the stretch reflex and by forcing the contraction processes to operate in conditions of full stretch, thereby bringing into play more contractile fibres.

Investigation

4.10: Mobility training

Task One—initial assessment

1. The four mobility tests shown in Figure 4.43 are completed.
2. Results are recorded in Table 4.21.

Figure 4.43a–d Mobility tests.

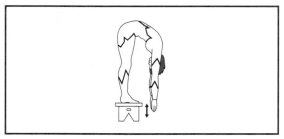

a Hamstring stretch: distance of fingertips below soles of feet is measured.

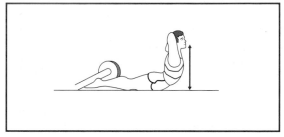

b Spinal hyperextension: feet are held, and height of nose above floor is measured.

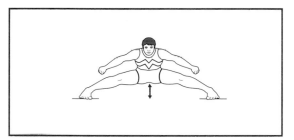

c Hip mobility: height of pubic bone above floor is measured.

d Shoulder mobility: nose in contact with ground; height of fingers above ground is measured.

Task Two—the exercises

1. About 15 minutes of exercises are completed per day for 2 weeks.
2. The mobility exercises can be put into three categories:

- *Active mobility* (Figure 4.44): exercises in which joints are moved in as full a range as possible by the action of agonists and relaxation of antagonists. The exercise is done slowly without jerking or using body weight or a partner to extend the range of movement. Each exercise is performed five times by pulling, using muscle action only (hands must not grip another part of the body in the end position). The end position is held for 5 seconds each time.

- *Passive mobility* (Figure 4.45): again slow careful movements, but now by relaxation of all muscles, with increase of joint movement by a partner assisting or the sportsperson pulling him/herself into extended positions. Again, the end position is held for 5 seconds for each of five repetitions per exercise.

Investigation

4.10 continued

Figure 4.44a–h Active mobility.

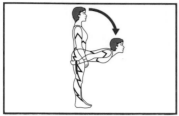

a

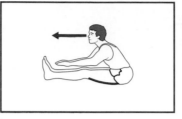

b

c

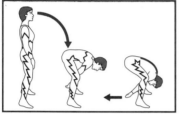

d

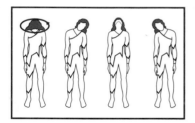

e

f

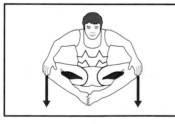

g

h

Figure 4.45a–f Passive mobility.

a

b

c

d

e

f

Investigation

4.10 continued

- *Kinetic or ballistic mobility* (Figure 4.46): this style of exercise uses body movement to extend joint range. Each movement is done five times per exercise.

3. The exercises are done in sets of five without rest—a total of about 15 minutes per day.

Figure 4.46a–e Kinetic or ballistic mobility.

a

b

c

d

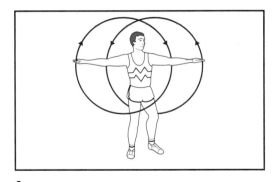

e

Task Three—final assessment

The mobility assessment test set out in Task One above is repeated and results are recorded in Table 4.21.

Table 4.21 : Results table

	Hamstring stretch	Spinal mobility	Hip mobility	Shoulder mobility
initial assessment				
final assessment				

Investigation

4.10 continued

Task Four—conclusions
1. Has there been an improvement in joint mobility? Use data from Table 4.21 to support your answer. Explain how the improvements in joint mobility have occurred.
2. Which type of mobility exercise would you think is most effective?

Skill training and game simulation
This is the repeated practising of the skills involved in a sport or game. The aim is to improve **specific motor fitness**, that is to improve effectiveness or capability at the sport by isolating skills and rehearsing game situations.

Although some skills can be practised in situations that do not need a substantial degree of fitness, it is more usual to incorporate the skills involved in a game into the anaerobic and aerobic training elements of a programme.

Investigation

4.11: Training programmes
This investigation puts into a practical situation the preparation of a training programme relevant to the student's own sporting interest.

Task One—selection of activities
1. Select *two* activities and/or games from:
- athletics (choose an event),
- basketball,
- tennis,
- gymnastics,
- swimming (select a stroke).

You will set out a training programme for your chosen activities.
2. Time allocation is 5 hours in total per week. The age of the sportsperson is 16 or 17.
3. Analyse the energy system demands appropriate to the chosen sport by using Table 4.13. Enter the percentage contribution for each system in the first row of Table 4.22.
4. Decide the **general** training elements and activities for each energy system. Make a list of these in the second row of Table 4.22.

5. Decide the **specific** training elements and activities relevant to the sport and the energy system demands. Make a list of these in the third row of Table 4.22.
6. Allocate time to warm-up and cool-down for each daily session.
7. Allocate time to each chosen activity over the weekly **microcycle**, according to the proportions required by the energy system demands of the sport (see first row of Table 4.22, as calculated at **3**, above). List activities and times in the fourth row of Table 4.22.

Task Two—choose details of activities
1. Decide on a battery of tests to determine what the loadings will be for each chosen activity.
2. Carry out the tests on yourself so that the actual loadings produced for the training programme are relevant to you.
3. Decide details of exercises, loadings, repetitions, distances run, rest, recovery times and so on.
4. Write down a programme of weekly activities to satisfy this—include warm-up and cool-down in each daily session.
5. Table 4.22 is a suitable *pro forma* in which the details of this investigation can be recorded.

Investigation

4.11 continued

Task Three—variations

1. Suggest *mesocycle* variations of loads for the schedule (a **mesocycle** is a training period of 3–8 weeks whose aim is to increase specific aspects of fitness and for which overload increases continuously).

2. Suggest variations in activities based on the mesocycle.

3. How would you modify the programme for progression to 17–18 and eventually 18–19-year-olds?

Table 4.22 : Results table

	ATP–PC energy system		LACTIC energy system		AEROBIC energy system	
% demand of sport						
Appropiate general activities						
Appropiate specific activities						
Time allocation to activities	activity	time	activity	time	activity	time
Weekly schedule of activities	activity	time	activity	time	activity	time
		reps		reps		reps
		load		load		load
Sun						
Mon						
Tue						
Wed						
Thur						
Fri						
Sat						

Task Four—self evaluation of programme

1. Having carried out the pre-programme tests on yourself, now carry out the programme itself for a period of at least 2 weeks.

2. Carry out a post-programme test on yourself. Evaluate its effectiveness in terms of:

- fitness benefit,
- skill learning,
- mobility and/or agility.

3. Explain your feeling of well-being and fatigue as the programme progresses in terms of:

- energy system demands,
- matching with food intake.

Review Questions

1. With regard to strength training, what is meant by:
a. 1RM,
b. the overload principle,
c. progressive resistance exercises?
2. a. What are the principles of circuit training?

b. Describe the stages you would go through in designing a circuit to develop the general strength of a sport performer such as a games player.
3. Discuss the advantages and disadvantages of active, passive and kinetic mobility.

Exam-Style Questions

1. Early increases in strength are more associated with neural adaptations, but later long term gains are almost solely the result of hypertrophy. Discuss. (15 marks)
2. a. What is meant by the term 1 repetition maximum (1RM) and how would you assess an athlete's strength? (3 marks)
b. You have been asked to devise a strength training programme for a fit 18-year-old sprinter.
i. Identify and explain the use of four important training principles that need to be considered when planning this athlete's training programme. (4 marks)
ii. Describe the activities within one strength training session for this athlete. (4 marks)
iii. How is ATP regenerated during maximal strength work? (3 marks)
c. i. What is the cause of muscle soreness after intense training? (2 marks)
ii. How can muscle soreness be prevented? (3 marks)
d. Explain the physiological advantages of a strength training programme for a practising athlete. (6 marks)
3. Study Table 4.23 which illustrates some outline interval training regimes for the training of different fitness components in a track athlete, before answering the questions which follow.
a. Briefly explain the meaning and purpose of the term 'set' in interval training. (4 marks)
b. What important information is missing from

the outline interval training regimes in Table 4.23? (3 marks)
c. Select two of the regimes in Table 4.23 and briefly explain how their particular fitness components respond to such training. (8 marks)
d. Discuss the relative importance of these three fitness components for performance in a 'game' type activity such as football or hockey. (5 marks)
4. a. Briefly explain:
i. How an organized fitness programme results in training effects. (2 marks)
ii. What is meant by the **reversibility** of training effects. (2 marks)
b. i. When an appropriate training programme stops, what happens to the cardiovascular system which helps to explain the reversibility of endurance training effects? (7 marks)
ii. Fast ball games require players to make quick decisions to cues and respond immediately with powerful movements. When training stops, what happens to the muscles and the nervous system which helps to explain the reversibility of these aspects of fitness? (5 marks)
c. Compared with the effects of a continuous training programme, explain why it is possible to improve sports performance when training is resumed after a rest due to injury, despite the reversibility of training effects which will have occurred during the rest period. (4 marks)

Table 4.23 : Outline interval training regimes

Component	Training regime
Alactic anaerobic	$3 \times (5 \times 50$ m$)$
Lactic anaerobic	$2 \times (2 \times 400$ m$)$
Aerobic	$1 \times (3 \times 1000$ m$)$

Summary

1. You should be aware that continuous training methods mainly utilize and enhance aerobic energy systems.

2. You should be aware of the applicability of interval training to the development of all types of energy systems, its organization in terms of repetitions, sets and intervals, and how intervals are measured.

3. You should be familiar with the concepts of weight training as an intervalized progressive resistance form of training, some of the exercises used, how they can be used to enhance the different energy systems, and the safety problems associated with this type of training.

4. You should be aware of the organization and principles of circuit, stage, mobility and skill-related training.

5. You should be able to construct a training programme for your personal fitness needs or those of a chosen sport.

Further Reading

Alter M.J. *Sport Stretch*, Human Kinetics, 1991.

Bowers R.W. and Fox E.L. *Sports Physiology* 3e, Wm C. Brown, 1992.

Clegg C. *Exercise Physiology*, Feltham Press, 1995.

Dick F. *Training Theory*, BAAB/AAA, 1991.

Dintiman G.B. and Ward R.D. *Sport Speed* 2e, Human Kinetics, 1997.

Hartmann J. and Tünnemann H. *Fitness and Strength Training*, Sportverlag, 1989.

Lamb D.R. *Physiology of Exercise*, Macmillan, 1983.

McArdle W.D., Katch F.I., Katch V.L. *Essentials of Exercise Physiology*, Lea & Febiger, 1994.

Pauletto B. *Strength Training for Coaches*, Human Kinetics, 1991.

Prentice W. *Fitness for College and Life* 5e, Mosby, 1997.

Sharkey B.J. *Coaches' Guide to Sport Physiology*, Human Kinetics, 1986.

Sharkey B.J. *Physiology of Fitness*, Human Kinetics, 1990.

Sharkey B.J. *Fitness and Health* 4e, Human Kinetics, 1997.

Westcott W. 'Strength Fitness'—*Physiological Principles and Training Techniques* 4e, Wm C. Brown, 1995.

Wirhed R. *Athletic Ability and the Anatomy of Motion* 2e, Mosby, 1997.

4.4 Children and Physical Activity

Keywords & concepts

balance
cardio/vascular/respiratory
functioning
children
co-ordination myelination

development
flexibility
growth
motor skill

performer
pre-adolescents
puberty
strength

Physical growth is a process that is associated with steady increases in height, weight and muscle mass. Development refers to the functional changes that occur with growth. With increasing popularity of sports, such as soccer, swimming, gymnastics and athletics, there is an increasing interest in paediatric exercise physiology. This section aims to examine age-related changes that are associated with the young performer (Figure 4.47).

The annual growth during early childhood (ages 3–8 years) is about 5 cm per year and the corresponding weight gain around 2.5 kg per year. During

"....AND THEY CALL IT A KID'S GAME......"

Figure 4.47

these years boys and girls follow similar growth patterns, have similar amounts of muscle, bone mass and body proportions, and progressively lose fat as they grow. During puberty, growth is under the influence of sex hormones. Increases in linear growth and skeletal muscle hypertrophy are responsible for increases in muscle strength and aerobic power. In addition, appropriate food intake is the most critical environmental factor that influences biological development. Physical activity is known to benefit growing bodies by reducing levels of body fat, increasing muscle mass and strengthening bone tissue. **Myelination** (the process of increasing the fatty substance within the sheath that surrounds neurones) is largely completed towards the end of early childhood, hence neural impulses are accelerated, thereby enabling the development of fast reactions and skilled movement. During late childhood (ages 8–12 years) the young performer progresses by improving perceptual abilities. Skills requiring visual acuity and tracking abilities (for example the ability to strike a cricket ball), develop along with the motor organization needed to accomplish the task.

Anaerobic aspects

The ability of young performers to work anaerobically is distinctly less than that of adolescents and adults, resulting in reduced peak and mean power outputs. This is because children have a much lower oxygen debt, due to a reduction in anaerobic glycolysis, and

therefore are unable to attain the same levels of fatigue found in older performers. The danger of working **pre-adolescents** too hard in training sessions could lead to total exhaustion and injury as body systems become overstressed and depleted of glycogen stores. On the other hand, it is possible to improve anaerobic parameters by appropriate interval training. **Strength** is measurable in many ways, such as by isokinetic dynamometry and the vertical jump. In young children strength training can be achieved by utilizing the child's own body weight as the resistance. A strength training programme is recommended at the frequency level of twice a week.

A typical strength training routine, for a young athlete, would be to start with a good warm-up, flexibility exercises that work through the full range of joints, followed by 10 maximal-effort flat and hurdles relays over 20 m, an introduction to long-jump technique and finally a cool-down. The emphasis of the session is on strength and skill development.

It is thought that any observable increases in strength that result from such a training regime are more likely to be the result of improved **motor skill co-ordination**, growth and increased **activation of motor units** than an increase in actual muscle mass.

Muscular strength improves with age and is a reflection of neural adaptation (as mentioned above) and increases in muscle size. During puberty, androgenic steroids, such as testosterone, cause a dramatic acceleration in muscle mass and associated strength in males, and to a lesser extent in physically active females. The net result is that peak and mean anaerobic power rise, and recovery reduces with chronological age.

During puberty, a strength session could incorporate the use of body circuits and weights that would stress the lactic acid system and therefore build up tolerance to muscle and blood lactate (Figure 4.20).

Flexibility usually decreases with age, especially during the growth spurt when increases in bone length stretch the attached muscles. Slow static stretching, in which stretched positions are held for several seconds, is most suitable for the young performer. Children do have a better sense of **balance** and **co-ordination**, mainly due to their smaller body size and lower centre of gravity, and hence they have an enormous capacity to learn complicated skills such as those required for gymnastics.

Figure 4.48

Aerobic aspects

Cardio/vascular/respiratory functioning is much the same in both sexes prior to puberty.

Blood pressure is lower in the child but progressively reaches adult values during adolescence. This is because of the child's smaller heart and reduced stroke volume, and because there is less peripheral resistance offered by blood vessels. During submaximal exercise, a child's heart compensates by working harder than that of the adult performer, and there is a bigger a-$\overline{v}O_2$ diff (due to increased blood flow to working muscles) which compensates for the reduced stroke volume.

Lung volumes, such as vital capacity, are significantly correlated to increases in body mass and therefore increase alongside growth patterns. Breathing rates are higher when compared with adolescents and adults at equivalent work loads.

Research evidence indicates that during puberty there are improvements in $\dot{V}O_{2max}$ for both males and females, with lower values for females. This would suggest that the adolescent growth period is a critical period for the development of aerobic fitness resulting from endurance-based training.

Aerobic training produces small increases in aerobic capacity, but must be limited by stroke volume, since any further increases in aerobic capacity depend on heart growth. When coaches are developing specific training programmes for the young male and female performer, they must take into account the growth and development of the young people. Training programmes have been shown to improve anaerobic and aerobic capacities, but they should be specifically designed for the appropriate age group.

An excellent resource that enlarges this brief section is a text called *Development Exercise Physiology* by Dr Thomas Rowland. This text provides a complete review of current knowledge about children's physiological responses to exercise.

 Review Questions

1. Identify some of the physiological changes that occur in children when training with submaximal and maximal work loads.
2. What advice would you give coaches should they want to improve the strength of young athletes within their coaching group?
3. How does regular training affect growth and maturation?

 Exam-Style Questions

1. What factors are responsible for the dramatic improvements in endurance performance from childhood through to puberty? (8 marks)
2. Muscle strength progressively improves from childhood through to adolescence. Discuss. (12 marks)

 Further Reading

Armstrong N. *New Directions in Physical Education*, Cassell, 1996.
Gallahue D.L. *Developmental Physical Education for Today's Children*, Brown & Benchmark, 1996.
Maffulli N. *Colour Atlas and Text of Sports Medicine in Childhood and Adolescence*, Mosby–Wolfe, 1995.
Rowland T.W. *Developmental Exercise Physiology*, Human Kinetics, 1996.
Wilmore J.H. and Costill D.L. *Physiology of Sport and Exercise*, Human Kinetics, 1994.

Chapter 5

Fitness For Life

People who exercise regularly, whether walking, jogging, swimming, cycling or playing team sports, are more likely to be able to carry on exhausting work for longer periods of time than sedentary people. This is due to the **adaptive** responses made by the body as a result of regular exercise (see Chapter 4, p. 131 onwards, for details of the long-term effects of exercise on the body).

Today's mass participation in jogging and distance running is a strong indicator that people generally value good health and work hard to keep their bodies in 'good working order'. On the other hand, modern day living with its sedentary life styles and increased leisure time has brought modern day illnesses such as **obesity**, **heart disease** and **cancers**.

This chapter will help you to understand the causes and consequences of obesity and heart disease and the role that regular exercise can take in the pursuit of **fitness for life**.

Figure 5.1

5.1 Obesity

 Keywords & concepts

basal metabolic rate	obesity
energy input	overeating
energy output	positive energy balance
glandular malfunction	skinfold measurements
negative energy balance	total metabolic rate
neutral energy balance	underwater weighing
nutritional balance	

Obesity is a severe overweight condition of the body, defined as when a person has an excessive accumulation of body fat that is more than 20% above the norm for his/her height and build. It is a serious form of **malnutrition** of the body (*mal*, of course, meaning bad).

Physical effects of obesity on the body

Because of the increase in body size, the cardio-respiratory system has to work much harder since more energy is used in just moving the body mass.

In addition, an increase in adipose tissue (fat under the skin) and a decrease in sweat gland density make it much harder for the vascular system to remove waste heat energy, produced as part of the process of conversion of food fuel into useful work or energy in the body's muscles and organs. This heat energy has to leave the body from the skin surface, and therefore a thick insulating layer under the skin will tend to restrict flow of heat outwards. This means that the heart has to work harder to pump blood faster round the circulatory system, so that heat energy, carried by the blood, can be released more rapidly near the skin surface.

Also, a relatively poor circulatory system within adipose tissue means that the blood (and therefore heat energy) cannot reach the skin surface in large enough quantities to release its heat as effectively as it would in a thin person.

All these factors result in **heart overload** and increased respiratory functioning, to keep pace with the increases in total metabolic functioning.

Obesity and disease

Obesity has been strongly associated with a number of modern day cardiovascular diseases, such as atherosclerosis, hypertension, and coronary and cerebral thrombosis.

An obese person has an increased risk of suffering from mature diabetes, hernia, and gall bladder diseases, cirrhosis of the liver, and mechanical injuries to the body—such as backache and damage to joint structures. In addition, there are greater surgical risks and complications during pregnancy.

Causes of obesity

Positive energy balance

Carbohydrates and fats are the fuels needed for energy production. The major cause of obesity is that energy intake (eating carbohydrate and fat) is far greater than energy output. In other words, there is a lack of energy expenditure, so the obese person will continue to gain weight. This concept is known as a **positive energy balance** and can be expressed as:

ENERGY INPUT > ENERGY OUTPUT

Excess carbohydrate is stored as glycogen. When all the glycogen stores are filled, carbohydrate is converted to fatty acids and glycerol together with the excess fat content in the diet. Excess fatty acids and glycerol are stored as triglycerides (fat) in adipose tissue around major organs such as the heart and stomach, underneath the skin and in skeletal muscle.

Glandular malfunction

A small percentage of obese people suffer from a **glandular malfunction**, which results in a hormonal imbalance in the body. This tends to create adipose tissue abnormally.

Overeating and overweight

There is a strong relationship between a positive energy balance and being overweight. The latter is often associated with poor eating habits and imbalanced diets containing a high proportion of fat. This results in an individual becoming exhausted through work (exercise) more quickly than someone with a higher proportion of carbohydrate in his/her diet.

Figure 5.2

Over-indulgence in food is also associated with psychological, social and cultural factors. For example, the overeater may eat in an attempt to relieve anxieties. It has been shown that childhood obesity is strongly linked to adult obesity, i.e. the fat child grows into a fat adult!

Figure 5.3

The development of fat cells begins during the first 2 years of life. The fat cells in young children who are overfed may proliferate to five times the normal number of cells. So as the child grows she/he has thousands of extra fat cells just waiting to fill with fat. In the adult the number of fat cells remains constant, but the cells increase in size as weight is gained. Once this weight is gained it will be maintained unless a negative energy balance (described in detail below) is achieved.

Figure 5.4

Obesity and lack of exercise

There is strong evidence to suggest that overweight children and adults are far less active than their thinner counterparts. Obesity has the long-term effect of limiting the mobility of joints, thus restricting the person's ability to co-ordinate movements. It also places an additional strain on the cardio-respiratory system, as described earlier. Bodily strength, endurance and speed are impaired as a result of weight gain. So a combination of physical and psychological factors (such as self-image) often inhibit the person from participating in sport and leisure activities.

Figure 5.5

How to lose weight

The only method of controlling obesity is to shift the energy relationship so that energy output exceeds energy intake. This concept is known as a **negative energy balance** and can be expressed as:

ENERGY OUTPUT > ENERGY INPUT

The result is that the body will mobilize the potential energy reserves stored in the fat deposits.

A combination of **balanced diet** and **regular aerobic exercise** is known to be the most effective means of weight control.

A balanced diet

While dieting may be one effective way of losing weight, drastic dieting often leads to lethargy and illness as energy levels drop and resistance to infection decreases, as a result of vitamin and mineral deficiencies. The key to dieting is that a diet must be **well balanced**, i.e. containing all the nutrients for good health. Weight reduction will be achieved only when the normal proportions of fats, carbohydrates and proteins are maintained, but amounts are reduced.

Regular aerobic exercise

The long-term effects of aerobic exercise in alleviating obesity are well established. Long-term systematic exercise increases energy output, as **fat mobilization** takes place in the liver. Exercise causes lipids (fat-like molecules, insoluble in water, which form large parts of fat cells) to decrease and metabolic rate to increase. For example, an energy increase of approximately 5000 kJ per day through exercise will burn off 1 kg of body fat in 1 week. The result of such an excess of energy output through exercise, against input via food, is a steady progressive long-term weight loss.

As **weight decreases**, physiological functioning and physical fitness improve, and so the obese person is **able to** increase the intensity, duration and frequency of exercise. In addition, there is a small reduction in the risk of heart disease.

Figure 5.6 A balanced diet

Figure 5.7

Energy balance

When energy input is equal to energy output a **neutral energy balance** is achieved, as a result of which a person's weight remains constant. This concept can be expressed as:

ENERGY INPUT = ENERGY OUTPUT

Body fat and its measurement

Body composition has two basic components:

1. **Body fat** or accumulated adipose tissue.
2. **Lean body mass** or the fat-free mass, including the mass of other tissues such as muscle, bone and skin.

Measurement of the proportion of body fat is one of the measures of physical fitness discussed in Chapter 4 (p. 122). It is possible to estimate the proportions of body fat and lean body mass by underwater weighing. The subject is weighed in air and reweighed under water while breathing out (see McArdle's *Essentials of Exercise Physiology*, p. 461 for details of this method).

Preparing a weight control programme

The principles of preparing a weight control programme involve a knowledge of the relationships between:

a. The quantity and types of nutrients required by the individual for perfect health.
b. Energy expenditure needed for **basal** and **total metabolic rates**.
c. The concept of **energy balance** and **body weight**.

Investigation

5.1: The preparation of a weight control programme

Task One—calculation of energy intake over 24 hours

Record all details of food and drink taken in 24 hours in Table 5.1. Quantities of each item will need to be estimated so that energy values can be calculated using food energy tables from a standard table or chart such as that found in McArdle's *Exercise Physiology*, 1991, Appendix B.

Task Two—calculating energy expenditure over 24 hours

1. Using Table 5.2, and the information that the Basal Metabolic Rate (BMR) for a male is 100 kJ kg^{-1} perday and for a female is 90 kJ kg^{-1} perday, calculate your total metabolic requirements and insert the value in Table 5.3 .
2. Specific Dynamic Action (SDA) accounts for the extra energy needed for digestion, absorption and transport of the nutrients to body cells. To calculate the SDA, refer to the food intake Table 5.1 and work out 10% of the kJ in food consumed. Now add this value to Table 5.3. You will observe that the total energy output is the result of the BMR + *all* energy requirements above BMR + SDA.
3. Discuss the relationship between your energy intake and energy expenditure. What type of energy balance is there?
4. Using the information from Tables 5.1 and 5.3, describe the different ways in which positive and negative energy balances could be achieved.

Task Three

Write an equation reflecting energy relationships for:
a. maintaining body weight,
b. losing weight
c. gaining weight.

Table 5.1 : Kilojoule intake

Meal	Food	Quantity	Kilojoules
Breakfast			
Snack			
Lunch			
Snack			
Evening meal			
		Energy total	kJ

Table 5.2 : Energy expenditure for various activities

Subject's weight (kg): _____

Activity	kJ kg^{-1} min^{-1} over BMR requirements
Sitting at rest	0.14
Walking	0.2
Jogging and swimming (moderate)	0.6
Cycling (moderate)	0.46
Vigorous exercise	0.8

Table 5.3 : Energy expenditure table

Activity	Duration of activity	kJ/kg above BMR needs	Total kJ for body mass
			+ SDA =
			+ BMR =
			TOTAL MR _____

Review Questions

1. What are the effects of obesity on health and what are its causes and its cure, based on energy considerations. Describe the most effective way of reducing weight.
2. What do you understand by 'Healthy Eating'? How can this concept be applied to dieting?
3. How could an evaluation of body composition assist in:
a. The control of body weight?
b. Aiding sportsmen and women preparing for competitions?
4. How can exercise be used as a means of weight control?

Further Reading

Allsen P.E., Harrison J.M., Vance B. *Fitness for Life—An Individualised Approach* 6e, Brown & Benchmark, 1997.

McArdle W.D., Katch F.I., Katch V.L. *Exercise Physiology* 3e, Lea & Febiger, 1991.

McArdle W.D., Katch F.I., Katch V.L. *Essentials of Exercise Physiology*, Lea & Febiger, 1994.

Prentice W. *Fitness for College and Life* 5e, Mosby, 1997.

Sharkey B.J. *Fitness and Health* 4e, Human Kinetics, 1997.

5.2 Cardiovascular Diseases

Keywords & concepts

angina	**cardiovascular disease**
atherosclerosis	**coronary thrombosis**
cardiac arrest	**hypertension**

Cardiovascular diseases include diseases of the heart and blood vessels. The majority of patients suffering from cardiovascular diseases have hypertension or high blood pressure (this is diagnosed when the diastolic pressure consistently reads over 95 mmHg or 11.9 kPa). Hypertension is a major contributing factor in **atherosclerosis**, **coronary heart disease** and **strokes**.

Atherosclerosis, commonly described as **furring up of the arteries**, is caused by lipid deposits accumulating in the inner lining of arteries, resulting in a narrowing of the arterial lumen, thereby impeding blood flow. When the deposits silt up one of the coronary arteries, a coronary heart attack results—illustrated in Figure 5.8b and c.

Figure 5.8a–c

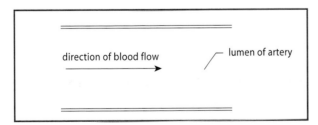

a Normal artery.

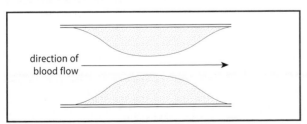

b Narrowing of the arterial lumen.

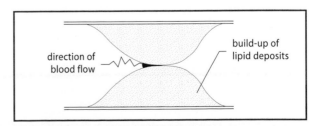

c Artery blocked by lipid deposits.

Coronary heart disease (CHD) is one of Britain's greatest killers and encompasses diseases such as angina and heart attacks or coronary thrombosis. The first symptoms of coronary heart disease are often manifested as a result of an increased heart rate caused by physical exertion or excitement. Heavy, cramp-like pains are experienced across the chest. This kind of pain is known as **angina** and is normally treated and controlled with drugs and relaxation. A person suffering from angina has a higher risk of suffering from a **coronary thrombosis**.

A **coronary thrombosis** or heart attack is a sudden severe blockage in one of the coronary arteries, cutting off the blood supply to the cardiac tissue. This blockage is often caused by a blood clot forming in an already damaged, furred-up coronary artery, as illustrated in Figure 5.8c. Heart attacks can be severe or mild, depending on the positioning of the blockage.

In Figure 5.9 a severe blockage has occurred in a descending coronary artery. The amount of heart tissue involved is great, causing a major heart attack. The mild blockage is towards the end of the coronary artery and therefore the amount of heart tissue involved is minimal. In this instance the patient would have a better chance of full recovery.

In a severe blockage the heart may stop beating. This is called a **cardiac arrest**. About half of all cardiac arrest cases die.

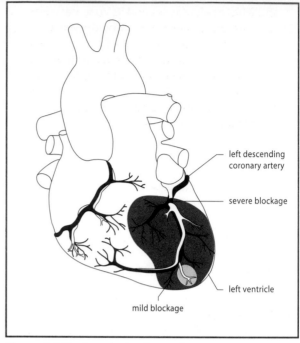

left descending coronary artery

severe blockage

left ventricle

mild blockage

Figure 5.9 Blockage in the descending coronary artery.

 # Investigation

5.2: To examine death rates from coronary heart disease

Task One
Coronary heart disease accounts for 30% of all deaths in the UK to people aged under 75 years. Suggest possible reasons and causes for this.

Task Two
Figure 5.10 shows different death rates from heart disease for those aged 35–74 years in different countries of the world.

1. Using examples from this chart, suggest reasons why the death rate from coronary heart disease varies so much from one country to another.

2. Suggest reasons why men are more likely than women to suffer from coronary heart disease.

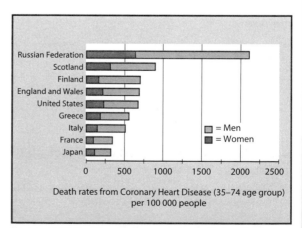

Death rates from Coronary Heart Disease (35–74 age group) per 100 000 people

Figure 5.10 Death rates from coronary heart disease.

Protection against coronary heart disease

The advice usually given is to watch your weight, do not smoke, do not drink too much alcohol, reduce your salt intake and relax, but take regular exercise. This is because, although some individuals who smoke, eat too much and drink too much, live to old age without heart trouble, a higher proportion contract heart disease than the average for the population as a whole. There is therefore a higher statistical risk of heart disease among people who drink, smoke, eat too much and take salt in their food.

Exercise and coronary heart disease

There is good evidence that regular exercise can have a protective effect on the heart. Stamina-building activities such as jogging, cycling and swimming will improve the efficiency of cardiac tissue and circulation.

Regular exercise reduces resting heart rate and increases heart stroke volume because of a stronger, more efficient, heart. Resting blood pressure is lowered and the balance of cholesterol (a constituent of animal fat in the diet) and triglycerides (fat) is improved. Amounts of cholesterol and triglycerides that reach the fuel transport system of the body are statistically associated with a high incidence of atherosclerosis, and therefore there is an increased probability of heart disease and coronary thrombosis. Diets should therefore include less animal fat (saturated fats) to reduce this risk.

In addition to the positive physiological effects of exercise on the body, a person will feel and look better.

The type of exercise undertaken to protect your body from coronary heart disease will depend on your present physical condition. The major questions to be asked in devising an exercise programme are: how often, **frequency**; how much, **intensity**; and how long, **duration**.

1. **Frequency:** at least two to three times a week.
2. **Intensity:** hard enough to make you breathless. This should mean that your heart rate should be at least 60% of your maximal heart rate and increase in proportion to your maximal heart rate as your fitness improves.
3. **Duration:** the length of each session will depend on the intensity of the exercise, but should last between 20 and 60 minutes for it to be beneficial to the body.
4. Finally, **what activity?** Something that you enjoy doing! It is important that the selected mode of exercise is aerobic and uses large muscle groups so that stamina is improved.

Figure 5.11

Investigation

5.3: To devise an activity programme

Task One
Consider the information in the stamina rating chart (Table 5.4) and devise two exercise programmes—one for a male and one for a female aged 42 years. Give reasons for your selection of activities, frequency, intensity and duration of the schedule.

Task Two
Why would a medical examination be advised for anyone who decides to start regular exercise at this age?

Task Three
Why should an exercise session be preceded with a warm-up and finished with a cool-down?

Table 5.4 : Stamina rating chart

	Stamina rating		Stamina rating
Badminton	●●	Mowing the lawn by hand	●●
Canoeing	●●●	Swimming	●●●●
Golf	●	Tennis	●●
Jogging	●●●●	Walking (briskly)	●●
House work (moderate)	●	Yoga	●

KEY

not much effort	●	very good effort	●●●
beneficial effort	●●	excellent effort	●●●●

Investigation

5.4: The application of energy concepts

Task One
Select a team game and individual sport and briefly describe the ways in which energy is supplied to working muscles. How can an understanding of the ways in which energy is produced help you in devising a training programme for your selected activities?

Task Two
How can an understanding of energy production enable us to find out about the causes of fatigue and how it can be delayed or even avoided during competitive performance?

Task Three
How does information regarding nutrition and its potential energy supply assist performance?

Task Four
What principles of body weight need to be applied to energy requirements of the body?

Task Five
Why is it important for the athlete to keep a stable body temperature?

Review Questions

1. Describe the ways in which exercise can reduce the risk of getting coronary heart disease.
2. How might changes in life style go some way to preventing coronary heart disease?

Summary

1. You should understand the causes, cures and effects of obesity on health; and appreciate the long-term effects of exercise on weight control.
2. You should understand the concepts of neutral, positive and negative energy balance; be able to compare energy intake with energy output using investigational procedures; and relate this information to the concepts of the role of exercise and nutrition in body weight control.
3. You should be able to understand what is meant by a 'balanced diet'.
4. You should appreciate the two components of body weight through investigational procedures.

5. You should appreciate the effects of changes in modern life styles on the general state of health of populations.
6. You should understand what is meant by coronary heart disease; appreciate its risks and causes; and be aware of the long-term effects of different types of exercise in protection from coronary heart disease.

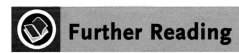

Further Reading

Robbins G., Powers D., Burgess S. *A Wellness of Life*, Brown & Benchmark, 1997.

5.3 Ageing and Physical Fitness

Keywords & concepts

biological ageing	**osteoarthritis**
body composition	**osteoporosis**
flexibility	**target zone**
HR$_{max}$	**$\dot{V}O_{2\,max}$**

Ageing includes all the changes that occur in the body with the passage of time. A major problem for researchers in this field is to distinguish between **biological ageing** and physical inactivity. This section aims to examine the effects of ageing on body systems and the effects of physical activity in slowing down the ageing process (Figures 5.12 and 5.13).

The rate of ageing is the change in function of organs and systems per unit of time and it is often associated with quite dramatic physical changes. For example, both sexes lose height as a result of compression of the fibrocartilage between the vertebrae and loss in bone density. Often these changes are due to dietary deficiencies and lack of

Figure 5.12

Figure 5.13

physical activity. In women this process occurs much faster following menopause when oestrogen levels fall, accelerating the onset of **osteoporosis** (Figure 5.14).

Figure 5.14

Joint flexibility becomes severely restricted if mobility work is not done on a regular basis and diseases such a **osteoarthritis** cause abnormal thicknesses and fluid-filled pockets in joints resulting in impaired joint functioning.

Body composition continues to change throughout life. Young males and females have roughly 15–25% body fat and around 35–45% of muscle, respectively. Over the following decades the ratio of body fat to muscle steadily changes until mean values for fat in men and women in their 70s are 25% and 40%, respectively. Increases in fat levels and decreases in muscle mass cause substantial decreases in anaerobic and aerobic capacities (Figure 5.15).

Anaerobic aspects

Reduced strength output and movement speed are largely attributed to loss of muscle mass (in particular fast twitch fibres), loss of motor units, changes in synapse/neuromuscular junctions and a reduced myelinated sheath, which surrounds the neurones. As nerve conduction velocity decreases, there is an associated increase in reaction time. Loss of central and peripheral neurones particularly affect short-term memory and muscle co-ordination respectively (Figure 5.14).

Aerobic aspects

The most observable physiological change that accompanies the ageing process is a decline in maximum heart rate, which can be estimated by using the following equation:

$$HR_{max} = 220 - age$$

(Depending on state of fitness, individual values can deviate by more than 20 beats per minute.)

Other changes include an increase in resting pulse rate owing to a decrease in stroke volume, an increase in resting systolic blood pressure (due primarily to a thickening and hardening, and therefore loss of elasticity, of the aorta and other main arteries), an increase in peripheral resistance (often caused by diseases such as atherosclerosis) and a deterioration in glucose and lipid metabolism. During exercise the heart rate of older people remains higher and recovers more slowly following maximum exercise.

$\dot{V}O_{2max}$ declines at a rate of about 10% per decade (starting in late teens for inactive females and in the mid-20s for inactive males) mainly due to reductions in stroke volume and maximun heart rate. Within the physically active ageing group, maximal oxygen consumption can be maintained at much higher levels. When older people take regular aerobic and anaerobic exercise most of the changes that are associated with ageing are lessened. A summary of some of these benefits is to be found from p. 131 onwards.

Figure 5.15

Investigation

5.5: A training programme for health-related fitness

The aim of this investigation is to build an exercise/training programme based on improving fitness for health, as opposed to a particular sporting activity.

The student should choose a single subject for the investigation from among parents, brothers/sisters or friends.

Task One—initial assessment

Decide on a battery of tests from Section 4.1 on fitness testing and energy balance that would determine the fitness levels of the chosen subject. Take into account:

- **age and sex**
- **general build of individual**
- **physical fitness assessment (the duration of any step test must not be so long as to initiate heart failure!)**
- **body composition tests**
- **dietary intake**
- **energy demands of occupation.**

Task Two—the programme

1. Decide on a **gradual, progressive** exercise regime that would help the health needs of your subject **without overstrain**. You can calculate your subject's maximum heart rate (220 – age) and then select an appropriate working intensity within the **target zone** from Figure 5.16 (selection of the target zone will depend on your subject's current state of health and personal fitness goals). When your subject begins the exercise programme, start at the lower end of the target zone and, as his/her fitness levels improve, vary the exercise intensity within the selected target zone. Work within the target zone for 20–30 minutes.

2. Research one of the many available texts to help in sorting this out.

3. Set out in detail the day-to-day activity programme for the subject for a period of 4 weeks.

Make this realistic for the subject to contemplate. There is no doubt that he/she would definitely not co-operate with an exercise regime thought to be too difficult or time-consuming.

DO NOT TRY TO IMPLEMENT THE PROGRAMME BEFORE CONSULTATION WITH YOUR TEACHER—WE DON'T WANT FATALITIES AS A RESULT OF YOUR EFFORTS!

4. Explain in your programme how warm-up and cool-down are incorporated.

5. Using the information in Figure 5.16, sketch a graph to show the expected changes in your subject's heart rate from resting, through to: warm-up; target (HR) zone exercise period; cool-down; and resting for the duration of one training session.

Indicate on your graph the fat-burning zone, aerobic zone and maximum heart rate.

6. Draw a second curve on your graph to indicate expected changes in exercise heart rate values following 3 months of regular aerobic training.

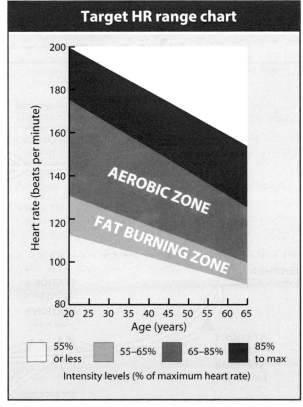

Figure 5.16 Chart of target heart rate ranges.

Chapter 6

Biomechanics: Linear Motion

Figure 6.1 All motion and no speed!

Chapters 6 to 8 deal with the study of **biomechanics**. This area of study applies the concepts of physics and mechanics to the way in which the human body moves, and how it applies forces to itself and other objects with which it comes into contact.

6.1 Linear Motion

Linear means **in a straight line**. This chapter attempts to put into perspective concepts involving movement in a single direction such as speed, velocity, acceleration and force (through Newton's Second Law of Motion).

Distance, position and displacement

Speed and **velocity** (see p. 182 for an explanation of the difference between these two concepts) are ideas that involve a body or object changing its **position**. For example, if an athlete starts a race—the stopwatch or electronic timer starts also—and he runs 10 m in 2 seconds, his **position** has changed by 10 m from the start line; the **distance** moved is 10 m, and the average speed over this distance is 5 metres per second.

The same idea could be used in a game situation, but now the **position** of the centre-forward might be 20 m out from the opposing goal, on a line 10 m to the left of the left hand post. At this point he might shoot for goal, and the ball travels 25 m—the **distance** from the striker to the net at the back of the goal—in 0.5 seconds. In this case the speed of the ball would be 50 metres per second.

So, you can see that **distance** is usually measured from one point to another point, and the **position** of the points tells us where they are in space (or on a pitch or court). This distinction becomes important

176

in races or games where starts and finishes are fixed. The **displacement** of a sportsperson from the start of an event may also be important in some cases. For example, a triathlete may swim, cycle and run huge distances, but he/she may only be **displaced** at most 2 km from the start position. So the **displacement** of the triathlete is the distance (as the crow flies!) between the start position and the position of the triathlete—usually the **direction** is also taken into account.

Investigation 6.1 attempts to apply the ideas of distance, time, speed, velocity, acceleration and force to a practical situation.

Investigation

6.1: Motion of a sprinter during a 100 m run
This investigation comprises the bulk of the work in this chapter and requires the use of a video camera (with on-screen timing facility), a tape measure (50 m), ten traffic cones or markers, bathroom scales, and a video playback machine with slow and stop facilities.

Task One—Production of video film
Work in groups of at least four.
1. Mark out a 100 m (or 50 m) stretch of straight track with cones (or other easily visible objects) at 10 m intervals down the track.
2. Set up your video camera, viewing at right angles to the screen, at about 50 m from the track.
3. Student A then performs the run from a standing start (flat-out from the start—otherwise important features of the exercise will be lost; Figure 6.2); Student B calls the start commands; Student C operates the video camera (which will need to follow the runner as he/she runs down the track); Student D has the very important task of operating the timer start on the on-screen timer display of the camera.
4. The latter facility is essential for all practical uses of a video camera in measuring the motion of a sportsperson.
5. Trial runs of the investigation showed that only a couple of 'takes' were needed to obtain very usable film.
6. An alternative method of obtaining the data is to station a student armed with a stop-watch at each cone, who then measures the time from the start to the moment the runner passes.

Figure 6.2a and b Performing the exercise.

a The start.

b The finish.

Investigation

6.1 continued

Task Two—production of primary data from the film

1. Locate the beginning of a suitable run on the film.
2. Using the pause and frame advance facility on the video machine, move the film forwards until the runner is level with the first 10 m marker (i.e. at 10 m from the start line) and record the time in the second column of Table 6.1.

3. Continue this process, moving the runner to successive 10 m points down the track and recording the times on the chart. Note that it will be important to allow for the fact that the camera is not alongside the runner. Therefore you will have to estimate when he/she passes each marker, and then not line up the marker with her/him in the field of view.
4. Now complete the third column of Table 6.1, 'time interval for the previous 10 m' (by subtraction of times).

Table 6.1 : Times at 10 m intervals during the run

Distance moved (m)	Time at this point (sec)	Time interval for previous 10 m (sec)
0	0.0	
10		
20		
30		
40		
50		
60		
70		
80		
90		
100		

Task Three—graph of distance against time

1. Plot a graph of distance (*y*-axis) against time (*x*-axis) from the second column of Table 6.1. *Note*: For the purpose of this text the *y*-axis is the vertical axis and the *x*-axis is the horizontal axis of a graph (Figure 6.3).
2. Mark on your graph any straight (or almost straight) portions—note that when drawing a line through your graph points, **do not** connect up the points but draw a smooth curve or line that best fits the motion that is represented.
3. Mark on your graph any obviously curved portions.
4. Write a brief description of what you understand may be happening during the straight and curved parts of the graph.
5. Using the equation below, work out the slope (gradient) of the graph at 1.0 and 5.0 seconds after the start. What do these values

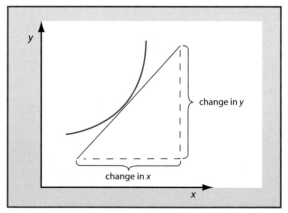

Figure 6.3 Sketch graph of a gradient.

tell you about the motion of the runner?

$$\text{gradient} = \frac{\text{change in } y \text{ value of graph}}{\text{corresponding change in } x \text{ value}}$$

Investigation

6.1 continued

Task Four—computation of the speed of the runner
1. Using a calculator and the information that:

$$speed = \frac{distance\ moved}{time\ taken}$$

[units—metres per second (m s^{-1})]
calculate the speeds of the runner for successive 10 m intervals. Record these values in the second column of Table 6.2.

Table 6.2 : Speed against time for the runner		
Section of race (m)	Speed for the section (m s^{-1})	Time at the middle (sec)
0-10		
10-20		
20-30		
30-40		
40-50		
50-60		
60-70		
70-80		
80-90		
90-100		

2. Now work out the average time at which each speed was reached. For example, for the 10–20 m section of Table 6.2, calculate the time half way between the 10 m and the 20 m times. This should be done for all sections of the run, and entered in column three of Table 6.2.

This can also be done approximately by taking the times at 5 m, 15 m, 25 m, 35 m and so on from the **distance–time** graph produced in Task Three above.

3. This may seem complicated, but it is necessary so that the average speed over each 10 m distance is linked to the average time at which this speed was achieved.

Task Five—speed–time graph
1. Now plot a graph of the speed of the runner (*y*-axis) against the time at the middle of the section (*x*-axis), using the data from columns two and three of Table 6.2.
2. Try to make the graph as large as possible within your paper—include the origin of the graph (0.0).

Note: remember that the distance moved is always 10 m and the time taken is the time recorded in the third column of Table 6.1.
Also, you should draw a smooth curving line of best fit to your points on the graph; **don't** connect up the points (as this will result in a graph showing rapid and sharp changes in speed, which cannot be the case). A smooth curve of this construction averages out the errors made in taking measurements.

Task Six—analysis of motion
Now put into writing what you understand, on the basis of your graph, actually happens to the athlete during the run. This should be between half and one side of A4 paper in length and include comments on:
1. What happens between 0 and 2 seconds after the start?
2. When does the athlete reach maximum speed?
3. What happens to the athlete in the last three-quarters of the run?
4. Does the athlete slow down at any time during the run in spite of maximum effort?
5. When is the biggest **net** force being applied to the runner (to enable him/her to accelerate)?

Investigation

6.1 continued

Task Seven—calculation of initial acceleration
1. From your speed–time graph, write down the speeds at time = 0.0 seconds, and time = 1.0 seconds.
2. These two values give you the change of speed in one second, which is the acceleration of the athlete at the start of the run. Write down the value of this acceleration:

acceleration = change of speed per second
unit of answer = metres per second per second (m s^{-2})

Task Eight—calculation of final deceleration
1. During the last part of the run the runner will be slowing down. Why do you think this is?
2. Deceleration is very similar in definition to acceleration, only slowing down instead of speeding up. Complete the following sequence to calculate the final deceleration of the runner. Use values from your speed–time graph.
3. Calculate the speed at 2.0 seconds from the end of the run and the speed at the end of the run. Calculate the deceleration using:

deceleration = change of speed per second

Task Nine—forward force at start of run
1. Use Newton's Second Law of Motion to compute the accelerating force on the athlete at the start of the run. Newton's Second Law of Motion says:
Force (in newtons) = mass (kg) × acceleration (m s^{-2})
(provided the mass that is accelerating remains constant, which in this case it does).
2. Find the mass of the runner **in kilograms** (using bathroom scales).
3. Compute the force at the start of the run using:
force = mass × acceleration
[unit of answer—newtons (N)]
4. What is the nature of this forward force acting on the athlete?
Note: it must be a forward force since the athlete is accelerating forwards, but the athlete pushes **backwards** on the ground.
5. Does friction play a part in this force?
Note: the runner probably would not be able to accelerate as quickly if he/she wore flat shoes instead of spiked ones. How could we test if friction is the cause of this forward force, and in

any case how does this friction force manage to push the runner forwards when he/she obviously pushes backwards?

Task Ten—forces acting on the runner
1. Consider Figure 6.4—our runner is one second into the run. Copy this diagram and sketch on him/her the forces that might be acting.

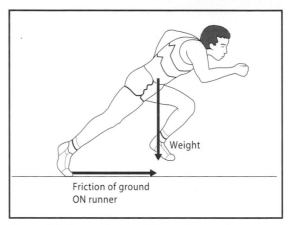

Figure 6.4 Forces that might be acting on the runner.

2. To extend the list a little, remember that gravity acts downwards (towards the centre of the earth) on all objects on the surface of the earth and the **force** due to gravity is called **weight**.
3. Newton's First Law of Motion says that an object that is not accelerating has **no net force** acting on it. Our runner is **not** accelerating vertically, therefore there can be **no net** vertical force acting on him/her.
4. Using the bathroom scales again, stand still on them and read the force (or, better still, have a partner read the force) you are exerting on them.
5. Bend your knees very slowly until they are at about 90°, then jump violently upwards (making sure you don't land on the scales, thereby breaking them or your ankle!).
a. What do the scales read during the act of jumping? (It will be important here to have a partner read the scales.) More or less than your weight?
b. Why should the scales read more, since your weight obviously remains the same?

Investigation

6.1 continued

c. Perhaps the fact that you push hard down on the scales means that the scales push hard up on you and enable you to accelerate upwards off the ground?

This is Newton's Third Law of Motion—that for every action there is an equal and opposite reaction.

6. This means that when the athlete pushes hard against the ground during the start, the ground pushes back on the runner with an exactly equal force, but in the opposite direction.

Now extend your force drawing to include all the forces that might be acting on the runner (Figure 6.5).

Task Eleven—does air resistance affect the runner?

1. Near the end of the race (when the runner is moving at considerable speed) another force may come into play; what could this force be, and how does it depend on the speed of the runner?

2. Air resistance (or fluid friction) crops up in various forms in other sports and sporting situations. Write about one side of A4 paper to describe this, mentioning as many examples as you can. (Hint—water has a much bigger fluid friction than air, and very fast-moving objects, such as golf balls or motor cars, generate much more fluid friction.)

3. What about the shape of the moving object?

Streamlining occurs naturally in fish, birds and some animals, and less naturally in cars and planes; boats also are streamlined to reduce water fluid friction.

4. Look at the drawing of our runner (Figure 6.6), which includes the forces acting on the runner **near the end of the run**. Will the friction force now be as large as it was at the start?

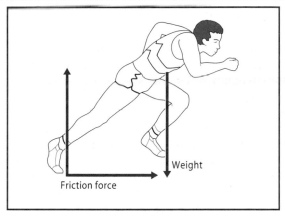

Figure 6.5 Forces acting on the runner.

Note: since the runner is running at almost constant speed, Newton's First Law of Motion can be used to answer this question.

At the end of the run, the fact that the runner is going at almost constant speed means that the forces (although each is large) cancel out to produce almost zero net (or resultant) force.

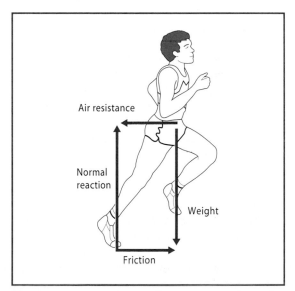

Figure 6.6 Forces acting on the runner near the end of the run.

Speed and velocity

At this point it is worthwhile explaining the difference between these two apparently similar concepts.

Although both are expressed as metres per second and are defined by the same formula (v = distance/time), **velocity** is a **vector** and has value **and** direction, whereas **speed** is a **scalar** and has value only. There is a discussion on vectors in Chapter 7 (p. 188 onwards), when we look at the concept of **force**, which is also a vector.

In Investigation 6.1, it doesn't actually make any difference whether we use speed or velocity to describe the motion of our sprinter, because he/she always moves in the same direction. But once the direction changes, then it is important to use **velocity** to describe the motion. This is because the definition of acceleration is:

change of VELOCITY per second

So if the **direction** changes, so will the velocity and there will be an acceleration and a **force** (by Newton's Second Law).

Note: remember Newton's First Law, which says that an object on which no net forces are acting has no change in velocity; and Newton's Second Law, which gives a value for the force needed to provide an acceleration: ***F** = **m** × **a**.*

For example, imagine a football, soccer, tennis or rugby player swerving (Figure 6.7). The friction force of the ground on his/her feet causes a change of direction but **no change of speed**. The fact that there has been a change of direction means that there has been an acceleration in the **direction of the force**.

Another sporting example in which this idea is important is the hammer throw (Figure 6.8). As the hammer head moves in a circle, its direction is continually changing, so there is a force causing this change **along the hammer wire towards the thrower**; also the hammer head is continuously accelerating towards the thrower, as the hammer head continuously changes **direction** towards the thrower.

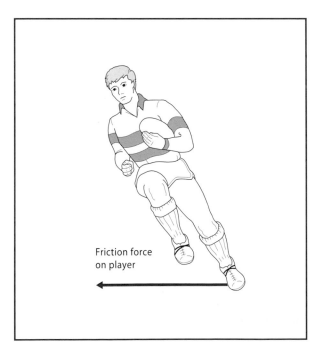

Figure 6.7 Friction force on a swerving player.

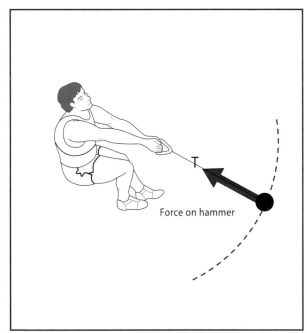

Figure 6.8 Force on a hammer.

Review Questions

1. Sketch a pin-man drawing of a sportsperson standing still, showing all the forces acting on him/her.
2. Sketch a second diagram showing all the forces acting on a runner accelerating.
3. Sketch a third diagram showing the vertical forces acting on a high jumper just before take-off. Clearly mark the relative sizes of any forces you show, representing the size of the force by the length of arrow.

4. Use this third diagram and your understanding of Newton's Laws of Motion to explain why the high jumper is able to take off.
5. If the vertical upward ground reaction force on the jumper is 1400 N, and the weight of the jumper is 600 N, estimate the net upward force acting on him/her.
6. If the mass of the jumper is 60 kg, calculate his/her upward acceleration during this part of the jump.

Further optional reading on linear motion

Linear motion can be described by a set of equations called **equations of motion**, some of which we have come across already:

$$\text{speed/velocity} = \frac{\text{distance travelled}}{\text{time taken}} = v = \frac{s}{t}$$

$$\text{acceleration} = \frac{\text{change of velocity}}{\text{time taken}} = a = \frac{v - u}{t}$$

where s = **distance travelled**
t = **time taken**
u = **starting velocity**
v = **finishing velocity**
a = **acceleration**

Further equations can be derived from these:

$$v = u + at$$
$$s = ut + 0.5at^2$$

$$\text{average speed} = \frac{u + v}{2}$$

$$v^2 = u^2 + 2as$$

all of which apply to uniformly accelerating motion of acceleration a.

The student who wishes to use these formulae to describe the motion of people or objects should obtain advice from a physics text book (see bibliography at the end of Chapter 8)—since this is more a physics matter than a biomechanics matter.

 Review Questions

1. Define the terms force, mass, velocity and acceleration, and give the unit of measurement for each.
2. State Newton's First Law of Motion.
3. An ice hockey puck is struck by a player, and travels across the ice to rebound from the far wall of the rink.

   Assuming that both the friction between puck and ice and the air resistance are negligible, and that the puck travels from

right to left as you look at it, sketch force diagrams to show what forces act in each of the following situations:
a. While the puck is stationary before being struck,
b. While the stick is in contact with the puck,
c. While the puck is travelling across the ice before it hits the wall,
d. While the puck is in contact with the wall.

Work, energy and motion

The discussion in Chapter 3 (p. 89) on human energy systems outlines the ways in which the human body as a machine can transform energy from food as fuel (from chemical energy) into movement of the skeleton. The implication is that energy can be neither created nor destroyed, but only transformed from one form to another (this is the Law of Conservation of Energy). One of the forms into which energy can be transformed is **motion energy** or **kinetic energy**.

Kinetic energy (KE) is mechanical energy possessed by any moving object or body **by virtue of its motion**. This motion can be **linear** (in a straight line) or **rotational** (spinning or turning). A formula for KE can be derived from the **work** definition:

work = force × distance moved in the direction of the force

$$\textbf{KE} = \tfrac{1}{2} \times \textbf{mass} \times (\textbf{velocity})^2$$
$$= \tfrac{1}{2} \times m \times v^2$$

(Answer in joules)

Note that this concept includes dependence on the mass as well as the speed of the moving body.

An application of this idea to a sporting context is in the throwing of an implement (such as a shot or javelin or ball). Mechanical work is done by the thrower, who applies a force over a distance in order to accelerate the thrown object:

$$\textbf{work} = \textbf{force} \times \textbf{distance}$$
$$= F \times s$$

At the point of release, this energy has been transferred into kinetic energy:

$$\textbf{KE} = \tfrac{1}{2} \times m \times v^2$$

So it can be seen that in order to make the release velocity (v) of the thrown object as large as possible, it is necessary to **increase** the **force** (F) or **distance** (s) over which the force is applied. This is the reason throwers do so much weight training (to increase strength and hence F) and mobility and skill training (to improve the distance over which force is applied).

Looking at Figure 6.9, it can be seen that the skilful shot-putter starts applying force on the shot from a position where the shot lies on a vertical line that passes outside the back of the circle, to a point on a vertical line that passes outside the front of the circle, and therefore applies force over the greatest distance possible.

Power

Another concept useful in the above context is that of **power**. Power is defined scientifically as the rate at which energy is used or created from other forms, or:

$$\textbf{Power} = \textbf{energy used/second} = \frac{\textbf{energy used}}{\textbf{time taken}}$$

(measured in watts or joules per second) and following from the equivalence of energy and work

$$\textbf{Power} = \textbf{done/second} = \frac{\textbf{force} \times \textbf{distance}}{\textbf{time taken}} = \textbf{force} \times \textbf{velocity}$$

since

$$\textbf{velocity} = \frac{\textbf{distance}}{\textbf{time taken}}$$

So this means that power is not only a measure of how much energy is created (in a movement or activity) in each second that passes, but also a measure of the size of force applied and the velocity at which it is applied. In the example of the shot-putter, large forces applied at high speed are required to put the shot a long way, i.e. the most powerful athlete is one who can apply the largest force at the highest possible speed—the objectives of training for throwers are to maximize both force and speed during training movements.

Power is also the relevant concept when discussing anaerobic capacity. Therefore, when undertaking the Wingate anaerobic power cycling test, the output measure is that of the maximum power output of the sportsperson taking the test measured in watts, i.e. the maximum energy expenditure per second—see Chapter 3, p. 90.

Figure 6.9 Action of a skilful shot-putter.

Exam-Style Questions

1. Consider the data in Table 6.3, obtained during an athlete's 100 metres sprint race at an international championship meeting in 1987:
a. i. Work out the athlete's average speed over successive 10 m sections of the race and complete the blank column E of Table 6.3. (3 marks)

$$\text{speed (E)} = \frac{10}{\text{time (C)}}$$

ii. Plot a speed–time graph (with time along the *x*-axis) of this motion using the last two columns of Table 6.3. (3 marks)
iii. Explain what the shape of the graph means. (3 marks)
iv. By using the data at time = 0 seconds and at time = 0.93 seconds (or otherwise), calculate the athlete's initial acceleration. (2 marks)

Table 6.3 : Data for 100 metres sprint

A Distance (m)	B Time at this distance (sec)	C Time for previous 10 m	D Average distance at which measurement is taken (m)	E Speed at this point (m s⁻¹)	F Time at this point (c)
0	0	–	0	0	0
10	1.86	1.86	5		0.93
20	2.87	1.01	15		2.37
30	3.80	0.93	25		3.34
40	4.66	0.86	35		4.23
50	5.55	0.89	45		5.11
60	6.38	0.83	55		5.97
70	7.21	0.83	65		6.80
80	8.11	0.90	75		7.66
90	8.98	0.87	85		8.55
100	9.83	0.85	95		9.41

Note: the time shown in column F is half way along each 10 m section

b. The athlete has a mass of 75 kg.
i. Calculate the net force acting on him at the start of the race. (2 marks)
ii. Draw a pin diagram to show all the forces acting on him at the start of the race, and explain the nature of these forces. (4 marks)
c. Before 1968 all major athletic championships were held on a cinder surface. How do you think this might have affected this athlete's performance and explain how the wearing of flat shoes instead of spikes might

have affected his acceleration? (3 marks)
d. Later in the race, from 6 to 8 seconds, a different pattern of forces acted upon him.
i. Draw a pin diagram to show all the forces acting on him at this later stage, and explain the nature of any extra forces now acting which were not evident at the start of the race. (3 marks)
ii. What can you say about the resultant (net) force acting in a forwards direction on him during this later part of the race? (2 marks)
(Total 25 marks.)

Exam-Style Questions

continued

2. Table 6.4 shows the speed of an 18-year-old female sprinter during a 200 m race.
a. i. Plot a graph of speed against time during this race. (5 marks)
ii. When does she reach maximum speed, and what happens to her speed between 8 and 27 seconds? (2 marks)
iii. Use the graph to establish her speed at 0.5 seconds and 1.5 seconds, and calculate the average acceleration between these times. (3 marks)
iv. If her mass was 50 kg, what was the net forwards force acting on her between 0.5 and 1.5 seconds? What is the nature of this force? (3 marks)
v. Sketch pin diagrams of the athlete to show the forces acting on her at the start and at the end of the race. (5 marks)
b. What physiological reason could you give for the fact that she begins to slow down from about 7 seconds after the start, assuming that she is going 'flat-out' all the way? (2 marks)
c. A hockey player at constant speed is able to swerve and change direction:
i. Sketch a diagram to show the direction of the force acting on her which would have this effect. (Show on your diagram the direction of the force relative to the direction of travel.) What is the nature of this force? (3 marks)
ii. What factors would enable her to swerve more effectively? (2 marks)
(Total 25 marks.)

Table 6.4 : Data for 200 m sprint	
Speed (m s⁻¹)	Time (sec)
0.0	0
5.0	1
7.1	2
7.8	3
8.0	4
8.1	5
8.1	7
8.0	8
7.9	10
7.8	13
7.7	18
7.6	22
7.5	27

3. **a. i.** Define the term 'velocity'.
ii. For movements that take place along a single line of motion, what is the significance of positive and negative velocity values? (2 marks)
b. The diagram (Figure 6.10) shows a linear velocity curve (of the centre of gravity—centre of mass) for a volleyball blocker during the take-off ground contact phase of a vertical jump.
Examine the curve and explain what is happening to the jumper at points P, Q, R and S. (8 marks)
c. Copy the diagram and sketch a continuation of the graph to show what would happen to the player's velocity during the period of flight. (2 marks)
d. If it assumed that air resistance is negligible, identify which forces will cause the changes in velocity when the jumper is:
i. on the ground,
ii. in the air. (4 marks)
e. At which points on the graph is the net force acting on the jumper zero? Explain your answer. (4 marks)
(Total 20 marks.)

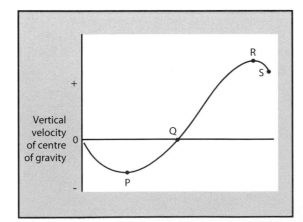

Figure 6.10 Linear velocity curve for a volleyball player.

Summary

1. You should be able to calculate speed, acceleration and deceleration from primary data:

$$\text{speed} = \frac{\text{distance moved}}{\text{time taken}}$$

$$v = \frac{s}{t}$$

acceleration = change of speed per second

$$a = \frac{v - u}{t}$$

2. You should be able to plot distance–time and speed–time graphs, and understand the meaning of the slope (gradient) of each.

3. You should be able to apply Newton's Second Law to accelerating sportspeople and objects:

$$\text{force} = \text{mass} \times \text{acceleration}$$

$$F = m \times a$$

4. You should be able to apply Newton's First Law to stationary or constant velocity systems.

5. You should begin to understand Newton's Third Law and how this leads to the idea of reaction forces.

6. You should begin to be able to appreciate the place of air resistance and streamlining.

7. You should be able to distinguish between the concepts of speed and velocity.

8. You should be familiar with the concept of the conservation of energy as applied to thrown objects, and be aware that:

$$\text{kinetic energy} = \tfrac{1}{2} \times \text{mass} \times (\text{velocity})^2$$

$$KE = \tfrac{1}{2} \times m \times v^2$$

9. You should be familiar with the concept of power as the rate of energy conversion or expenditure.

$$\text{Power} = \frac{\text{energy used}}{\text{time taken}} = \text{force} \times \text{velocity}$$

Further Reading

Carr G. *Mechanics of Sport: A Practitioner's Guide*, Human Kinetics, 1997.

Dyson G. *The Mechanics of Athletics* 7e, ULP, 1980.

Ecker T. *Basic Track and Field Biomechanics*, Tafnews Press, 1985.

Hay J.G. and Reid J.G. *Anatomy Mechanics and Human Motion* 2e, Prentice Hall, 1988.

Hochmuth G. *et al. Biomechanics of Athletic Movement* 4e, Sportverlag, 1984.

Page R.L. *The Physics of Human Movement*, Wheaton/Pergamon, 1978.

Walder P. *Mechanics and Sport Performance*, Feltham Press, 1994.

Watkins J. *An Introduction to Mechanics of Human Movement*, MTP Press, 1983.

Wirhed R. *Athletic Ability and the Anatomy of Motion* 2e, Mosby, 1997.

Chapter 7

The Nature and Application of Force

Figure 7.1 'Grunt'.

Very broadly speaking, force involves the idea of 'pushing' or 'pulling', the idea that one object exerts a force on another object, and the idea that a force will cause motion (that is, accelerated motion).

7.1 The Nature of Force

 Keywords & concepts

air resistance	gravity field	resultant force
Bernoulli effect	impulse	scalar
component	laminar flow	streamlining
drag	Magnus effect	the newton
fluid friction	mass	vector
force	momentum	weight
friction	net force	
gravitational field strength	reaction force	

Force as a vector

Force is also a **vector**, and therefore has a **direction** as well as a size, or value. This point is very important to anyone thinking about what happens when forces are applied, because it enables a force in one direction to cancel out completely an equal force in the opposite direction, so that—in spite of very large forces being involved in a given situation—forces can cancel out to give a zero (or very small) **net** or **resultant** force.

For example, consider the weight-lifter in Figure 7.2. As he pulls upwards on the bar, he exerts a force of 1000 newtons (N) **upwards** on the bar and gravity exerts a force of 980 newtons **downwards** on the bar. (See section below on measurement of force for a definition of the newton as the unit of force.)

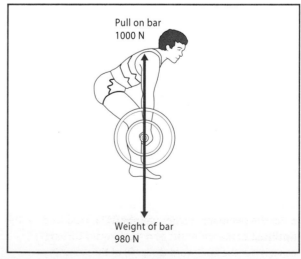

Figure 7.2 Forces acting on a weights bar.

The **resultant** or **net** force acting on the actual bar is therefore only about 20 N **upwards**—just enough to accelerate the bar off the floor.

The idea that **net** force causes **acceleration** is linked with Newton's First and Second Laws of Motion, and is a fundamental property of force.

Also, it is possible for many forces acting in all sorts of different directions to cancel one another out. When this happens, from Newton's First Law we know that the object (or sportsperson) on which the forces act will either be stationary or moving at constant velocity (in a straight line). This situation is called **equilibrium**—where the object is stationary this is **static equilibrium**, and where it is moving at constant velocity this is **dynamic equilibrium**.

Further notes on vectors

There are specific mathematical rules that enable you to add together vectors that are **not in the same direction**. You may notice from Figures 7.3a and 7.3b that the resultant of two forces at an angle has been drawn by completing a parallelogram (in Figure 7.3a) or a rectangle (in Figure 7.3b, where the forces are at right angles). The **resultant** then lies along the **diagonal** of the parallelogram.

It is also possible to calculate the size and direction of resultant vectors using trigonometry. Looking at Figure 7.3d, in which R (the reaction force) and F (the total friction force) are at right angles, we note that angle α lies between F and the resultant X of the two vectors as drawn.

Figure 7.3a–e Resultants of forces.

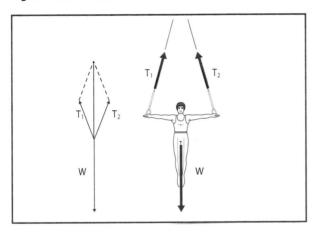

a The resultant of the forces in the wires (T_1 and T_2) supporting the gymnast **upwards** cancels out exactly his/her weight (W) **downwards** (static equilibrium).

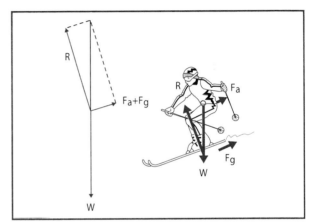

b Again, the resultant of the normal reaction force (R) and the combined friction forces (air resistance and friction with the ground) exactly cancels out the weight of the skier—note the geometric vector diagram (dynamic equilibrium).

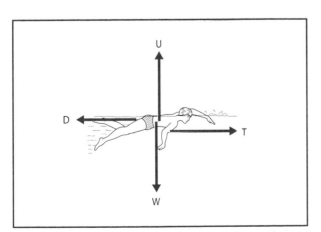

c For the swimmer, his/her **weight** (W) is balanced by the **upthrust** of the water (U) and the forward **thrust** (T) cancels out the backward **drag** (D) of the water (again dynamic equilibrium).

(See overleaf for Figure 7.3d–e.)

Figure 7.10a–d (*continued*)

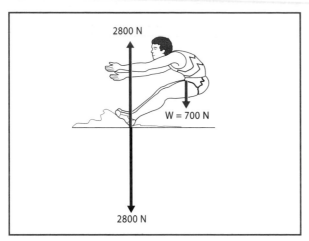

c As the jumper lands, he pushes **into** the sand at 2800 N, which in turn pushes **upwards** on him at 2100 N. The **net upwards** force is now 2100 N—producing a deceleration of 30 m s^{-2}. (Again, using $F = m \times a$, with and m = 70 kg.)

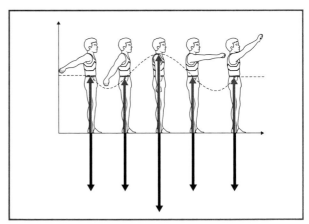

d The total reaction force is the resultant of the **normal** reaction (i.e. at right angles to the ground) and **friction** forces (parallel to the ground). In this example, the **reaction resultant (R) on the athlete** is a reaction to the athlete pushing both **backwards (F) and downwards (N)** on the ground.

Reaction forces with the **ground** (or from the ground **on the athlete**) are caused as the athlete pushes hard downwards on the ground. These forces enable the **ground** to **push upwards** on the athlete and hence cause acceleration upwards of the athlete. The skilful person can vary this force by swinging or moving any body segment, such as the trunk, arms or legs, as demonstrated in Figure 7.11.

A detailed discussion of reaction forces is to be found in Wirhed (1997, pp. 102–108).

Figure 7.11a and b Reaction forces on the body.

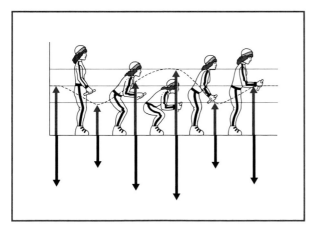

a As the skier in this example moves her body down and then up, as shown in the sequence, the downward force she exerts on the ground (black arrows) changes, and hence the reaction force of the ground **upwards on** her (red arrows) varies.

b A similar example to that in **7.11a** is of a person swinging his arms. As the arms accelerate downwards or decelerate upwards (!), the force exerted on the ground is less; as the arms swing violently at waist level the effect is to pull down on the shoulders and hence increase the force on the ground. The reaction force **upwards** on the body exactly mirrors this.

Reaction forces during the strike of a ball

Reaction forces can also be applied to the impact between sportsperson and ball, as in striking a ball with the foot, golf club, tennis racket, etc. The force forwards on the ball is equal and opposite in direction to the reaction force backwards on the foot and so on. In Figure 7.12, the force forwards on the ball is marked in red and the reaction in black.

Figure 7.12a–c Reaction forces during the strike of a ball.

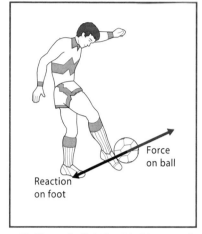
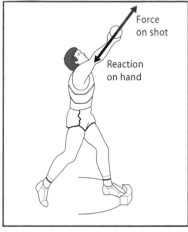
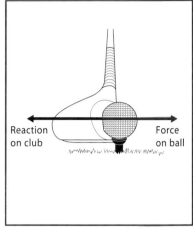

a Kicking a ball. (*After Watkins, 1983.*)

b Throwing the shot-put. (*After Watkins, 1983.*)

c Hitting a golf ball.

Reaction forces within the body

Action and reaction forces within the body are caused when any muscle contracts. The two ends of the muscle pull equally on one another. In Figure 7.13 the **insertion** of the muscle is pulled to the **left**, and the origin to the **right**. The effect this has on the body shape or relative position of the different limbs and attachments depends on which of these are able to move.

Examples of muscle contraction causing changes in body shape, as origins and insertions are pulled towards one another, are shown in Figure 7.14 overleaf.

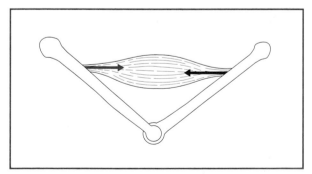

Figure 7.13 Reaction forces within the body.

Investigation

7.1: The effect of different footwear and surfaces on friction forces

Aim: to demonstrate how friction forces change as footwear and surface change.

Task One

1. There is an almost unlimited number of combinations of the two factors; in fact, any combination from:

spikes	rubber track surface
flat trainers	shale track surface
studs	grass
ridged trainers	sand
walking boots	mud
climbing boots	ice
discus shoes	concrete
etc.	etc.

2. Some measure of comparability can be gained from a timed run over 20 m.
3. Each student can perform the 20 m run with a range of footwear and surfaces.

Task Two—tabulation of results

Complete Table 7.1 by putting the fastest time at the top of the chart and the slowest at the bottom.

Task Three—analysis of results

1. Obviously, it will be difficult to prove anything scientifically from this investigation, but it should be possible to place the footwear–surface combinations in some sort of grouped order—the most friction to the least.
2. What factors increase friction?

Table 7.1 : Results table

Time for 20 m	Footwear	Surface

a. It would be simple to say clean, dry fixed surfaces (with no loose material), but is it always the case that ridged, spiked or studded shoes have the most friction?
b. What about the effect of smooth-soled shoes on concrete?
c. What effect does surface water have?
d. Why are rock-climbing boots completely smooth soled?
e. Does the area of contact between shoe and surface play a part?
f. Do spikes completely eliminate the effect of surface?

Pressure

Another concept useful when looking at footwear and surfaces is that of **pressure**. Pressure connects together the force applied to a surface, and the area of surface it is applied to.

For example, the traditional cases of snowshoes and skis having a **large surface area** means that the person wearing them doesn't sink into the snow as readily as someone wearing ordinary shoes. This is because the pressure is less the larger the area of contact, and the less the pressure, the less the tendency to sink into the snow. This can equally be applied to the sportsperson with big feet not sinking into the mud as easily as one with small feet (and having the same weight), and explains why spikes work so well on rubberized tracks.

The formula for pressure is:

$$\text{pressure} = \frac{\textbf{force per unit area of surface}}{\textbf{(applied at right angles to the surface)}}$$

$$= \frac{\textbf{force applied to surface}}{\textbf{surface area of contact}}$$

(unit = Pascal = N m^{-2})

Take an example of a sportsperson of mass 60 kg (and therefore whose weight $= 10 \times 60 = 600$ N) wearing size 9 training shoes. When running, the area of sole in contact with the ground is, say, 40 cm^2 ($= 0.004$ m^2). The pressure of his foot on the ground is given by:

$$\frac{\textbf{his weight}}{\textbf{area of sole}} = \frac{\textbf{600}}{\textbf{0.004}}$$

$$= \textbf{150 000 N m}^{-2} \textbf{ or 150 000 Pascal (Pa)}$$

If, on the other hand, he were to wear spikes, the surface area of the point of the spike (this could be applied to studs or ripples also) is the area in immediate contact with the ground.

If we estimate this area as 6 mm^2, assuming six spikes each with a point of the area of 1 mm^2 (6 mm^2 = 0.000006 m^2—i.e. 6 millionths of a square metre), then the pressure now on the ground at the point of contact is given by:

$$\frac{\textbf{his weight}}{\substack{\textbf{area of points}\\\textbf{of spikes}}} = \frac{\textbf{600}}{\textbf{0.000006}} = \textbf{100 000 000 Pa}$$

This new pressure is now large enough to penetrate the track surface—hence there is an enormously improved grip.

Investigation

7.2: Flight of a ball or thrown or struck object
Aim: to consider the flight paths of different objects. The word object is meant to include badminton shuttles, discuses and javelins, as well as light and heavy balls.

Task One
Work in threes—one acting as thrower, one as catcher and the other as viewer and/or sketcher.
1. Throw or strike the following objects outdoors—remember that you are watching the flight path, not playing a game:
a. shot,
b. discus,
c. football,
d. tennis ball,
e. golf ball,
f. cricket or hockey ball,
g. javelin,
h. frisbee.
To obtain the most simple shapes, try to make the release height as near as possible to the landing or caught height.
2. In each case sketch the flight path as you see it **from a position some distance from the flight and observed at right angles to it**. The stress is laid on this because we want a view of the flight undistorted by the perspective of the thrower (or striker) or receiver of the ball or object.

3. It may be helpful to take a video film of these flights, so that the shape of the flight path can be assessed more carefully. This would then be viewed indoors later and corrected versions of the flight paths drawn up.

Task Two
1. The same sequence is repeated indoors, this time with a gently thrown or struck:
a. badminton shuttle,
b. tennis ball,
c. indoor shot,
d. squash ball.
2. This lends itself more to observation by video film.
3. Drawings of flight paths should be sketched.

Task Three—analysis of flight paths
1. Collect together drawings (from the whole group) into groups:
a. flight paths almost exactly symmetrical or parabolic in shape;
b. flight paths nearly symmetrical but obviously not so;
c. flight paths definitely asymmetrical.
2. i. What characterizes groups **a**, **b** and **c**?
ii. Make a list of factors that might affect the shape of flight for each group. Consider effects like: weight of the object, speed of the object, spin of the object and so on.

Investigation

7.5 continued

Task Seven—changing the angles
1. Taking the biceps group as an example, explore what happens when the angle between the effort and the lever arm (in this case the forearm) changes, as in Figure 7.44.

Figure 7.44a and b Changing angle between effort and the lever arm.

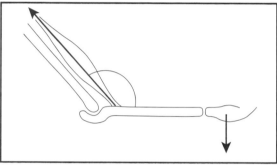

a Extended.

2. You will need to measure the angle between the 'pull' of the biceps and the forearm and note whether the force at the hand changes.
3. This task is left open for the student to explore the best method of displaying his/her results, and deciding on a conclusion from these.

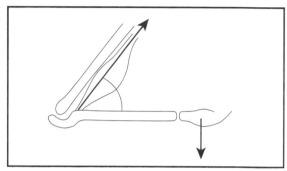

b Flexed.

Classification of levers
Another way of looking at lever systems is to classify them in the following way.

Class 1 lever
The **fulcrum** lies **between** the **effort** and the **load**, as in Figure 7.45a. Note that if the system is in balance the principle of moments applies.

An example from a human joint complex is the action of the **triceps** muscle on the elbow joint—the **effort** lies in the muscle, the **fulcrum** at the elbow joint and the **load** at the hand exerting a force, as shown in Figure 7.45b. This particular arrangement has the load smaller than the effort (effort is closest to the fulcrum).

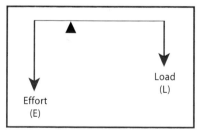

a General case.

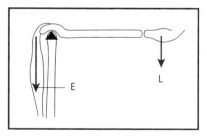

b Triceps–elbow complex.

Figure 7.45a and b Class 1 lever.

Class 2 lever

In this type of lever the **fulcrum** is at **one end** of the lever arm, the **effort** at the **other end** and the **load** is **between** fulcrum and the effort (Figure 7.46).

The example of this in the human body is the ankle joint, as discussed in Task Four of Investigation 7.5. Here the load is larger than the effort (effort is further from the fulcrum).

Class 3 lever

The **fulcrum** and **load** are at **opposite ends** of the lever arm, with the **effort** somewhere in the **middle**. In this case the effort is **always** larger than the load, since the effort is nearer the fulcrum (Figure 7.47a). This is the most common class of lever to be found in human joint complexes.

The simplest example from the human system is the biceps–elbow complex (Figure 7.47b), used frequently in the discussions above.

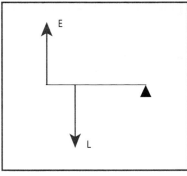

a General case.

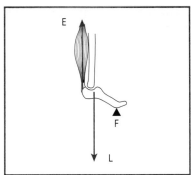

b Ankle joint.

Figure 7.46a and b Class 2 lever.

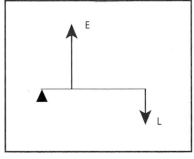

a General case.

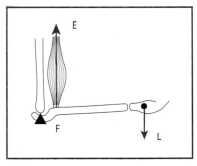

b Biceps–elbow complex.

Figure 7.47a and b Class 3 lever.

ⓡ Review Questions

1. Classify the lever systems mentioned in Task One of Investigation 7.5.

2. Research the human joint complexes and classify the lever class of as many groups as you can.

A more advanced lever representation

In the interests of simplicity, the discussion above has been restricted to those cases where the muscle (effort) action and the load direction are at right angles to the lever arm. This is because the definition of a moment includes the idea that all distances from the fulcrum are to be measured at right angles to the force involved.

In practice, of course, it rarely if ever happens that these angles are 90°, so it is necessary to be able to represent diagrammatically in a simple way real muscles and joints as they would naturally operate. From such diagrams it is possible to calculate the forces acting in muscles in the same way as in Investigation 7.5. Figures 7.48–7.51 show how this can be done.

In each case:
'a' shows the location and directions of forces (**load** and **effort**) and **fulcrum**,
'b' shows the simplified lever representation.
The load is, in each case, the weight of object, limb or head.

In Figure 7.51, we have two antagonistic muscle groups working on opposite ends of the lever arm; the forces exerted by these muscles are marked M_1 and M_2, respectively, and perpendicular distances from the fulcrum x_1 and x_2 (after Hochmuth *et al.*, 1984).

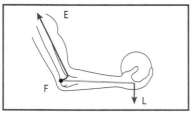
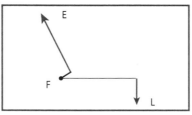

a Location and direction of forces.   **b** Simplified lever representation.

Figure 7.48a and b The biceps–elbow system.

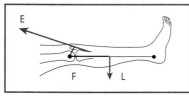
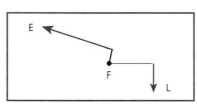

a Location and direction of forces.   **b** Simplified lever representation.

Figure 7.49a and b The patellar tendon–lower leg system.

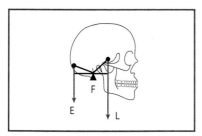
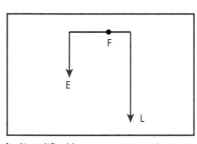

a Location and direction of forces.   **b** Simplified lever representation.

Figure 7.50a and b The neck muscles–head system.

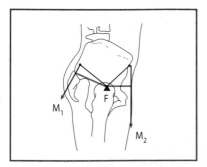
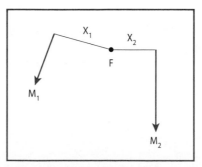

a Location and direction of forces.   **b** Simplified lever representation.

Figure 7.51a and b The pelvic system.

Centre of gravity—centre of mass

This is the idea that the mass of a body behaves as if it is all at one point in the body instead of spread out across the arms, legs, torso, head, etc.

Strictly speaking, the concept is **not** dependent on gravity and is relevant in weightless situations as well as on the surface of our planet. We therefore use the term **centre of mass** from now on.

Consider the simplified object in Figure 7.52 in balance (equilibrium) at the fulcrum marked. This is where the moment of the left-hand weight (anti-clockwise) balances the moment of the right-hand weight (clockwise). If we were now to apply a force to the system as a whole it would behave as if the mass was entirely at the balance point instead of in two parts.

Therefore, you can see that the definition of the position of the centre of mass is that at which the body would balance at any angle, if suspended at that position.

Also, if the body were suspended or hung from a point, the centre of mass would lie vertically below the point, since if it were not there would be a **moment** of the weight tending to turn it towards this position—as shown in Figure 7.53.

The idea of **centre of mass** can be extended to any body (or object) spread out in space—such as the human body. This is obviously much more complicated than the simple example above, but the same principle applies—only now with variable masses and distances from the fulcrum.

In Figure 7.54a the dots mark the approximate positions of the centre of mass of the body segment, with the numbers representing the percentage of the total length of the segment on each side of the centre of mass. Figure 7.54b shows the percentage of total body mass of each body segment (after Wirhed, 1997).

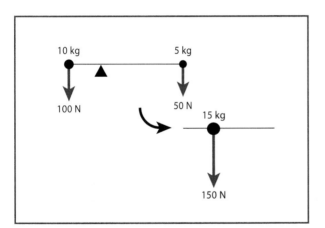

Figure 7.52 Centre of mass is the balance point of all parts of the body.

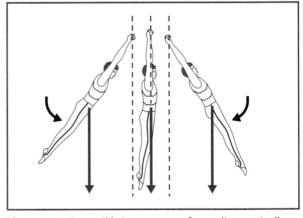

Figure 7.53 In equilibrium, centre of mass lies vertically below point of suspension.

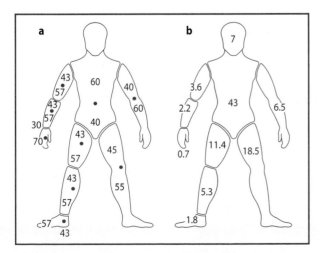

Figure 7.54a and b Centre of mass for the body segments.

a Red dots mark centre of mass for the body segments, with percentage length shown on either side.

b Percentage of total body mass for each body segment.

The application of the concept to the human body revolves around the fact that the position of the centre of mass will change as the shape of the body changes (Figure 7.55). The red dots in Figure 7.55 mark the position of the centre of mass.

The detailed position of the centre of mass can be calculated (and computerized) using the method of Wirhed (1997, p. 122) or Hochmuth (1984, p. 96).

It is also possible to use a mannequin [cardboard model, with jointed movable limbs weighted in proportion to actual body parts—see Hay and Reid (1988, p. 397)] to simulate body shapes and discover the position of the centre of mass. This is done by hanging the mannequin from at least two points, determining a line vertically below the point of suspension and finding the intersection of the lines from each suspension.

It is now possible to simplify the mechanics of any given sporting situation to a single mass and a single net force (and a **couple**, which is a turning moment, as explained in Task Two of Investigation 7.5, p. 215).

Figure 7.55 Position of centre of mass (red dot) changes as body shape changes. (*After Watkins, 1983.*)

 Review Questions

1. Explain the concept of **centre of mass** (centre of gravity). Illustrate your answer using sketches of the human body.
2. Research and describe an experiment you could use to determine the position of the centre of mass of a person who is adopting a sporting pose.

3. What effects do changes in body position have on the location of the centre of mass?
4. Explain with drawings how a high jumper changes the position of his/her centre of mass by changing body shape after take-off.

Motion of a jumper

We use the example of a jumper to illustrate how the **mechanics** of a sporting situation involving the human body can be simplified. Whether a high jumper, long jumper, basketball dunker, gymnast or trampoline tumbler, the mechanics can be split into two sections, **before take-off** and **flight after take-off**.

Before take-off

While in contact with the ground (or trampoline) the combination of **reaction force**, **friction force** and **weight** produces a **net** force on the jumper, as shown in Figure 7.56.

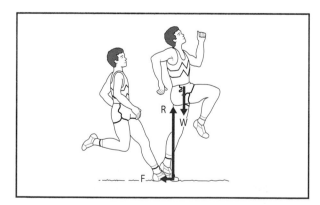

Figure 7.56 The resultant of **R**, **W** and **F** will be upwards and slightly backwards.

This **net** upward force produces an upward acceleration on the body, which can be increased by the skilful swinging or moving of trunk, arms and legs—as discussed in the section on reaction forces (p. 196). We can therefore represent the vertical motion of the athlete on a velocity–time graph, as in Figure 7.57.

So at the instant of the foot leaving the ground the jumper has a velocity of 3 m s^{-1} (in this example). In fact, the **centre of mass** of the jumper has an upward vertical velocity of 3 m s^{-1}, and it will follow a flight path similar to (and following the same rules as) that of the objects in flight discussed in Investigation 7.2 above.

Flight of the jumper after take-off

In flight the force diagram (Figure 7.58) consists of just two forces: **weight** and **air resistance**. Since the jumper is moving relatively slowly (so that air resistance is relatively small), the force is almost entirely the weight acting vertically downwards; hence the centre of mass of the jumper's body will accelerate vertically downwards at 10 m s^{-2}, and will describe a parabolic path of the sort discussed in Investigation 7.2.

This is where the **flexibility** of the human body affects the pattern of the activity in the air. As you can see from Figure 7.58, the body changes shape

considerably during flight, but the path of the centre of mass remains parabolic.

In the case of the high jumper, a skilful performer can actually have the centre of mass pass underneath the bar while clearing the bar with his/her body—in Figure 7.59 this is not quite achieved.

Similarly, the basketball dunker can gain extra height for his dunking hand by lowering the arm and free leg rapidly near the top of the jump (Figure 7.60). Note that the centre of mass still follows a parabolic path.

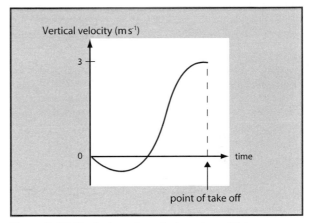

Figure 7.57 Vertical motion of a jumping athlete on a velocity–time graph.

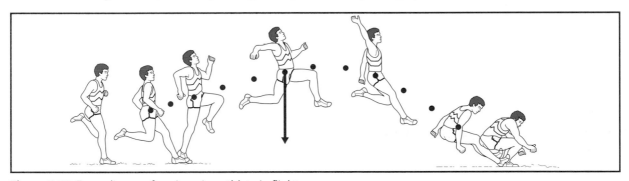

Figure 7.58 Force diagram for a jumping athlete in flight.

Figure 7.59 Path of centre of mass (red dots) in a high jump.

Figure 7.60 Path of centre of mass (red dots) in a basketball dunk.

223

Effect of direction of net force on motion of jumper

In Figure 7.61, of a jumper before take-off, the basketball player has the **resultant** (of reaction and friction) force of the ground on him/her acting in a direction **through** the centre of mass, whereas the high jumper has this force acting in a direction to the **left** of the centre of mass.

The effect of this is for the basketball player to keep the same body orientation throughout the jump, whereas the high jumper's body rotates in a clockwise direction.

In the case of the high jumper this is because the **net** force has a **moment** about the jumper's centre of mass, which will cause rotation about this point as a fulcrum or axis of rotation.

This process is more or less violently initiated by a tumbling gymnast or vaulter, and it is the skill of being able to apply forces to the body **before take-off** in this way which makes one athlete more successful than another.

Once the athlete (jumper) has taken off, then the **path** of the centre of mass **and** the **rotational momentum** of the body have been determined and **cannot be changed** (assuming the effect of air resistance can be ignored).

Figure 7.61a and b The jumper taking-off.

a For the high jumper the resultant force acts in a direction away from the centre of mass.

b For the basketball player the resultant force acts in a direction through the centre of mass.

(R) Review Questions

1. Sport performers adopt strategies to improve height in situations such as basketball tip-off, rugby line-out, soccer header, etc. State the shape of the flight path of the centre of mass of the jumper once he/she has taken off, and briefly explain why this cannot change once he/she is in the air (assume air resistance is so small as to be negligible).
2. How does the jumper change the position of his/her centre of mass relative to the centre of his/her torso during the jump?
3. The size and direction of forces applied before take-off can affect the subsequent flight—sketch diagrams or briefly explain how this is done in the cases of a high jumper and of a basketball player executing a jump shot.

Stability

Another issue related to the concept of centre of mass is that of **stability**.

As mentioned above, a body suspended from a point will tend to hang so that the centre of mass is vertically below that point. This is called stable equilibrium, since whichever way the gymnast is pushed he/she will tend to return to the same position (Figure 7.62a).

On the other hand, a gymnast doing a handstand would fall over if pushed, although in balance (equilibrium) while he/she holds the handstand: this is called **unstable equilibrium** (Figure 7.62b).

Neutral equilibrium is where, on pushing the system, it immediately adopts a new equilibrium position—as for the gymnast lying on the floor (Figure 7.62c).

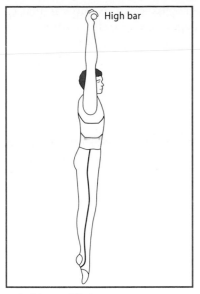

Figure 7.62a–c Stability.

a Stable equilibrium.

b Unstable equilibrium.

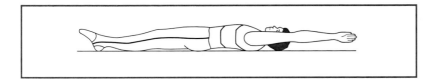

c Neutral equilibrium.

In practice, all sportspeople need to perform movements in balance, which is done by ensuring that the line of action of his/her weight lies between his/her **base of support**. In other words, the centre of mass lies **above** the base of support. If, on the other hand, the centre of mass lies above a point **outside** the base of support, then the sportsperson will lose balance and be unstable.

For example, in Figure 7.63 the martial arts player adopts a stance with his/her feet wide apart, so that the opponent has to apply a large force to move the player's centre of mass to a position in which it lies over one of his/her feet—this is then unstable equilibrium, and he/she can be thrown.

In order to increase stability the martial arts player can bend his/her legs, thereby lowering his/her centre of mass and increasing the moment needed to tip him/her off balance.

Figure 7.63a and b Stance of martial arts player.

a Stable equilibrium.

b Unstable equilibrium.

Similarly, the rugby or football player about to make a standing tackle will adopt the stance in which the centre of mass must be moved further in order to be above a point outside the base of support (Figure 7.64).

A slightly more sophisticated example is that of the beam gymnast who needs careful control of the position of her/his centre of mass if she/he is not to fall off (Figure 7.65).

Figure 7.64a and b Stance of football or rugby player about to make a standing tackle.

a Easily made unstable.

b Difficult to make unstable.

Figure 7.65a and b Gymnast on beam.

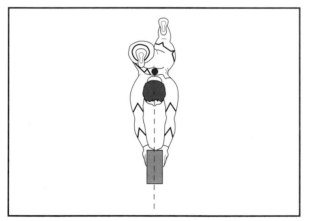
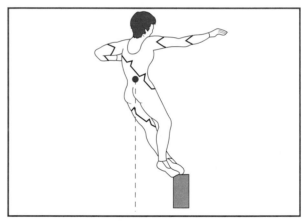

a Centre of mass above beam and so stable.

b Centre of mass to side of beam and so unstable.

Exam-Style Questions

1. a. Figure 7.66 shows an elbow joint of a person performing an exercise. Work out the **clockwise** moment provided by the force of 160 N about the elbow as a pivot/fulcrum, then, assuming the arm is stationary, use the **principle of moments** to calculate the force F exerted by the biceps muscle. Show your working. (6 marks)

b. The results from an experiment on various joints and muscles of the same person are given in Table 7.2.

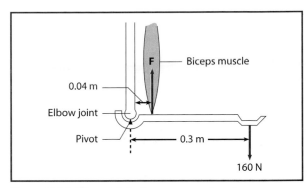

Figure 7.66 Elbow joint of a person performing an exercise.

Table 7.2 : Results table

Muscle	Force exerted by muscle/N	Cross section of muscle/cm^2
biceps	x	30
gastocnemius	1400	40
triceps	1000	25
quadriceps	2000	70

i. Plot a graph of force exerted by muscle against cross-sectional area of muscle using your answer x from **a.i.** above. (3 marks)

ii. What is the physiological reason for the shape of this graph? (2 marks)

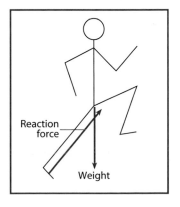

Figure 7.67 Force diagram for a runner at the start of a race.

c. What feature of the ankle joint and its associated calf muscles enables it to be more efficient in exerting force to the body than almost any other joint in the body? (2 marks)

d. A sprinter uses her calf muscles to push hard on the blocks at the start of a run. Explain, using Newton's Laws, how this enables her to accelerate forwards out of the blocks. (5 marks)

e. Figure 7.67 shows the forces acting on the runner at the start of the race.

i. Use a vector diagram to show how you could work out the **resultant** force acting. (3 marks)

ii. If the resultant force was 200 N and the runner's mass was 50 kg, what would be her acceleration? (2 marks)

iii. What would be the speed of the runner after 2 seconds, assuming that the acceleration is the same over that period of time? (2 marks)

(Total 25 marks.)

Exam-Style Questions

continued

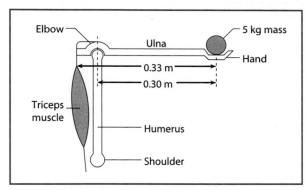

Figure 7.68 The elbow joint and triceps muscle when supporting a load behind the head.

2. a. Figure 7.68 shows the elbow joint and the position of the triceps muscle in relation to it when supporting a load behind the head.
i. Draw a simplified sketch to show the lever system, indicating the various forces that are operating. (4 marks)
ii. Using the values show in Figure 7.68, calculate the load. Neglecting the mass of the

ulna, estimate the effort needed to balance the system. (Take the gravitational force on 1 kg to be 10 N.) (4 marks)
iii. What anatomical factors would affect the value of the maximum load that this system could support, given that the angle between the long bones does not change? (3 marks)
iv. How would you expect the load to change as the arm extends and briefly explain how this change of load affects the use of the arm in a sporting situation. (2 marks)
b. Sketch two other types of lever system within the body, labelling the effort, fulcrum and load in each case. (6 marks)
c. i. Briefly describe an experiment or investigation which would show the relationship between the forces exerted by different muscles and the muscle area of cross-section or girth. (2 marks)
ii. Sketch a graph to show the relationship which might exist between cross-sectional area of muscle and muscular strength. (2 marks)
iii. Relate the graph to muscle anatomy. (2 marks)
(Total 25 marks.)

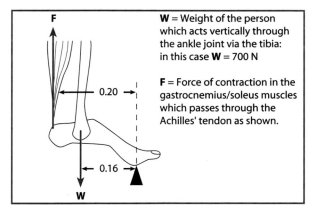

Figure 7.69 Sportsperson's foot pivoting at a point under the ball of the foot.

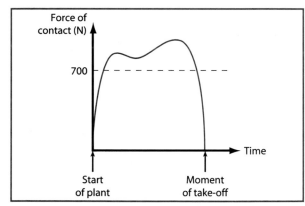

Figure 7.70 Graph showing how the force of contact on a high jumper's foot changes up to the point of take-off.

3. a. Figure 7.69 shows a diagram of a sportsperson's foot pivoting at a point under the ball of the foot.
i. Use your knowledge of the **principle of moments** applied to this lever to calculate the force *F*. Show **all** your working. (4 marks)
ii. Sketch the lever system which would represent the action of the biceps muscle in **flexing** the arm. (3 marks)

iii. Explain why the biceps–radius lever system is much less efficient at exerting force on the surroundings than is the ankle–calf muscle lever system. (3 marks)
b. A high jumper firmly plants her foot on the ground before take-off. Figure 7.70 shows how the force of contact on the foot changes up to the point of take-off. *Note:* Positive forces are acting upwards. The weight of the jumper is 700 N.

Exam-Style Questions

continued

i. Sketch a **force diagram** to show all vertical forces acting on the jumper. (2 marks)

ii. Explain why it is necessary for the foot contact force to be greater than 700 N. (3 marks)

iii. Use your understanding of **Newton's Laws of Motion** to explain why it is necessary for the jumper to push her foot as firmly as possible into the ground just before take-off. (3 marks)

c. I. Briefly explain the meaning of **centre of mass** as applied to the human body and explain the effect if the line of action of the upwards force acting on the foot of the high jumper does not pass through her centre of mass? (3 marks)

ii. Sketch a diagram and briefly explain how the centre of mass of the jumper can pass under the bar, while the jumper successfully clears it. (4 marks)

(Total 25 marks.)

Summary

1. You will be aware of the concept of **moment** of a force:

$$\text{moment of a force} = \text{force} \times \begin{array}{l}\textbf{perpendicular distance}\\\textbf{from fulcrum to line}\\\textbf{of action of force.}\end{array}$$

2. You will be able to apply the **principle of moments** to lever systems, and to classify such lever systems:

$$\frac{\text{clockwise}}{\text{moment}} = \frac{\text{anticlockwise}}{\text{moment}}$$

3. You will be able to describe some of the lever systems within joint complexes of the human body.

4. You will understand how **Internal forces** are applied within the body and some of the effects produced by them.

5. You will be aware of the concept of **centre of mass**, and how its position in the body can be changed by changing the shape of the body.

6. You will understand that the weight and mass both appear to act at the centre of mass, and that the centre of mass of the body follows a parabolic path when in flight.

7. You will be aware that the **stability** of your body position depends on the position of your centre of mass relative to your base of support.

Further Reading

Carr G. *Mechanics of Sport: A Practitioner's Guide*, Human Kinetics, 1997.

Dyson G. *The Mechanics of Athletics* 7e, ULP, 1980.

Ecker T. *Basic Track and Field Biomechanics*, Tafnews Press, 1985.

Hay J.G. and Reid J.G. *Anatomy Mechanics and Human Motion* 2e, Prentice Hall, 1988.

Hochmuth G. *et al. Biomechanics of Athletic Movement* 4e, Sportverlag, 1984.

Jardine J. *Mass in Motion*, Longman, 1970.

Page R.L. *The Physics of Human Movement*, Wheaton/Pergamon, 1978.

Walder P. *Mechanics and Sport Performance*, Feltham Press, 1994.

Watkins J. *An Introduction to Mechanics of Human Movement*, MTP Press, 1983.

Wirhed R. *Athletic Ability and the Anatomy of Motion* 2e, Mosby, 1997.

Chapter 8

Rotating Systems

Figure 8.1

This final chapter on biomechanics deals with some examples of rotating systems in sport, and the physical concepts involved.

8.1 Angle and Angular Displacement

Keywords & concepts

angular displacement	angular velocity	radian

Angle is a familiar concept to most people, so you readily understand what is meant by 30°, 90°, 180° and 360°. In scientific terms, angle is measured in **radians**—the radian as a unit of angle is defined in Investigation 8.1, Task Two, part 2—suffice it to say at this point that 1 radian is approximately 60°.

Angular displacement is defined similarly to displacement for linear systems, and is the relative angle compared to some fixed position or line in space. For example, if a golfer starts his/her drive from the presentation position (i.e. with club just touching the ball), and backswings to the fully

extended position with the club behind his/her back, the club shaft would have an angular displacement equal to the angle between the starting position and the fully extended position of the backswing. This would be a measure of the fluency and range of the swing, and could be anywhere from 180° to 290° (or 3.142 to 5.06 radians!). Another example occurs in Investigation 8.1, where the angular displacement of the tumbling gymnast in Figure 8.2 between landing and starting is approximately 335° or 5.85 radians; it is less than 360° because he is leaning back as his feet touch the floor.

Investigation

8.1: Rate of turn of a tumbling gymnast
Aim: to examine the concepts of angle, angular velocity and the law of conservation of angular momentum in the context of a gymnast (or trampolinist) performing a somersault. Further study will enable the student to extend application of the concepts to other sporting situations.
Materials: a video camera with timer, together with a 360° protractor and a video playback machine with stop and slow controls, and a

turntable (for standing on—standard physics apparatus) or office swivel chair.

Task One—production of video film
1. The video camera is set up so that the field of view is at right angles to the tumble to be performed and far enough away for the student performing the action to fit within the field of view.
2. The student performs a variety of straight, piked and tucked forward or backward somersaults. If you have an expert student who

Investigation

8.1 continued

can perform double somersaults, even better.
3. The student doing the filming will need to follow the action with the camera—**with the on-screen timer running**.

Task Two—information on angle
1. Although we are used to measuring angles in degrees, this is not adequate for scientific measurements.
2. To avoid adding to the complications of this investigation, we use a simple conversion factor from degrees into **radians**. The radian is the scientific unit of angle.

    1 radian = 57.2958 degrees
    1 degree = 0.017453 radians

3. Convert 30°, 60°, 105°, 360°, 47° into radians (use a calculator—some have automatic conversion).

Task Three—analysis of video of motion
1. Locate the beginning of a suitable piece of film.
2. Using the pause and slow forward facility on the video machine, position the gymnast at the point at which his/her feet are just about to leave the floor (or trampoline bed). Note the time on the auto on-screen timer at which this occurs.
3. Measure the angle of the **gymnast's upper body** to the vertical at this time (Figure 8.2).
4. Record in Table 8.1: the angle (in degrees) against time (actually recorded on the film), and elapsed time (the difference between the film time and the answer to **2** above).

Make your measurements with a protractor on the screen for every 30° of turn of the upper body of the gymnast. This is so that measurements are made at regular intervals of angle, and the time is just sufficient to register a difference on the tenth of a second timer on the video film.

Figure 8.2 A gymnast tumbling. (*After Watkins, 1983.*)

Table 8.1 : Angles against time

Angle (degrees)	Time (film) (sec)	Elapsed time (sec)	Angle (radians)	Time for previous 30° or 0.523 radians
30			0.5236	
60			1.0472	
90			1.5708	
120			2.0944	
150			2.6180	
180			3.1416	
210			3.6652	
240			4.1888	
270			4.7124	
300			5.2360	
330			5.7596	
360			6.2832	

Investigation

8.1 continued

Note: the first angle recorded, i.e. answer to **3** above, needs to be in the first row of the angle column. This will not necessarily be 0°, since at the instant the gymnast's feet leave the ground he/she may be leaning into the action of the tumble.

(We are aware that the measurement of the upper body angle does not reflect the true averaged whole body angle of the gymnast. However, this is an attempt to simplify the process without losing sight of the basic idea behind the investigation.)

You will need a bigger chart if the gymnast does a double somersault!

5. Complete the fifth column of Table 8.1 (p. 231) by subtraction of successive times.

Task Four—calculation of angular velocities

1. Now comes the hard bit. Angular velocity is defined as 'angle moved through per second' and is measured in radians per second. A formula would be:

$$\text{angular velocity} = \frac{\text{angle turned through in radians}}{\text{time taken}}$$

2. Using your calculator and the data from Table 8.1, complete Table 8.2 of angular velocity against time for each segment of the somersault.

Note: each segment of 30° is approximately 0.52 radians. Apart from the first calculation, this figure will appear on the top of the formula (the numerator).

Table 8.2 : Angular velocity against time		
Segment of tumble	Angular velocity (rad s⁻¹)	Average time for segment
-30		
30–60		
60–90		
90–120		
120–150		
150–180		
180–210		
210–240		
240–270		
270–300		
300–330		
330–360		

3. Finally, compute an elapsed time half-way between the elapsed times for the beginning and end of each segment for column three of Table 8.2.

For example, if at 30° the time is 0.2 seconds, and at 60° 0.3 seconds, the average time at the middle of the segment will be 0.25 seconds.

Investigation

8.1 continued

Task Five—graph of angular velocity against time

1. Plot a graph of angular velocity, from the second column of Table 8.2 (*y*-axis or vertical axis) against time, from the third column of Table 8.2 (*x*-axis or horizontal axis). Use as large a scale as possible so that the graph occupies as much of the paper as possible.

2. Draw a smooth curve through the points on the graph.

Task Six—interpretation of results

1. What does the graph drawn in Task Five show? Angular velocity means rate of spin—can you relate the rate of spin to body shape?

Examine again the video film from which the data were taken—the tucked or piked position adopted by the gymnast during the middle part of the somersault somehow made him/her spin faster. Why?

2. Examine a few textbooks (Wirhed, Watkins, Walder) on spinning sporting systems. See if you can come up with a general rule that governs changes in rates of spin during a movement.

3. Sketch pin-men diagrams of body positions that lead to high rates of spin and compare them with similar diagrams for body positions within the **same** activity that lead to low rates of spin.

4. For example, with our tumbler the tightly tucked position seems to lead to a higher rate of spin than the open or straight position (see Figure 8.3)—what happens with the spinning skater?

Figure 8.3a and b Styles of tumbling.

a Tucked.

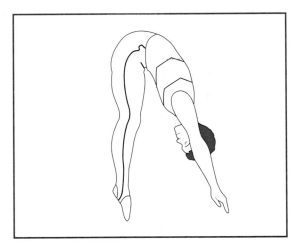

b Piked.

Investigation

8.1 continued

Task Seven—the spinning skater

1. Take a small turntable and stand on it with arms outstretched. (An alternative piece of apparatus would be an office swivel chair that is capable of being rotated freely.) Another student should now spin you as quickly as possible.

2. The spinning student should now bring his/her arms to the side—what happens?

3. The experiment can continue with various positions being adopted: hands overhead; one leg held out at right angles; body adopting a sideways 'V' shape (>) and so on (see Figure 8.4).

4. Each position should be drawn with a pin-man diagram, and relative rates of spin mentioned.

5. What factor induces change of spin?

Figure 8.4a–g Styles of spinning.

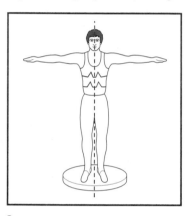

a

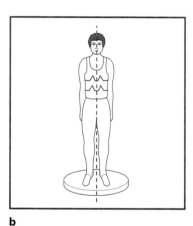

b

c

d

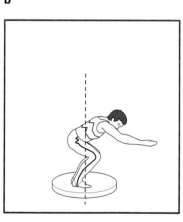

e

f

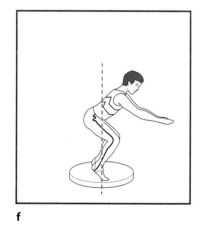

g

8.2 Moment of Inertia

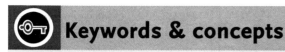

Keywords & concepts

angular acceleration   axis of rotation   rotational energy
angular momentum   moment of inertia

Definition of moment of inertia

Various texts have a lot of detail about this concept—see intermediate level physics and mathematics books, and Watkins (1983, pp. 118–122), Wirhed (1997, 135–138) Page (1978, pp. 45–56), or Walder (1994, p. 103) for application of the idea to the sporting situation.

Basically, moment of inertia is the resistance to rotational motion (directly comparable with mass inertia for objects moving in straight lines—see p. 193 above for an explanation of this).

The bigger the *moment of inertia*, the bigger the **moment of force** (or **couple** or **torque**) needed to provide the same **angular acceleration** in the body, and vice versa. This is the same as in the linear situation only here, instead of moving in a straight line, the object spins about an **axis**; instead of acceleration (in m s^{-2}) we have **angular acceleration** (in radians s^{-2}); and instead of force we have **turning moment of force**.

Angular acceleration is the change of (increase of) angular velocity per second of the spinning body—see p. 241 below for expansion of this idea, and applications to sporting situations.

The concept of **moment of inertia** (MI—usually the symbol I is used) depends on the distribution of mass about the axis of rotation of a spinning system, i.e. the further away from the axis a mass is, the greater the moment of inertia, and the harder it is to make it spin, or stop it spinning if it is already doing so.

A simple example of this idea applied to a sport is that of the leg action during running. As the leg drives through at the moment of leaving contact with the ground, it is (or should be) as straight as possible to maximize the range of movement in the stride (see position 2 of Figure 8.5).

The next action that needs to be performed is to bring the leg through as rapidly as possible to the fully forward position (as in position 9 of Figure 8.5). The most efficient way of doing this would be to use the least possible force in the abdominal muscles—which would produce the least possible **moment of force** applied to the femur of the leg in question rotating about the hip joint. If the leg is as bent as possible and therefore has the **least possible moment of inertia** about the hip joint as an axis of rotation, then the least force would be required to rotate it. This is why the more efficient sprinter will have his/her heel as close to his/her backside as possible (as in position 7 of Figure 8.5) at this point in the stride pattern.

To relate to the tumbling gymnast in Investigation 8.1, the act of spinning in a straight position (as opposed to a tucked position) means that some of the gymnast's mass is further away from the axis of spin and therefore the **moment of inertia** is larger (Figure 8.6).

Similarly, for the skater, if the body is straight with no bits sticking out, the moment of inertia is low—but as soon as a leg or arm is put out at right angles to the body, the moment of inertia increases, since more of the person's mass is further from the axis of spin (Figure 8.7).

Figure 8.5 Leg action during running.

Figure 8.8a–k (*continued*)

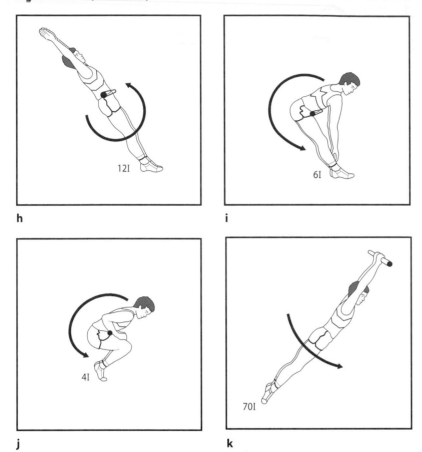

h   12I

i   6I

j   4I

k   70I

Rotational kinetic energy

This is defined by:

$$\textbf{rotational energy} = \tfrac{1}{2} \times \textbf{moment of inertia} \times \textbf{(angular velocity)}^2$$

It can therefore be seen that the spinning energy stored in a system depends on both the **moment of inertia** and the **angular velocity**.

Angular momentum

Angular momentum is defined as:

angular velocity × moment of inertia

This very difficult construct combines our two most difficult concepts in a slightly different way to the rotational energy concept outlined above. However, it enables us to explain why the rate of spin changes when the moment of inertia changes. This is because:

Angular momentum of a system remains constant throughout a movement provided nothing outside the system acts with a turning moment on it.

This is known as the **Law of Conservation of Angular Momentum**, and as far as is known it is obeyed by all rotating systems. (There is a similar universal law in linear dynamics—see p. 211—this is **not** the same law.)

In simple terms, this 'conservation law' means that if our gymnast or skater, **when already spinning**, changes his/her moment of inertia (by changing body shape), then the rate of spin will also change.

So, if the skater spins rapidly with arms and legs held near the body and then the moment of inertia is **increased** (e.g. by sticking out an arm), the rate of spin will **decrease** (and, in fact, the angular momentum will remain the same; see Figure 8.9a).

Similarly the tumbler goes from an open shape with large moment of inertia into a tucked position with small moment of inertia—and in doing so speeds up the rate of spin (see Figure 8.9b).

Other examples of this law applied to sporting situations are illustrated in Figures 8.10–8.13.

Figure 8.9a and b Conservation of angular momentum.

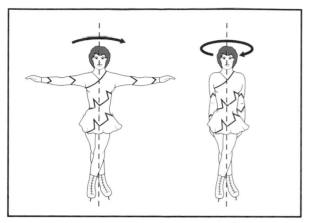

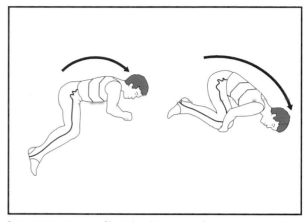

a Large moment of inertia, slow rate of spin (left). Small moment of inertia, large rate of spin (right).

b Large moment of inertia, slow rate of spin (left). Small moment of inertia, large rate of spin (right).

Figure 8.10 The dancer begins her movement with arms wide, and therefore a large moment of inertia. As she jumps and turns, she brings her arms to her side, reducing her moment of inertia and increasing the number of turns possible in the air before landing.

Figure 8.11 The discus thrower kicks his leg wide at the start of the turn, thereby giving his lower body rotational momentum with a large moment of inertia. As he moves to the centre of the circle he brings his leg closer to the body, reducing his moment of inertia and increasing the rate of spin of the lower body so that it moves ahead of the upper body in the movement.

Figure 8.12 The slalom skier begins his turn in a low, squat position with a high moment of inertia and, as he passes the gate, straightens his body into a shape with half the moment of inertia, doubling the rate of turn past the gate. After passing the gate, he reverts to the high moment of inertia position in order to slow down the rate of turn again.

(*See overleaf for Figure 8.13.*)

Part Two

The Performer as a Person

So far in this book we have considered the way in which the body works when we perform physical tasks. In physical education the body is central to what we do; if it is not trained and functioning properly we cannot achieve our intentions. But we must not ignore the mind in our studies, for in complex skills and movements, such as we employ in physical education and sport, body and mind work together. Next time you hear a sportsperson interviewed on television or radio, note how he or she talks about the mental aspects of preparation and performance as well as the physical aspect.

The science which studies how people's minds work, and how they behave, is called psychology. Behaviour is a result of how people think and feel in a situation, and may or may not be an 'automatic reaction'. So when we are interested in what sportspeople do to prepare for competition and how they react in the competition itself, or when we study dancers as they perform and choreograph, or when we observe and analyse what motivates the water sportsperson or mountaineer, then we use psychological theories and methods. You will be introduced to some of these aspects as you work through this section.

People have a number of different motives for participating in sport: to stay fit, to meet the challenge of competition and prove themselves, to share an enthusiasm with friends. But research has shown that what people tend to put high on their list of reasons for involvement in sports is the desire to improve skill and achieve excellence. So it is impor-

tant for students of sport to understand how we become skilful in physical activities; in other words, how we learn or acquire skill, and the factors which makes this process easy or difficult. Chapters 9–11 deal with this topic, which is referred to in the literature as skill aquisition, Chapters 12 and 13 consider how sportspeople prepare themselves for performance or competition; we look at some of the things that could go wrong and what coaches, teachers and the performers themselves can do to optimize their performance. We look at the performance itself, how people behave, how they achieve success (or failure) and what factors influence their performance in physical activities. Although we tend to focus our attention on sport, and most of the additional reading you do will be about sport, you should remember that the ideas apply equally to any form of physical activity—dance or outdoor pursuits, for example. They apply when anyone is learning and trying to do something to the best of her or his ability.

Associated with each section of work are suggestions for practical activities, which either illustrate the theory presented or else form the basis for investigations. At the end of each section are some review questions and some examples of questions typical of those you will find in GCE 'A'-level examinations. Additional reading is suggested, and the ideas contained therein might prove useful when you come to discuss your practical work, its results and your observations, or prepare answers to the questions. This reading will also help to extend your knowledge and understanding of the key concepts and issues.

The Nature and Classification of Skill

Chapters 9–11 consider how we acquire skill. The chapters introduce you to the nature of skill, to some ways in which skills may be classified and to a consideration of the way in which people learn to become skilful in an activity. A theoretical model is presented which sets out to analyse performance and learning in terms of the way in which information is processed, and we also look at learning from the teacher's or coach's point of view.

Student Learning Outcomes

When you have completed the work in Chapter 9 you should be able to:
- define skill and say what makes a performance skilful;
- describe the bases of four different classifications of skill and analyse physical tasks in terms of their characteristics;
- distinguish between 'skill' and 'ability'.

* * *

9.1 Skill Defined

 Keywords & concepts

cognitive skills	learning	performance
consistency	motor skills	predetermined results
efficiency	perceptual skills	psychomotor skills
economy of effort	perceptual–motor skills	skill
fluency		

The concept of 'skill' is used in several different ways:
- We use the word to mean an element of a game or sport, a technique—for example, passing, volleying or somersaulting.
- Later in this section we refer to sports themselves as 'skills'; for example, diving, archery or tennis.
- Also, we use the word 'skill' to imply a quality which a sportsperson possesses.

We use the word 'skilful' in the same way. In using the concept of skill in this way we must ensure also that we are differentiating 'skill' from 'ability', for in the literature on motor learning and skill acquisition these mean different things.

Let us first identify three different types of skill:

1. When you do arithmetic in your head (for example, when you are computing a darts score) you are employing intellectual (cognitive) skill. **Cognitive skill** is the ability to solve problems by thinking.

2. If you look at Figure 9.1 you can probably see two different images. With practice you will be able to switch between these two images at will. You are employing **perceptual skill**. Perception is the process by which you sense things and interpret them. In sport, you use this skill, for example, to determine where and when to pass the ball or in judging the type of shot to play in golf.

3. As you write your name, your hand is moving across the page and you are thus using essentially motor skill. You could probably do this with your eyes closed. **Motor skills** are those in which voluntary movement is predominant, and perception plays a less important role.

The skills we employ in PE and sport usually incorporate elements of all three types, and certainly include perception and movement. They are thus called **perceptual–motor or psychomotor skills**, but often this is shortened to **'motor skill'**; the perceptual element is usually implied, however.

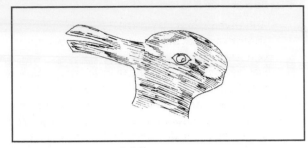
Figure 9.1 Perceptual skill.

 # Investigation

9.1: To identify the characteristics of skill

Task One
Work in pairs. One person demonstrates a perceptual–motor skill which can be performed very well; for example, a badminton serve. If you are short of space or equipment, throw and catch one or two tennis balls.
Observations: Note down all the things about the performance which enable you to describe it as 'skilful'. In other words, what is it about the performance which suggests that 'skill' is being demonstrated? You may find it helpful to contrast this performance with one where lack of skill is evident; for example, you might ask your partner to try to juggle two or three tennis balls with one or two hands
(Figure 9.2).

Task Two
If possible, watch a video of an experienced performers in action. What is it about their performances which tells us they are top class?

Discussion
From your observations, outline the characteristics of skilled performance.

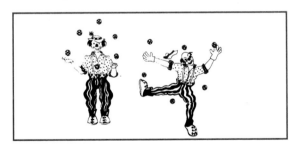
Figure 9.2 Skilled performance.

The characteristics of skilled performance (Investigation 9.1), which are summarized in the 'key points', lead us to definitions of skill, of which there are several. One useful one states that skill is

'the learned ability to bring about pre-determined results with maximum certainty, often with the minimum outlay of time or energy or both.' (Knapp, 1977, p. 4).

Key Points
- **Skill is learned.** It requires practice and results from experience. Learning is usually defined as a relatively permanent change in behaviour and/or performance which persists over time. We recognize this idea when we refer to an early success as a 'fluke' (accidental, or not the usual performance) and when we acknowledge a skilful gymnast as one who can reproduce, for example, a vault successfully time after time.

- **Skill has an end result.** We refer to it as 'goal-directed'. It is obviously important that the learner is aware, before the skill is attempted, of what this goal is and the reasons for aiming to achieve it. These are the 'predetermined results'. There is usually a 'best way' to achieve these results and the skill will thus be based on a technically sound model.
- Skilled performers achieve their goals **consistently**. There is much more likelihood than

not, that a skilful racket sports player will place shots exactly as intended; there is 'maximum certainty'.

- Skill results in **economic and efficient movement**, which is well co-ordinated and precise. A skilled performer can vary the timing of the movement, performing it quickly or slowly according to the demands of the moment. A beginner may use a lot of energy and still not succeed, but an experienced performer is able to fit the energy required to the demands of the task. The movement is efficient. It therefore appears fluent, controlled and in many instances aesthetically pleasing.

- A skilled performer makes accurate analyses of the demands of a sport situation and **appropriate decisions** about how to deal with these. Skill is not just about being a good technician, but about being able to use techniques at the right moment.

Notice that two terms keep occurring in this description: **learning** and **performance**. You will come to a clearer understanding of these concepts as you progress through Part Two (in particular, Chapter 11), but we need to be able to distinguish between these terms at this stage.

Performance is a demonstration of the solving of a problem or task at a given moment in time. Learning is shown by relatively permanent incremental improvements in performance over time.

Learning is a process, a life-long process. Even top-class sportspeople claim that they are still learning about their sport and aiming to improve. But a sport has definable elements or stages of learning associated with it, and so a gymnast, for example, can be said to have learned to perform a back somersault. What we mean is that her early performances were unsuccessful (or that she was reliant on her coach for support), but that with practice she became able to produce a well-formed somersault that would achieve good marks in a competition and was able to produce this performance consistently. A good coach or teacher defines stages of learning (i.e. intermediate goals) within a learning process so that the gymnast knows which elements of the skill have been mastered and which need further refinement. Learning is thus shown by improvements in performance—we have learned a skill when we can show a relatively permanent improvement. Of course, what we mean by 'relatively permanent improvement' depends to some extent on the accuracy requirements of the task. We do not say that a professional golfer had not learned to putt just because she/he occasionally misses! This subject is dealt with further in Chapter 11.

9.2 Skill Classified

 Keywords & concepts

balance	co-ordination	learning
classification of skill	discrete skills	open skills
closed skills	externally paced skills	self-paced skills
continuous skills	fine skills	serial skills
continuum	gross skills	

Let us return to the idea of skills being activities, such as climbing, dancing or playing a shot in badminton. Clearly, these are very different and may well have to be learned in different ways. Teachers, coaches and performers themselves, therefore, find it useful to be able to classify skills so that differing characteristics can be taken account of. **Classification** is the process of grouping similar skills together and giving them a generic label. You are already familiar with the 'cognitive–perceptual–motor' classification (see Section 9.1). As you complete your further reading, see how many different classifications you can

find. For example, Singer (1982) classifies skills in terms of:
- bodily involvement,
- duration of movement,
- pacing conditions,
- cognitive involvement,
- feedback availability.

Stallings (1982) has a similar list:
- continuity,
- coherence,
- pacing,
- environmental conditions,
- intrinsic feedback.

We consider here a classification system which has four elements: body involvement, environmental conditions, continuity and pacing.

Each of these elements can be thought of as a **continuum**. This means that the two ends of the continuum are opposites and that there is a gradual change in characteristics from one end to the other.

Body involvement continuum

Fine skills are those which involve small movements of specific body parts. Rifle shooting, for example, involves the movement of just the trigger finger (though considerable perceptual ability and steady posture) and is an example of a fine skill.

Gross skills involve large muscle groups and movement of the whole body; an example of this would be the high jump.

In between these two extremes are skills which have greater or lesser body involvement. For example a basketball or netball free shot has a major postural element (it is important to be steady, with a firm base), but the arm and shoulder muscles are fully used (Figure 9.3).

Continuity continuum

Continuous skills are those which have no obvious beginning or end (Figure 9.4); in theory they could be continued for as long as the performer wished. The end of one cycle of the skill becomes the beginning of the next.

Discrete skills, on the other hand, have a clear beginning and end; the skill can be repeated, but the performer 'starts again'.

Serial skills are composed of several discrete elements, strung together to produce an integrated movement. The order in which the elements are performed is important; for example, in a high jump or a triple jump, the run up, take-off and the

components of the jumping phase happen in a particular order. Note that whereas we refer to these as serial skills, they are also clearly discrete, so the two terms are not mutually exclusive.

Pacing continuum

The **pacing** continuum (Figure 9.5) is concerned with the extent to which the performer has control over the timing of the action. Actions are said to be 'self-paced' or 'externally paced' (or somewhere between these two extremes) according to the extent to which the performer can decide when to start the action.

Self-paced skills are those in which the performer has control over the rate at which the action takes place. Some examples are: a tennis player determines the timing of the action of the serve; some floor-work moves in men's gymnastics may be done slowly or quickly, depending on the effect required; a climber may move up a pitch slowly and carefully, savouring the technical problems posed, or may decide that the weather is closing in and it would be better to hurry. In others the start of the action can be controlled, but thereafter the movement takes place at a given rate; for example, a diver decides when to start his dive, but once he has left the board he cannot slow down his rate of progress to the water!

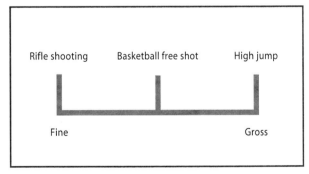

Figure 9.3 The 'body involvement' continuum.

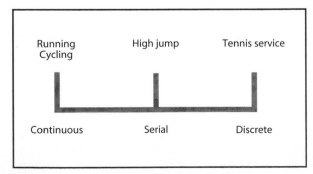

Figure 9.4 The continuous/discrete continuum.

Externally paced skills are those in which timing and form are determined by what is happening elsewhere in the environment; for example, a sailor adjusts the trim of the sails and the direction to be taken according to the wind.

Environmental requirements continuum

The 'pacing' continuum leads us to an important classification proposed by Poulton (1957) and developed in relation to sport skills by Knapp (1977). The continuum is based on the extent to which environmental conditions affect the performance (Figure 9.6).

Open skills are those in which the form of the action is constantly being varied according to what is happening around the performer.

Closed skills are pre-learned patterns of movements which can be followed without (or with little) reference to the environment.

At first sight this seems to be a fairly straightforward idea, but as one tries to identify skills as more or less open or closed, complexities arise. For example, one might identify soccer as essentially an open skill because players are constantly reacting to other players, but within the game there are skills which are clearly closed, for example taking a penalty. We call these 'closed skills in open situations'. It is very important that performers, teachers and coaches recognize where on the continuum a skill lies, because open skills need to be practised differently from closed skills.

When learning and practising a closed skill, such as in trampolining or athletics, the performer and coach have a model of the required movement pattern in mind and the task of the performer is to make the performance conform as closely as possible to that model. Practice therefore entails gradually refining performance and, once the movement pattern has been established, repeating it until it becomes habitual and the performer can reproduce the movement consistently without having to give too much attention to it.

Self-paced   Externally-paced

Figure 9.5 The pacing continuum.

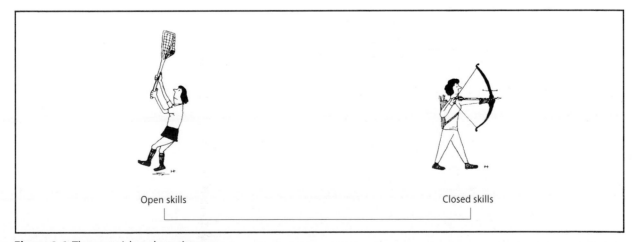

Open skills   Closed skills

Figure 9.6 The open/closed continuum.

Open skills, on the other hand, require practice which takes into account the many different ways in which the techniques are to be used. For example, a fielder in cricket, rounders or baseball must be able to throw an infinite variety of distances to ensure the ball reaches the receiver at just the right height.

Key Points

Fine	BODY INVOLVEMENT	Gross
Continuous	CONTINUITY	Discrete
Self	PACING	External
Open	ENVIRONMENTAL REQUIREMENTS	Closed

 # Investigation

9.2: To explore the classification system
Method: Work in pairs. Each makes a list of physical education skills. Exchange the lists and place the activities you have been given on to the four continua we have studied so far.
Observations: As you think about these classifications, you will realize that to assign a particular activity a place on a continuum can be a complex task. Much depends on the circumstances. For example, skiing could be open or closed depending on the state and gradient of the piste. And one could argue that whereas a game such as tennis clearly demands open skills, once a player has decided what sort

of shot to make, has positioned him/herself correctly and has read the pace and spin of the ball, then the resulting stroke is closed, hence the idea of 'closed skills in open situations'.
Discussion: Try to come to some agreement with your partner about the placing of the various activities. Suggest what some of the implications of this classification for sportspeople might be. In spite of the difficulties you may have identified, the idea of classifying skill is an interesting one and gives us food for thought when deciding how a skill should be practised. We return to this in Chapter 11.3.

 # Review Questions

1. Give a definition of skill.
2. Define and give an example of (a) a perceptual skill and (b) a motor skill. Why are sport skills referred to as 'psychomotor' skills?

3. Give an example of a sport skill which is both discrete and closed.
4. How are open skills different from closed skills?
5. What is 'a closed skill in an open situation'?

9.3 Skill and Ability

 Keywords & concepts

ability	perceptual ability	trunk strength
dynamic precision	psychomotor ability	speed
dynamic strength	static strength	stamina
explosive strength	extent flexibility	static precision
motor ability		

We need at this stage to distinguish between two terms, **skill** and **ability**, which are often used, in everyday language, to mean the same thing; but to sport psychologists these are technical terms that mean two different things.

Skill is acquired. Skills must be learned, and the process of this learning is considered in Chapter 11.

Ability (for example, to react quickly) is a stable, enduring, mainly genetically determined characteristic (or trait) that underlies skilled performance and can be used in a variety of skills (Schmidt, 1991, p. 283). Abilities develop through maturation; they are modified by experience, but are generally considered to be innate and enduring (though some psychologists question this). As with skills, abilities can be essentially perceptual, essentially motor or a combination of the two. Since most abilities to do with action are a combination, they are referred to as **psychomotor abilities**.

Abilities underpin and contribute to skills. For example, someone with good natural balance, shoulder flexibility, upper body and wrist strength has the prerequisites to perform a handstand. The handstand is a skill and the gymnast has to learn to use and co-ordinate these abilities effectively to learn to do a handstand.

Maturation, the result of growth and development, varies with individuals and causes differences in the rate at which individuals learn. A second factor which leads to individual differences in rate of learning is psychomotor ability; this may also set limits on the level of performance in any one skill that an individual is capable of achieving. For example, if you have not inherited enough fast-twitch muscle you will never make a top-class sprinter, no matter how hard you train.

It is important to remember that there is as yet no definitive list of psychomotor abilities. Different researchers categorize ability in different ways and even the terms used to describe the abilities vary slightly.

Stallings (1982), for example, selects her list on the following grounds: that each ability has been identified in a number of studies; that they can be developed and assessed; and that they are relevant to physical educators (Figure 9.7).

Fleishman (1972) identified the characteristics of motor performance, in a major research programme that involved over 200 tasks and many thousands of subjects, as follows (Figure 9.8):

- A series of psychomotor abilities derived from limb co-ordination tasks: reaction time; response orientation (i.e. choice reaction time); speed of movement; finger dexterity; manual dexterity; response integration (i.e. making sense of a variety of sources of information, as in interactive games).
- Nine 'physical proficiency abilities', referred to later as 'gross motor abilities'.

Guilford (1958) had earlier produced a similar list: impulsion, speed, static precision, dynamic precision, co-ordination and flexibility. There are some interesting differences between the two theories.

Figure 9.7a–e Stallings' (1982) motor abilities.

a Muscular power and endurance.

The contraction capacity of muscles

Short-term, high intensity, anaerobic

Long-term, low intensity, aerobic

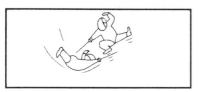

b Flexibility.

The range of movement in a joint or group of joints

Static—range of motion

Dynamic use of range of motion within a movement task

c Balance.

The maintenance of position and equilibrium

Static—fixed position

Dynamic—whilst in motion

Rotational—whilst turning

d Co-ordination.

The integration of all aspects of an action

Timing

Agility

e Differential relaxation.

The selective adjustment of muscle tension

EXTENT FLEXIBILITY:	flexing or stretching the trunk and back muscles as far as possible in any direction.
DYNAMIC FLEXIBILITY:	making repeated rapid movements in which the ability of the muscles to recover is critical.
EXPLOSIVE STRENGTH:	expending a maximum amount of energy in one or a series of strong, sudden movements.
STATIC STRENGTH:	the maximum force which can be exerted for a brief period.
DYNAMIC STRENGTH:	exerting muscular force repeatedly or over a period of time.
TRUNK STRENGTH:	dynamic strength specific to the abdominal muscles.
GROSS BODY CO-ORDINATION:	co-ordinating the similtaneous movements of different body parts whilst involved in whole body action.
GROSS BODY EQUILIBRIUM:	maintaining balance whilst blindfolded.
STAMINA:	continuing to exert maximum effort over time.

Figure 9.8 Fleishman's gross motor abilities.

Investigation

9.3: To consider the abilities required for particular skills

1. Discuss with a friend the similarities and differences between Fleishman's and Guilford's inventories of abilities. Check up on the meanings of the terms if you are not sure.

2. Look at the photographs of PE skills in Figure 9.9. List the abilities which you think are very important for good performance in each skill.

Figure 9.9 Physical education activities.

You have probably found that several abilities keep being mentioned over and over again. Strength, speed and co-ordination seem to be requirements for most motor skills, which has lead some writers to argue for the idea of a general motor ability. We hint at this when we say that someone is a 'natural' games player, meaning that they are good at most sports. But research tends to show that this is not the case and that specific skills require specific abilities. The co-ordination required to kick a ball is not the same as that required to execute a complex dance step. There are more than 100 motor abilities, so when we talk about a 'natural' sportsperson we mean someone who has inherited and developed a large number of the abilities which underpin skill in sport, including the ability to learn motor skills efficiently. This implies that, in addition to motor abilities, we could also argue that there are perceptual abilities that are important in sport, concerning the way in which we notice significant things that are happening around us and how quickly and effectively we make decisions about how to deal with them. These abilities, which Stallings (1982) identifies as visual, auditory, tactile and kinaesthetic, are discussed in more detail in Chapter 10.

Key Points

- Skills must be learned.
- Abilities are usually thought of as stable and enduring traits which underpin skills and contribute to the speed with which individuals learn psychomotor skills and to the quality of their performance.
- There is no such thing as general psychomotor ability. Specific skills require specific abilities and individuals vary in the range of abilities they possess. The 'natural', all-round athlete possesses a number of abilities appropriate to sport.

The measurement of psychomotor abilities

If psychomotor abilities are fundamental to the learning and performance of skills then it is useful for us to be able to measure ability in sportspeople for research purposes, to add to our knowledge of how skill works or to find out our own personal ability make-up. Arnot and Gaines (1984), in their book *Sports Talent*, show how a knowledge of the specific tasks of an activity such as windsurfing or tennis can lead to participants being able, with simple 'home-made' tests, to measure the strengths and weaknesses of relevant abilities in their profile. They can then choose activities they have the potential to be good at, or compensate for, say, lack of strength with good co-ordination.

Investigation

9.4: Measurement of psychomotor skills
In the three tasks below, work in pairs. The scorer has a stop-watch.

Task One—to measure static balance (gross body equilibrium)
Method: This test measures the ability to balance using the inner ear mechanism only; that is, not using the considerable positional information provided by the eyes. It is quite difficult and not suitable for young children; if you find difficulty in scoring, perform the test with eyes open.

The subject stands as in Figure 9.10. It is best to wear 'trainers' and to be standing on a hard surface. Stand on your preferred leg; keep your bent knee well out to the side. The experimenter starts timing as soon as you close your eyes (don't cheat!). The watch is stopped when you open your eyes, move your hands, take your foot off your knee or move your standing foot from the spot. Wobbling is permissible as long as you don't do any of the above. Take the test three times (with rests in between) and record your best time.

Results: Use Table 9.1 to find your score in points; record your points score.

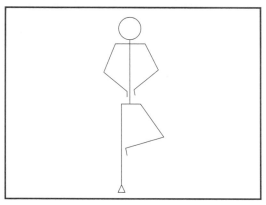

Figure 9.10 Stork balance.

Table 9.1 : Blind-stork balance

Men		Women	
Best time (sec)	**Points**	**Best time (sec)**	**Points**
60	20	35	20
55	18	30	17
50	16	25	14
45	14	20	11
40	12	15	8
35	10	10	4
30	8	5	2
25	6		
20	4		
15	3		
10	2		

(Arnot and Gaines, 1984, p. 175)

Task Two—to measure co-ordination (agility)
Method: Measure out a 66 cm-per-side hexagon on the floor as shown in Figure 9.11. Cover the lines with masking or plastic tape so that the outside edge of the tape becomes the outside of the hexagon.

Stand in the middle of the hexagon, facing side A; face this way throughout the test. On the command 'go', when the watch is started, jump with both feet across line B and immediately back into the hexagon (remember to keep facing front). Then jump over side C and back and continue until you are back in the hexagon, having jumped over side A. This is one complete

Investigation

9.4 continued

circuit; do three circuits altogether. The watch is stopped when you have completed the third circuit. Record your time. If you make a mistake, by treading on a line or jumping over the wrong line, start the trial again. Count the times for successful trials only. Have three 'goes' with rests in between and note your best time.

Results: Use Table 9.2 to record your points score.

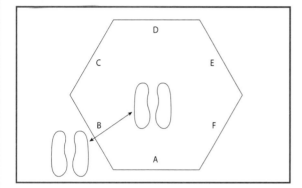

Figure 9.11 The hexagon.

Task Three—to measure the endurance strength of the quadriceps

Method: The subject stands with his/her back against a smooth wall. Do the test barefoot or in trainers that do not slip, as your feet will tend to slide. When you are ready, gently slide your back down the wall until you are in the position shown in Figure 9.12. Your feet should be comfortably apart. There should be angles of 90° at the hip and knee.

Lift one foot about 5 cm off the ground. Your partner should start timing now. The watch is stopped when you put your foot back down on the floor. Stand up by putting your hands against the wall by your hips and pushing forwards slowly. Stand up gently. Record your time. Take a rest and then repeat the test with the other leg supporting. Again record your time.

Results: Taking the lowest of the two times, record your points score using Table 9.3.

Discussion

Look at your profile of points for the three tests. Which is your highest points score? Is this what you would have expected?

Table 9.2 : Hexagonal obstacle

Best time without sides (sec)		Points
Men	**Women**	
9.0	9.0	10.0
10.1	10.6	9.0
11.2	12.2	8.0
12.3	13.8	7.0
13.4	15.4	6.0
14.5	17.0	5.0
15.6	18.6	4.0
16.7	20.2	3.0
17.8	21.8	2.0
18.9	23.4	1.0
20.0	25.0	0.0

(Arnot and Gaines, 1984, p. 145)

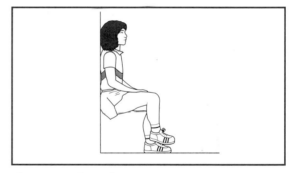

Figure 9.12 The wall squat.

Table 9.3 : Wall squat

Time (sec)		Points
Men	**Women**	
120	70	8.0
111	65	7.6
102	60	7.2
93	55	6.8
84	50	6.4
75	45	5.6
66	40	4.8
57	35	4.0
48	30	3.2
39	25	2.4
30	20	1.6
21	15	0.8

As you read further you will find many examples of psychomotor ability tests other than those in Investigation 9.4. Sometimes you will recognize that these measure more than one ability, for it is often difficult to isolate abilities in simple tests. The three tests in Investigation 9.4 measure the motor aspect of ability, i.e. the work that the muscles are doing.

In your further reading you will find tests that measure the perceptual aspects of ability.

Ability testing is a useful addition to fitness testing, but because of the complex interaction of abilities in sports skills, such testing is inappropriate for predicting how good an athlete will become.

Review Questions

1. List four differences between abilities and skills.
2. Why is there 'no such thing as a general motor ability'?
3. Why is it important to distinguish between ability and skill?
4. To what extent do abilities limit the level of acquisition of skills?
5. What are the advantages and difficulties of measuring motor abilities?

Exam-Style Questions

1. **a.** Here is a list of activities drawn from a variety of sports: basketball free throw; jogging; swimming; high jump; gymnastics sequence.
i. Classify each of these activities in terms of whether they are discrete, continuous or serial tasks. (3 marks)
ii. Justify your decisions in the case of the first two of these activities. (2 marks)
b. Define a serial task and explain it by using an example. (3 marks)
c. Another way to classify movement is in terms of pacing.
i. Explain what is meant by self-paced skills. Illustrate your answer from a sport. (2 marks)
ii. Explain what is meant by externally-paced skills. Illustrate your answer from a sport. (2 marks)
2. Figure 9.13 shows a profile for the racing start in swimming scaled across five continua that represent certain characteristics of skilled movements.
a. With reference to the profile, briefly describe the swimming racing start in terms of each of the five characteristics of skilled movement. (5 marks)
b. i. Using the same five continua, sketch a profile to describe the characteristics of a tennis serve.
(3 marks)
ii. Justify your choice of position on the continua for **coherence** and **environmental conditions**. (5 marks)

iii. Explain briefly how your profile of the tennis serve might help a coach decide how to organize practices for players learning this skill. (7 marks)
3. **a.** You are observing a number of badminton players being coached. They are of mixed ability. Some players cannot seem to improve their skill level, no matter how hard they try.
i. Define the terms **perceptual ability** and **motor ability**. (2 marks)
ii. Give two motor abilities required for performing a serve in badminton. (2 marks)
iii. Some performers have a large number of abilities, which gives the impression of 'natural ability'. Why is this impression misleading? (2 marks)

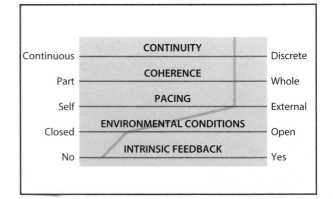

Figure 9.13 Profile for the racing start in swimming. (*Adapted from Stallings, 1982.*)

Summary

1. The terms **ability** and **skill** mean different things. Skill is learned; it the efficient attainment of a pre-specified goal; it involves speed, accuracy and the adaptation of movements to the requirements of the task. Ability is largely a function of inheritance; though it may be developed and extended with use, it is not learned. Abilities underpin skills. There are a limited number of abilities, but an infinite number of skills.

2. Skills may be **classified** in a variety of ways.

Four of the most useful classifications in terms of an understanding of how skills are acquired relate to (i) body involvement, (ii) continuity, (iii) pacing and (iv) environmental requirements.

3. The learning and performance of skills is affected by the stage of development of **motor abilities**. It is possible to measure the extent to which any ability has developed at a given moment; however, we must remember that it is not always easy to isolate motor abilities and tests often measure several at once.

Further Reading

References

Arnot R. and Gaines C. *Sports Talent,* Penguin, 1984.

Fleishman E.A. The structure and measurement of psychomotor abilities. In: Singer R.N. (ed) *The Psychomotor Domain: Movement Behaviour,* Lea & Febiger, 1972.

Guilford J.P. A system of psychomotor abilities. *American Journal of Applied Psychology,* 1958; 71: 164–174.

Knapp B. *Skill in Sport,* Ch 1, Routledge and Kegan Paul,1977.

Schmidt R.A. *Motor Learning and Performance: From Principles to Practice,* Ch 1, 11, Human Kinetics, 1991.

Singer R.N. *The Learning of Motor Skills,* Ch 5, Macmillan,1982.

Stallings L.M. *Motor Learning From Theory to Practice,* Mosby, 1982.

Further reading

Beashel P. *Advanced Studies in Physical Education and Sport,* Nelson, 1996.

Bull R. *Teachers' Guide and Answers to Skill Acquisition,* Jan Roscoe Publications, 1996.

Honeybourne J. *et.al. Advanced Physical Education and Sport,* Stanley Thornes, 1996.

Magill R.A. *Motor Learning: Concepts and Applications,* Brown & Benchmark, 1993.

Schmidt R.A. *Motor Learning and Performance: From Principles to Practice,* Ch 1, 11, Human Kinetics, 1991.

Scottish Sports Council. *Acquiring Skills,* Coach Education Module 1, Scottish Sports Council, 1987.

Sharp B. *Acquiring Skill in Sport,* Ch 2, Sports Dynamics, 1992.

Information Processing in Perceptual-Motor Performance

So far we have defined skill by describing it. Knapp's approach is thus a 'descriptive definition'. Let us now consider a different form of definition—one which analyses **how** the skill is performed. This is known as an 'operational definition'.

When you have completed the work in Chapter 10 you should be able to:
- understand how information is transmitted through the central and peripheral nervous systems;
- use an information processing model to analyse a skill;
- understand the relationship between sensory input, perception, decision making, memory and motor output in the performance of skilled actions and in the learning process;
- measure reaction time and test hypotheses using reaction time data;
- understand the difference between open and closed modes of motor control;
- define, and apply to physical education activities, the keywords listed at the beginning of each section.

10.1 Introduction to Information Processing

 Keywords & concepts

central nervous system (CNS)	**information processing**	**perceptual mechanism**
cognitive system	**input**	**peripheral nervous system**
decision making	**intrinsic feedback**	**physiological system**
decision mechanism	**memory**	**receptor system**
display	**muscular system**	**response programming**
effector mechanism	**output**	**sensory system**
extrinsic feedback	**perception**	**translatory mechanism**

 Investigation

10.1: To examine the concept of 'information processing'
Method: Watch a video (preferably played in 'slow motion') of a player receiving or catching and making a pass or shot (net or invasion game). Alternatively, while playing a game concentrate on what you are doing while you yourself are receiving and sending.

1. Note down everything that you do (or the player does), from first picking out where the ball is as it approaches to assessing the effectiveness of the shot or pass.
2. Group the activities you have identified into:
a. those concerned with identifying what is happening to the ball,

Investigation

10.1 continued

b. those concerned with making decisions about where to move and what to do,
c. those concerned with making an appropriate movement.

You will go through this process twice—one set of activities is concerned with receiving and one with sending.

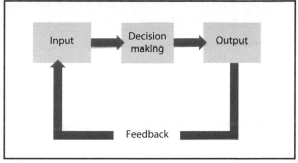

Figure 10.1 A simple information processing model.

In Investigation 10.1 you need to identify the three main stages by which players take in information about the game being played, make decisions about how to respond and programme their muscles to produce the skilled movement required. This can be represented by a simple model of information processing (Figure 10.1)

There are many such models, some of which you will come across in your further reading, but they all contain these three basic elements. You should remember that these models are only representations of what psychologists think is going on within a player's **CNS**. We can assess what is entering the system and we can observe what the player does to respond, but we can only hypothesize the processes in between.

Key Points
- **Input** is the information from the environment which the player is aware of and uses to decide on a response to the situation.
- **Decision making** refers to the combination of recognition, perception and memory processes used to select an appropriate response to the demands of the situation.
- **Output** is the response which the player makes. In sport this is usually in the form of a movement of some kind. Output becomes a form of input in that the player perceives the outcome of his/her response and this in turn becomes the basis for further decision making.

The definitions given in Key Points suggest that we need to expand the model further:

- **Perception**. As the player receives information from the environment he/she needs to make sense of it, i.e. to perceive it, interpret it and identify elements in it which are important, for example whether the ball is spinning or not, what the flight path of the shuttle is, whether there is a gap in the defence which can be exploited.
- This recognition and interpretation relies on previous experience and **memory** of that experience;
- Following decision making about what to do, the muscles needed to carry out the required movement must be activated. This is referred to as **response programming** (Schmidt, 1991).

An expanded model is shown in Figure 10.2.

Welford's (1968) model gives even more detail to show the difference between the **physiological systems** of the body and the **cognitive mechanisms**, in addition to differentiating between **intrinsic** and **extrinsic feedback**.

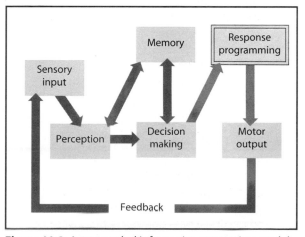

Figure 10.2 An expanded information processing model.

Investigation

10.2: To use an information processing model to analyse a skill

Method: Work in pairs. Use your knowledge of a striking skill (tennis, badminton, hockey, football, etc.) to analyse the action of striking using Welford's model (Figure 10.3).

1. Define all the terms in Figure 10.3, using the striking skill as the exemplar.
2. Give a practical example of what is happening in each of the processes identified in the model.

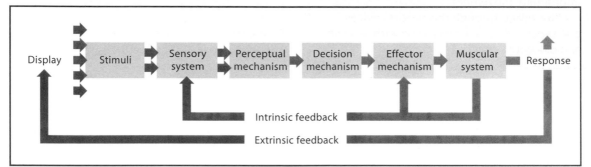

Figure 10.3 Adapted from Welford's model of information processing. (*After Welford, 1968.*)

Another model, which is essentially the same but which uses different terms, is given in the examination questions at the end of this chapter (Whiting, 1969). Compare Whiting's and Welford's models.

Whiting uses the term **receptor systems** for Welford's 'sensory system' and **translatory mechanisms** for 'decision mechanism'.

Key Points

- Display—The surroundings or environment.
- Stimuli—The aspects of the display which the player is attending to.
- Sensory and receptor system—The part of the CNS which passes information from the sense organs to the brain.
- Perceptual mechanism—The process by which the interpretation of stimuli takes place.
- Decision and translatory mechanism—The process which deals with receiving the interpretation of the input and using the memory of previous similar situations to decide upon a response.

- Effector mechanism—On the basis of the decision made, a motor plan or programme is constructed which informs the muscles of the movement requirements.
- Muscular system—The nerves and muscles which are involved in the particular movement.
- Response—The movement which results from the whole information-processing sequence.
- Intrinsic feedback—Information performance about the movement provided by proprioception (see Section 10.2).
- Extrinsic feedback—Information about the outcome of the response.

Skilled movement thus relies on the transmission of information though the nervous system. The nervous system as two elements:
- the **CNS**—the brain and the spinal cord;
- the **peripheral nervous system**—the nerves that connect the spinal cord with all parts of the body, radiating from and returning to the CNS.

To understand how this transmission of information works you should read Chapter 1.6. Sections 10.2–10.4 deal with the three elements of the information processing model—sensory input, perception, and selective attention and memory.

Exam-Style Questions

1. **a.** The items in the boxes In Figure 10.4 represent the elements of a simple information processing model of skill. Arrange the boxes and add lines and arrow heads to represent the flow of information during the execution of an **open** skill. (3 marks)
b. With reference to open passing skills, what difficulties might a beginner expect to experience with each of the elements of the model? (8 marks)

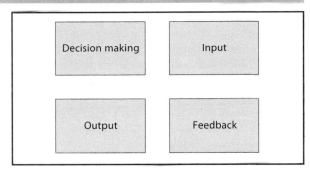

Figure 10.4 Simple information processing model of skill.

10.2 Sensory Input

Keywords & concepts

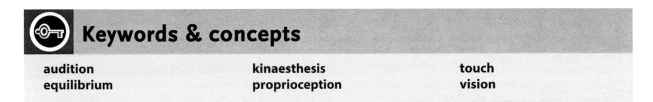

audition	**kinaesthesis**	**touch**
equilibrium	**proprioception**	**vision**

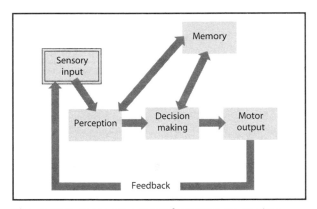

Figure 10.5 Sensory input in information processing.

When we are doing any physical activity we are aware of our surroundings. We use all our senses to locate ourselves in space and to decide on the requirements of the task, whether it is to pass a ball or perform a gymnastic or dance movement. Taste and smell are not used to any great extent in physical activity, but vision, hearing and proprioception are (Figure 10.6).

Vision and hearing (audition) deal with information from the external environment. We also receive information from the internal environment—that is, from within our own bodies.

Proprioception is the means by which we know how our body is oriented in space and the extent to which

muscles are contracted or joints extended—it allows us to feel the racket or ball. The three components of proprioception are **touch, equilibrium and kinaesthesis**.

Touch (or the tactile sense) enables us to feel pain, pressure and temperature. In sports and dance we are mostly concerned with the pressure sense to tell us how firmly we are gripping a racket, for example, or whether our climbing partner is on a tight rope, or whether we struck the ball hard or

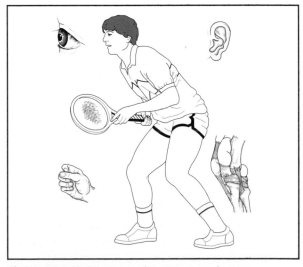

Figure 10.6 Major sensory input systems in games.

'stroked' it. If we are sensible we take heed of any pain warnings we receive.

Equilibrium is the sense which tells you when your body is balanced and when it is tipping, turning or inverting. It is obviously important for divers, gymnasts and trampolinists, as well as dancers, to be able to orientate themselves in space. This is done by means of the sense organs in the vestibular apparatus of the middle ear.

Kinaesthesis is the sense which informs the brain of the movement or state of contraction of the muscles, tendons and joints. A skilled performer knows whether a movement has been performed correctly or not, not only from seeing its effect, but also from sensing how the movement felt to perform. You may have experienced a foot or a limb 'going to sleep' and you will know how difficult it is not only to move the limb, but to know what is happening to it. The messages to and from the muscles have been interrupted and kinaesthetic sense impaired. Investigation 10.4 illustrates how we use our kinaesthetic sense.

 # Investigation

10.3: To investigate the effects of sensory deprivation on performance

1. Vision
Task One
Method: Play a game of five-a-side soccer or basketball (or any passing or striking game). One team plays as normal. Players in the other team have one eye covered with a medical eye patch. Do not continue this activity for too long.
Observations: What are the effects on the visually deprived players? What does it feel like to play like this?

Task Two
Method: Reverse team roles so that the other team is visually deprived. This time restrict peripheral vision (your ability to see 'out of the corner of your eye' things which you are not looking at directly). You can do this by cutting a strip of card (8 cm × 60 cm,) stapling the narrow ends to form goggles and attaching it around your eyes with elastic or string (Figure 10.7).

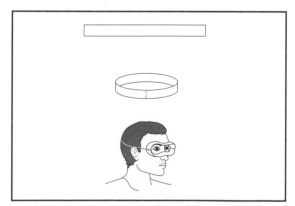

Figure 10.7 Goggles to restrict peripheral vision.

Observations: What is the effect of the goggles? What does it feel like to play like this?

Task Three
Method: Try a gymnastic or dance sequence with which you are familiar, using the same vision restrictors.
Observations: What are the problems? What does the sequence feel like?

We use vision a great deal in physical activities. Imagine the difficulties for a blind or partially sighted person. Discuss with a partner any knowledge you have of visually handicapped people participating in sport or physical activity. How do they compensate?

2. Audition
Task Four
Method: Select an activity in which sound is an integral part (for example, the sound of the ball against the racket in tennis or the bed in trampolining). Try this activity when wearing headphones or ear plugs to block out the sound.
Observations: How does this affect your performance? To what extent do we use sound in these activities?

3. Proprioception
Task Five
Method: Play a ball-handling game such as basketball, netball or softball in thick gloves. Perform a gymnastic or dance sequence, with which you are familiar, in stiff trainers.
Observations: It will obviously feel strange, but what are the particular problems?
Discussion: Explain the difficulties in terms of your loss of some tactile sense.

Investigation

10.4: To illustrate kinaesthesis

Method: Make a loop of fairly strong elastic and loop it round your fingers, as in Figure 10.8. Your partner holds a ruler horizontally and you stretch the elastic to a length specified by your partner. You relax the elastic, your partner removes the ruler and you try to repeat the exact stretch again, but this time with your eyes closed. Repeat this several times, each time with a different length to reproduce.

Observations: How accurate were you? Calculate your percentage error each time.

Discussion: Discuss with your partner how kinaesthesis is being used.

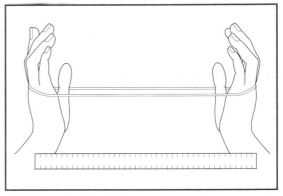

10.8 Equipment to illustrate kinaesthesis.

We take our sense organs very much for granted in sport and recreation and do not always appreciate that our ability to make appropriate decisions is based on receiving the right information. Whether or not we get the right information depends on:

- the efficiency of our sense organs,
- the intensity of the stimulus,
- our ability to interpret the stimulus correctly, i.e. our perceptual capability.

Exam-Style Questions

1. The **Information Processing** theory sheds light on the actual processes which take place during the learning of motor skills. Whiting's model (1969), shown in Figure 10.9, is a well-known illustration of the Information Processing theory.

a. i. Input data comes from the display. What is meant by the term **display**?
ii. Identify the **three** main receptor systems used by the performer in a **named** motor skill. (4 marks)

Figure 10.9 Whiting's model of information processing. (*After Whiting, 1969.*)

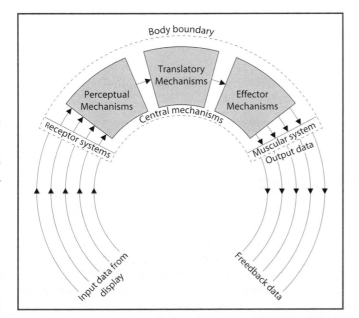

10.3 Perception

Keywords & concepts

comparison	noise	stimulus identification
detection	recognition	
memory	stimulus	

Perception (Figure 10.8) is the process by which the brain interprets and makes sense of the information it is receiving from the sensory organs. Perception consists of three elements:

- Detection,
- Comparison,
- Recognition.

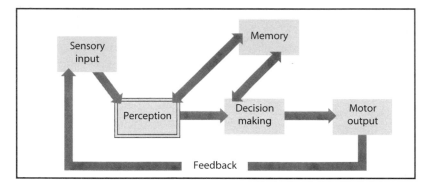

Figure 10.10 Perception in the information processing model.

Detection is the process by which the brain identifies that a stimulus is present. The brain detects many more stimuli than we are aware of. It registers everything that the sense organs are capable of detecting for a brief moment. If we concentrate on that information, then it is passed on for further processing, but if we do not attend to it then it quickly fades out of the system. For example, when playing an invasion game, all the players within our range of vision are detected, but if you concentrate on the player you are closely marking, you will not be aware, in detail, of what the others are doing.

Comparison is what happens when we attend to something we have sensed. The image, sound and feel of the stimulus is coded and passed through the memory and compared with similar codes that have been stored in memory.

Recognition occurs when the code of the incoming information matches a code stored in memory and the stimulus is then perceived, i.e. identified and recognised.

This process is considered in more detail in the next section and in Chapter 11, which deals with the learning of skills.

Investigation

10.5: To investigate perception in physical activities
Method: Participate in (or imagine you are participating in) any open skill. Remember that an open skill is one in which the important aspects of the environment are constantly changing. As you participate, be aware of those aspects of your surroundings to which you pay particular attention.

Observations: List all the things that you take notice of in order to perform well. In a ball game you need to note the flight of the ball as it comes towards you; as you climb a rock or wall, you attend to the changes in the surface; as you canoe, you watch for waves, rocks and currents.
Discussion: Talk these over in detail with a colleague.

Each of the factors you noted in Investigation 10.5 is a **stimulus**: the spin of a ball, the flight path of a shuttle, the size of a hold on a climb. The word 'stimulus' is used here to mean any item of information that stands out from background information and to which the player pays more attention. The 'background' is those aspects of the display that are not directly relevant to the task in hand, but which nevertheless enter our sensory system. Examples of 'background' are the surroundings of the court, or the audience. Psychologists refer to this background information as 'noise'. Noise used in this sense is information that is present and that we might be aware of, but it is not directly relevant to the task in hand. We usually try, therefore, to ignore it and concentrate on the important stimuli. Later it is shown that the ability to differentiate background from stimuli is partly learned, but partly a personality trait, and also that noise can be a problem in decision making.

We are more likely to perceive something if it is intense, i.e. loud, bright, large, contrasting, fast-moving, unusual. Hence the referee's whistle is shrill, team strip is distinctive and sight screens are used in cricket to help the batsman pick out the ball.

Investigation

10.6: To investigate the effect of background and ball colour in tennis
Method: Play two games of short tennis, one with balls that contrast with the surroundings and one with balls which blend with the court and wall colour. (Dye a few tennis balls to find a colour which blends with your particular sports hall.)
Observations: How did the colour of the balls affect your game?

Investigation

10.7: To investigate the effect of early and late stimuli identification in the catching and returning of a ball

Task One
Method: Work in threes—a 'feeder', a 'catcher' and a 'scorer'. Mark a cross in chalk or tape on the ground about one metre from the catcher's feet. First, the feeder bounces the ball on the cross for the catcher to receive. You will need to adjust your position and that of the cross so that the ball can be received comfortably by the catcher. Have ten trials. The feeder should try and make the bounces consistent. The scorer notes successful catches out of ten.

The catcher then has a further twenty trials, but this time the catcher has closed eyes until the feeder shouts 'Now!'. This should be done at varying points on the trajectory of the bounce, ten times early (i.e. shortly after it has left the feeder's hand) and ten times late.
Results: What are the effects on catching of early and late opportunity for stimulus identification?
Discussion: How do you explain the results you obtained?

Task Two
Repeat the experiment playing badminton or volleyball, with a server, two or more receivers and a scorer as before.

Task Three
Discuss examples from a variety of sports by which a player can inflict late signal detection opportunity on an opponent.

10.4 Selective Attention and Memory

 Keywords & concepts

long-term memory	**selective attention**	**short-term sensory store**
memory	**short-term memory**	

Perception depends on three processes:
- **D**etection,
- **C**omparison,
- **R**ecognition.

These are integrated into the information processing model in Figure 10.11.

Detection

All the senses feed a vast amount of information into the CNS. Think for a moment of all the aspects of your surroundings and your body on which you can focus your attention if you choose. The games player can switch attention from the opponent to the ball to the grip on the stick or bat (for example) very quickly. She/he is able to do this because all the information that enters the sensory system is held for a very short time (less than a second) in a section of the memory known as the **short-term sensory store** (see Figure 10.11). We can concentrate only on a very small proportion of all this information at any given moment.

If we are looking out for some particular stimulus, or if a particular happening catches our interest, then we focus on that by the process of **selective attention**. This focusing of attention passes the information into the short-term memory and allows the stimulus to be **detected**. That information which is not attended to is almost immediately lost from the memory. The short-term sensory store has a very large capacity, but a minimal storage time.

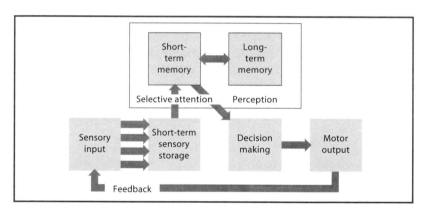

Figure 10.11 Memory and selective attention in the information processing model.

 Investigation

10.8: To investigate selective attention

Task One
Method: Listen through stereo headphones to an audio tape that has been recorded with two separate passages of prose on the two tracks of the tape.
Observations: Can you listen to them both simultaneously? What strategies did you adopt to make as much sense as you could of both passages? What aspects of the passages made you switch your attention?

Task Two—To investigate the effect of selective attention on the performance of a motor skill
Method: You need five yellow tennis balls and one of a contrasting colour. A catcher stands 2 m from a line of six throwers, each of whom has a tennis ball held so that it cannot be seen.
A. On the command 'throw', given either by one of the throwers or by the scorer, the throwers throw simultaneously and gently to the catcher, who attempts to catch the contrasting ball. Score successful catches out of ten trials.

Investigation

10.8 continued

B. The instructor gives the command 'throw'—and the name of one of the throwers. All throw; the catcher is to catch the ball thrown by the nominee. Score successful catches out of ten.
C. The instructor gives the command as in **B** above, but only the nominee throws. Score successful catches out of ten.
Results: Draw a bar chart to illustrate the mean scores for the whole class on each of the three tests (an example is given in Figure 10.12). Note that a bar chart, with spaces between the bars, is used because the horizontal axis shows three separate trials: it does not represent a scale, as it would if a histogram was drawn.

Discussion
In which of the three tests is selective attention easiest? Suggest reasons.

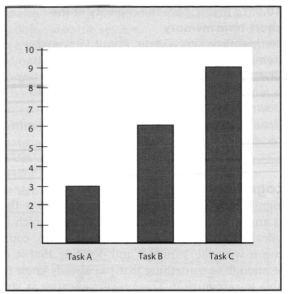

Figure 10.12 Hypothetical group mean scores on three tests to illustrate selective attention.

Key Points
Selective attention (SA) is the process by which information important for performance is 'filtered out' for further processing. It is very important in sport when accuracy or fast responses require concentration on the goal of the action without letting other aspects distract, e.g. the full-back catching a high ball in rugby needs to ignore the on-rushing forwards. SA is an instinctive process, but its effectiveness can be improved through learning from past experience.

As we learned earlier, intensity of the stimulus may attract our attention—for example, loudness, brightness, colour contrast, speed of movement; but we are also attracted to unusual stimuli (we try to make sense of them) or to stimuli in which we are particularly interested, as in Task Two of Investigation 10.8.

Task One of Investigation 10.8 indicates that our capacity to attend to several stimuli at once is severely limited. The process of selective attention ensures that only a small amount of information can be processed at a time. We see later that this is not necessarily a disadvantage, for it means that the decision making system is not overloaded. Imagine what it would be like to decide when and who to pass to in a team game if, before making a move, we had to analyse all the available information coming in through our senses!

Comparison
The **short-term memory** (see Figure 10.11) is the 'workplace' of the information processing system. Once a stimulus has been detected, it must be recognized if it is to be of use. This is done by **comparing** the characteristics of the stimulus as it is held in the short-term memory with similar stimuli previously learned and stored in the **long-term memory** (LTM). Learning is the process of storing information in the LTM by practice and rehearsal. For example, tennis players learn where a ball is going to bounce and where they must position themselves to return it effectively by having lots of practice at seeing balls bounce and then storing in the LTM the visual picture of what happened when their positioning was right. Any future similar event is compared with this memory.

Chapter 11

Principles of Learning and Teaching

In working through this chapter you will:
- become familiar with some theories about what learning is and how we learn;
- use information processing models to analyse aspects of motor learning;
- understand the implications of motor programmes and schema theory;
- examine the processes of transfer of learning and mental rehearsal;
- realize the importance of feedback to learning;
- examine the way in which styles of teaching, modes of presentation, forms of guidance and types of practice can affect learning.

11.1 Introduction: Learning, Performance and Learning Curves

 Keywords & concepts

cognitive strategy	learning curve	performance
decreasing errors graph	linear graph	plateau
learning	negative acceleration curve	positive acceleration curve

In Chapter 9 we defined learning in general terms and contrasted it with performance. Let us look again at the definitions of learning and performance.

> *Learning may then be considered to be a more or less permanent change in performance associated with experiences but excluding changes which occur through maturation and degeneration, or through alterations in the receptor or effector organs.*
> (Knapp, 1973.)

> *Performance may be thought of as a temporary occurrence ... fluctuating from time to time because of many potentially operating variables. We usually use performance to represent the amount of learning that has occurred, for the process of learning must be inferred on the basis of observations of change in performance.*
> (Singer, 1975.)

Activity
11.1: Meaning of learning and performance
Work in groups of two or three. Discuss the meaning of the two definitions given in the text to make sure you understand them. In particular, explain:
- permanent change in performance,
- associated with experiences,
- maturation and degeneration,
- alterations in the receptor or effector organs,
- potentially operating variables,
- inferred on the basis of observations of change in performance.

Investigation

11.1: To distinguish between learning and performance

Method: Work with a partner. One is the pupil, the other his/her instructor. The instructor, out of sight of the pupil, composes a sequence of movements, chosen at random. Keep the movements simple and 'nonsense'. About 10 separate movements are sufficient. The instructor practises this sequence so that it can be demonstrated fluently to the pupil. The sequence is then taught to the pupil by demonstrating it in full **once only**; the pupil then performs it as best he/she can. This performance will probably contain some errors or omissions. Without any explanation or correction, the instructor shows the sequence again and requests another demonstration. Repeat this procedure, without verbal coaching, until a completely correct sequence is produced.

Results: Note how many mistakes of movement pattern or sequencing are made at each performance. Draw a graph as in Figure 11.1.

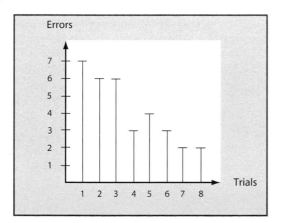

Figure 11.1 A graph of decreasing errors to demonstrate learning.

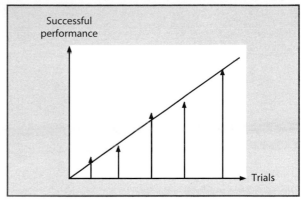

Figure 11.2 A graph of increasing gains in learning.

Each attempt at the task is a **performance**, a demonstration of the learner's ability in that task at that time. While a person is learning, each performance is likely to be different from (and hopefully better than) the last. As the skill is learned, performance becomes more consistent. So learning is the process by which performance is refined in such a way that it represents a permanent change of behaviour.

Learning curves

If you smooth out the fluctuations in performance shown in Figure 11.1, as has been done in Figure 11.2, you obtain a **linear** representation of the rate of learning in which learning (improvement in performance) is directly related to the number of trials (performances). Graphs of real learning experiences are seldom, if ever, as simple and symmetrical as this. People differ in the rate at which they learn. Some skills can be learned quickly, which produces a very 'steep' graph; others take more practice, so the graph is flatter.

Usually, however, the rate of learning changes throughout the learning of the skill and so plotting a graph over a period of practice time usually produces, not a straight line, but a series of **learning curves**. Figure 11.3 shows two such curves for two different skills.

The graph you drew in Investigation 11.1 is one of **decreasing errors**—one way of measuring learning and showing that it has occurred. Another way would be to measure how much better your partner was getting at an activity by measuring increases in performance, i.e. the number of successful catches in a juggling task. The graph might then look like that in Figure 11.2.

Key Points
- If a **negative acceleration curve** is produced when rate of learning is plotted, this shows that rate of learning is faster in the earlier stages than in the later stages.
- If a **positive acceleration curve** is produced, this shows that learning starts slowly, with only small improvements in performance early on, but then speeds up towards the end of the learning period.

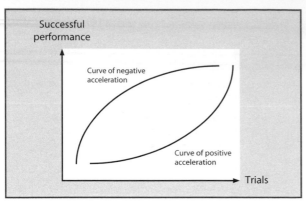

Figure 11.3 Curves of positive and negative acceleration.

Activity

11.2: A learning curve

Draw a hypothetical (not based on reality, but on your imagination) learning curve to represent the efforts of a learner who initially finds it hard to make progress, starts to learn quickly, but then faces a learning 'block' or '**plateau**' in which he/she maintains the standard of performance but makes no further improvement.

Why do you think the plateau might have occurred? What could the teacher or coach do about it?

Causes of plateaus

Plateaus usually indicate a period of transition in the learning or development of the skill, or changes in the lifestyle of the athlete.

Christina and Corcos (1988) categorize causes of plateaus as:

- **Psychological factors**—anxiety, lack of motivation, boredom, emotional problems.
- **Physical fitness deficiencies**—inadequate or inappropriate training, fatigue, lack of physical ability.

- **Changes in technique**—as a learner focuses on a new aspect of the technique or tactic, established routines may deteriorate temporarily or the skill as a whole may not progress. For example, as a discus thrower introduces the turn (after first learning a static throw) his/her distances may not improve for a while, or may even get worse, but once the new technique is incorporated into the action, performance will start to improve again, often at an increased rate.
- **Changes in cognitive strategy**—the way in which the athlete thinks about the skill, both before and during performance, affects learning. If this is changed, performance is affected. For example, if the coach introduces the athlete to a new visualization technique, the athlete needs time to learn and adapt to this and progress may be delayed in the short term while this adjustment is made. Similarly, if a teacher asks a beginner breaststroke swimmer to think about swimming through a narrow tube (in order to make the stroke more streamlined), concentrating on this may temporarily disrupt co-ordination and the swimmer may feel he/she is not making progress.

The teacher/coach can help the learner overcome these difficulties by:

- explaining that plateaus are a normal part of the learning process;
- explaining the cause of the plateau and reassuring the learner that the plateau can be overcome;
- planning appropriate goals to ensure continued progress;
- structuring training and practice appropriately;
- providing psychological support and not putting the learner under pressure if stress is a possible cause of the plateau.

 # Review Questions

1. Define 'learning ' and 'performance' and show how they are related.
2. Draw a series of learning curves which show positive acceleration, negative acceleration and a plateau of learning.

3. What causes plateaus and what can teachers or coaches do to help the learner overcome these?

Exam-Style Questions

1. a. You see a novice complete a number of tennis serves over a period of 20 minutes of **massed practice**.

i. Sketch a graph, with time in minutes on the horizontal *x*-axis and success rate on the vertical *y*-axis, showing the possible changes **in performance** of the novice over the practice period. (3 marks)

ii. Explain the shape of the performance curve on your graph. (4 marks)

iii. What **strategies** might the teacher employ to help improve the performance of any closed skill by a novice during a 20 minute practice session? (4 marks)

11.2 Learning: Principles and Theories

Keywords & concepts

association theory	instrumental conditioning	reflex
classical conditioning	law of effect	reinforcement
cognitive map	law of exercise	response
cognitive theories	law of readiness	reward
conditioned response	modelling	shaping
conditioned stimulus	motivation	social learning theory
connectionist theory	negative reinforcement	stimulus
drive theory	neutral stimulus	stimulus–response (S–R)
executive programme	observational learning	subroutine
feedback	operant conditioning	transfer
gestalt	positive reinforcement	unconditional response
habit	punishment	unconditional stimulus

In Chapter 10 we considered learning to be the commitment of skills and knowledge to memory. We discussed 'input', which can also be termed 'stimulus', and how this is processed to produce an appropriate 'output' or 'response'. We saw that this process requires that we view what is to be learned as relevant, that we are attentive to what we are doing and that we are prepared to practise so that the information or movement becomes 'grooved' in memory. In other words, we must have the will, or the need, to learn; effective learning cannot take place without this. This will or need to learn may be termed **motivation**.

Motivation and drive theory

Motivation has been defined as 'the internal mechanisms and external stimuli which arouse and direct behaviour' (Sage, 1977, p. 457).

There are many theories of motivation. One, derives from **drive theory** and views learning as the development of 'habits', i.e. in this case the most appropriate behavioural responses to movement problems which need to be solved. This is illustrated in Figure 11.4.

This is a very complex theory in its totality, but stated simply and applied to physical activity it suggests that as a movement problem arises, for example in dance choreography or the performance of a particular skill in a game, this generates a need for competence, a need to solve that problem. This need in turn develops a **drive** and an incentive to learn to solve the problem and also a habit (the way of performing the

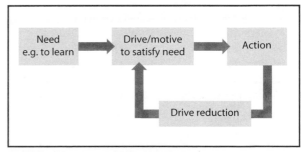

Figure 11.4 Drive reduction theory.

285

skill). So we start to practise. At first the performance is not effective, but as success comes it is perceived as a **reward** and thus acts as **reinforcement**. As a result a memory bond is forged between the **stimulus** (the problem) and the **response** (the effective performance; Figure 11.5). The two become associated in the memory and a 'habit' (a successful performance) is developed.

As our performance improves, so the habit is strengthened and the drive to go on learning reduced. At this point the teacher or coach needs to extend the problem to maintain interest and motivation. The important point this theory makes is that learning depends on drive, i.e. the incentive to be competent and master the skill or solve the problem; without drive, learning does not occur. We consider motivation in a broader context in a later section.

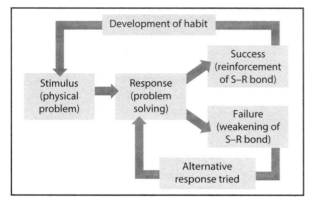

Figure 11.5 The stimulus–response bond.

Association theories

Hull was by no means the first psychologist to notice the importance in learning of the relationship between a stimulus (the task or problem) and the response to it (the performance). Theories of learning which focus on this are variously known as 'stimulus–response (S–R)' or 'association' or 'connectionist' theories.

Figure 11.6.

Classical conditioning

This is a basic form of S–R learning. It was studied by Pavlov, an eminent Russian physiologist, who used dogs as his subjects. In a controlled experiment, he presented food to a hungry dog, first ringing a bell a few seconds before giving the food (Figure 11.6). The smell and/or sight of food causes dogs to salivate automatically, as a reflex. At first, the bell had no effect on the dog (neutral stimulus), but within a few trials the dog started to associate the sound of the bell with food, and began to salivate as soon as the bell sounded, even before the food was produced.

It is important to recognize what has been learned in this example—not new behaviour, but to behave in the same way to a new stimulus through association of the first stimulus with the second.

Key Point

Classical conditioning is the pairing of a neutral stimulus with an unconditional stimulus so that an association is formed between them and the original unconditional response becomes a conditioned response. The important point to remember about classical conditioning is that for it to be termed 'classical' the response must be a reflex (or unconditional response). A reflex is an involuntary, unlearned response to a particular stimulus. It is not controlled by any conscious thought and has an evolutionary basis and purpose in helping the animal to adapt to the environment or be protected (Miller, 1972).

Activity
11.3: Reflexes
- Write down at least three human reflexes—make sure they really are reflexes.
- What are the purposes of these reflexes in evolutionary or protective terms?
- Which are particularly important to us in physical activity?

Humans can learn through classic conditioning. For example, if a puff of air is blown into someone's eye to make them blink and this stimulus is paired with a bell, the person soon learns to blink when they hear the bell. But human reflexes are limited in number. Most of our learning depends on developing new responses and skills, not on association with innate, unconscious reflexes.

Some writers (Davis *et al.*, 1986) refer to 'learned reflexes', i.e. movements which have been learned, but which are not under conscious control. Withdrawing your hand from a hot surface or ducking if something is thrown near your head are two examples. If we accept this notion (not all psychologists do), we can extend the range of behaviours which we could claim to be 'classically conditioned'. We could learn irrational fear responses by this form of conditioning. This might explain some children's (and adults') fear in a swimming pool. But it is still an association between two stimuli which is being conditioned, not the behaviour. As physical educationalists or sport scientists, it is the behaviour we are interested in. So where do completely new skills, for example performing a somersault, come from?

Operant (instrumental) conditioning

Skinner (1974) suggested that, even though much of our behaviour is not reflexive, it can still be conditioned, but not by classic methods. Naturally occurring, learned behaviour is called 'operant' behaviour. If this behaviour is rewarded in some way, then there is an increased likelihood of it occurring again; we seem to be programmed to seek reward or satisfaction.

A young swimmer is learning a tumble turn. The first attempts at the somersault (the operant behaviour, already learned) are not successful, but sooner or later, perhaps accidentally, his/her feet touch the wall and the push-off is effective. This is a good feeling, particularly if the coach gives praise and encouragement. This satisfaction acts as a **positive**

reinforcer. It strengthens the connection between the stimulus and the response (Figure 11.7).

Positive reinforcement is a relatively straightforward concept. Feelings of satisfaction can be generated by the outcome of the response, as illustrated in the tumble turn example given above, or can be given by the teacher in the form of praise (bear in mind that praise only acts as a reinforcer if it gives satisfaction to the learner).

Negative reinforcement is rather more difficult to understand. Look again at the definition; an example may help. The coach has been working with the soccer team on some defensive drills. The team has been working hard, but is keen to put the drills into a 'real game'. The coach is trying to set up a conditioned game, but the players are anticipating the excitement of competition and are not paying attention. The coach wants them to listen (desired response). She/he stops the explanation, waits for attention and says, 'Until you stand still and listen to what we are going to do, we are not going to start. It's your playing time we are wasting.' Not allowing the coaching session to continue is the negative reinforcement; it's unpleasant because the team are keen to play. Paying attention to the coach is the required response. Once the team are doing so, the negative reinforcement is removed, i.e. the coach stops holding up the game. Hopefully the players learn that if they want to have plenty of time in the game they must listen to the coach.

It is important not to confuse negative reinforcement with punishment. Punishment is given as a **consequence** of a response, and to **prevent** the response occurring again. To extend the example, if one of the team continued to 'mess about' the coach might say, 'Sam, I've warned you once. You're still not doing what I asked, so you're not going to play for the first ten minutes. Go and get your tracksuit on.' The punishment of not playing is designed to stop Sam misbehaving in future.

Skinner extended his theory of operant conditioning to include the concept of '**shaping**'. He recognized

Key Points

- Operant conditioning—process by which the desired response (selected from a range of naturally occurring responses) is reinforced and so developed. Note that in operant conditioning the focus is on the relationship between the response and the reward; the stimulus is less important. It is the environment that is manipulated to produce new behaviour.
- Reinforcement—the process of increasing the desired behaviour by giving satisfaction to the learner.
- Positive reinforcement—providing a feeling of satisfaction to increase the likelihood of the desired response being repeated.
- Negative reinforcement—removing an unpleasant experience in order to increase the likelihood of the desired response being repeated.

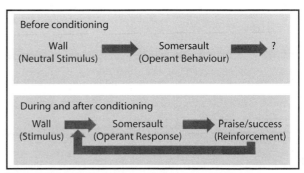

Figure 11.7 Operant conditioning: learning the tumble turn in swimming.

that with complex skills, for example a tennis serve, you cannot immediately reinforce the whole action because it is unlikely to be produced in the first trial. So the coach might:

- break the skill down into small, easily learned parts and progressively reinforce these, building the whole skill up; this is sometimes called '**chaining**';
- or introduce the whole skill, but 'shape' it by reinforcing actions which are along the right lines, even if not quite right. By reinforcing actions which are closer and closer approximations to the desired end result, the overall correct movement is gradually learned.

Operant conditioning facilitates the initial learning of the skill. Once a skill is learned, there is no need to continue reinforcement and so it can be gradually withdrawn and transferred to the learning of a more advanced skill. As long as this withdrawal does not happen before the skill is learned, the S–R bond will not be weakened.

Thorndike's laws of learning

Thorndike (1932) was an extremely influential S–R theorist. He established three laws of learning (of readiness, of effect and of exercise) which are particularly important in skill learning.

Law of readiness

Learning can only take place when the nervous system is sufficiently mature to allow the appropriate S–R connections. Basic body management skills, such as simple gymnastics, should be developed before the implementation of striking and catching skills. This concept of nervous system readiness is in addition to issues of muscle strength and skeletal maturity, which are also very important considerations.

Law of effect

Learning occurs when a particular response has an effect on the person, i.e. when the response is reinforced. Satisfying reinforcers increases the strength of the S–R bond and increase the likelihood of the response being repeated. Thus, to enable early success it is important for a coach or teacher to use positive feedback to reinforce correct attempts.

If the learner knows what he/she is trying to achieve, then observed success can serve as a positive reinforcer and failure as a punishment, without a teacher or coach being there to provide supplementary reinforcement. This process has become known as 'trial and error' learning. It depends on the learner being able to recognize success and to feel satisfaction with the response or alternatively to admit that a

response is not appropriate and to try another. The problem of this approach to skill learning is that it can allow learners to establish 'bad habits', i.e. responses that are immediately successful at the beginner stage, but that do not allow further development.

Law of exercise

Repetition strengthens the S–R bond, hence the importance of practice. Even though a skill may have apparently been learned effectively, practice beyond this point leads to 'mastery learning'. Mastery learning ensures that a skill is not easily forgotten and can be performed under varied and difficult circumstances.

Key Points
- Classical conditioning emphasizes the connection between a stimulus and a reflex response.
- Operant (instrumental) conditioning emphasizes the connection between the response to a stimulus and effect of the response on the person.
- Learning depends upon repetition of S–R connections and reinforcement.
- Reinforcement is most effective when it immediately follows the response and when it is positive, i.e. satisfying to the learner.
- Learning is most effective when learners are both motivated and physiologically ready to learn.

Cognitive theories

S–R theory has been very influential in helping us to understand how people become skilful, but many psychologists, particularly today, do not believe it is the whole answer. They argue that the extent, variety and richness of human learning cannot be explained solely by S–R bonding. A number of alternative theories, known as 'cognitive' theories, have been put forward. These are called cognitive because they place a greater emphasis on thought processes and on understanding how concepts relate to one another than is evident in S–R theory.

Tolman (1946) believed that behaviour is driven by purpose and expectation, so learners are motivated to work towards goals of which they are aware. In sport and PE these are the skills and understandings which make up the particular activity. Learners progress towards the goal (for example, being able to intercept a pass in football) by recognizing cues, using past experience and forming what Tolman referred to as a 'cognitive map' of the activity, which becomes more complex and sophisticated as the learner becomes more skilful.

A group of psychologists known as the 'gestaltists' proposed two principles of learning:

- Learning can be accelerated by using 'insight' or 'intuition' to solve a problem. For example, a gymnast and her coach might want to link two moves in a floor sequence, but are not sure how to do it. The gymnast may experiment with several ideas (trial and error) which help to clarify the problems and possibilities, and might then suddenly say 'I know, how about ...' and produce the movement solution—a moment of insight.

- Learning is most effective when a problem is seen as a whole or when the whole pattern of a movement can be practised. This enables the learner to understand all the issues and relationships which need to be considered. Gestaltists therefore advocate that learners practise a tennis serve as a whole, without breaking it down into parts.

Activity

11.4: Advantages and disadvantages of the Gestalt approach

- Discuss and write down some further examples of skills or activities which could be learnt as a whole.
- Identify some tactical problems in a game of your choice which you could present to a group of learners to solve.
- Identify some skills which you think should not be taught as a whole, but should be broken down into parts. Discuss why part learning is more appropriate for these skills.

Social learning theory

Social learning theory explains how our behaviour is influenced by the behaviour of other people. Coaches and teachers are using this theory when they employ demonstration as a learning tool. Demonstration is a powerful teaching tool in skill acquisition.

Demonstration is the application of 'modelling' or 'observational learning'. This theory maintains that much social behaviour is learned through **observation** of models, and skilled behaviour is no exception to this. One problem of observational learning is that teachers and coaches cannot always control what players are learning. A youngster might learn a lot about skill from watching his football hero, but he may also pick up some bad habits too!

Bandura (1977) suggests that there are four processes in observational learning (see p. 364):

- **attention** and **retention**, which relate to the acquisition of the skill;
- **motor reproduction** and **motivation**, determining performance.

Coaches and teachers use this model when they:

- Demand that players **attend** to instructions, or provide cues about how best to perform ('Don't watch where the ball goes, watch how my racquet swings through at waist level and where it finishes').
- **Retention** is the process of remembering the modelled behaviour. Good coaches help this process by repetition, by making learning interesting, by encouraging mental imaging of the skill and by 'catch phrases': 'step-step-step-lift' helps the hurdle step in springboard diving.
- **Motor reproduction** refers to the attempt by the learner at the modelled skill. It is important that the coach has demonstrated correctly and also that the learner has the physical make-up to be able to do the task. Further guidance is usually helpful at this stage.
- People tend to imitate what they are interested in and be **motivated** to achieve. Good coaches understand what motivates their players and use this as an important coaching tool. They use reinforcement to enhance motivation.

 Review Questions

1. Explain the difference between classical and operant conditioning. Give some sport-related examples of each.
2. What is meant by 'shaping'? Select a closed skill and explain how a coach might 'shape' the learning of it.
3. Why are Thorndike's three laws of learning important in skill acquisition?
4. Explain the difference between negative reinforcement and punishment.

 Exam-Style Questions

1. Discuss the advantages of the **whole and part** methods of learning and comment on any general factors the coach should consider when determining the appropriate way of coaching a new skill. Illustrate your answer with examples of sports skills. (20 marks)

11.3 Motor Learning and Motor Control

 Keywords & concepts

associative phase	immediate feedback	recognition schema
autonomous phase	internal feedback	schema
ballistic skills	intrinsic feedback	sequential programming
closed loop theory/control	knowledge of performance	supplementary feedback
cognitive phase	knowledge of results	terminal feedback
concurrent feedback	open loop control	verbal motor phase
delayed feedback	phase theory	
external feedback	recall schema	

Motor programmes

In Section 10.4 we considered the concept of motor programmes as an element of information processing. We here consider motor programmes as an aspect of learning.

Open loop theory

This theory suggests that when a skill is being learned, an overall plan or programme of that skill is built up in long-term memory. This is called the **executive programme**, which consists of **subroutines**. The whole programme is organized **hierarchically**, i.e. the executive programme is made up of a number of subroutines, which in turn consist of small subroutine units.

Activity

11.5: Executive programmes and subroutines
- Identify the executive programmes and the subroutines in Figure 10.26.
- What smaller subroutines would make up the 'throw'?

The programme is also ordered **sequentially**, i.e. it is able to tell the muscles in what order to produce the appropriate subroutines.

Learning the tennis serve means practising the skill so that the subroutines are properly sequenced and co-ordinated, and also become increasingly automated until the whole executive programme is also automatic. By 'automatic' we mean that the performer does not have to think about the performance. Once the programme has been put into operation, the motor programme commands the entire movement.

In teaching a serve, a teacher therefore needs to ensure that the subroutines are well-established and then that the whole skill is practised, emphasizing the timing and co-ordination of the subroutines.

Once the skill is learned, open loop theory suggests that it can be put into action without feedback being used to control the movement. Knowledge of results is used **only** at the end of the movement to give the learner feedback on the outcome. For example, as the team's penalty-taker you will have practised shooting for a considerable amount of time, so that once you have decided on a particular shot it will be performed under open loop control (Figure 11.8). The outcome feedback will be very apparent (to everyone!).

Another example of open loops is the case of **ballistic** skills, in which the limbs swing fast and move temporarily under their own momentum, e.g. in a fast cartwheel. Golf is a difficult game partly because the golf swing is ballistic and not controllable once it has started.

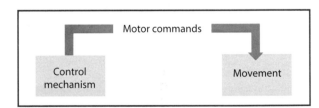

Figure 11.8 Open loop control.

Closed loop theory

If a skill is under closed loop control (Figure 11.9), then the motor programme is structured in the same way but its commands can be countermanded by the need to correct errors. Kinaesthetic feedback is used to do this.

If, for example, a gymnast is learning a slow, controlled cartwheel, it is possible to sense that the body is not properly aligned and to make adjustments while the skill is being performed. Of course, this can only happen once the gymnast has learnt enough to know what the correct body alignment feels like.

Adams (1971), in discussing closed loop theory, suggested that as a particular movement is reinforced

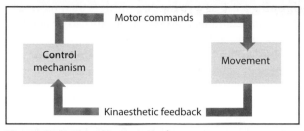

Figure 11.9 Closed loop control.

during learning, it is stored in the long-term memory as a 'memory trace'.

You should refer back to the section on information processing to remind yourself how this memory trace develops, see Chapter 10. It is strong if:

- the movement has been extensively rehearsed;
- the information has been stored in 'chunks' so that relationships between individual subroutines are well-established;
- the movement or stimulus has strong emotional intensity, i.e. it is important to the learner;
- the kinaesthetic image of the movement is reinforced by visual imagery (mind pictures).

This memory trace includes both the subroutines and the executive programme of the movement. For example, a gymnast learning a cartwheel on the beam has a memory trace of the whole movement and the various elements of it—the leg extension, the hand positions, the landing, the timing, etc. As the cartwheel is performed, a 'perceptual trace' is recorded in the short-term memory and compared with the memory trace. If the match is good, the movement continues; if there is a mis-match, the learner tries to correct the error (for example, by adjusting the foot position as it lands to achieve a better balance). Adams (1971) suggests that the closed feedback loop operates throughout the movement and thus allows correction during the movement.

Some sports psychologists are dissatisfied with this polarized view of motor control; they believe that performance involves both open and closed loop processes. Schmidt (1980) suggests that both are used at different points in an action. Consider a serve in tennis—which elements do you think might be under closed loop control and which under open loop control? Evidence from experiments involving continuous tracking movements (e.g. using a joy-stick to play a computer game) indicates that short bursts of activity may be programmed centrally and the outcome checked (peripherally) for error and correction before the next burst of activity is initiated (Schmidt, 1980, p. 127).

Key Points
- Skills are stored in memory as motor programmes.
- A motor programme is organized hierarchically and sequentially, and consists of an executive programme and levels of subroutines.
- If a skill is not being moderated by feedback it is said to be under open loop control.
- Closed loop control allows kinaesthetic feedback to compare the stored memory trace of the motor programme with a perceptual trace of what is happening during the performance of the skill, thus allowing error correction.

Activity
11.6: Open and closed loops
- Make sure you understand the difference between open and closed loop models of motor control and learning.
- Take a sport or PE example of your choice and explain how a learner recognizes errors in performance using both open- and closed-loop theory.
- Which theory do you think best fits your example?

Schema theory

A second theoretical alternative to the 'open loop versus closed loop' perspective is schema theory. One of the problems with Adams' closed loop theory is that it requires movements to be stored as separate units. When you think of how many separate memory traces this requires, memory capacity would seem to be a problem. Schema theory (Schmidt, 1977) claims that what is stored in memory is not a fixed pattern of movement (programme), but a set of relationships or rules that determine the performance of the skill. This is the '**schema**'. This 'set of relationships' could be thought of as a programme of sorts, but a generalized one which can be run differently according to the demands of the situation.

A schema is made up of two elements—recall and recognition. The **recall schema** is the schema responsible for the production of the movement. It is made up of information stored in the long-term memory about:

- the initial conditions under which the movement is to be produced, i.e. 'where am I in relation to the ball?'.

- the required response specifications, i.e. the movement requirements, i.e. 'what have I got to do and how do I do it?'.

The **recognition schema** is the schema responsible for evaluating the movement response. Initially this information is stored in the short-term memory for comparison with the recall schema. The two elements of information are:

- the sensory consequences, i.e. the kinaesthetic feel of the movement;
- the response outcomes, i.e. what happened as a result of the movement.

When a movement is completed, all these elements are stored in long-term memory for use in future movements which may be the same or similar.

You may have noticed similarities with Adams' theory of memory and perceptual traces, but you should note the important differences.

Key Points
- In open or closed loop theory, the motor programme is stored as an **exact model** of the movement to be produced in the future.
- In schema theory the motor programme is stored as a **generalized model** or set of rules about how a skill is to be produced given the conditions at the time.

Activity
11.7: Comparison of the schema and the open loop and closed loop theories
Discuss how (i) open and closed loop theory and (ii) schema theory analyse how a cricketer or baseball player learns to throw a ball into the wicket or base from thirty metres out.

In order to develop a schema for kicking or throwing (for example) a player practises to establish the rules for a relationship between the distance the ball is to be sent and such variables as muscular force, l imb speed, angle or direction of release, etc. This schema is adapted to his/her perception of the specific requirements of the task.

Schema can apply at any part of the skill hierarchy (see Figure 10.24). Thus, you developed a schema for

throwing a ball as a youngster, which is then refined to throw, for example, a basketball; it can also be generalized to help you learn a new throwing action, for example the javelin. Schema theory sees learning as the generation of increasingly more comprehensive general programmes. You should be realizing that schema theory fits in with several ideas we discussed earlier, for example the need to teach open skills by stressing variety of practice and decision making. Schmidt (1977) developed some important implications of his schema theory for the learning of motor skills:

- People learn from errors. Where appropriate, errors could even be included in practice to up-date and strengthen the schema. For example, how far can you 'lean' on your paddle before capsizing your kayak? There's only one way to find out!
- Terminal feedback is important in learning, because it strengthens the schema in memory.
- Practice must be varied and relevant to the game or competition. In open skills, in particular, do not spend too long practising a specific move or stroke over the same distance and in the same direction. The learner must have plenty of opportunity to establish rules such that a strong schema is developed, which takes into account all the possible situations. This is known as 'variability of practice'.

Motor control is an aspect of skill acquisition, the theory of which is still developing, so it is important to view the various theories as hypotheses still to be tested. Whereas these can be usefully applied to the practical problems of learning skill, equally we need to be aware of their limitations.

Motor learning and feedback

We have seen:

- how reinforcement is an important aspect of S–R learning theory;
- how kinaesthetic feedback plays an important role in motor learning.

We now consider the role of feedback in skill learning in a little more detail, in particular how the teacher or coach can structure feedback to help learners.

There are a number of different types of feedback—Figure 11.10 summarizes these.

Investigations such as 11.2 can tell us a great deal about how feedback affects learning, but it is important to recognize that the theories that emerge are merely guidelines for action and may not apply in every instance.

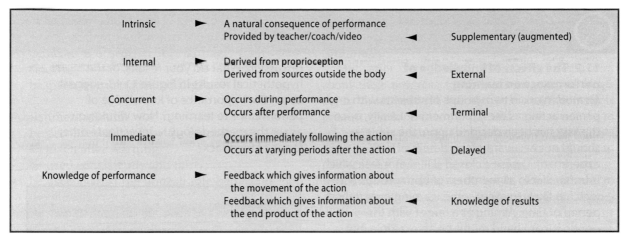

Intrinsic	►	A natural consequence of performance		
		Provided by teacher/coach/video	◄	Supplementary (augmented)
Internal	►	Derived from proprioception		
		Derived from sources outside the body	◄	External
Concurrent	►	Occurs during performance		
		Occurs after performance	◄	Terminal
Immediate	►	Occurs immediately following the action		
		Occurs at varying periods after the action	◄	Delayed
Knowledge of performance	►	Feedback which gives information about the movement of the action		
		Feedback which gives information about the end product of the action	◄	Knowledge of results

Figure 11.10 Categories of feedback.

Feedback for information

Information feedback can be either intrinsic or augmented. Augmented feedback should be structured by the teacher or coach such that it gives (i) reinforcement of correct performance and (ii) help with correcting errors. It should include:

- the outcome of the performance (if not clear to the learner);
- correct and incorrect aspects;
- what the correct movement response should feel like;
- explanation of the cause of errors;
- changes in technique or tactics to correct the errors;
- why these changes are suggested.

The good coach gives positive information feedback first, followed by error correction (Figure 11.11) and finally some motivational comment. Before giving feedback, the coach also gives the learner a moment or two to evaluate and come to conclusions about his/her own performance. Sometimes questions can be used: 'What did that feel like?', 'Why do you think that happened?'. This gives control to the learner, identifies to the coach the ability of the learner to analyse his/her own performance and ensures the coach does not tell the learner what he/she already knows.

> **Key Points**
>
> Feedback has four functions (Christina and Corcos, 1988):
> 1. Information about performance or outcome.
> 2. Reinforcement (either positive or negative).
> 3. Punishment.
> 4. Motivation.

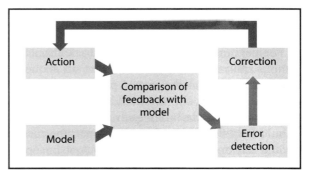

Figure 11.11 Feedback as error detection.

> **Key Points**
> - Knowledge of performance (Figure 11.12) is feedback which gives the performer information about the movement aspect of the action. It may be kinaesthetic (internal) or augmented (given by the teacher).
> - Knowledge of results (Figure 11.12) is feedback which gives information about the end product of the action. It may be intrinsic (what he learners themselves perceive about the outcome) or augmented

Figure 11.12 Knowledge of performance and ... knowledge of results.

Associative–verbal motor phase

The learner now understands the aim of the activity. Movement patterns are now more fluent and integrated. Simple aspects of the skill are becoming well learned and there is scope to refine the more complex aspects. The aim of the learner is to begin to associate the 'feel' of the movements with the end results. Feedback should be specific and focus on both knowledge of performance and knowledge of results to allow the association of kinaesthetic feedback with outcomes.

Autonomous motor phase

Movement patterns are now well integrated and automatic; they can be performed without the performer giving conscious attention to the movement, unless it is required. The performer can concentrate on the external demands of the environment and give a lot of attention to subtle cues. For example, a tennis player can use the opponent's wrist and racket action to judge what kind of spin is being put on to the ball, a task impossible for a novice because there is too much else to think about. There is less need for feedback from the teacher, because the performers are able to judge their own performances, but any information feedback can now be very detailed and specific.

Fitts and Posner (1967)		Adams (1971)
Cognitive (early) phase	Understanding of the nature of activity.	
	Analysis of techniques.	
	Establishment of 'models'.	
Associative (intermediate) phase	Focus on movement.	Verbal-motor phase
	Comparison of action with model.	
	Error detection and correction.	
	Movement is variable and inconsistent.	
Autonomous (final) phase	Action has become automatic.	Motor stage
	Attention can be given to environmental aspects of game/activity.	
	Strategy can be focussed on.	

Figure 11.14 Phases of motor learning.

The rate at which a learner progresses through the phases is determined by practice, effectiveness of information processing and the nature and extent of the reinforcement, guidance and feedback available.

Review Questions

1. Give examples of closed loop control and open loop control in sport.
2. How is a motor schema formed in memory?
3. Differentiate between knowledge of performance and knowledge of results.

4. Give four functions of feedback.
5. What points should a coach consider when giving feedback?
6. Describe Fitts and Posner's three-phase theory of motor learning. What are the characteristics of a learner at each phase?

Exam-Style Questions

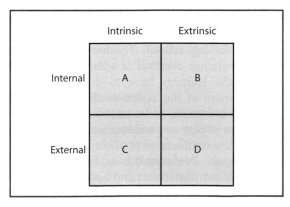

1 a. Define the term feedback, and briefly describe three functions of feedback. (4 marks)
b. Figure 11.15 illustrates two ways of classifying sources of feedback. Where possible, explain the kinds of feedback available to a performer that would be classified as A, B, C and D respectively. (4 marks)

Figure 11.15 Classifying sources of feedback

Exam-Style Questions

continued

2. One of the fundamental elements of successful training is **motivation**.

a. Define the term motivation, and using examples from sport, explain what is meant by **extrinsic** and **intrinsic** motivation. (4 marks)

b. **Feedback** can affect motivation. What type of feedback is appropriate to motivate the novice and how might this change for the skilled player? (3 marks)

c. As learning progresses, the performer passes from the **cognitive**, through the **associative** to the **autonomous** phase of learning. With reference to the skill of dribbling a ball (e.g. basketball, hockey or football), describe how the predominant type of feedback used in the **cognitive** phase of learning differs from that used in the **autonomous** phase. (4 marks)

d. What other conditions concerning the provision of feedback should a coach bear in mind when helping performers to improve their level of skill? (7 marks)

3. Discuss the idea that improvement in skill performance is dependent on the nature and the frequency of feedback provided by the coach. (20 marks)

11.4 Transfer of Learning

Keywords & concepts

negative transfer
proactive transfer

positive transfer
retroactive transfer

zero transfer

Schema theory (see above) seems to imply that certain aspects of a skill learned in one situation can determine performance in another similar situation. Singer (1982) refers to this as 'relating the now with the then' and suggests that we rarely learn a totally new skill after our early years. This is named 'transfer' in the skill acquisition literature.

Transfer is defined as the effect of the learning and performance of one skill on the learning and performance of another. If this effect is on a skill that is about to learned it is referred to as **proactive transfer**. **Retroactive transfer** occurs on skills already learned. It is important to note that not all transfer enhances learning.

Teachers and coaches attempt to use positive transfer whenever possible. Stallings (1982) identified a variety of forms of transfer in addition to the general categories listed below (Figure 11.17).

Key Points

- **Positive transfer** occurs when learning in one task is promoted by previous learning in another; for example, you may initially be better able to throw a ball with a lacrosse stick if you have a good basic throwing action with your hand.
- **Zero transfer** (no transfer at all) may occur, even between skills which appear on the surface to be similar.
- **Negative transfer** (Figure 11.16) occurs when the learning of a new task is interfered with by knowledge of a similar activity; for example, the flexible use of the wrist in a squash or badminton shot may interfere with learning the firm wrist needed for a tennis drive, or vice versa.

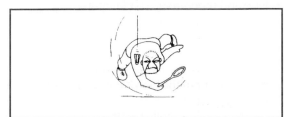

Figure 11.16 Negative transfer.

1.	Skill-to-skill	Between two skills. Evidence suggests little long-term positive transfer.
2.	Practice-to-performance	Positive transfer likely only to occur if environmental conditions are similar in both situations. Practices should simulate the stimuli and cues which occur in performance.
3.	Abilities-to-skill	Abilities do not transfer totally to the performance of skills which they underpin, but contribute significantly.
4.	Limb-to-limb (bi-lateral)	Positive transfer of learning and training occurs between limbs (hand–hand; leg–leg). Effect most obvious in transfer from preferred to non-preferred limb.
5.	Principles-to-skill	Under particular learning conditions (*Stallings, 1982, p. 213*) knowledge of a skill principle, e.g. body shape/speed of rotation, will enhance the learning and performance of the skill.
6.	Stage-to-stage	Motor skill development depends on building each new skill upon those learned previously. See Sections 10.4 and 11.1 on fundamental motor patterns and hierarchy of motor control.

Figure 11.17 Categories of transfer. (*Adapted from Stallings, 1982.*)

Transfer is a complex concept and is not easy to apply in the learning–teaching situation. What can we learn from the research literature?

- The greater the actual similarity between skills, the greater the possibility of positive transfer.
- The greater the dissimilarity, the less likelihood exists of positive transfer.
- Where skills share some similarities but have important differences, there is the danger of negative transfer.
- Athletes learn new techniques and tactics more effectively if new learning builds on and is related to skills already learned.
- Coaches or teachers should emphasize the similarity between skills when teaching for transfer (e.g. by letting players practice throwing the ball by hand before attempting an overhead pass in lacrosse).
- Tactical understanding can be transferred (e.g. zone defending in basketball and netball).

Activity

11.8: Examples of transfer types

Put the following pairs of skills into one of three categories—(i) very similar; (ii) likely to cause interference; (iii) dissimilar:

- tennis serve and volleyball serve,
- long and short serve in badminton,
- golf drive and ten-pin bowling,
- straight arm pull and bent arm pull in back crawl,
- Rugby League and Rugby Union,
- dismounts from the high bar and the rings in men's gymnastics,
- Scottish and Irish folk dancing,
- ice hockey and field hockey.

- General principles of attack and defence play can be transferred in invasion games.
- The more thoroughly the first skill has been learned, the more effective is the transfer.
- In activities where bilateral transfer is encouraged (e.g. basketball dribbling, soccer kicking), it is important that the skill is well learned on the preferred limb before transfer is attempted to the other.

Let us consider transfer of learning in a broader context by taking the example of a good gymnast who goes to college and follows a beginners' dance course as part of his or her 'A'-level or undergraduate studies. To what extent does successful experience in gymnastics aid learning in dance? Using Figure 11.17 to analyse the situation:

- The student's attitude to the new activity contributes considerably to early learning. Our gymnast will be confident about his/her body image in a movement task and will enjoy showing a competent individual performance. In this respect there is likely to be positive transfer. On the other hand, a gymnast is used to having performance choreographed by a coach or trainer and may approach the creative element of dance with trepidation. The rule- and technique-governed nature of competitive gymnastics may even cause negative transfer initially.
- In skill-transfer terms, evidence suggests that the actions he/she has learned as a gymnast do not transfer readily to dance unless the choreography is particularly gymnastic in style. In this respect there is no obvious transfer effect.
- In terms of ability–skill transfer, there is much more likely to be some positive effect. Balance, co-ordination, flexibility and many other abilities developed in gymnastics can be used very

Investigation

11.3: Positive transfer effects in skill learning

Method: Select one form of transfer from categories 1–5 in Figure 11.17. Select two groups of subjects, Group 1 and Group 2, matched for motor learning ability as far as possible. Devise two novel tasks (A and B) by which you might expect learning in Task A to transfer positively to learning in Task B. Make your tasks relevant to the category of transfer you have chosen. Ensure that the tasks are 'learnable' in the time you have available, but they should present some degree of difficulty.

Decide on the criteria to use to determine that learning has taken place; for example, you might decide that seven accurate shots out of ten in a novel aiming task constitutes learning.

Group 1 learns Task A and then Task B; Group 2 learns only Task B.

Results: Determine which group learned Task B more quickly.

Discussion: Assuming all other variables have been controlled (a dangerous assumption under the circumstances of a class experiment), what do your results tell you about the possibility of transfer between Task A and Task B for Group 1? How might you improve the experiment so that you could be more confident of your results?

---

effectively in dance. The rhythmic ability so necessary for dance may or may not be present.

- Practice-to-performance transfer depends on how well the gymnast has learned to use later practice sessions as a rehearsal for the 'real thing'. If this strategy is also used in preparation for dance performances, then positive transfer could occur.

- Repetition and variation are two important dance choreography principles. One way of both repeating and varying the movement is to use both sides of the body in a dance phase. If the gymnast has developed this skill, then positive transfer to dance occurs; however, gymnasts tend to be 'one-sided', for example, by always using the same foot for take-off, which may be a difficulty in dance work.

- Movement principles are universal, although they are analysed and expressed differently. The gymnast's knowledge of, for example, biomechanics, transfers directly to the production of good technique in dance. Research does, however, show that we must have reservations about the extent to which the performance of an action is aided by knowledge of the principles of that action.

For teachers and coaches to undertake transfer work positively, they must make a careful analysis of the relevant tasks and the teaching environment, to ensure that all the potential points of transfer are stressed.

To summarize our work on learning, use Investigation 11.4 to study the relationship between stage of learning and appropriate feedback.

Investigation

11.4: Stages of learning and feedback

Method: Work in threes, with roles of 'learner', 'teacher' and 'observer'. Before the start of the investigation, each member of the trio selects a simple, novel psychomotor skill to teach; a short sequence of hopping and stepping would be appropriate, or a mirror-tracing task if such a task has not been used before. Exchange roles for each of the following learning episodes (if videoing the episodes is possible, this will aid your analysis and discussion):

Method A. The teacher demonstrates the skill to the learner, who practises it. No feedback is given, but the skill is demonstrated by the teacher at intervals. The observer attempts to identify when learning changes from 'cognitive' to 'associative' to 'autonomous'. A video of the learning allows review.

Method B. The teacher demonstrates the skill to the learner, who practises it. The teacher focuses on giving instructions appropriate to the phase of learning, i.e. demonstration and general verbal guidance in the cognitive stage, error detection and specific guidance in the associative stage and a focus on style and/or speed in the autonomous

Investigation

11.4 continued

stage. The observer checks the appropriateness of the instruction given.

Method C. The teacher demonstrates the skill to the learner, who practises it. The teacher has identified beforehand examples of supplementary feedback which give (a) knowledge of results and (b) knowledge of performance and uses these during the learning episode. The observer notes these and attempts to identify which are intended as knowledge of results and which as knowledge of performance.

Discussion:
- Were the skills essentially open or closed?
- How does instruction in the different stages differ between open and closed skills?
- What evidence did the observer use to identify the different stages of learning?
- How effective was the teacher in giving appropriate instructions?
- Do teacher and observer agree about the examples of knowledge of results and knowledge of performance?
- How helpful did the learner find the instruction and the feedback in terms of amount, timing and specificity?

Review Questions

1. Give a sport-related example of (a) positive transfer and (b) negative transfer.
2. List the six categories of transfer and give an example of each.

3. List four requirements for positive transfer to occur.
4. Give an example of a coach using positive transfer to develop a technique.

Exam-Style Questions

1. **a.** Define the terms **positive transfer** and **negative transfer** in the context of someone learning a sport skill. (2 marks)
b. Figure 11.18 shows different extents of transfer in different situations labelled A, B and **c.** For each of the situations, A, B and C, give examples of one pair of **games type** skills which illustrate the kinds of transfer indicated, briefly explaining the reasons for your selections. (10 marks)
c. Describe how a coach could help **positive transfer** to occur during the learning of sports skills. (8 marks)
2. Describe and evaluate the use of video playback in the **learning** of sport skills. (20 marks)

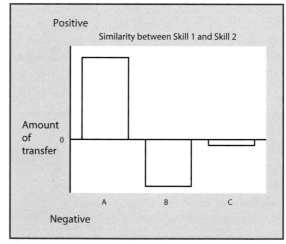

Figure 11.18 Extents of transfer in various situations

11.5 Teaching

Keywords & concepts

command style	negative transfer	task analysis
discovery style	organization	trail and error
distributed practice	part practice	variable practice
fixed practice	practice style	verbal guidance
guidance	problem solving	visual guidance
manual guidance	progressive part presentation	whole method
massed practice	progressive parts practice	whole practice
mechanical guidance	pure part presentation	whole–part–whole method
mental rehearsal	reciprocal style	whole–part–whole practice
modification of display	spectrum of teaching styles	

So far in this chapter we have considered some elements of the learning process. This section focuses on how learning may be structured so that it is achieved efficiently. You should bear these points in mind when planning your own practice or training, or when helping others with theirs. We have referred to teaching and coaching as if they are the same activity. Whereas some would argue that they have different aims and purposes, current approaches suggest that teaching physical education and coaching sport share much common ground, so we treat them as one process.

The teaching process

Most learning is achieved by being taught in one way or another, although 'trial and error' learning or 'learning by experience' also occur. Teaching others is a process we are all involved in, even though we may not consider ourselves to be teachers. Teaching is about giving experiences or advice which aids learning.

The teaching process can be summarized as in Figure 11.19, which echoes an old Chinese proverb about learning, attributed to the philosopher Confucius:

I hear and I forget;
I see and I remember;
I do and I understand.

Current theory suggests there are **four** elements of the teaching process—instructing, demonstrating, applying and confirming—and good teaching progresses through each in turn.

Instructing

In the instructing (telling) phase, teachers make sure that learners understand the task and have enough information to allow them to start practising. Usually this is done verbally, though written practice schedules or worksheets are sometimes used. The danger in this phase is that the teachers give too much information (in their eagerness to ensure that the learners completely understand). Unless the information given is clear and concise, most of it is quickly forgotten.

Demonstrating

As we have seen, demonstrating (showing) is an important aspect of skill learning because of the need for the learner to establish a model of the skill in memory. It needs to be carefully planned so that both teacher and the learner are clear about the purpose of the demonstration and what exactly is to be learned from it. A bad demonstration may be worse than no demonstration at all.

Applying

Applying (doing) is the opportunity for the learner to practise the skill—without plenty of time for this, effective learning is unlikely to take place. The teacher's role is to structure this practice effectively and by appropriate guidance to help learners to

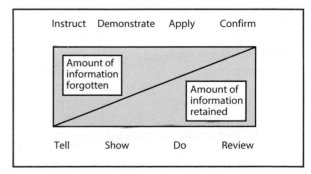

Figure 11.19 The teaching process. (*Adapted from Priest and Hammerman, 1989.*).

apply what they have learned from instruction and demonstration to the activity itself.

Confirming

Confirming (reviewing) is the feedback process, which is covered in detail in an earlier section. It is an essential part of the learning process, but is sometimes omitted by teachers, to the detriment of learning. An important part of reviewing is to question the learner about what he/she has learned and the progress made. This not only helps the teacher to confirm what has been learned, but also encourages the learner to be self-evaluative and reinforces learning.

Styles of teaching

Within the four elements of the teaching process described above there are many different ways to teach. These are known as **styles** and have been analysed and classified in much the same way that we have classified skill, that is by observing action, noting the characteristics of that action and devising a theoretical framework to fit the observations.

Mosston and Ashworth (1986) produced a classification (based on observations of physical education, but applicable to all teaching) which they have labelled the 'spectrum of teaching styles' (Figure 11.20). They suggest that teaching and learning are essentially about making decisions: what to teach–learn; when to teach–learn; how to present and acquire the ideas and skills, etc. Their model suggests that at one end of the spectrum the teacher makes all these decisions and at the other end the learner makes them all. In between are a range of styles in which the teacher and learner are both involved in decision making. The styles are distinct and Mosston and Ashworth (1986) give them letter labels and names (for example, Style A = Command Style).

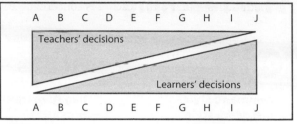

Figure 11.20 The spectrum of teaching styles.

The teacher in Investigation 11.5 was probably nearer to Style A, the one in which the teacher makes all the decisions. It is very difficult to teach for long in this style and it is not advisable to do so, because we usually want to hand some of the decisions to the learner, e.g. 'start when you're ready'. Style A is known as the 'command style' and is used when a teacher wants tight control over what the learner is doing, or wants uniformity in a class. A lot of aerobics and keep-fit teaching is done in command style. Style B is 'practice style'—the teacher sets the task, but the students work on it in their own time.

Style C is an interesting style. Pupils work in pairs—one is the 'doer' and the other the 'observer'. In this style the teacher hands over all contact with the learners (the 'doers') to fellow pupils (the 'observers'). The teacher makes sure, either by a worksheet or by very explicit instructions, that all the pupils understand the task and the criteria for successful completion of it. It is then up to the observer to help the doer; the teacher helps the observers with their teaching. This is known as **reciprocal** teaching; it is a useful style with large groups because it allows each learner a lot of immediate feedback. Look back to p. 300 to remind yourself of the advantages of this. No doubt you can think of some disadvantages, however.

 Investigation

11.5: Decision making in teaching and learning

Method: Work in pairs—one is the teacher and one the learner. The teacher devises a simple task to teach the learner. It may be something the learner can already do and wishes to improve. It can be classroom or sports hall based, but it should have a motor component. Spend some time teaching and practising the task. This period of time is known as an 'episode'.

Discussion: When the episode is over, discuss with each other and list all the decisions which were made by both the teacher and the learner:
- before the episode,
- during the episode,
- when the episode was over.
1. Who made each decision?
2. What was the ratio of teacher decisions to learner decisions?
3. Do you think the teacher was nearer to Style A or Style J?

In both Styles A and C the teacher is concerned not only with what the learners learn, but also with how they learn it; a specific product and process. At other times the teacher may focus on 'how to learn' and adopt a problem-solving style. A task or problem is set which the pupils have to solve in their own ways. The problem may be defined by a single solution which the teacher wishes the pupils to **discover** (Style F); or there may be several possible solutions (not all of which the teacher may have thought of) and the pupils' task is to investigate these and select the one which most interests them (Style H). Teachers of creative dance and educational approaches to gymnastics use these styles a lot; so, in a different way, do teachers of outdoor pursuits.

There is not the space here to discuss the whole spectrum of styles, nor to go into much detail about each, but it is important that you begin to grasp that there are many ways of learning and therefore of teaching, and the skilful teacher selects appropriately from the range. So when you are next helping a friend or group of juniors with an activity, consider ways in which you can vary your approach.

Modes of presentation

Teaching style is concerned with the way in which a teacher opts to deal with the range of decisions that the teaching process imposes. One of these decisions is, 'How do I present this new information or skill to my pupils?'. The answer to this question depends on the teacher's analysis of two important factors, which is illustrated in Figure 11.21

Task analysis involves deciding what the important elements of the task are—information processing theory helps here:

• What are the perceptual requirements?
• What are the decision making requirements?
• What techniques does the performer need?
• What feedback is available?

Answers to these questions indicate the complexity of the task. Note that complexity relates to the nature of the task; whether a task is simple or difficult depends upon the amount of attention/processing space that needs to be given to it, and the experience of the learner.

Analysis should also indicate the extent to which the skill is organized. Skills which are not easily broken down into constituent parts are said to be highly organized. Swimming strokes are examples of low organization, because the leg, arm and breathing actions are all different and separate, although obviously they need to be well co-ordinated for effective performance (Singer, 1982).

This **task analysis** should be compared with an analysis of the state of readiness and the capabilities of the learner. The good teacher and coach consider age, previous experience, physical abilities, preferred learning style, motivation and goals.

Whole practice
Ideally, a skill should be taught as a whole. The learner can then appreciate the end product and can develop a feeling for the flow of movement necessary for a smooth, efficient production of the skill; he/she can see the relationship between the movements which constitute the whole action.

Part practice
However, for some skills it is not appropriate or sensible to teach the whole all at once, such as:

• when the skill is too complex and/or difficult for the learner, i.e. a lot of information processing is required;
• when there is an element of danger.

In these cases the skill is broken down into its constituent parts (subroutines); these parts are taught as separate actions and then put together, which can be done in a variety of ways (Figure 11.22).

Part methods of teaching are useful when the skill is complex and/or difficult, not highly organized and the mechanics of the movement are important. Closed skills, such as those in gymnastics, diving and trampolining, are usually taught in this way. It lessens fear and risk in dangerous skills and allows the teacher to focus on key elements of the skill. It may help motivation, as the teacher can structure the teaching of the parts as 'mini wholes', thus giving the

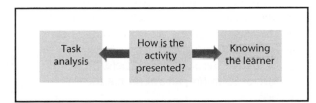

Figure 11.21 Deciding on presentation.

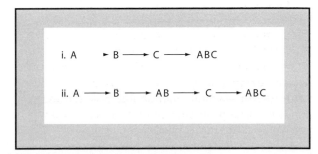

Figure 11.22 'Part' methods of presenation

Investigation

11. 6: The effectiveness of whole and part methods of teaching a novel sequence of movement

Method: The class is divided into four groups; four group leaders are appointed. The class teacher has previously devised and taught to the group leaders a sequence of movements which flow into one another and which contains some complex (but not impossible) moves. The constituent parts of the sequence are agreed.

- Group A learns the sequence by the 'pure parts' method (Figure 11.22i).
- Group B learns the sequence by the 'progressive part' method (Figure 11.22ii).
- Group C learns the sequence as a whole.
- Group D learns by the whole–part–whole method.

Discussion:

1. Which group takes the longest to learn?
2. Which group performs the sequence best?
3. What seems to be the best method of teaching for this particular skill?
4. You have been investigating teaching methods, but what are the 'confounding variables' in this experiment, i.e. factors other than teaching method which may have affected the result?

learner a feeling of success and progress. The main problem is one of transfer, for it is essential that the separately taught elements be practised in the same way as they are performed within the whole skill, which is not easy to achieve. It is also important that the whole skill be demonstrated to the learner initially so that the end product can be appreciated in terms of its purpose, pace, flow and organization.

Whole–part–whole practice

Many skills can be taught by the whole–part–whole method, whereby the learner first tries out the whole skill to get the feel of its performance requirements and to identify the easy and difficult elements. These may be different for each individual. By careful observation the teacher can isolate the difficult elements and teach them as parts, finally integrating them into the whole again.

Whole and part methods assume that the parts of the skill are taught as if they were being performed within the whole, and they rely on positive transfer. If, however, the whole is complex, but not easily broken down into parts that are meaningful, then the task itself may be simplified. A good example of this is the current focus on the 'mini-game' for youngsters. Short tennis and pop lacrosse have many of the elements of the full adult game, but are played with modified rules and equipment.

If simplification of this kind is inappropriate, the idea of shaping the performance may be used. This is an aspect of operant conditioning as described earlier. The coach or teacher rewards aspects of the performance as the correct technique is approached and so the performer gradually acquires the skill. This is also known as **gradual metamorphosis** of the skill.

Forms of guidance

When we practise or experience a skill or activity, some learning inevitably takes place; but we learn most efficiently by a combination of experience and guidance. Sharp (1992) differentiates between 'practice' (which is **without** guidance) and 'training' (which is practice **with** guidance), but not all writers make this distinction.

Activity
11.9: Practice and Training
Using Sharp's distinction between practice and training, which do you think is the most efficient way to learn? Discuss and justify your conclusion.

Key Points
- Practising for long periods without guidance may be demotivating; it also allows errors to creep into the skill that may be difficult to eradicate.
- Learners need time to practise without feeling under pressure from the teacher or coach, so that they can work out their own solutions to problems.
- Guidance should be given before and after, but rarely during an attempt at the skill or task.

Bearing the key points in mind, a second set of decisions a teacher must make is about the type of guidance to give. There are three basic forms of guidance or methods a teacher may use to transmit information about performance:

- visual;
- verbal;
- manual or mechanical.

Guidance is received by the learner through the senses; because we have several of these, information can be communicated to us in a variety of ways. Two points are important here:

- the senses interact, so a combination of forms of guidance can be effective;
- people differ as to the type of guidance they prefer.

Visual guidance

This is used at all stages of teaching and learning, but is particularly valuable in the early (cognitive) phase to introduce the task and set the scene.

Demonstration

Demonstration relies on imitative learning and/or modelling (Bandura, 1977), and is a powerful tool. It is efficient, 'on-the-spot' and interesting to learners, but it must be accurate and relate to their age, experience and gender. It must show the activity as it occurs in real life. Teachers should avoid talking too much as a demonstration is taking place (remember channel capacity), but it is necessary to focus the learners' attention on important performance cues.

Visual aids

Visual aids can be of value if constructed and presented thoughtfully. Photographs, charts and models are cheap and readily available; they can be tailored to the exact requirements of the particular situation, but they are static and thus limited. Video is generally agreed to be more beneficial, particularly if action can be slowed down, but playback equipment is expensive. Video can be used either in place of demonstration or to provide information feedback on the learners' performances.

There is now a great deal of opportunity for off-air recording of top-level sport performances which can be used in the coaching or teaching situation. Camcorders have extended the usefulness of video to record learners' progress, but it is time-consuming to video and analyse large groups.

Modifying the display

Sometimes it is appropriate to give assistance by enhancing perception of the important aspects of the surroundings. We discussed signal detection in Section 10.3 and the way, for example, the colour of tennis balls might affect play. Areas of space might be highlighted; for example, a coach might mark a target on a court for serving practice, or chalk the points on a gymnastic mat where the hands should be placed for a cartwheel. Coloured bibs or different strips not only help the referee, but they help player identification in a team game.

Verbal guidance

A great deal of teaching and coaching is done using verbal guidance. A good coach is able not only to set the task clearly and unambiguously and to describe the actions; he/she is able to highlight the important performance cues. With advanced learners these cues are detailed and technical. With beginners it may be more appropriate to express the cues in ways that may not be entirely accurate, but that will convey the feel of the movement to the learner: 'Climb with your eyes!'; 'Stretch your toes to the ceiling!'. The advantages of using verbal guidance are that it is 'on-the-spot' and, when used by a knowledgeable and perceptive teacher, is directly relevant to the problems and capabilities of the individual learner.

 Investigation

11.7: To produce a visual aid
Method: Select a skill or aspect of an activity with which you are especially familiar. Decide on a particular aspect which you might focus upon when helping a friend to learn the activity. Produce a visual aid to support your proposed coaching. Try making a video if you wish, but this is a time-consuming task so you are probably better advised to avoid the technicalities of filming and concentrate on producing a good chart or model. Think about:

- simplicity;
- clarity;
- use of colour;
- highlighting the important performance cues.

Try out your visual aid on a friend and invite constructive criticism of it.

There are some difficulties which a teacher must work to overcome:

- Does the learner understand the instructions?
- Can the learner remember what has been said (remember the capacity of the short-term memory)?
- Can the learner translate from the spoken word to movement?

Manual or mechanical guidance

This form of assistance involves physical contact, for example by the coach supporting and guiding the movement (as in the practice of a gymnastic vault) or by the support of a device such as a swimming armband, a trampoline belt or a 'tight rope' in climbing. It allows the learner to discover the timing and spatial aspects of the movement, but does not help acquire knowledge of the forces that act on the body or of the movement cues. The aim is to reduce error and fear—important when there are safety considerations. Such support is therefore generally used with youngsters and people with special needs. Two forms of manual guidance have been identified:

- physical restriction—a person or an object confines the moving body of the performer to movements which are safe, e.g. a trampoline belt;

- forced response—the learner is guided through the movement, e.g. a coach may physically guide a player through a forehand drive in tennis.

Types of practice

The concept of open and closed skills also gives the teacher guidance in deciding how to structure the practice of a particular activity. We saw, in an earlier section, how, as a general rule, open skills should be practised with as much variety as feasible (**variable practice**), to allow a general schema to be developed; whereas in closed skills (in which the replication of a specific movement pattern is the aim), **fixed practice**, with repetition to allow the movements to be over-learned, is appropriate.

A third decision about practice which the teacher needs to make concerns the length of the practice periods and the extent to which the learners need rest during practice. For teachers, these decisions relate to how they structure practice within a lesson, how long each episode should be and how to change the focus of practice while maintaining the pace of learning. For a coach, the decision also includes how many times a week the athlete should train and how long the training period should be, as well as what the training should consist of.

If learners need rest during a practice or training session, how long should the rest periods be and

what should the learners do in them? This is an important question for, as you probably know from your own experience, if fatigue or boredom set in, learning decreases markedly.

> **Key Points**
> - **Variable practice**—practising a skill in a variety of different contexts and experiencing the full range of situations in which the technique or tactic might be used in competition.
> - **Fixed practice**—a specific movement pattern is practised repeatedly. Often known as 'drills'.
> - **Massed practice**—the skill is practised until learned without taking any breaks.
> - **Distributed practice**—practice is interspersed with breaks, which can either be rest or the practice of another skill.

What is the best form of practice organization? There is not a straightforward answer. **Massed practice** appears to be most suitable for activities in which:

- the skill is simple;
- motivation for learning is high;
- the purpose of the practice is to simulate fatiguing conditions that might be experienced in competition or performance;
- available practice time is very short;
- the learners are experienced, able and fit.

Thus if the performers are highly skilled, fit and well-motivated, massed practice may be the most appropriate form of organization. This means that the learners work continuously at an activity without any breaks until the skill is mastered or time runs out. Massed practice is efficient and allows concentration and over-learning.

Distributed (spaced) practice should be used for activities in which:

- the skill to be learned is new and/or complex;
- there is a danger of injury if fatigue sets in;
- attention spans are short, i.e. with young learners;
- motivation is low;
- learners are not fit enough;
- weather conditions are adverse.

In distributed practice organization, the total practice session is split into several shorter periods with intervals between. These intervals may be rest periods or the teacher may set alternative tasks. From what you now know about negative transfer, what must the teacher be careful about in organizing alternative tasks in the intervals?

In general, both researchers and teachers agree that distributed practice is the most effective in the majority of cases. One of the advantages of distributed practice is that the rest intervals can be used for **mental rehearsal**. This is the process whereby the performer, without moving, runs through the performance in his/her mind. The learner can do this in several ways:

- by watching a demonstration or film,
- by reading or listening to instructions,
- by mental imagery, if the skill is established.

Obviously, this is a useful strategy for experienced performers, and many use it in preparation for competition, but interestingly it also appears to enhance the learning process. Research cited by Cratty (1973) suggests that when mental rehearsal occurs, the muscular neurones fire as if the muscle is actually active. Because of this, it is suggested, mental rehearsal has a real learning effect. Though few sports psychologists would claim that a skill can be learned entirely by mental rehearsal (Figure 11.22), evidence suggests that a combination of physical and mental practice is beneficial. Mental rehearsal is dealt with as a cognitive preparation strategy in Chapter 12.

Whatever methods of practice are used by coaches, an indisputable fact is the amount of practice needed

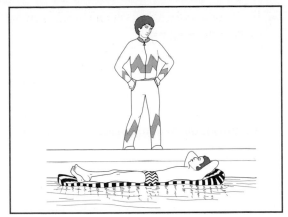

Figure 11.23 'But coach, you told me to include mental rehearsal in my training!'

to produce top-level performers. Research evidence indicates a close relationship between the level of skill and the total number of hours of practice. Kottke *et al.* (1978) suggest that by the time a professional quarterback reaches his peak he will make 1.4 million passes; a 10-year-old female gymnast needs about 8 years of daily practice to reach an Olympic final (some countries start serious training of their gymnasts a lot younger than this). This suggests that Olympians may not so much be super-men and -women as people who are prepared to devote a considerable proportion of their life to training for their sport.

 ## Review Questions

1. Draw Priest and Hammerman's model (1989) of the teaching process. What constitutes confirming and reviewing?
2. What are the essential differences between teaching by command and teaching by discovery?
3. Under what conditions would you teach (a) a whole skill and (b) by the progressive parts method?
4. Briefly describe four types of guidance.
5. Why is variable practice of open skills important?
6. Give an example of the use of mental practice.

 ## Exam-Style Questions

1. **a.** Mosston and Ashworth (1986) classified teaching styles in terms of **decision making** in the learning process. This spectrum of Teaching Styles is shown in Figure 11.20.
   i. Identify the teaching style at 'A'. What are the advantages and disadvantages of this teaching style in gymnastics? (5 marks)
   ii. What is meant by the term **reciprocal** teaching style? (2 marks)
   iii. A **problem solving** approach may be employed by the teacher. Using an example from sport, explain the main benefits of a problem-solving approach. (4 marks)

Summary

1. In order to learn we must be motivated—effective teaching relies upon this motivation. The relationship between motivation and learning has been highlighted in 'drive reduction theory'. There are many different theories of learning. One group, the S–R theories, consider learning as a process of conditioning, i.e. the establishment of a connection between stimulus and response, with success seen as a reward or reinforcement. Feedback is an important part of S–R bonding and is therefore an integral part of the learning process. It provides motivation and reinforcement and thus effects changes in performance. But if feedback is to be effective, there must be a frame of reference, a model by which error detection can function. There are several forms of feedback and much research has been done into its effects on learning.

2. Feedback is central to the concept of motor control. Closed- and open-loop theories of control give rise to different coaching philosophies but modern thinking tends to integrate the two; an important outcome of this is schema theory which suggests that what is stored in memory is not a fixed pattern of movement but a set of relationships. An important practical implication of this is the need for the practice to be as varied as possible.

3. There are many factors which teachers need to consider in structuring learning for their pupils. Possible transfer from previously acquired to new skills is one, and teaching style is another. Decisions on what material to present and how to present it lead to a need for task analysis and a knowledge of the stage of motor development of the pupils. Skills which a learner may find relatively straightforward can be taught as a whole, but more complex skills may need to be broken down into, and taught as, parts. The interaction of task complexity and learner capability also necessitates consideration of the kind of guidance which is most appropriate, and the way in which practice of the activity may be structured.

Further Reading

References

Adams J. A closed loop theory of motor learning. *Journal of Motor Behaviour,* 1971; 3: 111–150.

Bandura A. *Social Learning and Theory,* Prentice Hall, 1977.

Christina R.W. and Corcos D.M. *Coaches Guide to Teaching Sport Skills,* Human Kinetics, 1988.

Davis D. *et al. Physical Education and the Study of Sport,* Macmillan, 1986.

Fitts P.M. and Posner M.I. *Human Performance,* Brooks Cole, 1967.

Gentile A.M. A working model of skill acquisition with application teaching. *Quest,* 1972; 17: 3–23.

Knapp B. *Skill in Sport,* Routledge and Kegan Paul, 1973.

Miller G.A. *Psychology: The Science of Mental Life,* Penguin, 1972.

Mosston M. and Ashworth S. *Teaching Physical Education,* Merrill, 1986.

Priest S. and Hammerman D. Teaching outdoor adventure skills. *Journal of Physical Education, Recreation and Dance,* 1989; 63(1): 64–67.

Sage G.H. *Introduction to Motor Behaviour: A Neuropsychological Approach,* Addison Wesley, 1977.

Schmidt R.A. Schema theory: implications for movement education. *Motor Skills: Theory into Practice,* 1977; 2(1): 36–38.

Schmidt R.A. Past and future issues in motor programming. *Research Quarterly,* 1980; 51: 122–140.

Sharp B. *Acquiring Skill in Sport,* Sports Dynamics, 1992.

Singer R.N. *Motor Learning and Human Performance,* Macmillan, 1982.

Skinner B.F. *About Behaviourism,* Vintage Books, 1974.

Stallings L.M. *Motor Learning,* Mosby, 1982.

Thorndike E.L. *Fundamentals of Learning,* Columbia University Press, 1932.

Tolman, E.C. Studies in spatial learning. *Journal of Experimental Psychology,* 1946; 36: 221–229.

Wallace S.A. and Hagler R.W. Knowledge of performance and the learning of a closed motor skill. *Research Quarterly,* 1979; 50: 265–271.

Further reading

Bull R. *Teachers' Guide and Answers to Skill Acquisition,* Jan Roscoe Publications, 1996.

Bunker L.K. *et al. Sport Psychology,* Mouvement Publications, 1985.

Christina R.W. and Corcos D.M. *Coaches Guide to Teaching Sport Skills,* Human Kinetics, 1988.

Gill D.L. *Psychological Dynamics of Sport,* Human Kinetics, 1986.

Magill R.A. *Motor Learning: Concepts and Applications,* Brown & Benchmark, 1993.

Mosston M. and Ashworth S. *Teaching Physical Education,* Merrill, 1986.

National Coaching Foundation. *Planning Your Programme,* NCF, 1992.

National Coaching Foundation. *Improving Techniques/ Planning and Practice: Introductory Study Packs 4 & 6,* NCF, 1993.

Schmidt R.A. *Motor Learning and Performance,* Human Kinetics, 1991.

Sharp B. *Acquiring Skill in Sport,* Sports Dynamics, 1992.

Chapter 12

Psychology of Sport: Individual Differences

12.1 The Nature of Sport Psychology

In Chapters 9–11 we considered the processes by which people become skilful and the factors which influence motor skill learning. We now turn our attention to the idea of performance, and study what is happening while people take part in physical activity for recreation and competition, once they have become proficient (though, of course, we never stop learning).

We call this study the psychology of sport. Psychology is the study of the behaviour of individuals. Most researchers in this area have dealt with behaviour in a sports context, though many of their findings apply to other physical activities such as dance and outdoor pursuits. Currently, sport psychologists are extending their field of study to encompass fitness and exercise psychology (Willis and Campbell, 1992). Sport psychology (as it is usually called) has a great deal to offer sportsmen and sportswomen; indeed some claim that it will be a key factor in future improvement in performance.

Our biomechanical, physiological and sports medicine counterparts will all contribute—but ultimately it will be the athlete's ability to control his or her own body and mind in action and in all areas of life that will determine the level of ultimate athletic performance (Bunker and McGuire, 1985, p. 13).

The field of study of sport psychology covers a range of topics, some of which we deal with in this book. Sport personality is an important area; we study how psychologists have attempted to identify what makes up personality and whether the kind of person you are affects your performance in sport. We develop this further in Section 12.2. We also take our study of motivation further, and in Section 12.6 consider the effects of stress on sportspeople and how they can optimize their performances. In Chapter 13 we examine how being part of a team or group affects behaviour.

The knowledge we have about the psychological aspects of physical activity derives from research by an 'army' of psychologists, teachers and coaches, as well as sportspeople themselves. This research uses, for the most part, social science methodology, so it is important that you understand the basis of this in order both to carry out your own investigations and to appreciate how others have derived their theories. The practical work in Chapters 9–11 (and in other chapters of the book) introduces you to this methodology, but as you work through this chapter you should further develop your awareness of the importance of:

- asking appropriate questions,
- deriving hypotheses and identifying variables,
- selecting a method of enquiry, such as interview, questionnaire, test or measurement, observation and analysis,
- choosing your subjects appropriately,
- analysing, presenting and evaluating your data.

As an example, look back to an investigation in which you have been through the process outlined above (e.g. Investigation 11.2). Identify, for that particular investigation, each of the stages. For example, what were the variables you were interested in; what data collection techniques were used; how was the sample chosen; how were the data presented and analysed; and what were the issues for discussion which arose? These questions ask you to describe what you did; to 'tell the story' of your investigation. You must also evaluate and ask:

- How representative was my sample of the general group (population) I was interested in?
- Were the data collection techniques I used valid, i.e. did they actually measure what was intended?
- Were my methods reliable, i.e. likely to produce similar results in similar circumstances?
- Were my observations objective, i.e. free of variation or bias due to the experimenter, or was there an inevitable element of subjectivity?
- Did I respect my subjects' rights to refuse, to remain anonymous and to have their physical and emotional well-being protected?

12.2 Personality

 Keywords & concepts

body image	models	psychometric methods
character	neuroticism	self-concept
constitutional theory	roles	self-esteem
EPI/Q	significant others	self-report questionnaires
extroversion	social learning theory	Sheldon's constitutional theory
intellect	stability	16PF
interactionist approach	state measures	source traits
introversion	STEN score	surface traits
psychometric methods	temperament	trait theories
physique	trait	

What is personality and why is important that we understand it? As a player, captain, teacher or coach, you need to be aware of how different people are and how they react differently to the same situation. Some people train with single-minded determination; others are easily distracted or 'put off' by difficulties. Some players react badly to defeat or apparent unfairness; others seem to take it all in their stride. Knowing and understanding yourself and the people you train and play with is likely to help you produce the best out of yourself and others.

On completion of this section you will:

- be able to define personality and understand its structure;

 Investigation

12.1: To derive a common sense definition of personality

Method: Work in groups of three or four. Think of a televised sport with which you are all familiar. Select two 'personalities' within that sport who contrast in the way they behave as they play.

Discussion: What is it about them that differs? What characteristics do they show through their responses to things that happen in the game or competition?

You have been talking about a pattern of characteristics which makes each of these two people different. You have begun to define their personalities.

- know how personality might be measured and understand the limits to the interpretation and use of such measurement;
- know what research tells us about the relationship between personality and performance or participation;
- appreciate the importance of personality as a major variable in learning and performance;
- understand the relationship between learning, performance and the development of self-concept.

Key Points

- Personality has been defined as a person's unique pattern of traits. A **trait** is a general, underlying, enduring predisposition to behave in a particular way each time a given situation occurs. So if you always believe you have a good chance of winning the competitions you enter, you could be said to show the trait of 'optimism'.
- Eysenck (1969) suggests that personality is the 'more or less stable and enduring organization of a person's **character, temperament, intellect** and **physique** which determines the unique adjustment to the environment.'

Note the use of the term 'unique' in both the definitions in Key Points, and the range of attributes which Eysenck (1969) says contribute to personality. Note, also, that Eysenck claims that personality **determines** how people react to their surroundings.

Theories of personality structure and development

There are many different theories about what personality is and how it develops. A good review, which considers those theories most applicable to sport and physical activity, can be found in Cox (1994) or Gill (1986).

Most theories in current use view personality as being structured in 'levels'. These levels refer to how deeply rooted a particular personality trait is in our psyche. Figure 12.1 illustrates this structure. It represents an individual who, as part of his/her core personality (level 1), is highly achievement oriented—wants to succeed in everything. As a games player this gives him/her a tendency to show aggressiveness when under pressure (level 2). When made captain, however, this drive to achieve remains (it is stable and enduring), but becomes transferred to the need for the team to have a good model, so the aggressiveness disappears (level 3).

> **Key Point**
> - Personality can only be **inferred** from **behaviour** or from what a person tells us about him/herself. In Figure 12.1, we can see evidence of the aggressiveness and the good behaviour model, but the underlying achievement motivation is abstract.

There are a number of different theories of personality—Sheldon's constitutional theory, trait theories, social learning theory and interactionist approaches—which operate at the different levels of Figure 12.1. The first two are concerned with the psychological core.

Sheldon's constitutional theory

Sheldon's constitutional theory has never been fully accepted, but maintains credibility partly because it has a certain 'folklore' validity. In working through Chapter 4, you measured body type by means of a process known as somatotyping. Sheldon and Stevens (1942) associated each of the three somatotypes with a personality type (Figure 12.2).

Trait theories

Trait theories assume that a **trait** is a general, underlying, enduring predisposition to behave in a particular way each time a given situation occurs. For example, if we always feel nervous before a competition we could be said to possess the trait of 'competitive anxiety'. Trait theories suggest that our personality is made up of many traits. Two theorists in particular (Eysenck and Cattell) suggested that these traits are organized in a hierarchical way. Their research led to a model of personality in which those traits which seem to cluster together are given a label that summarizes a group of behaviours. For example, think of a sportsperson whom you would label as 'extrovert'. Now list some words which describe his/her behaviour and which define the term 'extrovert' in this case. Did you think of words like outgoing, confident, talkative, publicity seeking?

Trait theory was very important in the early years of sport personality research, largely because it provided a straightforward way of assessing personality (by means of self-report questionnaires), which sport psychologists and coaches could use with their athletes. However, although the tests themselves have been shown to be valid and reliable, they do not appear to **predict behaviour** consistently. For example, a young swimmer might be confident and sociable within his sport and with his friends in the club, but shy and

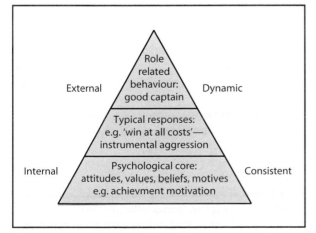

Figure 12.1 The structure of personality. (*Adapted from Martens, 1975.*)

SOMATOTYPE	PERSONALITY TYPE
Ectomorphy Linearity	Cerebrotonia Tenseness, introversion
Endomorphy Plumpness	Viscerotonia Sociability, affection, comfort-loving
Mesomorphy Muscularity	Somatotonia Risk taking, adventure-seeking, extrovert

Figure 12.2 Sheldon's somatopersonality typology. (*Adapted from Carron, 1981.*)

lacking in confidence when required to make a speech at a club function. His core personality is probably somewhere between shy and confident, depending on how he views himself. Because psychologists like to use measures of personality to try and predict behaviour, this lack of predictive validity is a problem.

Another problem with trait theory is that it tends to suggest that personality is innate, i.e. we inherit a predisposition to develop certain traits, which largely determine our behaviour. Eysenck's evidence for this comes from research which relates introversion and extroversion with physiological functioning. Critics of trait theory refute this and claim that we learn our behaviour entirely from how we interact with our environment.

Social learning theory

Social learning theory explains behaviour in terms of our reactions to specific situations. An extreme view of this is stimulus–response (S–R) theory, which we studied in Chapter 11. S–R theory suggests that our behaviour is controlled by reinforcement alone—personality plays no part in the process.

Bandura's (1977) social learning theory is not so extreme and acknowledges the role of personality in behaviour, in so far as a person comes to a situation with certain preconceptions. Bandura (1977) claims that we learn to deal with situations by observing others (or by observing the results of our own behaviour on others) and by modelling our own behaviour on what we have seen. Social approval or disapproval reinforces our responses. Thus behaviour is determined largely by the situation, and the role of personality is played down. You should note, therefore, that social learning theory is not a theory of personality, but a theory about behaviour.

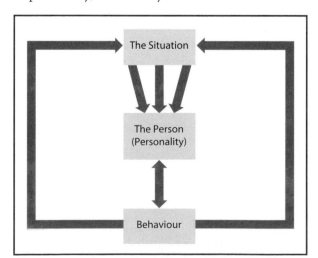

Figure 12.3 Personality, behaviour and the situation: an interactionist model.

Interactionist approaches

Most sport psychologists today acknowledge the existence of traits and the fact that traits to some extent determine behaviour, but recognize that their effects can be modified by particular situations, as shown in Figure 12.1. They take an **interactionist approach**, represented in Figure 12.3, which brings together trait and social learning theories.

Activity
12.1: Interactionist theory
A young tennis player shows promise, but worries about playing in important tournaments and underperforms in these situations. Her coach works with her on anxiety management strategies and in her next tournament she wins. How would you explain this, using interactionist theory?

Key Point
* Behaviour (B) is a function of both the person (personality, P) and the environment (E) (Lewin, 1935):
  B = f(P,E)

How is personality assessed?

Just as there are many theories of personality, so there are several distinct ways in which personality can be assessed. The most widely used in coaching, of course, is **observation**—'getting to know you'. Good coaches and teachers observe their athletes carefully, noting when they are consistent in their behaviour and when the situation seems to affect what they do, i.e. taking into account both traits and situations. Good coaches or teachers are good communicators and, particularly, good listeners, and so they get an all-round understanding of their athletes.

The methods most usually used in sport research are known as **psychometric methods**; that is, they set out to quantify personality—to say, for example, just how extrovert someone is. This is normally done by means of self-report questionnaires.

Trait measures

Trait measures assess a person's general disposition to behave in a particular way. Some of these measures focus on a complete personality profile, e.g. Cattell's Sixteen Personality Factor Questionnaire (known as the **16PF**), which has been widely used in sport research (Figure 12.4). Cattell first identified 171

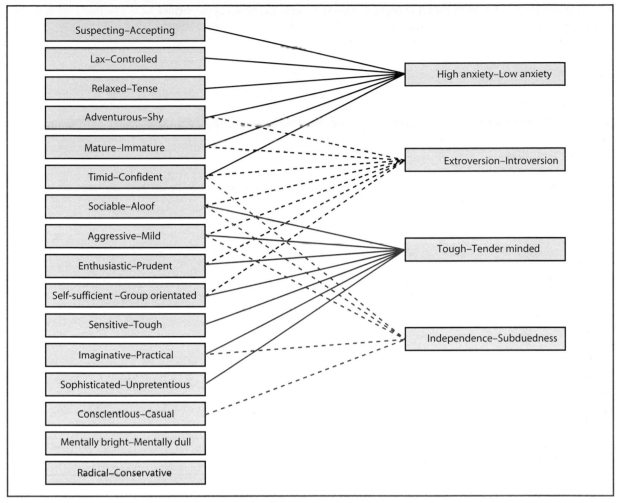

Figure 12.4 The structure of Cattell's 16 personality factors.

behaviours, which he believes we all exhibit to a greater or lesser extent. He grouped these into 16 clusters, which he labelled source traits or first-order (primary) factors. He then constructed a questionnaire which, after considerable preliminary work, he proved to be a valid and reliable measure of these 16 surface traits. The scoring system allows, if the researcher wishes, further grouping of the source traits into four surface traits or second-order (secondary) factors.

There are 141 statements in the 16PF questionnaire, each assessing a particular trait. The statements are similar to the following example:

I feel the need every now and then to engage in tough physical activity:
a) Yes.
b) In between.
c) No.

When the scoring of the questionnaire is completed, the subject has a standardized score out of 10 (known as a **STEN score**) on each of the 16 factors and his/her profile might look like that in Figure 12.5.

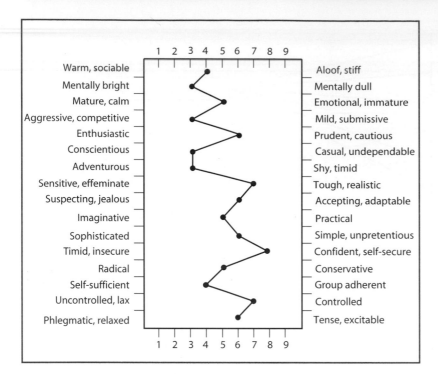

Figure 12.5 The 16PF profile of an athlete.

 Investigation

12.2: To analyse a 16PF profile
Method: Imagine you have collected data on an athlete's personality using the 16PF questionnaire and have constructed a profile as in Figure 12.5.
Observations: Analyse the profile, noting particularly those traits in which the athlete's scores fall outside the range 3.5–6.5. We consider the implications of scores such as these later in the section.

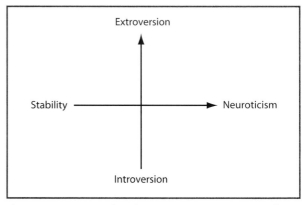

Figure 12.6 Personality dimensions: extroversion and neuroticism.

Eysenck developed a similar self-report questionnaire, shorter and with a 'Yes/No' answering format in contrast to Cattell's three-point scale. This is known as the Eysenck Personality Inventory (or Questionnaire), the **EPI** or the EPQ. There is also a version for children. The major difference between this and Cattell's questionnaire is that Eysenck's directly identifies second-order factors; the two most usually referred to are extroversion and neuroticism (Figure 12.6).

Neuroticism is associated with emotionality and is characterized by a tendency to worry, to exhibit physical symptoms associated with anxiety and to tend to experience unstable mood states. Its opposite construct is '**stability**'. **Extroversion** is a tendency to be outgoing, sociable and to enjoy physical action; **introversion** is its opposite.

Figure 12.7 summarizes the structure of personality according to trait theory and also points to the differences in the labelling of categories by Cattell and Eysenck.

Other trait measures which you may come across in your reading and which have been used in sport are the Profile of Mood States (POMS) (McNair *et al.*, 1971), Nideffer's (1976) Test of Attentional and Interpersonal Style (TAIS), Spielberger *et al.*'s (1970) State–Trait Anxiety Inventory (STAI) and Martens' (1977) Sport Competition Anxiety Test (SCAT).

State measures
As the interest in interactionist theory grew, there developed a number of situation-specific measures, designed to assess a person's state-of-mind at a

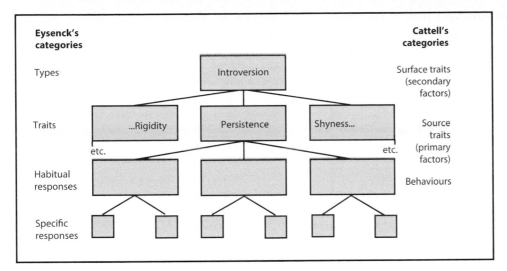

Figure 12.7
Eysenck's and Cattell's hierarchical models of personality.

particular moment in time. These are useful for sport psychologists who want to plot changes in athletes' mental approach to competition, for example. Some such tests that you may come across in your further reading are: The Competitive State Anxiety Inventory (CSAI-II Martens *et al.*, 1990) and The Tennis Test of Attentional and Interpersonal Style (TTAIS; Van Schoyck and Grasha, 1981).

Key Points
- Trait measures give information about an athlete's typical way of behaving in general. They are likely to reflect the 'psychological core' (see Figure 12.1).
- State measures give information about an athlete's state of mind at a particular moment and in a specific situation, i.e. 24 hours before the final of a major table tennis tournament.

Activity
12.2: Identifying confidence problems
You are a golf coach with a sport psychology qualification. You are concerned about a young golfer whose putting goes well in practice, but becomes inconsistent in competition. You think you know him well; he is normally a confident, relaxed person and appears to enjoy competitions; but you suspect he may lose confidence or concentration at crucial times in his game. Discuss how you might use (a) observation, (b) trait measures and/or (c) state measures to help identify the problem.

Note that the coach in Activity 12.2 is qualified in sport psychology. If coaches use such tests they should be aware of the limitations as well as be able to interpret the results appropriately. They should be aware of the ethical guidelines for test administration. They should always use the results for the benefit of the athlete and not for purposes of team selection. There is no evidence that personality tests can predict success in a sport.

What does the research tell us about personality?
During the 1960s and 1970s a great deal of research was carried out, using mostly Cattell's and Eysenck's inventories, into the relationship between personality and sport. Sport scientists were interested in answers to three questions:
- Is there an athletic 'type'?
- Can success in sport be predicted from measures of personality?
- Does personality change as a result of participation in sport?

Is there an athletic type?
Do certain groups of sportspeople, performers or recreationists differ from the norm in terms of their personalities (for example, do they have scores which fall outside the 3.5–6.5 range in the 16PF)? The results of research into these questions are very unclear, largely because of theoretical and methodological problems associated with the research itself. The most clear-cut evidence seems to emerge when second-order factors are considered. A good review of the great wealth and variety of data is given in Butt (1987). When studying research data we must remember that it is mean scores which are reported and within any group of athletes there is a wide variety of

personalities. However, what does seem to emerge is that both male and female sportspeople show traits of extroversion, dominance, enthusiasm, confidence, aggression and high activity levels (Butt, 1987).

Is a particular personality profile necessary for performance at the top level?

In some countries psychological testing is used, in addition to measures of performance and body composition, to identify children who are suitable for intensive training in a sport. You may be aware of the increasing use of personality testing in the selection of people for executive positions in industry and commerce in the UK. Evidence to support such selection processes is not conclusive, however; there is **no** consistent personality profile which discriminates athletes from nonathletes (Weinberg and Gould, 1995). Morgan (1980) identified a relationship between athletic success and mental health, suggesting that successful athletes have a significantly more positive mental health profile than either less successful athletes or the general population (Figure 12.8).

Does personality change as a result of participating in sport?

Morgan's research (1980) begs the question as to whether athletes are successful because they have a particular personality profile or whether their success has given them this profile. As with other questions, research has not yet adequately given us an answer. Traditionally, sport and tough physical activity have been associated with the development of 'character' and 'team spirit'.

Recent research into exercise participation (jogging, aerobics, swim-fit programmes, etc.) does suggest beneficial effects of regular exercise on psychological well-being as well as for physical improvement. Girdano *et al.* (1990) claim that personality characteristics associated with stress, tension and cardiovascular disease can be modified by exercise programmes, with resulting improvements in health; Sonstroem (1984) has shown that improvements in self-esteem have been associated with exercise. Self-esteem as a particular aspect of personality is discussed in the next section. Willis and Campbell (1992) offer a useful review of exercise participation research in much more detail than can be given here.

> **Key Points**
> - Research has had little success in **predicting** achievement in sport from personality profiles.
> - There is some evidence of particular personality profiles being associated with specific sports, but this is inconclusive.
> - There is stronger evidence that successful athletes have a more positive mental health profile than less successful athletes or the general population.
> - There is evidence of a relationship between psychological well-being and regular exercise participation.

The self concept

An interesting element of personality, and one which certainly affects the way in which we participate, learn and perform in physical activities, is the self concept. As you read you will find many different terms and definitions in this area—we confine ourselves to two: self concept and self-esteem.

- The self concept is the descriptive picture we have of ourselves. It includes physical attributes, attitudes, abilities, roles and emotions. It is important to remember that it represents how we see ourselves, which may not reflect reality or the way others see us.
- Self-esteem is the extent to which we value ourselves. Again, this may or may not match up to the expectations of others. For example, a player may take pride in an ability to tackle hard, whereas the referee and the coach may see it as unnecessary aggression.

Several theories that describe the structure of the self concept exist, summarized in Fox (1988). Here we assume that the self concept is built in levels, as illustrated in Figure 12.9.

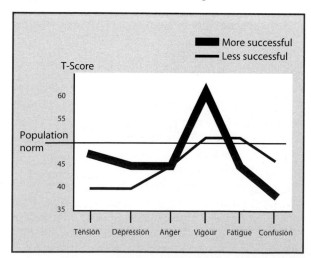

Figure 12.8 The 'Iceberg profile'. (*Adapted from Morgan, 1980.*)

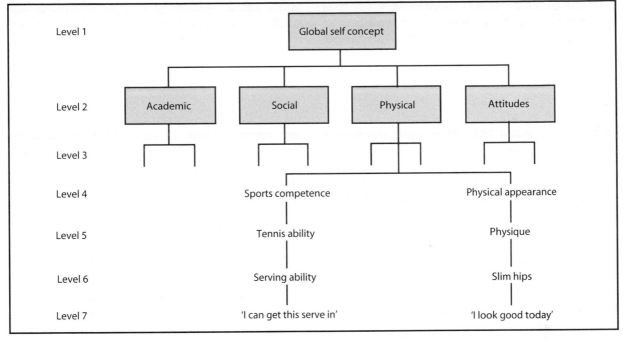

Figure 12.9 The structure of the physical self concept. (*Adapted from Fox, 1988.*)

The development of the self concept

Developmental psychology tells us that the newly born child cannot distinguish between itself and its environment. Growth and maturation bring an increasing awareness of self, of other people and of control over the surroundings and events. At this point the self concept comes into existence. Some aspects of the self concept are enduring; others change as our experiences, our roles and our position in society change.

Factors which influence the self concept

Figure 12.10 represents the internal and external factors which give rise to a particular self concept and self-esteem. Some are objective—they are aspects of yourself which can be measured or readily agreed upon. But others are socially developed and depend upon how you and other people view or value the objective characteristics. This is illustrated in Figure 12.11 in relation to body image, which is the view a person has of his or her body and physical make-up.

Let us consider in a little more detail the social or interactional view of the development of the self concept, referred to in Figures 12.10 and 12.11. We are interested in how other people see us and we take note of their reactions to things we do and say. In this sense other people act as a mirror to reflect

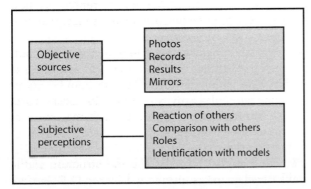

Figure 12.10 Factors affecting the self concept and self-esteem.

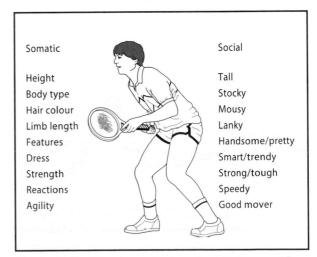

Figure 12.11 Objective–somatic and subjective–social aspects of body image.

us and we internalize what we perceive. If you have received praise and encouragement as you learned to participate in physical activity, then you are likely to have begun to think of yourself as good at sport, or dance or gymnastics. As this picture of self begins to clarify we ask ourselves, 'Well, how good am I?'. We start to compare ourselves with others to see how we 'measure up'. Interestingly, we appear to be sensible about this, and in order to obtain a reasonable evaluation we do not compare ourselves with others who are 'out of our league'. For example, if you are a good college tennis player you will, for the moment, compare yourself with your team-mates and those above you in the club ladder, not the Wimbledon champion!

Our roles in society determine very much how others see and react to us. A role is a set of behaviours associated with our position in a family, group or organization. The longer and more fully we play a particular role, the more we internalize it. You are interested in sport or dance or other forms of physical activity. Others begin to think of you as a sportsperson, or dancer or climber. You may like the idea of being seen in this role and reinforce it by, for example, wearing clothes which identify you with it and adopting the associated role behaviours.

 Investigation

12.3: To identify aspects of role
Method: Each member of the group makes a list of the roles they play—examples might be sister, team captain, student. Select six or so which are common to all members of the group. Each person then writes down the behaviours which are inherent in that role. In groups of two or three devise a 'role play' to illustrate one of the roles, but which does not directly name it. Other members of the group have to identify the role being acted out.
Discussion: What were the behaviours and attitudes that most obviously characterized each role?

Part of learning to play a particular role is the way in which we identify with others who we see to be playing the role successfully (this is assuming that we want to). Sports heroes act as models in this respect, which is partly why sports authorities believe it to be important that players at the top of a sport behave in a way which 'sets a good example' to youngsters.

The establishment of self-esteem

The process described above allows us to develop a particular view of ourselves and also to place a value on that view. If the majority of our experiences with people and of events are enjoyable and satisfying we develop a positive self concept and high self-esteem. If we often feel 'put down' and incompetent, we may have a correspondingly negative self concept and/or low self-esteem. In fact, it is not quite as simple as this for two reasons:

- Self-esteem is a reflection of how significant others value us. We do not seem to be so interested in the evaluations of people who are not important to us. So if parents, teachers or coaches treat our efforts with respect and support, self-esteem rises independently of how competent we actually are or even perceive ourselves to be. People are significant at different periods of our life—early

on it is parents, but later the evaluations of our peers become much more important to us.
- Self-esteem in relation to a particular activity or attribute is a reflection of how important we see it to be. So friends laughing at you for being 'hopeless' at soccer when you are not very interested in it does not have as much effect on your self-esteem as it would if you really wanted to be seen as a good player. This is illustrated in Figure 12.12.

The effects of levels of self-esteem on learning

Research has shown that differing levels of self-esteem give rise to differing personality profiles. People with high self-esteem tend to be optimistic, resilient, adventurous and to enjoy challenge. People with low self-esteem tend to lack confidence, to be self-protective and to be critical of others. It must be remembered that self-esteem can be specific to one particular activity or area of life, or it can be global, but high or low global self-esteem colours all our ideas about ourselves. Once self-esteem is established, it predisposes us to view new experiences in particular ways. This is known as attribution and is considered in more detail in Section 12.5, but we should note the contribution of the self concept to this process. This is shown in Figure 12.13.

This relationship, together with the personality factors we know to be associated with high and low self-esteem, suggest that self-esteem is an important variable in learning and that self concept is important in the avoidance of or adherence to physical activity. It seems to be a cyclical relationship (Figure 12.14).

If this is the case and if we believe that physical activity is something which everyone should have the opportunity of enjoying and being successful in, then what are the implications for the way in which we present, teach and coach physical activity?

Discuss this question in terms of:
- the range and type of activities offered to young people;
- the teaching and coaching styles used;
- the place of competition in physical education;
- the place of fitness training in physical education;
- the role of dance and adventure activities in physical education;
- the use of award schemes, e.g. Royal Life Saving Society.

	Perceived competence	Perceived importance	Self-esteem
Basketball	L	L	O
Fitness	L	H	L
Gymnastics	H	L	O
Dance	H	H	H

Key: L = Low rating
H = High rating
O = Little effect

Figure 12.12 The effects of perceived competence and perceived importance of self-esteem.

	Existing positive self concept	Existing negative self concept
Positive experience of PE	Self concept enhanced	Self concept may become positive
Negative experience of PE	Self concept may become negative	Self concept reinforced

Figure 12.13 The relationship between experiences and the self concept.

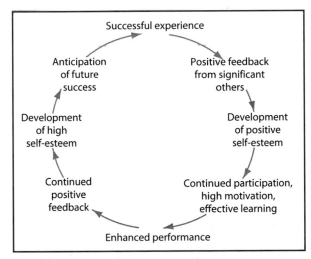

Figure 12.14 The self concept wheel.

Key Points
- A significant way in which individuals differ in how they learn and perform is in their personalities and the way they view themselves.
- Research into personality and sport has tended, in the past, to focus on finding an 'athletic type', but more recently sport psychologists have been trying to find ways of using sportspeople's self-knowledge to help them get the best out of themselves.
- The extent to which we value ourselves seems to play a large part in effective learning and a satisfying performance.

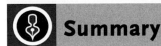 # Summary

1. Personality is defined as a person's unique pattern of traits. Some psychologists view personality as stable and enduring, others see it as dynamic.

2. There are a number of theories of personality development and structure. We considered constitutional theory, trait theory, social learning theory and interactionist approaches.

Summary

continued

3. Behaviour is a function of both personality and the environment: B = f(P,E).
4. Personality is assessed by observation and psychometric measures, particularly trait questionnaires. These have been used extensively in sport research; outcomes have been ambivalent

in terms of defining a particular sport personality, but have successfully identified the characteristics of successful athletes and the relationship between exercise and mental health.
5. An important aspect of personality is the self concept, which appears to play a large part in determining learning and performance.

Review Questions

1. Define the term 'personality' and outline the 'trait' approach and the 'social learning' approach to personality theory.
2. Why has it been difficult to obtain consistent information from research about the relationship between personality and sports participation?

3. Name one sport-specific and one general personality questionnaire. Which might a coach find most useful and why?
4. List six ways in which a coach might use personality theory to help an athlete during training and competition.

Exam-Style Questions

1. Figure 12.15 shows attitude scores for boys and girls aged 11 and 15 years. The attitude scores were measured using the Children's Attitude Towards Physical Activity Scale and shows the results of the health and fitness enjoyment, aesthetic and vertigo scores. (Vertigo refers to attitudes towards risky or adventure sports like white-water canoeing or hang-gliding.)
Note: maximum possible score = 25; minimum possible score = 5
a. i. Comment on the attitudes of the children by making specific reference to age and sex differences that may exist. (4 marks)
ii. Discuss the figures in the context of socialization. (4 marks)
b. What are attitudes? List three components of attitude. (4 marks)
c. i. How can attitudes be formed or changed (illustrate your answer from physical education)? (8 marks)

ii. Comment briefly on the statement that 'attitudes predict behaviours'. (5 marks).

Attitude area	Age 11		Age 15	
	Male	Female	Male	Female
Health and fitness enjoyment	21.7	22.3	20.4	21.0
Vertigo	18.9	17.6	20.1	16.6
Aesthetic	18.0	20.8	16.4	20.1

Figure 12.15 (*Adapted from Schultz* et al., *1985.*)

2. a. For a **team coach** to be effective, it is important that each member of the team is known

Exam-Style Questions

continued

and recognized as a separate **personality**. Give a definition of **personality**. (1 mark)

b. Eysenck identified **two** dimensions of personality as illustrated in Figure 12.16.

i. Describe the characteristics of players **A** and **B**. (4 marks)

ii. What are the disadvantages of the **trait theory**? (2 marks)

c. Outline the **social learning theory** of personality by using an example from sport. (3 marks)

d. How can personality be related to **personal choice** and **performance** in sport? (4 marks)

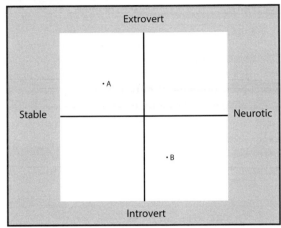

Figure 12.16 (*Adapted from 'Trait Theory' by Eysenck, 1975.*)

12.3 Attitudes in Sport

Keywords & concepts

affective component	**behavioural component**	**persuasive communication**
attitude	**cognitive component**	**scale**
attitude object	**cognitive dissonance**	**stereotype**

On completing this section you will be able to:

- define the term **attitude** and describe how attitudes are measured;
- state the three components of attitude and indicate how attitudes are developed;
- link attitudes to behaviour in sporting contexts;
- show how attitudes in sport might be changed by means of persuasion and cognitive dissonance techniques.

We saw in Section 12.2 how our 'core' personality is made up of a combination of attitudes, beliefs, values and motives. The study of attitudes in and to sport and physical education is important because of the way in which attitudes seem to influence our behaviour. Thus, if I feel angry about being constantly fouled by my opponent I may well behave aggressively towards her; more positively, if you believe it to be important to keep fit and enjoy

exercise, then you are likely to participate in sport, or an exercise programme, regularly.

> **Key Points**
> - Attitudes are a combination of beliefs and feelings about objects, people or situations (known as '**attitude objects**') which predispose us to behave in a certain way towards them.
> - Attitudes are learned, or organized through experience (Allport, 1935).
> - Attitudes are evaluative, i.e. they lead us to think and behave positively or negatively about the attitude object.
> - Attitudes tend to be deep-seated and enduring, but can change or be changed.

The three components of attitude

Some theorists (e.g. Triandis, 1971) suggest that attitudes consist of three elements (Figure 12.17). The implication of this model is that an attitude consists of:

- a **cognitive component**—the knowledge and beliefs held about the attitude object, i.e. fitness training;
- an **affective component**—the positive or negative feelings and emotions towards the attitude object, i.e. enjoyment of training;
- a **behavioural component**—the intended behaviour towards the attitude object, i.e. attending training sessions regularly.

Note that the behaviour is **intended**. The inter-relationship between beliefs, emotions and intended behaviour is usually quite strong. Thus, if you value physical fitness, you intend to keep yourself fit. The relationship between attitudes and **actual** behaviour is not as strong, though research does indicate that if you intend to do something, there is a likelihood that you will do it. Can you think of any examples from your own experience when having a particular attitude about something (a) means you usually act out that attitude and (b) does not necessarily mean you do anything about it?

Attitudes to sport and participation

Research into attitudes to and in sport (e.g. Smoll and Schutz, 1980; Deaux and Lewis, 1984) has traditionally tended to focus on establishing the views of particular groups about issues or situations. Some examples are:

- children's attitudes to their school PE programmes;
- women's views on the availability of sport opportunities in their area;
- athletes' attitudes to training;
- teachers' attitudes to the physical and intellectual abilities of black children;
- general attitudes to women in sport.

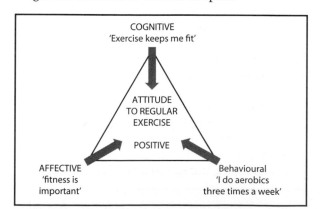

Figure 12.17 The three components of attitude.

The results of this research show no general patterns of attitude to sport, i.e. it is not straightforward to predict attitudes to sport from other variables such as gender or age. Research into the value of physical education in schools has shown generally positive attitudes of teachers, parents and pupils, though pupils are somewhat more critical of the content of the programme. Society seems to be becoming more egalitarian in its view of women in sport, though evidence of gender stereotyping still exists, as does racial stereotyping.

People with positive attitudes to sport and physical activity:

- have had some success in or satisfaction from participating;
- believe in the value of the activity in promoting health and well-being;
- have been encouraged by 'significant others';
- have opportunities to continue participation;
- are likely to participate in physical activity regularly;
- are likely to be willing to try new activities;
- have a positive physical self-concept.

People with negative attitudes to sport and physical activity:

- may have had negative experiences in sport or PE;
- find sport frustrating or boring;
- do not believe in its value for health and well-being;
- lack encouragement or have been discouraged;
- are unlikely to participate regularly, if at all;
- have lifestyles which make regular physical activity difficult;
- may have a negative physical self-concept.

Sport stereotypes

A stereotypical attitude in one that leads the holder to expect people characterized as belonging to a particular group to behave in a certain way. In sport this usually leads to expectations about what people are or are not able to achieve. Although stereotypes can be positive, negative stereotyping has been instrumental in holding back particular groups by limiting opportunity or access. This happens either because provision is not made for such groups or because the public (including coaches and teachers) have stereotypic attitudes which encourage low expectations. Examples of such negative stereotyping are or have been:

- women in contact, strength, endurance sports;
- participation of the disabled in physical activity;
- older age groups' interest and ability in sport;
- participation of particular ethnic groups in specific sports or positions within teams.

Measurement of attitudes

Research into attitudes to sport is based on measurement of attitudes. This may be done in a variety of ways. Since attitude tends to be linked to behaviour, we can observe, record and analyse people's behaviour in situations which are likely to reflect their attitudes, and then infer their attitudes from that behaviour.

Can you think of some sport and nonsport examples of how you might do this? For example, how might you collect information about students' attitudes to the meals provided in your school or college canteen?

There are problems of validity with such methods, however, so the most usual form of attitude measurement is a scale. A scale is a questionnaire which has been carefully constructed to be valid and reliable and to give a score for an individual on a particular attitude. There are three major types of scales, named after their authors: **Thurstone scales**, **Likert scales** and **Osgood semantic differential scales**. They differ slightly in their construction, but all consist of asking respondents to indicate the extent to which they agree or disagree with a particular statement.

Osgood's semantic differential scale asks respondents to rate the attitude object on a series of continua between bipolar constructs, such as:

Gymnastics lessons are:

good	1	2	3	4	5	6	7	bad
boring	7	6	5	4	3	2	1	fun
easy	1	2	3	4	5	6	7	easy

(scoring not included in questionnaire)

Gill (1986, p. 98) gives a useful comparison of the different types. Investigation 12.4 contains an informal example of a **Likert** scale.

Investigation

12.4: To measure schoolchildren's attitudes to PE

Method: Obtain permission to gather data from a mixed class of school pupils (boys and girls) of any age, from your own school or a neighbouring one. Use the **Likert scale** below or construct your own. If you construct your own you should do a pilot study initially to choose those items which best differentiate the sample, i.e. produce both high and low scores. Do not include the scores on the questionnaire.

Make sure you understand how the scoring works; you must take the minus signs into account. The higher a positive score, the more positive is the pupil's attitude to PE.

Calculate each pupil's total attitude score and then calculate: (i) a whole group mean score; (ii) a boys' mean score and (iii) a girls' mean score.
1. What do you notice about the differences (if any) between these three means?
2. How might you explain them?
3. How could you improve the scale?

Attitudes to PE Questionnaire

For each statement, tick the extent to which you agree.

1. Most PE lessons are enjoyable
   - ☐ strongly agree (+2)
   - ☐ agree (+1)
   - ☐ don't know/neutral (0)
   - ☐ disagree (−1)
   - ☐ strongly disagree (−2)
2. I miss PE lessons whenever I can
   - ☐ strongly agree (−2)
   - ☐ agree (−1)
   - ☐ neutral (0)
   - ☐ disagree (+1)
   - ☐ strongly disagree (+2)
3. I want to get a good report in PE
   - ☐ strongly agree (+2)
   - ☐ agree (+1)
   - ☐ don't know/neutral (0)
   - ☐ disagree (−1)
   - ☐ strongly disagree (−2)
4. PE doesn't really teach you anything important
   - ☐ strongly agree (−2)
   - ☐ agree (−1)
   - ☐ don't know/neutral (0)
   - ☐ disagree (+1)
   - ☐ strongly disagree (+2)

As with personality scales, the most useful published scales for researchers interested in attitudes to sport are those which have been constructed with a sport-specific attitude object. Examples of these are:
- Kenyon's (1968) 'Attitudes towards Physical Activity'.
- Sonstroem's (1978) 'Physical Estimation and Attraction Scale'.
- Smoll and Schutz's (1980) 'Children's Attitudes to Physical Activity'.

There are two important points to remember about attitude scales.

- They appear simple to construct, but in fact it is very difficult to ensure that you have composed a valid and reliable measure. If you wish to use an attitude scale in an investigation it is sensible to use one that has already been constructed and validated for the attitude which you are interested in.
- Although scales are composed of a number of questions, each scale represents the same attitude (though you may have more than one scale in a questionnaire). Ensuring that you are only dealing with one attitude with the questions you have constructed is one of the problems that affects validity.

Changing attitudes

PE teachers are familiar with the need to change negative attitudes towards physical activity into positive ones. For coaches and activity leaders this is less of a problem, but they may find it necessary to work on changing attitudes, for example to winning and losing or to aggressive behaviour.

Persuasive communication

Persuasive communication theory suggests that for an attitude to change the person must attend to, understand, accept and retain the message (Hovland *et al.*, 1953). Persuasion to change an attitude in sport works best when:

- The coach/teacher is perceived as:
  – expert,
  – trustworthy;
- and the message is:
  – clear,
  – unambiguous,
  – appropriately balanced between:
    emotion and logic,
    pros and cons.

Cognitive dissonance theory

Cognitive dissonance theory (Festinger, 1957) claims that people appear to need to be **consistent** not only in the three components of attitude (knowledge, feelings and behaviour), but also within the cognitive (knowledge) element. If any elements conflict, then **dissonance** is set up. For example, you might reject the need for instrumental aggression in your sport (belief 1), but think that in order to win against a particular team you must physically intimidate your opponent (belief 2). The two beliefs conflict. This dissonance is resolved by telling yourself that it's all right to play hard against these particular opponents because they play that way too, so that is what you do (modification of belief 1).

In this situation a coach might use cognitive dissonance theory by re-creating the conflict: 'Skilful players don't need to resort to that sort of behaviour—they can win the ball without it. You're a skilful player, so why are you playing like a thug?' The coach is trying to persuade the player to resolve the dissonance by changing belief 2 and thus the behavioural outcome.

> **Key Points**
> Gill (1986) specifies two methods of attitude change:
> - **persuasive communication**;
> - **cognitive dissonance theory**.

> **Activity**
> **12.3: Changing attitudes to training**
> You are a swimming coach. Your squad believe that the only way they will be successful is to train in the pool for longer and longer periods. You believe that it is the quality of training that counts and you want them to cut down on their pool time and do more general conditioning and cognitive strategy work. Discuss how you would use persuasion theory and cognitive dissonance theory to change their attitude to training.

 # Summary

1. Attitudes are a combination of beliefs and feelings about attitude objects which predispose us to behave in a particular way. They are learned, evaluative, deep-seated and enduring.

2. There are three components of attitude— cognitive, affective and behavioural.

3. Attitudes are measured by attitude scales, but can also be observed by listening to people and by watching them behave.

Summary

continued

4. Attitude research in sport tends to centre on athletes' and children's attitudes to their sport and their PE programme. Attitudes of spectators and of the public towards sport and sportspeople are also of interest.

5. Attitudes affect performance in sport, so teachers and coaches may wish to change attitudes. Techniques such as persuasive communication and cognitive dissonance may be tried.
6. Stereotyping is an outcome of attitude development and can be detrimental so some groups' participation in sport.

Review Questions

1. Define the term 'attitude'. How are attitudes measured?
2. Describe the three components of attitudes.
3. What is meant by the terms 'stereotype' and 'prejudice' in attitude terms? Give some examples from sport.
4. Describe the 'persuasion' and 'cognitive dissonance' methods of attitude change.

Exam-Style Questions

1 **a.** If young people are to participate fully in physical education and sport, then it is essential that they hold positive attitudes towards physical activity.
i. What features would reflect a **positive attitude** to physical education? (3 marks)
ii. Explain the factors which could have **influenced** the formation of this positive attitude. (4 marks)
iii. Use practical examples to explain how you might **change** a young person's negative attitude to physical education. (4 marks)
b. Setting goals is one way to help motivate a sports performer:
i. Use an example of a sport of your choice and identify **two** short-term goals and **two** long-term goals. (2 marks)
ii. Discuss the factors which should be taken into consideration when setting these goals. (4 marks)

• •

12.4 Aggression in Sport

Keywords & concepts

aggression	**frustration–aggression**	**instrumental aggression**
assertiveness	**theory**	**interactional theory**
bracketed morality	**hostile aggression**	**moral reasoning**
catharsis	**instinct theory**	**social learning theory**
drive theory		

The aggressive behaviour of players or spectators is one aspect of group interaction in sport which is currently attracting particular attention. As the rewards of winning become increasingly more substantial, at both professional and amateur levels, so emotions tend to run high, and some players (and coaches) believe that almost any means can justify the end—that of winning. That is not to say that this is a modern phenomenon (look at some of the photographs of mob games in the 'history' section of this book!), but the organization and codification of games during the 19th century was designed to bring a spirit of control and 'fair play' to potentially violent activities.

On completing this section you will be able to:

- define aggression and differentiate it from assertion;
- discuss theories of aggression—instinct, frustration–aggression and social learning theories;
- describe the antecedents of aggression in sport contexts and discuss ways in which aggression can be eliminated from sport.

Definitions of aggression

One of the main difficulties in studying this area from a psychological viewpoint is that there can be confusion in defining the term, since we use the word extensively in everyday life. A good starting point for your study of aggression would be to video a game and then identify, and discuss as a group, all the incidents of aggressive behaviour you find. This will raise some interesting questions:

- Is a strong but fair tackle aggressive?
- Is it aggressive to shout at the referee?
- What about throwing your racket to the ground after a bad line call?
- Are some soccer fans' chants aggressive?

The answers you arrive at will depend on how you define 'aggression'.

In this section we differentiate between aggression (as defined below) and assertion (which is forceful, decisive play). Sport psychologists generally agree that **aggression is behaviour in which a deliberate intent to harm or injure others is evident** (Gill, 1986, p. 196). Gill goes on to identify several issues which arise from this definition, listed in the Key Points, and further clarification was given by Baron (1977), as summarized in Figure 12.18.

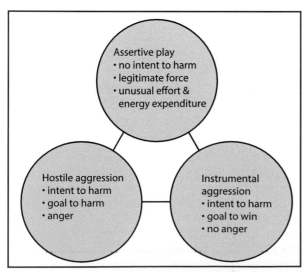

Figure 12.18 Aggression and assertion from the player's perspective. (*Adapted from Cox, 1994.*)

> ### Key Points
>
> - Aggression is behavioural, so willing or wishing harm to someone is not aggression and neither is anger, unless it is expressed as intention to harm.
> - Aggression must be intentional, so accidentally causing injury or harm is not included in the definition.
> - The inclusion of the idea of 'harm' in the definition implies that aggression can be verbal if the words are such that they are intended to embarrass or hurt, but it seems to rule out 'eyeballing' an opponent.
> - This definition refers to other people, so it does not include smashing your racket into the ground.

Hostile (reactive/angry) aggression is an act in which the main purpose is to hurt or harm the other person, purely for the satisfaction gained from inflicting hurt. Instrumental aggression is an act that also intends to cause harm but in which the main aim is not to cause suffering, but to achieve dominance or a point/goal. Assertiveness is the use of legitimate force to achieve the goal, with no intent to cause harm. If injury results, this is of course very regrettable, but the act is not aggressive because there was no intent to injure.

Taking this view of aggression we can see that the frequency of **hostile** aggressive acts in sport is less than we might have at first thought. There may well be players who set out with the intent to injure, because their coach has told them to, or because they have a score to settle, or perhaps because they enjoy hurting others. But it is likely that these are very much a minority.

What is probably more worrying to governing bodies of sport, and to those who value the socializing potential of sport, is the apparent increase in **instrumental aggression**. Invasion games and contact sports offer plenty of scope for this kind of behaviour. The difficulty is the boundary between hostile aggression (always illegal), instrumental aggression (which is normally illegal, in all sports except boxing) and **assertiveness** (which is normally legitimate) is not easy to distinguish. During play this is a task for referees and officials; it becomes more difficult as cynical coaches (particularly in professional sport) train players in how to be aggressive without it being noticed and how to feign being a victim of aggression (e.g. 'diving' in soccer). Coaches and teachers must take as their main concern the task of encouraging nonaggressive attitudes and behaviour in players.

Sports commentators and interviewees should use unambiguous language when they are applauding assertive play, for there is no escaping the fact that, using the definitions of aggression that we have described, aggressive behaviour is wrong and should not be condoned under any circumstances.

Theories of aggression

> **Key Points**
> There are four main groups of theories about aggression and each warrants further reading to fully appreciate what they have to say:
> - Instinct theories.
> - Frustration–aggression (drive) theories.
> - Social learning theory.
> - Revised frustration–aggression theories.
> (*Note:* In some texts social learning theory and revised frustration–aggression theory are combined.)

Instinct theories

Instinct theories (Lorenz, 1966) are based on the believe that aggression is innate and instinctive, developed through evolution to help us survive as a species. According to this assumption, we all from time to time experience a build-up of aggression which must be released in some way. Sport is seen as an appropriate way of dissipating pent-up aggression; it acts as a **catharsis**. This is an interesting idea, but it does not have general recognition. From your own experience, what flaws can you see in it?

Drive theories

The best known of the drive theories is the frustration–aggression hypothesis (Dollard *et al.*, 1939) which suggests that frustration (being blocked in the achievement of a goal) causes a drive to be aggressive towards the source of the frustration. As frustration mounts, so does the drive to remove the block to achievement. If this is an opponent, and she/he is consistently beating you, then aggression automatically follows. Whereas this idea makes sense in some examples, there are problems with it as a general theory. Can you suggest what these problems may be?

Social learning theory

Social learning theory (Bandura, 1973) claims that aggression is learned, in the same way that much other behaviour is learned. Bandura's experiments suggest that aggression is learnt by observation and social reinforcement. This suggests that if players (and spectators) are frequently exposed to the aggressive behaviour of others, and particularly if they are praised or rewarded (either directly or indirectly) for their own aggression, then they are likely to develop aggressive responses to some situations in sport. However, this theory also indicates a positive factor; an individual can also learn nonaggressive ways of dealing with the same situations; hence the importance of teachers and coaches in establishing clear, unambiguous behavioural codes for themselves and their players, so helping players to deal positively with sources of frustration.

Revised frustration–aggression (interactional) theory

Berkowitz (1969) combined the original frustration–aggression theory with social learning theory to suggest that frustration increases the likelihood of anger, which in turn creates a 'readiness' aggression. This readiness is mediated, however, by social learning. The important point here is that anger is not a drive (which has to be resolved), but an emotion which people can learn to deal with. Thus aggression only occurs as a response to frustration *if* that is the response which has been observed, reinforced and thus socially learned. If alternative responses have been learned (for example, changing tactics or using stress management strategies), then aggression is not the automatic outcome.

> **Activity**
> **12.4: Aggression**
> View a video of aggressive and/or assertive behaviour in a sport context. Unfortunately, televised, professional sport will provide many, some infamous, examples of aggression. Using the four theories described in the text, speculate on the causes of the behaviour that you have seen. Did you judge the behaviour to be assertive, hostile aggression or instrumental aggression?

Causes of aggression

Cox (1994) cites two main causes of aggression.
- Physiological arousal. Research has shown that to feel anger towards another person, the individual must be highly motivated and thus physiologically aroused and ready for action. There is thus an increased danger of aggression in sports where high pre-game arousal is encouraged, such as invasion team games.

- Underdeveloped moral reasoning (Bredemeier, 1985). This theory suggests that players with low levels of moral reasoning are more likely to be aggressive than players with well-developed morality. Bredemeier concludes that participation in sport in which aggressive behaviour is tacitly condoned may retard players' moral development, because it teaches a confusing 'double standard' ('aggression is wrong in real life, but OK in sport'), known as **bracketed morality**.

More specific causes of aggressive behaviour have been listed by Cox (1994) and Weinberg and Gould (1995):
- high environmental temperature,
- home or away,
- embarrassment,
- losing,
- pain,
- unfair officiating,
- playing below capability,
- large score difference.
- low league standing,
- later stage of play,
- reputation of opposition ('get your retaliation in first'!).

Eliminating or preventing aggressive behaviour

Coaches, teachers, officials, parents and players themselves have a responsibility to help prevent and eliminate aggression in sport, while maintaining a healthy 'will to win'. Professionals who appear frequently in the media have a particular responsibility in this respect, because they are the models whom young players seek to emulate; they set the standard. The following recommendations are derived from the literature (Gill, 1986; Cox, 1994; Weinberg and Gould, 1995) and from the experience of coaches.

Spectator aggression, particularly in large, partisan crowds, is a broad issue and has its roots in social issues which may be only indirectly associated with the game itself. However, evidence shows that spectators are more likely to demonstrate physical and extreme verbal aggression if:
- players are aggressive to each other;
- the officiating is perceived as poor or biased;
- alcohol is available prior to and during the game;
- there is opportunity for racial or national abuse;
- the crowd is composed largely of adult males.

Aggressive behaviour on the field needs to be tackled at a variety of levels and can be prevented when:
- governing bodies of sport establish and enforce a nonaggressive code of conduct with officials, coaches and players;
- governing bodies of sport work with the media to inform commentators of this code and emphasize the importance of using appropriate terminology to describe assertive play;
- coach education programmes emphasize the necessity to eliminate aggressive behaviour and teach strategies for controlling it;
- coaches work with players to develop stress management strategies and 'prosocial' or ethical behaviour in anger-producing situations;
- coaches and players develop respect for the opposition and interaction before and after the game is encouraged;
- the concept of 'sporting behaviour' includes the possibility of sacrificing success;
- parents and/or supporters avoid showing and advocating aggression and do not respond to aggression on the field;
- players take responsibility for their own actions and develop self-control strategies so that levels or arousal do not rise too high.

 Summary

1. Aggression in sport is currently an important issue. The term aggression is used in everyday life, so confusion arises as to what exactly it means.
2. In sports psychology aggression is the intent to harm, whether for the sake of hurting an opponent or in order to block them, win the ball or otherwise achieve a goal.
3. We thus distinguish between hostile aggression, instrumental aggression and assertiveness. Assertiveness is positive and to be encouraged.
4. Boundaries between the three types of behaviour are not easy to distinguish, either in discussion or in practice.
5. There are a number of theories of aggression; we have considered instinct theories, drive or frustration–aggression theories and social learning theories.

Summary

continued

6. There are two main antecedents of aggression in sport—physiological arousal and low level of moral reasoning. More specific causes of aggression can be identified— analysis of these can be used by coaches and teachers to prevent aggressive behaviour in athletes.

7. Governing bodies, officials, teacher or coach educators, coaches, spectators and athletes themselves all have a role to play in eliminating aggression from sport.

Review Questions

1. Give a definition of 'aggression'.
2. Differentiate between 'hostile aggression', 'instrumental aggression' and 'assertiveness', using examples from sport.
3. Briefly outline the 'frustration–aggression (drive)' theory of aggression and show how it has been modified by social learning theory.
4. How can coaches reduce the likelihood of aggression being shown by their athletes?

Exam-Style Questions

1. You will have played in a team game and you may have had some players in your team who have been aggressive. They may have displayed aggression frequently and this would probably have been detrimental to your team's performance.

a. What does the term **aggression** mean when related to sports psychology? Explain the **possible causes** of aggressive behaviour in these team players. (4 marks)

b. Briefly discuss the view that aggression is learned rather than an instinctive response. (4 marks)

c. What strategies could be employed by these players to control their aggressive tendencies? (3 marks)

2. a. Define the terms **aggression** and **assertion** in relation to sports performance. (4 marks)

b. Explain how competitive game situations can create aggression, referring to the appropriate theory in social psychology. (4 marks)

c. Describe the **social learning theory** of aggression, using examples from sport to illustrate your answer. (8 marks)

d. What can a referee do to control aggression in sporting competitions?

3. It has been suggested that aggression in sport is the result of frustration, as shown by the simple model in Figure 12.19.

a. Name the theory represented by this model. (1 mark)

b. What are the similarities and differences between **assertive** and **aggressive** behaviours in sport? (5 marks)

c. Discuss the theory of **social learning** of aggression. (10 marks)

d. State **two** methods, each with a relevant example, that a games coach might use to control aggression in players. (4 marks)

4. With particular reference to football crowds, give an account of how and why violent behaviour can occur. (20 marks)

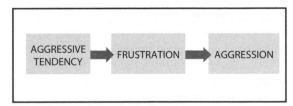

Figure 12.19 Causes of aggression.

12.5 Motivation

Keywords & concepts

ability	intrinsic motivation	personality
achievement motivation	inverted-U theory	risk taking
attribution	learned helplessness	self-confidence
avoidance	locus of causality	self-efficacy
direction	luck	self-fulfilling prophesy
drive theory	modelling	situational factors
effort	motives	stability
emotional arousal	need to achieve	task difficulty
expectancy	need to avoid failure	verbal persuasion
extrinsic motivation	performance	vicarious experience
intensity	performance accomplishments	

Motives and motivation

In a previous section we briefly considered motivation as a factor in the learning process. In this section we study it as a factor in performance, particularly in terms of the role it plays in people's continuing participation in physical activity.

On completing this section you will be able to:

- define motives and motivation;
- give examples of extrinsic and intrinsic rewards;
- interpret motivation in terms of arousal levels and associate these with personality, ability level and task differences;
- describe drive theory and the inverted-U theory and use these to predict the effects of motivation on sport performance;
- discus the role of achievement motivation in sport;
- use attribution theory to interpret how athletes view success and failure and describe how inappropriate attribution can lead to learned helplessness;
- show how self-confidence and self-efficacy affect performance and can be developed.

Key Points

- Motivators are the reasons why sportspeople think and behave as they do.
- Motivation has five components: direction, intensity, persistence, continuity and performance.
- Early theories focussed on the notion of 'drive'.
- Current theories are based on social perception and goal orientation.

Activity
12.5: Participation motives
Individually, write down the reasons why you enjoy participating in sport or other physical activity. As a group, pool these reasons and then put them into categories, e.g. all those to do with fitness. List these categories (not the individual reasons) and ask all members of the group to rank them in order of personal importance: for example, if the main reason you play sport is because it is important for you to stay fit, rank this as '1'. Combine these ranks to see which are the most important participation motives for your group.

In the Key Points, 'direction' refers to the acts of seeking out or avoiding situations. For example, an ambitious athlete might be motivated to attend additional training sessions, whereas a demotivated, burnt-out player might start to skip practices. 'Intensity' refers to the amount of effort expended. Highly motivated people put in a lot of effort.

Research into motives for participation has shown the patterns of motives outlined in Table 12.1.

Intrinsic and extrinsic motivation

Figure 12.20 identifies a continuum between two forms of motivation, intrinsic and extrinsic. People who are intrinsically motivated pursue an activity for its own sake, for the pride and satisfaction they achieve, regardless of what anyone else thinks of their efforts. Extrinsic motivation stems from other people, through positive and negative reinforcement, and from tangible rewards such as trophies, badges and payment (for professionals).

Behavioural psychologists have, for many years, recognized the power of extrinsic rewards to develop and modify behaviour. A very basic principle of human behaviour is the **law of effect**, which states that rewarding a particular behaviour increases the probability that the behaviour will be repeated. Coaches and teachers recognize this and many of the governing bodies of sport have produced award schemes which encourage youngsters to work at skills in order to increase their proficiency and thus be awarded a badge or certificate (Figure 12.21).

Investigation

12.5: To identify a range of governing body award schemes

Method: Go to your local school or college library and look up the magazines and journals produced by the governing bodies of sport, e.g. *The Swimming Times*. Note details of any award schemes which are described. As a class group write to several governing bodies, asking for details of their award schemes.

Analyse these schemes in terms of:

1. Age range for which the award is designed.
2. Level of difficulty of each stage of the award.
3. Nature of the award (certificate, badge, etc.).
4. General attractiveness of the presentation.
5. Potential interest which the award might generate in its target population.

Until recently, few would have questioned the appropriateness or effectiveness of such schemes. It was assumed that extrinsic rewards would encourage initial participation, and that adding an extrinsic reward to a situation in which youngsters were already intrinsically motivated at best increased motivation, and at worst did no harm.

Recent research has led us to question this, however:

intrinsic motivation + extrinsic reward = ?

Deci (1971) and Lepper *et al.* (1973) showed that, in certain circumstances, adding external reward to a situation that is already intrinsically motivating actually decreases that intrinsic motivation and may eventually replace it, so that when the reward is no longer available, interest in the activity wanes.

Can you suggest some explanations for these findings? Can you think of any occasions when you have found the receipt of an extrinsic reward irrelevant or even demotivating?

Table 12.1 : Major motives (Weinberg and Gould, 1995)	
Youth sport participation	**Adult exercise participation**
improving skills	health factors
having fun	weight loss
being with friends	fitness
experiencing thrills and excitement	self-challenge
achieving success	feeling better
developing	fitness

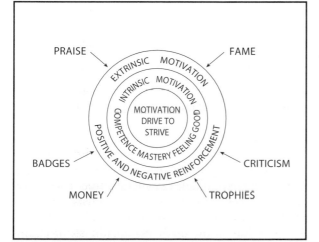

Figure 12.20 Intrinsic and extrinsic motivation.

Extrinsic rewards			Intrinsic sources
Tangible	**Intangible**		
Badges	**negative**	**positive**	Satisfaction
Trophies	criticism	praise	Achievement
Certificates	defeat	fame	Feeling good
Money		winning	

Figure 12.21 Extrinsic rewards and intrinsic sources.

Explanations which have been suggested are:

- The reward acts as a distraction to the sportsperson's intrinsic desire to work at his/her own pace.
- Individuals may feel that being given a reward turns what they thought of as play into work and thus changes the nature of:
  (i) the relationship between themselves and the person giving the reward;
  (ii) the activity itself.
- People like to determine their own behaviour; participating for the sake of a reward makes them feel that someone or something else is in charge.

Does this mean that we should scrap all award schemes, leagues, certificates, etc.? Certainly not—rewards do not automatically undermine intrinsic motivation. They may be used to attract youngsters to an activity they might not otherwise try, or to revive flagging motivation, or to help an athlete over a bad period in his/her training. The psychological borderline between intangible extrinsic rewards, such as praise and fame, and the intrinsic rewards of satisfaction and sense of achievement is by no means clear. Thus, if extrinsic rewards provide information about levels of achievement and competence, they enhance motivation. However, current thinking does suggest that as intrinsic motivation and participation for its own sake develop, so tangible rewards become redundant and should be withdrawn or used very sparingly.

Developing and enhancing motivation in sport and physical activity

One of the most important aspect of the teacher's or coach's role is to help the athlete develop intrinsic motivation. To do this effectively requires considerable understanding of a very complex phenomenon. Weinberg and Gould (1995) suggest some principles to guide a coach's thinking and planning, as summarized below:

- Motivation is a combination of personal characteristics and situational aspects. Motivation is highest when the performer is keen to participate and learn or perform effectively and when the motivational climate is right, e.g. the training programme is interesting and varied.
- People have multiple motives for involvement. People share motives, as we have seen in Activity 12.5, but each individual also has a unique motivational profile and participates for more than one reason. Sometimes these motives compete and cause an apparent decrease in interest—for

example, a school squad swimmer may become interested in badminton and find it difficult to sustain training for both at the level she/he wants.

- Motives change over time—the profile of motives for youth sport participation differs from that of adults.
- Teaching and coaching environments need to be structured to meet the motivational needs of all participants. This means that a coach or teacher must treat all participants as individuals and try to understand the motivational profile of each.
- Training and competition need to be varied in terms of intensity and competitiveness—routine tends to lessen motivation.
- Teachers and coaches are themselves important motivators.

Achievement motivation

So far we have considered motivation in terms of the sportsperson's interest in participating in physical activity. In taking this stance, we recognize that an important part of intrinsic motivation stems from perceived success in achieving competence and mastery. An individual's drive to achieve success for its own sake is known as achievement motivation. In sportspeople this is closely related to competitiveness; in other aspects of physical activity, this is the persistence of a climber in the face of difficulties, for example, or the striving for perfection of a dancer. Achievement motivation is about what happens when we are faced with a choice to seek out or to avoid situations where we might or might not be successful. For example, you might have a choice of routes to climb on a rock face, or of opponents to make up your school or college fixture list. Which or who do you choose? Research shows that two factors contribute to the decision—personality and situation.

Personality factors

Atkinson (1974) suggests that there are two personality factors that contribute to achievement motivation (Figure 12.22):

- the need to achieve (*Nach*);
- he need to avoid failure (*Naf*).

We all have both characteristics, but those with a high need to achieve usually tend to have a low need to avoid failure (subject 'A'), and those who have a high need to avoid failure generally have a low need to achieve (subject 'B'). What is not so clear to sport psychologists are the characteristics of people who might appear in the other two quadrants of Figure 12.22 (Gill, 1986).

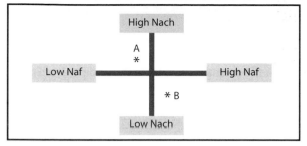

Figure 12.22 The personality components of achievement motivation.

This aspect of personality explains why some people seek out success while others avoid situations where they might be seen to fail, but it does not give the full picture or account for behaviour in those situations where someone is committed to participate, but can choose the level of task difficulty; for example, deciding on an easy or difficult rock route once a climber has arrived at the base of the cliff.

Situational factors
We judge the situation in terms of:
- the probability of success;
- the incentive value of that success.

This is shown in Figure 12.23 and is derived from the work of Atkinson (1974). The model shows that if the probability of success is low (for example, if you are playing squash against a world-class player), the incentive value of success is high (you would be very excited if you won). Similarly, if you play against weak opposition, winning doesn't mean so much to you.

Research (e.g. Roberts, 1974) shows that people with a low achievement orientation (high failure avoidance) tend to choose tasks which are either very easy or very difficult. Can you suggest why this is? High achievers, however, tend to select tasks where there is a fifty–fifty chance of success. Thus, high achievers tend to be risk takers.

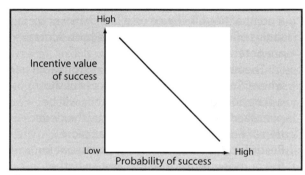

Figure 12.23 Situational factors in achievement motivation.

 Investigation

12.6: To investigate the hypothesis that high achievers are high risk takers
Method: Select a group of subjects who are not aware of the nature of the experiment.
1. Measure the achievement motivation of your subjects either by using the Lynn Survey of Achievement Motivation (Carron, 1981) or by means of the following scale (circle the score which most represents your feelings about each of the paired statements):

a. Success in sport is very important to me.　5 4 3 2 1　Winning doesn't matter; its the game that counts

b. I prefer to play opponents I know I can beat.　1 2 3 4 5　I like playing opponents who are about my level.

c. I enjoy a challenge.　5 4 3 2 1　I like doing things I know I will succeed in.

d. I don't enjoy close games.　5 4 3 2 1　I enjoy a close game.

e. I don't worry about the result of a game.　1 2 3 4 5　I don't like having to tell people I lost a game.

f. I tend to make errors when I'm under pressure.　5 4 3 2 1　I play best when I'm under pressure

Individual differences

> **Activity**
> **12.6: Arousal curves**
> In Figure 12.29, what do the arousal curves depicted tell you about the three athletes?
> 1. Who is capable of the best performance?
> 2. Who needs to be really psyched up before he performs at his best?
> 3. Whose level of arousal needs to be very carefully controlled for good performance?
> Your answers should be: 1, Sam; 2, Jon; 3, Ted. You should note, however, that these are stylized graphs. Actual arousal–performance curves are much more variable than these.

Task differences

It is not possible to predict exactly what level of arousal is best for any one sport activity—so much depends on circumstance and the personalities of the competitors, but there are some general rules which help competitors and coaches:

- **Simple and complex tasks**—we consider it to be easier to kick a penalty in rugby from in front of the posts than from the side-line. What we usually mean in saying that a task is easier is that there is a greater margin for deviation from the movement plan, while still staying within the boundaries of successful execution. Note that we are referring here to inherently simple and complex tasks. Obviously, a task becomes easier for an individual to perform as he/she becomes more practised at it. Thus, simple tasks have a broader optimal arousal zone than complex tasks; i.e., individuals can tolerate greater arousal levels before successful turns into unsuccessful performance.

- **Fine and gross tasks**—as with complex tasks, fine motor tasks have less margin for error than gross motor tasks; they require precision of movement. Compare putting in golf with weightlifting. If you watch these two sports on television you will notice that a golfer tries to relax and calm down before putting, while the weightlifter really tries to 'psych himself up'. Individuals tackling gross motor tasks can tolerate greater levels of arousal before errors appear than those dealing with fine motor tasks.

- **Strength or endurance and information processing tasks**—another difference between golf putting and weightlifting is that the former has information processing as a key component. High arousal levels seem to interfere with information processing; thus skills in which this is important are more likely to be adversely affected than skills such as weightlifting in which the performer's concern is to summon as much of his/her strength and/or endurance as possible.

Figure 12.30 illustrates the optimal arousal levels for the six types of task discussed, but again you should note that these are largely hypothetical and that obtaining research data which confirms the relationships indicated is not easy. What seems to be clear from experience (Gill, 1986), however, is that:

- optimal arousal levels can be identified;
- these vary across individuals and activities;
- ability to control arousal is the key to successful performance.

Martens (1989) put forward an interesting critique of arousal theory, suggesting that it is more useful to think in terms of positive and negative psychic energy. Such discussion is outside the scope of this book, but interested students might like to follow up his ideas by reading further.

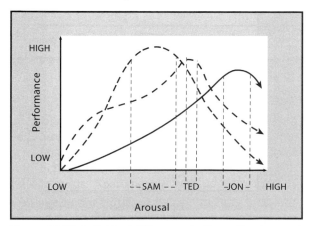

Figure 12.29 Individual differences in the optimal arousal zone. (*Adapted from Martens, 1989.*)

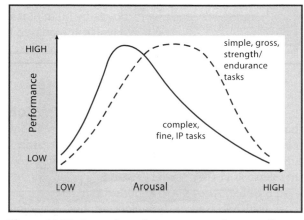

Figure 12.30 Arousal–performance curve for gross/fine, simple/complex and strength/IP motor tasks.

The attribution process

Investigation

Investigation
12.7: To introduce the concept of attribution
Method: Play a small-number-a-side game, such as basketball, netball or five-a-side soccer. Play to a win/lose situation, i.e. avoid a draw. After the game, the players individually write down four reasons why they think their own team won or lost. In addition, each states whether or not he/she would like to play against the same team again, with the same team-mates, in the near future.
Discussion: As a class group, pool these statements. Categorize them into groups of similar reasons, e.g. 'we played well as a team' with 'we had some good players'. These reasons are known as attributions.

1. How many categories did you construct?
2. Consider the relationship between wanting/not wanting to play again and winning/losing—does any pattern emerge?

The process of ascribing reasons for, or causes to, events and behaviours is known as **attribution**. When something significant happens to us, such as winning or losing an important game, we ask ourselves 'why?'. Sport psychologists have asked two important questions about this:

- What sorts of reasons do sportspersons give?
- How does this affect their future participation and chances of success?

Weiner's (1974) attributional theory of achievement behaviour has been widely applied to sport contexts. He suggests that one of the differences between high and low achievers (Weiner, 1974, p. 307) is the way in which each group develops attributions about success and failure. He proposes a model with four types of attribution (though recognizes that these are not the only attributions), as shown in Figure 12.31. Weiner's four types of attribution are:

- **Ability**—the extent of the performer's capacity to cope with the task.
- **Effort**—the amount of mental and physical effort the performer gives to the task.
- **Task difficulty**—the extent of the problems posed by the task, including the strength of the opposition.
- **Luck**—factors attributable to chance, such as the weather or the state of the pitch.

To what extent did the categories you derived in doing Investigation 12.7 correspond to these?

Weiner also organized his categories into two dimensions (Figure 12.31), which he termed **locus of causality** and **stability**. The word 'locus' is derived from the Latin 'place'; thus the 'locus of causality' indicates where the individual perceives the cause of success or failure to lie. In this case, the two categories are internal (ability and effort) or external (task difficulty and luck) to the individual. The stability dimension implies that two of the factors (ability and task difficulty) are relatively stable, i.e. not subject to change (in the short term at least), whereas the other two (effort and luck) can vary from competition to competition or even within an activity.

Weiner did not claim that these dimensions were exclusive and further research (Weiner, 1979) identified a third, that of controllability. This is the extent to which the outcome of a situation is under control (by the individual or others) or is uncontrollable (Figure 12.32).

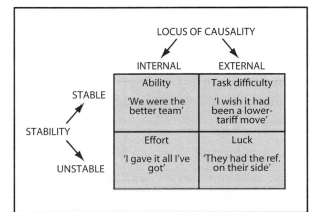

Figure 12.31 Weiner's model of causal attribution.

Figure 12.32 The control dimension!

Key Point

These attributions affect a sportsperson's view of his/her sport in three important ways:

- Feelings of pride and satisfaction.
- Expectancy.
- Learned helplessness and avoidance.

Feelings of pride and dissatisfaction (affective responses)

Figure 12.33 shows the results that were obtained when two teams of basketball players were asked to state the extent to which they felt satisfied with their performance after a game, in terms of the four categories of attribution. These results appear to be fairly typical (Weiner, 1974) and suggest that if we attribute our success in an activity to internal factors, such as ability and effort, we are more likely to feel satisfaction with our performance than if we put our winning down to luck or the ease of the task. In the same way, we experience greater feelings of disappointment if we perceive our losing to be due to internal rather than external factors.

Expectancy

In addition to predicting the probability of a performer feeling satisfaction or disappointment with the outcome of an activity, attribution theory attempts to explain the way in which we come to expect certain things to happen.

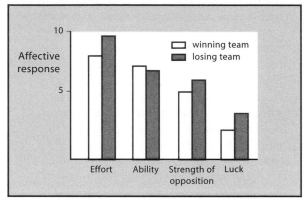

Figure 12.33 Affective responses and attributions.

 Investigation

12.8: To investigate the effect of attribution on the expectation of subsequent success or failure

Method: Select a group of students who do not know the purpose of the task. Divide this group into four.

1. Devise four motor tasks, one for each group. The tasks should have a clear goal to be attained and should be as follows:

a. Luck plays a major part in success or failure; e.g. throwing a dice for a specified number (code letter U).

b. Effort plays a major part; e.g. improving previous performance on a simple strength task (code letter U).

c. Ability is of importance—any novel motor task (code letter S).

d. Task difficulty is central—this can be simulated by selecting a relatively simple task, but distracting the performer during it (code letter S).

The code letters refer to whether the task is likely to produce stable or unstable reasons for the result.

2. Measure the subjects' performance in their

particular task by noting whether they succeed or fail.

3. Suggest to them that they are going to do the task again (in fact they are not). Ask each subject whether they think they are going to succeed or fail at the second attempt.

4. Mark each subject in one of the boxes in Figure 12.34: for example, if they succeeded in their task, but couldn't predict the outcome of the proposed second attempt, they would be marked in box 'C'. Mark the subject with the letter that corresponds to the attribution task they did, as in Figure 12.34.

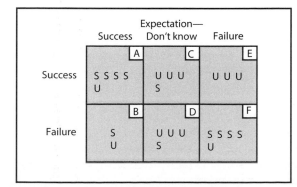

Figure 12.34 Result of Investigation 12.8.

Investigation

12.8 continued

Discussion: Theory suggests that you might obtain results as in Figure 12.34. If you did not, can you offer an explanation? Do you think the hypothesis is faulty, or was there something different or special about your sample or your method? For example, do you think it is legitimate to assume that the subjects would attribute success or failure in the way suggested by the tasks?

Figure 12.34 suggests that people who attribute success or failure in an activity to stable factors are more likely to expect the same outcome next time they perform than if unstable attributions are made.

Learned helplessness and avoidance

Why is it that some people seem to give up very easily if a task is difficult? If you ask some of your non-sporting friends why they don't join, for example, the badminton club, the initial response may well be 'I don't like sport', but if you persist you may get answers such as 'I'm no good at badminton', 'I never was any good and I never will be' or 'I'm useless at all sport'. Dweck (1980) calls this learned helplessness and sees the cause as the individual attributing early difficulties to internal, stable and global factors. The global–specific dimension relates to whether failure is seen to be specific to the particular activity or generalized to other areas of sport ('I'm useless at sport' is a global attribution). People who suffer from learned helplessness in sport tend to attribute failure to causes which are internal, unchanging and apply to most situations.

The application of attribution theory

The attribution process can be summarized as in Figure 12.35. Clearly, the theory carries implications for coaches and trainers. Performers are more likely to do well if they think they are going to do so, which in turn depends on how they attribute their success and failure in the past. It is part of the coach's job to help the performer achieve initial success and then attribute this to stable, internal and controllable factors.

Coaches need to be aware that athletes do not always make logical attributions, based on the evidence of the competition. Even if attributions are logical, coaches need to help the athlete to ascribe success to internal, stable factors and failure to unstable factors.

Athletes with low self-esteem tend to ascribe internal and stable causes to failure and unstable causes to success, and confident athletes the reverse. For example:

- 'I lost because my backhand is just not good enough at this level' (internal–stable: ability).

- 'Well, I won that game, but only because she was serving so badly' (external–stable: task difficulty or ease).

These are typical attributions of a player who has lost confidence—they are not helpful, because they emphasize stable factors, i.e. factors which cannot be changed easily. They may not be an accurate reflection of the games, in which case the coach should offer an alternative assessment (with evidence), so changing attributions from stable to unstable, or emphasizing internal control:

- 'No, your backhand's fine normally; you were just not getting into position quickly enough.

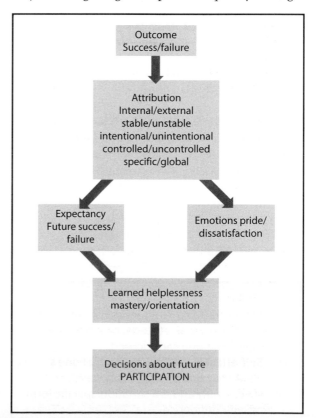

Figure 12.35 The attribution process.

Make that extra effort when you see it coming onto the backhand' (internal–unstable: effort).

- 'No, it wasn't weak serving; it was your good returns. Keep returning the ball deep, as you are, and you've got him/her' (internal–stable).

'Even if the player's attributions are an accurate reflection of what is happening, the coach should try to attribute failure to unstable causes and success to internal causes:

- "Yes, we need to work on your backhand, but I know what the problem is, and it's easily put right; work your strong forehand for now' (internal–unstable: effort).
- "OK, she had some uncharacteristic double faults, but that shows you've got her worried. Keep the pressure on' (internal–stable: ability).

Attribution training is becoming increasingly important in sport—you can hear the positive outcomes of this when you listen to debriefing with athletes and sportspeople on television. On the whole they make internal attributions, which is a sign of competitive maturity. If an athlete is consistently making external attributions for defeat, then this is likely to have long-term negative effects on performance, so the coach needs to consider attributional re-training. This might be done by a programme of:

- 'recording, classifying and discussing attributions for success and defeat;
- 'using video to analyse performance and adjust attribution;
- 'devising a clear goal-setting programme which includes appropriate attribution strategies.

Self-confidence and self-efficacy

In Section 12.2 we studied self-esteem as an aspect of personality and recognized the importance of the 'self-concept wheel' (see Figure 12.14) in enhancing performance and ensuring success. In this section we study self-confidence and self-efficacy as aspects of self-esteem.

Self-confidence is probably one of the most important psychological prerequisites for success in

sport. Self-confident athletes believe in their ability to develop the knowledge, skills and attitudes to succeed; athletes who lack self-confidence doubt their abilities, or assume that opponents inevitably 'have the edge' over them. This represents what has been termed the '**self-fulfilling prophesy**', i.e. that expecting something to happen tends to cause it to happen. We all recognize this phenomenon in ourselves and others, but how does it happen?

Weinberg and Gould (1995, pp. 301–302) outlined the psychology of self-confidence:

- 'Confidence arouses positive emotions, allowing the athlete to remain calm under pressure and assertive when required.
- 'Confidence facilitates concentration and a focus on the important aspects of the task. Lack of confidence causes stress under pressure and thus concentration on outside stressors, i.e. mistakes or spectators.
- 'Confidence affects goal-setting. Confident athletes set challenging but realistic goals. Athletes lacking in confidence set goals for themselves which are either too easy or too difficult.
- 'Confidence increases effort.
- 'Confidence affects game strategies. A confident player plays to win, even if it means taking risks. A nonconfident player tries to avoid mistakes.
- Confidence affects psychological momentum. Nonconfident athletes find it difficult to reverse negative psychological momentum, i.e. once things start to go wrong they find it difficult to think positively, whereas confident athletes take each point or play at a time and never give up, even when defeat stares them in the face.

Of course, overconfidence or false confidence is dangerous because it leads to inadequate preparation and low motivation and/or arousal, both of which are difficult (though not impossible) to correct once the competition is under way.

There are a number of theoretical models of self-confidence (see Cox, 1994, pp. 219–227), of which the most widely reported is that of Bandura (1977) and shown in Figure 12.36. This model brings together several ideas that have been discussed separately in this section. Bandura theorizes that there are **four factors** that affect the expectations of future success which an athlete holds and thus determine self-efficacy. These are performance accomplishments, modelling (sometimes referred to as **vicarious experience**), verbal persuasion and emotional arousal. All are important. We discussed in Chapter 11 the coach's role in helping the athlete to **model** performance on someone who is already skilled and

---

Key Points
- **Self-confidence** is an aspect of self-esteem—it is an attitude, based on the belief that one can succeed.
- **Self-efficacy** is the perception of one's ability to perform a particular task successfully and is a situation-specific form of self-confidence.

successful. Good demonstration by a successful model not only assists skill acquisition, but helps the athlete to think 'if I can perform like that, I'll be a good player too.'

We also discussed the role of **persuasion** in changing attitudes. In Bandura's model the coach establishes a positive attitude by convincing athletes that they are capable of performing well. **Emotional arousal** refers to the motivational component of all performance situations, discussed above.

Many sport psychologists claim that the most important of the four elements in developing self-efficacy is the '**performance accomplishments**' element. This is because success (and failure) in sport is very obvious and clear-cut. It gives the athlete very direct feedback and is an indication of current status and a signpost for the future. If you are successful in one competition, you will feel confident about the next; if you fail, you may worry about the next.

> **Key Points**
> The coach or teacher has a fundamental role to play in developing self-confidence and self-efficacy through successful achievement:
> - to ensure early and continued success during the learning process by the careful selection of goals, tasks and levels of competition,
> - by focusing on successful personal performance and not on winning.

The second Key Point is a fundamental one in all coaching and teaching and cannot be overstated. Success should be defined by how well athletes play or perform in relation to their ability and their 'personal best', and not by whether or not they win. Such an attitude was typified by the British men's

4×400 m track relay squad, interviewed after their run in the Atlanta Olympic Games. They had hoped to win gold, and thought they could, but in coming second took pride in having broken national and European records and were bubbling with confidence and optimism for future races.

Weinberg and Gould's (1995, p. 313) recipe for building confidence is shown in Figure 12.37.

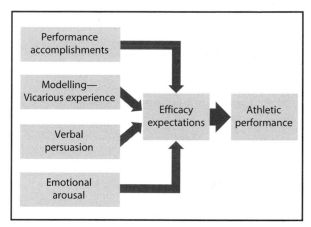

Figure 12.36 Bandura's (1977) theory of self-efficacy.

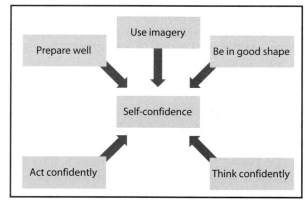

Figure 12.37 Developing self-confidence. (*Adapted from Weinberg and Gould, 1995.*)

 # Summary

1. Motivation can be categorized into intrinsic and extrinsic forms. Extrinsic rewards have a powerful effect in developing and modifying behaviour. In certain circumstances, adding an external reward to a situation that is already intrinsically motivating decreases that motivation. Rewards do not automatically undermine intrinsic motivation, but current thinking suggests that as intrinsic motivation and participation for their own sake develop, so tangible rewards become redundant and should be withdrawn or used very sparingly.

2. An individual's drive to achieve success for its own sake is known as achievement motivation. Four factors contribute to this: two personality factors—the need to achieve and the need to avoid failure, and two situational factors—the probability of success and the incentive value of that success. Research shows that people with low achievement orientation tend to choose tasks

Summary

continued

which are either very easy or very difficult, whereas high achievers tend to select tasks where there is a fifty–fifty chance of success.

3. The process of ascribing reasons for, or causes to, events is known as attribution. Weiner (1986) suggested that one of the differences between high and low achievers is the way in which each group develops attributions about success and failure. He developed two dimensions of attribution: locus of causality and stability. Later, other dimensions were added. If success in an activity is attributed to internal factors, such as ability and effort, satisfaction with performance is more likely to be felt than if external attributions, e.g. task difficulty or luck, are involved. In addition to the emotions of pride in, or dissatisfaction with, performance, certain expectations of outcome (future success or failure) accrue. Sportspeople who attribute success or failure in a task to stable factors are more likely to expect the same outcome next time than they would if unstable factors are involved. Attribution theory contains many implications for coaches.

4. Arousal is the state of alertness and anticipation that exists before, during and after a sports performance—and, indeed, throughout our lives. It has physiological and cognitive components.

5. Drive theory suggests that as arousal increases to meet the demands of a task, so the dominant motor habit is increasingly likely to be reflected in performance

6. The inverted-U theory suggests that as arousal increases, so up to an optimal level does potential performance, after which that performance deteriorates. Coaches and sportspeople accept that optimal arousal levels can be identified, but that these vary between individuals and with the type of task. Ability to control arousal seems to be a vital aspect of successful performance.

7. Self-confidence (a general personality trait) and self-efficacy (a situation-specific form of self-confidence) are essential for success in sport and physical activity generally. Coaches and teachers can increase self-confidence by careful planning of their teaching and by sensitive use of teaching or coaching style and interactions.

Review Questions

1. Define the terms 'motivation' and 'motives' and distinguish between intrinsic and extrinsic rewards in sport, using examples.

2. Sketch a graph which shows the relationship between motivation (arousal) and performance of (a) a simple and (b) a complex task.

3. Sketch Weiner's (1974) model of attributions and give sport-related examples of each component of the model. Explain 'locus of causality' and 'stability'.

4. What is meant by 'self-efficacy' in sport? Give at least five ways in which a coach can build an athlete's positive approach to competition.

Exam-Style Questions

1. **a.** It is assumed that there is a relationship between the levels of a person's motivation-induced arousal and the quality with which he/she performs a sport skill. Draw appropriately labelled sketch graphs to illustrate how each of the following theories represents this relationship:

i. Drive theory. (2 marks)

ii. Inverted 'U' theory. (2 marks)

b. Briefly describe how **each** of the two theories explains the relationship between arousal and the quality of performance. (6 marks)

c. Comment on the ability of these two theories to explain how changes in the level of motivation may affect the level of performance in the competitive situation. (10 marks)

Exam-Style Questions

continued

2. **a. i.** Briefly define **self-confidence** in a sports performer. (3 marks)

ii. Contrast the ways in which **high** and **low** levels of confidence might affect a sportsperson's performance. (5 marks)

b. A sport participant's performance has deteriorated because of a loss of confidence.

i. Explain possible sport-related causes for this loss in confidence. (6 marks)

ii. How might the coach attempt to **improve** the self-confidence of the performer? (6 marks)

3. **Motivation** is a central issue in sports psychology.

a. The **theory of attribution** suggests that attribution can affect a player's or team's motivation to succeed and to persist with a sport. Figure 12.38 partly illustrates **Weiner's** model of attribution.

i. Give a definition of attribution **in a sporting context,** and explain what is meant by **internal** and **external** locus of causality. (3 marks)

ii. Explain the **stability** dimension. (2 marks)

iii. Redraw the model and put **one** appropriate attribution into each of the **four** boxes. (4 marks)

iv. As a coach, how would you use this model to decide what to say to your team if they had just lost, but played well? (5 marks)

b. An individual's motivation to achieve success for its own sake is known as **achievement motivation**.

i. What are the characteristics of a young person who is motivated to achieve in sport, and give an example from sport of someone who has a high motive to **avoid failure**. (4 marks)

ii. Given that there are motives to succeed and motives to avoid failure in sporting activities, identify the **factors** which might **affect** the **adoption** of these **two** types of motives. (2 marks)

iii. As coach, how would you try to ensure that your players have **motives to succeed**? (5 marks)

4. **a.** Coaches use a number of different techniques to raise the level of performance of their athletes. Differentiate between **rewards** and **goals,** both of which may be used by a coach. (4 marks)

b. Explain the difference between **intrinsic** and **extrinsic** types of reward, giving a sport example of each. Comment briefly on the relative value of each of these types of reward. (6 marks)

c. i. Define **goal-setting** and briefly describe its purpose in attempting to improve sport performance. (3 marks)

ii. Discuss the procedures a coach should try to adopt to try to ensure that the setting of goals will result in improved sport performance. (7 marks)

5. **a.** Figure 12.39 shows two hypothetical relationships between the level of motivation and quality of performance. With reference to the diagram:

i. Name the **two** hypotheses represented by the graphs. (2 marks)

ii. **Briefly** explain the relationship between motivation and skilled sport performance as proposed by each of these hypotheses. (5 marks)

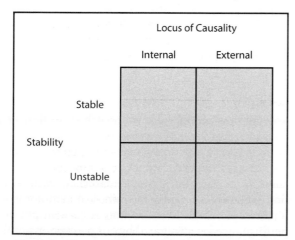

Figure 12.38 (*Adapted from 'Causal attribution model' by Weiner, 1980.*)

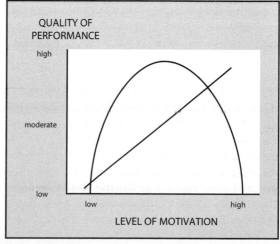

Figure 12.39

Exam-Style Questions

continued

b. i. Based on your answer to **a. i.** sketch **two** hypothetical graphs to illustrate differences in the motivation–performance relationship for fine and gross motor skills. (2 marks)

ii. Give a sport example for both **fine** and **gross** categories of motor skill. (2 marks)

iii. Discuss the implications of the graphs you have drawn for the precompetition psychological preparation of the performers. (5 marks)

c. Large financial prizes have often been blamed for unsporting behaviour during competitions. Critically discuss this opinion in relation to motivation theory. (4 marks)

6. Figure 12.40 shows the kinds of **attributions** thought to be common in sport.

a. What are **attributions**? (2 marks)

b. How are emotional reactions thought to be related to the types of attributions made in sport? (7 marks)

c. With reference to sport examples, explain what is meant by the **self-serving bias** in attribution theory. (4 marks)

d. Those who fail in sport may, at some time, experience **learned helplessness**. What is learned helplessness and what role do attributions play in its development? (6 marks)

Figure 12.40 Sport attributions. (*Adapted from Weiner, 1972.*)

12.6 The Nature of Stress

Keywords & concepts

anxiety	galvanic skin response	short-term goals
biofeedback	goal-setting	state anxiety
cognitive stress	imagery	stress
management	intermediate goals	stressor
competitive state and/or	long-term goals	trait anxiety
trait anxiety	mental rehearsal	zone of optimal
electromyography	progressive relaxation	functioning
eustress	training	

On completion of Section 12.6 you will be able to:

- 'define stress and differentiate stress and anxiety;
- 'understand the need to manage stress in sport situations;
- 'define trait and state anxiety and give examples of each from sport contexts;
- 'describe how stress can be monitored, using a range of physiological and psychological measures;
- 'describe how stress can be managed and controlled in sport or performance contexts, including cognitive and somatic techniques and goal-setting.

Anxiety

You are now aware, from your work in Section 12.5, that a certain level of arousal is necessary for your best possible performance in sport. Arousal responses are generated by a variety of means—some are automatic, some are associated with emotion (you will recognize the physical symptoms of, for example, anger). Those associated with physical performance are generated by our perceptions of the demands of the situation. We know that in a practice or recreational game it is less important that we do not fail. In a championship game, however, it is very important that we live up to the demands of the situation, of our team-mates, and of our supporters; even the most confident of us has occasional doubts. These doubts can, if we dwell on them, generate high arousal, and may lead to **anxiety**.

Key Points

- **Anxiety** is an emotional state, similar to fear, associated with physiological (somatic) and psychological (cognitive) arousal and with feelings of nervousness and apprehension. Anxiety has two components—trait anxiety and state anxiety.
- **Trait anxiety** is 'a behavioural disposition which predisposes a person to perceive objectively non-dangerous circumstances as threatening and to respond to these with state anxiety levels disproportionate to the level of threat' (Weinberg and Gould, 1995, p. 94).
- **State anxiety** is an emotional response to particular situations, characterized by feelings of nervousness and apprehension.

Trait anxiety is a personality variable. If a person has high trait anxiety, he/she tends to be fearful of unfamiliar situations and to respond with obvious anxiety symptoms.

State anxiety is an emotional response, often temporary, which exists in relation to particular situations. For example, if you become nervous before a dance production but not a team game, you are showing state anxiety in relation to dance. People with high trait anxiety usually have higher state anxiety in competitive or evaluative situations than those with low trait anxiety.

Spielberger *et al.* (1970) developed a self-report inventory to measure levels of state and trait anxiety in general situations. It is known as the State Trait Anxiety Inventory (STAI). It is not easily obtained, but an excerpt from it can be found in Carron (1981). Martens (1977) developed a sport-specific competitive trait anxiety measure, the Sport Competition Anxiety Test (SCAT). This has proved more helpful in investigating anxiety in sportspeople because it deals specifically with sport. You should note, however, that it is a test of competitive trait anxiety; that is the tendency to be anxious in sport contexts in general. The state anxiety version of this test is the Competitive State Anxiety Inventory (CSAI) (Martens *et al.*, 1990).

 Investigation

12.9: To investigate the relationship between competitive trait anxiety as measured by SCAT, and state anxiety prior to an important sport event

Method: Select a group of people who are involved in competitive sport at a high level, for example your school or college first team or a local club team. Obtain their permission to administer two simple questionnaires, at a mutually convenient time. Use SCAT (Roberts *et al.*, 1986, p. 68) to obtain a trait anxiety score, and the following question (adapted from Roberts *et al.*, 1986, p. 66) to obtain a crude state anxiety score for each player:

'Imagine that it is a few minutes before a very important league or championship game or event. You have been beaten only once this season, by today's opponent(s). How do you feel with a few minutes to go before the start of the game or event?'

Very anxious 9 8 7 6 5 4 3 2 1 Not at all anxious

Results: Follow the scoring system for SCAT in Roberts *et al.* (1986). Using each respondent's SCAT and state anxiety (SA) scores, compute the Spearman's Rank Correlation Coefficient. *Discussion:* What does the correlation coefficient tell you about the relationship between SCAT and SA scores? Discuss the implications of this for the team's coach or for the sportspeople themselves.

Research along the lines of Investigation 12.9 (Scanlan and Passer, 1979) suggests that:

- competitive trait anxiety and pre-game state anxiety are correlated;
- high trait anxiety tends to cause high pre-game state anxiety;
- winners tend to experience less post-game anxiety than do losers.

SCAT and STAI are self-report, psychometric approaches to anxiety measurement. In this sense they are equivalent to the personality tests (Eysenck and Cattell) discussed in Section 12.2.

From Section 12.5 you know that achieving optimum levels of arousal before and during performance is not easy. The extrinsic factors which are likely to affect what Hanin (1980) called the '**zone of**

optimal functioning' (A–B in Figure 12.28) are: complexity of the task; the open–closed (information processing) nature of the task; the importance of the result. To these we must add the intrinsic factors—the ability and experience of the athlete and his/her **level of trait anxiety**.

What this means is that if a coach is working with a young, relatively inexperienced figure skater on the compulsory figures (closed skill) for an important competition and the skater's levels of trait anxiety are high, then the prime task of the coach is to work on relaxation and stress management strategies to bring her arousal level as far down as possible, so that state anxiety prior to competition does not have a detrimental effect.

Conversely, a weightlifter with low trait anxiety levels probably cannot be too psyched-up before an important lift.

Stress

So far we have used the term 'anxiety' to refer to the negative aspects of arousal. Another term which you will come across in your reading and with which you are familiar is 'stress'. Often the two terms are used interchangeably. Arriving at a generally agreed definition of stress is difficult because of the differing theoretical perspectives adopted by researchers. For example, is stress a stimulus, a response or an interaction between stimulus and response? Is it what causes us to feel sick before an exam, or is stress the resultant 'butterflies'? Current usage, led by the work of Selye (1976), tends to favour the latter.

Key Point
- Stress is defined by Selye (1976) as 'the non-specific response of the body to any demand made on it'. The sources of stress are referred to as stressors.

Some stressors are universal—everyone would be worried by a loud, unexplained noise in the night. But others, for example performing in front of an audience, may be stressful to one person but not to someone who is used to the experience and enjoys the challenge.

Stressors come in many forms. Pargman (1986) lists the following:
- social,
- chemical or biochemical,
- bacterial,
- physical,
- climatic,
- psychological.

Those involved in physical activity are very aware of the last three. The physical pain resulting from a sports injury, ill-fitting dancers' shoes or the final stages of a long-distance race or walk causes the participant considerable stress, as perhaps you know.

The weather can be a stressor. Heat stress is something that marathon runners have to be able to deal with, and very cold, wet weather brings the danger of hypothermia for those involved in outdoor pursuits.

Psychological stress results from a mismatch between a person's perception of the demands of a situation and a self-assessment of his/her ability to cope, given that the outcome is important, as illustrated in Figure 12.41.

Selye's (1976) theory of stress proposes that the body reacts to all these stressors in the same way. He suggests that there is a General Adaptation Syndrome (GAS) which has three stages, as illustrated in Figure 12.42. In the alarm reaction stage, the body is alerted to deal with the stressor. This is when breathing and heart rate quicken and adrenaline is released.

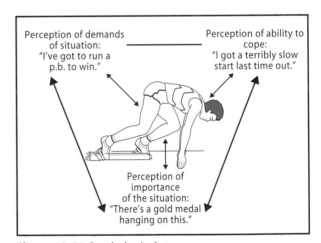

Figure 12.41 Psychological stress.

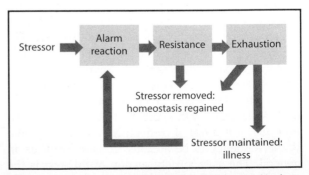

Figure 12.42 The General Adaptation Syndrome. (*Seyle, 1976*).

During the resistance stage, a series of hormonal and chemical changes attempt to maintain homeostasis, that is, the delicate biochemical and fluid balance which allows our body to function effectively. Selye (1976) defines a stressor as anything which disturbs this balance.

The final stage is that of exhaustion, when the product of the strength of the stressor and the length of time during which it acts is such that the body can no longer put up any resistance. Exhaustion is the body's last defence. If this stops the stressor (if, for example, you have been pushing yourself too hard in a 13 km run and you drop out), then the body recovers homeostasis. But if you drop exhausted in a blizzard on Ben Nevis without having gained shelter, then the stressor (the cold) persists in spite of your body having stopped, and you may well not recover.

Psychological stressors do not have as powerful an effect on the body as the others, but over a long period of time will take their toll on general health.

You should note at this stage that several writers (e.g. Harris and Harris, 1984) discuss **eustress**, or 'good' stress, associated with thrill and excitement. This should not be confused with optimal levels of arousal. The stressor is there and the body is resisting, but the individual enjoys, and may even seek out, the sensation (Figure 12.43). Mo Anthoine, a climber and mountaineer, has said:

> *The truth is, I like an unforgiving climate where if you make mistakes you suffer for it. That's what turns me on. I think it's because there is always a question mark about how you will perform.*

> (Alvarez, 1988, p. 151.)

In general, however, stress is something to be avoided in sport, for its effects, as with anxiety, may inhibit performance:

- It may act directly on the information processing and motor elements of skill. Muscles tense, muscular control is reduced, concentration is difficult, our span of attention is narrowed and we don't attend to the things we should (Figure 12.44).
- Our awareness of being under stress may itself act as a stressor (Figure 12.45).

Martens (1989) suggests that there are three forms of stress symptoms—physiological, psychological and behavioural:

- **Physiological symptoms**—increased heart rate; increased blood pressure; increased sweating; increased respiration; decreased flow of blood to the skin; increased oxygen uptake; dry mouth.
- **Psychological symptoms**—worry; feeling overwhelmed; inability to make decisions; inability to concentrate; inability to direct attention appropriately; narrowing of attention; feeling out-of-control.
- **Behavioural symptoms**—rapid talking; nail biting; pacing; scowling; yawning; trembling; raised voice pitch; frequent urination.

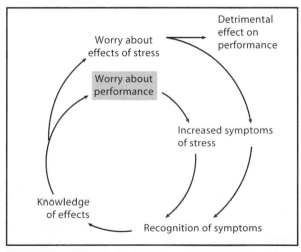

Figure 12.44 Attentional narrowing.

Figure 12.43 Climbers as stress-seekers?

Figure 12.45 The stress spiral.

Measurement of stress

These symptoms are used to identify and measure stress. There are essentially three types of stress measurement:

- **Self-report questionnaires**—two examples of these (STAI and SCAT) are dealt with above; there are many other similar inventories.
- **Observation techniques**—these are used extensively by coaches and consist of observing and monitoring the behavioural aspects of stress listed above in relation to particular aspects of competition and training; thus, over a period of time the coach learns what the athlete finds stressful and can work to avoid or overcome this.
- **Physiological responses**—many of the physiological responses listed above can be measured directly; for example, heart rate, temperature, oxygen uptake, sweating by a galvanic skin response apparatus. Under appropriate supervision, blood analysis can be carried out to measure hormonal responses. All these are useful to establish pregame levels of stress, but it must be remembered that exercise itself produces similar responses and therefore to measure stress during or immediately after performance is very difficult.

The management of stress

It should now be clear to you that, in sport and other physical activities, the most damaging form of stress is that which is self-induced through worrying about the performance to come. Physical activity is inherently arousing, so in most cases becoming adequately 'psyched up' is no problem; the difficulty is in limiting anxiety to manageable levels. This means breaking the 'stress spiral' (see Figure 12.45). Since we know that the mind and body work in very close harmony in the production of skilled movement, it is no surprise that there are two places we can break the spiral; we can deal with the mind by replacing negative thoughts with positive ones (**cognitive management**) and we can eliminate many of the harmful physiological responses to stress by persuading the body that the stressor does not exist (**somatic management**). For this we use relaxation. There are four forms of relaxation:

- imagery,
- self-directed,
- progressive relaxation training,
- biofeedback.

Imagery relaxation involves picturing yourself in a place where you feel very comfortable and safe. You should try to see yourself there as vividly as you can, relaxed, warm, at ease; evoke the sounds, the smells, the whole 'feel' of the place. It helps if you are in a quiet and comfortable setting in reality, but eventually you learn to use the technique whenever you feel stressed. To make imagery relaxation work well, you need to (Martens, 1989):

- think of a place which has clear associations of warmth and relaxation;
- possess good imagery skills;
- practise the technique initially in nonstressful situations, before using it to control competitive stress.

Self-directed relaxation is a simplified form of progressive relaxation training (PRT), developed in the 1930s. PRT involves learning to tense and then deeply relax separate muscle groups. Tensing a muscle is not difficult, but thoroughly relaxing it is, and takes several weeks of practice. Self-directed relaxation involves focusing on each of the major muscle groups in turn, simultaneously allowing the breathing to become slow and easy. As you focus on each muscle, visualize the tension flowing out of it until it is completely relaxed. Work through all the muscle groups in this way. Whereas initially you need to relax muscles separately to obtain the required relaxation effect, as you become more proficient you can combine groups and achieve total body relaxation very quickly. Martens (1989, p. 123) gives a useful script which you can ask someone to read to you, or can tape, to help start. Alternatively, there are several relaxation audio tapes on the market.

A similar technique is suggested by Benson (1976), but his focus is just on breathing and hence is closer to meditation than relaxation. You should find a quiet setting and concentrate totally on your breathing. As you breathe out, silently repeat a single syllable word which has no particular meaning for you. If you find your attention wandering, just bring your mind back to your breathing.

You may find that it is difficult to feel the difference between tension and relaxation in your muscles. In this case, biofeedback may be helpful, for it is a technique which gives you direct information about what is happening in your body. We have suggested that physiological responses to stress can be measured. Biofeedback does this and teaches you how to use your mind to change the reading. There are three main types of biofeedback:

- **Skin temperature**—when muscles are relaxed, more blood flows to the skin and skin temperature rises; this can be detected by sensitive electrothermometers taped to the skin. If you are stressed, blood is diverted from the skin to the tense muscles so the skin becomes cold. As you relax, using imagery relaxation techniques, the reading changes, which provides feedback and reinforces the relaxation.

- **Galvanic skin response**—a means of measuring the electrical conductivity of the skin, which increases when the skin is moist. When the muscles are tense, sweating occurs to remove the heat generated, thereby increasing the skin conductivity, which can be measured using a simple battery-operated device. This device provides immediate feedback on how successful you are at relaxing.
- **Electromyography (EMG)**—electrodes are taped to the skin over specific muscles whose state of tension or relaxation can then be monitored. This is very helpful if you have a problem with tension in a specific muscle group during performance.

Relaxation techniques can be invaluable for reducing stress prior to an important sport event. They sound easy, but in fact it takes some time to learn to do them really effectively. The drawback is that whereas you do wish to remove stress, you do not want to remove all muscle tension before your game or event. Your aim, therefore, is to prepare the body to remove unhelpful tension, so that you can then effectively direct your thoughts and attention to the task in hand.

Mental preparation for performance

Cognitive stress management involves controlling emotions and thought processes prior to, during and after competition or performance, and is closely linked to the achievement and attribution processes discussed in Section 12.5. It is about eliminating negative feelings about oneself and the sports situation, and developing confidence. Coaches and performers use a great variety of methods—there is not scope here to go into these in any depth, but many recent sports psychology texts, written for sportspeople and coaches (e.g. Bull, 1991; Nideffer, 1992) deal with these issues in detail.

Self-confidence is an important aspect of our personality in everyday life. As with any aspect of character, if taken to extremes it can be annoying to others; but there is no doubt that, if you believe in yourself and your ability, you are more likely to succeed in reaching your goals than if you do not. Ways of developing self-confidence are discussed in Section 12.5.

Mental rehearsal (sometimes referred to as mental imagery or mental practice) is increasingly being recognized as an important skill and many top class sportspeople use it in some form, although it takes some time to learn how to rehearse effectively. In essence, it involves consciously imagining the performance, either by re-running a past experience, as if in 'action replay', or by previewing a hoped-for success. Sharp (1992) gives a fuller explanation of the concept.

Evidence shows that mental rehearsal can help a sportsperson concentrate before an event, can create self-confidence, help him/her focus on strengths and weaknesses, and also assist in the learning and improving of skills. However, Nideffer warns that 'no amount of mental rehearsal will help you perform well if you lack technical skill. There is no substitute for actual practice' (Nideffer, 1992, p. 4).

Research (e.g. Hird *et al.*, 1991) suggests that mental rehearsal is not as effective in skill acquisition as well-structured physical practice, but can still have a positive effect on learning.

Goal-setting is an important aspect of any sportsperson's preparation, whether for competition or performance. If performer and teacher or coach are aware of what is being aimed for, then success is more likely. This is because:
- learning is focused;
- uncertainty is reduced;
- confidence is increased;
- practice is planned and structured;
- evaluation and feedback are specific.

If goals are structured so that they are relatively easily attained initially and then progressively become more difficult, the early success necessary for confidence-building is more likely.

Goals should be identified and training planned, first by specifying a long-term goal, something that can be worked towards over the next 9–12 months. You might, for example, be aiming for a place in an Olympic team or for a particular competition score. This is then broken down into intermediate and short-term goals which lead to the long-term goal. For example, a skater might have the long-term goal of becoming the national junior champion in 12 months' time. One of the intermediate goals might then be to learn a routine which would catch the judges' eye and be awarded a high score, so the short-term goal would be practising particular sections of this routine.

Goals should be:
- stated positively;
- specific to the situation and the performer;
- time phased;
- challenging;
- achievable;
- measurable;
- negotiated between the sportsperson and coach;
- progressive, from short term to long term;
- performance-orientated rather than outcome-orientated.

This last point is important and relates our earlier discussion in Section 12.5 about reinforcing good performance rather than focusing on winning.

Goals should also be:

- written down;
- reviewed regularly (with downward adjustment if necessary, e.g. in the case of injury).

Goal-setting is increasingly used not only as a means of ensuring that training targets are met, but also so that a sportsperson feels prepared for, and therefore confident about, an event. There is a wealth of literature now on optimizing performance and managing stress in sport; the National Coaching Foundation (1990; 1992) material is a useful and interesting starting point, particularly in terms of goal-setting.

As we have already indicated, being a good performer involves training the mind as well as the body, so that both work together in harmony. Understanding and helping sportspeople achieve this are important contributions of sport psychology to physical endeavour.

> **Activity**
> **12.7: Setting goals**
> Select a sport or physical activity in which you participate regularly. Individually, plan a series of short-, intermediate- and long-term goals, to a specific time plan, under the following headings:
> - individual skill;
> - fitness;
> - psychological skill.
>
> Ensure that these goals meet the criteria indicated in the text. See if you can implement them and evaluate your progress.
> 1. What difficulties do you encounter in (a) goal setting and (b) implementing the goals?
> 2. How might you overcome these difficulties in the future?

 # Summary

1. Anxiety is an emotional response which causes physiological reactions similar to, but less specific than, fear. Two forms have been identified—state and trait anxiety. Competitive trait anxiety has been shown to correlate with state anxiety in competitive situations, as measured by self-report questionnaires.

2. Stress is the nonspecific response of the body to the demands made on it by stressors. Stressors have many forms, but the three most applicable to sportspeople are physical, climatic and psychological. Selye's (1976) general adaptation syndrome outlines three stages in the body's response to stressors. Symptoms of stress may be behavioural, psychological or physiological and are used to monitor stress in athletes by means of self-report questionnaires, observational techniques and physiological measurements.

3. In controlling stress, coaches and athletes use two types of technique—somatic and cognitive stress management. Somatic techniques deal with the physiological effects of stress. The two examples given are self-directed relaxation and biofeedback.

4. Cognitive stress management techniques deal with emotions and thought processes prior to, during and after competition or performance. The development of self-confidence, mental rehearsal and goal-setting is used as an example of this. It is emphasized that, whereas the development of these skills is often initiated by the coach or trainer, the long-term aim is for the athletes themselves to understand and learn the principles of stress management and sport preparation, and thus to use them to manage their own performances.

 # Review Questions

1. Define 'stress'. What is the relationship between stress, motivation and anxiety?
2. What is the difference between 'state' and 'trait' anxiety and why is it important for coaches and athletes to recognize the difference?
3. List the techniques which can be used to manage stress in sport situations.
4. Draw a model to show how short-, Intermediate- and long-term goals are structured.

Exam-Style Questions

1. 'Stress can occur in a sportsperson when an imbalance is **perceived** between the performance demands of competition and the performer's ability to meet those demands successfully' (Martens, 1977).

i. What is the significance of the word **perceived**. Give **two** psychological symptoms of stress. (3 marks)

ii. High levels of **arousal** have often been linked with stress. Sketch a graph showing the relationship between performance of complex skill and low, moderate and high levels of arousal. Show how this relationship might change for the performance of **simple** skill by adding and labelling a second curve to your graph. (3 mark)

iii. Outline **two** methods of **measuring** stress in a sportsperson. (2 marks)

iv. What **strategies** might the coach employ to help a team member to cope with high levels of stress? (3 marks)

2. **a. i.** Define **trait anxiety** and **state anxiety**.

ii. Explain the implications of high **trait** and high **state** anxiety for performance in a competitive sport situation. (5 marks)

b. Briefly describe Martens' Sport Competition Anxiety Test (SCAT) and Spielberger's State Trait Anxiety Inventory (STAI). (5 marks)

c. A national squad gymnast, who has been performing very well, develops high state anxiety in the competitive situation.

i. Sketch a graph to illustrate the kind of results you would expect and an appropriate schedule for use of Spielberger's STAI with this gymnast, over a 1 month period prior to a competition. (3 marks)

ii. Suggest procedures the coach might use to help the gymnast reduce high levels of state anxiety. (4 marks)

3. **a.** Define the terms **state anxiety** and **sport competition anxiety**. (4 marks)

b. Figure 12.46 shows the levels of **state anxiety** reported by two wrestlers at intervals prior to a competition. One of the wrestlers is high, the other low in sport competition anxiety. Sketch the graph and extend each curve by suggesting **two** further points to show the levels of state anxiety experienced by each of the two wrestlers just after beginning a competition against:

i. A tougher opponent,

ii. A weaker opponent. (3 marks)

c. Give reasons to explain your extensions to the two curves. (7 marks)

d. Describe procedures a coach might employ in an attempt to ensure that each of these wrestlers is mentally prepared to compete at his optimal level. (6 marks)

4. Discuss the idea that a coach's half-time 'pep talk' significantly influences the performance of team members. Support your answer with reference to relevant theories and the use of appropriate examples from sport. (20 marks)

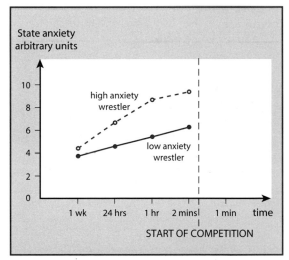

Figure 12.46 (*After Gould, Horn and Spreeman, 1983.*)

Further Reading

References

Allport G.W. Attitudes. In: Murchison (ed) *Handbook of Social Psychology*, pp. 798–844, Clark University Press, 1935.

Alvarez, A. *Feeding the Rat*, Bloomsbury, 1988.

Atkinson J.W. The mainsprings of achievement—oriented activity. In: Atkinson J.W., Raynor J.O. (eds) *Motivation and Achievement*, Halstead, 1974.

Bandura A. *Aggression: A Social Learning Analysis*, Prentice Hall, 1973.

Bandura A. Self efficacy: toward a unifying theory of behavioural change. *Psychological Review*, 1977; 84: 191–215.

Baron R.A. *Human Aggression*, Plenum Press, 1977.

Benson H. *The Relaxation Response*, William Morrow, 1976.

Berkowitz L. *Roots of Aggression*, Atherton Press, 1969.

Bredemeier B.J. Moral reasoning and the perceived legitimacy of intentionally injurious sport acts. *Journal of Social Psychology*, 1985; 7: 110–124.

Bull S.J. *Sport Psychology: A Self-Help Guide*, Crowood, 1991.

Bunker L.K. and McGuire R.T. Give sport psychology to sport. In: Bunker L.K. *et al. Sport Psychology*, Mouvement Publications, 1985.

Butt D.S. *Psychology of Sport*, Van Nostrand Reinhold, 1987.

Carron A.V. *Social Psychology of Sport: An Experimental Approach*, Mouvement Publications, 1981.

Cox R. *Sports Psychology: Concepts and Applications*, Brown & Benchmark, 1994.

Deaux K. and Lewis L.L. The structure of gender stereotypes: inter-relationships among components and gender label. *Journal of Personality and Social Psychology*, 1984; 46: 991–1004.

Deci E. Effects of externally mediated rewards on intrinsic motivation. *Journal of Personality and Social Psychology*, 1971; 18: 105–115.

Dollard J. *et al. Frustration and Aggression*, UP, 1939.

Dweck C. Learned helplessness in sport. In: Nedeau C. *et al.* (eds) *Psychology of Motor Behaviour and Sport*, Human Kinetics, 1980.

Eysenck H.J. *The Biological Basis of Behaviour*, Thomas, 1969.

Festinger L.A. *A Theory of Cognitive Dissonance*, Harper & Row, 1957.

Fox K. The child's perspective in physical education: Part 5, the self-esteem complex. *British Journal of Physical Education*, 1988; 19(6): 247–252.

Gill D.L. *Psychological Dynamics of Sport*, Human Kinetics, 1986.

Girdano D.A., Everly G.S., Dusek D.E. *Controlling Stress and Tension: An Holistic Approach* 3e, Prentice Hall, 1990.

Hanin Y.L. A study of anxiety in sports. In: Straub W.F. (ed) *Sport Psychology: An Analysis of Athlete Behaviour*, pp. 236–249, Mouvement Publications, 1980.

Harris D.V. and Harris B.L. *The Athlete's Guide to Sports Psychology*, Leisure Press, 1984.

Harris P. *Designing and Reporting Experiments*, OUP, 1986.

Hird J.S. *et al.* Physical practice is superior to mental practice in enhancing cognitive and motor task performance. *Journal of Sport and Exercise Psychology*, 1991; 8: 281–293.

Hovland C.I. *et al. Communication and Persuasion*, Yale University Press, 1953

Kenyon G.S. Six scales for assessing attitudes towards physical education. *Research Quarterly*, 1968; 33: 239–244.

Lepper M., Greene D., Nisbett R. Undermining children's intrinsic interest with extrinsic rewards. *Journal of Personality and Social Psychology*, 1973; 28: 129–137.

Lewin K. *A Dynamic Theory of Personality*, McGraw-Hill, 1935.

Lorenz K. *On Aggression*, Harcourt Brace and World, 1966.

McNair D.M., Lorr M., Droppleman L.F. *EDITS Manual for POMS*, Educational and Industrial Testing Service, 1971.

Martens R. *Sport Competition Anxiety Test*, Human Kinetics, 1977.

Martens R. *Coaches Guide to Sport Psychology*, Human Kinetics, 1989.

Martens R., Vealey R.S. and Burton D. *Competitive Anxiety in Sport*, Human Kinetics, 1990.

Morgan W.P. The trait psychology controversy. *Research Quarterly for Exercise and Sport*, 1980; 51: 50–76.

National Coaching Foundation. *Mind over Matter: Introductory Study Pack No. 5*, NCF, 1990.

National Coaching Foundation. *Mental Skills: An Introduction for Sports Coaches*, NCF, 1996.

Nideffer R.M. Test of attentional and interpersonal style. *Journal of Personality and Social Psychology*, 1976; 34: 394–404.

Nideffer R.M. *Psyched to Win*, Human Kinetics, 1992.

Pargman D. *Stress and Motor Performance: Understanding and Coping*, Mouvement Publications, 1986.

Roberts G.C. Effect of achievement motivation and social environment on performance of a motor task. *Journal of Motor Behaviour*, 1974; 4: 37–46.

Roberts G.C., Spink K.S., Pemberton C.L. *Learning Experiences in Sport Psychology*, Human Kinetics, 1986.

Scanlan T.K. and Passer M.W. Sources of competitive stress in young female athletes. *Journal of Sport Psychology*, 1979; 1: 151–159.

Selye H. *The Stress of Life* (rev. edn), McGraw Hill, 1976.

Sharp, B. *Acqiring Skill in Sport*, Sports Dynamics, 1992.

Sheldon W.H. and Stevens S.S. *The Varieties of Temperament: A Psychology of Constitutional Differences*, Harper & Row, 1942.

Smoll F.L. and Schutz R.W. Children's attitudes toward physical activity: a longitudinal analysis. *Journal of Sport Psychology*, 1980; 2: 137–147.

Sonstroem R.J. Physical estimation and attraction scales: rationale and research. *Medicine and Science in Sports*, 1978; 10: 97–102.

Sonstroem R.J. Exercise and self esteem. In: Terjung R.L. (ed) *Exercise and Sport Science Reviews*, pp. 123–155, Collare, 1984.

Sonstroem R.J. and Bernardo P.B. Individual pre-game state anxiety and basketball performance: a re-examination of the inverted U curve. *Journal of Sport Psychology*, 1982; 4: 235–245.

Spielberger C.D., Gorsuch R.L., Lushene R.F. *Manual for the State–Trait Anxiety Inventory*, Consulting Psychologists Press, 1970.

Triandis H.C. *Attitude and Attitudes Change*, Wiley, 1971.

Van Schoyck S.R. and Grasha A.F. Attentional style variations and athletic ability: the advantages of a sport-specific test. *Journal of Sport Psychology*, 1981; 3: 149–165.

Weinberg W.S. and Gould D. *Foundations of Sport and Exercise Psychology*, Human Kinetics, 1995.

Weiner B. *Achievement Motivation and Attribution Theory*, General Learning Press, 1974.

Weiner B. A theory of motivation for some classroom experiences. *Journal of Educational Psychology*, 1979; 71: 3–25.

Weiner B. *An Attribution Theory of Motivation and Emotion*, Springer-Verlag, 1986.

Willis J.D. and Campbell L.F. *Exercise Psychology*, Human Kinetics, 1992.

Further Reading

Further reading

Backley S. *The Winning Mind*, Aurum Press, 1996.

Biddle S. *Psychology of PE and Sport—A Practical Teachers Guide*, FIT Systems, 1994.

Biddle S. European *Perspectives on Exercise and Sport Psychology*, Human Kinetics, 1995.

Bull S.J. *Sport Psychology: A Self-Help Guide*, Crowood, 1991.

Cox R. *Sports Psychology: Concepts and Applications*, 1994.

Gill D.L. *Psychological Dynamics of Sport*, Human Kinetics, 1986.

Hackfort D and Spielberger C.D. *Anxiety in Sports: An International Perspective*, 1990.

Hardy L. and Fazey J. *Mental Training Package*, NCF, 1990.

Harris D.V. and Harris B.L. *The Athlete's Guide to Sports Psychology*, Leisure Press, 1984.

Jones G. and Hardy L. (eds) *Stress and Performance in Sport*, Wiley, 1990.

Kremer J. and Scully D. *Psychology in Sport*, Taylor Francis, 1994.

Martens R. *Coaches Guide to Sport Psychology*, Human Kinetics, 1989.

National Coaching Foundation. *Mind Over Matter: Introductory Study Pack No. 5*, NCF, 1990.

National Coaching Foundation. *Mental Skills: An Introduction for Sports Coaches*, NCF, 1996.

Nideffer R.M. *Psyched to Win*, Human Kinetics, 1992.

Roberts G.C., Spink K.S., Pemberton C.L. *Learning Experiences in Sport Psychology*, Human Kinetics, 1986.

Roberts G.C. *Motivation in Sport and Exercise*, Human Kinetics, 1992.

Silva J.M. and Weinberg R.S. *Psychological Foundations of Sport*, Human Kinetics, 1984.

Weinberg W.S. and Gould D. *Foundations of Sport and Exercise Psychology*, Human Kinetics, 1995.

Willis J.D. and Campbell L.F. *Exercise Psychology*, Human Kinetics, 1992.

Chapter 13

Psychology of Sport: Social Influences on Performance

On completion of this chapter you should be able to:
- show how young people may be socialized through and into sport and physical activity;
- define the role of significant others in this socialization;
- use social learning theory to describe observational learning;
- discuss the factors which lead to a cohesive sports team or group;
- discuss motivational factors within groups, including social loafing and the Ringelmann effect;
- describe coaching strategies that will ensure maximum effort from group or team members;
- analyse the effects of an audience and co-actors on performance for different skill levels, personalities and types of task (social facilitation);
- describe how a coach might control social facilitation effects;
- understand the nature of leadership and cohesiveness within a group context;
- analyse the characteristics of good leaders in a number of different situations.

Keywords & concepts

audience	interaction	situational factors
autocratic style	interactive others	social cohesion
co-actors	leadership	social facilitation
cohesion	members' characteristics	social loafing
democratic style	passive others	sociogram
emergent leader	person-centred style	sociometry
evaluation apprehension	prescribed leader	task-centred style
group processes	Ringelmann effect	task cohesion

13.1 Social Learning

It is often claimed that physical education and sport have a variety of positive social effects: they build character, encourage team-work and team spirit, develop the notion of fairness, teach adherence to rules, and provide opportunity to let off extra energy and aggressive feelings in socially acceptable ways. While we do not have a great deal of research evidence for this, our common sense and experience suggests that sport and physical activity do have a **socializing effect**. In other words, we become socialized into the some of the norms and values of our society **through** participation.

Sport itself has been, since the 19th century, a very important subculture of Western society; it is becoming a global subculture, as the modern Olympic Games demonstrates. A second socializing effect for youngsters entering sport is socialization **into** sport culture, that is learning how to be a sportsperson. As in any culture, sport has rules and values which must be learned and internalized. Some of these rules and values are formal, written down and public, such as the laws governing the playing of a particular game or the members' rules posted on the clubhouse notice-board. Sanctions are likely to apply if these are not followed. Others are accepted by the sport community, but are unwritten, such as applauding your opponents into the changing room in rugby union. Flouting these rules may be judged to be 'bad manners', but normally sanctions do not apply.

There are also the norms and values, certainly unwritten and often unexpressed, associated with being a member of a particular team or club: wearing the team kit in a particular way; always questioning the referee's decisions; playing 'hard but fair'. Some of these norms and values may be socially acceptable, others less so. A newcomer to the group must identify these characteristics of the group and decide (i) to accept them and become an integrated member of the group, (ii) to reject some but still stay a member or (iii) to leave the group. This sounds like a conscious decision process, but it is not necessarily so.

How do these socialization processes work? There are a number of theories which explain socialization. The one we use frequently in this text is Bandura's (1977) **social learning theory**. We have used it to explain skill learning from demonstrations, the development of personality, aggressive behaviour and the development of self-efficacy.

Social learning theory has three component processes:

- modelling—observational learning: athletes learn by behaviour (good and bad) by watching others;
- reinforcement—this behaviour is reinforced or penalized;
- social comparison—behaving in the same way as the peer group.

Let us say you have accidentally tripped your opponent; you have seen your captain, who you respect, offer a hand to an opponent to help him/her up in similar circumstances and you do the same (modelling). The opponent says 'thanks' and doesn't attempt retaliation during the rest of the game. As you pass the captain in running back into position for the free hit, she/he says 'nice gesture' (reinforcement).

The key process in social learning is observation of other people (models) and imitating their behaviour. Bandura refers to this process of observational learning as 'modelling' (you may see it referred to as 'vicarious experience' in some texts). Observational learning is a very powerful learning tool and much early learning depends on it. Young children learn very quickly and easily by observing adults. A diagram of the process is shown in Figure 13.1 in the examination questions at the end of this chapter. This model can be used to analyse skill learning, as in Chapter 11, or the learning of social behaviour.

In social learning, the role and status of the model is of prime importance. For learning to be effective, the model must be a 'significant other', i.e. a person of importance to the learner or playing a role the learner aspires to. Young sportspeople have different significant others as they mature. Initially parents and siblings provide the model. Children with family members who participate in sport are more likely to be attracted to it. Then teachers become important in their lives; this is why it is so important that primary school teachers are positive about physical education. As children watch sport on television, they acquire 'heroes' who become very powerful models; children imitate their heroes' behaviour faithfully (the good and the bad), as well as practising their skills and wearing their strip. As the youngsters move into secondary school, PE teachers become models. They remain an important influence, but are usually superseded for the talented youngster, who moves into club sport, by the coach who often remains a model, mentor and friend for the person's sporting life.

 Review Questions

1. Define social learning theory (Bandura, 1977).
2. Draw Bandura's model of observational learning.
3. Describe how observational learning theory explains how youngsters become socialized into a sport club.
4. Show how observational learning theory is used in skill acquisition.
5. Why is it important that professional players and/or athletes set good examples of behaviour in sport?

Exam-Style Questions

1. We use demonstrations a great deal in physical education and Bandura (1977) has suggested that we learn many of our behaviours through the observation of others.
a. The model in Figure 13.11 is of Bandura's **Observational Learning**:
i. Explain this model and apply it to the teaching of a specific individual activity skill. (6 marks)
ii. Give an example of a specific video you might watch to try to motivate yourselves in a particular game. Would you always use the same video for instilling confidence in skill development? Explain your decision. (5 marks)
b. Bandura's **Social Learning Theory** also suggests that **self-efficacy** is an important factor in developing and changing behaviours. Explain in a sporting context the terms:
i. **Social Learning Theory.** (4 marks)
ii. **Self-efficacy.** (2 marks)
c. You are coaching an athlete in the high jump and he/she has just fallen off the landing area. The athlete is not physically injured, but has obviously suffered psychologically from the experience. Explain how you would help the athlete by using the four stages in Bandura's self-efficacy theory. Ignore the technical advice you might give on adjustments to the run up. (8 marks)

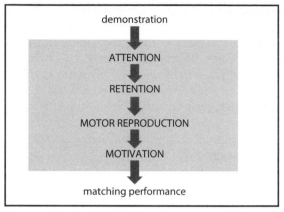

Figure 13.1 Model of Bandura's observational learning.

13.2 Groups and Teams

Most sports and activities take place within a social context. While there certainly are people who derive satisfaction from training and competing alone, dependent upon their own psychological and physical resources, most are drawn to activity because of the opportunity to join people who share their enthusiasm. Personal experience and research tell us that we tend to react differently when we are in a group from when we are alone, and thus investigating these differences and considering their implications for teams and squads is an important.

Key Points
What is a group?
• Shaw (1976, p. 11) defines it as 'two or more persons who are interacting with one another in such a manner that each person influences and is influenced by each other person.'
• McGrath (1984, p. 7) states that 'groups are those social aggregates that involve mutual awareness and potential interaction.'

Both definitions in the Key Points highlight the importance (whether actual or potential) of interaction. Shaw sees influence as an important component; McGrath prefers awareness.

Activity
Group discussion
If you accept these definitions, would you consider a crowd at a football match, or a collection of people at a public swimming session, to be a group?
  Select some other examples of groups and nongroups in sports and activity contexts. Don't be concerned if you have some difficulty in deciding—the borderline between group and nongroup is not clear-cut.

Of interest to sports psychologists and coaches is the question of how people interact in sports groups and how that interaction can be made most productive. Gill (1986) used Steiner's model of group productivity to suggest that:

$$\begin{matrix} \text{team} \\ \text{success} \end{matrix} = \begin{matrix} \text{potential} \\ \text{for success} \end{matrix} - \begin{matrix} \text{co-ordination and} \\ \text{motivation problems} \end{matrix}$$

or

$$\begin{matrix} \text{actual} \\ \text{productivity} \end{matrix} = \begin{matrix} \text{potential} \\ \text{productivity} \end{matrix} - \begin{matrix} \text{losses due to} \\ \text{faulty processes} \end{matrix}$$

These equations are explained below.

- **Potential for success**—in general, the most skilful individuals make up the best team. Jones (1974) correlated the individual success of members of a team against the overall success of the team and found high positive correlations in all his cases. The lowest correlation (0.6) was in basketball, a sport in which there is a great deal of interaction.
- High interaction presents **co-ordination problems** for players (Figure 13.2)—if one player is being selfish or aggressive, or if a defence is not working together, overall team performance suffers.
- **Motivation problems**—people seem to work less hard in a group than they do on their own. For example, in the 1972 Olympics, the time of the winning double sculls was only 4% faster than that of the single sculls, and the eights only 6% faster than that of the fours. Obviously, there might be a technical explanation for this in terms of the sizes and weights of the boats, but the effect seems to be general and is known as the Ringelmann Effect (Gill, 1986) or 'social loafing' (Figure 13.3).

Social loafing

Social loafing (Latane, 1979) is the tendency for individuals to lessen their effort when they are part of a group. Work by Williams *et al.* (1981) suggests that this is eliminated if players think that their contribution within the team is identifiable. Thus team coaches who are aware of this develop strategies for recognizing individual performance in a game—the use of player statistics in American football is an example.

Interaction

In some teams, the need for interaction between players is high; basketball has already been suggested as a game that requires a lot of co-operation. In other teams, such interaction is not as important.

Investigation

13.1: Interaction within sports teams
Method: Make a list of sports included in the Olympic Games. Construct a continuum, based on the extent to which the members of a particular team in each sport need to interact with one another during competition.
Results: You might have, for example, volleyball near one end (as a highly interactive sport) and archery near the other.
Discussion: Compare your list with those of others in your group and discuss any discrepancies.

Cohesion

In sports where the need for co-operation between team members is high, coaches take the interactional skills of players into account and so may sometimes select a slightly less able player who 'fits in' better than a more skilful, but selfish, colleague. The nature of these interactional skills in sport has not been extensively researched. Cratty and Hanin (1980) suggest that players like and value each other more when the team is doing well. Strong competition for places on a team can lead to personal rivalry and even hostility. Friendships within a team can aid team spirit and cohesion. Cohesion is the extent to which members of a group exhibit a desire to achieve common goals and group identity. But friendship groups can have negative effects; some research (Klein and Christiansen, 1969) shows that passing patterns in team ball games reflect friendship groups, though

Figure 13.2 Co-ordination and co-operation may be a problem.

Figure 13.3 'Social loafing'.

observation suggests that this does not happen at the top level or in professional sport.

Friendship patterns in a team can be measured by a technique known as sociometry. You will find more details of this in methodology textbooks, but essentially it involves asking members of a group to nominate, in confidence, two or three other members who they would choose in the situation being investigated. The situation might be a friendship choice or it might be a task; the ways in which the technique can be used are very varied. These choices are then represented on a diagram, known as a sociogram.

Several researchers (Carron and Ball, 1977; Williams and Hacker, 1982) have studied the relationship between success and cohesion in sports teams. The results of this research are equivocal. Some studies show that high group cohesion leads to better performances; others suggest that good performance leads to increased cohesion. There would seem to be a 'cause and effect' problem in interpreting the data. This may be resolved if we consider cohesion to have two facets, i.e. 'social' and 'task' elements. Social cohesion refers to interpersonal attraction within the group; task cohesion is determined by how well the group works together to achieve their goals.

Research shows that teams who are high in task cohesion (i.e. they are willing to work together, whether or not they 'get on' personally) have the potential to be successful. Teams who have high social cohesion but low task cohesion are less likely to be successful. The relationship between team performance and cohesion also depends on the type of teams. Interacting teams (e.g. hockey, football, basketball) need high cohesion for success, whereas for co-acting teams (e.g. skiing, judo, diving), cohesion is less important, once the team has been selected.

 Investigation

13.2: To interpret a sociogram
Method: Look at the sociogram in Figure 13.4. The arrows represent choices, for example 'N' has nominated 'K' as a friend.
1. Identify the following individuals and subgroups:
a. A 'star'—someone who is chosen by many others.
b. An isolate—someone who is not chosen by anyone else.
c. A mutual pair—two people who choose each other.
2. What effect might friendship patterns such as this have on the way the players interact as a team?

3. How would you rate the cohesion of this group?

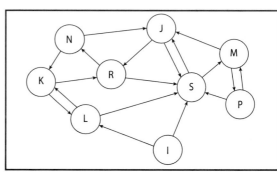

Figure 13.4 A friendship sociogram within a sports team: social cohesion.

 Investigation

13.3: To investigate the relationships between social cohesion, task cohesion and team success
Methods: Do either of the following:
- Use one of the learning experiences described in Carron (1981) or Roberts *et al.* (1986).
- Organize a tournament in your class or college in a small-team sport, such as basketball or volleyball, so that the teams can be ranked at the end. Select the teams

so that intra-team friendship groups are avoided as far as possible. Ask the individual members of the teams who were ranked highest and lowest to complete the following simple questionnaire to assess task cohesion (Q1) and social cohesion (Q2).
- Q1. Did the members of your team play well together?

9	8	7	6	5	4	3	2	1
very much								not at all

Investigation

13.3 continued

- Q2. Do the members of your team like one another?

9   8   7   6   5   4   3   2   1

very much   not at all

Results: Calculate a mean score on each question for each team. From your results, draw a bar chart similar to that given in Figure 13.5. *Discussion:* What do your results tell you about the relationship between task cohesion, social cohesion and team success?

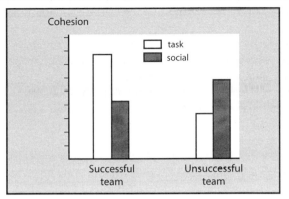

Figure 13.5 Task cohesion, social cohesion and team success.

Most coaches accept that members of a team interact more effectively in task-oriented situations if they like, or at least respect, one another. This does not apply in sport only. Consider the implications for a climbing team or a dance company if excessive rivalry develops between its members.

Review Questions

1. Define a 'group'.
2. What are the factors that make a team or dance group 'cohesive'?
3. What is meant by the equation: actual team productivity = potential productivity – faulty processes?

4. **a.** What is meant by (**i**) the 'Ringelmann effect' and (**ii**) 'social loafing' in a sports context.
b. How may these effects be overcome?
5. List at least five ways in which a coach might set about developing 'team spirit'.

Exam-Style Questions

1. **a.** On paper, your team looks good with several outstanding players, but you lose more times than you win. The formula below has often been used to identify problems associated with team performance:
actual productivity of team = potential productivity – faulty processes
i. What is meant by potential productivity? (1 mark)
ii. There may be motivational problems which contribute to the faulty processes. What is meant by the Ringelmann Effect? (2 marks)
iii. Latane (1979) identified one motivational problem as social loafing. Using your team as an example, briefly explain the concept of social loafing. What strategies could your coach use to stop social loafing occurring? (6 marks)

b. **i.** What two main personal qualities do you feel are important in a team captain? (2 marks)
ii. Using your knowledge of attribution theory, what reasons might you encourage your team members to give for losing a game? (3 marks)
2. **a.** Explain what is meant by the term group cohesion. (4 marks)
b. Briefly identify two methods of measuring the cohesiveness of a sports team. (2 marks)
c. 'Two heads are better than one'; 'Too many cooks spoil the broth'. Discuss these apparently contradictory statements in relation to sports groups, with specific reference to group size and cohesion. (8 marks)
d. Are cohesive groups in sport always more successful? Explain your answer. (6 marks)

13.3 Social Facilitation

Most of us involved in sport or dance recognize the effect that the presence of spectators has on the way we play or perform. This is known as social facilitation. People watching us may tend to make us nervous, but their presence often means that we try a little bit harder. In this sense it is the opposite of 'social loafing' (p. 358). Investigating these effects experimentally has interested sports psychologists for a long time, but there is still some difficulty in isolating the different variables that operate. Early research, which contrasted performance with an audience with performance without one, proved unexpectedly inconclusive, until Zajonc (1965) clarified the terms which were being used. He first defined different kinds of audience, as shown in Figure 13.6.

It is important for you to note that, in this model, the audience and co-actors are completely passive; i.e. not communicating in any way with the performer.

Competitors and supporters interact with the performer in a variety of ways. Co-actors are involved in the same activity at the same time as the performer, but are not competing directly.

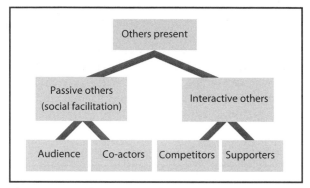

Figure 13.6 Different types of audience. (*Adapted from Zajonc, 1965.*)

Investigation

13.4: To interpret Figure 13.6
Method: Study Figure 13.6—take each of the four categories of audience, co-actors, competitors and supporters, and give sport-related examples for each category. Remember that 'audience' and 'co-actors' do not interact or communicate in any way with the performer. You may have to select particular periods in a game or event to illustrate these categories.
Discussion: Compare and discuss your ideas with others in the group.

Investigation

13.5: To investigate whether performance of a simple endurance task is improved by the presence of an audience or co-actors
Method: For the task, use a wall squat as illustrated at Figure 9.12. Divide the subjects available into three groups—A, B and C. Arrange your data collection so that all the subjects are timed on their ability to hold a wall squat under three different experimental conditions: (**i**) alone; (**ii**) in the presence of co-actors; (**iii**) in the presence of an audience. Measurements are taken in the following order:
- Group A: audience, alone, co-actors.
- Group B: co-actors, audience, alone.
- Group C: alone, audience, co-actors.
Once you have got results from the three groups for the three conditions, treat all three groups as one.

Results: Obtain a mean score for the three conditions and plot these on a bar chart, as in Figure 13.7.

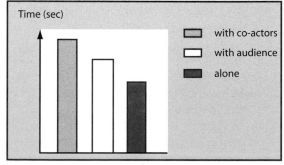

Figure 13.7 The hypothetical relationship between scores on an endurance task, under three different experimental conditions.

Investigation

13.5 continued

Discussion:
1. To what extent do your results match those in Figure 13.7? Explain any discrepancies.

2. What is the reason for collecting the data in groups?
3. Does the presence of an experimenter pose a problem of validity?

On the basis of work such as in Investigations 13.4 and 13.5, Zajonc (1965) suggested that an audience affects a performer differentially, according to the part of the learning curve he/she is in (Figure 13.8).

Experiments show that learners perform better alone than with an audience, but that experienced performers do better with an audience. Zajonc explains this in terms of an increase in psychological arousal caused by the audience (Figure 13.9). For the inexperienced performer, still in the associative phase of learning, this increase causes interference with the production of the skill, but for the expert the increased level of arousal is motivating, as discussed in an earlier section.

Thus, according to Zajonc, the mere presence of others creates arousal which then affects performance. Cottrell (1968) disputes this model and suggests that it is not 'mere presence' which creates arousal, but the fact that the audience may be perceived as evaluating the performance, thus creating what Cottrell calls **evaluation apprehension**.

There is still a lot of work for sports psychologists to do in this area. We do not fully understand audience effects, particularly aspects such as the 'home advantage', which is very obvious in professional football.

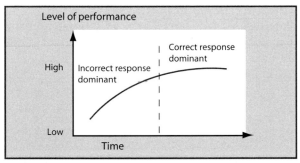

Figure 13.8 A learning curve to show the development of a correct dominant response.

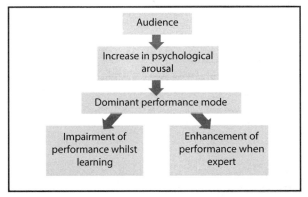

Figure 13.9 The relationship between audience, arousal level and performance.

 Review Questions

1. **a.** Define the term 'social facilitation'.
b. What different groups of 'others' in sport or dance does the theory define?
2. Draw a diagram of Zajonc's drive theory of audience effects. What are the implications of this model for competition in sport?

3. Explain Cottrell's evaluation apprehension theory.
4. How should a coach and/or performer prepare for audience effects in competition or performance?

Exam-Style Questions

1. You are the coach of an individual activity club and you are concerned with top level performance, increasing participation in your sport and understanding your role as coach.

   One of your athletes performs well in training, but in competitions, where there is a sizeable crowd, she underachieves.

   a. What is the term used to describe the influence of the **presence of others** on performance and what is the main effect of an audience on a skilled performer? (2 marks)

   b. Using psychological theories, give reasons for the different effects that the presence of spectators may have on performance. (4 marks)

   c. What strategies could you employ to help an athlete in situations where there are spectators present? (3 marks)

2. **a.** Briefly explain what is meant by social facilitation. (4 marks)

   b. Some people seem to perform well in sport in front of an audience, while others perform badly, 'choking' under pressure. Use social facilitation theory to explain this observation. (8 marks)

   c. Describe the practical implications that arise from social facilitation theory for coaching:

   i. Performers in the early stage of learning. (4 marks)

   ii. Performers in the later stages of learning. (4 marks)

13.4 Leadership

The development of team cohesion often depends on the **leadership** of the coach or team captain. Leadership has been defined in a variety of ways, but most definitions view it as the process by which a particular individual is instrumental in fulfilling the expectations of a group or team, and develops an environment in which the group is motivated, rewarded and helped to achieve its goals. Martens points out that it should not be confused with management, which deals with routine organization— leadership is about vision.

Early research into leadership, both in sport and generally, suggested that leaders are 'born not made', i.e. they possess personality traits that suit them to a leadership role. This theory has been largely superceded by the idea that there is not a particular set of personality traits which mark out a leader, but that certain combinations of traits might be useful in particular situations. The more modern version of this theory is that good leaders match their behaviour and approach to the situation. For example, a good team coach will treat players as individuals, being tough and demanding on some players and more encouraging with others, whilst maintaining a fair, supportive approach to all. These behaviours can be learned, so everyone has the potential to be an effective leader.

Leaders tend to come forward in one of two ways (Carron, 1981): **emergent** leaders are those who come from the group itself, either informally because of their skills and abilities, or formally through nomination and/or selection; **prescribed** leaders are those appointed by the organizing body. What do you see to be some of the advantages and difficulties for leaders themselves of being in each of these two categories?

Characteristics of leaders

The characteristics of effective leadership are difficult to pin down, but it is generally recognized that there are three main factors which interact to affect a person's capacity to lead, as represented in Figure 13.10. Chelladurai's (1984) theory is that the more the leader's actual behaviour matches the expectations and preferences of the **members** of the group, and the specific demands of the **situation**, the greater the group's satisfaction, enjoyment and performance is.

The problem is, however, that each group, and each activity context, is different, so defining just what these behaviours are is very difficult. The results of research and your own experience of leading and being lead help us to clarify these factors.

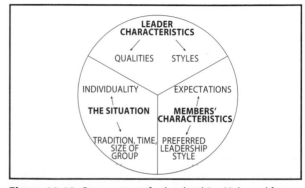

Figure 13.10 Components for leadership. (*Adapted from Chelladurai, 1984.*)

Investigation

13.6: To identify the qualities of an effective leader

Method: From your own experience, make a list of the qualities you would associate with a good team captain. Compare your list with those of others and derive a definitive list of about 12 qualities which you all agree on. Think of opposites for these. For example, if you choose 'self-confident', the opposite might be 'diffident'. Construct a questionnaire by separating your opposites on a five-point scale,

for example:

| self-confident | 5 | 4 | 3 | 2 | 1 | diffident |
| unfriendly | 1 | 2 | 3 | 4 | 5 | friendly |

Try out your scale on yourself. To obtain an overall score you need to reverse the scoring on some items, e.g. unfriendly–friendly.

Discussion: How did you rate as a leader? Of course, you may have all these qualities and not be your team's captain—there are many other factors involved.

Leadership style

Investigation 13.6 identifies leadership qualities or characteristics. Fiedler (1967) summarized leadership characteristics as a continuum between two styles. He labelled these task-centred leadership and person (or relationship)-centred leadership (Figure 13.11). It is possible for a leader to adopt either style or a combination, and a good coach or captain does the latter. Fiedler suggests that effective leadership also depends on the situation.

Situational factors

Fiedler related leadership style to what he called 'situational favourableness'. If things are going well for the coach and the team, or alternatively, if the situation is unfavourable (e.g. poor facilities, little support) then a sports leader needs to be very task centred. If the situation is moderately favourable then a person-centred approach is likely to work best.

There are a range of situational factors which a leader needs to be aware of in selecting an appropriate style. Research has shown that players in team sports look for a captain or coach who is directive and uses his/her authority to organize and structure the group in order to complete the **task** or achieve the group's ambitions (e.g. promotion to a higher

league). Individuals, for example skaters and athletes, prefer a more **person-oriented** leader. This seems to relate to the size of the group—the more team members there are, the less easy it is to take each person's individual needs and preferences into account. Similarly, if decisions have to be made quickly an autocratic style is usually adopted. Another interesting research finding, probably backed up by your own experience, is that groups tend to be traditional—once they have become used to a particular style they resent change.

Members' characteristics

This leads us to the third section of the model (see Figure 13.10). We tend to think of captains, coaches and leaders as influencing the behaviour of the group members, but of course it works the other way too. If, for example, a team captain senses that the team is hostile, he/she tends to develop a more autocratic style than if the team is friendly and co-operative. A team or group working towards a particular goal, an important competition, expedition or performance, looks towards the leader to help it succeed, and has ideas about how this should be done—particularly if its members are experienced. Problems can arise if the strategies for training and preparation adopted by the leader do not match members' expectations. Good leaders are sensitive to the expectations, knowledge and experience of group members.

Figure 13.12 represents Chelladurai's interactional model of leadership more specifically. It is known as his 'multidimensional model of leadership'. He indicates that the athlete's **performance and satisfaction** are the required outcomes of the coaching process and that the extent to which these occur depend on the way in which three aspects of leader behaviour interact. 'Prescribed leader behaviour' refers to the expectations that team management have of the coach

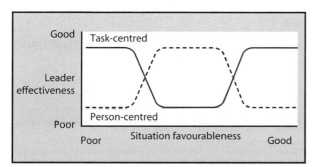

Figure 13.11 Fiedler's (1967) contingency model.

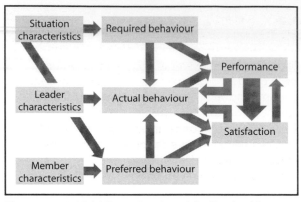

Figure 13.12 Multidimensional model of leadership.

or captain. 'Actual leader behaviour' refers to the way in which the coach/captain normally goes about his/her job, i.e. interaction with the team, coaching style, etc. 'Preferred leadership behaviour' is the way in which the athletes like their coach/captain to relate to them. The ideal team situation is when all three beahviours are congruent, i.e. when the coach/captain acts in ways that both management and the team like. If the coach behaves in a way that neither the management nor the athletes approve of, he/she is unlikely to last very long; an ambitious sport leader will ensure that either management or the athletes (and preferably both) are satisfied with how he/she deals with the team. Professional football management offers some interesting examples of this.

Chelladurai developed his multidimensional model to focus on preferred leadership behaviour and identified five types of coaching focus:
- training and instruction,
- democratic approach,
- autocratic approach,
- social support,
- rewards.

Athletes seem to prefer a coaching focus that is strong on technical and tactical aspects (training and instruction) and in which the coach gives plentiful feedback and reward. Least preferred is an autocratic approach by a coach who only relies on authority and does not demonstrate an awareness of athletes' needs and preferences.

It is important to bear in mind, however, that different groups will have different preferences. For example, youngsters prefer and need a coach who provides plenty of social support; male athletes are more prepared to tolerate an authoritarian coach than are female athletes. This does not imply that other focuses are inappropriate; it is a question of emphasis.

 # Review Questions

1. List at least three different leadership roles in a sport context—indicate whether each is 'emergent' or 'prescribed'.
2. Discuss whether leaders are 'born' or 'made'.

3. Differentiate between a 'task-oriented' leadership style and a 'person- or relationship-oriented' leadership style.
4. When should a coach adopt a task-oriented style and, when, a person-oriented style?

 # Exam-Style Questions

1. a. i. What are the main differences between the selection of a prescribed leader and an emergent leader? (2 marks)
ii. What are the main characteristics of the autocratic and democratic leadership styles? (4 marks)
iii. What factors would influence your choice of a particular style of leadership with respect to: the type of activity; level of skill; personality of the performer; and the size of the group? (6 marks)
b. Figure 3.12 shows a multidimensional model of leadership. Explain each part of the model by using examples from sport. (8 marks)
c. It is often said that 'good leaders are born not made'. Discuss the extent to which you agree or disagree with this statement in the light of related psychological theories. (5 marks)
d. As an effective coach, you are perceived as a **leader** by the performers.
i. What is a **leader** in this context? (1 mark)
ii. Fiedler (1967) looked at the interaction of **leader characteristics** and **situational factors**. Name the two types of leader that Fiedler identified and describe the **environmental** situations in which each is the more effective. (5 marks)
iii. Identify and explain an important factor, other than leader characteristics and environmental situations, which must be taken into account when assessing the effectiveness of leadership. (2 marks)

Summary

1. Most sports and activities take place within a social context, in groups. Young people are socialized into these groups through the process of social learning. Sport thus has a socializing influence and also requires athletes to conform to its norms and values. Social learning takes place through observation, modelling and reinforcement.

2. A group is defined as two or more people who are interacting with each other. In general, the most skilful individuals make the best sports team, but co-ordination and motivation are controlling factors. In sports where the need for co-operation between team members is high, coaches take the interactional skills of players into account and try to develop social cohesion since it appears that members of a team interact more effectively during the game if they like and/or respect one another.

3. Sports groups show many of the characteristics of other social groups, but for a team, cohesiveness is particularly important.

There can be problems in obtaining maximum productivity from a team because of interactional and motivational factors. Coaching and teaching strategies need to take these into account.

4. Performance can be affected by a variety of factors, one of which is the presence of others, either as an audience or as participants. This is known as social facilitation. Effects on performance, negative and positive, are associated with levels of arousal brought on by either the mere presence of others or by apprehension of their evaluation.

5. Leadership is an important concept, particularly in sport, where coaches, managers and team captains have particular roles to play. Whereas there is no generally accepted definition of good leadership, certain characteristics of effective leadership have been identified, but these must be seen in the context of the situation and the requirements of the group. The essence of good leadership appears to be flexibility.

Further Reading

References

Bandura A. *Social Learning Theory*, Prentice Hall, 1977.

Carron A.V. *Social Psychology of Sport: An Experimental Approach*, Mouvement Publications, 1981.

Carron A.V. and Ball J. An analysis of the cause–effect characteristics of cohesiveness and participation motivation in inter-collegiate hockey. *International Review of Sport Sociology*, 1977; 2: 49–60.

Chelladurai P. Leadership in sports. In: Silva J.M. and Weinberg R.S. (eds) *Psychological Foundations of Sport*, Human Kinetics, 1984.

Cottrell N.B. Performance in the presence of other human beings: mere presence, audience and affiliation effects. In: Simmell E.C. *et al.* (eds) *Social Facilitation and Imitative Behaviour*, Allyn & Bacon, 1968.

Cratty B.J. and Hanin Y.L. *The Athlete in the Sports Team*, Love Publications, 1980.

Fiedler F.E. *A Theory of Leadership Effectiveness*, McGraw-Hill, 1967.

Gill D.L. Individual and group performance in sport. In: Silva J.M. and Weinberg R.S. (eds) *Psychological Foundations of Sport*, Human Kinetics, 1984.

Jones M.B. Regressing group on individual effectiveness, *Organisational Behaviour and Human Performance*, 1974; 11: 426–451.

Klein M. and Christiansen G. Group composition, group structure and group effectiveness of a basketball team. In: Loy J.W. and Kenyon G.S. (eds) *Sport, Culture and Society*, Macmillan, 1969.

Latane B. *et al.* 'Many hands make light work'. *Journal of Personality*, 1979.

McGrath J.E. *Groups: Interaction and Performance*, Prentice Hall, 1984.

Roberts G.C. *et al.* *Learning Experiences in Sport Psychology*, Human Kinetics, 1986.

Shaw M.E. *Group Dynamics*, McGraw Hill, 1976.

Williams K. *et al.* Identifiability and social loafing: two cheering experiments. *Journal of Personality and Social Psychology*, 1981; 40: 303–311.

Zajonc R.B. Social facilitation. *Science*, 1965; 149: 269–274.

Further Reading

Backley S. *The Winning Mind*, Aurum Press, 1996.

Butler R.J. *Sports Psychology in Action*, Butterworth & Heinemann, 1996.

Cox R.H. *Sport Psychology: Concepts and Applications*, Brown & Benchmark, 1994.

Gill D.L. *Psychological Dynamics of Sport*, Human Kinetics, 1986.

Kremer J. and Scully D. *Psychology in Sport*, Taylor Francis, 1994.

NCF. *Psychology and Performance*, National Coaching Foundation, 1996.

Silva J.M. and Weinberg R.S. *Psychological Foundations of Sport*, Human Kinetics, 1984.

Weinberg R.S. and Gould D. *Foundations of Sport an Exercise Psychology*, Human Kinetics, 1995.

Part Three

The Performer in a Social Setting

It is very easy for us to turn to the sports pages and consider that information about players' performances is all there is to know. If we are to gain a useful knowledge and understanding of physical education and sport we must recognize that any group activity involves relationships between people, and that any group activity is influenced by the society to which it belongs.

There are three main dimensions to be examined under the title of **The Performer in a Social Setting**. These consist of **contemporary sociocultural aspects**, **historical perspectives** and **comparative studies** of physical education and sport.

The **contemporary sociocultural** and **comparative studies** have been deliberately integrated because of the international nature of much of physical education and sport. The section starts with a critical analysis of concepts, ranging from play to professional sport, and involves the reader in the process of understanding words and notions. Having established what we mean by certain concepts, it is useful to review the administration of these in a number of countries. The third phase involves an examination of physical education and sport using a number of sociological techniques at both intra- and inter-group level. Finally, these components are integrated to examine a number of contemporary issues in physical education and sport.

The **historical perspective** consists almost entirely of British sports history, on the grounds that this represents the nucleus from which most

international developments have stemmed. It is presented in four phases: popular recreation, public school athleticism, rational recreation and elementary school physical training, and can be readily linked with the contemporary scene.

Bibliographies are presented at regular intervals to encourage additional reading, and a large number of models and illustrative material are offered to involve the student in decision-making activities.

Inevitably, a text is dated almost as soon as it is written and so this 3rd revised edition includes changes that have occurred in our field of study since 1994 as well as elements that have emerged as a result of reflective study by teachers and young people.

The main additional input is the decision to include Australia in the countries being reviewed. This is partly because Russian studies remain in a state of flux and partly because the build-up to Sydney 2000 makes Australia a most interesting country to study, made easier by the common language and the amount of published material available.

It is presumed that developments in the former USSR will eventually stabilize and so the content is retained because it gives a useful analysis of a communist society to compare with Western democracies. It also gives us a chance to look at Russia as an emergent country, with all the pressures on nation building, integration, health and defence, reflected in the commitment to physical culture and sport, following the political and economic U-turn of the 1991 reforms.

Chapter 14

Important Concepts in Physical Education and Sport

Introduction

You have read about the structure and function of our subject through the eyes of the scientist and the social scientist. It is now time to also look at physical education and sport in a social setting. If we put this in the form of a model, it should look something like that shown in Figure 14.1.

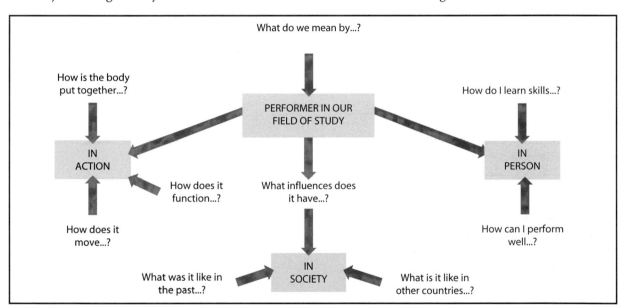

Figure 14.1 Model to show a thematic framework, whereby we can understand the multi-disciplinary basis of physical education and sport.

Do you understand what each of the nine questions is trying to show? Can you give a brief answer to each of them? You need to know the meanings of the words and notions and be able to express them accurately. Get into the habit of asking two basic questions whenever you meet new words or situations: 'What do we mean by?' and 'How do we know?'.

What do we mean by?

If you can answer this, you will be able to sort your definitions out, which will allow you to discuss things rationally.

How do we know?

If you go on to this second level of questioning and establish authoritative back-up to what you have said, you have changed a point of view into a worthwhile, public statement that will stand up to a certain amount of scrutiny.

So, what does this model tell us?

It would seem that most of what you have been reading has been centred on the **performer** and his or her involvement in a family of activities that we variously call **physical education**, **sport** or **physical recreation**.

You have looked at the **performer in action** through the eyes of the physiologist; at the **person involved in the activity** using the techniques of the psychologist; and you are about to examine the nature, structure and function of **physical performance in a social setting**. This implies that you should know about physical education and sport in your own country; that it helps to know what it is like in other countries; and that it is important to know what influence the past has had.

Let's try to establish some **terms of reference**:

• We are concerned with a particular **field of study** that we have called **physical performance**.

• Our initial task, therefore, is to establish the boundaries of *this* term in *this* book.

• Our definition of physical performance is limited to activities that fall within the categories of **play**, **physical recreation**, **sport** and **physical education**.

• Other forms of physical performance exist and may have common features with those categories we have identified, but they are outside our present **field of study**.

All four categories can also be experienced in the natural environment, where alternative motives arise and different types of challenge have to be met, producing recreative and educative sub-categories.

Having identified four categories we now apply our questioning technique by asking, **what do we mean by them?** Figure 14.2 shows what they *might* mean.

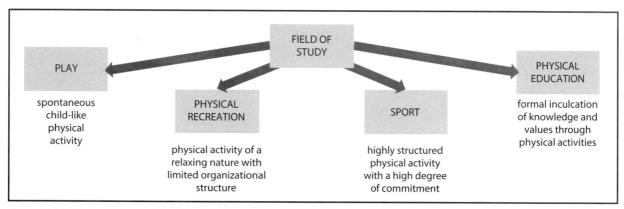

Figure 14.2 The four categories of our model and what they might mean.

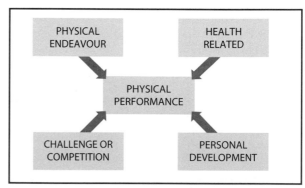

ℝ **Review Questions**

To test the definitions

1. See if you can think of an experience you have had in each of the categories in Figure 14.2.

2. Put the following activities into these categories:

a. two children playing hopscotch in the street,

b. Miami Dolphins playing the Redskins in the Superbowl,

c. a school gymnastics lesson,

d. a group of backpackers rambling in the English Lake District.

3. Make sure that you understand the words in each definition, and try to find some exceptions.

If you have tackled the Review Questions in the right way, you will be starting to come up with some **characteristics** that all four categories **share**, but you will also be aware that each has certain characteristics that make it **different** from the others. Do you agree with the **shared characteristics** shown in Figure 14.3?

Figure 14.3 Possible shared characteristics of the four categories.

Now let's look at a few other physical performances which we suggest are outside our terms of reference: acting in a play; playing chess; pulling a tooth out; and gardening. It is suggested that none of these fits into our notion of play, physical recreation, sport or physical education because they don't have a sufficient number of the shared characteristics we expect to find in our field of study.

See if you can establish why these four activities are outside our terms of reference. What you will find is that there is a core of activities that can be applied to all four categories, and others that may fit into only one. Motor racing, for example, is certainly a sport, but it is hard to see it as play, physical recreation or physical education. Football, on the other hand, can consist of some children kicking a tin can down the road; being taught it at school; playing a game in the park with coats for goals; or fulfilling a league fixture. It is all football, but each of these examples fits into a different category of physical performance.

Most of the examples we are going to use will be like football; in other words, it depends on the players and the way they play as to whether they are involved in play, a formal educational experience, a sport or a recreation. Figure 14.4 identifies some of these core activities and 'dares' to classify them into five major groups.

We are suggesting that all these activities belong to the same family or field of study, but that they have a number of unique features that make them rather like the fingers of one hand.

Try to identify some of these unique features. You will probably come up with words like game, combat and conquest; you might decide that some are objective while others have subjective elements; you might conclude that the key lies in the number of players and their relationship. It is always easier if you relate your definition to a specific activity and test it.

A combat, for example, involves you in beating an opponent in a stylized war game. Do you agree, or is there more to it than that? Test your definition by looking at judo or fencing. What do you think about archery being in this category?

Can you define a conquest activity? Does it involve competition or challenge? Is it against man or nature? Does it have to be the first time? What are its physical and psychological components? Is it basically an objective or a romantic experience? If you ask these questions and link them with an acknowledged conquest activity like mountaineering, you should come up with certain characteristics that will give you a clearer understanding of the term.

You are still left with the difficult notion of what a game is. For example, you might agree that basically it is a contrived competitive experience existing in its own time and space. That is quite a difficult statement. Can you simplify it and then pick a game to test it?

However, in Figure 14.4 the games are divided into partner and team. We also know that there are invasion games, such as hockey and football; court games, such as tennis and squash; and target games, such as cricket, baseball and golf. Can you set up some sets of characteristics to differentiate these types of game?

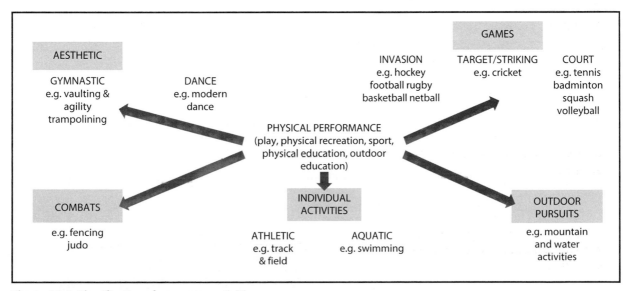

Figure 14.4 Classification of some core activities.

Unfortunately, this degree of analysis simply takes us into another round of what do you mean by and how do you know? For example, can you differentiate a contest from a game? Or what is the notion of combat? Is it a description of certain activities or a potential feature of all contests? Can you establish the difference between a competition and a challenge? We are probably raising more questions than answers by this point. Don't worry too much; the debate itself is valuable, and the more we question, the more you will realize that there are very few absolutes.

Let's make a decisive statement and if it holds we are ready to make a start.

> Our field of study includes a number of specific activities that share a number of characteristics. There would seem to be four main categories within this field of study: play, physical recreation, sport and physical education. Most of the core activities can exist in each category, dependent on the attitude of the performer and the level of performance and organization.

Test this statement by using different examples and different situations.

We now have one more basic step to take. Having just used the word situation, we need to recognize that we are concerned with a dynamic experience that is complete in itself, an intrinsic whole. Like a watch, once it is put together successfully, it works independently. Let's not forget, however, that we are not just a machine: our battery is an independent mind!

In model form, the components of this working dynamic can be arranged as in Figure 14.5. Can you make this model more meaningful by putting it into a real situation? For example, if you are performing, what are you performing? Where are you performing? Why are you performing? These are the most important components. Now, what about the influence of the coach, the spectators and the administrators? They all have a direct bearing on you as a performer and on the direct function of the activity.

However, this activity does not exist in a vacuum. All the time, outside forces are acting on it. In the case of the watch, someone winds it up, wears it, looks after it, uses it, looks at it and values it. These outside influences are what we have called the social setting, or they could be called extrinsic factors.

Terms like 'spheres of influence' and 'affective horizons' can help to explain the way in which society changes the performer and the performance. You probably belong to a sports club. What factors outside the club influence it? Are they human, financial, geographical or perhaps political? Or all four?

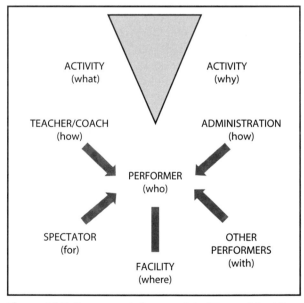

Figure 14.5 Components for a model of the social setting of sport.

Figure 14.6 identifies the main extrinsic factors which influence the performance situation. It is often said that performance situations reflect the society and culture they exist in, but there are occasions where such is the impact of sport on society or physical education on education that the opposite occurs, so our field of study changes aspects of society as well as some of its cultural patterns.

The extent to which this interaction takes place varies from a local influence to an international one, in waves of reaction which have been variously called 'spheres of influence' and 'affective horizons'. At a local level, you probably belong to a sports club and are aware of the influence of the local community on it. Conversely, you may be able to recognize the influence your club has on the town. Similarly, but on a wider scale, you could assess the wave-like impact of the 1992 Olympic Games not only on Barcelona itself, but also on Spain, Europe and ultimately the whole world. These examples of interaction remind us that to understand the performance situation we must be aware of its social setting. These relationships do not always reflect intrinsic values—for example, the selection of Atlanta instead of Athens for the Centenary Olympic Games may well have hinged on the influence of the Coca Cola™ Company.

If these are the dimensions in which our field of study operates, we must appreciate the Contemporary Scene; but we then need to unravel both traditional behaviour, through the **time** perspective of historical knowledge, and environmental influences, through the **spatial** perspective of comparative study, to understand parallel developments in other countries.

Clearly, for play, local influences are likely to predominate, whereas the impact of high-level sport can be world-wide. England being allowed to re-enter European football is one example, but the exclusion of South Africa from the Olympic Games had even wider implications.

In addition to dimensions, we need to be aware of perspectives if we are to obtain a coherent picture of the social setting. We will understand our own contemporary society more fully if we use historical perspective to establish what has **caused** the present; and a comparative perspective to understand parallel developments in other countries.

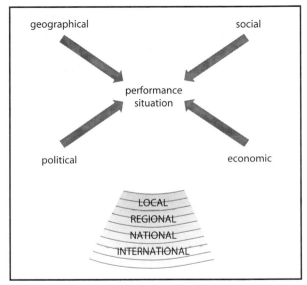

Figure 14.6 Main extrinsic factors that influence the performance situation.

14.1 Towards a Concept of Leisure

The ordinary citizen has to work for a living. He or she then has certain obligatory activities that have to be performed, such as sleeping and eating. What is left is leisure time.

All the activities in our field of study either take place in leisure time, are themselves leisure activities or prepare us for active leisure, and it is therefore essential that we understand what is meant by the term leisure. Let's start by making a list (Figure 14.7).

How clever are you at recognizing differences between these activities? Well, there would seem to be two major variables.

1. Not all leisure involves physical performance; for example, watching TV sport.

2. Physical performance is not always a leisure-time experience; for example, professional sport has work connotations.

It looks as if it might not be as simple as we thought! Let's play safe and look at what other people think leisure is.

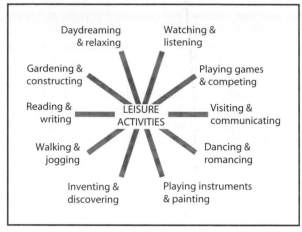

Figure 14.7 Leisure activities.

Leisure is time in which there is an opportunity for choice.

(Arnold, 1968)

Leisure has three functions: relaxation of energies consumed by daily life; free development—compensation for the specialization of movement and knowledge imposed by modern industrial life; and recreation—relief from the boredom and restrictions of daily life.

(McDonald, 1965)

Leisure helps people to learn how to play their part in society; it helps them to achieve societal or collective aims; and it helps the society to keep together.

(Parker, 1971)

Leisure is a mental and spiritual attitude—a condition of the soul, not the inevitable result of spare time.

(Pieper, 1965)

A necessary prerequisite for practising the more civilized virtues—the adoption of a critical attitude to life and developing a taste for excellence.

(Bell, 1947)

Leisure is the complex of self-fulfilling and self-enriching values achieved by the individual as he uses leisure time in self-chosen activities that recreate him.

(Miller and Robinson, 1963)

Leisure is an activity—apart from the obligations of work, family and society—to which the individual turns at will.

(Dumazedier, 1967)

Leisure consists of relatively self-determining activity-experiences that fall into one's economically free-time roles.

(Kaplan, 1975)

Review Questions

1. Remember, anyone can select quotations to make a biased case. Look for quotations by other authors and make an attempt at your own definition of leisure.

2. Before reading on, pick out the keywords in each quotation and assemble them in a model.

   These keywords should represent characteristics of leisure and you should try to fit them into a number of categories if you can.

Compare your presentation (see Review Questions) of the concept of leisure with the analysis in Figure 14.8. Don't worry too much if your format differs from ours, as there are many ways of presenting characteristics of a complex experience like leisure. However, we tend to use the same order of presentation with all models: structure (what); function (how); interpretation (why); conclusion (key).

Well, we have produced a list of words in Figure 14.8, characteristics of leisure, maybe, but now you need to establish what each word means and explain it in a physical performance situation that you have experienced.

Figure 14.8a–d Leisure!

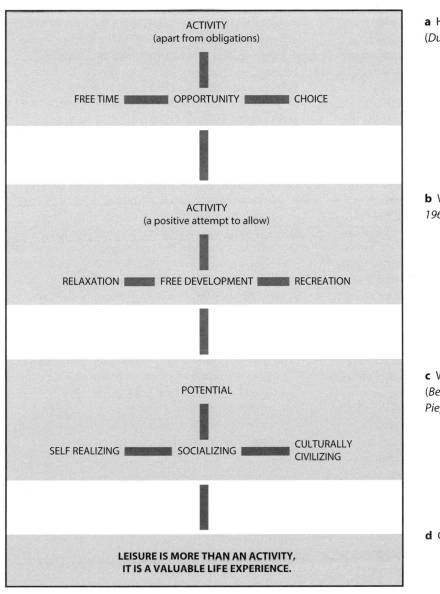

a How can we recognize it? (*Dumazedier, 1967; Arnold, 1968.*)

b What is its function? (*McDonald, 1965.*)

c What is its humanistic potential? (*Bell, 1947; Miller & Robinson, 1963; Pieper 1965; Parker, 1971.*)

d Conclusion?

Figure 14.9 Don't be a 'jock' all your life! Remember the reflective and the sportive should complement each other.

Investigation

14.1: The potential value of leisure

Read this short case study.

I'm John and I spend much of my leisure time gardening, but my wife, Jane, prefers the theatre and my two children love swimming.

We all pursue our favoured activities when we have the free time to do so, but once in a while we share each other's hobbies. Both my wife and I work, but on summer evenings I am able to visit my allotment, while she settles down to a good play on the TV. We don't have to do either of these things, but we enjoy them and respect each other's right to choose. Similarly, the children swim whenever they have the chance, which amounts to two or three times a week. Mary is a little more serious than Bill and so she tends to train quite hard while he just plays around. Either way, they come home tired, but happy.

Our hobbies certainly take us away from the boredom, conformity and stress of the working day and we find that we can relax within a few moments of tasting the atmosphere of our chosen activities. Funnily enough, although we often feel quite jaded when we start our various activities, the tiredness falls away as we accept the responsibilities of our chosen activity. There are always new situations which are totally unpredictable and my wife tells me that her greatest joy is to experience a play unfolding for the first time. Nor is she limited to watching plays on the TV, as she belongs to a small amateur company, which puts on plays twice a year, and she also visits the West End in London occasionally, as a special treat.

It is as if we are genuinely part of the experience. I sometimes feel that I am actually growing with the plants and Jane says that she often loses herself in the story she's watching.

The children, of course, with their practical activity, are able to express themselves physically, as well as test their temperament in the hurly-burly of the swimming baths, and they invariably come away from the pool exhausted but glowing inside.

Unfortunately, we find that our work is not very fulfilling. I work on a conveyor belt in a car factory and my wife is a typist in an office. We seem to spend each day doing the same thing, surrounded by the same noises and petty anxieties. Only our leisure activities seem to give us a chance to achieve something as individuals. I've learnt so much more about myself as a result of my leisure activity, sometimes reflecting on life's many foibles as I dig the ground each Autumn; at other times realizing, as I pick my own strawberries, that I am totally responsible for their existence; and, honestly, is there anything to equal the peace and quiet of a garden on a balmy summer evening?

Not that any of my family particularly want solitude—gosh, on the contrary, we seem to spend most of the time chatting to friends, sharing and caring, as they say, with a kind of sincerity that doesn't seem to occur very often at work.

I know I'm a better person as a result of the time I spend on the garden and the allotment; it's as if nature is slowing me down and actually giving me roots.

No one can tell me that gardening is just an activity. It is a diversion which is at once relaxing and invigorating; it broadens my experiences and has given me lasting friendships; it really is the free exercise of my creative capacity; and it's the only time in my life when I feel I actually taste excellence.

OK, so my family is involved in a pretty purposeful approach to leisure, but if I can paraphrase John Ruskin:

True creative fulfilment comes from the exertion of body or mind to please ourselves.

1. Pick out the key words that reflect the potential value of leisure. It is only a question of looking at Figure 14.8!
2. Establish your own role-play groups so that you can 'score points' in illustrating characteristics of leisure.

Always remember, however, that an activity is only the vehicle which allows a person to experience leisure.

Leisure in a Cultural Setting

At first sight, it would seem that leisure is a universal concept. However, all activity-experiences are influenced by their cultural setting, and so where there are societal differences between countries there will also be variables in the structure and function of leisure. Kaplan (1975) produced a six-model analysis, but we will use the less sophisticated approach suggested by Jelfs (1970).

Leisure is spare time

The most common concept of leisure is the negative view that leisure is non-work. It presents work as the valued ethic in society and tends to devalue leisure, presenting it as a means of restoring individuals for work. This leaves leisure with little or no independent identity and minimal cultural status.

This view still exists in the United Kingdom as a result of the industrial revolution and the Protestant work ethic. To paraphrase Huizinga (1964), 'Work was first of all the IDEAL and then the IDOL of the age.'

This sums up 19th-century English industrial society, and the ethic can still be seen today. Less evident in France and what was once the Soviet Union, it does have links with capitalist economics and so has found some favour in the United States.

Try to explain Figure 14.10, establishing what each term means and illustrating it wherever possible.

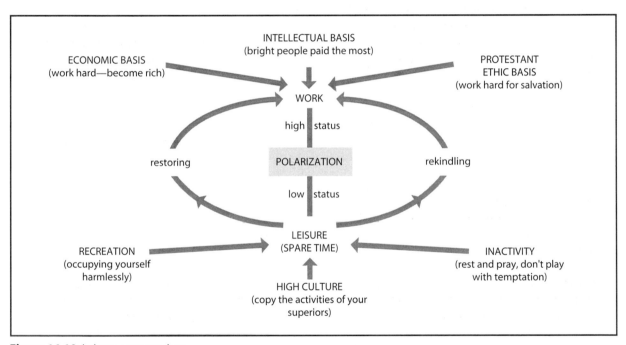

Figure 14.10 Leisure as spare time.

Leisure as an economic condition

This second concept of leisure is very closely identified with the first. An expression that describes it is: leisure as a reflection of cultural life-style—the point being that any inherent form of social inequality will be evident in a society's pattern of leisure.

See if you can explain Figure 14.11 using illustrations from your experience.

If we look at the British and American leisure scene we find a high and a low culture, which are partly determined by status in society. This may reflect social class variables, racial discrimination or gender inequalities. In England it is evident in the group who play polo, as against those who play soccer. In the USA a comparison might be made between golf and baseball. Even in activities that involve a mixture of social groups, cultural demarcation is often evident, even if this is only a vestige of the past. The English Derby, for example, has the Grandstand and Enclosure for 'Society', and the Downs, where popular culture continues to thrive.

As egalitarian trends reduce these traditional boundaries, fewer leisure activities are completely exclusive, but the traditional conservatism of many leisure activities gives them a permanence that resists change.

Leisure as a form of social control

This is identifiable in a society where social equality is very important, but also where deviance from a culturally acceptable pattern of behaviour is not tolerated. The key phrase here is purposeful leisure.

So far, we have seen leisure as an optional extra and as a feature of privileged groups in society. In both cases the values have tended to be intrinsic, which means the activities are seen to have little value outside themselves. This view is common to most of the Western World, and most strongly evident in Britain.

However, the former Soviet Union and other 'socialist' societies reflected this third concept much more strongly than America or the Common Market countries, because the former Soviet Union tended to be, and still is, more authoritarian, even though committed to an egalitarian political system. Such statements as 'good socialist principles' and 'for the good of the State' were commonplace until the break-up of the Union. Leisure was given considerable

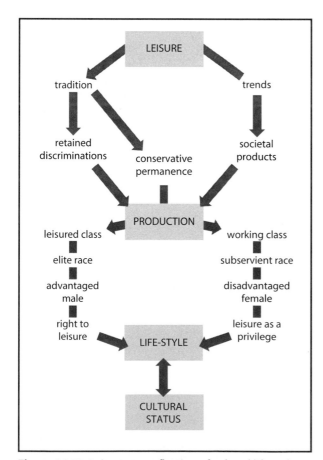

Figure 14.11 Leisure as a reflection of cultural life-style.

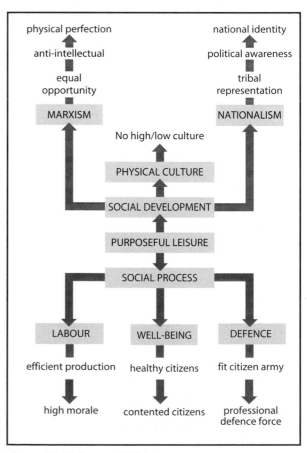

Figure 14.12 Purposeful leisure.

social status, designed to reinforce sociopolitical values and based on the belief that leisure had extrinsic value—which meant that it could influence the social development of a society and also exist as a social process in its own right.

See if you can work your way through Figure 14.12 and try to grasp why leisure had such prominence in societies like the former Soviet Union.

Leisure as a basis of self-realization

Finally, we have the most difficult concept to look at. We need to pick up the comments made by several of the authors we quoted earlier, where they wrote about humanistic values such as self-realization and socialization.

The potential of leisure as a medium for creative fulfilment is being increasingly recognized. It takes the social conditioning of the third model an extra step, where, in addition to the extrinsic usefulness of leisure, it is felt that in the modern world of sedentary jobs, packaged goods and repetitious work, the only creative moments may arise in our leisure experiences; that only leisure can give us all a taste of excellence. Though you might think that all this is pretty revolutionary, the notion goes back to Aristotle, who argued that leisure is the most serious human occupation or activity. If you combine this with Ruskin's comment in the 19th century that leisure is the exertion of body or mind to please ourselves, we have an enlightened view of leisure as the key to personal development in a democratic society and as an art form in the context of cultural advancement. Select a leisure experience you have had and trace it through Figure 14.13.

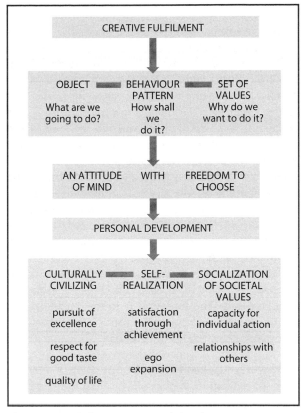

Figure 14.13 Leisure as personal development.

 Exam-Style Questions

1. Leisure is more than an activity; it is a valuable experience. Using examples:
a. How can you recognize leisure? (3 marks)
b. What is its function? (3 marks)
c. What is its potential as an experience to improve the quality of our lives? (3 marks)
2. The concept of leisure has a number of interpretations:
a. What are the limits of a work–leisure analysis? (4 marks)
b. How does the traditional view of leisure in Britain reflect its social class system? (4 marks)
c. Explain ways in which leisure can be a form of social control, where a society presumes that leisure is purposeful. (4 marks)
d. Explain leisure as an attitude of mind with freedom to choose. (4 marks)
(Total 25 marks.)

Summary

Leisure:
1. Freedom; relaxation; choice; opportunity; recreation.
2. Leisure time is time without obligation; an activity that is also an experience; a performance depending on attitude.
3. It is a non-work experience; an economic condition; a social process; and a basis for self-fulfilment.

14.2 Towards a Concept of Play

It is very important to understand what we mean by the term play. We use the word all the time and yet when we read about it in psychology books we find a highly complex area. Let's take it gradually.

Play is something we do. It involves ourselves and others in action. It tends to make us feel good, but it has little or nothing to do with the real world; in fact, we often play to get away from the real world. Children play much more than adults, and if it was not for the use of the word in the theatre and in sport we would probably feel that it concerned children only. Play is not necessarily a physical experience, but because it normally involves the whole person there is often a physical component.

When we are playing, we are behaving in such a way as to retain attitudes that have their origin in play; and when we are playful we are having fun (Figure 14.14).

Let's compare war and a football match for a moment. War is real. You fight and the consequence may be death. The intention is to kill. Jokingly, you might suggest that you have seen football matches like that! Well, first of all, football is kicking a ball about, it is fun. A match is contrived to test the temperament and skill of one group against another, through football. It is played according to fixed rules with playing area and timing strictly controlled. When the whistle goes it is over.

These are all characteristics of play, but occasionally rules are broken, violence breaks out and aggression goes on after the whistle. When this happens the game has left the world of play and become real; it can even become war!

Similarly, playing the game means you have made an undertaking to 'play the game'. If you cheat or commit fouls, you have stepped outside the play concept. We would argue that you have also stepped outside the moral concept of the game. The result of such behaviour will lead to the destruction of the play element immediately, and of the game situation eventually.

Can you identify any characteristics of play in Figures 14.15 and 14.16?

Figure 14.15 It's mine!

Figure 14.16 Let's go!

Figure 14.14 Go on! Enjoy yourself!

If you have an opportunity, do a critical review of the film Rollerball to explain what has happened to the twin concepts of play and game.

Finally, you will find that theorists invariably look at a pure form of play, largely because it is much easier to categorize. However, when you see play operating, it is clear that you are looking not at a pure form of it but at elements of play mixed in with moments of reality. This is almost always the case in our field of study.

Try to pick out the keywords that help to identify this thing called play from what has been written above. We have come up with the model in Figure 14.17. Compare it with your own.

Let us have a look at what other people think play is. Identify the key words in the following definitions and use a play activity to explain what is being suggested.

Play consists of activities for immediate gratification.

(Spencer)

Play is play because the observer thinks it is.

(Ellis)

If it's fun it's play.

(Biesty)

Play requires an achievement of a social self.

(Biesty)

Play serves as adaptive problem solving for children.

(Johnson and Snyder)

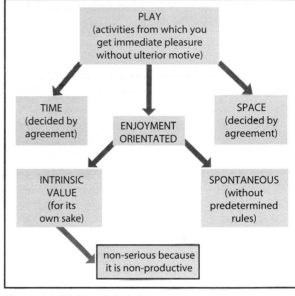

Figure 14.17 A model of play.

Review Questions

There has been a lot of theory written about play. What we need to do is to test some of these views against our own experiences.

1. Divide the following notions between members of the group, establishing the meaning of the different phrases and giving examples: civilization preparation; role rehearsal; surplus energy; recreation; instinctive practice; recapitulation; transmission of culture; personality development; cathartic function; ego expansion.

Alternatively, take a simple play activity like hide-and-seek and see how many of these interpretations can be linked with it.

What we are discovering is that play has many sides to it and, therefore, can have a wide range of interpretations and uses.

2. Now explain Figure 14.18.

3. The final test as to whether we understand the term play in the context of physical performance is to turn to Huizinga (1964).

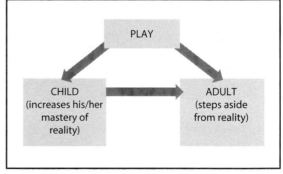

Figure 14.18 Functions of play.

Select a physical performance activity that you have played. Test the extent to which you were really playing from the following criteria:

a. Play is a voluntary activity, never a physical necessity or a moral duty. It is not a matter of leisure and free time, it is freedom.

Review Questions

continued

b. Play is not ordinary or real life, but this is not to say that play may not be intense or serious ... an interlude in our daily lives, an end in itself.
c. Play is a temporary world within and marked off from the ordinary world. It begins and is over in a specific moment and functions within limitations of time and space.
d. Play creates order; in fact it is order. Slight deviation from the rules spoils the game.
e. The play community tends to become permanent, because in the course of playing

you become part of an 'in-group', sharing a common existence.

If you have managed to understand these principles in the context of your chosen activity, you will realize that many of the components of play are immediately identifiable in physical recreation and sport. The more structured and commercially orientated sport is, the less play is evident, and one might argue that the sheer joy of participation is often lost because of the work-orientated values that exist in high-level sport, resulting in an obsession with a 'win-at-all-cost' ethic.

And so we end with the Huizinga (1964) definition: Play is an activity which proceeds within certain limits of time and space, in a visible order according to rules freely accepted, and outside the sphere of necessity or material utility. The play mood is one of rapture and enthusiasm and is sacred or festive in accordance with the occasion. A feeling of exaltation and tension accompanies the action; mirth and relaxation follow.

You will no doubt recognize these characteristics from your own experiences of games, individual activities and outdoor pursuits, and so there is every justification for us to continue to use the word play freely in our field of study and to expect sport for all to live up to the qualities that are an inherent part of the play concept.

It may not be obvious, but the application of play theory to playing games takes us away from the original emphasis by Huizinga (1964) and Caillois (1961) in that they stressed the temporary nature and spontaneity of play, largely discounting its developmental potential. The concept of play that we are adopting presumes that, given a retention of play attitudes, rules can facilitate rather than destroy a play situation. Secondly, that whether the game is won or lost, the experience can yet increase a person's ability to know themselves and others with greater emotional and social skill.

This explanation is very much part of the education in physical education and the test of temperament that exists in most sporting situations. It is also a counter to the 'win-at-all-costs' ethic, which presumes that only winners gain from a sporting competition.

Exam-Style Questions

You will have seen play activities taking place in the playgrounds of schools. They may be recognizable by their intention, such as 'hide and seek', or by the equipment being used, such as a ball or skipping rope.

1. Play has been defined as 'activity from which you get immediate pleasure without ulterior motive':

a. Explain this definition, using a play activity to illustrate you answer. (2 marks)

b. In what ways would you expect spontaneity to exist in your play activity? (3 marks)

c. Explain how time and space constraints may operate in your play activity. (3 marks)

2. It has also been said that 'play is a voluntary activity, never a physical necessity or moral duty':

a. How is this reflected in adult recreation? (3 marks)

b. Explain the suggestion that in play a child increases mastery of reality, but an adult escapes from it. (4 marks)

c. Figure 14.19 summarizes the characteristics of play and physical recreation:

i. How might a good physical education teacher make use of some of these characteristics of play? (4 marks)

ii. Use this diagram to identify why professional sport is different from physical recreation. (6 marks) (Total 25 marks.)

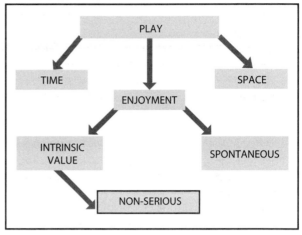

Figure 14.19 Characteristics of play and recreation.

Summary

Play:

1. Free time; free space; spontaneity; intrinsic; enjoyable; unreal.

2. Play is something we do: it is an activity-experience.

3. It is associated with children, but vestiges are retained into adulthood.

4. Play is non-serious because it is non-productive, and yet it may be a major factor in self-development.

14.3 Towards a Concept of Recreation

Recreation is a positive aspect of leisure and is widely used in the Western World to describe active leisure.

Two major problems with its universal acceptance concern its traditional association with the privileged classes, and the built-in presumption that it has intrinsic value only. 'Socialist' societies have tended not to use the term on these grounds. Let's see how others define it.

Activity voluntarily engaged in during leisure and motivated by the personal satisfactions which result from it ... a tool for mental and physical therapy.

(Kaplan, 1975)

Recreation embodies those experiences or activities that people take part in during their leisure for purposes of pleasure, satisfaction or education.

Recreation is a human experience or activity, it is not necessarily instinctive, it may be considered purposeful.

(Zeigler, 1964)

Recreation carries away the individual from his usual concerns and problems. The attitudes derived from this are those involving feelings of relaxation. Contentment not complacency might best describe an attitude which is a product of a recreative experience.

(Vanderswaag, 1972)

Recreation is a concept closely related to play ... It means literally to re-create or to refresh oneself in body and/or engagement. Recreational activity is also limited in time and space by the actor and requires no preparation or training. Recreation is also non-utilitarian in product.

(Edwards, 1973)

If you go through the same exercise of selecting key words, you will notice strong links with the analysis we have already done on leisure, but also be aware of the conflict between those who label recreation non-utilitarian and others who acknowledge that it can be purposeful. Significantly, all the authors quoted are American, and yet they cannot agree. Little wonder writers in the now disbanded Soviet Union find it an outmoded concept!

You will find that the four basic conceptual models we used to analyse leisure apply also to the slightly narrower field of recreation. We have taken characteristics mentioned in the quotations and built a model (Figure 14.20). Take a particular recreation and identify it in the context of each stage.

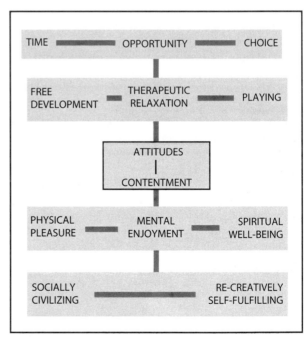

Figure 14.20 Towards a concept of recreation.

14.4 What do We Mean by Physical Recreation?

To date, you have been asked to identify the characteristics of leisure and recreation from a series of models and the occasional photograph. It is important that you should now get some practice in recognizing the characteristics yourself, from a series of statements that we will call notional propositions. It is for you to think them through and decide whether you accept them or wish to question them. At the end of the exercise, however, you should have a list of the central characteristics of physical recreation.

Having made the progression from the general concept of leisure to the narrower experience of recreation, it should be a relatively straightforward step to reduce the field that much more to include only physical recreation. This notion of narrowing is an important one, because the conceptual elements identified in the leisure analysis still hold true, but also because some of the cultural bias evident in recreation continues to operate in physical recreation.

The former Soviet Union, for example, tended to suspect that discrimination and non-functional values were still applied to the term physical recreation in the West. They chose to use the term *massovost*, which avoided these limitations. In Britain and France, the slogan sport for all is extremely popular and tends to be replacing the term physical recreation to describe physical performance opportunities for all members of the community, where emphasis is on participation rather than performance standards. Loy (1968) in the United States has coined the phrase game occurrence to describe physical activity that is playful, competitive and strategic, uses physical skill and prowess, but is played at a relatively unsophisticated level.

Probably the main reason why the term physical recreation is still used is simply tradition, but it would also seem that none of the other expressions are able to replace it completely. It is a wider concept than game; and the recreative can be at odds with the sportive. Similarly, how can we still incorporate the concept of outdoor recreation, which is very much in vogue, when we are suggesting that the concept of physical recreation is outmoded?

Outdoor recreation

This term survives not only because of the traditional romanticism associated with the countryside, but also because it invariably involves the challenge of self in the natural environment, which is more obviously recreative than the contrived competition of a game.

Outdoor recreation and the frontier spirit remain symbolic features of American ideology; also the former Soviet Union gave considerable political and national recognition to its outdoor policy, under the heading of tourism.

Participation for its own sake

This is the key to the identity of physical recreation and is also the reason why academics and politicians have claimed that it is non-serious. The assumption here is that if there is no intellectual or commercial value, it is not functionally important in a society.

The fact that, in the 19th century, recreative opportunity was to some extent limited to wealthy people who had the 'right', the money and the time to participate is no more than an accident of history, but may yet remain as a vestige of those times.

The privilege of a few has now become the right of the majority and so the social impact of physical recreation is that much broader. Now that almost everyone has the opportunity to recreate physically, we are increasingly motivated to gain from it—as a therapeutic experience; as a frontier experience, where we learn more about ourselves; and as a social experience, where we can make lasting friendships.

The key democratic factors are the right to choose; the opportunity to participate; and the provision to facilitate that freedom.

Little wonder that the Soviet Union was prepared to take these intrinsic elements and give them cultural status, on the grounds that here was an experience that would influence productivity and social well-being by improving health and increasing group morale.

American writers such as Slusher (1967), Vanderswaag (1972) and Hellison (1985) all argue that the self-realizing potential of physical performance makes it a vital element in personal development. This would seem to be particularly true in a country where individual decision-making is a cornerstone of the culture.

There may even be a case for using the term physical recreation in a more general context, where sport is identified as one specialized aspect of it.

In societies where taking part is more highly valued than winning, the recreative component may be stronger than the competitive one (Figure 14.21). After all, there is not so much a conceptual difference between physical recreation and sport, as a gradually increasing intensity of efficiency at the professionalized end of the continuum.

Figure 14.21 This is my idea of heaven.

Hold on a minute: surely professional sport, as a means of livelihood, can hardly be identified as a physical recreation!

We have already made the point that physical activities can be recreational, sporting or educational, depending on the level of commitment. Furthermore, certain words specifically identify activities at a recreative level. For example, rambling, pony trekking, hill-walking, paddling, cycle touring and boating reflect outdoor activities as pastimes rather than as sports; jogging, bathing and aerobics are recreative forms of individual activity; in addition, there are phrases like kick about at football, knock about at tennis or a friendly game of golf that imply that a game is being played at a low competitive key.

These words and phrases tell us that the physical activity is recreative and being enjoyed with minimal organization. We have now gathered enough characteristics of physical recreation to produce our own conceptual model as a framework to test our understanding.

It is most important that you should be able to operationalize this framework, so take a physical activity that you have experienced at a recreative level and use it to illustrate the key words in Figure 14.22.

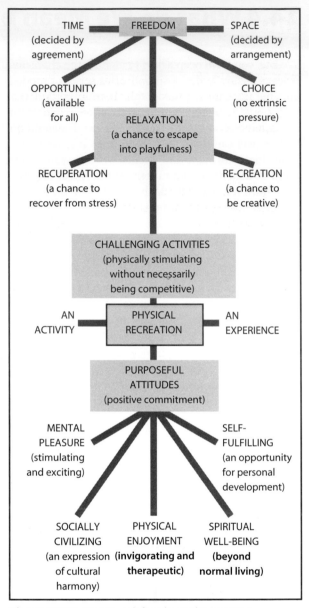

Figure 14.22 Framework for physical recreation.

Review Questions

You have your experience of recreating; you have made a systematic analysis of leisure characteristics earlier in this chapter; and you now have a range of notions outlining the qualities one would expect in physical recreation.

1. Using this knowledge, select one outdoor activity, one individual activity and one game from Figures 14.23–14.25, and describe the characteristics you would expect to find if you were playing these at a physical recreation level.

a. Outdoor activities. Study Figure 14.23 and identify what these outdoor pursuits have in common.

Figure 14.23 Outdoor activities.

b. Individual activities. Why are the individual activities in Figure 14.24 'recreative' rather than 'sporting'?

c. Games. What clues are there in Figure 14.25 to suggest that the players have a recreative attitude? Could we be wrong?

Figure 14.24 Recreative activities.

Figure 14.25 Various games.

Exam-Style Questions

1. a. Outdoor recreation allows man and woman to re-create in ideal surroundings.
i. What qualities are you likely to find in the natural environment that could lead to the use of the term 'romanticism'? (4 marks)
ii. Use any one photograph in Figures 14.23–14.25 to explain the association of freedom and adventure. (6 marks)
b. i. Explain how therapy appears to result from considerable effort in the outdoors. (6 marks)
ii. Why do you think bonds of friendship are so strong after expeditions similar to those shown in Figures 14.23–14.25? (9 marks)
(Total 25 marks.)
2. a. Individual activities do not have to be based on competition.
i. Explain the idea of being 'free to move'. (3 marks)

ii. Select any one picture from Figures 14.23–14.25 and discuss the 'health related' qualities depicted. (3 marks)
iii. What can you learn about yourself if you become involved in an individual activity at a recreative level? (4 marks)
b. The most important element in a game is the enjoyment that arises from taking part.
i. Why do you think a game should always be 'friendly'? (3 marks)
ii. Why is participation in a game so rewarding even when the standard of play is low? (4 marks)
iii. We say that we 'play' a game. Explain the elements of play that can exist in any one of the games in Figures 14.23–14.25. (8 marks)
(Total 25 marks.)

 Summary

Physical recreation:
1. Free time; free space; enjoyment orientated; recuperative; spiritual well-being.
2. Physical recreation is a part of recreation. It can include most sporting activities, but also includes physical activities that are not competitive.
3. Participation is invariably more important than results where the recreative component is dominant.

14.5 Towards a Concept of Sport

Sport is commonplace and yet always controversial. It is universal in the sense that every country practises it, and yet it does not always take the same form in each country. Everyone seems to know what it means, but it doesn't always mean the same to everyone.

There are three levels at which we can attempt to explain these apparent contradictions:

1. Sports and pastimes are as old as civilization and many features and values of modern sport are vestiges of the past.

2. Sport reflects the culture to which it belongs and, therefore, it also reflects cultural variables.

3. Sport is a sophisticated concept and, while it is relatively easy to identify its universal characteristics, the more we refine our definition the more varied the cultural interpretation.

Let's first of all clarify the historical connotations. You must be well aware that sports and pastimes are as old as civilization itself. There is ample archaeological evidence that ancient societies indulged in physical activities ranging from bull-leaping in the Minoan culture of Crete to the football game of Tsu Chu played in China over 3000 years ago. You will be aware of the Ancient Greek Olympic Games, but you may not realize that Olympian Games also took place in Medieval England, as witnessed by the Dover Games; and re-emerged in Victorian England with the Much Wenlock Olympian Games, well before the 1896 modern Olympic Games were revived.

 Review Questions

1. Do you know a sport when you see one?
- Under the heading of games, football, hockey, baseball and tennis, for example, all seem to be acceptable—but what about poker, chess or table skittles?
- Individual activities, such as track and field, swimming and gymnastics, are unquestionably sports, but what about sunbathing, skipping or body building?

- We have no doubts about outdoor pursuits such as canoeing and rock climbing, but what about cycling, motor racing, hunting, angling and horseracing?

Take some of these activities and discuss your reservations about them being part of sport.

2. Look at Figures 14.26 and 14.27. What characteristics determine whether these are sports or not?

Figure 14.26 How many for tennis?

Figure 14.27 And they're off!

In answering the Review Questions here, you have been determining what is necessary for an activity to be a sport. This is the first level of definition.

If, on the other hand, we look briefly at the cultural factors, there is ample evidence that different primitive cultures have evolved sports and pastimes that reflect their needs. The sports of the Canadian

Eskimo may have little in common with those of the Australian aborigine. Even where cultures are geographically related, there are major differences. In Polynesia, for example, the war-like contests in Fiji are very different from the land-diving festival in the New Hebrides.

Controversially, a case has been made by Elias (Elias and Dunning, 1970) that these ancient and primitive sports are not sport in the modern definition of the term. He suggests that the Genesis of Sport is the product of the European industrial revolution in the 19th century, and is consequently a highly sophisticated institution matching the technology of such advanced societies as those in the United States and Western Europe.

Having made our own attempt to classify sport, let's find an authoritative view.

The International Council for Sport and Physical Education (ICSPE) (1964) has suggested that:

Any physical activity which has the character of play and which takes the form of a struggle with oneself or involves competition with others is a sport.

Did you pick out elements such as physical, play, struggle with self, and competition when you were identifying those activities earlier?

Michener (1977) has a similar definition of sport:

An athletic activity requiring physical prowess or skill and usually of a competitive nature.

Should we take the Kaplan (1975) notion on board again and suggest that sports are more than activities in that they are also experiences? Certainly, we could argue that participation in a sport can be a most worthwhile experience.

The notion of sport as an experience is supported by Inglis (1977) when he suggests that:

Sport is a scrapbook of memories which defines life. It involves a peculiar and intense awareness of yourself, a self-consciousness, in which the point of awareness is to get something right which is quite outside yourself.

Let's not forget our definition of physical recreation and the associated term, game occurrence. We have not defined anything which is exclusively sport as yet, have we? However, it is worth making the point that we are reinforcing the notion that sport is at one end of a physical recreation continuum (Calhoun, 1987).

Don't worry if you are still unsure whether some activities are sports or not. Many others have also tried to define what are sports or not with only limited success.

Caillois (1961), in his analysis of *paida* to *ludus* (play to games), classified sports into four main categories:
- Agon (competition).
- Mimicry (pretence).
- Alea (chance).
- Ilinx (vertigo).

Huizinga (1964) extended these to eight:
- Pursuit (chase).
- Enigma (mental).
- Chance (gamble).
- Vertigo (heady).
- Strategy (planning).
- Imitation (pretence).
- Dexterity (skill).
- Exultation (excitement).

McIntosh (1987) suggested:
- Competition.
- Aesthetic.
- Combat.
- Chance.
- Conquest.

There is considerable overlap between these three attempts at classification. It should also be clear that, whereas some activities or experiences fall within one criterion alone, other sports fall into two or more.

If you use the Huizinga (1964) classification, it also seems reasonable to suggest that the more criteria that operate in any particular activity, the more secure its status as a sport.

Test these propositions by describing the sport criteria evident in:

1. horseracing,
2. rowing.

We are now ready for a second level of analysis. Are there any set conditions as to how an activity should be performed before it can be accepted as a sport?

The ICSPE (1964) claimed that:

If this activity involves competition, then it should always be performed with a spirit of sportsmanship. There can be no true sport without the idea of fair play.

The assumption is that sport and sportsmanship are inseparable, definitive components of the sporting experience.

Noel-Baker (1965) suggested that:

Fair play is the essence, the sine qua non, of any game or sport that is worthy of the name.

Similarly, the following words of Baron de Coubertin are displayed at all the modern Olympic Games:

The most important thing in the Olympic Games is not to win but to take part, just as the most important thing in life is not the triumph but the struggle.

This moral intention is further reinforced in the Olympic oath, where reference is made to:

... respecting and abiding by the rules that bind them, in the true spirit of sportsmanship, for the glory of sport and the honour of our teams.

Before you point to the cheating and corruption, the drug abuse and the political intrigue that are commonplace in the modern Olympics, remember we are trying to establish what sport ought to be. Time enough later to recognize all the shortcomings.

An explanation of this moral requirement is best achieved at the three levels used earlier: historical, cultural and ideological.

Ancient and primitive societies have consistently used sport festivals as a ritual expression of their cultures. The Ancient Olympic Games reflected the Man of Action concept held by citizen Greeks; the Tournament reinforced the Chivalric Code in 12th-century Europe; the Courtly Mould was a cornerstone of Tudor England and Renaissance Europe; and the emergence of the Gentleman Amateur in 18th- and 19th-century England reflected the lifestyle of a leisured class.

In each case, the elite members of a civilization used sport to reflect the ideals they held most dear. It is important to recognize that sport was the arena in which physical prowess and temperament were tested.

There were various times when these ethics were closely tied to religious beliefs: Greek gods were idealized humans; the chivalric code fuelled the Crusades; and muscular Christianity was inspired by Gentlemen Amateurs who were also social Christians. Nor must we forget that 19th-century Athleticism in the English Public Schools was a duality of physical endeavour and moral integrity, not one or the other.

The bonding through tradition, therefore, is very clearly defined. However, we need to recognize that cultures differ and this means that, in addition to sport differing, the values associated with it vary from one country to another.

Gardner (1974) examined the American 'Win' ethic, linking it with the 'Lombardian' commitment of American professional sport and the pressures of capitalism and commercialism in American society.

See if you can discover who Vince Lombardi was and why he is quoted so much by American sports commentators.

Little wonder that the European ethic of 'doing your best' has been regarded as an excuse for weakness. Mind you, professional British sport is equally sceptical of this amateur ethic. Lombardism, on the other hand, defends the view that only winners matter in sport and society, turning the Olympic model on its head and emphasizing the triumph rather than the struggle. If you want to continue this dialogue, it is probable that the humanist would reply that the struggle to do one's best is socially desirable and open to all, but that triumph is a reward for a few and a mark of failure for the rest.

There is a very interesting relationship here with rewards. The Greeks had a laurel wreath and 19th-century amateurs had medals—token reminders of the struggle. Today, an elite group of athletes receives great wealth, because commercialism idealizes the champion in order to sell products to the envious. We find emergent cultures promoting their champions for such reasons as giving their citizens a sense of national pride or, more questionably, as an opium to forget hardship or revolution.

The Soviet culture, interestingly, needed winners to reinforce its political identity and yet could not justify the promotion of individualism in a so-called socialist society. Consequently, 'to do your best' was a very real Soviet concept, but it had to be for society rather than for self.

Fair play, therefore, is under attack from professional and commercial forces. Sport and sportsmanship have become political instruments and expedients. In both instances they represent a dominance of extrinsic factors that undermine the intrinsic values.

We must defend sport from these external excesses, if we believe that the essence of sport is sportsmanship.

As early as 1968 Lüschen pointed out that sport had the potential to be functional or dysfunctional. It is an arena where 'man' is tested and may fail to cope with the situation. How many of you have fouled in a game in the heat of the moment, hopefully to regret it later?

If you want to achieve the highest moral experience from sport, you should be able to play to the rules regardless of having a referee present. Jimmy White, the professional snooker player, repeatedly acknowledges when he has committed a foul stroke, regardless of whether the referee has seen it. Here is the principle of 'walking at cricket'.

In life, there are those of us who would not steal on principle, while others do not steal because they are afraid of being caught. Similarly, some of us need the referee to be there to make decisions for us. Hopefully, we accept his decision even if we don't agree with it, but there are times when we argue with the referee or even retaliate against an offending player. When we do this the experience is detrimental to us as a person and detrimental to the game.

Nash developed this concept in the context of Recreation and Leisure—Figure 14.28 is an adjustment of his model to match the sporting situation.

The third level of analysis is the one which allows us to distinguish between physical recreation (a game occurrence) and sport.

You will recall that Inglis (1977) identified an 'intense awareness ... to get something right'. Similarly, McIntosh (1987) wrote about 'striving for superiority against man and/or nature'. Weiss (1969), Loy (1969) and Howell and Howell (1986) all define sport as a highly organized game requiring physical prowess.

This is the identification of sport as an institution. To understand this we need to take it through three stages:

1. As an administrative feature. To paraphrase Dunning (Elias and Dunning, 1970)—sport has a stringent organization; fully standardized codification; a high level of permanence and regularity; and technological sophistication.

2. It requires a performer to embark on a high level of physical preparation, involving fitness and skill ability.

3. It invariably demands an attitude of commitment, a struggle to focus the mind and body on attaining the goals of the competition or challenge situation.

high 3 (functional)	personal decision in the true spirit of the game	creative participation	inventive player/coach
2	personal decisions regarding the rules of play	active participation	playing the part: role-play
1	acceptance of the referee	emotional participation	observational appreciation
0	reluctant acceptance of the referee	entertainment amusement escape from monotony of killing time	antidote for boredom
-1	arguing with the referee	injury or detriment to self	excesses
-2 (dysfunctional)	retaliation	violence against other players	crime

Figure 14.28 Application of Nash's model.

We need look only at great athletes like Don Bradman (Australia), Daley Thompson (UK), Mark Spitz (USA), Jean-Claude Killy (France), and Ludmilla Turishcheva (former USSR) to identify the time and attitude commitment; the outstanding quality of performance; and the administrative support system necessary for them to have achieved their optimum level of performance.

What we have, therefore, is a three tier analysis: certain activities or experiences involving a spirit of fair play at the highest level of personal excellence.

What will have become obvious is that the more professionalized the sport, the less affinity there is with Huizinga's play criteria. Edwards (1973) goes so far as to say that sport has nothing in common with play, but this seems too categorical. Howell and Howell (1986) seem nearer the mark when they write that:

> An individual has to have satisfaction from playing the sport, otherwise it ceases to be a sport. A professional athlete whose only concern is money and who does not care for the activity itself would no longer be engaged in sport, but work.

It might seem that this combination necessarily excludes the Sport for All concept. However, though attention is automatically drawn to a professionalized elite, the term personal excellence has been deliberately chosen because it describes any person with the commitment to strive for his or her own optimum level of achievement. The Sport for All campaign is designed to give everyone this opportunity, and if they choose to retain a recreative attitude, so be it, but the provision, opportunity and esteem are all there to be grasped in the fullness and freedom of a leisure-time decision.

It is important that you should be able to illustrate Figure 14.29 from your own experience of a sport. You could trace a sport at which you have competed and then take the likely path of a successful professional performer. Comparing these two pathways is worthwhile, but it is also important that you refer back to Figure 14.22 and compare it with

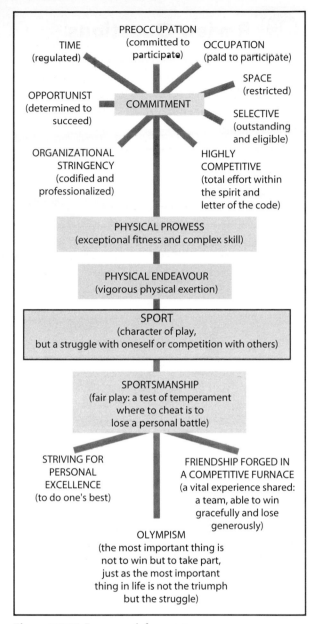

Figure 14.29 Framework for sport.

Figure 14.29, explaining the extent to which the concepts of physical recreation and sport can differ.

Test your understanding of the concept of sport

Select a specific sport with which you are acquainted and use it to explain the following definition of sport:

> Sport is an institutionalized competitive activity that involves vigorous physical exertion or the use of relatively complex physical skills by individuals whose participation is motivated by a combination of the intrinsic satisfaction associated with the activity itself and the external rewards earned through participation.
>
> (Coakley, 1982)

Review Questions

1. Test your understanding by identifying one of your own experiences in each of the labelled boxes in Figure 14.30, briefly explaining what is happening as you move from top left to bottom right.

2. This is a good time to reaffirm that no classification in our field of study is going to be perfect—and so have fun trying to point out the errors in this one. Then, if you are brave enough, produce your own format and defend it.

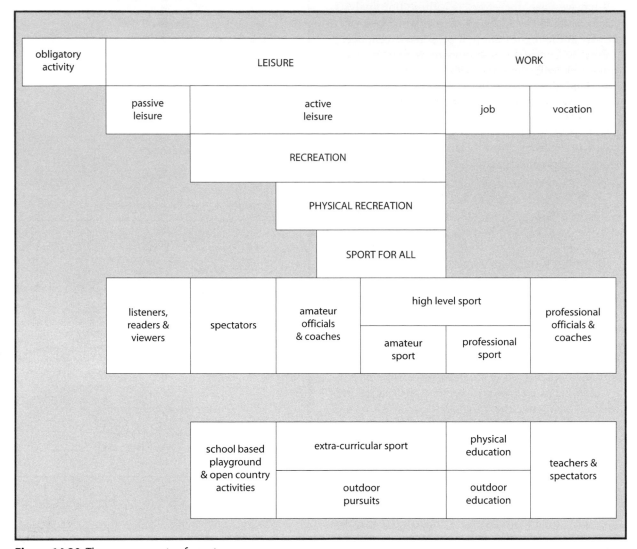

Figure 14.30 The many aspects of sport.

Exam-Style Questions

Sport may be defined as a highly structured physical activity with a high degree of commitment. Use this definition and the model in Figure 14.31 to answer the following questions.

1. a. In terms of sporting commitment, what is the difference between preoccupation and occupation? (4 marks)

b. How does the use of time and space differ in sport from children at play? (4 marks)

c. Explain the differences between physical prowess and physical endeavour. (4 marks)

2. Describe the main features of organizational stringency in sport. (3 marks)

3. Attitudes are a central factor in sport:

a. What do we mean when we talk about the letter and the spirit of the game? (2 marks)

b. Explain ideal relationships between competitors during and after a competition. (4 marks)

c. Distinguish between sportsmanship and gamesmanship. (4 marks)

(Total 25 marks.)

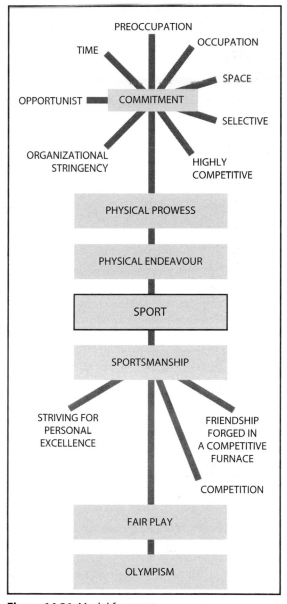

Figure 14.31 Model for sport.

Summary

Sport:

1. Sport for all or sporting excellence; amateurism and professionalism; commercialism and spectatorism; sport and sportsmanship.

2. Sport consists of contests, conquests, games and chance.

3. Sport is an activity-experience, reflecting dynamic attitudes.

4. Sport and society are intertwined.

5. Sport is an institution and a social process.

14.6 What is Physical Education?

It might help to begin with to establish where the term is used:

- numerous Universities award degrees in physical education (PE);
- it is a subject taught in all schools and is part of the core curriculum;
- the main administrative body is the Physical Education Association (PEA);
- the term is used to describe several GCSE and Advanced level GCE syllabuses.

However, authors tend to write about physical education and sport, and so presumably they are not one and the same thing. And although the term appears to have a similar currency in the United States, France and Britain, this is less the case in the diverse group of countries, federation of republics, etc., that once comprised the Soviet Union.

Let's look first at the situation in the former USSR. Though the term physical education is used, physical culture is a more common expression. Riordan (1977) suggested that this more general concept could be defined as:

> *The sum total of social achievements connected with man's physical development and education.*

If this is to be accepted, what was once the Soviet Union has a collective term for the whole of our field of study.

We intend to work from a very narrow definition of physical education, in which it is limited to:

> *The formal inculcation of knowledge and values through physical activity and/or experiences.*

As a direct result, physical education is most likely to be practised in educational institutions. The Leeds Study Group (1970) defined physical education as:

> *A term used to describe an area of educational activity in which the main concern is with bodily movement.*

(where the words 'educational activity' are presumed to mean the formal inculcation of socially desirable knowledge and values). The actual activities are often common to those already identified in play, physical recreation and sport, and are those found in the school curriculum.

1. a. Using your own school as an example, explain Figure 14.32 in terms of curriculum PE, extra-curricular programmes and recreational activities.
b. Why is a pyramid such a useful analogy?

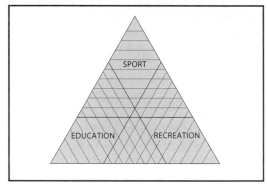

Figure 14.32 Pyramidal model of physical performance opportunities in schools.

2. a. Again using your own school as an example, explain Figure 14.33 in terms of relationships.
b. Why are circles such a useful analogy in this context?

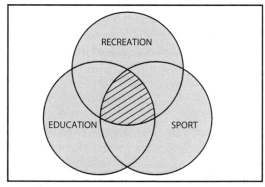

Figure 14.33 Relationships within physical performance opportunities in schools.

3. List the activities on your curriculum under two headings: core subjects and options.
4. Select one of your favourite physical education activities and use it to explain the three ways of knowing and understanding physical performance shown in Figures 14.32 and 14.33.

The core subjects will probably be common to most schools and include major games, gymnastics, track and field, and swimming. These are normally compulsory activities, but may vary according to gender and age group.

It is very important at this point to recognize that curriculum physical education is only one of a number of physical performance opportunities in the average school. Groves (1972) produced two diagrams to illustrate this relationship between physical education, physical recreation and sport in schools (Figures 14.32 and 14.33).

The optional subjects will probably be less common because they have not been a traditional part of the curriculum, because they are less physical or because they are too expensive in terms of time, space or cost. Some of the activities we have recognized as sports may not be included in the school curriculum for these reasons, but some sports may not be suitable for children; for example, they may be too dangerous to be pursued at school.

There are a number of traditional reasons why certain activities are included in the PE curriculum. For example, gymnastics has military and therapeutic roots; games owe much to the character building ethic of the English public schools in the 19th century; and swimming has had links with cleanliness and safety.

There is also a very strong cultural association. Examples of high prestige activities dominating the curriculum for economic and popularity reasons include American football and basketball in the United States; gymnastics and skiing in the one-time Soviet Union; and cricket and football in England.

However, the overriding reason for teaching a particular activity should be its potential as a medium for education. Lüschen (1967), for example, subdivided sports into functional and dysfunctional, meaning that the latter had a detrimental influence on society. In England today, the behaviour associated with professional soccer might lead educationists to the conclusion that the game should not be taught in schools. Conversely, it can be argued that there is an even greater need to teach it, to reform its popular image.

It would seem that certain activities have more potential as a vehicle for the inculcation of desirable values. Currently, in England, gymnastics is regarded as an ideal medium by educationists, whereas table tennis is generally presumed to have only recreative value. These are dangerous presumptions as most sporting activities can become educational vehicles in the right hands.

A great deal also depends on the knowledge and values being promoted; for example, the choice of gymnastics in England is linked with heuristic, therapeutic and individualistic values, currently in vogue in educational circles. Alternatively, the importance of football in the American high school is tied to the significance of the sports ethic in the community and the socio-economic importance of competition and manliness.

We certainly need to tease out these societal variables before we can suggest what physical education ought to be in any one particular country. What we need to do, therefore, is to produce a series of models that can easily be adjusted to meet the needs of different societies.

First of all, we will look at knowledge. We teach physical education because we think it is a useful body of knowledge, the implication being that having this knowledge will make us better people and enhance our life-style.

We can assess its usefulness at three levels:

1. **Knowing about** physical activities should help us to understand them and enable us to talk about them.

2. **Knowing how** to perform allows us to express ourselves through physical skills and competitive performance.

3. **Knowing how it feels** to perform gives us an enriching experience that is possible only in a performance situation.

We teach physical education because we can promote desirable values both as an intrinsic experience and to achieve extrinsic ends. Let's look at these values under four main headings. Where you can, illustrate each one from your experience of a game, an individual activity, a contest and an outdoor pursuit.

1. **Instrumental values**: those directly linked with physical performance (Figure 14.34).

2. **Economic values**: those which are useful in everyday life and valuable to the community (Figure 14.35).

3. **Humanistic values**: those which help in the development of a wholesome personality (Figure 14.36).

4. **Quality of life aspects**: those which carry experience beyond the ordinary in terms of awareness and commitment (Figure 14.37).

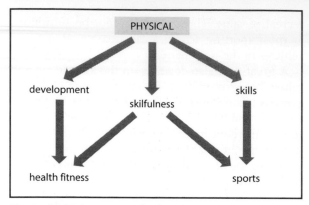

Figure 14.34 Instrumental values.

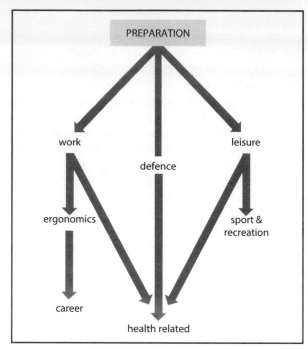

Figure 14.35 Economic values.

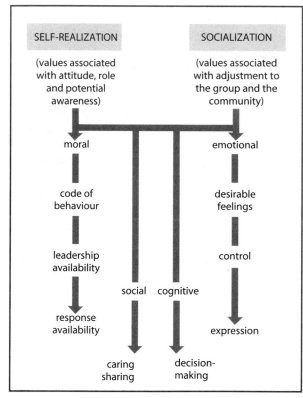

Figure 14.36 Humanistic values.

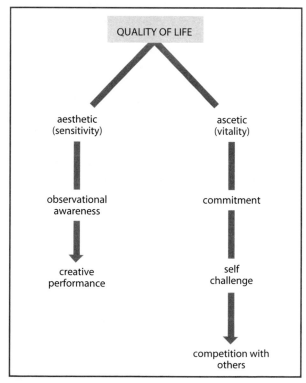

Figure 14.37 Quality of life.

If you have explained each of these models in the context of a particular physical education activity, you should be aware of the potential range of intentions in the mind of a teacher. It is not enough to claim that this experience is physical education because the children are learning skills. Performance skills have obvious values in active leisure terms, but a good teacher looks for an opportunity to educate the performer at each of the four levels identified.

Remember, the first concern of a sports coach is performance, but for the physical educationist it is the person. The all-important factor is that if a comprehensive knowledge and a wide range of values are inculcated through physical education during the formative years of childhood, it is more likely that physical recreation and sport will have a functional rather than a dysfunctional influence on adult life-style.

When looking at the concept of physical recreation, a special case was made for outdoor recreation. A similar situation arises between physical education and outdoor education. Conceptually, outdoor education is a part of physical education in that outdoor pursuits are sports that are included in the physical education curriculum, and the use of the term education implies that both involve the formal inculcation of knowledge and values.

However, we make special mention of outdoor education because, whereas games, contests and individual activities function in controlled surroundings, outdoor pursuits tend to be undertaken in a natural environment that is not entirely predictable. Also, in most physical activities, the environment simply regulates the activity, but in outdoor education the natural environment stimulates the activity.

A series of definitions may be useful at this point:

Outdoor education is learning in and for the outdoors.

(Patmore, 1972)

Outdoor education contains within it a combination of outdoor pursuits and studies in the rural environment, but it is not necessary for them to be practised simultaneously or even in proportion to one another.

(Parker and Meldrum, 1971)

Outdoor education is a means of approaching educational objectives through guided direct experiences in the environment using its resources as learning materials.

(NAOE, 1974)

Mortlock (1984) advanced the understanding of outdoor education in his book *The Adventure Alternative*. His analysis of natural examination, the instinct for adventure and an awareness of risk suggests that outdoor education has an advantage over games and individual activities because it places the individual at the decision-making frontier.

Bonnington (1981) examines this powerful element of adventure, an experience that is not always evident in other physical activities; and Mortlock (1984) suggests that it requires an individual to differentiate between real and perceived risk, and this helps a person to become a part of nature rather than a conqueror of it.

The word 'escape' is often used in sports history, where people have tried to find an alternative experience. In our urbanized society, the need for an escape to the simplicity of the natural environment has never been greater.

Review Questions

1. Select an outdoor activity and use it to examine one of Mortlock's propositions (Figure 14.38).

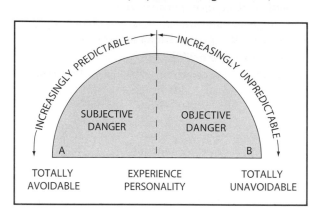

Figure 14.38 Danger diagram. Subjective danger: that potentially under the control of the human being, e.g. correct choice and use of equipment. Objective danger: that over which the human being has no control, e.g. avalanches, blizzards, floods, storms. Beginners will be working at the left end of the base line AB. Committed experts will be taking on challenges at the right end of the base line.

2. We have now analysed the concepts of leisure, play, physical recreation, sport and physical education. As we have progressed from one to the other, relationships between them have been discussed. Test your understanding of these conceptual relationships by writing a critical evaluation of the model in Figure 14.39.

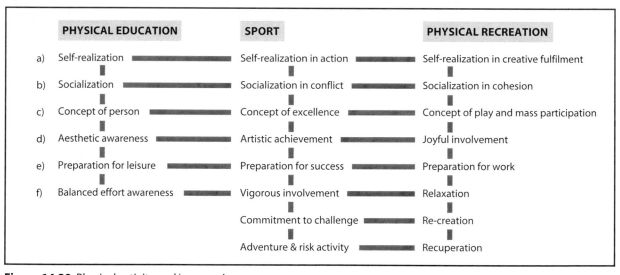

Figure 14.39 Physical activity and/or experience.

Exam-Style Questions

1. Figures 14.32 and 14.33 are diagrams which show that curriculum physical education is only one of a number of physical performance opportunities in the average school.
a. What does the outside perimeter to Figure 14.32 represent? (3 marks)

b. What administrative units do the three main inner triangles represent? (3 marks)
c. Explain the decision to overlap the triangles, using a PE curriculum activity as an example. (5 marks)
d. Why would it be better to describe Figure 14.32 as a pyramid? (3 marks)

Exam-Style Questions

continued

e. Explain the additional relationships the set of circles shows in Figure 14.33, using your own school or college as an example. (3 marks)

2. Figure 14.38 illustrates different types of danger in outdoor adventure activities.

a. Using an outdoor adventure activity as an example, establish the difference between objective and subjective danger and explain how this varies according to the difficulty of the challenge. (4 marks)

b. You are leading a group of young people on an extended walk or down a white water river in canoes. Explain the difference between real and perceived risk in one of these situations. (4 marks)
(Total 25 marks.)

Summary

Physical education:

1. Formal inculcation of knowledge and values; an educational instrument.

2. May include outdoor education.

3. Fundamentally a physical experience, it is also concerned with cognitive and moral development.

Further Reading

Armstrong N. (ed) *New Directions in Physical Education*, vol 1, PEA, Human Kinetics, 1990.

Arnold P.J. *Education, P.E. & Personality Development*, Heinemann, 1968.

Arnold P.J. Notes on use and meaning of the term leisure. *Bulletin of P.E.*, 1978; 14(1).

Beisty P. If its fun, is it play? In: Mergen B. (ed) *Cultural Dimensions of Play, Games and Sport*, Human Kinetics, 1986.

Bell C. *Civilisation*, Pelican, 1947.

Bonnington C. *Quest for Adventure*, Hodder & Stoughton, 1981.

Caillois R. *Man, Play and Games*, Free Press, 1961.

Calhoun D.W. *Sport, Culture and Personality*, Human Kinetics, 1987.

Coakley J.J. *Sport and Society: Issues and Controversies*, Mosby, 1982.

Dumazedier J. *Towards a Society of Leisure*, Collier-Macmillan, 1967.

Edwards H. *Sociology of Sport*, Homewood, 1973.

Elias N. and Dunning E. *Sociology of Sport*, Frank Cass, 1970.

Ellis M.J. *Why People Play*, Prentice Hall, 1973.

Fine G.A. (ed) *Meaningful Play, Playful Meaning*, TAASP, vol II, Human Kinetics, 1987.

Gardner P. *Nice Guys Finish Last*, Allen Lane, 1974.

Groves R. PE, recreation and competitive sport. *PE Bulletin*, 1972; 9(3).

Hellison D. *Humanistic PE*, Prentice Hall, 1975.

Hellison D.R. *Goals and Strategies for Teaching Physical Education*, Human Kinetics, 1985.

Howell R. and Howell M. *Physical Education Foundations*, Brooks Waterloo, 1986.

Huizinga J. *Homo Ludens: A Study of the Play Element in Culture*, Beacon, 1964.

ICSPE. *Definition of Sport*, International Council of Sport and PE, 1964.

Inglis F. *The Name of the Game*, Heinemann, 1977.

Jelfs B. *Towards a Concept of Leisure*, ATCDE (PE) Conference Papers, 1970.

Johnson E.P. and Snyder K. The lighter side of play. In: Mergen B. (ed) *Cultural Dimensions of Play, Games and Sport*, Human Kinetics, 1986.

Kaplan M. *Leisure, Theory and Policy*, Wiley, 1975.

Kenyon G.S. and Loy J.W., Jr. *Sociology of Sport*, Chicago, Athletic Institute, 1969.

Kretchmar, R.S. *Practical Philosophy of Sport*, Human Kinetics, 1994.

Leeds Study Group. *Physical Education Journal*, 1970; 1(4).

Loy J.W. The nature of sport. *Quest*, 1968.

Lüschen G. *Sociology of Sport*, Mouton, 1968.

McIntosh P.C. *Fair Play. Ethics in Sport and Education*, Heinemann, 1979.

McIntosh P.C. *Sport in Society*, West London Press, 1987.

Michener J.A. *Sports in America*, Fawcett, 1977.

Miller N.P. and Robinson D.H. *The Leisure Age*, Wadsworth, 1963.

Morgan R.E. *Concerns and Values in PE*, Bell, 1974.

Mortlock C. *The Adventure Alternative*, Cicerone Press, 1984.

Parker S.R. *The Future of Work and Leisure*. MacGibbon & Kee, 1971.

Parker T.H. and Meldrum K.I. *An Approach to Outdoor Activities*, National Association of Outdoor Education Publishers, 1971.

Patmore J. *Land and Leisure*, Penguin, 1972.

Pieper J. *Leisure and the Basis of Culture*, Fontana, 1965.

Riordan J. *Sport in Soviet Society*, Cambridge University Press, 1977.

Slusher H. *Man, Sport and Existence*, Kimpton, 1967.

Vanderswaag H. *Towards a Philosophy of Sport*, Addison & Wesley, 1972.

Weiss P. *Sport: A Philosophic Inquiry*, South Illinois University Press, 1969.

Winnifrith T. and Barrett C. (eds) *Leisure in Art and Literature*, Macmillan, 1992.

Zeigler E. *Philosophical Foundations of Physical Health and Recreation*, Prentice Hall, 1964.

Chapter 15

The Social Setting of Physical Education and Sport in Five Countries

We need to have a knowledge of the **cultural background** before we can hope to understand how organized physical activity functions in different societies. We will call these influences **cultural determinants** and look at them under **three** main headings: **geographical**, **historical** and **socio-economic**.

15.1 Geographical Influences on Physical Education and Sport

Geography is a very broad field of study, but is limited in the analysis here to comments on population, land area, topography, climate, urbanization and communications in the context of sport and physical education.

United Kingdom

Population

The population growth for the UK from 1851 to 1991 is shown in Table 15.1—the ethnic minority (Afro-Caribbean and Asian) was approximately 2% in 1981. Over the past decade the anticipated population increase did not occur, but there were shifts in population from old industrial areas into rural districts, suburbs and new towns. There are also urban centres where there is a disproportionately high concentration of ethnic minorities.

Size

The area of the UK is 94 247 square miles.

Topography

England has mainly rolling country with the Pennines and the Cotswolds as its major hill features. The hills and meadows are ideal for rambling and field sports. The East Anglian Fens are very flat and popular for boating, angling and ice skating. Mountains in the UK are limited to the Lake District, the Scottish Highlands and the Welsh Mountains, and are attractive for climbing, game fishing and shooting, with skiing in Scotland. There are extensive coastal waters which are ideal for sailing and other water sports and, traditionally, the British have an annual holiday by the sea. Numerous rivers make angling the most popular sport in the country, but there are also a large number of canoe and inland-sailing clubs.

Table 15.1 : UK population growth							
Year	1851	1881	1921	1951	1961	1981	1991
Population (millions)	20	29	42	49	51	54.1	53.9

Climate

The weather is temperate—western maritime, with a moderating influence from the Gulf Stream Drift. Generally, there is less rainfall on the east coast, which also has colder winters as a result of the continental influence.

The four clearly identifiable seasons have shaped the pattern of sport, but the weather is so changeable and unpredictable that it may account for the durable British temperament, particularly in the context of sport. Though the area is small, the climate and terrain is so variable that the diversity of sporting opportunity is considerable, with the possible exception of winter sports.

Urbanization

The population density is very high, 596 per square mile, with many urban–industrial conurbations, surrounded by green belts.

Communications

There are six international ports. The railways were reduced after 1945, but there is a fast inter-city service, which includes a 'cross-channel' link with France. Roads include major motorways, with A-roads radiating from London. There are airports serving each of the major cities. All areas in Britain can be reached in the same day for sporting fixtures and tourism.

France

Population

The population growth for France from 1931 to 1989 is shown in Table 15.2—the ethnic minority (so-called foreign residents) was approximately 2% in 1982, mainly North African Arabs and Portuguese.

Size

The area of France is 210 000 square miles. In comparative terms, France and the UK have populations of approximately the same size, but France is twice as large, with the result that Provincial France retains its rural nature.

Topography

A wide plain covers half the country, with the Massif Central, a mountainous plateau, in the centre. The Alps are famous for winter sports and climbing and there are numerous canoeing rivers in the Massif Central. An extensive coastline makes sailing and other water sports as popular in France as in Britain.

Climate

This is much more varied than in Britain, with western maritime in Normandy and Brittany; Continental inland from Paris; Alpine in the mountainous areas; and Mediterranean along the south coast. The French follow a clear pattern of winter skiing holidays in the Alps and seaside summer holidays on the Landes (Atlantic) and Mediterranean coasts.

Urbanization

The population density is 260 per square mile (less than half that of Britain). France is dominated by Paris, but there is an industrialized north east, where soccer is popular, and extensive vineyards in the south west, where the main game is rugby football. Ethnic activities include Breton wrestling, kick boxing or 'savate', boule or petanque (a form of street bowls), pelota and bull fighting.

Communications

These are totally dominated by Paris, with roads and railways radiating from it. Marseilles, Le Havre, Nantes, Bordeaux and Rouen are the main ports, with numerous ferry ports along the English Channel. The country is geared for tourism, but the French themselves tend to have fixed holidays at Eastertide and in July and/or August.

Table 15.2 : French population growth

Year	1931	1954	1962	1982	1989
Population (millions)	42	43	47	54	56.2

United States of America

Population

The population growth for the USA from 1930 to 1988 is shown in Table 15.3—in 1980, there were 188 million Caucasians, 26.5 million Afro-Americans and 12.5 million others.

Size

The area of the USA is 3 539 289 square miles. In terms of different individual States in 1980:

- Texas—population of 14 million with an area of 262 000 square miles,
- California—23.6 million with an area of 156 000 square miles,
- New England—12.3 million with an area of 63 000 square miles.

In comparative terms, the UK is about two-thirds the size of California, but has well over twice the population; France is four-fifths the size of Texas, but with over four times the population. Geographically, therefore, each State is equivalent to a European country.

Topography

Every type of terrain occurs, from wide plain and deserts to the high mountains of the Rockies. There are wide expanses of 'frontier country', with back-packing and winter sport provision, and extensive coastal waters, with New England being the centre of ocean sailing.

Climate

There are ten climatic zones:

- Pacific Coast, ranging from polar to warm temperate to desert in the south.
- Mountain States, with relief and latitude factors,
- High Plains, cold continental, ranging from blizzards to dust bowls,
- Central Plains, temperate continental and high rainfall,
- Mid-West, continental with hot summers and cold winters,
- Great Lakes, similar to the Plains, but very cold winters,
- Appalachian Mountains, with cool temperate moving south to warm temperate, but very high rainfall,
- Gulf Coast, subtropical,
- Atlantic Coast, temperate maritime (similar to UK),
- New England, cool temperate with severe winters and warm summers.

All sports and recreational pastimes are possible with such a complex pattern of climate, but distance can be a problem.

Urbanization

Population density is 65.3 per square mile. Massive areas are virtually unpopulated, while some areas, such as parts of California, have huge urban sprawls and air pollution problems.

Communications

Sophisticated inter-state air travel and trans-continental railways, with complex freeways and Greyhound coach services. There is extensive car use, with a custom of travelling long distances compared to Europeans.

Table 15.3 : US population growth

Year	1930	1950	1960	1980	1988
Population (millions)	106	151	179	227	245.8

Australia

Population

The population growth for Australia since 1901 is shown in Table 15.4. On 31st December 1993, the population was 17 745 800, and in 1986 85.4% of the population was urban.

1991 census figures recorded 257 333 Aboriginal or native Australians. They have only been included in population statistics since 1967, which reflects their limited political status. Almost all native Australians now have mixed blood, but it is presumed that the statistics refer to those who identify with the Aboriginal culture.

For comparison, on 31st March 1993, New Zealand had a population of 3 494 000 and the Polynesian minority (mainly Maori) represented 18% of the population.

Australians were almost exclusively of British or Irish descent before 1945, but by 1980 there was a 30% non-British minority. This was the result of two policies: a recognition of Asia as a market rather than Europe; and the need to populate or perish.

The expansion policy was entirely racially based. In the 1940s and 1950s Britons were preferred, but displaced Europeans were accepted; in the 1960s people from the Middle East were accepted; and in the 1970s, Asians were admitted. This marked the end of the White Australia policy, which had been established against the so-called 'yellow peril'. These controlled phases of expansion have influenced racial stratification in much the same way as similar policies in the USA.

The 1994–1995 quota for new settlers was 86 000 and was strictly observed.

Table 15.4 : Australian population growth

Year	1901	1921	1947	1961	1981	1991
Population (millions)	4	5	8	11	15	16.9

Size

The area of Australia is 2 966 151 square miles. The population in terms of different individual States in 1980 is given in Table 15.5 [ACT is the (Federal) Australian Capital Territory of Canberra, similar to Washington DC in the USA]. Figures 15.1 and 15.2 are useful for comparative purposes.

In comparative terms, Australia is a similar size to the USA if Alaska is excluded. The five Australian States are much larger than any of the 50 American States. Western Australia is four times larger than Texas; New South Wales is as large as France and the UK combined; and Tasmania is as large as England and Wales.

Table 15.5 : Australian state population figures

State	Area (nearest 1000 sq. miles)	Population (nearest 100)
New South Wales	300 000	6 025 500
Victoria	180 000	4 468 300
Queensland	680 000	3 155 400
South Australia	394 000	1 467 500
Western Australia	971 000	1 687 300
Tasmania	67 800	427 500
Northern Territories	518 000	170 500
Australian Capital Territory of Canberra	800	299 400
(New Zealand	175 000	3 494 400)

Figure 15.1 Australia superimposed on Europe.

Figure 15.2 Australia superimposed on the USA.

Topography

There are three broad zones. Firstly, three-quarters of Australia is a great flat plain, which is largely desert and unpopulated. Australians commonly refer to this as the Red Centre, consisting as it does of outcrops of exposed rock that has sacred significance to Aboriginal culture.

Secondly, running north–south from the Kimberley Mountains in the Northern Territory to the Eyre Peninsular in South Australia, there is a swathe of grassland that separates deserts to the west and east.

Thirdly, there is the Great Dividing Range running down the east of the country, with its foothills running down to the Eastern Coastal Plain and round the south coast of Victoria as far as Adelaide in South Australia.

Climate

The significance of Australia being in the southern hemisphere is that seasonal sports can be played all the year if international players have the money to travel. This is particularly relevant to professional sports such as cricket and, more recently, athletics and rugby; and for sports of the wealthy, such as skiing and tennis.

The sheer size of the land mass is such that North Queensland is within 10 degrees of the equator and experiences a tropical climate which includes summer monsoons and dry winters.

The southern belt of Victoria and Tasmania is in the westerly wind belt and is well into the cool temperate zone with cold winters and heavy rainfall, but hardly any of this rain reaches the interior. High precipitation just inland has produced large areas of temperate rain forest, where protected gullies have examples of ancient tropical vegetation. In the arid interior, however, the only saviour is the underground water of the Great Artesian Basin.

The climate down the east coast reflects its latitude, with sub-tropical in the north and warm temperate in the south.

The coast is influenced by the usual wind variables, and the rising slopes of the Great Dividing Range have considerable rainfall as well as rapidly decreasing temperatures with altitude. It is reputed that within an hour of surfing in Pacific breakers, it is possible to be skiing in the Southern Alps.

Urbanization

The population density of Australia is lower than that of any other major country and far below the other four countries studied herein. The 3 per square mile density has little meaning, however, as 84% of all Australians are urbanized, leaving vast tracts of emptiness in the Red Centre. The cities of Sydney, Melbourne, Brisbane and Adelaide have a total of 9 million, and Perth is the only other city with a million inhabitants.

Additionally, a map of Australian towns shows a whole string close to the Pacific Highway, from Brisbane south to Cape Horn on the Tasman Sea. It is significant that, despite its size, some economists suggest that Australia cannot successfully support a much higher population than it already has.

Communications

Road communication is dominated by a series of superb freeways on the American pattern. They link the major cities, which means that most are along the east coast. The size of Australia is best appreciated when it is realized that it can take two days to drive from Melbourne to Sydney, even on the freeways. The Red Centre has a few cross-continental freeways, but consists of mainly dirt roads. Rail travel is more popular, where there are similarities with the Trans-Siberian Railway in Central Russia. However, the distances are such that air travel is preferred by the business community and tourists, so, as with the USA, each major town has its own civil airport with regular internal flights. At the moment one variable is the relatively high cost of inter-state flights in Australia, which is determined by limited franchising.

Former Soviet Union

Population

The population growth for the former Soviet Union since 1970 is shown in Table 15.6—the most important 'ethnic' comment is the former Soviet policy of encouraging Russians to settle in all the other republics.

Size

The area of the former Soviet Union was 8 649 490 square miles. Before its dramatic disintegration, the Soviet Union consisted of 15 republics, each of which might be compared with an American State or European country. West of the Ural Mountains is much more technically developed, with a more rapidly expanding population than on the east, or oriental, side of the Urals, which remains rural and underdeveloped.

With the break up of the Union in 1991, it is important to provide data for at least some of the individual republics:

- Russia—a population of 147.4 million with an area of 7 625 000 square miles,
- Ukraine—51.7 million with an area of 174 412 square miles,
- Georgia—5.5 million with an area of 26 611 square miles,
- Lithuania—3.7 million with an area of approximately 26 000 square miles.

In comparative terms, Russia covers seven-eighths of the old Soviet Union, but has about only half its population. It is over twice the size of the USA with around two-thirds the population. The Ukraine is about the same size as California, but has similar population figures to France or the UK.

Topography

Covering one-sixth of the earth's land surface, there is a full range of land features, similar to that in the USA, but with a limited seaboard, mainly in the Arctic Circle.

Climate

There is a full range of climates, but with no tropical conditions. Mainly, it is very much Continental, giving cold winters and hot summers, but with large areas in the colder latitudes making winter sports a central feature. The Steppes have a traditional reputation for equestrianism; and wrestling is very popular in certain southern republics (Georgia, etc.). The extreme cold of the Siberian winter delayed development until the advent of the 'Sunshine Cities' policy in the 1970s.

Urbanization

Population density is 31 per square mile (half that of the USA, but with more uninhabitable areas). Major cities are in the west, with Leningrad (St Petersburg) and Moscow, and there is a large population on the Black Sea, where many of the tourist resorts are situated.

Communications

Complex road and rail networks in the European republics, but only two trans-continental rail links to the east coast. Air travel is the only hope for speedy communication. Many of the Asian republics are isolated by distance and primitive roads.

Table 15.6 : Former Soviet Union population growth

Year	1970	1979	1983	1989
Population (millions)	242	262	273	286.7

Conclusion

It is important that these statistics be updated regularly—there are numerous year-books available in most libraries. The two used for this material were Paxton (1991) and Lane (1986).

Review Questions

1. Explain the contradiction that, despite the average populations of France and Australia, France is normally described as rural while Australia is referred to as an urbanized society.
2. Explain the significance of the Frontier Spirit in the USA, the former Soviet Union and Australia in the context of Wilderness.
3. Compare links between the size of a country, communications and sport in any two of the countries reviewed.

Summary

Geographical:
1. Population; size; topography; climate; urbanization; communications.
2. UK: small, densely populated; western maritime.
3. France: larger, same population as UK; diverse climate and topography.
4. USA: isolated from the world; large, with diverse climate, topography and ethnic groups.
5. Australia: large, underpopulated landmass of the Red Centre, with dense urban population centres on the Pacific coast.
6. Former Soviet Union: double the size of USA with similar population; massive diversity, but limited coastline.

Further Reading

Bale J. *Sport and Place*, Hurst, 1982.
Lane H.V. (ed) *The World Almanac*, Newspaper Enterprise Association, 1986.
OPCS. 1991 Census. Preliminary Report for England and Wales, HMSO, 1991.

Paxton J. (ed) *The Statesman's Year Book, 1988–89* 127e, Macmillan, 1991.
Regional Surveys of the World. *The Far East and Australasia* 25e, Europa, 1994.

15.2 Historical Influences on Sport and Physical Education

United Kingdom
Chapters 19–22 examine the development of sport and physical education in the United Kingdom as a major area of study.

France
The first comment about sport in France must belong to the high culture of Louis XIV, and with it the extension of the 'courtly mould' and the art of fencing, associated with the sophistication of real tennis in the 17th century.

This elite culture finally collapsed as a result of the French Revolution, which in turn led to the Napoleonic period. From this time, militarism and nationalism have dominated French physical activity, reflecting the phrase 'every Frenchman is born a soldier'.

As early as 1817, Amoros was invited to Paris to open a gymnasium to match the German and Scandinavian developments. It was built at Joinville and destined to be the centre of French military and sporting endeavour for well over a century.

By 1845 Clias was at Joinville, training school PT instructors as well as military personnel. Drill was central, particularly after France had lost a war with Prussia, but in 1887 Demeny identified therapeutic exercises, and in 1906 Hebert introduced his 'Natural Method', a lasting influence partly because it so closely reflected the philosophy of Rousseau.

Teacher training, as we know it today, began at Joinville in 1920 and, in 1934, despite Hebert's condemnation of sport, attempts were made to quantify PE with a series of Brevets Sportives (tests).

Throughout these years sport had been excluded from PE and even today PE is known as 'la Gym'. Sports development consisted of popular recreations, as in England, but very clearly provincially orientated.

Conversely, rational recreations radiated from Paris and, stimulated by such aristocrats as Baron de Coubertin, amateur sport spread among the middle classes in the last quarter of the 19th century, based very much on the Olympic ideals (Figure 15.3).

Although professionalism did not occur in games, there were semi-professional cycling races between Rouen and Paris as early as 1869, which eventually developed into the Tour de France.

Sporting links with schools were established with the formation of the Association du Sport Scolaire et Universitaire (ASSU—School and University Sports Association), where university sports clubs helped in the coaching of school children, changing to the Union National du Sport Scolaire (UNSS—National Union of School Sport) in 1978.

The collapse of France in the Second World War, followed by failure in the 1952 Olympics, led to an upsurge of nationalism, which was encouraged by President de Gaulle.

M. Herzog, alpinist, led a High Commission for Youth and Sport in 1958 to improve the organization and finance of sport, and this was followed in 1961 by a four-year plan and £46.5 million to improve sports facilities nation-wide.

United States

In the 18th century, only the eastern seaboard had been settled—by Europeans—but a primitive version of lacrosse was already being played by a number of Indian tribes. European culture steadily took over and, according to Baker (1988), the geography of colonial sports reflected the varied origins of the settlers. In the English colonies, courtly activities such as hunting and horse racing were evident, as well as popular recreations; international cricket matches were being played by 1751.

As in Europe, many of the popular recreations suffered at the hands of Puritanism. Following the War of Independence, field sports continued in the east, but the phrase 'frontier sport' reflected the spirit of survival and individualism through such festivals as 'barn-raisings'.

The Civil War took American society yet another step away from the 'courtly mould' of the English gentry, and sport became a key element in the emergence of an American identity. Both codes of English football were played at American universities in the 1870s, but it was the rugby style at McGill and Harvard that became more popular. At Princeton in 1879,

Figure 15.3 Breton wrestling. (*125 Sports in France, 1985.*)

Figure 15.4 The American National Game of Baseball. A print by Currier and Ives dating from 1866. (*Baker, 1988.*)

'guarding the runner' marked the first step towards the Grid Iron game. Amateur rowing and athletics were also part of a collegiate input that established the tradition of collegiate sport.

Alternatively, the 'American National Game of Baseball' was well established by the 1860s, with the National Association of Professional Baseball Players coming into being in 1871, marking the popular replacement of cricket (Figure 15.4).

The great John L. Sullivan and Jack Johnson made USA the centre of world professional boxing, a status it still retains.

Although American sport was extremely masculine, the traditional role of the female was less entrenched than in Europe, and so lawn tennis, croquet and cycling were popular among middle-class women, with bloomers and rational dress accepted much earlier than in England.

The influence of the Young Men's Christian Association (YMCA) was also considerable and the combination of James B. Naismith and the Springfield YMCA University led to the birth of basketball in 1891, followed by volleyball in 1895. Significantly, women were encouraged to play both games from the beginning.

Gymnastics and physical training were very popular among German and Scandinavian ethnic communities, to the extent that both activities were well established in Massachusetts by the 1820s, with fully qualified civilian instructors. However, such was the significance of sport in the universities and high schools that it was games rather than gymnastics which emerged triumphant, epitomized by the American cry of 'health and sport' as against 'health through physical education!'.

The frontier was a reality until 1918, personified by the dynamic life-style of President Theodore Roosevelt. When it finally disappeared, the rugged scenery became the vehicle whereby national pride was sustained through back-packing in wilderness environments, with well-administered National and State Parks.

Australia

Aboriginal tribes probably entered Australia during the last Great Ice Age via land bridges and a short stretch of water from Southeast Asia, some 30 000 years ago. Over this period tribal societies developed, with different languages and dialects evolving across Australia. Aboriginal society was highly organized, extremely well disciplined and spiritually rich, with territorial boundaries respected despite their semi-nomadic existence as hunters. Many of these features are still evident in the Northern Territory and Western Australia, despite exploitation by European colonialists. To legitimize European occupation of Aboriginal land, a 'legal fiction' known as Terra Nullius (empty land), presumed that the country was unoccupied before colonization; this has remained a foundation of Australian law and even today there are doubts about the legality of Aboriginal land claims.

Much is made of Australia's initial function as a penal colony from 1788; indeed, in 1830, 90% of the population of New South Wales (NSW) and Van Dieman's Land (Tasmania) were convicts, former convicts or relatives. However, by 1840, with transportation abolished, free settlements were flourishing and Anglo-Scottish protestants worked alongside ex-convicts and Irish labourers.

The rest of the century was dominated by three themes. Firstly, there was migration expansion and economic growth arising from a series of 'gold rushes', especially in Victoria, which resulted in a rapid urbanization process. It is suggested that by 1891 Australia was the most urbanized country in the world and with this came a very powerful middle class.

The second theme was the expansion of responsible democratic government, with a spirit of independence from Britain, such that, by the 1850s, most of the States had separate constitutions that included wide adult male franchise. The negative experience of the American War of Independence may have convinced the UK not to resist this trend.

Thirdly, there was a major attempt to invent and popularize a distinctive Australian nationalism. It is probable that the sporting ethic, which started at this time, was part of this movement, and was coined 'our sporting obsession' by Keith Dunstan (1973). He goes on to recognize three factors that bind Australia as a nation: Federation, the tragic loss of life at Gallipoli and cricket. In the case of the last, there is the reminder of the roots of the people's game and the incentive to beat the 'old enemy'. In 1877, 24 years before the Federation, the divided Australian colonies combined to play the first match against England as the 'Australian' team. The English immigrants had brought the game with them and there was a cricket club in Sydney as early as 1826. The All-England XI, which had done so much for cricket in the English counties, toured Australia in 1861 and had a similar stimulating impact.

The 20th century saw the rise of swimming as a national sport. The three main causal factors were probably the climate and beaches of the south Pacific coast; urbanization, the emergent middle class and their views on cleanliness and athleticism; and the invention of the 'Australian crawl', which revolutionized speed swimming. The emergence of lawn tennis as an elite game had similar supportive elements, where Anglo-Saxon status was expressed through this urbanized game in an ideal climate, but there is also the role-model effect of such great champions as Hoad, Rosewall and Laver. There have always been strong female swimmers and in tennis the feminist cause was expressed through Margaret Court and, even more significantly, Evonne Goolagong, an Aboriginal women's world champion.

Of all sports only football divides Australia, but the exclusivity of different codes makes this a world issue.

New South Wales and Queensland are dominated by rugby league and rugby union, while Victoria, South Australia and Western Australia have a preference for 'Aussie' Rules football. Significantly, the game of Association Football did not develop as it had in Britain, probably because of the relative absence of industrialization; but more recently

Italian and Greek immigrants have brought soccer to Australia, complete with its spectator hooligan tendencies. In historical terms, colonial links with Rugby School and Melbourne Cricket Club led to the birth of the handling game, but Celtic links may account for the eventual adoption of Aussie Rules with its similarity to Gaelic football. Meanwhile, the development of the rugby code around Sydney and Brisbane probably owes much to the high proportion of settlers from England and Wales in these areas.

The history of sport in Australia, therefore, reflects developments in the UK, but middle-class developments remained dominant because there was hardly any industrial working-class influence. Private clubs stimulated by school athleticism produced a decentralized sporting system with State teams dominant and minimal Federal support. Test matches and the Olympic Movement stimulated nationalism, but Federal involvement was delayed until the 1970s.

Failure at the Montreal Olympics by Australia (one silver and four bronze medals) led to widespread criticism and a review of the national administrative structure and Federal funding. Particular note was made of the successes of East European and Soviet state sponsorship, and the selection and the training methods of their sporting elite. Significantly, it also became a political instrument of the Australian Labour Party.

Soviet Union

Whereas the UK had an industrial revolution in the 19th century, Russia was very much a feudal society until the October Revolution in 1917. This meant that there were nobles who pursued the 'courtly' activities of field sports and horse racing, and peasants who retained their occasional festivals. These folk activities were tribal, with horse riding on the Steppes, troika in the north and wrestling in the south.

The emergence of rational recreation was restricted to a wealthy elite, except in a few industrial towns such as St. Petersburg (Riordan, 1977). Gymnastics and drill did develop as a part of the European Movement, with Swedish influences from 1835 and the Czech Sokol Movement from 1870. It was soon after this that Lesgaft introduced a system of drill gymnastics, which was adopted in most grammar schools by the 1880s.

The second phase of development followed the 1917 Bolshevik Revolution, but sporting developments were limited because of the poverty of the people, the political focus on education, industrialization and militarism, and the ravages of a civil war which continued until 1921.

Lesgaft became a cult figure and the Sokol Movement was encouraged because of its social basis. Lenin recognized the need for 'improved health for the young' and in 1920 the Supreme Soviet of Physical Culture was established. This led to the formation of the Pioneer Movement in 1927 and the Preparation for Labour and Defence (GTO) in 1931. Meanwhile, the trade union movement had started to encourage sport for the workers and sports clubs were formed by such societies as Dynamo and Spartak.

The first Moscow Spartakiad was held in 1928, and school spartakiads were established from 1935. It was around this time that Sportsmen's Awards were introduced.

Alongside the GTO and sport, there was a strong military component and the encouragement of ethnic sports (Figure 15.5).

All this was internal and designed to be politically conforming as well as to bring the republics together in friendly competition. After the Second World War, Moscow Dynamo Football Club toured Britain, and in 1956 the Soviet Union felt ready to compete in the Olympic Games for the first time since 1908.

This process of nation building and the formal political and economic integration of the 15 republics continued until the appointment of Mikhail Gorbachev as general secretary of the Soviet communist party in 1985. Though apparently a confirmed communist, he was unhappy with the old-style authoritarian form of government and concerned about the Soviet economy. By 1989, two words symbolized the reforms he started to enact. *Glasnost* reflected a policy of public frankness and accountability, and *perestroika* was a policy whereby Soviet institutions and the economy were modernized and westernized.

The political consequences were that after nearly 70 years of authoritarianism, free speech was

Figure 15.5 Traditional archery is still seen. (*Yearbook USSR, 1987.*)

encouraged among groups of people, the newspapers and the media. At republican level, this released all the old nationalist and racist hates held in check by the communist regime, resulting in calls for independence by different republics. The Baltic States of Latvia, Lithuania and Estonia led this fight for political freedom and, though there was pressure for Gorbachev to subdue this nationalism by force, he allowed them to achieve independence.

It was only a very short time before all the remaining republics called for levels of independence, so the Supreme Soviet ceased to be the centralized controlling body. Gorbachev tried to keep this revolutionary trend in check by establishing an elected Soviet President to hold the various republics together, while allowing the individual republics to make their own decisions on how far down the democratic path they wished to go. However, the emergence of nationalist leaders, such as Boris Yeltsin of Russia, led to the removal of Gorbachev and the emergence of individual Presidents for each republic. By 1996 no single, stable political pattern had emerged as the liberals competed with the old-style communists in the battle for power.

There is little doubt that democratic policies would have the support of the majority in the old Soviet Union in the name of *glasnost*, but *perestroika* is meeting opposition because linking liberal politics and racial enmity with a market economy is causing extreme hardship. (This pattern can be seen at its worst in the former Yugoslavia, with its combination of racial hatred, territorial bitterness and religious bigotry.) The same thing could easily happen in a number of the old-style Soviet republics, resulting in civil war and the abhorrent 'policy' of ethnic cleansing.

The end of authoritarian rule by the Supreme Soviet was welcomed as a step towards democracy, but there was a security in the old regime, where decisions were made for you in an atmosphere of full employment. Many initial enthusiasts for the reforms are now looking for a return to that security, having witnessed an increase in crime, unemployment and food shortages and a rise in nationalist dissent. There might yet be a reversion to an authoritarian form of socialism, run by 'reformed' communists and supported by an older generation, or a disenchanted youth might be attracted to right-wing political groups.

Review Questions

1. Explain the dominance of gymnastics in French physical education.
2. The development of sport in the USA reflects a nation adapting games to meet its cultural needs—discuss.

3. Explain the extent to which Australian sport has been influenced by colonialism.
4. Explain the function of physical culture in the former USSR as a vehicle to produce a superpower.

Summary

Historical:
1. Ancient traditions and popular recreation.
2. Industrialization and the rise of rational recreation.
3. Influence of colonialization on sporting

tradition.
4. Changes in physical education and sport, caused by war, civil war and revolution.
5. Continuing political and economic reform in the name of *glasnost* and *perestroika*.

Further Reading

Baker W.J. *Sports in the Western World* 2e, University of Illinois, 1988.
Cashman J. *Paradise of Sport*, Oxford University Press, 1996.
Dunstan K. *Sports*, Cassell Australia, 1973.
Holt R. *Sport and Society in Modern France*, Macmillan, 1981.

Howell R. and Howell M. *A History of Australian Sport*, Shakespeare Head Press, 1987.
Lucas J.A. and Smith R.A. *Saga of American Sport*, Lea & Febiger, 1978.
Riordan J. *Sport in Soviet Society*, Cambridge University Press, 1977.

15.3 Socio-Economic Factors Influencing Sport and Physical Education

Nationalism

United Kingdom: decentralized civil administration

The UK consists of four major racial groups, the English, Scots, Welsh and Irish. A number of nationalists in Scotland and Wales would prefer more independence than in a Union dominated by London.

Sports fixtures between the four countries have been held annually for over a century and remain highly emotive, but the sporting ethic normally prevails and so they may be seen to act as a safety valve in the long term. In these traditional international confrontations, England is invariably the 'old enemy' and constantly finds itself involved in the defence of ancient transgressions, well in excess of normal rivalry. Rugby against Wales, soccer against Scotland and cricket against Australia are all ritual battlefields.

In the Irish context, the Republican cause has been identified with Gaelic Football; we have the divisive rivalry in soccer where Northern Ireland and Eire have separate administrations, but there is also the bridge-building situation of players from both sides of the border playing for the Irish Rugby Union.

Large numbers of Afro-Caribbean and Asian immigrants have settled in Britain since the Second World War, and although they are British citizens they retain links with their mother countries. This is never more evident than during cricket tours by the West Indies, India and Pakistan. This can be seen to be separatist, but at the same time it allows cultural identity to be expressed.

Despite some initial discrimination, the Afro-Caribbean contribution to British athletics and both codes of football is considerable, as is the Pakistani influence on hockey and squash. Significantly, Afro-Caribbean women have successfully broken into British sport, but cultural barriers still prevent Muslim girls from widespread participation.

There is also a tradition of regional loyalty being expressed through sport. The county championships in cricket and rugby are highly competitive and charged with territorial pride. Similarly, the sense of belonging to an urban community is achieved through loyalty to a professional soccer club, although the football fan may also be attracted for a variety of other reasons.

France: centralized civil administration

France has a very strong sense of national identity, largely because of the constant threat from outside. In sporting terms this is more closely associated with amateur representation, as in rugby union, than with professional soccer and cycling, which are seen to be commercially based. Even in the case of rugby, however, appearances are deceptive. The French cockerel is displayed with great pride against England, but a closer scrutiny shows that the players are largely drawn from provincial clubs in the south of the country, suggesting that the game has national appeal only when representing the 'tricolor'. There are similarities here with rugby league in the north of England.

In France, as in Britain, there are powerful ethnic minorities, like the Basques and the Bretons, who are trying to maintain a cultural and a political identity; in addition to retaining their own language, there is a major attempt to revive many of the old ethnic sports.

A second comparative point is that sport and nationalism have never had political ties in England, but President de Gaulle made French sport a rallying point for the revival of national pride.

Unlike the British, the French have always regarded their colonies as part of Greater France. Consequently, there is a substantial North African minority resident in the country with little evidence of discrimination in terms of sport participation. Significantly, middle-distance runner Said Aouita, the Moroccan Olympic gold medallist, received a great deal of his coaching in France.

United States: decentralized civil administration

The USA has a 'pluralist' policy, unlike Britain and France, whose policies are 'assimilative'. This means that every cultural group living in the USA is encouraged to keep its ethnic identity, on the grounds that this is one of the basic freedoms in the 'Land of the Free'. The various racial groups retain a cultural identity; they seem to dominate certain geographical areas and vary considerably in terms of economic wealth and social status.

Generally speaking, the last group to enter the country has the lowest status. Consequently, Caucasians tend to have a higher status than members of the black community, but they in turn are

411

higher up the social ladder than the Puerto Ricans, Mexicans and Vietnamese. Each of these racial groups has been identified with particular sports— for example, there have always been strong links between the Italian community and baseball, and there are a disproportionate number of black professional basketballers. To some extent this may reflect the social exclusivity of certain sports; for example, track and field has a very broad racial input, but the majority of top golfers and tennis players are white.

The autonomy of the 50 states is another obstacle to a national identity. Federal control is resented and the diversity of life-styles is such that a State identity is far more relevant than a generalized national character, which tends to be meaningless except in international affairs. It can be seen, therefore, that national pride is not easily established in a young country, particularly one which has a decentralized administration and is practising pluralism.

Yet another problem has been the country's history of isolationist policies. However, the post-Second World War role of America as the champion of the Western World has brought the country into the international arena.

Sport most certainly plays its part in all these facets of nationalism. In addition to being a vehicle for ethnic and racial identity, activities such as professional boxing have allowed individuals to climb out of the social gutter. American football, baseball and basketball are uniquely 'American', culturally fashioned to meet the needs of a confident, get-up-and-go society, and endowed with a status that makes sport one of the unifying features in a country where competitiveness is an esteemed quality, and where the mass media are the main conforming agency.

The extent to which the honour of citizenship is respected, and the ritual associated with the Oath of Allegiance and the Star-spangled Banner, reflect a country that is striving to achieve the American Dream.

It is important to recognize that loyalty functions on a continuum from support for the local community to concern for the starving world. For example, New Yorkers can choose to support either the Jets or the Giants, but when one of them plays any other football team the whole city rallies behind them. Probably, if this happens to be a game against a Californian team, they will gain not only the support of the State of New York, but of the whole East Coast. Should they reach the Super Bowl, they are now representing a Conference, in other words half the American football public. As

for the rest of the world, the game is a spectacle of excitement and athleticism; a mixture of showbiz and gladiatorial combat. Like Hollywood, it is a dream rather than a reality: symbolizing American competitiveness and commercial enterprise, but not necessarily reflecting the conscience of the American people.

Australia: decentralized civil administration/centralized Federal dominance

A decentralized civil administration is in transition to a centralized Federal dominance, but this trend is being resisted by individual States. As with the USA, Australia is a young country, with a population that is increasingly pluralistic, seeking to establish a national identity.

As a colonial country that denied Aboriginal culture, Australia developed a British pattern of democratic government, but generally of a more radical nature after Dominion status had been achieved. This was evident in a Liberal dominance from 1949 to 1972. The growth of the Labour Party was influenced by concern over communist involvement and religious friction involving a large Irish Roman Catholic minority. Since 1972 Labour has become the leading party and in 1990 held power in five States and won three Federal elections, 1984, 1987 and 1990, but lost power in 1996. The ex-Labour Prime Minister, Paul Keating, considers that nationalism is essentially linked with republicanism.

The Labour Government reforms in 1972 has led to a centralized policy, with national planning coming from the Australian Sports Commission and extensive Federal funding. However, the high level of independence maintained by individual States is reflected in the structure of their sport. Each State has its own Sports organization at elite and mass participation levels, which should not be seen as just an extension of the Federal Australian Institute of Sport, but as standing in its own right. This appears to mirror the pattern found in the USA and is even more evident in the independent republics that had been part of the Soviet Union.

In terms of Australian attitudes to National and State sport, Dunstan (1973) quoted Mrs Ed Clark, the wife of a former American Ambassador: 'Living in Australia is like living in a gymnasium— there's always somebody practising something'. In similar vein, Saturday radio in Australia has continuous sport on all four channels and there is regularly 25 hours of sport televised each week. There are obvious similarities here with the American sporting ethic, but it is also important to recognize that counter cultures exist in both countries.

Former Soviet Union: centralized civil administration

The former Soviet Union was faced with even greater problems of national identity. Many of the 15 republics that constituted the Union had been independent countries previously. It was acknowledged that within these republics there were at least a hundred distinct nationalities and 180 spoken languages. In literacy terms, 60 of these were taught in schools; there were 65 newspaper languages, and books were published in 76 languages.

The political uniformity and authoritarianism of the Soviet Union did tend to cement relations between the constitutionally autonomous republics, but attempts had also been made to establish a cultural unity through the policy of making the Russian language compulsory in schools. Inevitably, this 'Russianization' programme met with a great deal of opposition from the various republics.

Most of Eastern Europe has in recent years moved dramatically from single-party communist authoritarianism to multi-party democracies, a process which has been part of the break-up of the Soviet Union. With the three Baltic States leaving the 'Union', the remaining 12 republics are tied only temporarily by trade agreements and specific treaties. As a result, the centralized civil administration between the republics no longer exists in a formal sense, but various arrangements, such as the Commonwealth of Independent States (CIS) grouping for the 1992 Olympic Games, were in place in the interim. Each republic is now entering international competitions as an individual State. However, there is little likelihood that the administration of sport and physical education within each republic will become decentralized in the short term. On the one hand, they have more pressing issues to occupy them, and on the other, former Soviet sport is changing to a nationally based system as found in Russia and the Ukraine.

Howell (1975) used the phrase 'sport and politics intertwined', which expresses the dual role of sport to reinforce a Soviet identity on the one hand, and to allow continued ethnic expression on the other. The significance of ethnic minorities remains in the independent republics, but politics is being take out of sport as liberalism overtakes communism. The association between sporting excellence and communism may yet cause a backlash, in which the replacement of authoritarianism by 'people power' may lead to an emphasis on popular and ethnic sport.

It remains to be seen whether the nationalistic significance of excellence in sport, evident in France and Germany, is adopted by Russia and the other republics. The infrastructure already exists and so it depends on the strength of nation building and integration intentions.

 Review Questions

1. How have the USA, the former Soviet Union and Australia used sport to help establish a national identity?
2. Compare the ways used by the United Kingdom and France to establish nationalism through sport.

Internationalism

United Kingdom

Ireland retains special links with the UK, particularly at a sporting level: Cheltenham Races is probably the best example.

The United Kingdom contribution to world sport is extended by the influence of Commonwealth countries. They have perpetuated and even developed many of the British games and activities, resulting in international competitions such as the Commonwealth Games and Test matches.

France

Undoubtedly, the Common Market has drawn Western Europe together in sporting and tourist links. More recently, commercial interests have broadened with several European soccer competitions and the European Athletics Grand Prix.

France also has the Tour de France cycle race, which is probably the biggest annual international event in Europe and which includes a UK stage—emphasizing, with the Channel Tunnel, the ever-growing European unity. This is reflected in the number of European leagues and championships.

As a Continental country, France has close sporting and recreative ties with various European countries—for example, the special relationship with Britain and Ireland in rugby union and horse racing; the shared winter sports and tourist amenity of the Alps; and the business of attracting tourists to its Mediterranean resorts and casinos.

United States

As the major power in the North American subcontinent, the USA has attempted to keep an economic and political hold on the other countries. This is particularly true of Mexico and Central America, but their policy suffered a considerable setback when Fidel Castro gained control of Cuba.

The international political status of the USA has meant that it has had to defend its reputation on the sports field.

In terms of games, the greatest threat in ice hockey and basketball until the recent past came from the Soviet Union. For Americans, to be beaten in games which they originated has always been the bitterest of pills to swallow. The same attitude has applied to Cuban and Soviet successes in track and field athletics, boxing and volleyball.

Australia

Britain and Australia have a bond forged by common roots and the sacrifices of two world wars; this is enhanced by the regular opportunity to compete against each other in sport.

Despite moves towards republicanism, the Commonwealth Games does much to bind countries in 'friendly' competition and it is probable that the new centralized policy for sport in Australia is a copy of the Canadian approach. However, in economic terms, the past few years has seen Australia forming increased links with Southeast Asia and the degree of Americanization is evident from the amount of TV basketball. Finally, there is no doubt that Olympic success is a major national objective and the high level of sponsorship together with the sporting obsession of the people gives Australia a level of success far above their demographic expectations.

Former Soviet Union

The former Soviet Union supported international communism and used sport as a vehicle to promote accord, but also to allow nationalistic rivalries to be released in the relatively harmless sporting arena. This was achieved through contests against Eastern Bloc countries.

The Soviets also poured money and coaching expertise into Cuba to beat the Americans on their own doorstep. Cuba remains a communist power at the moment, but from 1992 has, of course, had to retain its political stance as well as its sporting excellence without money from 'Mother Russia'. It may well be that several of the old-style 'Soviet' republics will remain communist and continue to use sport as a shop window, or perhaps, like China, try to embrace a market economy without relaxing communist control.

International boycotts

When the USA and the Soviet Union boycotted each other's Olympic Games they were using sport as a pawn in international politics. That the boycotts were made in the context of the Olympic Games, a festival which supposedly involves individuals rather than nations, is a sad reflection on both the USA and the USSR and its satellites. In Britain and France athletes were allowed to choose in each case.

The principle of political boycott in international sport is nowhere more evident than in links with South Africa. All communist and non-white countries exercised a total boycott, but, though the majority of white countries would not send national teams, individuals could still play in South Africa from choice in certain sports.

The political reforms taken by the South African government, symbolized by the release of Nelson Mandela and his appointment as President, together with the steps taken by governing bodies of sport in the country to make their activities multi-racial, have resulted in the international boycott being called off and South Africa being re-admitted to the Olympics.

 Review Questions

1. Explain the notion of 'shop window' and sport in the former USSR, the USA and Australia.

2. Discuss the role of different football codes in international relations in Europe.

Political

United Kingdom

The monarchy, with wealth and romantic influence but little political power, has a strong impact at Commonwealth level. Sporting members of the Royal Family include Prince Philip, Prince Charles and the Princess Royal, who have a considerable impact on national and world sport. The Queen Mother and the Queen have maintained a lifelong love of horse racing.

With two Houses of Parliament, the Lords and the Commons, with an elected lower House, opposition parties function at local and national level. There is a Minister of Sport with limited executive powers and a Sports Council that remains politically autonomous (Figure 15.6).

Conservative governments over the past decade have dramatically changed many features of the welfare state, moving it towards a market economy.

United States

A republic with an elected president and two elected Houses, the Senate and the Representatives, there is a two-party system with the Democrats and Republicans, both on the political right. Socialism remains a political taboo in a strongly capitalist economy.

State legislation is highly significant, with the State Governor having as much power as most national leaders in Europe.

As a relatively young society, the USA is still striving for an identity. It continues to admire the 'macho' image and has romantic associations with the 'frontier spirit of the Wild West' (Figure 15.7), much as the English warm to the notion of 'Merrie England' at the time of Shakespeare. This promotes an energy in America to forge a modern, unified nation from a melting-pot of exiles and immigrants.

Figure 15.6 Who is really running the show?

Figure 15.7 Playing the American Way.

France

A republic with an elected president, it tends to be identified as a bureaucracy. It is a Western democracy, but has a larger number of minority parties than in the UK and a much wider political spectrum. There is a disturbingly influential right-wing Nationalist Party and an equally large Communist Party. This results in moderate parties having to establish coalitions with extremists to gain a majority. It is very much a mixed economy.

Australia

The political system was based on the British model with two Houses, but when the Federation was established in 1900 there was a move towards the American model with both Houses being elected, an upper House or Senate and a lower House of Representatives. The party system remains similar to Britain's with a Country or Conservative Party, and a strong Liberal Party; these two parties fought the 1996 election as a coalition to unseat the powerful Labour Party, which had been dominant over the past decade, despite numerous internal problems. A Democratic Party, though relatively small, has the potential to control the balance of power at State and Federal levels.

The three most significant political steps made over the past decade by the Labour Government have been the ending of the 'White Australia' policy;

a change of their economic focus from Europe to Southeast Asia; and the disproportionately high funding of sport from Federal and State budgets.

The result of the 1996 election was a landslide victory for the Coalition Parties. There are a number of possible explanations in a country where a desire for a change is favoured, but there is a strong middle-class support for retention of a European culture, even if it exists in a Southeast Asian economy, and this may well have been reinforced by an anti-republican mood. The significance of Sydney 2000 would seem to suggest that the high profile of sport will continue, perhaps with an increase in commercial sponsorship with the new Government.

Former Soviet Union

Politics was intertwined with sport in the Soviet Union, and was responsible for the USSR not sending a team to the Los Angeles Olympic Games.

Tsarist elements ended with the 1917 Revolution. Until the recent break-up of the Soviet Union, the Marxist ideology ruled, implemented by Lenin on the basis of socialism working towards communism, . Being an egalitarian society, mass participation in sport was central and part of a 'collective' system. It is still too early to say whether communism is finished in the independent states that once formed the Soviet Union. It is likely that the old-style authoritarianism has become outmoded, but various forms of 'socialism' might well emerge in some States while others might revert to a form of democratic socialism, having found the market economy and capitalism unpalatable.

If it is unlikely that single party politics will re-appear, some of the Marxist precepts may survive, including man as a social animal; working for the State; living in a changing world; and the spread of international 'socialism'. The old protectionist consumer-based society is being replaced by a market economy in Russia and the Ukraine that idealizes the entrepreneur and a supply-based society. Whether this can be maintained in the face of efforts to slow down the change or even initiate a counter reform has yet to be settled.

What has now to be decided is whether the image of the manual worker or the bourgeois intellectual is going to dominate Russian thinking and whether sport will continue to be the shop window (Figure 15.8). Much depends on whether sporting excellence is linked with the old order.

ℝ Review Questions

1. Explain the phrase that sport and politics are intertwined in the former USSR.
2. Briefly describe the impact of capitalism on sport in the USA.

Figure 15.8 Traditional dancing. (*Yearbook USSR, 1987.*)

Finance and resources
United Kingdom

The UK owes its status to industrialization, to the raw products of coal and iron ore, but most of all to its skilled workforce and business expertise. The 1980s saw a decline in heavy industry, and now it is technological advance that holds the key to the future.

Depression and resultant unemployment are major social problems that might promote a more enlightened view of leisure in the future. The increasing importance of tourism is also highly relevant.

The Sports Council publication *Into the 90s* (1988) gives detailed figures of grant aid from central government and local government, as shown in Table 15.7. It is anticipated that there will be a rise in revenue from tourism and from the commercial and voluntary sections.

Feeling exists that the revenue from the football pools should go directly to sports aid rather than to the general exchequer.

The National Lottery was introduced in 1994 and has averaged first prizes of over £8 million each week, with an additional mid-week draw, which commenced in January 1997. Although it is argued that the Exchequer benefits most and many charities lose from it, sports' estimated share is some £320 million a year. Initially, money was only made available for capital projects, where the applicant had to find 30%. However the initiative has been expanded into what is called the 'four-pack', where money is also allocated for coaching, for promising athletes to be sponsored and for schools to apply for special 'sports college' status. To put this into perspective, the Sports Council now receives £48.9 million a year.

France

Much less urban than the UK, France depends a great deal more on agriculture and the tourist industry. The significance of sport in France can be measured in the increases in the size of the sports budget since 1958 (Figure 15.9).

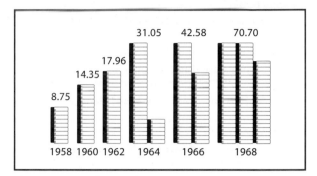

Figure 15.9 Evolution of the French sports budget (francs).

1982 French Sports Budget

It is expected that the Ministry of Youth and Sport will receive 1626 million francs as compared with 1300 last year.

In addition, the Ministry of Leisure is to receive 587 million francs as compared with 423 last year.

Sport itself will get some 168 million instead of 148 but this is less than inflation. Top level sport will get approximately 28 million with Sport for All receiving 134 million francs.

Sports grants for clubs (FNDS) will get up to 102 million francs from 76 last year. This money is outside the sports budget.

(Extract from *L'Equipe*, Nov. 16th 1981.)

A Sports Lottery began in 1985 involving soccer, tennis, rugby and cycling with an expected three billion francs available for sports federations and clubs each year.

Table 15.7	
	£m
Sports Council	7.1
Local Authorities	4.0
Governing Bodies (net of Sports Council grants)	16.0
Sponsorship	109.5
Sports Aid Foundation	0.5
British Olympic Appeal	2.0
TOTAL	£139.1

United States

The capitalist economy is based on the self-made man who has risen 'from rags to riches'. This is a key factor in American competitiveness, tying in closely with the 'win-at-all-costs' philosophy (Figure 15.10):

Winning isn't the most important thing—it's the only thing.
(Vince Lombardi, professional football coach)

How can you be proud of a losing team?
(Jim Tatum, college football coach)

If it's under W for Won, nobody asks you how.
(Leo Durocher, professional baseball manager)

A team that won't be beaten can't be beaten.
(Bill Roper, college football coach)

[Some American sports slogans taken from Paul Gardner's (1974) *Nice Guys Finish Last.*]

Advanced technology and material wealth give the USA the confidence to accept its role as the major world power, with the demise of the Soviet Union. It also takes its responsibility as a benevolent society seriously through aid to the Third World and American support for the Voluntary Overseas Service.

Affluence is also evident in the extent to which Americans travel abroad on business and tourist visits. Europe is a major attraction for many Americans as they attempt to find their roots.

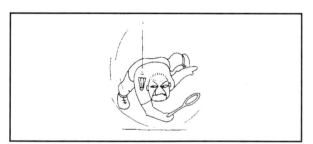

Figure 15.10 'A winner never quits, a quitter never wins'. (*Anon.*)

Australia

An apparently rich country in material wealth and positive attitudes, Australia has two permanent problems of a high rate of unemployment and a huge foreign debt. Underneath the surface is the danger of arousing racial hatreds and ethnic tensions in a pluralist society reaching the end of Anglo-Celt dominance.

Unlike the UK, Australia owes little to industrialization. Its export of wool, meat and wheat to Britain has declined since the development of the European market and competition in Southeast Asia is against countries with cheaper labour.

Australia is well endowed with energy resources, being a major exporter of coal and is almost self-sufficient in petroleum. A century ago Australia had a gold rush similar to that in America, and minerals remain an important source of income.

The free enterprise focus of Thatcherism and American-style commercialism is reflected in media moguls such as Kerry Packer and Rupert Murdoch, who have revolutionized professional sport in Australia. However, Olympic sports have been advanced by a French and Soviet-style centralized funding policy in a determined attempt to produce elite performers in a wide range of activities (Figure 15.11). It is worth noting that the £49 000 000 budget of the British Sports Council with a 56 million population pales alongside the Aus$63 363 000 contribution by the Australian Government in 1993–1994 for a mere 17 million citizens (the exchange rate in 1996 was approximately $2 to the pound).

The Tattersalls Lottery has a weekly top prize of approximately Aus$8 000 000, half that of the UK lottery, but reflects the level of gambling in a country with a much smaller population. There are also additional State and private lotteries, as well as a major casino industry, all of which rival Tattersalls.

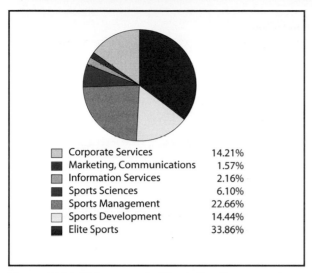

Corporate Services	14.21%
Marketing, Communications	1.57%
Information Services	2.16%
Sports Sciences	6.10%
Sports Management	22.66%
Sports Development	14.44%
Elite Sports	33.86%

Figure 15.11 Disbursement of Australian Government appropriation. (*Australian Sports Commission Annual Report, 1993–1944.*)

Former Soviet Union

This was a socialist economy in which the source of money was from the State with the bulk of its distribution through work and trade unions. Wealth did not lie in the hands of the individual or private enterprise, but not all workers had the same wages. The industrialization of the European USSR led to population growth in towns and increased wealth—hopefully this trend will not only continue but will spread to the Eastern republics.

Raw materials are abundant in the Urals and elsewhere. The amazing speed at which industrialization took place was the result of authoritarian, directed labour policy emanating from the Stalin era. Sputnik and the success of the USSR in space demonstrated a technological advance which at the time shocked the USA.

Considerable sporting and tourist developments were sponsored by the trade unions through the factories and collective farms. Each union had its own holiday camps and sports facilities, where workers were rewarded with holidays which reflected their level of productivity. The economic reforms will probably mean that the factory owners or management panels will take over organization and sponsorship, given that State and union money is no longer available. The principle of rewards for working hard, however, could still apply as an incentive.

In the past, every Soviet citizen who wanted to take up a sport had to pay a token 30 kopecks admission fee to use the local facility. Any representative expenses were paid by the sports society or the USSR Sports Committee. This is standard procedure in all advanced countries, but there will certainly be some difficult times still to come as the transition continues and before adequate commercial money can be negotiated, given the beleaguered state of the economy that still persists despite the disunification of the Union.

The opportunities made available to Soviet citizens has produced an even spread of popularity across five sports (Figure 15.12).

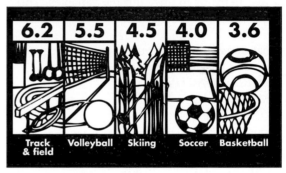

6.2	5.5	4.5	4.0	3.6
Track & field	Volleyball	Skiing	Soccer	Basketball

Figure 15.12 The most practised sports in the former Soviet Union in the 1980s (number of people involved, in millions).

Some commercial money has already become available within Soviet sport, such as come from gate receipts, the sale of sports goods and publications, and the promotion of various lotteries. It is likely that these lotteries will continue, given that the rest of the Western world has now followed the Soviet example.

One can also expect an extension of the American win-at-all-costs philosophy as Russia and the Ukraine change to adopt professionalism and the commercialism attached to television advertising. Not only are Soviet sports stars and coaches being lured abroad by high wages, but performers like Sergei Bubka have considerable international advertising credibility.

Review Questions

1. Discuss the influence of government aid on sport in France or Australia.

2. How has a market economy determined the funding of sport in the USA and what is the likely influence of sport in Russia following the 1991 Reforms?

3. Discuss the likely advantages to sport of the National Lottery in the UK.

Discrimination

Cultural variables have inevitably led to certain groups being discriminated against in a specific community and in a society. Normally, whatever form this takes, it is reflected in a country's sport.

In order to compare one community or society with another it is useful to have a structural framework that helps us to tease out the variables. Three basic questions need to be asked:

- What opportunities do you have to participate in sport and physical recreation?
  CHOICE OF ACTIVITY
  TIME TO PLAY
  MONEY TO PAY
  SUITABLE STANDARD
  ACCEPTABLE COMPANY

- What provision is there for you to participate in sport and physical recreation?
  VARIED TYPES
  ACCESSIBLE
  REASONABLE COST
  SUFFICIENT SPACE
  EQUIPMENT FOR USE
  SOCIAL AMENITIES
  DEGREES OF PRIVACY

- Do you have sufficient esteem to play a full part in sport and physical recreation?
  SELF (how do you see yourself?)
  OTHERS (how do others see you?)
  STATUS
  EXPECTATIONS
  RESPECT
  SELF-FULFILLING
  SOCIALLY STRATIFIED

Western Europe
Regional
In the UK, regional differences have always existed between England, Scotland, Wales and Ireland; and between the industrial Midlands and the North, the rural South West and South, and suburbanized London and the Home Counties.

This has influenced the pattern of sport, largely on a class and/or occupation basis, but with the decline in the industrial economy there is now a north–south divide in wealth terms, which directly influences the pattern of leisure. France has a similar division between north and south and between Paris and provincial France.

Class
Clearly identifiable cultural patterns, particularly in tourism, become a major problem when associated with racial and gender discrimination. Traditional divisions are:
- Upper-class: exclusivity, land ownership and schooling: dominance of rural sports.
- Middle-class: salaried, urban influence; dominates many sports with strong club control.
- Working-class: wage earning, traditional sports; soccer spectator dominance.

There is a gradual breakdown of elitist divisions, evident in such sports as rowing and sailing.

Gender
The pattern is linked with the class variable. Upper-class women are fully emancipated, but Victorian values have delayed equal opportunity for other women. Some problem areas remain in sport, e.g. girls and soccer; femininity and aggressive sports; and payment of professionals.

Religion
Divisions still exist in Northern Ireland and Scotland with the separatism between Catholics and Protestants. This influences community recreation and determines sporting loyalty. However, sport does have a bridge-building potential, for example the Irish Olympic Boxing Team (1988) was drawn from Northern Ireland and Eire and included boxers from both religious groups. The rivalry between Glasgow Rangers and Celtic is a classical example of religious allegiance being expressed on the terraces.

There is still some conflict over sport on Sundays (Sabbatarianism) in Britain, but the 'Continental Sunday' is very much a day for sport. The limited sporting opportunities for Muslim females is an area for concern.

Race

Until 1948, there was only a very small non-white community in the UK and sports like professional boxing helped Jewish and black boxers to improve their social status.

This picture has changed dramatically since 1948, with the influx of Afro-Caribbean and Asian immigrants into Britain, Algerians into France and Turkish workers into what was then West Germany. Legally, there is no discrimination, but colour, language and cultural variables result in social discrimination still being practised. The baiting of professional black soccer players and cricketers still occurs in England (even though it is the country of their birth). Generally it is not simply colour, rather the combination of race and lower class in traditional activities that has prevented black performers from having access to certain sports.

Age

As the countries are welfare states in the Common Market, all age groups should be catered for equally. Schools are of a high standard nationally, but the British have failed to make the strong links between youth and sport which France and Germany have done (Figure 15.13). In sporting terms, the post-school 'gap' reported by the Wolfendon Report (1960) is still evident in the UK.

Disabled

There is an increasing awareness that physical education, sport and physical recreation concerns the whole of society, not just the able-bodied. If we start from our own interest and ability, it should be possible for all of us to express ourselves through a physical experience. To exclude those with special needs is unfair and fails to recognize the potential of our field of study to make life more worthwhile. Most of us are disabled in some way or other and it is for society to help us through these problems. Regrettably, in Western Europe, societies seek to separate, forget and even deny the disabled.

The Sports Council publications *The Next Ten Years* (1982), *Which Way Forward* (1987) and *Into the 90s* (1988) identify 'target groups' that do not make full use of Britain's sports provision. These groups are invariably the ones that are still discriminated against socially.

Investigation

15.1: Discrimination
1. One of the most necessary tasks for you to undertake is to establish the extent to which our society handicaps the disabled.
2. This involves all problems of discrimination. You must attempt to assess the suitability of separation, pluralism and/or assimilation in any discriminatory situation.

United States
Regional

The historical division of America is north–south and the racial variable remains much more evident in the south. However, there is also a major differential east–west, in which the eastern seaboard has a much greater affinity with Europe.

The most important regional comment is that there is no such thing as an American view, only a Californian or a New Yorker view, suggesting that it is always dangerous to generalize whenever you comment on American attitudes and traditions.

The underprivileged group varies according to the region, in that it is the Mexican in California, but the Puerto Rican in New York. The general principle is that the latest immigrant group finds itself at the bottom of the social ladder.

Class

There is no clearly defined class element in the USA, but early English settlers took the concept to the eastern seaboard. There is a clear meritocracy based on wealth, and this is also linked with old families such as the Dutch families of New Amsterdam (New York) and the Irish families around Boston.

Gender

Feminism is strong in the USA. The frontier spirit gave the American woman a more dynamic role, but it also produced a society with chauvinistic tendencies, epitomized in the masculine sports scene. Women's rights have been fought for at a political and an educational level, but it is the extent to which women have inherited wealth that has made some

Figure 15.13 'If only I'd been given a chance to participate in organized sport!'

commentators suggest that America is a matriarchal society. There is less traditional separation of the sexes in terms of occupations and community games. Lapchick (1996) and others have analysed the feminine image in America, where, in the major games, girls appear to accept the limited role of cheerleaders.

Title IX of the Education Amendment Act of 1972 stated:

> *No person in the United States shall, on the basis of sex, be excluded from participation in, be denied the benefits of, or be subjected to discrimination under any education programme or activity receiving federal financial assistance.*

Where competitive women's sport existed in the early 1970s, it was often financed with a budget of less than 1% of the men's athletic programmes. Title IX required equality of opportunity, facilities, practice time, coaching and travel—though it is important to recognize that private organizations can opt out.

Religion

In a pluralist society, with so many religious minorities, decisions are left to the communities themselves, sometimes resulting in individuals losing various freedoms for religious reasons.

Race

The subjugation of the Red Indian and the slavery of black Americans have resulted in a form of racial inequality, which continues to exist despite legislation. Wealth, education and sport have helped to break this down, but there are very few black quarter-backs at top level; only one leading black golf professional; and a few black female tennis professionals. On the other hand, there is a black dominance in basketball, athletics and positions in American football other than quarter-back. This suggests that freedom of opportunity is still being denied in certain privileged sporting situations.

A considerable amount of research is being carried out in this area. There are two basic hypotheses being tested. One is concerned with **centrality**: that the dominant male WASP (white Anglo-Saxon protestant) society tends to control all the central and/or decision-making playing positions in professional football and baseball. This research is also being undertaken in England in the context of rugby, soccer and cricket. The second research area

is concerned with **stacking**: that certain playing positions are directly linked with promotional prospects, on the grounds that, as decision-making positions, the successful player has a capacity for management. This would appear to hold for American football, baseball and basketball at a professional level. The vast majority of players in these privileged positions are white and so this limits the prospects of ethnic minorities reaching coaching or management status.

Finally, the views of Professor Harry Edwards are worth noting. He suggests that, in any discriminatory situation, there are three groups of people: a small group of conservatives who do not want change and, therefore, seek to retain the dominance of one minority group; the reformists at the other end of the scale who actively seek equal opportunity; and the mass of people in the middle who, apathetically, go along with the existing system as a self-prophesying admission of their own inadequacies.

Age

Though undoubtedly the wealthiest country, with the highest level of recreational provision, the highest standard of performance and the largest Olympic team in 1988, television news coverage has shown a New York scene of young black boys tumbling on old mattresses in a derelict building site. Without wishing to make too much of a spontaneous street activity, it would seem that a self-help policy inevitably means that the most talented and the wealthiest gain most. The plight of the loser in the competitive society, identified by Arthur Miller in *Death of a Salesman*, could also be referring to a social administration that pays little attention in recreative terms to the underprivileged, except as a law and order issue or as a source of potential commercial profit. A similar criticism could be levelled at Britain.

Disabled

America has a very active physical activity policy for disabled people, particularly in education. They call it an adaptive programme on the grounds that they are helping those with special needs to adapt to and to cope with their particular disability, but also to alert able-bodied people to the needs of others. There is an active programme of assimilation, but also an awareness that special needs sometimes need special attention.

Australia

Regional

The arid plateau of central Australia is the centre of Aboriginal culture and there is still poverty in these areas. The heart of the problem lies in European colonialization in which, as in the USA, white settlers considered existing tribal cultures to be hostile and inferior. The native Americans and the Aboriginals were shot indiscriminately, dispossessed of their land and denied franchise. In fact, Aboriginals have only been included in Australian population statistics since 1967 and the Native Title Act that set up a system for assessing land claims only came into effect in 1994, but the failure of some recent claims suggests that there are ways round it. As with North America, these ancient tribes are in resurgence, but a typical example is the tourist abuse of Ayers Rock, *Ulura*. This is a sacred place in Aboriginal culture and yet, despite appeals from Aboriginal leaders, white tourists insist on the right to climb over it.

Class

The total dominance of British settlers for nearly 200 years has led to a variation of the English class system being adopted. This does not include an upper class of landowners, nor an industrial working class, but there is a very strong conservative rural society and a powerful urban middle-class liberal society. Finally, there is the caricatured brash, chauvinist, lower class 'Bruce' who makes for a very boisterous spectator at cricket or football and is mentally and physically tough as a competitor.

Gender

Australia and the USA have a great deal in common in the context of the status of women. The Anglo-Saxon core, with its Victorian ethic of the dependent female, is combined with the 'frontier' attitudes of a dynamic young country to produce a chauvinistic Australian male stereotype.

Predictably, sport has been a male preserve, which is still reflected in the dominance of male professional sports and the media coverage of them. Any breakthroughs by females have been influenced by cosmetic as well as athletic factors, by the independence of middle-class women, and by the occasional irresistible talent of individuals like Kathy Freeman.

There is a very strong feminist counter-culture in Australia, with considerable publicity being given to women in sport at Federal and State levels, see Figure 15.14. In the case of Kathy Freeman and Evonne Goolagong, it is also important to recognize that they were fighting for Aboriginal culture as well as gender identity.

Religion

The White Australia Policy limited religious friction to the Protestant and Catholic divide and, as in the USA, the WASP hegemony prevails, a product of the English middle classes compared with the Catholic influence of Irish and Italian communities. The divide has been emphasized by political association, reflecting Anglo-Protestant Liberals and a Labour Party with a strong Irish Catholic minority supporting republicanism. The admission of Middle

---

- One hundred and twenty female administrators, players and coaches attended the 'Focus on Marketing and Management' seminar series conducted in Queensland, the Australian Capital Territory and Western Australia and with softball and basketball administrators.

- Eleven NSOs initiated activities or conducted planning seminars specifically targeted at increasing the involvement of women and girls in their sport under the Gender Equity Planning Program.

- The Active Girls Triathlon Series was extended from 21 events in 1992–1993 to 29 events in 1993–1994.

- The 3rd annual Prime Ministerial Women and Sport Awards was conducted to acknowledge special initiatives taken to encourage greater involvement of women and girls in sport, including those with special needs.

- Resource materials including four issues of the national magazine Active were produced to provide a communication vehicle for women's sport and greater recognition of women's sporting achievements.

- The ASC participated in the first international conference on women and sport, conducted in the UK, which agreed to an international set of principles aimed at developing a sporting culture that enables and values the full involvement of women in every aspect of sport. These were endorsed by 280 delegates from 82 countries.

Figure 15.14 Women and sport, Australia. (*ASC. Programme Performance, 1993.*)

East and Asian communities has further increased the religious mix and has led to state education becoming secular.

Race

The White Australia Policy was an Anglo-Celtic creation to keep Australia safe from the so-called yellow peril. Its colonial base also served to keep other Europeans out and it was not until the 1950s that large groups of displaced persons were accepted from mainland Europe. Given an expansionist policy and a relatively low response from this source, the migration policy was extended in the 1960s to people from the Middle East and to Asians in the 1970s. The result is a pluralist society, similar to that in the USA, but produced in a small fraction of the time. Class remains the major form of stratification, but there is racial ranking that generally reflects the changing migration policy. As in the USA, non-British Europeans are rapidly building themselves a place in the social order, but there are racial concerns over non-integrated Aboriginal Australians existing as a submerged class, while oriental communities, encouraged to settle on economic grounds, are resented by some conservative elements.

Attempts are being made to give Aboriginal Australians more status and their life-style, including their ethnic sports, is receiving recognition, but the dominance of certain sports is linked with racial identity, reflected by the Anglo-Celt games of cricket, rugby and Aussie Rules. The proportion of Aboriginal professional players, for example, in no

way matches the Maori involvement in New Zealand. Association football, on the other hand, is strongest in the Italian and Greek communities. As in the UK laws exist to prevent racism, but even in sport, wealth and traditional rivalries cause elements of exclusivity and dissension

Age

The notion of being a young, dynamic country bodes well for youth culture, as reflected in the support given to young athletes at Federal and State levels. This includes a careful monitoring of young athletes so that there is less commercial exploitation of young people than in the USA.

Alternatively, one might have expected the aged to be ignored in sport terms, but the strength of the Healthy Outdoor Australian ethic is a lifetime obsession, one which only the recent fear of skin cancer has curbed. Private bowls, tennis and golf clubs abound in urban areas, where space still does not seem to be a problem, and every small town has similar facilities, with organized walking trails. All these facilities are widely used by the elderly.

Disabled

As with Britain, a great deal was learned about physical disability as a result of wartime injuries and this in combination with the Australian concern for health and activity has resulted in, predictably, a major integrated adaptive programme in education; the Aussie Able Program (Figure 15.15) is a well developed sports programme in most urban areas.

- The ASC completed an examination of its role in funding and supporting disabled sport in Australia.

- Two additional Coaching Athletes with Disabilities (CAD) manuals were completed, bringing the total number of finalized manuals to six. Sport-specific coaching resources for the disabled (videos, manuals and courses) were developed in consultation with swimming, athletics, gymnastics and tennis coaches.

- Sixteen Level One coaching courses were conducted, and mainstream sports continued to include CAD material in the Level One coaching curriculum.

- Twenty-three elite athletes with disabilities were granted AIS Scholarships and training camps were held for swimming, athletics, weightlifting and basketball.

Figure 15.15 People with Disabilities—Aussie Able Program. (*ASC. Programme Performance, 1993.*)

Former Soviet Union

Regional

The standard of living in the European republics was higher than that in the East, but this is more a case of emergence than discrimination.

Class

The presumption is that, with the Bolshevik Revolution in 1917, the class system was destroyed. Such is the nature of humans that the ambition to get on and do the best for their children inevitably leads to an undercurrent of meritocracy. This was called the 'white collar cult' in the Soviet Union. Party policy was directed against this in the past, but the new era of *glasnost* may change this. Sport was one of the few areas where individualism was encouraged, but even here the rewards of success tend to be wrapped up in social benefits.

Physical aptitude was the key factor in sporting achievement. Societal status came as a result of this, and was not a prerequisite.

In a political system based on economics, the value of an individual lay in his/her contribution as a worker. Unions had a range of holiday camps and choice was linked with effort.

> Soviet trade unions show particular concern for the organization of holiday activities for working people and their children. In the summer of 1983, for example, nearly 14 million children spent their holidays in 68,000 Young Pioneer camps. The cost of maintaining a child at a camp for one shift (26 days) is 100 roubles. But half the accommodations at Young Pioneer camps is free, for the other half parents pay only 20% of the actual cost. The past few years have seen an expansion of facilities for the summer holidays and recreation of parents with their children. In 1985, trade union-sponsored holiday homes and hotels have three times more accommodation for families than ten years ago.
>
> (Novosti Press, 1985)

It is probable that, if Russia and the Ukraine continue to introduce a market economy, the old infrastructure of full employment and a narrow differential between rich and poor will be eroded. The Soviet Union had already built up a wealthy class of high-ranking party officials, but the reforms are producing a new class of rich entrepreneurs. However, in the long term, the old 'white collar tradition' will probably re-emerge. The consequence of these trends may be a widening of the wealth continuum, resulting in a large deprived sub-class; also, if jobs become scarce there may be a backlash associated with the ethnic minorities, similar to events in Britain and France.

Gender

The Soviet Union attempted to adopt universal female equality. In a society based on both parents working there was no differential and, therefore, no discrimination. To some extent this accounted for the success of Soviet and East European female athletes. They were not handicapped by traditional myths and roles as is the case in Western democracies.

However, having quoted Articles 34 and 35 of the Soviet Constitution on sexual equality, the text *Women in the USSR* went on to explain that:

> Unlike several Western countries, such popular men's sports as football, judo and boxing are not cultivated.

This was supposedly on health grounds, but the suggestion was made that women had many other alternatives. To some extent, this was cultural pressure to deter women from taking part in these activities and it may well be that there was more freedom for women to play soccer in Britain than in the Soviet Union. There is certainly more freedom for girls to play soccer in the USA than anywhere else in the world.

Religion

There was a political policy of atheism, but it was based on education rather than a destruction of churches. It was hoped that religion would die with the older generations, but a strong Christian and Muslim minority still exists and *glasnost* has allowed more religious freedom in Russia and the Ukraine.

Race

There has been a level of discrimination against the Jewish community. This was partly because they were accused of putting their race and religion before 'socialism', but also because the Soviets feared a 'brain-drain' to Israel. *Perestroika* has allowed Jews to go to Israel, but the future may yet bring a re-emergence of anti-Semitism in Russia and the Ukraine.

Even in the case of the Jewish problem, there was no question of discrimination influencing sporting opportunity. The desire to maintain the economy and to produce champions was far too strong to allow racial discrimination to exist in sport.

It might be argued that individuals who were not party members lost some of the advantages associated with pioneer palaces and workers' camps, but even in this context appeasement was a vital factor in an authoritarian society, and recreation was regarded as a conforming instrument.

Age

> *Every Soviet child, regardless of the financial state of its family, enjoys equal opportunities for physical and intellectual development. Apart from free medical care and universal free education, the state fully finances the development of the interests and abilities of every child at art studios, music and sport schools, young technicians' and young naturalists' centres, etc.*
>
> (Novosti Press, 1985)

The Soviet Union was politically aware that the future of its community ideology lay in the hands of its children. From a very early age, therefore, the State was presented as a benefactor. Children's groups from the Octobrists (young children) to the Pioneers (adolescents) were given the best possible facilities, complete with a high level of political education. The Komsomol, which represented the politically active youth of the country, had considerable influence on impressionable young people.

With both parents employed, the State recognized the need to keep children occupied in a positive way, and sports' palaces and outdoor camps were very popular inducements to keep young people 'off the streets', complete with a reward system of competitive 'pins' and prestige camps available for those who tried hardest.

Finally, the 'Olympic Reserve' policy encouraged the identification and promotion of young talent in sport, with a view to selection and special treatment—an attraction to children and parents alike.

It is important to recognize that this appealed to the politically committed citizen, and also to ambitious parents who saw a chance of using the system for their own ends.

Perestroika has removed the political indoctrination motives and this, together with the end of funding, has led to a breakdown in organizations for young people. In time, there may be a re-emergence of scouts and guides, but in the meantime children are increasingly being left on the streets, encouraging deviance and lawlessness. It will be a tragedy if the superb pioneer palaces for young people fall into disrepair before an alternative programme can be implemented.

Disabled

In the dark days of the Cold War, the Soviet authorities would not have admitted to the existence of a handicapped group in their society. However, *glasnost* has shown that this is just as big a problem in Russia and the Ukraine as it is in the rest of Europe. The problem is that if these 'new' republics continue to descend into economic depression, the less able are likely to suffer most.

 # Review Questions

1. How does class stratification still influence sport in the UK?
2. Racial stratification still exists in the USA. Compare the chance of reaching the top in sport with obtaining a top career.

3. Discuss the exploitation of young sports stars in the USA and the former Soviet Union.
4. How does media coverage of sport reflect the status of women performers in the context of English rugby, Australian swimming and French climbing?

Summary

Sociocultural:

1. Ideology reflected in sport; pluralism and the survival of ethnic sports.

2. Centralized administration in France and the former Soviet Union; decentralized administration in the UK and the USA. Australia may have found a compromise between these two extremes, where central sports administration is balanced with regional responsibility at State level.

3. Political influence in all countries, but was strongest in the Soviet Union.

4. Financial aid determined by ideology: ranging from subscriptions and commercial sponsorship to state aid.

5. Elements of discrimination reflected in the sporting inequalities that exist in different cultures.

6. As a result of the reforms republics such as Russia and the Ukraine are going through a transition that is largely unpredictable, but in 1993 they showed signs of becoming increasingly democratic and market led.

Further Reading

Calhoun D.W. (ed) *Sport, Culture and Personality*, Human Kinetics, 1987.

Cashman J. *Paradise of Sport*, Oxford University Press, 1996.

Cashmore E. *Making Sense of Sport*, Routledge, 1990.

Daly J.A. *The Quest for Excellence*, Australian Government Publishing Service, 1991.

Davis D. *et al. Physical Education: Theory and Practice*, Macmillan, 1986.

Dunstan K. *Sports*, Cassell, 1973.

Edwards H. *Sociology of Sport*, Homewood, 1973.

Gardner P. *Nice Guys Finish Last*, Allen Lane, 1974.

Houlihan B. *Sport and International Politics*, Harvester Wheatsheaf, 1994.

Howell R. The USSR: Sport and politics intertwined. *Comparative Education*, 1975; 11(2).

Lapchick R.E. (ed) *Sport in Society*, Sage, 1996.

McPherson B.D. *et al. The Social Significance of Sport*, Human Kinetics, 1989.

Miller A. *Death of a Salesman*, Viking, 1977.

Rigby F. The place of PE and sport in a centralized system—France. *PE Review*, 1978; 1: 53–58.

Riordan J. *Sport in Soviet Society*, Cambridge University Press, 1977.

Sage G.H. (ed) *Power and Ideology in American Sport*, Human Kinetics, 1990.

Sports Council. *Into the 90s*, Sports Council, 1988.

Sports Council. *New Horizons*, Sports Council, 1994.

Sport in France. *France Information Services*, 1985; 125.

Vamplew W. *et al. Oxford Companion to Australian Sport*, ASSH, 1992.

Women in the USSR, Novostl Press, 1978.

Report of the Wolfenden Committee. *Sport and the Community*. CCPR, 1960.

Chapter 16

The Administration of Physical Education and Sport in Five Countries

16.1 The Administration of Physical Education

United Kingdom

Traditionally, the British educational system has been divided into a private sector for a social elite and a State sector for other children. At the end of the Second World War, a major building programme was necessary following the widespread destruction due to bombing. The victory resulted in a general feeling of well-being and a need for an extension of recreational opportunity, and a tripartite system of education allowed some children to receive a free grammar or technical education. In the 1960s, the tripartite system was largely replaced by comprehensive schools, but the old style grammar schools persisted in some authorities and the private schools continued as a separate system, functioning as private institutions or as charitable trusts (Figure 16.1). Then, in the 1980s, central government encouraged schools to consider becoming independent from local authority control as grant maintained schools.

Throughout these changes, the British educational system has remained **decentralized**. This means that the basis of decision-making is in the hands of the teacher responsible for physical education in the individual school. That person can select from a variety of objectives, activities and teaching styles. There are a number of common features that operate, however. Teachers appear to retain habits and interests from their own school experiences; they often select colleges which reflect these interests, but they are also influenced by innovations experienced at college; they are very much at the mercy of local attitudes and provision in the school; and, although they are 'responsible', the Head of the school always has the final word (Figure 16.2).

The considerable increase in the quality of physical and human resources in physical education has had a marked effect on the PE curriculum. On the physical resources side, the new sports halls and

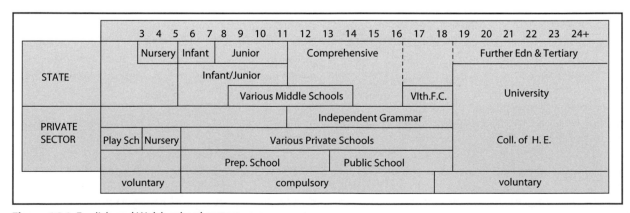

Figure 16.1 English and Welsh school system.

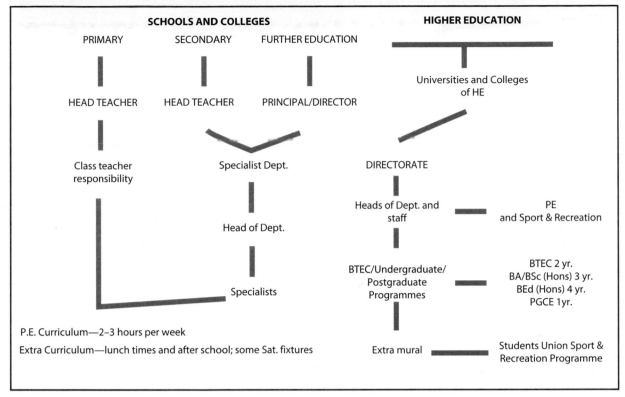

Figure 16.2 Institutions.

swimming pools have broadened PE beyond gymnastics and field games, and the introduction of an all-graduate profession has increased the general quality of input and the status of the subject.

Another major area of change arises from the cluster of ethnic minorities. In certain schools, the proportional dominance of Asian and Afro-Caribbean children is such that the traditional PE programme is being questioned. The overall trend of increased co-educational PE is being criticized by Asian parents; they also prefer their boys to play hockey rather than traditional soccer and rugby; and swimming for Muslim girls is a particular problem.

The local authorities, which represent shire counties and urban conurbations, are the pivot on which decentralized administration functions. They have the communicative role of relaying government policy and maintaining local standards. The personnel involved are professionally qualified and highly experienced and, despite the recent move to give them inspectorate status, their traditional role has always been as advisers—helping teachers with their problems; initiating in-service programmes; recommending and supplying equipment; and stimulating innovation.

Finally, central government is responsible for general educational legislation and has maintained this decentralized policy. However, the 1988 Educational Reform Act resulted in a number of major changes being directed by the government which, apparently, reduce the level of decentralized autonomy. The 1988 Act introduced a National Curriculum; increased the extent to which schools are open to public scrutiny, through the increased powers of school governors; increased the influence of parents; and increased the extent to which market forces can determine the success of schools. While on the one hand this would appear to increase governmental control, it significantly reduces the powers of local government, particularly where schools decide to 'opt-out' of local government control (Figure 16.3).

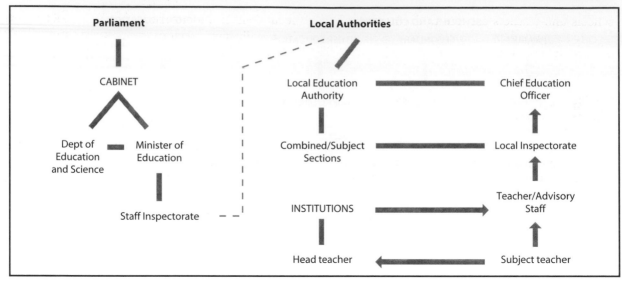

Figure 16.3 Government and Local Government Authorities.

There was an initial adverse affect on physical education as the local managements of schools (LMS) made policy decisions on the basis of costs rather than benefits, such as reducing the priority of swimming, closing school facilities to the public, and selling off part of their playing fields.

This policy has now been checked as a result of pressure from the Sports Council, PE associations and parents. It has become obvious that sports facilities can generate a steady income for a school; that a successful record by sports teams and PE examinations can increase status and improve admissions; and that, as a subject on the core curriculum, PE remains a vital part of education.

This last has become increasingly apparent as attainment targets and programmes of study have been written for PE (The Education Order, 1992), where the purpose of the attainment target for PE is to 'demonstrate the knowledge, skills and understanding involved in areas of activity encompassing athletic activities, dance, games, gymnastic activities, outdoor and adventurous activities and swimming.' There are four Key Stage Tests; Stages 1–3 came into effect in August 1992 and Stage 4 in August 1995. Stages will take place in years 1, 3, 7 and 10 of schooling, respectively, and be followed by the national examinations of General Certificate of School Education (GCSE) and Advanced GCE (A-level), at an optional level.

Courses for young people in the 16–18 age group have been rationalized under the general title of General National Vocational Qualifications (GNVQs), which are vocationally orientated programmes for those not taking A-level courses.

Key Stage 1 programmes meet the needs of children aged 5–7 years and includes five areas of activity: athletic activities, dance, games, gymnastic activities, and outdoor and adventurous activities, but if the school wishes, swimming can also be included. Stage 2 is for children aged 8–11 years, where the six activities include swimming. Stage 3 is for 12–14 year olds and requires children to cover four areas, one of which must be games, with choices from the other areas. Stage 4 is for 14–16 year olds and has still to be fully rationalized, but it will run for children not doing GCSE in PE, and two activities will be selected.

GCSE PE has been under some Government criticism because of the variations in content and standard, but these were rationalized by the School Curriculum and Assessment Authority (SCAA) in 1996. The two A-level programmes, Physical Education and Sport Studies, which had been administered by the Association of Examining Boards (AEB) since 1986, were merged into one syllabus and the Oxford and Cambridge Board (OCEAC) introduced a new Physical Education Syllabus in 1996 and, given the support for diversification by SCAA, there may be other new syllabus presentations in 1997. In 1996 more than a thousand centres were teaching A-level in Physical Education and Sport Studies, which amounts to more than 10 000 candidates a year.

With the worst abuses of LMS now in the past, the value of accountability in raising standards in schools and departments could make the National Curriculum a positive step, provided testing does not reduce learning and as long as the ambitious schools and teachers are free to do more than the national requirement. It would seem, however, that the ambitious content of the PE attainment tests will require either the provision of specialist PE teachers in the Primary sector or increased professional training in PE for prospective general teachers.

 Investigation

16.1: The administrative levels
Trace the following three administrative processes from ministerial level to the child in the school:

1. A particular school is in need of a new swimming pool.
2. A parent asks a teacher about safety regulations in the gymnasium.
3. A pupil wants to do an A-level PE programme.

Local administrative framework

Having produced a structural framework for the administration of physical education in the United Kingdom, we now want you to examine the level at which it operates in your own school. Four research models are presented in Investigations 16.2–16.5—we suggest that the class should be separated into four sets, with each set researching one Investigation.

These exercises should help us to obtain a balanced picture of what is actually happening in our own institutions, but will also be useful when we try to look across at physical education in other societies.

If we visit a school we see a curriculum in action; if we read articles on curriculum theory, we begin to appreciate what the curriculum ought to consist of; but most important, we should be able to use our theoretical knowledge to draw the most out of the limited provision in any given situation. This can be simplified into a model called **the credibility gap** (Figure 16.4).

We can't always achieve what **ought** to happen, because of limitations in staff ability, provision, finance, children's attitudes, etc., but with effort we could probably improve upon what we are doing at the moment (Investigation 16.2).

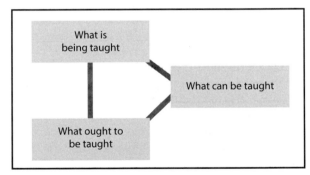

Figure 16.4 The credibility gap.

 Investigation

16.2: Session organization
You will have all played either basketball or hockey. You know quite a bit about how an ideal session should be organized.
You go to another school and you see 30 children being given a one hour lesson in basketball or hockey. Throughout the period they use only one ball in a game situation, with those not selected in the teams acting as spectators.

Suggest what limitations may have brought this situation about and then describe how you would use your knowledge of what **ought** to be happening to produce the best experience for the children that the limitations will allow.

If we are going to understand the British PE curriculum, it should be possible to produce a model which will act as a series of 'coat-pegs' for us to analyse what **is** happening, or what **might** happen in any given school (Investigation 16.3).

Investigation

16.3: Curriculum theory analysis
Select an individual pursuit (athletics, swimming or gymnastics) and show how each of the conditions in Figure 16.5 can be met in a half hour practical session.

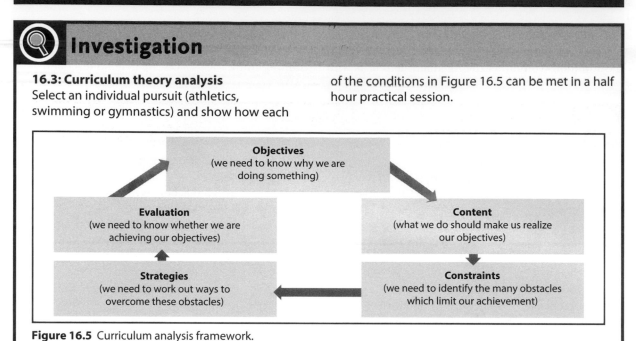

Figure 16.5 Curriculum analysis framework.

In the early 1970s, the Schools Council researched the PE objectives favoured by teachers of secondary school boys and girls. They asked the teachers to rank in order nine objectives—the results are listed in Table 16.1.

We are going back some 25 years for this information. Very few PE teachers were graduates in those days and most of the teacher-training programmes were practical in content. In addition, general attitudes have changed as regards the role of the female in society; and there has been an extensive campaign by the Sports Council in the shape of Sport for All (Investigation 16.4).

Table 16.1 : Teachers' rank order of PE objectives

Boys	Girls
1. Motor Skills	1. Emotional Stability
2. Self-realization	2. Self-realization
3. Preparation for Leisure	3. Preparation for Leisure
4. Emotional Stability	4. Social Competence
5. Moral Development	5. Moral Development
6. Social Competence	6. Organic Development
7. Organic Development	7. Motor Skills
8. Cognitive Development	8. Aesthetic Appreciation
9. Aesthetic Appreciation	9. Cognitive Development

Investigation

Investigation
16.4: Rank order of PE objectives
1. Ask all the members of your PE staff to make their own rank order.
2. Ask the group to rank order these objectives.

3. See if you can account for the changes that have occurred over the 25 years as well as for the differences you might find between the views of staff and students on the rank order of these objectives.

Finally, let's put all this together with the framework in Figure 16.6 produced by Layson (1971) (Investigation 16.5).

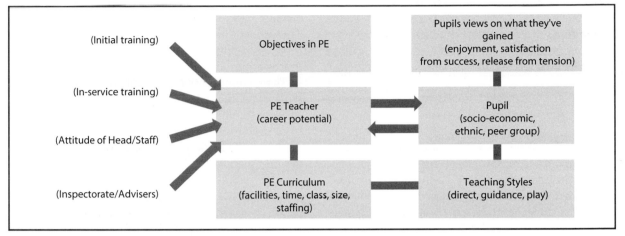

Figure 16.6 Objectives and outcomes of the British PE system.

Investigation

16.5: Objectives and outcomes of physical education

With the help of the staff, see if you can gather the information to explain the relationships between objectives, programme and outcomes in the teaching of physical education in your school or one PE class in your school.

Things you ought to know about british physical education

Local Authority

With senior advisers increasingly involved in the inspection of standards arising from the central directive on accountability, a number of advisory teachers have been appointed to retain the close liaison between the local authority and individual schools. Finance for courses and in-service training was distributed by local authorities, but is becoming the responsibility of individual schools.

Teachers

In-service is now a compulsory part of the teacher's contract. There is concern at the degree of wastage, as a large proportion of PE teachers leave the profession.

There have been problems over a reduction in the birth rate which has led to a cut-back in the number of teachers being trained and also a number of redundancies and job-reallocation. New contractual regulations for teachers are having a detrimental effect on extra-curricular activities.

Exams

The introduction of GCSE and A-level examinations in PE has led to more graduate knowledge being brought into play.

In-service

National in-service courses are held annually at Liverpool, Worcester and Winchester on an optional basis, with financial aid from local authorities, schools and the National Coaching Foundation (NCF).

Increasingly, local authorities, colleges and schools are also structuring in-service programmes at a local level.

Teacher training

Although physical education is a graduate profession, there are still a number of older teachers who are only certificated.

Undergraduate programmes have changed dramatically over the past 10 years in terms of the increased proportion of theoretical study, and also in the delay of professional studies until the third or fourth year. It is felt in some quarters that this has had an adverse effect on teaching standards.

Extra curriculum

City schools have established league fixture programmes in most sports, whereas their rural counterparts tend to retain friendly fixtures with schools in the locality. The **English Schools Sports Associations** are very well organized and there is a creaming system in most games and sports from area level through to national representation in each of the four home countries.

There are a number of dynamic changes occurring in sport education; however, it is difficult to separate policy from implementation at the moment. The NCF, as part of a ministerial strategy, initiated **Champion Coaching** in 1991. All the major administrative sports bodies were involved, including the **British Council for Physical Education** and the **National Council for Schools' Sport**. This was a major breakthrough, reducing the rivalry between sports coaching and physical educators. Twenty schemes went into operation, two in each of the 10 regional Sports Council areas in England. Each scheme provided six weeks of top-quality coaching in a number of target sports and involved around 3500 children. Progress was published in 1992 as *Champion Coaching: School-Age Sport, 24 Recipes for Action*, and the success of the project brought more funding and a second phase, which was in turn evaluated in 1993 in the publication *More Recipes for Action*. Meanwhile, the other three National Sports Councils are following suit; Northern Ireland, for example, has already produced a **Corporate Plan, 1993–1997** to raise standards in Sport for children aged 11–14 years.

It is in the context of these projects that the political initiative, known as the John Major Initiative, July 1995, must be viewed. John Major, as Prime Minister, endorsed the publication *Sport: Raising the Game*, by saying that his ambition is to 'put sport back at the heart of weekly life in every school. To re-establish sport as one of the great pillars of education alongside the academic, the vocational and the moral. It should not be relegated to be just one part of one subject in the curriculum.' These words need to be backed up with a detailed, fully sponsored programme. The Lottery is a potential source of money to pay for this and a strategic plan being operated in Victoria, Australia, **Physical and Sport Education**, may be the blueprint to work from. There are strategies to sponsor coaching courses for teachers and capital grants for schools and colleges hoping to specialize in sport.

Schools

The schools in the private sector still tend to give more credibility to PE and have PE lessons and games afternoons.

There remain but a small number of 'sports schools' in the UK. These include 'public schools' such as Kelly College, Llandovery, Millfield and Gordonstoun, where scholarships or special arrangements are made for talented performers. Alternatively, governing bodies are setting up 'schools' in conjunction with local education authorities. The Football Association (FA) soccer school at Lilleshall is an example of a Governing Body establishing a selective school. It was opened in 1984 and 16 boys per year are selected to spend two years at this boarding institution, where they have special coaching facilities and complete their normal schooling in Telford.

To date this experiment has had only limited success and it may be that community ventures like the Manchester United Soccer School and the Aston Villa Community Project will more closely meet the needs of aspiring young footballers.

Dual use and joint provision of major facilities are being encouraged to increase participant use and to share costs.

Parents

Parents are being encouraged to play a more active part in school management. There is a long history of support from Parent–Teacher Associations (PTAs), and parent governors will increase parental influence.

Curriculum

PE is one of 10 core subjects on the recently instituted National Curriculum. It recommends a minimum of 10% of the timetable for PE and some LMS committees have opted for this minimum. Market forces, particularly examinations, may lead to many schools offering more than the statutory minimum.

Gymnastics tends to be taught in most primary schools as 'movement' rather than formal skill gymnastics; games teaching is following this pro-active teaching style through 'games making' and 'games for understanding' approaches.

France

The traditional structure of the French educational system is similar to that in the UK in that it has a private and State sector, where private schools have tended to attract a wealthier clientele. However, French private schools and colleges are largely Roman Catholic institutions, whereas in Britain—though many private schools have church associations—only a minority are directly managed by church bodies. A second similarity has been the gradual change in the State sector from a tripartite system, where the lycée (grammar school) had considerable status, to a predominantly comprehensive system (Table 16.2). As in Britain, the private sector has been left relatively unchanged by successive governments and has retained the attraction of lycées in a society which values intellectualism.

The French educational system remains **centralized**, and as such it has a uniform, authoritarian basis which makes it totally different from the British model in decision-making terms (Figure 16.7). Any structural analysis, therefore, must start from the government and involves government-administered official instruction. The communication of these directives is carried out by regional authorities, but, unlike the British equivalent, policy is implemented and not initiated at this level.

The present organization of physical education dates from the 1967 Official Instructions, and in 1969 new provisions in respect of PE and sport in schools were made in a weekly timetable in primary and secondary schools. This is called the **programme** and is a syllabus equivalent. The credibility gap mentioned in the British situation certainly operates in the presentation of this programme. Schools are required to teach it, but human resources, such as the quality of teaching, and physical resources, such as equipment, do not always allow this to happen.

Central authority structure

Unlike the British system of virtual head teacher autonomy, administration is directed through bureaucratic channels (see Figure 16.7). Similarly, unlike the British local inspectorate and advisers, the French regional director and his inspectors have little autonomy.

The most obvious example is in the 'tiers-temps pedagogique'—primary instructions that six hours per week should be devoted to PE and sport (Table 16.3). A practising French teacher from Brive suggested in 1987 that this was a 'beautiful dream'. However, he did say that the problem over physical resources was much less than in the 1970s. He claimed that 'infant school children' in the area had about six hours of PE a week; and primary school children between one and three hours. He suggested that the most interesting developments were occurring in extra-curricular sport in the primary schools. Formerly, about 25% of the pupils took part in sport on a Wednesday afternoon, and about 30% within the tiers-temps programme. By 1987, this had increased to 50% during tiers-temps with only 7% on Wednesdays. It is important to note that primary school teachers assist programmes on a voluntary

Table 16.2 : The French School System

Age	Education	Establishment	Curriculum
2 to 5	Pre-School (non-compulsory)	Nursery School	All-round development, physical, motor skills, co-ordination of movement, special awareness
6 to 10	Primary	Primary School	
11 to 16	Secondary—1st stage	Collège	Wide range of developmental possibilities (in theory)—many schools still concerned with social control through physical situation
16 to 18	Secondary—2nd stage	Lycée	
18 +	Higher	University 'Grandes Ecoles'	

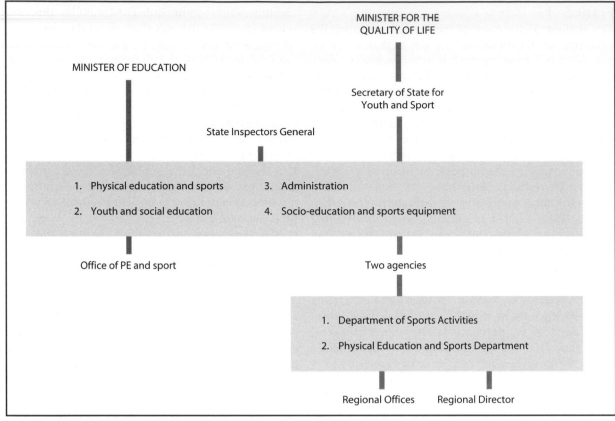

Figure 16.7 Central authority structure.

Notes:

1. Unlike the British system of virtual head teacher autonomy, French authority is directed through central bureaucratic channels.

2. Similarly, the British local inspectorate and advisory teachers have more autonomy than the French regional directors and inspectors.

3. The greater the distance from Paris, the less notice is taken of government directives. It remains to be seen whether the same will apply with respect to London for the national curriculum in Britain.

4. The key stage tests initially appear to be much more formal and ambitious than the 'brevets' in French PE.

5. The secondary PE curriculum retains a focus on 'la gym' as part of a long tradition, but over the past 10 years sport, in the sense of individual activities and games, has become an increasingly important part of the **programme**.

	Primary	**Secondary**	
		Stage I	**Stage II**
PE & sport (compulsory)	1/3 teaching time 6 hours	PE & sport 3 hours **SPORT** (CAS) 2 hours	PE & sport 2 hours **SPORT** (CAS) 3 hours
Sport (optional)	USEP 1/2 day	1/2 day UNSS (formerly ASSU)	

Table 16.3 : Weekly hours of PE and Sport

basis, and so there is a great range from one school to another. The *'tiers-temps'* programme is part of the teachers' paid commitment.

All these sporting activities are administered by an independent association (Union Sportive de l'Enseignement Primaire; USEP—Primary Schools Sports Union), acknowledged by the Ministry of Education and reflecting the centralization policy. In addition, agreements are being reached by which staff and coaches from individual sports federations go into schools to initiate interest in specific sports. In the Brive school this has so far involved rugby, riding, climbing and athletics federations. In the last few years a number of primary sports schools have been opened where children are selected on sporting ability (Smith, 1996).

France is even more 'examination conscious' than the UK and physical education is assessed formally at three levels: Brevet des Collèges—15-year-olds; Brevet d'Enseignement Professionel—17-year-olds; and Baccalauréat (Higher Education Entrance)—18-year-olds or older. In the Baccalauréat, besides the compulsory PE section, candidates who are specially gifted can take an optional complementary exam in a definite sport or activity, thus scoring extra marks which are added to their overall mark. This also occurs in music, art, handicraft and languages. In each of the three PE examinations, there is a system of continuous assessment throughout the final year, which mainly concerns practical performance—but also includes marks for general attitude and behaviour, goodwill shown and effort made.

The unfortunate consequence of these tests is that they can dominate the PE curriculum and act as a focus of interest for the candidates to the extent that attempts to extend the physical education experience are frustrated. It is hoped that the GCSE and A-level programmes in Britain will have the opposite effect because they are given additional time and also include extensive theoretical components.

If the overall impression is that the French PE curriculum is stilted compared with the British equivalent, then the opposite would seem to be the case in the context of **extra-curricular** sporting activities.

Britain has a tradition of games afternoons and school fixtures from a public school and grammar school system, but over recent years political and financial constraints have reduced these activities in many State schools. The opposite is the case in France. All French schools have had Saturday morning school and a games afternoon in the week as a long tradition. However, these sports afternoons, now normally a Wednesday, were optional and, therefore, extra-curricular, but instead of being administered by the individual schools they were controlled by a national sporting body, the Association du Sport Scolaire et Universitaire (ASSU, 1962–1978). More recently, the organization of school sport has been taken over by the Union National du Sport Scolaire (UNSS, Figure 16.8). Once again this is part of a centralized policy which takes the organizational responsibility away from individual schools. Nevertheless, it gives the children in poorly organized schools a better chance to participate, and ensures a pyramid structure for the promotion of talented performers.

One of the inherent problems of PE in schools was the lack of status of the PE teacher. Other teachers were answerable to the Ministry of Education, but PE teachers came under the Department for Youth and Sport. This was changed in 1982 and the status of the staff and the subject has increased since then.

There had always been a very restricted allocation of places for specialist teachers of PE at a specialist college (Ecoles Normales Supérieures d'Education Physique et Sportive; ENSEPS—Training Colleges for Sports and Physical Education), but in 1982 the ENSEPS stopped teacher training and became the National Institute of PE and Sport (Institute National de Sport et Education Physique; INSEP). ENSEPS had considerable influence on schools because it supplied all the specialist staff and was responsible for any new professional initiatives. INSEP still influences the schools, but now has a broader impact on research and sporting development in general. PE teachers are trained at special units attached to universities (Unites d'Education de Reserche de l'Education Physique et Sports; UEREPS—University Research Units for Sport and Physical Education).

The French equivalent to sports schools are called **sports study sections**. They consist of special classes for talented children, but these are not allowed to interfere with academic study. Schools specialize in certain sports and children are selected to attend them. Some centres cater for excellence in one sport, but others are multi-sport centres. Expert staff are appointed and facilities are well above average. These sections are on the increase and, though they are regionally based, they are centrally controlled.

The 1987 figures show that UNSS is flourishing:

- 890 000 licences and 1 200 000 participants;
- 90 000 sports associations (virtually one in each school);
- 2500 school coaches;
- 250 000 qualified officials in 44 sports;
- 8000 participants in the 1986 Jeux de l'UNSS.

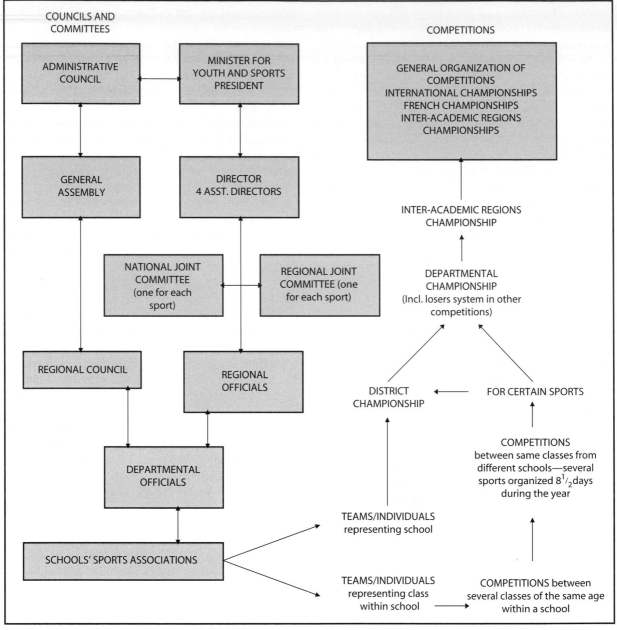

Figure 16.8 Structure of UNSS (formerly ASSU).

United States

American education and physical education is **decentralized**, but not to the same extent as in Britain (Figure 16.9).

It is very important for a European to recognize that each American State is comparable to a European country, and that Federal action by the American Government is rather like a confederation of European States agreeing to a unifying policy and constitutional foundations.

The size and population, together with a tradition of State autonomy, has resulted in each of the 50 States of America being responsible for the jurisdiction and general administration of their own education. However, the pluralistic, community-centred tradition means that control is administered at local board level.

Given these variables it is always dangerous to generalize. Certainly, each State is different and the relative affluence of a State determines the quality of its educational system. This also applies to the local school boards, some of which are in wealthy neighbourhoods while others are impoverished. In addition, some urban school boards are responsible for hundreds of schools, while some rural boards are responsible for just two or three.

American education has a private and a public sector, where the private sector is self-supporting and often associated with church groups. Though it tends to cater for a more affluent section of the community, this is more apparent at college level than in the schools. The American school system is outlined in Figure 16.10.

If we look at the school as the primary unit, there is a very important difference between an American school and the British equivalent. The American teacher responsible for physical education in the school does not produce his/her own programme. This is presented by the superintendent employed by the school board for the area. The teacher simply works through this set programme, much as the French teacher has to. The value of this approach is a guarantee of minimal content and planned progression; however, it tends to remove the elements of spontaneity and creativity evident among better teachers in the British system. It would also seem to promote an instructional approach, in that the heuristic style identified in **movement education** is not easily written into a fixed programme. Given that most of the teaching content is in fitness programmes and direct skill learning, it is not possible to write a programme of progressions, so the American system is flexible enough to allow individual differences, human and physical, to be recognized. Unlike the French and English syllabuses, the American programmes are localized, allowing for community variables. Additionally, there are avenues for review, where teachers can approach the superintendent and work towards innovation.

A programme exists for elementary and high school children, and specialist teachers teach the subject at both levels. Elementary schools average

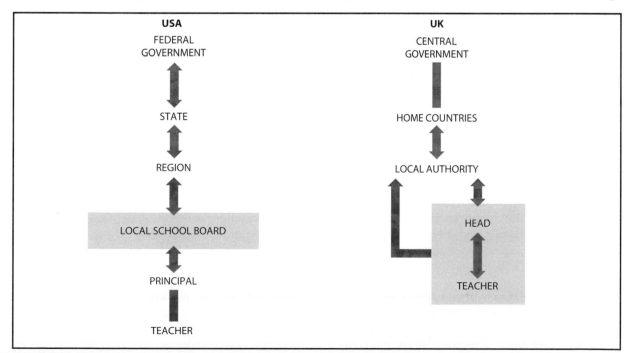

Figure 16.9 Diagrammatic comparison of decision making in the USA and the UK.

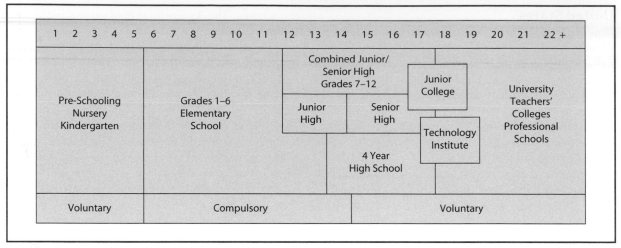

Figure 16.10 American school system.

Notes:

1. Mainstream route is for children to attend pre-schooling.

2. All children attend elementary school, normally progressing from Grade 1 to 6.

3. Most children attend junior high school (equivalent to the UK middle school), followed by senior high school, graduating from Grade 12.

4. At 17 years' old, approximately one-third leaves school; one-third goes to junior college (about half of whom progress to university); and one-third goes straight to university.

three 50-minute periods each week, but the larger high schools often work on a tri-semester basis limited to five subjects per semester. In the event, physical education may be taught daily for two terms, but excluded from the third term.

It is also important to recognize that the top-quality high school facilities are used extensively. An example of the use of an ice rink in Minneapolis high school is:

- 4.30am: individual ice hockey coaching.
- 7.25am: six one-hour PE lessons start.
- 2.30pm: ice hockey coaching recommences.

In Minneapolis, for example, the school day and bus travel are closely inter-related. The early start at the high school reflects the fact that the oldest children catch the first bus, followed by the junior high and then the elementary age group. The seniors are picked up first, followed by the others, to give each type of school an equal-length day.

The advantage of the early finish in the senior high school is that it allows for the implementation of not only a major athletics programme, but also programmes in drama, dance and other subject areas.

Federal administrative structure of education

Each of the 50 States is responsible for the establishment and maintenance of a system of free public education. Each State is responsible for the general instructional programme; the certification of

teachers; building standards; and financial support (Figures 16.11 and 16.12).

If we are looking for a set of objectives for American PE, four patterns are most common.

1. The traditional importance of sport in American society makes inter-scholastic athletics (in the general American sense of the term) by far the most powerful local objective, encouraged by ambitious parents and reflecting the commercial competitiveness of American society. This promotes skill-centred programmes, and may result in an elitist programme, where the physically able will have greater opportunities with better staff.

2. Certainly since the Kennedy administration, great importance has been placed on physical fitness and particularly measurements of this. Once again, in a society where accountability is significant, physical educators look for a measurable facet of their subject. An awareness of health-related fitness is also very popular in Britain, but one must always consider the value of the experience on the one hand, and the time taken measuring temporary outcomes on the other.

3. Educators who follow the Dewey tradition and who are aware of trends in Europe have introduced **movement education**, where task-orientated programmes encourage students to engage in decision-making situations. This approach has been adopted more readily by females, at least partly because they are not as committed to the competitive sports tradition. It

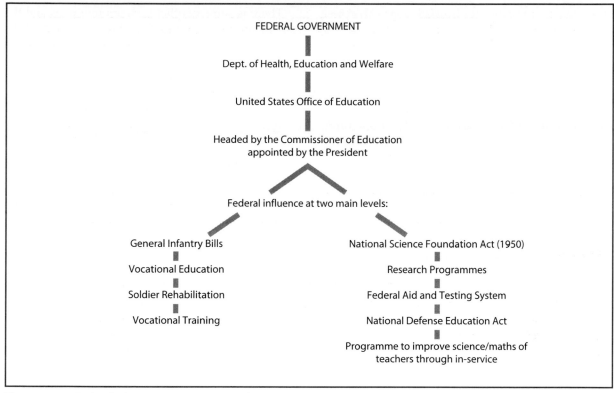

Figure 16.11 Federal administrative structure of education in the USA.

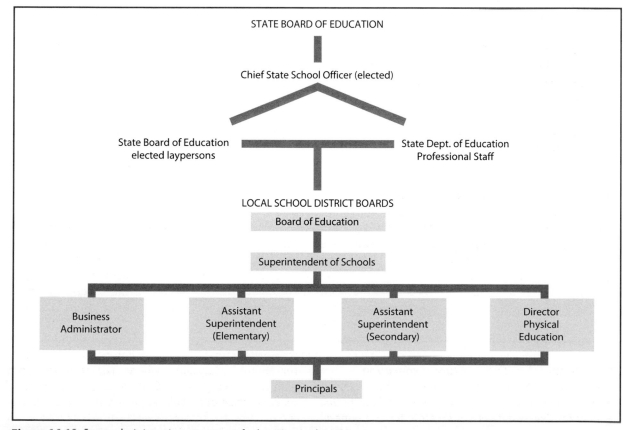

Figure 16.12 State administrative structure of education in the USA.

is because the **movement** or **heuristic** approach is seen to conflict with the competitive ethic that there are relatively few examples of this 'counter-culture' approach in boys' programmes, despite the number of books written on it.

4. The basis of American schooling is traditionally social education—the bringing together of pluralistic communities into harmonious, patriotic units. It also stresses the individuality of the American citizen, his/her ability to cope and his/her desire to make good. The more aggressive qualities fit well within the competitive sports concept, but many of the progress reports in high schools also include gradings for social attitudes such as co-operation, sportsmanship and leadership.

If we look at the specific objectives of certain schools, we can see the extent to which they identify with these suggested patterns (Figure 16.13).

The importance of the extra-curricular athletics programme cannot be overstated. The boys aspire to make one of the inter-scholastic squads; children compete to be part of the cheerleader support group; the reputation of the school and community rests on athletic success; and parents, in addition to the kudos gained, realize that success can mean a sports scholarship place in higher education.

There is some conflict between feminists and the role of girls in the male athletics arena. Certainly, **Title IX** (legislation which requires State educational institutions receiving Federal money to fund and staff boys' and girls' programmes equally) has dramatically increased the quantity and quality of girls' physical education and sport participation.

In the context of girls and the athletics programme, there has been a tremendous increase in the number of programmes in traditionally female sports, and the national reputation of women's athletics, swimming, basketball and volleyball has led to scholarship potential in higher education for girls as well as boys. However, in many senior high schools girls still have a tremendous enthusiasm to be selected for one of the cheerleader teams rather than actually participate as performers in their own right. Certainly, cheerleaders work extremely hard, and the number of girls involved is considerable, given that each competitive team in the major sport has its own cheerleader group. It may well be that more girls should be actively involved in school athletics as performers on the field of play—rather than playing a supporting role as entertainers confined to the sidelines. However, the admittedly limited possibilities of creative dance in schools allow at least some girls expression at a performance level.

Orange County School District (Benning, 1978)

Objectives of PE programme:

- Maximum motor development, commensurate with their physical abilities.

- Move with ease, confidence and a sense of well-being.

- Movement utilized as a means of self-expression.

- Develop and maintain a high level of physical fitness.

- Desirable social growth and development.

- Utilize motor skills in worthwhile leisure activities.

California State Board of Education (Benning, 1980)

PE goals:

- Motor skills.

- Physical fitness.

- Self-image.

- Social behaviour.

- Recreational interests.

Figure 16.13 Objectives of elementary school (Grades 1–6) and State pattern.

Physical education is required to be taught co-educationally; while this prevents some of the more aggressive athletic sports being played on the curriculum, it tends to make instructional method even less suitable, given the diversity of the class.

A similar comment might be made about the **adaptive programme**. A great deal of money has been spent on the education of children with special needs. They are given special help, but every attempt is also made to integrate them into the class and the community. While this objective is admirable, it is questionable whether an instructional approach from a formal programme with mixed groups is the most effective teaching style.

Europe has no equivalent to the American senior high school athletics programme, which makes a considerable amount of money from spectator support and is thus self-sustaining. It pays for the building of outstanding facilities, which are also available for curriculum classes, and pays the salary of coaches in each of the major sports. The Director of Coaching has a highly responsible post and usually a far higher salary than the PE teachers in the school. He is responsible for his team of coaches and for the administration of public occasions, and may also teach PE part time (Figure 16.14). However, his appointment, as is the case with all the coaches, depends very much on results.

The advantages to physical education of the status of sport in the high school have already been outlined, but there are also disadvantages. Inevitably, the objectives and the programmes in PE tend to be obscured by the pressure to build successful squads in the leading inter-scholastic sports. This leads to a focus on physical objectives rather than humanistic ones. This may be one reason why **testing** and **measuring** play such a vital part in American PE.

Another problem which tends to reduce the significance of physical education, as Europeans perceive it, is the misfortune that the profession is an ageing one, largely because a huge enrolment programme after the Second World War has resulted in a large number of teachers of pensionable age, in a profession which is far less mobile than the British equivalent. Full pension rights require 30 years minimum in the same State; the more outgoing teachers make it in coaching; and teaching a fixed programme can inhibit job satisfaction.

It is also important to remember, however, that the Kennedy Administration promoted a major fitness programme that was one of the few Federal projects that directly influenced physical education. This includes programmes for children with special needs.

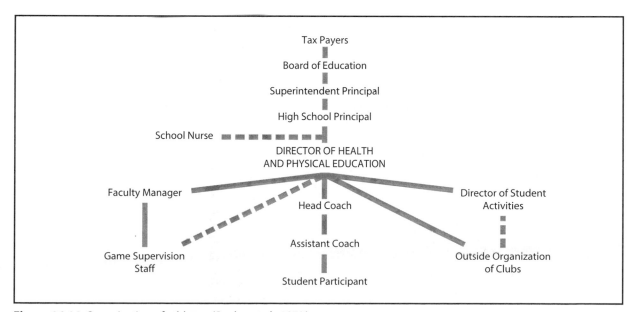

Figure 16.14 Organization of athletes. (*Bucher* et al., 1970.)

Australia

School system

As a British colony the 19th century education system in Australia was dominated by a parallel development of English public schools at a time when **muscular Christianity** and athleticism were at their height, culminating in the bravery, horror and human sacrifice of the 1914–1918 World War, epitomized by Australians at Gallipoli.

The diplomatic and commercial influence of upper middle class English gentlemen and the development of schools for their children resulted in the formation of elite 'public' and preparatory schools. To quote G.M. Hibbins, 'the Melbourne public schools varied not one whit from the English public schools in the growing passion for games.' In identifying the birth of Aussie Rules football in Melbourne, Hibbins pointed to the joint roots of Trinity College Cambridge and Trinity College Dublin, particularly as they were linked with Scotch College and Melbourne Grammar School in the 1850s. Without doubt, here is one factor which contributed to the Australian obsession with sport today.

The contemporary educational structure has been dramatically changed to a comprehensive national high-school system, but unlike in the UK, fee-paying independent, private schools are now almost entirely religious foundations. This secularization of Government schools is similar to that in France, but the high school system tends to resemble its American counterpart. These Government schools outnumber private schools by seven to one, but both sections receive Federal grants. Despite this centralizing influence, the administration of the educational system is controlled by individual States, where each is responsible for policy and operation, resulting in many variables between them.

It is important to establish that the private school system is very strong. Although it has a religious affiliation, it also has tradition and academic stringency that attracts middle class parents who are prepared to pay for what they consider to be an advantaged education for their children.

The structure of Government schooling is normally co-educational and is compulsory between the ages of six and 15 years (Figure 16.15). Pre-schooling is popular, but voluntary, and mainstream schools are divided into primary and secondary, similar to the English model. After Year 10 (15+), continued schooling is optional as children with ambitions to enter higher education commence a two year higher school certificate (HSC) programme. Federal Government operates a **Secondary Allowance Scheme** whereby grants, subject to a means test, are given to children to stay at school for their final two years to complete their HSC. In an attempt to meet regional needs, this national examination is now administered at State level, for example, Victorians now sit a Victoria Certificate of Education (VCE) which is set and assessed at State level. The size of Australia also makes it necessary for a special programme called the **Isolated Child Allowance Scheme**

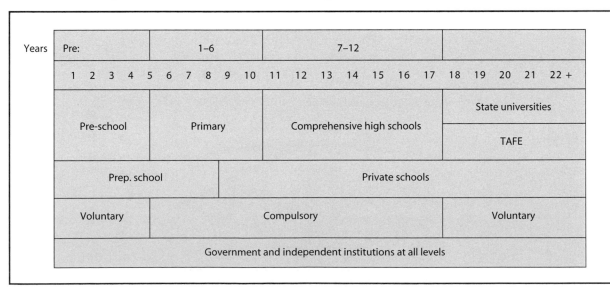

Figure 16.15 Australian school system.

Notes:

1. Mainstream route is for children to attend pre- schooling.

2. All children attend primary school, mainly co-educational, Years 1–6.

3. Compulsory secondary education, Years 7–10 with HSC Years 11–12.

to help children with travel expenses and to assist with financial support for using privately owned hostels. Other attempts to alleviate the distance problem are correspondence schools and schools of the air.

As with the UK, further education is also available for young people who do not follow the main academic route in the form of 250 Technical and Further Educational institutions (TAFEs).

Higher education institutes have degree and diploma courses that last from three to six years. Fees were abolished in 1974 and full-time students have allowances subject to means tests. This is in line with the British system, as is the merger of the three main units, universities, colleges of technology and teacher education colleges, into a single system of university higher education. Started in 1989, this is an on-going process, as is a recent trend to start a private university system. In both Britain and Australia, these trends seem to be linked with the USA system and privatization. In the Melbourne area, for example, there are four traditional universities, Melbourne, Deakin, La Trope and Monash, and two new universities, formerly the Royal Melbourne Institute of Technology (RMIT) and Victoria University of Technology (VUT), which had been polytechnics.

Physical education

Physical education has a traditional place on the curriculum that arises from the colonial system of 19th century public school athleticism and elementary school physical training. In addition, although there are national bodies that promote PE and Federal funding to support it, policy and programming is decentralized to State level and thence down to district and local school boards (Figure 16.16), similar to the system in the USA.

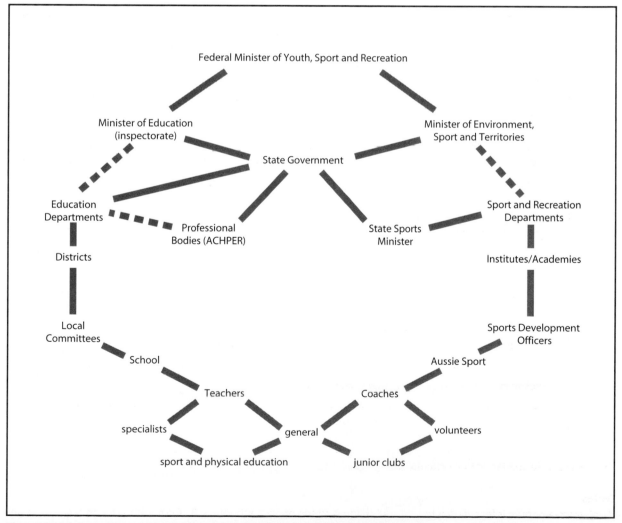

Figure 16.16 Australian administrative system for physical education and junior sport.

The period from 1945 to 1972 matched the expansion of educational principles of **movement education** seen in Britain and part of this trend was the setting up of colleges of higher education that specialized in physical education. This also marked an extension of the facilities in schools and the diversity of activities taught in PE. The next decade (1973–1982) marked a high point in physical education with the appointment of a PE inspectorate and a policy of training specialist teachers for primary and secondary schools. As in the UK, this also marked the emergence of a graduate profession. At this time a wide range of curriculum ideas came from the Ministry of Education and the professional PE Association (Australian Council for Health, Physical Education and Recreation; ACHPER).

Victoria was particularly progressive in education and physical education, but even this State found difficulty in sustaining a **Daily Physical Education Programme** for all primary children which was recommended in 1982 and supported by ACHPER. This was an attempt to establish a daily 30-minute PE lesson and to encourage teachers to use equipment and apparatus to increase children's games skills.

Unfortunately, this positive approach by physical educators was jeopardized in 1983 by general economic constraints and political reorganisation, including the closing of the PE branch of the Ministry and a series of in-service cutbacks. This led to a decline in the morale of physical educators, which was increased by the decision of the Federal Government in 1986 to put its weight behind an **Aussie Sport** policy promoted by the Australian Sports Commission (ASC) (Figure 16.17). This particular programme was designed to overcome the apparent lack of games skills among primary children and was initially directed towards the final three grades of primary schooling. Prior to this, sport in schools had reflected the British tradition of optional extra-curricular groups and teams, with skill learning as part of the PE curriculum.

Federal Government funds for the **Aussie Sport** scheme were to be distributed through State administrations and presented with a set of objectives which were largely acceptable to physical educators. However, the operation of the scheme was linked

Figure 16.17 Aussie Sport: its place in school and community.

with sport outcomes rather than personal development, even though the general aim was to offer every primary child in Australia the opportunity to realize his or her physical and personal potential. In 1988, as an extension of this project, the ASC suggested modified forms of netball, hockey, soccer, baseball and rugby with the major objective of improving the 'quality, quantity and variety of sports available to Australian children'.

As with the USA, it is important to separate Federal and State initiatives as well as discrepancies between policies and enactment in schools. With Federal funding on offer, State legislators looked very carefully at the Aussie Sport project; for example, the Victorian Ministry of Education made an initial statement on Sport Education as early as 1987 and a survey was made in 1989 to establish how much time should be given to physical activities in primary and secondary schools.

Also in 1989, an additional Aus\$12.3 million was provided from the Federal budget to expand **Aussie Sport** over a period of four years and to introduce a new programme, **Youth Sports**, for young people between the ages of 13 and 18 years (ASC, 1989).

In Victoria the Youth Sports initiative has been effectively implemented with an extension of the Aussie Sport programme to cover all school-age children.

However, these sport initiatives tended to reduce the status of curriculum physical education, closely reflecting the American emphasis on school sport; this appeared to be the Australian answer to the European sports school policy.

There were some initial problems with adopting **Aussie Sport** in Victorian schools, because educators were afraid of win-ethic objectives being applied by overzealous coaches and of focusing on a young sporting elite, so in 1992 a committee was set up to review **physical and sport education** (PSE). This review was published and put into operation in 1993. The committee was set up by the Directorate of School Education and the rationale established a sound fusion of educational and sporting objectives for all children aged five to sixteen years. Not all age groups were accommodated initially, but the scheme has become fully operational since 1995.

The intention is to give sport approximately one-third of the time allocated to physical activity on the curriculum. Though coaches may be used, every attempt is being made to qualify the teachers in a variety of sports to enable them to focus on specific sports skills in **sport education** and general personal development in the **physical education** lessons.

Emphasis on codes of behaviour throughout reflects the general educational intention of the combined programme. The recommended time allocation is 60 minutes' sport and 120 minutes' physical education per week in primary schools and 100 minutes' sport and 100 minutes' physical education in secondary school for Years 7–10. The overall objective at both levels is to achieve a daily lesson in either sport or PE and, though this is permissive legislation, every effort is being made to implement these intentions and make PSE part of the core curriculum with the full support of the Directorate of School Education.

Evidence to date suggests that additional sports funding has succeeded in the attainment of a daily physical activity session, whereas the educational criteria of ACHPER had failed in 1982.

To some extent these trends have been mirrored in the UK with the rivalry between PE teachers and sports coaches arising out of political support for the NCF, but in England and Wales physical education gained some initiative through physical education becoming a core subject in an imposed national curriculum, increased credibility through key stage testing, and increased status through the expansion of GCSE and GCE examinations in physical education. The recent tension between teachers and coaches regarding the John Major Initiative on School Sport, however, is a political strategy which might take Britain towards the Aussie Sport PSE school policy, but successful implementation will depend on adequate additional funding and rationalization.

Another similarity lies in the expansion of **sport science**. In both countries this is largely a higher education development which directly enhances the effective coaching and development of sport, but the funding in Australia is considerably higher than that in Britain, despite its smaller population. One outcome seems certain and that is the call for specialist PE teachers at primary and secondary level in both countries, either by increasing the proportion of physical educators in schools or by re-training teachers through coaching schemes in the Australian manner.

Years 11 and 12 are the optional examination years and, given that the Australian school year commences at the end of January, most children take this examination while they are still 17 years old. As a result the standards are acceptably lower than the English and Welsh A-level. The Australian HSC was a national examination which is now in the hands of State Departments of Education and presented by a Board of Studies.

In the case of Victoria the examination is the VCE and physical education is a subject which can be taken. Its aims are to:

- *understand the social, cultural, environmental and biological factors which influence participation in physical activity;*
- *analyse the processes associated with skill development in the performance of physical activity;*
- *examine the relationships between social, cultural, environmental and biological influences on participation in physical activity; and*
- *develop a critical perspective on physical activity.*

There is a great deal of common ground between the VCE PE and the OCEAC GCE PE syllabuses in terms of rationale, content and assessment, as well as in support documentation, where the VCE publishes common assessment tasks (CATs) which match the in-set material and answer schemes at GCE.

At a higher education level the **Australian College of Sports Education** (ACSE) is a joint venture involving the University of Canberra and the Australian Sports Commission. There are courses in sports administration, sports management, strength and conditioning, sports coaching and sports law. Facilities are at least equal to those of Springfield, Massachusetts, the Lesgaft Institute, St Petersburg, and the Paris INSEP, and generally superior to those of any British institution, particularly in the context of sport science.

The size of Australia and its Federal make-up militates against the ranking of university programmes found in England.

As with the UK, admission to university is on a grading system, but the Australian composite score is much more tightly structured according to specific subject requirements and, because VCE PE lacks some credibility, potential PE undergraduates are disadvantaged.

State universities appear to focus on different programmes rather than compete with each other as in the UK. In Victoria, for example, RMIT has a major Sport Science undergraduate and postgraduate programme; Deakin University has Bachelor of Applied Science degrees in Human Movement and Sport Coaching and Administration; and Melbourne University has a BEd (Primary) programme that produces specialist PE teachers.

In terms of undergraduate sport, inter-mural and inter-collegiate sport is almost entirely a social experience. Distance might be a cause, but, as in the UK, tutorial staff are not usually involved and coaches are employed by the student union sports associations. When student teams are needed for major competitions the administration is usually in the hands of elite sport institutions.

Given the British tradition of autonomous governing bodies of individual sports, the National Sporting Associations (NSAs) continue to have a major influence on Australian sport and the wealthier and more progressive governing bodies have established **Junior Development Programmes** to match the Federal initiatives. For example, in 1984, the Australian Athletic Union launched its **Athletics towards 2000 Junior Development Programme** which involved the formation of a national commission and the selection of a junior squad and junior events coaches, similar in many ways to the English FA initiative at Lilleshall. To clarify that this is a governing body programme rather than a Federal one, funding consists of Aus$50 000 from the ASC, but Aus$250 000 from the Australian Sugar Industry as a direct sponsor of Australian athletics.

Former Soviet Union and post-reform Russia

In the former Soviet Union education was free, universal and administered by the State after the 1917 Revolution. As a Union of so many different Republics and cultures, and as a conformist, authoritarian society, the Soviet Union had a centralized system of education, where the school was regarded as one of the most important agencies for the retention and promotion of Marxism. The break-up of the Soviet Union has led to each Republic becoming the highest level of government, but Russian education continues to be centralized and part of a 'socialist' if not a Marxist political regime.

Physical culture was considered to be of appreciable importance in a society which emphasized the role of the manual worker as against the part played by the intellectual. Physical education was a small part of this broad concept and referred to directed activities on the school and university curriculum.

A shortage of schools and teachers to keep pace with the rising population has remained a problem in some Republics and has resulted in a 'split-shift' system of schooling, requiring an early start for one group and an afternoon start for the other. This allows widespread use of some of the palaces, clubs and sports schools for the other half of the day.

There has also been an important educational role for extra-mural establishments like **Young Pioneer Palaces**, schoolchildren's clubs and centres for young technicians, naturalists and tourists. In 1985 there were some 5000 pioneer palaces and 6700 children's sports schools (Sport in the USSR, 1985). The political and economic crisis has resulted in the palaces losing not only their political justification, but also their automatic State funding.

Physical education continues to be a compulsory subject with a stipulated two hours per week. The general Soviet philosophy of exercise breaks also applied to schools and on occasions short exercise sessions were held between lessons. Exercise breaks are also practised by the Japanese and so the political changes may not affect these programmes if production rather than political motives are adopted. In addition, an emergent Russia will probably give health as well as production a high profile, retaining the status of regular exercise. The Soviet schools worked to a general syllabus, which was also the case in physical education. Speak and Ambler (1976), after a visit to several schools, commented that the common syllabus was not only recommended but observed. The Soviet school system and central administration are outlined in Figures 16.18 and 16.19.

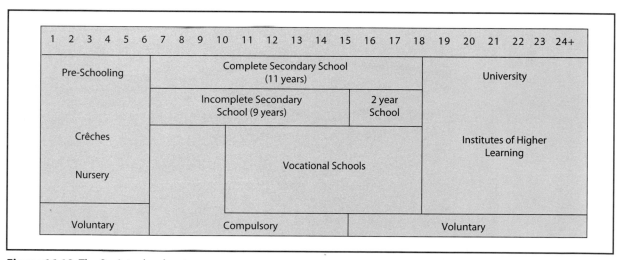

Figure 16.18 The Soviet school system.

Comments:

1. A primary objective of literacy, a fear of intellectualism, a need for economic advancement and a desire to lead the word for the sake of communism are intentions which do not easily coexist.

2. The intention continues to be to give free schooling for all through an egalitarian, polytechnic education.

3. Pre-schooling is still widespread, part of a policy to enable both parents to work.

4. The last two years of schooling are designed to link with industry and higher education.

5. Vocational schools continue to be of many kinds and include various types of sports schools.

A journal, *Physical Culture at School,* has been published monthly by the Ministry of Education, which contained articles on methodology, skill learning analysis and lists of GTO (preparation for labour and defence) standards around the country. Speak and Ambler (1976) were impressed with the quality of the articles and the value of the publication to practising teachers.

There continues to be a policy of co-education, at least up to the age of 15 years, with male and female staff involvement. The content of the syllabuses has regional alternatives to account for climate, but in the main the term physical education refers to a wide variety of gymnastics, games and athletics.

As with France and America, the existence of a set of instructions tends to result in direct teaching of specific skills, but all the work had an underlying political component. This political indoctrination is no longer a part of the educational system, but it will take some time before a new set of values is established; however, it is likely that in the foreseeable future the major concern will continue to be with exercise and basic levels of fitness.

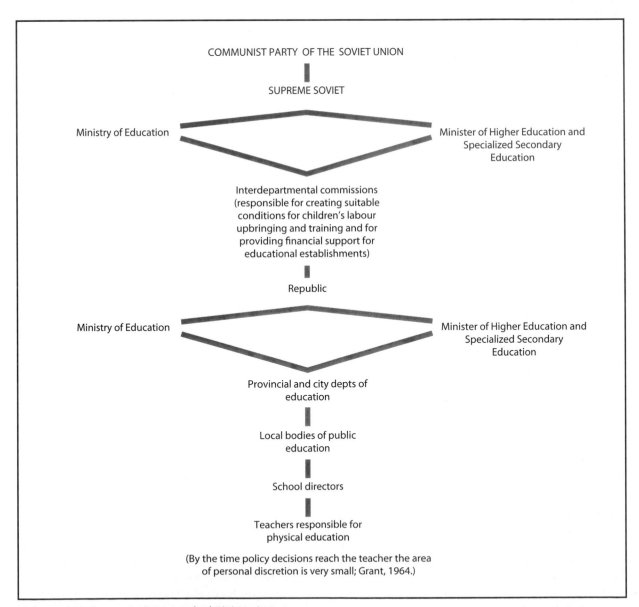

Figure 16.19 Former Soviet central administration.

The GTO award system (preparation for labour and defence)

The GTO classification was centrally organized and given priority in all schools. It catered for the young, through to middle age, and it was meant to encourage mass participation and not just record-hunting. It was a graded system of physical exercise which promoted health, ensured medical supervision and provided a unified system (Sullivan, 1964). The tables (see Figure 16.20) were revised regularly and the content was changed to match changes in political attitudes.

Though it was designed and categorized for all age groups, there were three sections for children of school age: boys and girls aged 10–13, 14–15 and 16–18 years.

There was some criticism that the tests exercised a time-consuming constraint on actual teaching, a problem which exists in most countries where assessment becomes more important than learning. Information coming out of Russia in 1993 suggested that the GTO is no longer operating. It was always likely to be interpreted as 'political' by reformers and it may be some time before a substitute fitness programme is put into effect, and when this happens it is much more likely to be linked with fitness for sport.

In 1975, the quality of school facilities was poor, a criticism already levelled against French schools, but in the intervening years there may have been improvements. The reason for the limited school provision reflected the importance of sporting facilities in the factories and community, leaving PE as a minimal health and social control provision. Once again there are parallels here with America, but in the Soviet Union the extra-curricular programme was often away from the general school. This view was substantiated by Speak and Ambler (1976), who found hardly any inter-school sport, but some school teams working towards knock-out tournaments which would lead to **spartakiads** at specific times of the year.

There was a major increase in the number of sports schools in the Soviet Union—figures for 1971 showed 4079 junior sports schools, whereas it was claimed that there were 6700 in 1985. Their function has been to search for and develop talent and they have been the key to Soviet athletic success. Administrators have referred to them as 'our Olympic reserve' (Sullivan, 1964). Their aim was for pupils to obtain their school leaving certificate with proficiency to 'Master of Sport' level in their chosen sport. Examples of facilities are shown in Figures 16.21–16.23.

The junior sports schools normally recruited 11-year-olds, but the age was lower in the case of some sports, e.g. swimming (7–8-year-olds) and gymnastics (9-year-old girls and 10-year-old boys). There were also youth sports schools with a four-year programme for 15–20-year-olds. While there has been specialization, a wide range of activities continued to be covered at a low level and academic schooling has not been interfered with.

Riordan (1977) refers to 'children's and young people's sports schools'. These would seem to be facilities which have been open to most enthusiastic children, maybe as part of a school, a factory provision or a pioneer palace, and making sports coaching available outside normal school. Different centres specialize, but they tend not to be exclusive. Riordan goes on to identify **sports proficiency schools** and **higher sports proficiency schools**. At these selective day schools talented children were given the best coaching available.

Finally, there continues to be a large number of **special sports boarding schools**, where the very best young performers are given a special educational programme in ideal surroundings. There is little evidence of pressure being applied by the authorities to recruit. On the contrary, parents and children work hard for selection and while teachers and coaches gain recognition for finding talent, many are reluctant to part with their most promising athletes. There is likely to have been at least a temporary breakdown in local sports schools, although there is evidence that factories are sponsoring local sports facilities. It would also seem that the prestigious sports boarding schools are too good to be abandoned by a society used to picking up Olympic medals.

In higher education, there continues to be two separate but co-operating bodies: the **Faculty of Physical Culture and Sport**, with the objectives of preparing students for the GTO and promoting massovost sport (mass participation); and the **Burevestnik**, or university students sports society, which caters for elite sport. With the GTO now defunct, it is likely that the Faculty of Physical Culture will focus on mass participation, similar to the intra-mural programmes in the USA.

The Moscow University Faculty of PC and Sport has around 100 staff belonging to eight departments or commissions. Facilities include ten sports halls, a swimming bath, indoor athletics track, eight open-air basketball courts, eight volleyball courts, a special soccer pitch and two practice pitches.

The premier institute of physical culture is the Lesgaft Institute in St Petersburg. It trains some 5000 students in physical culture with a specialist staff of 325 lecturers.

'Handgrenadier'
Strength & Courage
for Youths & Girls 16–18 years

Requirements: (pass examination)

1. Knowledge about physical culture and sport in Soviet Union.
2. Knowledge & carrying out of rules of personal and public hygiene.
3. Master programme of elementary battle-training, including section on defence against weapons of mass-striking-power and to remain one hour in a gas-mask, or to take a course on programmes of training specialist in organization—DOSAAF—or to have one of the practical technical specialities (for youths). For girls, to know the basic rules of civil defence and stay in a gas-mask for one hour.
4. To be able to explain meaning of and carry out the set of exercises relating to morning hygienic gymnastics.

Exercises & Standards.

Kinds of Exercise	BOYS		GIRLS	
	for silver badge	for gold badge	for silver badge	for gold badge
1. Running 100 m (sec.)	14.2	13.5	16.2	15.4
2. Cross-country				
500 m (min. sec.)	-	-	2.00	1.50
1000 m (min. sec.)	3.30	3.20	-	-
OR				
Skating (ordinary skates)				
500 m (min. sec.)	1.25	1.15	1.30	1.20
3. Long jump (cm)	440	480	340	375
OR				
High jump (cm)	125	135	105	115
4. Grenade throwing weight				
500 gram (m)	-	-	21	25
700 gram (m)	35	40	-	-
OR				
Putting the shot weight				
4 kg (m)	-	-	6.00	6.80
5 kg (m)	8	10	-	-
5. Ski racing 3 km (min.)	-	-	20	18
5 km (min.)	27	25		
OR				
10 km (min.)	57	52		

Kinds of Exercise	YOUTHS		GIRLS	
	for silver badge	for gold badge	for silver badge	for gold badge
In snowless regions				
Forced march 3 km (min.)	-	-	20	18
5 km (min.)	35	32		
OR				
Cross-country cycling				
10 km (min)	-	-	30	27
20 km (min)	50	46		
6. Swimming 100 m (min.sec)	2.00	1.45	2.15	2.00
or without timing (m)	200	-	100	-
7. Pulling-up on horizontal bar (no. of times)	8	12		
Lifting from a hand and holding by rolling* over or by strength. 3 4 (*revolution)				
Arms supported on gym bench, bend and straighten (no. of times)	-	-	10	12
Shooting small calibre rifle at 25 m (points)	33	40	30	37
OR				
at 50 m (points)	30	37	27	34
Shooting with battle-weapons: elementary exercises according to programme of elementary military training on assessment	satis-factory	good	satis-factory	good
9. A hike and test of hiking skills and ability to find one's bearings	1 hike of 20 km or 2 hikes of 12 km	1 hike of 25 km or 2 hikes of 15 km	1 hike of 20 km or 2 hikes of 12 km	1 hike of 25km or 2 hikes of 15 km
10. Sport rating for: Motorcar, outboard motor, motorbike, glider, parachute, aeroplane, heli-copter, under-water sport, all round sea-sport, modern pentathlon, machine-gun firing, radio, scouting (finding one's bearings), wrestling all kinds), boxing		III		III
11. Any other kind of sport		II		II

Figure 16.20 The GTO awards, USSR—ready for labour and defence sample table.

Note:

For the gold badge it was necessary to fulfil not less than seven standards at the level established, including a temporary swimming standard and two standards at silver badge level (excluding the tenth standard). Girls who passed a course for 'combatant medical orderly' were considered to have passed a tenth standard gold badge test.

Figure 16.21 Vocational School No. 68 in Baku is frequently called a sports school. It has 12 sports clubs in which activities are run by volunteer trainers—instructors and foremen employed at the school. Future cooks, sale assistants and other specialists in the services sphere successfully participate in city competitions in various sports. (*Sport in the USSR, August 1981.*)

Figure 16.22 Indoor stadium.

Figure 16.23 Athletics facilities—how do these compare with your school or college?

Review Questions

1. a. Compare the systems of assessment in France (with their brevets and the baccalauréat) with testing and measuring in USA senior high schools.
b. Compare the systems of assessment in Australia, with key stage testing, sports awards, with the GCSE/GCE A-level in the UK.
2. Compare preparation for high level sport at school level in Australia (with its Physical and Sport Education programme), France (with the UNSS and Sport Sections), the old Soviet Sport School system and inter-collegiate sport in American senior high schools with parallels in the UK.
3. Describe the Soviet GTO system and explain its function before the Reforms and suggest its possible future.

Exam-Style Questions

1. Figure 16.24 identifies the main administrative levels of the education and/or physical education systems in the USA and UK.
a. Use Figure 16.24 to explain the extent to which both countries have a decentralized system of decision-making. (2 marks)
b. Draw a simple outline of the administrative systems of PE in France or Australia to show the chain of decision-making. (2 marks)
2. Primary PE in France is dominated by a *tiers-temp* pedagogy, but distance from Paris tends to determine the extent to which it operates.
a. Briefly describe the *tiers-temp* pedagogy. (2 marks)

b. What is implied in the comment about Paris? (2 marks)
3. Compare sport in secondary schools in Australia or the USA with our own extra-curricular sport. (7 marks)
4. Teaching styles in primary PE vary according to the dominant ideology in the country concerned.
a. Compare the different teaching methods you would be likely to find in Australian, French and former Soviet Union primary schools and explain these in the context of respective ideologies. (10 marks)
(Total 25 marks.)

Exam-Style Questions

continued

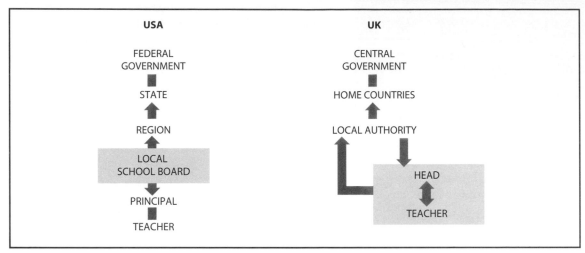

Figure 16.24 Main administrative levels of education and physical education systems in the UK and USA.

 Summary

UK, PE:
1. **Decentralized administration; autonomous institutions;** the institution of a national curriculum with PE as a core subject is intended to raise minimum standards and includes attainment tests to evaluate standards.
2. Credibility gap between what **ought to be, is,** and **might be.**
3. Curriculum theory based on **objectives, content, constraints, strategies** and **evaluation.**

France, PE:
1. **Centralized administration; fixed syllabus; examination based.**
2. *Tiers-temps* pedagogy in primary schools—six hours PE per week, but not always achieved.
3. UNSS a well organized sports programme for schools, one afternoon per week.

Australia, PE:
1. **Decentralized administration;** with Federal and State funding.
2. Tradition based on British system, but increasingly American, post 1945.
3. **Aussie Sport** programme to improve activity level of young children.

4. New policy of **Sport and Physical Education** as part of the curriculum.
5. Policy of sponsored coaching courses for teachers.

USA, PE:
1. **Decentralized administration**; power with **local school boards.** Great variations between different States.
2. PE dominated by sport.
3. Title IX legislation aimed to give equality to girls' PE in schools that receive Federal funds.
4. Emphasis on **health** and on **fitness testing.**
5. Major interest in adaptive PE.

Former USSR and Russia, PE:
1. Term **physical culture** widely used: more general than the term PE.
2. **Centralized administration** with polytechnic education.
3. **Fixed syllabus** with emphasis on the **GTO award programme**, until the political reforms curtailed it.
4. Development of sport and sports schools to establish **massovost** and an **Olympic reserve.**

16.2 The Administration of Sport

United Kingdom

The **Department of the Environment** used to be the government department primarily responsible for government policy regarding provision and public expenditure in the development of sport. Since 1962 there has been a **Minister *for* Sport**, with each of the Home Countries having their own Minister with responsibility for sport. It is important to note that they are not Ministers *of* Sport, and have only an advisory role in Britain's decentralized organization of sport. In 1990 the Ministry was moved to the Department of Education and Science, but in 1992 it achieved Cabinet status as part of the responsibility of the **Secretary of State for the National Heritage** (Figure 16.25).

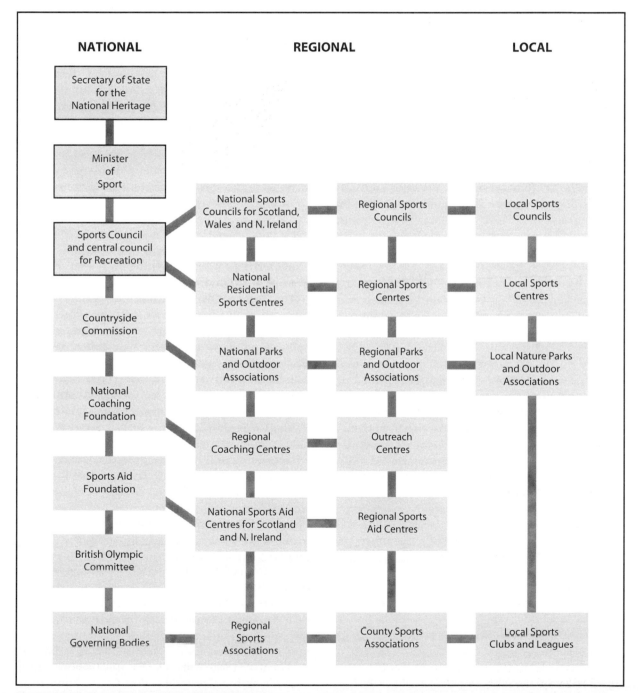

Figure 16.25 The administration of British sport.

The **Countryside Commission** is an independent statutory body, which reviews matters relating to the conservation and enhancement of the landscape and the provision and improvement of facilities of the countryside for enjoyment, including the need to secure access for open-air recreation.

The **Sports Council** was established in 1965 and received its charter in 1972. It is an independent statutory body with overall responsibility for British sport, but in effect there are separate Councils for England, Scotland, Wales and Northern Ireland. The Council has four main aims:

- To increase participation in sport and physical recreation.
- To increase the quality and quantity of sports facilities.
- To raise standards of performance.
- To provide information for and about sport.

The Sports Council has been given the responsibility of distributing lottery money for capital projects for sport and recreation provision.

The **English Sports Council** has nine regional offices which work closely with regional and county governing bodies, local sports councils and many other agencies to develop and implement regional strategies for sport.

The **Sport Aid Foundation** (SAF) is an autonomous fund raising body. It grants aid to individual established sportspeople for their financial needs in relation to training, preparations and medical treatment. It raises funds from commercial and industrial backing and distributes its grants through the governing bodies of sport. It aims to place Britain's talented performers on the same footing in relation to training and preparation as those in the USA and Eastern Europe (Figure 16.26). The SAF has national offices in Scotland, Wales and Northern Ireland and nine regional offices in England to encourage local fund raising and to help local competitors reach national standards. In 1997, the central role of sponsoring promising athletes and coaches will be taken over by the Sports Council, NCF and governing bodies, with the SAF supporting a second tier of performers.

Figure 16.26 Sport is all about getting it right on the day with a little help from others.

The **National Coaching Foundation** is the education service for coaches in the UK. Based in Leeds, the network comprises sixteen **National Coaching Centres** in different higher education institutions in England (11), Scotland (2), Wales (2) and Northern Ireland (1). Its function is to improve the quality of coaching in this country by providing introductory packs, a programme of key courses for practising coaches, advanced workshops and a diploma for experienced coaches, and a documentary resource. The NCF has been given many additional responsibilities as a result of the latest Government initiatives. These include sponsored courses for teachers and the negotiation of funds for elite performers and coaches.

The **Central Council of Physical Recreation (CCPR)** is an independent national voluntary organization representing over 240 governing and representative bodies of sport and physical re-creative activities. It is the 'collective voice' of British sport— a representative body which formulates and promotes measures to improve and develop sport and physical recreation in the UK and a consultative body to the Sports Council. The CCPR receives financial support from the Sports Council by contract, in addition to its members' donations. The Council has introduced a Community Sports Leaders Award scheme to encourage young people to assist in coaching sports groups.

The **British Olympic Committee** (BOC) enters competitors in the Olympic Games and the qualifying rounds. It is autonomous and must resist all political, religious and commercial pressures. It is also responsible for fund raising in conjunction with the governing bodies of sport. The BOC is one of several agencies that has applied to administer the proposed National Sports Academy.

The **Governing Bodies of British Sport** are completely autonomous. They are responsible for the organization and codification of their individual sport, and for financial solvency.

National Sports Centres

There are five national residential sports centres managed and financed wholly or partly by the Sports Council. Priority of use is given to national team training, competition and the training of leaders and officials. When these needs have been met, however, the centres are available for general courses to improve personal performance and to introduce beginners to new activities. The centres are:

- **Crystal Palace:** Established in 1964 in Norwood, London, it was Britain's first multi-sports centre, built by the Greater London Council and managed by the Sports Council. Facilities include swimming and diving pools to international standard, a separate teaching pool, a large indoor arena, cricket school, badminton courts, squash courts and a floodlit stadium with an international athletics track.

- **Lilleshall Hall:** Established in 1951, near Newport, Salop, it is set in secluded grounds. Lilleshall's facilities include a covered training track, a dance and gymnastics studio, squash courts, two indoor sports halls and outdoor pitches. In 1977 the Sports Council and the FA launched their development scheme to make Lilleshall the country's premier soccer school. There is also a sports injuries clinic.
- **Bisham Abbey:** Established in 1946, near Marlow, Bucks, it is a 12th-century abbey foundation adapted to the needs of 20th-century sport. Facilities include an extensive sports workshop, providing indoor training and tactical play facilities for all major sports, and a range of outside facilities, pitches and tennis courts. There is now an established tennis school for promising young players, which parallels the football and gymnastics at Lilleshall.
- **Holme Pierrepont:** Established in 1973 in Nottingham, this is a national water sports centre developed on derelict land as a joint project with Nottinghamshire County Council (Figure 16.27). Extensive water areas include an international 2000 metre rowing and canoeing course and separate lagoons for water-skiing and angling, all contained within a new country park. Lecture and conference facilities are also available.

Figure 16.27 Holme Pierrepont National Sports Centre.

- **Plas y Brenin National Centre for Mountain Activities:** Established in 1955 at Capel Curig, North Wales, it provides an outlet for adventure through the mountains and outdoor activities. Personal performance courses are given in rock climbing, canoeing, camping, skiing, fly fishing and field studies. Mountain leadership certificate courses for leaders and instructors are provided.

There was also the **Cowes National Sailing Centre**, which was established 1968, Cowes, Isle of Wight, as a national sports centre until it was sold in 1990. It now functions as a commercial sailing centre. There are plans to establish a new national centre with the Portland/Weymouth area as a possible site.

Future Developments

Subject to the resources being made available, the Sports Council will:

- *Seek the development of the following facilities for high level training and performance:*
  - *A national indoor velodrome (completed).*
  - *A national ice skating training centre.*
  - *A national centre and arena for movement and dance.*
  - *A national indoor athletics training centre.*
  - *A national outdoor competition centre for bowls.*
  - *Training facilities for judo, boxing, modern pentathlon, sailing, alpine skiing and hockey.*
- *Pursue in close co-operation with the governing bodies, the policy which it agreed early in 1987 for the future development, management and use of its national sports centres.*

[Source: *Into the 90s* (Sports Council, 1988.)]

Many of these projections have now been overtaken by the Government initiatives to promote sport using National Lottery Money. The so-called 'Four Pack' consists of capital schemes for sports provision; expansion of coaching; increased sponsorship for athletes; and capital schemes for the enhancement of sports colleges.

Review Questions

The Sports Council has published details on all governing bodies of sport, and the Palmer Report (CCPR, 1988) on **eligibility** is available from the CCPR.

See if you can use these publications to:
1. Build up an organizational structure for your own sport.
2. List the main regulations for amateur performers in your sport.

France

The sports movement is made up of two networks— **Federation** and **Olympic**.

The basic unit in French sport is the club and for the most part clubs are affiliated to federations (Figure 16.27). The point to be made is that this network has been built from the clubs up to the federations, very much as in Britain. These federations determine the technical and ethical rules in their respective sports. They are delegated by the Minister of Sport to organize competitions at which international, national and provincial titles are awarded. The federations issue licences to each registered performer. This makes it very much easier to obtain accurate statistics on regular participation.

There are four types of federation: **Sports Olympiques** (Olympic federations); **Sports Non-Olympiques** (non-Olympic federations); **Multisports** (associated federations); and **Scholaires & Universitaires** (school and university federations). These four bodies make up four 'collèges' within the French National Olympic and Sports Committee.

The Olympic network has been built the opposite way (that is from the top down), where the **National Olympic Committee** represents and promotes French sport and includes members from all the sports federations. This process of finding and promoting talented performers is achieved through **regional** and **county committees**.

Financial aid is controlled by the **French National Olympic and Sports Committee** in equal partnership with the State. This is divided into two sections, top class sport at national level and sport for all at regional level.

Sport currently comes under the **Ministry of Youth and Sport**. Regional and county directorates of youth and sport exist, but mainly to fulfil the objectives of the Ministry. A level of decentralization has been taking place since 1982, with the establishment of regional and general councils which have the power to finance local sports facilities. This suggests that similarity with the regional and local sports advisory committees in Britain is increasing.

The latest development is for the Government to set up three co-operative associations: the **National Council of Sport and Physical Activity**; a **National Committee for Research and Technology**; and a top class **Sports Commission**.

Table 16.4, from 1981, should give you some comparative insight into popularity variables with the UK. It is interesting, for example, to note that in 1981 golf had not yet become a popular game in France. This has changed dramatically over the past decade as a result of the high international media profile and its promotion as a commercial tourist attraction.

There are a number of national centres of excellence, such as the **National Institute of Sports and Physical Education (INSEP)** (Figure 16.29), the

Table 16.4 : Percentage of French people who practised each sport at least once in 1981. (From Marmet, 1987.)

Sport	Total	Male	Female
Jogging	18.0	21.5	14.7
Swimming	14.7	15.2	14.2
Football	11.1	18.3	4.4
Gymnastics	10.0	6.8	13.3
Tennis	9.5	11.7	7.4
Cycling	7.8	9.1	6.6
Skiing	7.5	8.4	6.5
Sailing	2.9	4.0	1.9
Table tennis	2.5	4.1	0.9
Horse riding	1.8	2.0	1.5
Judo	1.4	2.2	0.6
Dance	0.9	0.1	1.6
Boules	0.8	1.6	0.1
Motorcycling	0.7	1.4	0.1
Shooting	0.4	0.6	0.2
Golf	0.2	0.3	0.1
Archery	0.1	–	0.1
Other	3.5	5.2	1.9

National Yachting School, the **National Riding School** and the **Regional Sports and Physical Education** **Centres**. They all assist the Ministry in training officials and preparing athletes for top class competition.

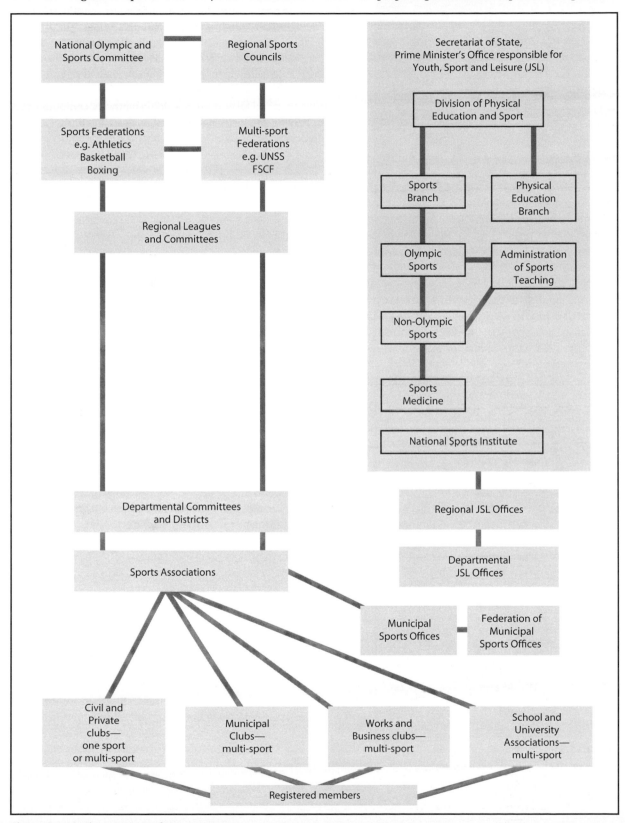

Figure 16.28 The structure of sport in France.

Figure 16.29 INSEP lies in Vincennes Park on the outskirts of Paris. Its facilities include:

- Six covered tennis courts, two swimming pools, outdoor track and field stadium, two straight tracks and a sprinter's track, one cycling track, two gymnasiums, football and rugby pitches, two fencing halls and the biggest judo hall in Europe.
- Europe's biggest research laboratory specializing in various fields: physiology, biomechanics, measuring instruments for anthropometrical tests, muscle building methods, computers to assist training and instruments to test and classify sports equipment.
- An audio-visual department and library containing video equipment and publications, some of which are in English, Spanish and Arabic.

Ethnic sports in the provinces are very popular (Figures 16.30 and 16.31). These range from a variety of folk activities in the Pays Basque to Breton wrestling and the ever popular street bowls (boules/petanque).

Figure 16.30 Scieurs de Long.

Figure 16.31 Course au Sac en Relais.

'Sport pour Tous' (sport for all)

Within everyone's reach; need to be physically active; a noble life style; mass participation in a wide range of activities; encourage multi-sport development; socialization of the family and community through sport; instil a love of the open air; a new approach as an alternative to elitism; part of the new image of the sports federations; and spontaneity as against the constrictions of professional sports.

(Free translation from Le Sport pour Tous. Une Dimension Nouvelle, 1976.)

United States

Three ethics appear to co-exist in American sport:

- The **Lombardian ethic**: winning is everything. The end result justifies the means of achievement.
- The **radical ethic**: the excellence of outcome is important, but more important is the way it is achieved.
- The **counter-culture ethic**: the process is more important than the result. A strongly anti-competitive view, with eco-sport an extreme example.

Structure and function exist within these conflicting ethics and remain sufficiently fluid to accommodate them.

It is important to remember that in America **athletics** is a term used to describe high-level sport and is often associated with professionalism and the Lombardian ethic. The term **lifetime sport** is associated with the European 'Sport for All' concept and tends to reflect the radical ethic; it is regularly associated with the intra-mural sports scene in educational institutions. The term **eco-sport** has been used to reflect sport which is healthy, fun and environmentally based, rather than competitive, and reflects the counter-culture ethic.

The structural basis of American competitive sport, athletics, lies in the specific club unit within an institution or a community. It is invariably private, in the sense that members subscribe to it, but at higher amateur and professional levels it is subsidized by sponsorship and gate money.

There are four main levels at which this administration functions: high school, collegiate university, amateur and professional (Figure 16.32).

The **National Federation of State High School Athletic Associations** (SHSAA) is a national advisory body which has branches in each of the States and controls inter-scholastic competition. Very little

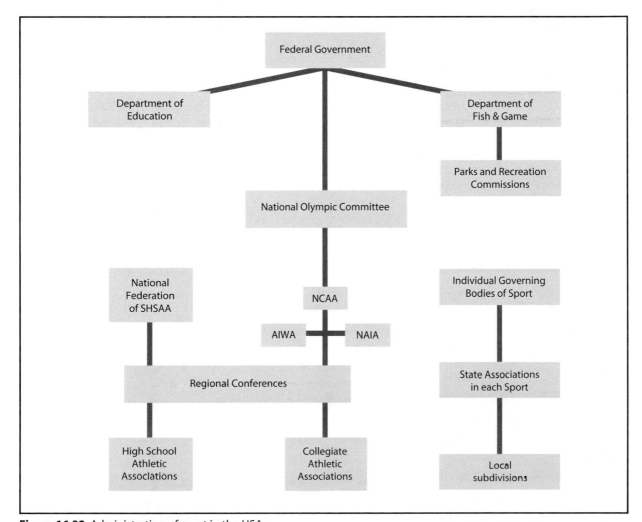

Figure 16.32 Administration of sport in the USA.

Federal money finds its way directly into sport. The exception is the sponsorship of the Olympic team. These individual organizations have met over many years and produced associations which act as governing bodies to maintain rules, regulations and competitions.

At the collegiate and university level, there are two organizations in operation. The **National Collegiate Athletic Association** (NCAA) is responsible for the inter-scholastic athletic programmes at larger institutions, and the **National Association of Intercollegiate Athletics** (NAIA) controls the athletic competitions between smaller colleges.

The surge of feminism in American colleges and the increase in the number of women athletes as a result of Title IX seems to have resulted in a counter-productive administrational move, where in 1981 the independent Association of Intercollegiate Athletics for Women (AIAW), which had been responsible for female athletic programmes, lost control and the male-dominated NCAA took over responsibility for all athletics. In addition to scholastic institutions, religious associations, like the YMCA, and larger industrial companies and trade unions have had considerable influence in the promotion of sport.

At a third level, there are the **individual governing bodies** of American amateur sport. As a result of the President's Commission on Olympic Sport (1977) and the subsequent Amateur Sports Act (1978), the powerful **Amateur Athletic Union** (AAU) was replaced by the creation of individual governing bodies of sport, for example **The Athletic Congress** (TAC) for track and field athletics, the **United States Gymnastic Federation** (USGF), the **United States Amateur Swimming** (USAS), etc. The rivalry between the NCAA and the AAU has thus been removed by legislation.

At a fourth level there is the professional scene. Each major professional sport has a separate controlling body or bodies (Figure 16.34). Such is the place of sport in America that to achieve success as a professional sportsperson is to guarantee heroic and financial status for life.

Formation of the United States Olympic Committee (USOC), 1950

The various Olympic developmental programmes—sports club based in Western Europe, sports school in Russia and Eastern Europe and armed services in developing countries—contrast sharply with the system of non-government involvement somewhat unique to the USA.
[Johnson, W. Secondary School Sports, *Gymnasion* XI(1), 1974.]

Children's sport in the community exists very much on the same lines as English "lad's and dad's" soccer. Parents and ex-players coach teams to play in leagues. The criticism is sometimes levelled that professional attitudes are encouraged at a time when recreational and educational values would be better. **Pop Warner Football** and **Little League Baseball** are the two best-known organizations (Figure 16.34), and to young Americans this may be the start of the glory trail to the Super Bowl or the World Series.

The huge commercial enterprise of collegiate football and basketball not only pays for the scholarships and seasonal costs of the whole athletic and intra-mural programmes, but also subsidizes other college projects (Figures 16.35–16.38). The American 'alumni' or 'old students' are a constant source of

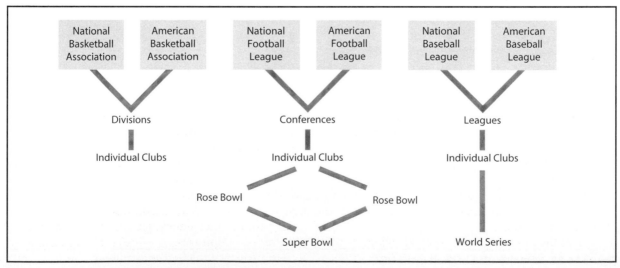

Figure 16.33 Professional Associations in the USA.

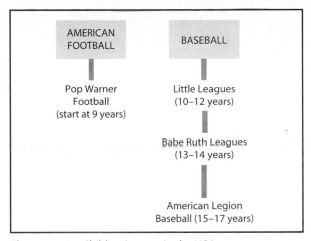

Figure 16.34 Children's sport in the USA.

Figure 16.35 Why are high-scoring games attractive to the American public?

patronage, but it is often a successful athletic programme which motivates their generosity. There are criticisms at intervals from 'academics' against the 'jocks', but such is the public and alumni commitment that there seems little likelihood that this tradition could be seriously threatened by any counter-culture revolution. Sports scholarship students should not always be blamed for their apparent disinterest in academic studies. Often the commitment required by the coaching staff prevents even the well-intentioned athlete from having enough time to study as well as train.

The college athletes in the major sports have sports scholarships which give them a free higher education, as long as they fulfil the requirements of the coach in their particular sport. Baseball tends to be the exception here, in that it is very much the inner-city game, and numerous community leagues exist to act as a proving ground for those aspiring to reach the professional ranks.

At a professional level, by far the largest amount of money is made through television and, as with any advertising franchise, this income is a direct reflection of success. Huge crowds attend professional American football games, but the facilities are of such a high standard that violence seldom breaks out. Baseball is again an exception here. The crowd is more volatile and the players are given to occasional fist-fights, suggesting some parallels with European soccer. It is also important to recognize that the distances travelled for away games result in most American professional games being played in front of home crowds.

Such is the pressure on winning at collegiate and professional athletics that coaches have a highly paid, but a very insecure, job. Reference is often

Figure 16.36 Why baseball and not cricket in America?

made to a 'hire and fire' policy. This means that, as with European soccer managers, you are retained only as long as you win regularly.

Amateur sport is very strong in the USA, possibly because of the status of professional sport, but also because to many Americans sport is the last frontier. The Americans consistently furnish one of the largest Olympic teams and invariably finish in the top three medal winners. The strength of American amateur sport reflects the quality and variety of collegiate athletics. With around 50% of 18-year-olds going into higher education and with a far higher proportion of promising athletes taking advantage of enthusiastic athletics departments, the American Olympic Committee has a ready-made selection process. Such is the intensity of competition between universities that there are also numerous sports scholarship places for promising athletes from Europe and Africa, to enable colleges to boast a winning team.

America differs markedly from Europe in that it does not have a strong private sports club system. This may be the result of the strong collegiate representation, which supplies quality athletes. However, this results in a rapid reduction in sports participation after college, except for the few who are good enough for the professional ranks.

The pro-draft system exists for American football and basketball. Well over 700 college football players are drafted into the professional ranks each year. This still represents less than one in a thousand college players making the professional game. The procedure is for the draft to be ranked and the lowest placed professional club has first choice. This system is not absolute, as wealthier clubs can break the draft by offering highly lucrative private deals with the clubs who have an early draft choice.

To some extent this frustrates the Sport for All idea and, even with exceptions like tennis and golf, many of the facilities for these two games are associated with country clubs where membership is very expensive. More recently, European soccer and rugby have become popular and clubs are springing up. It would be wrong to say that Americans have no sporting amenities for the less wealthy adult, but these tend to be recreationally based ice rinks and swimming pools, or outside basketball courts.

Figure 16.37 Can you explain why American females accept this role in sport?

Figure 16.38 Can you account for the high level of violence in some American games, but the low level of spectator violence?

Australia

In 1975 the **Department of Tourism and Recreation** made initial moves to establish a Federal involvement in sport. Until that time sport was largely controlled by autonomous governing bodies known as **National Sporting Organisations** (NSOs) and received no direct Federal funding. At that time the annual budget for the Tourism and Recreation Department was only Aus\$8 million per annum.

Federal involvement led to the formation of the **Sports Advisory Council,** which had a similar brief to that of the British Sports Council. Failures at the Montreal Olympic Games (1976) undoubtedly led to political pressure to establish the foundation of the **Australian Institute of Sport** (AIS) in 1980. A **National Outdoor Stadium** had been built in 1977 for the Pacific Conference Games. This was the first step to be followed in 1981 with the foundation of the **AIS** in Canberra as the administrative body to provide first class coaching and training facilities for promising

athletes. The initial programme catered for eight sports: basketball, swimming, weight lifting, track and field, gymnastics, netball, soccer and tennis, all of which had residential programmes at the Canberra centre.

Funding for the AIS came from Federal sources, administered through the reformed **Department of Sport, Tourism and Recreation**, and the budget was increased to Aus\$24 million in 1982. The following year momentum for a **National Sports Plan** came to a head following a major newspaper campaign. Strongly nationalistic, it called for a centralized Federal administration and increased funding to establish an Australian sporting elite.

By 1989 the sport administration had been absorbed into a new ministry, the **Department of the Environment, Sport and the Territories** which, as its first major act, established the **Australian Sports Commission**. Here was the start of a massive expansion in Federal funding, which reached Aus\$80 million in 1993.

The Australian Sports Commission, Canberra (ASC)

The ASC is governed by a Board of 12 Commissioners appointed by the responsible Minister. Its dual objectives are to increase participation in sport and sports activities by Australians and to establish excellence in sports performance. Its headquarters are in Canberra, but it has administrative offices in the different States. It is currently engaged in nine major strategies, many of which are linked with the **Sydney 2000 Olympic Games**.

In addition, the Sports Development Division of the ASC is responsible for **Aussie Sport** and **Youth Sport Programmes** as well as the **Australian Coaching Council** (ACC) and the **Australian College of Sport Education**.

National Australian Institute of Sport, Canberra (AIS)

Athletes receive scholarships to cover board and other expenses, including travel to sporting venues and coaching. An excellent sports science and medicine support service was also set up. No expense was spared in building this national facility for elite sport and at a cost of Aus$100 million it is ranked among one of the world's best training facilities. In addition, the AIS has Aus$11 million a year to cover administration costs and a further Aus$2.2 million to run the facilities. The Federal Government pays 95% of this with the remainder coming from commercial sponsorship.

As with the British National Centres of Excellence, there is a clause in the constitution of the AIS that the sports facilities are also available for use by individuals, community sports clubs and State and national sporting organizations. The common question is the extent to which the facilities are actually available to the public, given bookings by the resident elite groups as well as high fees.

By 1994 the scope of the AIS had been expanded to 20 sports, with scholarships for 500 athletes and a support team of some 70 coaches. To illustrate this from the sport of swimming, there were 37 full-time scholarships on one-year programmes in 1986. They were serviced by coaches, masseurs and physiotherapists, with support from sports science psychologists and physiologists, with education available for any young swimmers. In addition, the swimming unit had some 270 visiting scholarship holders on weekly visits and some 66 visiting coaches under the same arrangement.

The AIS has a basic function of supplementing and refining coaching in Australia, but also functions as a scientific research centre where performers are tested in an attempt to improve coaching effectiveness.

As a reflection of the size of Australia and as a gesture to Federalism, the AIS established out-reach centres in different major cities, where specific national squads were based and trained (Figure 16.39).

A number of activities also follow decentralized programmes in different areas, including baseball, rugby union, softball (female only), tennis, track and field, and water polo (female only).

Established in 1988, the **Cricket Academy** in Adelaide, with Rod Marsh as the chief coach, is probably the best known out-reach institution, largely because over the past few years Australia has produced an outstanding national team, where nine players are products of the Academy and England has capped two others with dual qualification (Figure 16.40). Fourteen of Australia's best young cricketers are on full-time scholarships, which includes professional coaching as well as access to sophisticated sport science technology.

Australian Institute of Sport. National Academies	
Canberra:	gymnastics, basketball, netball (f), road cycling (m), road and track cycling (f), rowing, soccer (m), swimming and polo, track and field.
Brisbane:	rugby, softball, diving, squash.
Adelaide:	cricket (m), track cycling (m).
Melbourne:	golf, baseball (m).
Sydney:	volleyball (m).

Figure 16.39 AIS academies and associated sports (f = female only; m = male only).

Figure 16.40 Professional cricket. Ex-Australian captain, Alan Border. (*Cricket Academy brochure.*)

Part of the AIS, there are two explanations for this being called an academy rather than an institute. One suggestion is that it may have been seen to be too academic, but another explanation is that the normal use of the word 'academy' in Australian sport is to signify the involvement of commercial sponsorship as well as government funding and, in the case of this cricket centre, there is a high level of funding from the Commonwealth Bank.

When the British Minister of Sport visited Adelaide in January 1995, he commented that he was impressed with the specialization and the scholarship system. He also hinted that lottery money might be used in Britain to follow this example.

In addition to the State academies, there is an **Intensive Training Centre** (ITC) programme which provides decentralized sport opportunities programmes for elite and potentially elite athletes. These programmes are often in smaller towns, supplementing the academies and acting as feeder programmes for AIS scholarships. ITC is a vehicle for recognizing promising talent and is supported by a full-time professional coaching system.

The **Australian Athlete Scholarship Scheme** (AASS) is the equivalent to the Sports Aid Foundation in the UK, but the Australian scheme has a much larger budget despite the smaller population and receives direct Federal grants. The aim of the AASS is to provide direct and timely financial assistance to elite Australian athletes. Scholarships are awarded to acknowledge the expenses and hardship elite athletes incur in the pursuit of excellence. The **National Sporting Bodies** (equivalent to the UK governing bodies) nominate athletes for scholarships, but they normally also have high national and/or international rankings. The money is paid directly to the athlete for individual activities and to the sporting body for team games.

There is also a parallel scholarship programme for coaches. In its second year, in 1995 the **National Coaching Scholarship** (NCS) programme had 37 coaches involved.

The **Australian Coaching Council** (ACC) is a programme of the Australian Sports Commission and is sponsored from the Federal budget. A centralized professional system, it also has State and Territorial centres with sub-offices at regional level. Its major function is to service the **National Coaching Accreditation Scheme**, a programme which is similar to the NCF scheme in the UK, but with substantially more funding (Figure 16.41).

Level	Course Format	Course Duration (minimum suggested)	Experience Required as a Practising Coach
0	Coaching principles and sport-specific practical	6 hours	This is a non-accreditation orientated course
1	Coaching principles	4 hours	1 season (or equivalent—at least 30 hours—decided by National Sporting Organization)
	Sport-specific theory and practice	14 hours / 10 hours	
2	Coaching principles	30 hours	2 seasons (or equivalent—at least 60 hours—decided by National Sporting Organization) in addition to Level 1
	Sport-specific theory and practice	60 hours / 30 hours	
3	Advance sport-specific information on the theory and practice of coaching	100 hours	3 seasons (or equivalent—at least 100 hours—decided by National Sporting Organization) in addition to Level 2
High Performance	Idividualized sport-specific programme to augment existing high performance coaching abilities	Determined by ACC and National Sporting Organization (generally 2–3 years depending on coaching commitments)	Must be coaching high performance athletes and be Level 3 (if available) qualified
Up-dating	Following accreditation under the NCAS, coaches are required to fulfill updating requirements over a four-year period as set down by their national sporting organization in order to keep their accreditation.		

Figure 16.41 National Coaching Accreditation Scheme in Australia.

The ASC, with its agency the AIS, engages in research and reform policies. Having established the schemes to accommodate athlete sponsorship and coaching, focus has now moved on to specific issues which influence sport in the context of Australian society.

SportsLEAP is a national programme, with organization at State level, which helps elite athletes in the areas of employment, education and personal development and helps them balance these long-term objectives with their immediate sport commitments. Part of this is to support athletes with their careers as their sporting opportunities decline.

Equal opportunity for **Women in Sport** (see Figure 15.14) is a world-wide issue, but has a particularly high profile in Australia, as it does in the USA, because of the male dominance of sport in a society where a macho image has stimulated a radical feminist movement. There is no doubt that Australian women's swimming, athletics, tennis and netball is world class and the male preserves of cricket, rugby and squash are being pressurized by successful women performers.

Each State has its own Women and Sport promotional schemes, complete with publications stating their case. An example of success arising from this progressive ASC policy is the central funding available for women's water polo, which helped to make them world champions in 1994 and 1995.

The **Aussie Able Programme** (see Figure 15.15) is equally positive as it strives to give people with disabilities equal opportunity for sport. This scheme is very similar to the American Adaptive programme and may well reflect the shared attitudes of young, successful, sophisticated democracies as they try to broaden the opportunities of disadvantaged groups.

The **National Aboriginal Sport Foundation** is an organization within the ASC. It has been responsible for the founding of the **Aboriginal Sport and Recreation Programme**, which employs some 24 development officers. The revival of Aboriginal culture is a flagship of the liberal Australian society, much the same as the Native American movement in the USA. In both cases it has become a political device; however, in sport, where ability rather than social status is the primary motive, talented individual Aborigines are able to socially and financially advance themselves and the Aboriginal cause as a result of success in international sport—Lionel Rose, MBE, predictably in professional boxing; Evonne Goolagong, MBE, an Aboriginal world tennis champion in a middle-class game, totally unexpected; and now Cathy Freeman, an international sprinter, with the education and will to use her status in sport to pro-

Figure 16.42 Aboriginal children playing war games. (*Traditional Aborigines. School Project Resource Book, Victoria.*)

mote Aboriginal causes. It is essential that the lifestyle of urban Aboriginals is differentiated from tribal communities living in the 'outback'. Figure 16.42 reflects a re-enforcement of old tribal activities and values, where children are role-playing the serious activities of their ancestors, as hunters and fighters.

Drugs and sport is a world issue and it is significant that the UK, Canada and Australia are at the forefront of athlete education in this problem. The **Australian Sports Drug Agency** is very active and the AIS and Academies, with their emphasis on sports science, are committed to promoting ethical and medical explanations for the exclusion of drugs in sport.

The Administration of Federal Sport in Australia

In addition to the AIS outreach centres working under the control of Canberra, there is an autonomous sports administration promoted by each State (Figure 16.43); it would be inaccurate to regard this as a direct extension of a 'performance pyramid'. Also stemming from a reaction from the Montreal Olympics in 1976, individual States introduced programmes, with the South Australian Institute being set up in 1982, Western Australia in 1984, New South Wales in 1985, Tasmania in 1987, ACT in 1988, Victoria in 1990 and Queensland in 1991. Their executive officers meet as the **National Elite Sports Council** (NESC), which includes AIS representatives.

In addition to the significance of autonomy, out-of-State programmes were seen to be a major problem, particularly for young performers, and there were also concerns that the AIS was a little too elitist. In reality, Canberra also had a very active **Federal (Commonwealth) Department for Recreation Development** in Canberra, but Sport for All objectives are best administered at a regional level, even if the State efforts are to some extent co-ordinated and financed nationally.

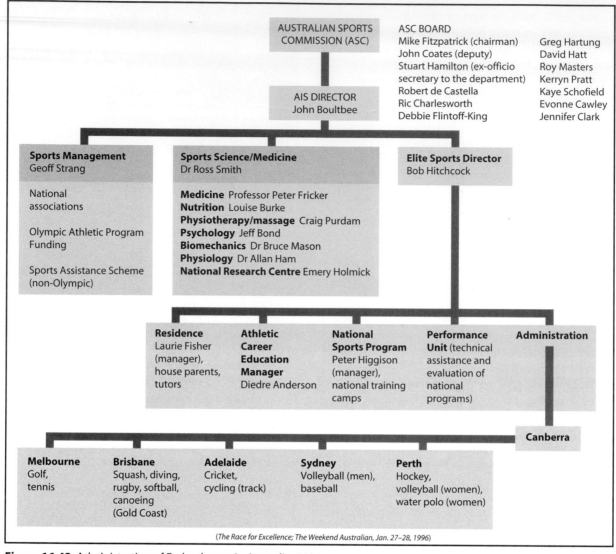

Figure 16.43 Administration of Federal sport in Australia, 1996.

The result is that Victoria, for example, has its own **Department of Sport and Recreation** (SRV), largely funded by State and commercial sponsorship, which is part of the **Department of Arts, Sport and Tourism** (Figure 16.44). The SRV administers and financially supports sporting associations, major sports facilities and recreation camps in the State and provides documentary information as well as a comprehensive coaching service.

At an elite level, the **Victorian Institute of Sport** (VIS) was established in 1990 to assist the most promising performers in Victoria. Its guidelines are to enable access to advanced coaching, to supply a service in sports science and sports medicine, to facilitate competitive opportunities and to assist career development. It is jointly financed by Government aid and private sponsorship, where

once again the Commonwealth Bank is the main contributor, and as such the individual centres of excellence are justifiably called Academies. In 1996 the VIS operated a major programme involving thirteen different sports and run from various facilities in the State by a Head Coach on a two- or three-year basis. In addition, there are six minor programmes of one year's duration and individual scholarships in 11 minority sports and 10 sports for disabled athletes.

Professional sport

The main professional sports bodies are business enterprises and represent the highest standard of performance in cricket, together with the four codes of football. Significantly, football is very much associated with certain States. Aussie Rules is centred on Melbourne (Victoria) but includes teams from

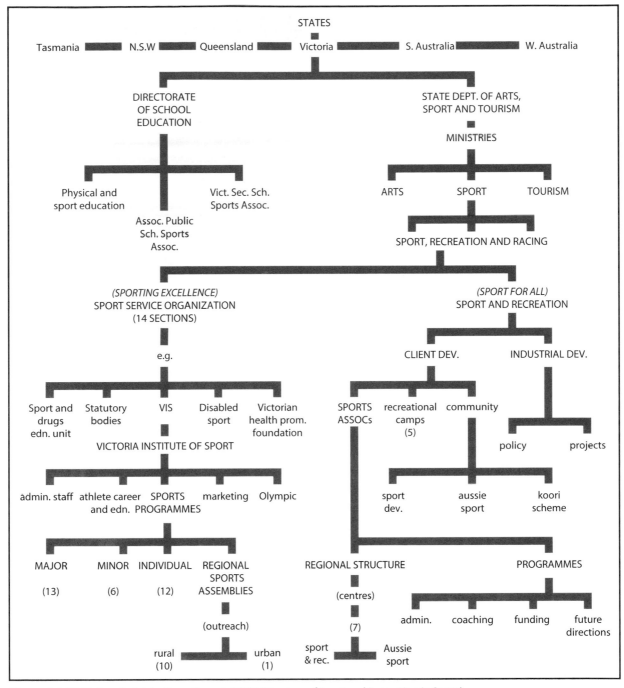

Figure 16.44 State administration of sport. (*1996 Directory of Sport and Recreation in Sport.*)

Western and South Australia; rugby union and rugby league are centred on Sydney (NSW) but are also major games in Queensland. They are all controlled by professional league administrations and the ability to prevent a super league commencing in rugby league reflects the power of the existing bodies against media moguls such as Packer and Murdoch.

Soccer is making rapid progress as a professional game and the latest developments are to reduce its ethnic associations. The development of basketball as a major American promotion is growing in popularity as a result of extensive TV publicity, but baseball and/or softball tends to be limited to the Sydney area. Other activities which tend to ignore the 'pro-am' variable, such as tennis and golf, exist at the highest level in each State.

The **draft system**, which is part of the American professional selection process, has existed in Aussie

to compete. This suggests that the older Soviet motives of displaying amateur qualities as a political image will now move across to presenting a nationalistic and commercial image by producing Russian or Ukrainian champions as the world's best performers.

The role of ethnic sport in the former USSR was vital, as it was so racially and culturally diverse, but it is just as important in the separate Republics, as they are also multi-racial; to prevent conflict it is important to encourage cultural activities which allow harmless tribal expression (Figure 16.52).

Non-Olympic activities continue to be encouraged because they extend the diversity of sporting experience. Rugby football is a typical activity in this context, and field sports, like hunting and shooting, are carried on without social exclusivity.

Finally, the technical activities such as parachuting, biathlon, and motor racing were the least universal in the Soviet Union, tending to be the preserve of military personnel. If they are to continue, given the new market economies they will need the commercial sponsorship of international companies and will probably be the first activities to become exclusive.

The Soviet Union was contemplating the establishment of professional soccer teams to compete on equal terms with the rest of Europe and South America. This trend was overtaken by the reforms and now all the major football clubs are being organized on a professional basis. With the authoritarian regime at an end, there is also the opportunity for the best players to join other European clubs, but, while this is very good for the players and their families, it may undermine the quality of the game in the Republics. This is a complete break with the Marxist tradition, because the concept of professionalism in the gladiatorial sense of American football, and the 'opium of the masses' sense of British football, can hardly be justified in a 'socialist' society. It may well be that amateurism is moving so fast along the path of fully sponsored training and playing time, together with trust funds to ensure that recognition is given to success, that there is just as little future for the old concept of professionalism as there is for amateurism. With social inequalities ostensibly removed, it may be possible for all athletes to strive for world champion status and receive rewards commensurate with their ability. If this is the case, and there is an opportunity to excel, with a parallel career base for those who fail, together with an efficient feedback into the sport, the Republics may be on the road to a far more socially desirable system.

Figure 16.52 A lasso thrower catching reindeer at an area competition for reindeer drivers, hunters, fishermen, and geologists in Naryan Mar, capital of the Jamalo-Nenets Autonomous Area. Other national sports, such as reindeer and dog-sled racing, jumping over sleighs and hatchet throwing, are also popular there. (*Sport in the USSR*, April, 1982.)

 # Review Questions

1. Compare the place of ethnic sports in each of the five countries.
2. How does the status of the professional performer vary in the five countries? Select sports to show how skill, gladiatorism and commercialism determine the image of the top performer.

3. What are the similarities and differences between strategies to achieve excellence in sport in any two countries you have studied? What cultural factors determine these variables?
4. Sport for All is an international policy, but opportunity, provision and esteem varies from one country to another. Discuss.

Exam-Style Questions

1. Contemporary studies

a. To achieve excellence in sport, a high level of commitment, resources and expertise is necessary:

i. Explain these three conditions, using illustrations from your own experience in a sport. (3 marks)

ii. Suggest three ways that a games club might be elitist. (3 marks)

b. There are only a limited number of sports schools in England and Wales compared with certain continental countries. Give three advantages and three disadvantages likely be to experienced at an existing residential school of excellence in Association Football or tennis. (6 marks)

c. The National Coaching Foundation was set up by the Sports Council in 1983:

i. Briefly describe the work of the National Coaching Foundation. (3 marks)

ii. Explain the Champion Coaching project in the context of the Major Initiative. (4 marks)

d. The UK has been largely responsible for the development of racquet games throughout the world. Why is Britain still not producing many performers of an international standard in tennis? (6 marks)

(Total 25 marks.)

2. Comparative studies

The escalation of violence in professional contact sports is an international problem.

a. Aussie Rules in Australia is one of the most explosive professional games in the world. Explain the features which may lead to outbreaks of extreme violence in this game. (4 marks)

b. The Soviet Union has produced world class ice hockey teams and players over the past decade, but their game has been based on skill. Suggest ways in which this approach might have reflected the political system that dominated Soviet life before the 1991 reforms. What tendencies would you expect to emerge in Russia today? (5 marks)

c. Analyse the cultural influences which may have caused American Football to differ from the rugby code which came from England. (6 marks)

d. Association Football has only recently been accepted in the USA:

i. Explain why female soccer appears to be much more readily accepted in the USA than it is in England. (4 marks)

ii. Discuss the causes of spectator hooliganism in British soccer and American baseball. (6 marks)

(Total 25 marks.)

 Summary

UK sport:

1. Decentralized administration, but increasing **central influence** due to funding pressures. Minister for Sport with a voice at Cabinet level since 1992.

2. Autonomous Governing Bodies of Sport with a regional network linking up with local clubs. Many anomalies still exist between these bodies.

3. Sports Council, assisted by the CCPR, has nine regions and five national sports centres.

4. Sports Aid Foundation sponsors top performers through its governing bodies and has nine regional offices.

5. National Coaching Foundation, with Regional Centres, established to promote coaching at all levels and improve information services.

French sport:

1. Centralized joint control—Federation and **Olympic** networks.

2. All regular performers are registered (licensed).

3. Strong links between **youth** and **sport**.

4. State aid for all Olympic sports.

5. Professional sports are commercially based.

6. Ethnic sports tradition very strong in the provinces.

USA sport:

1. Decentralized administration, with **autonomous** governing bodies.

2. Powerful professional sports, with considerable public support.

3. Commercial sponsorship and major media influence.

4. Lombardian 'win-at-all-costs' ethic arising through professionalism and capitalism, but a strong counter-culture at an intellectual level, in which excessive competitiveness is criticized.

5. College tradition acts as a sponsored nursery for professional and Olympic performers.

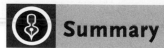
Summary

continued

Australian Sport:
1. Central structure with decentralized control.
2. The Australians are obsessed with sport.
3. Most sports reflect the colonial past.
4. Disappointment over failure at Montreal Olympics (1976).
5. Major innovations including ASC control of AIS and outreach programme of sports academies.
6. Each state with dynamic elite sport policy and sport for all.

USSR and Russian Sport:
1. **Centralized administration** from the Supreme Soviet, with a major political influence and State funding, changing to organization by individual Republics—but still with a centralized administration.
2. Masterstvo … communist world has changed only insofar as each Republic now has nationalistic ambitions.
3. Sport was a shop window for communism; it is now part of each nation-building process, as each organizes its economy and strives to build a reputation in the free world.
4. State-sponsored amateurism, which taught the rest of the world so much about effective training, has now opened the doors to professionalism as the Olympic Movement embraces a new concept of eligibility.

16.3 The Organization of Outdoor Recreation and Outdoor Education

United Kingdom

Outdoor recreation is taken to mean recreational activities in the natural environment. While it is fundamentally concerned with enjoying and appreciating natural scenery, there is an element of escape in that many outdoor recreationists are 'getting away from' the urban environment. There is also a concern for conservation, with environmentalists reminding us that abuse and excessive use of the countryside can lead to pollution and erosion.

When different ways of exploring the natural environment are considered, we are studying the area of **outdoor pursuits**. At the most recreational level, this can simply be the use of skills like canoeing or climbing to travel and reach places; or it can mean engaging in the challenge of nature and the elements, through canoeing on wild water or attempting classified rock climbs; finally, there is the sporting dimension, evident in sailing and canoeing, where contests are held on fixed courses.

The use of the term **outdoor education** implies the inculcation of educational values in the natural environment and may involve physical, personal and social development, as well as learning more about the natural environment.

The **Department of the Environment** (DoE) was established in 1970 and took over three existing ministries. It is led by the Secretary of State for the Environment and one area of responsibility is conservation of the countryside and the provision and upkeep of amenities (Figure 16.53). In Wales, the **Welsh Office** deals with all services affecting the physical development of the country.

National parks

The 10 national parks cover a total of 13 600 square kilometres, or more than 9% of the land area of England and Wales, much of it open countryside in the mountains or on the high moors. This is land considered to be of such great scenic importance that it has been given a special legal status to protect it against inappropriate development, but the fact that an area has been designated a 'national park' does not mean it is in public ownership. As in the rest of the country, all land in the national parks is owned, much of it privately, and farmed, forested or used in some other way, even on the moors. There is also no general right of public access simply because the land is within a national park and the normal rules about access to open land still apply (Countryside Commission, 1987).

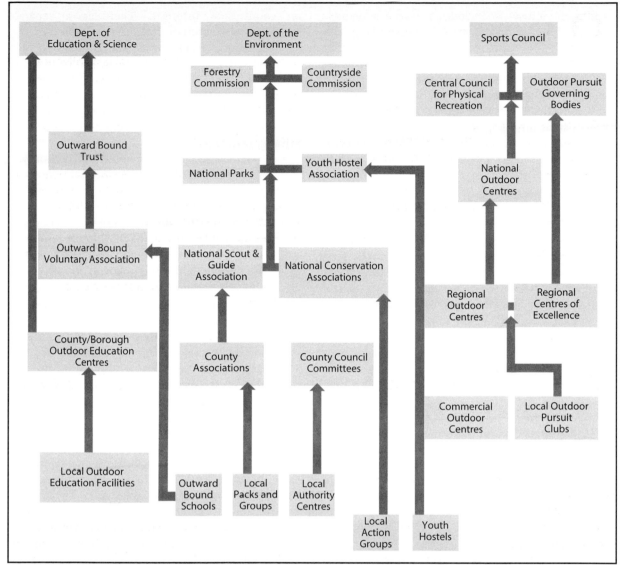

Figure 16.53 Structural framework of outdoor recreation and outdoor education in the UK.

Open country

'Open country' is just what the term suggests. It is any area consisting wholly or mainly of mountain, moor, heath, down, cliff, sea foreshore, beach or sand dunes. The term also includes woodland, as well as rivers and canals and their banks.

Although this is usually private land, local authorities are able to make access agreements or orders giving the public a legal right of access to it. Generally, access will be only on foot subject to certain restrictions. You may not be able to camp, for example, and you may have to keep a dog on a lead; and even where public access is guaranteed through an agreement or order, it may be suspended temporarily—for example, to reduce the risk of fire during very dry weather, especially in woodlands, or to prevent the spread of a livestock disease.

Picnic sites and country parks

Throughout England and Wales there are hundreds of picnic sites, some opened with the support and collaboration of the Countryside Commission, others provided by the Forestry Commission or bodies such as the National Trust. Each occupies a few acres, with seats and tables for picnics, and car parking nearby, and is chosen for the beauty of its surroundings.

There are about 170 country parks supported by the Countryside Commission, ranging in size from a few to several hundred acres. They cover a wide range of scenery, from open parkland and woodland to parks where abandoned industrial land or a worked-out quarry or gravel pit or even a disused reservoir has been transformed to create an attractive landscape. Depending on the site, it will have woods, streams and pools, good habitat for a variety of wildlife, and it may also include a golf course, enough open water for sailing and space for horse riding. The Countryside Commission advises with the planning of country parks and awards grants to help pay for them. A few are owned and managed privately, some by the National Trust for example, but most belong to local authorities or other public bodies. Country parks exist for the enjoyment of the public and within them you may go where you choose, although occasionally small areas may be reserved for wildlife (Countryside Commission, 1987).

Administration

Although there are number of very influential national bodies, like the **National Trust**, the **Youth Hostel Association** and various outdoor pursuit **governing bodies**, the emphasis is on a decentralized organization, which is controlled at local authority level and exercised with a great deal of freedom for individuals, families and organized parties. County councils and urban councils have **Town and Country Planning Committees**, responsible for matters to do with public access to the countryside. As with all British leisure administration, there is a mixture of State and private provision for community and school use.

The **Countryside Commission** is an advisory and promotional body which aims to conserve the landscape beauty of the countryside; to develop and improve facilities for recreation and access in the countryside (Table 16.5); and to advise government on countryside interests. There is a separate commission for each of the home countries.

The **National Trust** owns and protects 522 458 acres of Britain's finest countryside, 452 miles of unspoilt coastline and 276 houses which are open to the public. In 1987, the Trust had 1 193 946 members, who were entitled to free entry to its properties. Parks and areas open for rambling purposes may be privately owned (where access permission is needed), commercially based or belong to the local authority.

The **Duke of Edinburgh's Award Scheme** is an attempt to help young people to make the best use of leisure time. Established in 1956, it involves boys and girls aged 14–20 years in a series of challenging alternatives designed to help them with their personal development and their social awareness. There are bronze, silver and gold awards, which are valued by both participants and employers.

A wide range of **Outdoor Education Centres** is owned by Local Education Authorities (LEAs). The Centres are a fully subsidized part of the education system and the majority have residential facilities. The warden and staff receive children from the authority and the majority of State school children have an opportunity to attend at least one field week during their school career. Young children have programmes in environmental studies mixed with simple open country activities; older children have programmes in outdoor education involving outdoor activities; and youth groups have leadership courses involving outdoor pursuits.

Table 16.5 : Long distance routes in England and Wales

Long distance routes designated by the Countryside Commission	Length (km)	(miles)
Pennine Way	402	250
Cleveland Way	150	93
Pembrokeshire Coast Path	290	180
Offa's Dyke Path	270	168
South Downs Way	129	80
South-West Pennisula Coast Path:		
Somerset and North Devon	132	82
Cornwall	431	268
South Devon	150	93
Dorset	116	72
Ridgeway Path	137	85
North Downs Way	227	141
Wolds Way	127	79
Peddars Way and Norfolk Coast Path (opened 1986)	150	93
	2711	**1684**

The South Downs Way and parts of the Ridgeway and the North Downs Way are open to horse riders and cyclists as well as walkers.

In addition, college students and others attend award courses for proficiency and coaching, such as the **Mountain Leadership Certificate** and awards organized by the British Canoe Union (BCU) and Royal Yacht Association (RYA).

The **Outward Bound Trust** is a registered charity whose patron is the Duke of Edinburgh. It was formed in 1946 to promote personal development training for young people, and today administers five Outward Bound centres in the UK and has inspired some 35 centres of a similar type overseas. The Trust is supported by 35 Outward Bound Associations which consist of groups of people who voluntarily promote the Trust and raise funds to assist deserving cases financially.

A wide range of courses include Outward Bound, Expedition and Outdoor Skill Courses; the DoE Award; City Challenge courses, an urban equivalent to Outward Bound; the Gateway and Senior Gateway courses, which are associated with business management skills; and Contract courses, which can be arranged by individual companies and organizations.

All the programmes are 'intensive experiences involving personal development experience, designed for young people to develop skills, judgement and confidence to meet the future with its problems, uncertainties and new responsibilities' (Outward Bound Brochure, 1991.)

France

The whole concept of French outdoor recreation is expressed in the phrase *Le Plein Air*. Historically linked with twin European traditions of the '**spa movement**' and '**naturalism**', it has become a campaign to remove the young from the corrupting influence of the inner cities and to introduce them to the simple pleasures of life in the countryside. However, French administrators recognize that fresh air may not be enough and so they include physical exercise and strive to re-establish the '**rustic simplicity**' of being able to make the most of the natural environment.

A number of key variables need to be taken into account when looking at the French development of outdoor recreation.

The amount of open countryside and the range of climatic and topographical types give the French people greater opportunities than those available in Britain. They can ski in the Alps; walk in the Massif Central; bathe in the Mediterranean; fish and canoe on the many waterways; and sail on the extensive coastal waters (Figure 16.54).

The British have chosen to spread holidays over a three-month period to off-set crowding, but the French still cling to traditional holiday periods, which

Figure 16.54 Sea school in Brittany. Why are water sports so popular in France? (*France Information, 1985.*)

means that in the first week of August workers 'down tools' and start a grand exodus to the countryside. Inevitably, this concentration causes crowding in the more popular areas, but, as with British excursion trips, many holiday-makers appear to enjoy the bustle and social conviviality. At the centre of this ritual there is *le camping français*. Families swarm out of the cities and head for the sun, taking miniature homes along with them. Alternatively, the trains are filled to capacity twice a year to take skiers to the Alps at Easter and families to the sea in August, where 'beaches boil with Gallic bodies'.

The French family has changed a great deal since the Second World War (1939–1945). Mazeaud (1976) suggested that, with working wives and fewer children, spare time was becoming increasingly precious and parents were looking for more free time to pursue their own interests. This led local authorities and firms to sponsor holiday centres for children, **centres de vacances**. One example, the **colonie de vacances**, a rural institution, has much in common with the American camp school. In addition to freeing the parents, these 'colonies' are designed to take children out of the towns and, originally, many of the local authority centres made special efforts to cater for underprivileged children. Traditionally, wealthier children have tended to take private or commercial alternatives.

The programme in these residential centres includes educational, social and cultural elements as well as outdoor pursuits, with emphasis on promoting *le plein air*, a love of the open air. Children can stay at these residential centres for the whole summer holiday and are then returned to their parents.

Although reference has been made to residential *colonies de vacances*, there are many different types of leisure centre frequented by young people, some small and local, others of national significance, where outdoor pursuits are taught to a high level. For example, **Le Centre National des Sports de Plein Air** at Vallon-Pont-D'Arc is equivalent to Britain's Plas y Brenin, and there is a famous mountain school at Chamonix.

Alternatively, in the Nantes district, for example, there are leisure centres available for children to use on Wednesday afternoons; there are 10 or more local centres spread throughout the town for children aged 4–15 to use in the holidays; there are adventure playgrounds situated at various points; and, on a larger scale, there is a *village de vacances*, which is a permanent holiday complex for children and an urban equivalent of a *colonie de vacances*.

If these are holiday opportunities for French children, then the *classes* are outdoor experiences promoted as part of the school programme (Figures 16.54–16.56). As early as 1953 snow classes were started, where children were taken out of the towns to stay in the mountains for about a month under the supervision of their regular teachers, PE staff and qualified ski instructors. In addition to the snow classes, there are now classes in the countryside, also sea schools, and—as a result of government support and subsidies from Municipal and General councils—there has been a steady increase in the number of children involved. In 1984, for example, some 120 000 children attend a total of 4600 classes.

The full title of the programme is *Les Classes Transplantées: La Ville à la Campagne*, and the key to understanding its intention lies in the word 'transplanting'. Children are taken from the town to a country location in another region. It is an attempt to broaden the child's experience and knowledge about the natural environment, but also to take him/her to another part of France where traditions and customs may be different. It is a formal educational experience as parents have to be convinced that academic standards and health will not suffer as a result of a month away from formal schooling.

The Outward Bound Movement, though focused on the UK and Commonwealth countries, has been developed in Belgium and was started in France in 1986. However, in France it was still at the construction stage of its first centre in 1993 at Banassac in the Canourgue in southern France: to use its French title, **Hors Limites—Outward Bound**. Initiated by Alain Kerjean, he envisaged something like the British Outward Bound, but it is already taking its own cultural shape. This is probably because as many Belgian instructors were used as British to train the French **formateurs**, but the French commitment to their own national philosophies and the ideology of **rural simplicity** is already resulting in Rousseau's ideas on education in the natural environment having more influence than Kurt Hahn's philosophy of character building.

Consequently, there is already an emphasis on personal development in the outdoors as a form of therapy, rather than as a self-testing adventure experience. However, there is a wide variety of programmes for schools and universities (as well as those organized by the social services), and management and professional development training courses.

It is important to recognize the difference between the holiday and the school programmes. There are critics who believe that much of *le plein air* concept is lost in the formality of the *classes*: that it can be truly expressed only through a family holiday or as a leisure experience at a *centre de vacances*. There are others who see the value of the *classes* as the richest school experience, pointing to the social awareness of being taught in the natural environment. In both cases it would seem that the British outdoor education programme does not match up to the opportunities available to the average French child.

Figure 16.55 Snow school in Auvergne. Why has the French Government poured money into snow schools?

Figure 16.56 Class de vert. How does this compare with English environmental studies?

United States

The size and beauty of the USA natural resources are sufficient in themselves to make outdoor recreation one of the most rewarding elements in American culture, but there is also the legacy of Theodore (Teddy) Roosevelt. Acknowledged to have been one of the country's greatest presidents, 'T.R.' established a tradition of conservation and national pride for America's unspoilt wilderness. By 1909 he had set aside some 230 million acres of national forest, more than 50 Federal wildlife refuges and doubled the number of national parks. Despite tragic economic setbacks like the 'Dustbowl' in the 1930s,

this pride in the 'Great Outdoors' has remained part of the American Dream, nurtured no doubt by the heritage of the 'Frontier Spirit' which went with it.

In 1965, the Land and Water Conservation Fund Act ensured that the 'dream' could be a financial possibility, when the **Bureau of Outdoor Recreation**, as part of the **Department of the Interior**, was given the power to administer a fund for State, local and Federal outdoor education purposes (Figure 16.57). As a result, all 50 States now have park systems and every **State Highways Department** has to maintain roads into recreational areas.

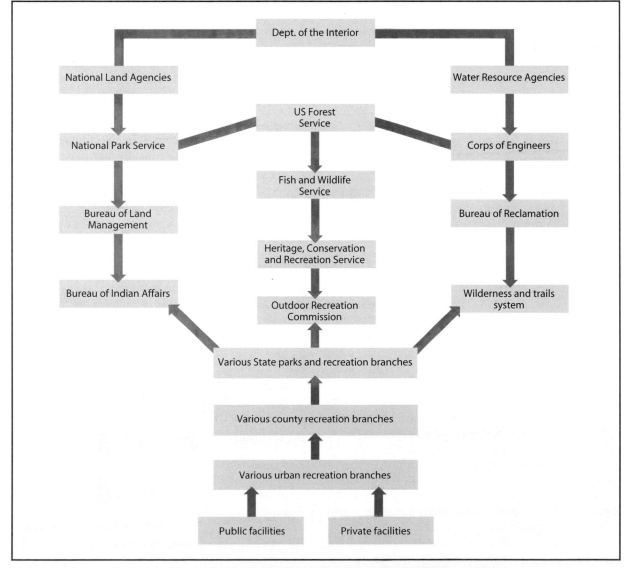

Figure 16.57 Agencies involved in outdoor recreation in the USA. (*For details, see Weiskopf, 1982.*)

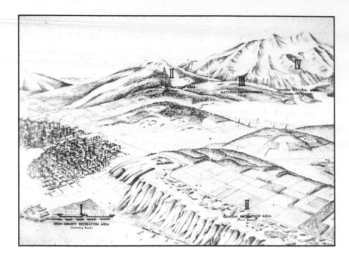

Figure 16.58 Classification of national park areas.
- Class I: Areas intensively developed near towns and designed for extensive use.
- Class II: Areas with substantial development for a variety of recreational uses.
- Class III: Areas which are suitable for recreational use in a natural environment, but which are within easy reach of habitation.
- Class IV: Areas of outstanding scenic beauty some distance from civilization.
- Class V: Undisturbed, roadless areas characterized by natural, wild conditions, including 'wilderness areas'.
- Class VI: Historical and cultural sites.

Given the status and scope of these natural parks, it has been necessary for the Bureau to produce a co-ordinated administration. It is difficult for Europeans to conceive wilderness areas so vast that, without a stringent organization, many hikers could become lost and die. Necessary regulations take away some of the freedom of action expected by hikers in Britain, but are essential to ensure safety standards. One method used to enlighten the public is through a classification of areas (Figure 16.58).

Wilson (1977) suggested that in the 1970s there was a major expansion in what was called 'wilderness sport participation', and research indicated that the two main reasons were a desire to escape from the technology and urbanization of modern living; and a desire to achieve a greater sense of self-awareness. These related attitudes were shared by mountaineers, backpackers, cross-country skiers and cyclists alike, and were also found by the National Park and Forest Services, as well as State Park Authorities.

Outdoor education has developed since the Second World War as part of an 'alternative' form of education. Very much in line with the philosophies of William James and John Dewey, it represented an experiential approach to learning and was readily associated with nature study and interdisciplinary study. Jenson and Briggs (1981) claimed that there were four main categories of outdoor education—personal growth programmes; interdisciplinary studies; socializing agencies; and recreational education.

In Britain, France and the USA there has been a desire to broaden the experience of urban children, but in America there is also a 'counter-culture' element operating, as an escape from the elitism and commercialism of the professional sports scene.

The **American Outward Bound Association** is an extension of the British Outward Bound Trust. It is a non-profit-making educational organization and

has the support of many senior high schools, where credit is given for attendance. Programmes range from standard 21–26 day experiences in the wilderness to shorter intensive adventure experiences; there are also courses in leadership skills and for potential business executives. These courses also include a variety of snow experiences, canoeing and backpacking, rock climbing and cycling, all with the intention of testing the resilience of the individual in an alien environment and group co-ordination in challenging situations (Figure 16.59). In 1981 there were seven centres: Dartmouth, Colorado, Hurricane Island, North Carolina, Northwest and Southwest. They are all situated in areas of natural beauty with wilderness characteristics.

In addition to outdoor education as a direct extension of schooling, and Outward Bound as an intensive adventure experience for those over 16 years of age, there is a wide-ranging provision of summer camps. As with the French system, it is important to distinguish between programmes with an educational basis and those with a recreational–vacational function. Examples of American children's camps go back to the 19th century; most of these were associated with taking impoverished children out of their depressed urban environment.

Since the Second World War camp schools have mushroomed in all the more scenic areas, particularly where there is a large supporting population within a convenient distance. These are essentially holiday experiences and there is a strong tradition of American children spending at least part of their long summer vacation in a residential camp school (Figure 16.60). These permanent institutions are run by a variety of groups and ownership tends to dictate the type of child involved. Many camps are run by the State or individual civic authorities; these tend to be heavily subsidized to allow poorer children to 'escape' to the countryside. Then, there are camp schools which are sponsored by firms, ethnic groups and religious bodies, and, finally, there are commercial camps, where the reputation of the centre tends to dictate cost and, consequently, the clientele. In all cases, the children are on holiday and every effort is made to give them a good time, but also a safe time.

Traditionally, there are numerous challenges designed to encourage personal growth, socialization and a love of the natural environment, combined with 'camp fire' and patriotic ritual.

There is little doubt that, as in France, there is a tendency for American parents to go on separate holidays while the children are under careful supervision at camp school. From the children's point of view, many make lasting friendships, particularly when they return to the same camp year after year.

A number of organizations, like Camp America and BUNAC, have the franchise to appoint staff from various countries, and many British students work as counsellors over the 6–8 week period.

Figure 16.59a and b What characteristics of the Outward Bound Movement do these photographs illustrate? (*Colorado Outward Bound brochure, 1979.*)

a

b

Figure 16.60a and b What do these photographs tell you about an American school camp? (*Colorado Outward Bound brochure, 1979.*)

a

b

Australia

The terms **Outdoor Recreation and Outdoor Education** have exactly the same connotations as in the UK, where they refer to positive physical experiences in the natural environment. At an administrative level, control in Australia is centralized through the Federal Department for the Arts, Sport, the Environment, Tourism and the Territories, with the Ministry of Education retaining responsibility for outdoor education as a part of physical education.

The size of Australia, with its variety of topographical and climatic conditions, makes it comparable with the USA, but because the population is so small and because the bulk of it is urbanized on the East Coast Plain, there are huge tracts of wilderness which have literally no townships and as such are readily comparable with central Russia.

In terms of attitude, there are many apparent similarities with the USA in so far that Australia is a young striving society with past links with Britain, but an increasingly pluralist society. Both the USA and Australia have come through a process of emigration and rolling back frontiers, with all the spirit of adventure linked with this.

As a young multi-cultural society, Australia is also striving to establish an identity which cannot be readily linked with historical roots and, as a Federation, it is difficult, politically, to bring a country together as a national unit. This need has already been linked with the significance of sport in Australia and the extent to which the Australian Government is prepared to fund sport, but, as with the USA, there is the potential to build national pride in the natural beauty of the Australian countryside.

Much is known world-wide about the beautiful beaches and an awareness of the interior has increased due to the *Crocodile Dundee* films, but the Australian Federal Government has now engaged in a comprehensive programme of promoting international tourism on a large scale to attract Japanese, European and American visitors. This has been sponsored at Federal level, but is organized by individual State departments and run by the National Parks and Wildlife Service.

It is important to understand that although Australia has National Parks, the term is really a misnomer as they are run by individual States and are not controlled at Federal level, as in the USA. Certainly, a similar process to that enacted by Theodore Roosevelt in America has happened in Australia and establishments like **Uluru Park**, which includes Ayers Rock (Figures 16.61), **Kakadu Park** in the Northern Territory and the **Barrier Reef** are world famous.

The stringent organization in the USA of grading outdoor recreation sites from urban picnic areas to wilderness has not yet been achieved in Australia. The British notion of freedom and romanticism has meant that provision is often very sparse off the beaten track and Australians have reserved the Aboriginal idea of 'going walkabout', where bushwalking is far less sophisticated than the backpacking American model. If you understand that huge areas of Australia are virtually wilderness country of the most hostile kind, with little or no marked roads off the superhighways, you can appreciate that a genuine frontier adventure situation still exists in Australia—indeed, places like the **Simpson Desert** and the **Kimberley Mountains** are barely mapped.

There is wide variety of natural facilities extending outward from each large city; these can take the adventurer into the wilderness in less than a hundred miles. Managed by **State Departments of Conservation, Forest and Lands**, the largest areas tend to be called National Parks, with State Parks covering an intermediate area and smaller Regional Parks being of about a five-mile radius. In the Darwin Region of the Northern Territory, for

Figure 16.61 Ayers Rock, Australia.

example, there are open country picnic sites within and beyond the city limits; within 30 miles there are nature parks which encourage rambling, mountain biking and horse riding; intermediate bushwalking and adventure environments at Litchfield Park and the Katherine Gorge National Park, some 50 miles away; and extreme wilderness conditions in the huge Kakadu National Park (Figure 16.62).

A difficult concept to understand is the attitude of the majority of Australians to their own beautiful, if frightening, outback. The vast majority of Australians are city dwellers, with the affluence of an economically advanced society and the creature comforts of modern urban living. Some young people regard bushwalking as a necessary life experience, but many Australians prefer urban sports and Channel 6. It is this love affair of Australians for the rigours of sport which physical recreationists and environmentalists hope to expand into the adventure and national pride dimensions of the Australian wilderness. At the moment, for example, many Australians have four-wheel drive vehicles, but very few of them take them onto the dirt roads of the outback.

The extremes of natural environment, combined with the emphasis on competitive sport, has led to outdoor pursuit enthusiasts reaching international standards. As the first winners of the America's Cup for ocean yachting outside America, the Australians broke a stranglehold Britain had not been able to break for well over 100 years. The eastern seaboard of Australia displays its wealth through its yachting community, but a beach society also excels at surfing and wind surfing as well as well-drilled beach rescue teams. Polynesian and East Asian influences have also led to the popularity of outrigger and dragon racing.

Rowing has long been a tradition in the older cities and remains part of the independent school sector, with Australian scullers among the world's best, and, farther inland, there are numerous graded rivers which have encouraged various types of canoe racing and rafting; also the mountains, particularly the Southern Alps, have allowed mountaineering clubs to flourish and numerous ski resorts to be opened up. As a massive land mass, it is also not unexpected to find cycle road-racing high on the Australian sports agenda with academies in Canberra for men and women.

In a young country with so many natural hazards, it is reasonable to expect **outdoor education** to be high on the school physical education agenda, if only to prevent unnecessary loss of life through uninitiated individuals and groups becoming lost or injured in the bush. It would appear that the urgency of this educational programme on safety, conservation and recreation grounds has not reached the levels found in the USA or France, but there has been a long-held colonial tradition of valuing the outdoors, even if this has been couched in terms of the freedom of the individual to 'do their own thing'.

Consequently, the older programmes in Australian schools have hinged on knowing **about** the outdoors in the nature study sense, rather than an experiential level involving physical activity. As new teaching styles evolved, so did the notion that first-hand experience in environmental studies was valuable and in 1980 the **Australian Curriculum Development Centre** produced a set of aims for **environmental education** which encouraged taking young people into the natural environment.

Parallel to this, there was a strong movement in the 1980s to encourage **education for leisure**, a campaign which had evolved in the UK a decade earlier; a major part of this was **leisure in the outdoors**. This movement was pioneered by ACT, where, for

Figure 16.62
Kakadu National Park, Australia.

example, the **Australian College of Education**, Canberra, started undergraduate programmes in leisure studies and schools in ACT were encouraged to develop leisure and outdoor education programmes.

In this way the work being done by physical educationists as part of their broad curriculum, where **education in the outdoors** included mountain and water activities, was reinforced by a central policy arising from this new awareness of the significance of leisure education. The physical education notion of field trips giving rise to greater understanding of the natural environment and the development of personal and social skills, which was part of the public school ethic, had not been entirely lost, but until the 1980s the majority of Australian physical educationists chose not to teach outdoor education. Today, however, given that the bulk of the school population lives within easy reach of the sea, you will find school minibuses ferrying children for scuba-diving and canoeing lessons.

The character-building notion imparted by public schools in Britain has continued in many of the Australian independent schools, the most famous of which is **Timbertop**. Founded in 1952, it is a branch of Geelong Grammar School, one of Australia's foremost independent schools. It is a forested mountain campus in the Victorian Alps, some three hours' drive from Melbourne.

In 1966 Prince Charles spent a year there as a teenager, while attending **Gordonstoun**. The reason for the extended visit may have been political, but it demonstrated the similar philosophy and curriculum operated by Gordonstoun and Timbertop. Though Gordonstoun's site on the Scottish coast results in a greater emphasis on water activities, they are both adventure schools and both independent, and both expound the philosophy of Kurt Hahn. Timbertop has self-contained living quarters for some 200 boys and girls who spend their ninth year at school (14–15-year-olds) in this mountain environment without telephone, television, video or compact disc provision. They live collectively in units of 16, adopting a spartan existence that requires personal responsibility and group co-operation. Furthermore, for a year the competitive sports they pursued at Geelong, such as cricket, rugby and football, are replaced by bushwalking, rock climbing, abseilling, cross-country skiing, canoeing and orienteering. There are additional

physical education classes, but focus is on co-operation rather than competition and gender integration through aerobics, weight training and recreative volleyball. Though research on the long-term effects on students is limited, claims are made that notions of self-esteem and a sense of community are instilled and recorded responses by the young people suggest that after the initial acclimatization problems, the year is seen to have been a valuable experience. The authorities of the school make three strong points:

- *That every decent Australian child must be interested in competitive sport is an idiocy which has caused a lot of unnecessary unhappiness to a number of children.*
- *Australia is one of the most urbanized societies in the world. It needed a protest and Timbertop supplied it.*
- *In the year in the bush a boy learns to know his capacity and discovers that it is much greater than he expected. He also perhaps learns his limitations when faced with the natural world, and this is also a good thing.*

[Taken from Montgomery and Darling (1967), the apparent gender bias being explained by girls not being included until 1975.]

The whole concept is identifiable in the support for Adventure Education in Britain, France and the USA, but is also recognizably a counter-culture movement supporting co-operative as against the competitive emphasis that is the dominant ethic in Australia and the USA.

There is evidence (McArthur and Priest, 1993) that this 'experiment' continues to be very popular with school authorities and pupils. Normal academic schooling continues successfully in this environment and evaluation of the adventure experience continues to be based on co-operative attitudes, initiative and leadership, and the safe application of skills in the natural environment.

There is little doubt that, in both Britain and Australia, the public school sector has the financial means to maintain outdoor education as a major feature of schooling, whereas State schools in both countries work on restricted budgets and limited aspirations of urban teachers. The inclusion of **adventure education** in the physical education core elements in Britain has been paralleled by directives from the Curriculum Development Centre in

Australia, which has led to the funding of residential centres in an attempt to give all Australian children a taste of outdoor education through organized field studies. These appear to exist at four levels:

1. **Centres as extensions of classrooms**: these are **outdoor schools** designed to facilitate a first-hand experience of the natural environment; for example, the outdoor school at Arbury Park in the Adelaide Hills.

2. **Environmental Centres**: these exist throughout Australia and focus on environmental studies rather than adventure education.

3. **Outdoor Pursuit Centres**: this is the largest group of field centres; they are outdoor activity centres mainly staffed by physical education teachers. In New South Wales, for example, McRae (1986) identified 12 Sport and Recreation Centres and five 'under canvas' sites.

4. **Outdoor Leisure and Environmental Centres**: these have a broader input than the outdoor pursuits centres, in that they also include environmental studies as part of an integrated study approach to the natural environment and its preservation.

It is easy to trace a similar range of centres in Britain and the level of successful uptake is similar, depending on local government support and the initiative of staff from specific schools. On the other hand, the Australian system lacks the organizational stringency, diversity and funding found in the USA and France, with their purposeful political, educational and domestic support for outdoor education. Similarly, although private camps exist, they have nothing like the uptake of the American summer camp system, although, as in the UK, many Australian students act as counsellors in American summer camps.

The **Outward Bound Trust** has existed in Australia since the 1960s, with the Outward Bound School at Tharwa in ACT; there has been an active research programme operating since 1972. The latter is typical of the Australian focus on sound scientific principles being developed in the educational and sport fields and is an ongoing research programme on staff training, programme design and implementation.

As an independent, non-profit-making educational organization, its objectives are the same as the parent organization in Britain, designed to promote self-discovery and social awareness in the natural environment.

The following courses are run at Tharwa:

- **Challenge Courses**: 22–28 days' duration—basic wilderness skills; community project; group discussion; solo periods of solitude and reflection. Includes Classic and Ultimate Challenge; Marine and Ski Classic Challenge. Involves canoeing, climbing and expedition skills in hazardous environments.

- **Adult Courses**: 9 days' duration—a chance to get away from urban living; includes mixed and women only courses; and marine, skiing and horse-riding courses.

- **Adventure Courses**: 8 days' duration—children aged 12–16 years; a fun and unique experience programme, linking in with the Duke of Edinburgh Award. Includes pack & paddle courses; horse adventure courses; and sailing adventure courses.

- **Courses for Past Participants**: 9 days' duration: children aged 14–16 years; involving: horse expeditions; marine and ski expeditions.

- **Family Courses**: 9 days' duration—for families of four; designed to strengthen family bonds.

- **Discovery Courses**: 9 days' duration—including disabled and able-bodied courses; intellectually disabled courses; and customized discovery courses of 1–22 days' duration.

- **Special Needs Programmes**: 10–12 days' duration—for young people with behavioural. problems.

- **Wilderness First Aid Courses**: 7 days' duration—a Leadership Wilderness programme.

- **Schools and Educational Programme**: 5–12 days' duration—with values which closely relate to British outdoor schools and includes programmes for schoolchildren and university students; and related programmes for educators and parents.

- **Management & Corporate Training Programme**: 1–16 days' duration—designed as a partnership between staff and client representatives to develop individual and team initiatives.

Like it? That would be one of the biggest understatements around. It's been one of the most incredible experiences I've ever had. Things that I'd never really contemplated doing before; here I was in the middle of the Snowy River. I just couldn't believe it!
(Discovery Course Participant.)

Tourism in the Soviet Union and post-reform Russia

As the Soviet Union considered itself an emergent 'socialist' society, it is important to recognize that recreation had bourgeois connotations and consequently the term **tourism** was more regularly in use.

The struggle for literacy and military preparedness meant that more dynamic aspects of physical culture had priority in the early years and that tourism became a priority only after 1968.

The term **tourism** implied a raising of the cultural and political awareness of the Soviet people. A major part of this cultural awareness concerned the natural environment but, with such a diverse and ancient country, there was also a considerable interest in the country's heritage. Pride in Mother Russia was framed in a political acknowledgement that, without communism, there would be no culture worth visiting. In the context of the reforms it is difficult to justify the continued use of the term 'tourism', as it has had so many political connotations, but its broad basis remains conceptually attractive. However, it is likely that, if progress continues towards a market economy, the label and concept of 'recreation' will become a part of the new order, hopefully without the negative characteristics of discrimination.

As a country which had industrialized during the past 50 years, working-class free time was many years behind the Western model. A five-day, 40-hour week was broadly established after 1972; and, up to 1968, 15 days' 'prescribed leave' was the annual holiday for the majority. In 1972, however, a legal minimum of 15 days was established, and an upper limit of 26 days. This led to a dramatic change in life-style, the weekend becoming a major leisure period, achieving a significance not unlike that of European countries. There was an inevitable shift of interest from explosive sports and spectatorism in the cities to a pattern of weekend excursions, where rural centres with a variety of sporting facilities were built.

In terms of the natural environment, the 15 Republics have the same diversity as the USA, but with at least twice the area of wilderness. However, the administration of the Soviet Union was totally different, with central control emanating from the **Supreme Soviet**, and policy exacted through a series of master plans. These were transmitted to the various Republics; the regions within the Republics; and down to individual districts. In addition, all Soviet Republics had their own voluntary nature protection societies with a reputed membership of one in five of the population. With the Republics now independent, it is unlikely that the administrative structure within each has changed in the short term, but it is likely that national interests will be more adequately served—even though there may be a halt in the expansion of recreational programmes until the respective economies are on a more sound footing.

It would seem that national support for conservation will continue. The **State (National) Forestry Committee**, for example, is not only responsible for all logging and felling, but it also controls the woodworking industry as a whole and is responsible for the protection of forests. At a rough estimate, almost a third of the old Soviet Union is forested, with timber reserves put at 82 000 million cubic metres in 1977. Very much the same is true of nature reserves in terms of conservation, but also the provision of facilities and communications to encourage tourism, sport and camps.

Given the importance of sport and active leisure, every opportunity was made to turn natural resources into outdoor pursuit facilities; most of these were administered and sponsored by individual factories (Figure 16.63). Parts of the old Soviet Union are naturally suited to specific outdoor pursuits: the Carpathian Mountains have numerous skiing centres; the Black Sea is famous for aquatics and sailing; and the Pamir Peaks are excellent for mountaineering and rock climbing.

The **tourism** aspect of **physical culture** made giant strides forward as a result of the National Economic Plan (1971–1975), when children's **Excursion-Tourist Stations** were set up; tourist sections were encouraged in the various sports clubs; and tourist centres were built throughout the Soviet Union, rather than just in the traditional holiday centres of the Black Sea and the Caucasus.

Though well behind the USA in the development of National Parks, there is a trend in this direction as witnessed by the Armenian National Park (Figure 16.64).

Angling is very popular, as in all European countries, and major efforts have been made to reduce the levels of river pollution in industrialized areas.

Figure 16.63 Trade Union Central Council of Tourism and Excursions. Why were the Soviets so anxious to link workers and tourism? (*Sport in the USSR, August, 1981.*)

Soviet holiday categories before the reforms

There were four main categories:

1. The majority of workers applied to attend camps run by their factory trade union. Normally, with the larger firms and farm collectives, a trade union had access to a number of camps of varying standards and the selection process involved an assessment of the worker's contribution to the firm over the year. In this way, a pass to a Black Sea resort was used as a work incentive. It is probable that factories will continue to sponsor these holiday camps, but it is more likely that the management or a joint committee will take on the funding. However, if the industries need money they might well sell these assets to entrepreneurs.

2. **Independent holidays** represent an increasing trend among the better-off urban white-collar workers. Although it would seem to be a political contradiction, there has been a strong tradition of financially secure families having a holiday home or *dacha*, which would be visited at weekends and holidays. It seems probable that with the increased freedom of *perestroika* more and more families will be hoping to organize their own holidays around hotels and *dachas*.

3. **The Communist Youth League (Komsomol)**—a political youth organization for 15- to 26-year-olds—organized holidays called **operational camps** (Figure 16.65). These involved a sizeable group of student volunteers working on major projects during the summer vacation. The largest was to assist in the building of the Baikal–Amur Railway (BAH), resulting in an alternative route to Siberia being established which opened up huge areas for population expansion. The break-up of the Soviet Union resulted in the Communist Party, and its youth wing, the Komsomol, losing most of their influence. The principle of encouraging young people to help develop major projects is a sound one, however, but with the removal of authoritarianism any new programme is more likely to be on the lines of the Voluntary Overseas Service which operates in the Western world.

4. **Children's holidays**. As with the other countries discussed in this section, there are two concepts operating—**outdoor education** and **holidays** in the outdoors. However, under the Soviet dictum of purposeful leisure, it was difficult to separate the two, all children's leisure having been to an extent educational, even if it was only a form of political education. Schools in the different Republics have clubs, which they call circles, and some of these involve outdoor activities. The pioneer palaces, which are community facilities for children, also have circles.

It is important at this point to identify the main children's organizations operating before the 1992 reforms. We have already mentioned the **Komsomol**, which was a highly political youth group that now exercises little power. There were two younger groups. The **Pioneers** (Figure 16.66) were boys and girls aged 7–17 years, and the **Octobrists** (after the October Revolution) were under seven years old. These political youth groups are now in disarray with their funding cut off and their political function rejected. However, care for the well-being of children is deeply rooted in Russian society and so families will probably promote a 'scouting' equivalent in the near future.

The Pioneers were much more politically orientated than scouts or guides, but shared several common features. These included a desire to reinforce a strong moral code; encouraging a sound understanding of the natural environment; performing tasks for the community; and instilling a sense of national pride. They wore a uniform and had

Figure 16.64 Dilijan Nature Park, part of the Armenian National Park. (*Soviet Weekly, 20th August 1977.*)

Figure 16.65 Operational Tourism. These youngsters spent their summer holidays at operational camps, helping archaeologists carry out excavations of ancient settlements.

organized activities at school and in the community palaces. Though centralized, their organization tended to work from the Republic down through regional committees to district level, and there was a direct link with political organizations at each level. Soviet children were not obliged to be Pioneers and many attended the Pioneer palaces and camps (Figure 16.67) without being members, suggesting that if a new source of funding could be found these excellent facilities could be utilized by the new outdoor education organizations.

Prior to the break-up of the Soviet Union, the majority of Soviet children attended a summer camp which had much in common with the American summer camp system. However, none of the Soviet examples were profit-making; they all had very close ties with the Komsomol and Pioneer organizations; they were run on much more authoritarian lines; and they were mainly sponsored and managed by trade union societies. Normally, parents had to pay about 30% of the cost, with the trade union covering the balance. Camps lasted for six weeks during the long summer vacation and most catered for about 400 children. Quality varied and schools were able to recommend their best pupils as a reward for effort. The most famous children's camp was probably Artek on the Black Sea.

The programme at the camp included some related school subjects, such as environmental studies, and some political lessons, but most of the time was spent exploring the natural scenery or engaging in other outdoor activities. As with the American camps, there was much 'camp fire' ritual and numerous group challenges. However, most of the

1. A Pioneer loves his Motherland and the Communist Party of the Soviet Union.
2. A Pioneer prepares himself to enter the Komsomol organization.
3. A Pioneer honours the memory of those who gave their lives in the struggle for freedom and for the prosperity of the Soviet Motherland.
4. A Pioneer is friendly to the children of all countries.
5. A Pioneer learns well.
6. A Pioneer is polite and well disciplined.
7. A Pioneer loves labour and is careful of public property.
8. A Pioneer is a good comrade: he cares for the young and helps the old.
9. A Pioneer is brave and unafraid of difficulties.
10. A Pioneer is honourable and values the honour of his detachment.
11. A Pioneer hardens himself, does physical exercises every day, and loves nature.

Figure 16.66 Extract for the Pioneer Principles. How does this differ from the UK Guide or Scout movement?

outdoor programme was structured to achieve the **Young Tourist Award** (children aged 12–15 years) and the **Tourist of the USSR Award** (those aged 16 years or more).

Finally, we must mention the historical features of tourism. Post-Revolution history was very important to the Soviet Union, particularly for the Russians; children were constantly reminded of the way the country had to struggle to achieve its status, and of the bravery of its people, especially in the

Figure 16.67 Artek Pioneer camp on the Black Sea. Only children with outstanding 'merit marks' had a chance to attend this showpiece.

fight against Germany in the Second World War. With independence and *glasnost* the history books may be rewritten, allowing the development of a free pluralist society that can grow to appreciate the natural environment without any political overtones being included.

Review Questions

1. Compare the American summer camps with the French *colonies de vacances* and the Outward Bound Movement which exists in both countries as well as in the UK and Australia.
2. How does the Outdoor Education programme in the UK compare with the *'transplantée classes'* in France?
3. Compare the development of National Parks in England with that in Australia.
4. Describe the links between the Soviet Pioneer movement and their camp schools and suggest likely changes as a result of the 1991 reforms.

Exam-Style Questions

1. Scenery is a major factor in attracting tourists to national parks:
a. What are the geographical similarities between the USA and Australia which might attract tourists to their national parks? (3 marks)
b. Examine the conflict between recreation and conservation in the British Isles and explain why this is not such a problem in France. (3 marks)
2. The structure and function of outdoor education is influenced by the dominant ideology of different cultures:
a. Compare the Scout and Guide movement in the UK with the pioneer movement in the Soviet Union in the context of their summer camps. (4 marks)
b. What cultural similarities might account for the UK, France, the USA and Australia all having Outward Bound Centres? (4 marks)
c. The USA has summer camps and France has *transplantée* classes and the *colonies de vacances*. Comment on the differences between them and explain the factors which determine these differences. (11 marks)
(Total 25 marks.)

Summary

UK, outdoor recreation:
1. **Outdoor education** is supervised in most schools.
2. **Outdoor pursuits** are controlled by governing bodies and individual enterprise.
3. **Outward Bound Trust:** residential schools to promote adventure and character building experiences.
4. **Countryside Commission** administers the **National Parks**, supported by the **National Trust**.
5. **Green Movement** on conservation is getting stronger.

France, outdoor recreation:
1. *Le plein air* is an important concept.
2. Significance of *les classes transplantées* which take the children into the countryside and teach them sailing and skiing.
3. *Colonies de vacances* are residential holidays, often used by the local authorities to give underprivileged children an extended open country experience.

USA, outdoor recreation:
1. **Federal** as well as **State** organization of **outdoor recreation**.
2. **Outward Bound Trust** also functions in the USA.
3. **State** and **commercial camp schools** very popular, attracting a wide range of children through the summer months.

Australia, outdoor recreation:
1. **Federal** as well as **State** organization of **outdoor recreation**.
2. Major similarities with the USA and the former Soviet Union with huge land mass and extensive areas of **wilderness**.
3. Full range of **outdoor pursuits** with emphasis on water sports but climbing, backpacking and skiing in Southern Alps.
4. Extensive **Outward Bound** programme, based at **Tharwa**, but with outreach centres across the country. Extensive development of outdoor education along East Coastal Plain.

Summary

continued

5. Well-developed organization of National and State Parks.

Outdoor recreation in the Soviet Union and post-reform Russia:
1. Soviet '**Tourism**' included all branches of outdoor recreation. Very much a politically motivated organization.

2. **Octobrists, Pioneers** and **Komsomol** were the political child and youth bodies.
3. **Pioneer palaces** were well-equipped youth centres and **Pioneer camps** were residential camp schools.
4. Conservation also had strong political support, with an increasing number of national parks being opened. This should continue in the independent Republics.

Further Reading

United Kingdom
Anthony D. *A Strategy for British Sport*, Hurst, 1980.
Armstrong N. (ed) *New Directions in PE*, Human Kinetics, 1990.
Cashmore E. *Making Sense of Sport*, Routledge, 1990.
CCPR. *The Howell Report, Sports Sponsorship*, CCPR, 1983.
CCPR. *Organization of Sport and Recreation in Britain*, CCPR, 1991.
CCPR. *The Palmer Report, Amateur Status*, 1988.
Coe S. *et al. More Than a Game*, BBC Books, 1992.
Coghlan J.F. *Sport and British Politics*, Falmer, 1990.
DES. *Physical Education in the Curriculum*, HMSO, 1992.
Hendry L.B. *Sport, School and Leisure*, Lepus, 1978.
Houlihan B. *The Government and Politics of Sport*, Routledge, 1992.
Macfarlane N. *Sport and Politics*, Collins & Willow, 1986.
McIntosh P.C. *Sport and Society*, West London Press, 1987.
Outward Bound Brochure. *It's a Beginning*, 1991.
Sports Council. *The Next Ten Years*, Sports Council, 1982.
Sports Council. *Which Ways Forward*, Sports Council, 1987.
Sports Council. *Into the 90s*, Sports Council, 1988.
Sports Council. *Sport: A Guide to Governing Bodies*, New Horizons, 1994.

France
French Embassy. Sports in France. *France Information*, 1985; 125.
Hantrais L. Leisure and the family in contemporary France. *Leisure Studies*, 1982; 1(1).
Le Sport pur Tous. *Une Dimension Nouvelle*, 1976.
Mairie de Paris, *La Direction de la Jeunese et des Sports en Chiffres*. 25, Boulevard Bourdon, Paris, 1992.
Mairie de Paris, *Sports et Jeunesse: 10 ans d'Action Municipale*. 1991.
Mermet G. *Francoscopie, Larousse*, 1987/88/90/91.
Platt J. The development of sport exchange. *Outdoors*, 1973; 3(4).
Rigby F. The place of PE and sport in a centralized educational system—France. *PE Review*, Spring 1978.
Smith P. *Philathletic Newsletter*, November 1996.

United States
Bucher C.A. *et al. Secondary School Physical Education*, Mosby, 1970.
Calhoun D.W. *Sport, Culture and Personality*, Human Kinetics, 1987.
Colorado Outward Bound Brochure, 1979.
Ewart A. The history of outdoor adventure programming. *Journal of Adventure, Education and Outdoor Leadership*, 1989; 6(4): 10–15.

Hellison D.R. *Goals and Strategies for Teaching P.E.*, Human Kinetics, 1985.
Jensen M. and Young A.B. Alternatives for Outdoor Education Programming. *Journal of Physical Education, Recreation and Dance*, 1981; 52.
McPherson B.D. *et al. The Social Significance of Sport*, Human Kinetics, 1989.
Sage G.H. *Power and Ideology in American Sport*, Human Kinetics, 1990.
Weiskopf D.C. *Recreation and Leisure*, Allyn & Bacon, 1982.
Wilson W. Social discontent and the growth of wilderness. *Sport Quest*, Winter 1977; 27.

Australia
Australian Sports Commission. Fact Sheets and Brochures on specific Academies, Aussie Sport, Women in Sport, etc. Belconnen, ACT 2616, 1995.
Crawford R. and Riley C. *Big Brother: Australian Physical Education and the ASC*.
Daly J. *The Quest for Excellence*, ASC, Australian Government Publishing Service, Belconnen, ACT 2616, 1991.
Dunstan K. *Sports*, Cassell Australia, 1973.
ISCPES. *Sport for All. Into the 90s*, vol 7, Meyer & Meyer Verlag, 1991.
McArthur A. and Priest S. Timbertop. *Adventure Education*, 1993; 10(1).
McRae K. Outdoor education 'down under' diversity; direction. *Adventure Education*, 1986; 3(3).
Montgomery E.M. and Darling J. *Timbertop*, F.W. Cheshire, 1967.
Neill J. *Outward Bound Australia, Tharwa Outward Bound School*, ACT 2620.

Soviet Union
Grant N. *Soviet Education*, Penguin, 1964.
Howell R. The USSR: sport and politics intertwined. *Comparative Education*, 1975; 2(2): 137–145.
ISCPES. *Comparative PE and Sport*, vols 3/4/5, Human Kinetics, 1986/7/8.
ISCPES. *Sport For All. Into the 90s*, vol 7, Meyer & Meyer Verlag, 1991.
Malkova *et al. Sport in the USSR*, Novosti Press, 1982.
Riordan J. *Sport in the Soviet Union*, Cambridge University Press, 1977.
Speak M.A. and Ambler V.H. *PE, Recreation and Sport in the USSR*, University of Lancaster, 1976.

Chapter 17

Sociological Considerations of Physical Education and Sport

17.1 Towards an Understanding of Sports Sociology

It is not intended to go into any detailed analysis of sociology as a discipline. The feeling is that in your reading you may need to be able to interpret certain sociological articles, and it will help you to understand some of the contemporary issues in our society if you can use sociology as an analytical tool. Unfortunately, the lay person is sometimes frustrated by the technical language and meanings used by some sociologists and so it is hoped to make you conversant with the main terms and concepts as they concern physical education, sport and outdoor recreation.

Two sociologists were asked to define their discipline:

1. **Sociology deals with the way individuals interact with one another to make up a social structure.** (Given that there is a great deal of group action in sport, there should be plenty to interest a sociologist!)

2. **Sociology is the scientific discipline that describes and explains human social organization.** The size of the human group under study can range from two people wrestling, to a sports club, a governing body, the leisure pattern of a community or the place of sport in a society. The sociologist is interested in the patterns that emerge whenever people interact over periods of time. Although groups may differ in size and purpose, there are similarities in structure and in the processes that create, sustain and transform the structure. In other words, although one group may be involved in aerobics while another is striving to win a football match, they will share many features. For example, they will have a **division of labour; a ranking structure; rules of procedure; punishments for rule breaking; special language and gestures**; and **co-operation to achieve group objectives**.

It is probable that most of you will want to adopt the first definition, and if you think the longer definition is rather repetitive and verbose, then you are probably right. However, if you take the second one step by step you will have a better working framework.

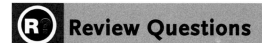 **Review Questions**

Take the two activities mentioned in the second definition, aerobics and football, and explain how they might share the six common features given in bold.

A sociologist makes an objective evaluation of what exists. Developmental treatment of what is established is left to 'professional' groups to interpret. Much of what follows includes both stages insofar that we are using sociology only to help us recognize how to achieve desirable social objectives.

Some basic sociological theories

1. **Relationships** (Figure 17.1) are what happens in a group or between groups. The study of **intrapersonal relationships** is a part of social psychology. It means looking at the interaction within a group and the resultant influence on individual members. The study of **interpersonal relationships** tends to focus on the influence of one group on another.

2. **Structure** (Figure 17.2) is the organization of a group—*what* it is. **Function** is the behaviour of the group—*how* it operates. **Deviance** is what occurs when members, or the group as a whole, break with the accepted structure and function of a group to achieve alternative objectives. In an **authoritarian** situation, **deviance** is automatically presumed to be **destructive**. In an **open** situation, it might be termed '**divergent thinking**' and result in **creative possibilities.**

The **structure–function** model (Figure 17.3) is useful when we classify the largest groups in a society down to the smallest.

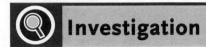

Figure 17.1 Relationships.

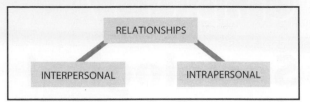

Investigation

17.1: Relationships
1. If you were observing your team in a basketball game, what intrapersonal features might be evident?
2. Explain what is happening when racist comments are made by sections of a home football crowd against a successful away team player.

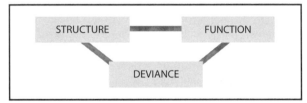

Figure 17.2 Structure, function and deviance.

 # Investigation

17.2: Deviance in structure and function
1. What is the structure of your school or college badminton club?
2. Explain what might happen when one partner in a pair is playing badly in a key game watched by the rest of the club.

3. What illegal or unethical means might be used to win the particular key game already mentioned?
4. You have already identified the disruptive elements of deviance in a formal game of badminton. Suggest a situation in gymnastics or in an outdoor pursuit where deviance might have positive results.

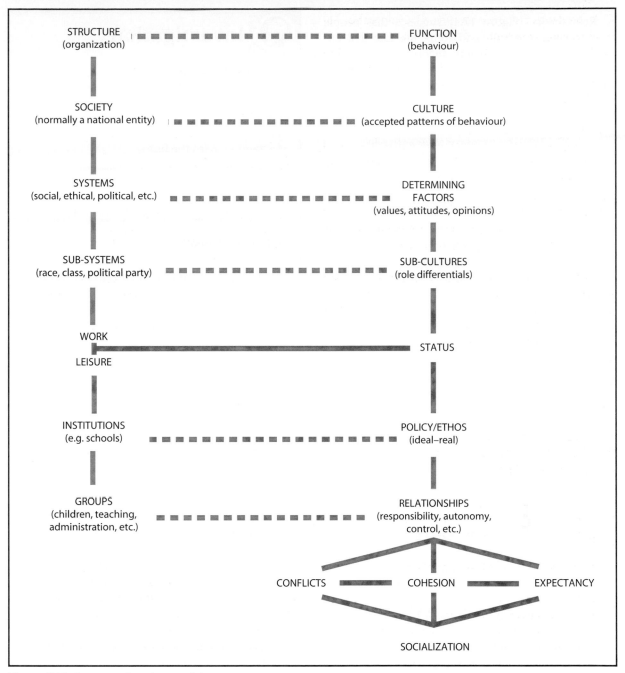

Figure 17.3 Structure–function model.

3. **Role theory** (Figure 17.4) suggests that people react to certain stimuli and adopt the role that circumstance dictates. **Action theory** suggests that though the stimuli are received by a person, he/she has the capacity to make an individual interpretation.

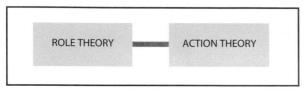

Figure 17.4 Role and action.

4. **Conflict theory** suggests that change and/or progress are made by one group at the *expense* of another. **Balanced tension theory** suggests that a degree of stress can be productive if it is controlled and channelled.

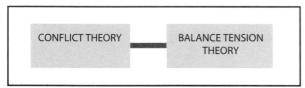

Figure 17.5 Conflict and balance.

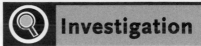

Investigation

17.3: Role and action theory
1. What did the Romans have to gain by slaughtering the Christians in gladiatorial games?
2. Why is it suggested that a boxer who loses his temper loses the fight?

Investigation

17.4: Conflict and balanced tension theory
1. Can you describe the action of a hockey umpire who sees an off-side? Is it predictable?
2. A climber has an injured friend several miles from civilization. What does the climber do? If you decide that he/she has several alternatives, identify them and justify one.

Summary

1. **Sociology** deals with the way people **interact**.
2. **Intrapersonal** and **interpersonal**.
3. **Structure—function—deviance**.
4. **Society—culture—systems—determining factors**.
5. **Role theory—action theory**.
6. **Conflict theory—balance tension theory**.

17.2 Society, Culture and Sport

You have been introduced to a number of sociological theories and each one has been examined in a sporting situation. We are now ready to look at a few of these in more detail.

We have decided that **society** is the structural composition of a community of people. We will be considering society as a national identity, in which a large group of people has an organization that is unique.

Secondly, we have decided that **culture** explains the way this society functions. It describes the unique patterns of a society, summarized in the term **life-style**. It reflects the customs, attitudes and values of the people and can be analysed at ethical, socio-economic and artistic levels.

Societies have **institutions** as organizations within their structure and these normally have a degree of autonomy with their own unique cultural interpretation.

Sport is one such institution. It has its own traditions and values, but these normally reflect the patterns in society at large. The same applies to physical education, but in this case we are concerned with a subject within a school institution, and so PE may be influenced by educational factors which do not directly apply to sport.

The intention is to look at different types of culture and to see how they affect organized physical activity. We haven't used the term 'sport' at this point because we might find that it is too sophisticated a notion to exist in some simple communal groups.

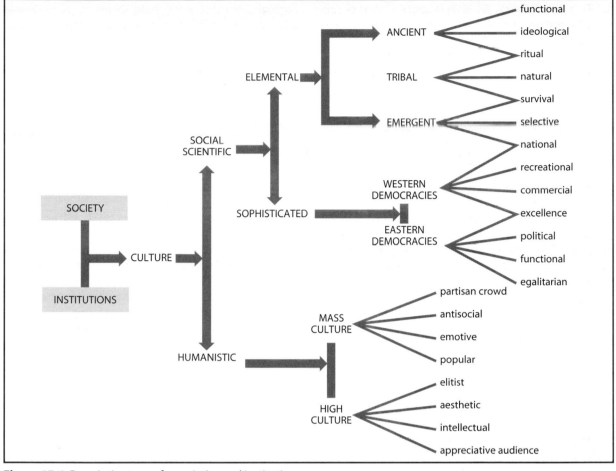

Figure 17.6 Descriptive terms for societies and institutions.

 Investigation

17.5: Sport in various societies and cultures
See if you can work your way through Figure 17.6 from left to right. Look at the social scientific section first.
1. To what extent was the sport of the Ancient Romans functional, ideological and concerned with ritual?
2. How was physical activity in the life of the American Red Indian ritualized, natural and concerned with survival?

3. Look at an emergent country such as Kenya and see if sport is linked with cultural survival and whether it is selective and nationalistic.
4. Take a Western democracy, Britain if you like, and decide whether sport is based on recreation and excellence, and explain how this is linked with commercialism.
5. Test your knowledge of Soviet sport by assessing the importance of excellence in the context of political ideology and purposeful intention.

In Investigation 17.5 you should have thought about five different cultures, using the key words to trigger your response. You may have agreed with the suitability of these words or questioned them. Most of your suggestions will have been **value judgements**, but you may have had some genuine evidence or obtained some information from a published article.

The important point to be made is that your own ideas are useful, but they do not represent social scientific evidence. A sociologist, archaeologist or anthropologist has systematically to collect and collate data and present them for public scrutiny. We need, therefore, to take this extra step and read what researchers have found. If we do this we are attempting to comment accurately on what is or was the situation in these cultures.

Ancient cultures, physical activity and archaeology

Minoan Crete

We have frescoes and vases which were retrieved from ruins. They show acrobats in the art of bull leaping, a ritual to please the Minoan god Minos who was half bull, half man. This type of bull fighting combined piety and courage, and reflected an affluent society, which used captives to fight the bulls while the citizens enjoyed the festival.

Ancient Egypt

There is considerable evidence in stone carvings on tombs. The best example is Beni Hasan's tomb (Figure 17.7) (2000–1500 BC), which shows the technical development of wrestling, and also boxing, fencing, swimming, rowing, running, archery and horse riding. These contests seem to have advanced beyond the level of religious ceremony to a sporting experience. Perhaps more directly linked with ritual, there are frescoes which show women engaged in various partner activities.

Ancient Greece

The earliest evidence concerns the funeral games, contained in Homer's *Iliad* and *Odyssey*, books which were written around 800 BC. They are legendary and so not an accurate record, but athletic feats, violent contests and chariot racing were part of a need to maintain fighting fitness, appease the gods and express the Greek ideology of 'Man of Action'. It is from these ancient myths and stories that the ancient Olympic Games derived as religious ceremonies connected with Zeus and lesser gods.

Formal contests were held between City States despite the fact that they were constantly at war. Evidence of the diversity of activities and the athletic form which was idolized is to be seen on a wide range of frescoes, painted objects and sculptures (Figure 17.8).

Ancient Rome

Recorded in written form, sculpture and as monuments like the Colosseum, evidence suggests that the Ludi or Roman Games were spectacles of extreme brutality, serving to illustrate the status of the patricians (ruling class) and the attempts to **appease** the plebeians (subject races). Affluence led the Romans away from vigorous participation to the spectator situation of the Games and the recreational pastimes of the thermae (baths).

Tribal societies, physical activity and the social anthropologist

General

The suggestion that tribal societies had **functional** physical activities is supported by the popularity of competitive foot racing among the Sioux tribe in North America, where the ability to cover large distances on the Plains was economically necessary. Log racing by the Timbira tribe in South America was not competitive, but assessed on team success in getting logs down the river, another economic strategy. In terms of **ritual**, the ball symbolized the supernatural in the case of the Aztecs, the Arizona Indians and in the old Celtic game of hurling. An extension of **ritual** into victory **ceremony** is demonstrated in the Red Indian game of baggataway, later refined into lacrosse. Similarly, Peruvian Indians played with a feathered object like a shuttlecock, in a simple version of badminton.

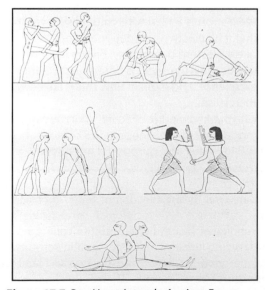

Figure 17.7 Ben Hasan's tomb, Ancient Egypt.

Figure 17.8 Sculptures of Ancient Greek wrestlers.

Samoans

Dunlap (1951) suggested that games were a central part of Samoan culture. In terms of the fulfilment of **social needs**, she identified social mixing, outlets for rivalry, opportunities for leadership, opportunities for prestige and honour to be won and an outlet for excessive emotions connected with birth, marriage and death. As a fulfilment of religious **ritual needs**, she suggested that erotic dancing was intended to stimulate the gods; fertility festivals were linked with nature and the tribe; and the flow of blood served to demonstrate devotion to the gods. Finally, at the third level, she identified fulfilment of **militaristic needs** partly through skill with weapons, and partly through the physical strength essential for military preparedness.

The significance of **outside influence** was also considered. **Missionaries** prevented the association of vigorous amusements with the old religion; certain sports like bonito fishing were denied their ritual and tribal status; and erotic dances and tumbling were banned. The **colonial** influences changed the method of warfare by introducing guns, reduced the freedom of travel between the islands, and introduced colonial games, some of which were eventually modified to meet local methods of play. The success of the Fijians and Western Samoans in rugby union, particularly at 7-a-side, is an interesting phenomenon. They have adopted the colonial game, but incorporated the aggression and flair of their culture to produce a unique variation of that game. The Haka is a typical re-emergence of ritual from a pre-colonial culture.

Polynesia

Jones (1967) looked at 10 Polynesian cultures, including Hawaii, New Zealand, Fiji and Tonga. He observed their games, which consisted of canoeing, hide-and-seek, spear throwing, dart games, bandy (primitive hockey) and sham fights. They played string games, and hand clapping, kites and surfboard riding were all in evidence. He found that the social and psychological need for group interaction was the major influence on the choice of activities; there were strong self-preservation and government control factors; very few family activities because of the Polynesian group culture; and a great deal of ritual significance.

Aborigines

Salter (1967) studied the Australian Aborigines. He suggested that group pastimes, such as tribal dancing, were most popular, followed by group games, which included hide-and-seek, mock battles, throwing the boomerang and plunging from a height. He felt that co-operational activities were much more common than competitions, because the Aborigines were few in number and needed one another to survive. Weapons were also necessary for survival and the various ritual dances were intended to please the gods.

Pueblo baseball

Fox (1969) noted that ancient Indian witchcraft was being mixed with a superimposed Catholicism to produce a non-competitive culture. With the importation of baseball, the competitive game conflicted with the culture and there was an emergence of witchcraft strategies within the game.

Emergent countries and sport as a national identity

Riordan (1988) suggested that all developing countries are in the process of **nation-building**, which normally entails the authoritarian **integration** of a variety of tribal groups to establish stability. In turn, this can be achieved only if the nation is healthy and strong, which leads to emphasis on the **health** of the people and their **military preparedness**. One outcome in the modern world is the recognition that **sport** is a competitive frontier which draws a nation together without bloodshed. However, technological and financial limitations mean that an **elitist** route is necessary, where focus has to be on a specific activity that is straightforward to establish. Funding and effort are then **disproportionately** allocated to achieve **excellence** in this one area. The reward for international success is the production of a **role model**, which at once **inspires** and **appeases** less fortunate members of the society under one banner and gives the developing country international **exposure** and **recognition**.

Africa

The world prominence of middle-distance and long-distance runners in East Africa and boxers in West Africa is out of all proportion to the sporting population of these countries. Tribal traditions and altitude have made athletics a natural choice in the East and the heavier build of Ghanaians and Nigerians has made boxing a natural choice for them. There is no need for sophisticated coaching methods or technological infrastructure, and both athletics and boxing have the world stage—resulting in a few elite athletes stimulating tremendous national pride as well as international respect.

499

Far East

The colonial impact on the old British colonies has had a widespread influence on the development and choice of sports. Success in these activities reflects the success of the family as a relic of colonial superiority. Cricket, hockey, badminton, table tennis and squash are games which have considerable cultural importance. Holding the Olympic Games in South Korea allowed it to express its particular form of nationalism; the use of the sports arena to demonstrate a political identity, and the opportunity of showing the world the richness of Korean culture through a variety of artistic displays gave a small country the world stage.

South America

Here, the sport and culture link lies in the pre-eminence of football. Each of the South American countries uses the game to express its national identity, to allow its volatile emotions to be expressed, to appease the underprivileged and to provide an escape route for a few of them to earn lasting fame and fortune.

West Indies

The popularity and success of cricket in the West Indies is an excellent example of the association between the natural life-style of tropical island communities and the pursuit of a colonial game which was initially elitist, but has now become an expression of the people, played in a style which is uniquely their own.

Advanced Western democracies and sport

You will be realizing that the roots of many of our games and individual activities lie in the inventiveness of ancient and primitive cultures and, more importantly, that changes which have occurred to those games are the result of changes in society in general. Three revolutions have been at the heart of this change: the **agrarian**, the **industrial** and the **urban**, leading to the present social structure of a sophisticated technological administration, based on a large population.

A sociologist looking at sport in such a country would be likely to say that sport is a solution to the problem of leisure; a release of physical energy and aggression in a harmless way; a challenge which is artificially created to give an ensuing sense of achievement; and a part of institutionalized education through physical education. The more complex social structure leads to a more sophisticated sporting system, but—as Loy and Kenyon (1969) have pointed out—sport exists as a **social institution**, thereby having a considerable influence on society at large; and as a **social situation**, so helping in the socialization process in a group, community or society.

The complexity of an industrialized society results in a number of **primary** determinants, such as the mode of production, relationships between rural and urban society, the division of labour and the distribution of power, in economic and political terms. It is also possible to produce a number of **consequential** determinants, such as the centralization of authority, the provision of communications, social class and racial divisions and the provision of specialized facilities, which are a necessary part of maintaining an advanced society. The tribal chief, elders and family could cope with all the social issues in a tribal community, but this level of administration would not work in the UK, France or the USA. Some sociologists might argue, however, that at a local level these simple, self-nurturing groups continue to operate even in an advanced society.

It is important to recognize the hypothesis by Lüschen (1968) and others that, in a sophisticated society, sport has a codification of rules which may not be the same as the cultural values outside sport. Things are done legitimately on the football field which would be common assault on the street. Critics of sport also say that it is excessively achievement-oriented, a situation which is already too strongly identified in our materialistic society. Finally, this **dysfunctional** possibility is carried to an extreme in the behaviour of some sports crowds, where it is suggested that antisocial behaviour is promoted in the sports situation and overflows into society at large.

 Investigation

17.6: Social influence on sport
Attempt to link Western sport with a social influence, e.g. how does commercialism influence high level sport in the USA?

Marxist democracies and functional leisure

The reforms in the Soviet Union do not mean an end to communist or 'socialist' influence in the world. China and Cuba still have communist political systems, even if they are increasingly adopting free market economics. Russia and the other old Soviet republics may yet revert to communist government or retain 'socialism' as a moderate version of stressing the community rather than the individual. It is also important to recognize that it might be single-party authoritarianism as against democracy which is critical, not right-wing or left-wing politics.

Today, we can see so much in common between the West and the East, but it is important to realize that the political principle of putting the individual or the community first can give rise to a different interpretation of the function of sport (Figure 17.9). Interestingly, Wohl (1966), a sociologist from Eastern Europe, came up with two cultural links similar to those identified by the American John Loy. He recognized **sport as a social influence**—stimulating social integration and overcoming cultural barriers, and **sport as a social process**—objectively improving work production, transportation and military needs (Figure 17.10). Yet the small print clearly establishes that the relative freedom of the individual to recreate in Western cultures differs from the more authoritarian association of the socially productive impact of physical activity as part of some grand ideological design.

 **Review Questions**

Explain why East European countries have used sporting success as a political agency.

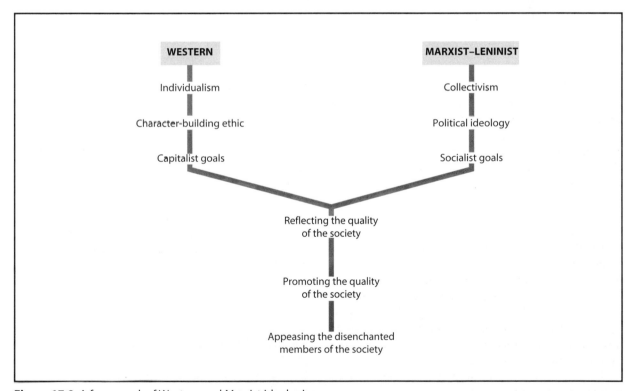

Figure 17.9 A framework of Western and Marxist ideologies.

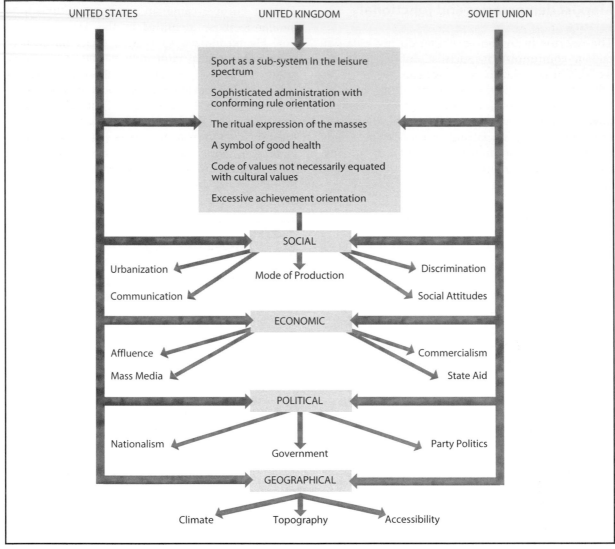

Figure 17.10 Try to put examples to each stage of this model.

Sport and low (mass) culture

An alternative way of studying sport and culture is to look at the behaviour of groups of people from a humanist viewpoint. Our basic model identifies two polarized patterns of behaviour: mass culture and high culture.

Mass culture is normally associated with modern industrialized societies with large population groups (Figure 17.11). It suggests that these groups can have common unifying values which may not match those held by other groups in the community. They are bound by a code of behaviour and emotional sharing, where a sport might bring them together as a group and stimulate them to act collectively. The behaviour of such a group represents the standard of the lowest member of the group, in a gravitation of standards permitted by the diminished responsibility of an individual in a crowd. It is generally felt that membership leads to a coarsening of human expression.

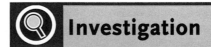

Investigation

17.7: Mass culture and sport
A mass culture sporting situation might be a fight between players in a rugby league game, a tag-wrestling contest or the football crowd at a local derby game.
1. Select one of these and use Figure 17.11 to establish any mass culture elements.
2. Link your popular sport with the four basic interpretations and then continue the analysis of sport as a mass medium.

In attempting to identify examples of mass culture operating in sport, you should be looking for situations with limited intellectual expression but considerable immediate excitement. Certainly, the most common example of mass culture in British sport at the present time is hooligan behaviour by members of a soccer crowd.

A great deal has been written on this topic, where almost everyone points to a different set of causes. Some blame society; others criticize the way the game is played and the attitude of players; some suggest that the facilities are at fault; others blame media hype and commercialism while probably most point the finger at the excessive use of alcohol. The Harrington, Popplewell and Taylor Reports made many recommendations, but the problem is still with us. We can argue it out with value judgements or we can attempt to produce a **sociogram** of the problem (Figure 17.12).

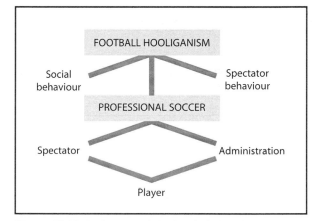

Figure 17.11 Elements of mass culture.

Figure 17.12 Sociogram of the football situation.

 Investigation

17.8: Mass culture and football

You could visit a ground and assemble some data. Then, armed with some facts, we might have more than points of view to offer.

1. a. Does my ground fit a **mass culture** classification?

b. Does a faction in my club bring violence to the ground?

c. Does the game trigger violence, or is it a combination of the two?

2. a. Is there a domination of certain **subcultures** in the hooligan element?

b. Can you identify a **youth cult**; a **class cult**; a **regional cult**; or/and a **religious cult**?

3. a. Is there an **interaction** of a **sub-system**?

b. Can you see the crowd being driven towards anti-social behaviour by the **code of the game**; by the **attitude of the players**; by the **condition of the facilities**; or by some other factor?

4. What are the **group dynamics** operating in the **crowd**. Can you pinpoint aggression, conflicting aspirations, collective bravado and protective reaction?

5. Is there evidence as to what incidents cause excessive stimulation or frustration, and to what extent is this loss of control carried into the streets?

6. Can you point to similar examples of group misbehaviour in the community at large and, if so, what evidence have you that this is a law-and-order problem in your town?

7. Is this a **territorial** issue, resulting from away fans invading and home fans protecting their territory?

Sport and high culture

High culture is the training, development and refinement of the mind, taste and manners in society. It identifies with the highest moral, social, intellectual and physical qualities of a culture (Figure 17.13).

In a society where there are differentials of class, gender or race, the underprivileged are unlikely to be included in the activities which make up this quality of life. It might be argued that such people have their own ethnic or communal qualities which off-set this. Arguably, in a 'socialist' State, such as the old Soviet Union, social discrimination should not exist and so these activities must be available and sought after by the whole of society. However, high culture tends to be based on affluence and intellect, and it may be that the Soviet Union did not have sufficient resources to fulfil high culture right across society; it may be that intellectualism and the stain of Tsarist culture stood in the way of its full expression. It now seems likely that there was so much corruption taking place that major inequalities continued to exist in the Soviet Union, which may have been one of the causes for its decline. Similarly, if we look at the commercialism and the competitiveness of American culture and particularly sport, there is a brashness which makes high culture activities part of the counter-culture. It is in the older cultures of Britain and France that high culture is at its strongest and where sport has had difficulty in achieving acceptance as a subject for aesthetic expression or as an art form in its own right.

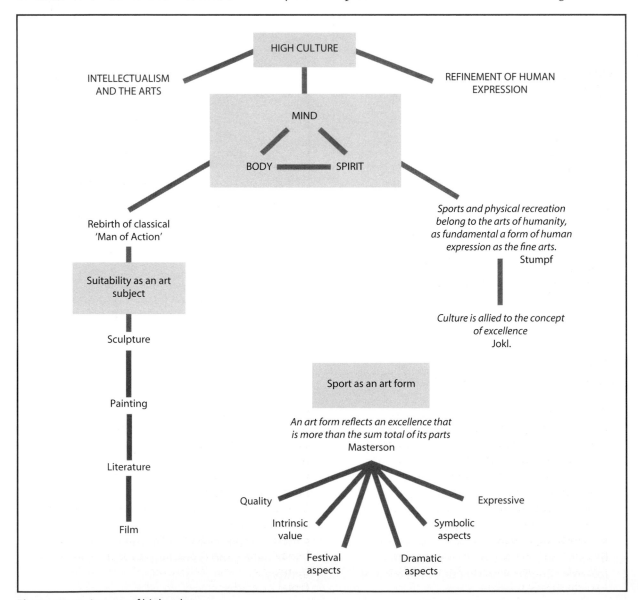

Figure 17.13 Aspects of high culture.

The biggest problem with sport being accepted as an art form has been the inability to capture it for public appraisal. In sport, the moment of beauty is transitory (Figure 17.14). Today, we have film and video to capture the moment and to relay it in slow motion, providing time for its moments of artistry to be appreciated and stand up to critical reflection.

Figure 17.14 'Children's Games', by P. Bruegel. Explain how the artist justified sport as an art subject.

Review Questions

1. Play is universal and yet each culture is responsible for the form and function it has. Suggest explanations why Aboriginal and Eskimo versions of hide-and-seek involve sending one person off to hide while the others seek, but in the British Isles we expect one person to find everyone else in the game.
2. Western Samoa and Fiji play a particularly committed game of rugby football. Attempt an explanation of this in the context of ethnic culture, colonialism and post-colonialism.
3. Many emergent and/or developing countries justify elitism in the name of stability, integration and aspiration. Explain this using at least one such country as an example and explain why this elitism may be only a temporary necessity.
4. Discuss the theory that the 'win at all cost ethic' in sport is strongly applied in both capitalist and communist societies, but that many of the motives differ.
5. Association football in this country can claim itself to be an art form on the one hand and a vehicle for the expression of mass culture on the other. Explain the duality of the English game identifying the good and bad of both cultural forms.

Exam-Style Questions

1. All societies have engaged in physical activities and these tend to reflect the level of cultural sophistication of the society. Figure 17.15 shows one model of this relationship.
a. How did the ancient Roman 'ludi' (gladiatorial games) meet the three characteristics of functional, ideological and ritual? (3 marks)
b. Wrestling appears to have been very popular in many primitive cultures. Use the relevant characteristics in Figure 17.15 to explain this. (4 marks)
c. Using the information in the diagram to help you, explain why Kenya has outstanding middle-distance runners. (5 marks)
d. Explain why Western democracies seem to have a commercial basis to their sport, while Communist democracies have tended to stress political ideology. (5 marks)
2. Figure 17.16 represents an alternative model of the relationships between Western democratic culture and physical activity. Explain the implied behavioural variables, using a soccer crowd and a gymnastics audience as examples. (8 marks)
(Total 25 marks.)

Exam-Style Questions

continued

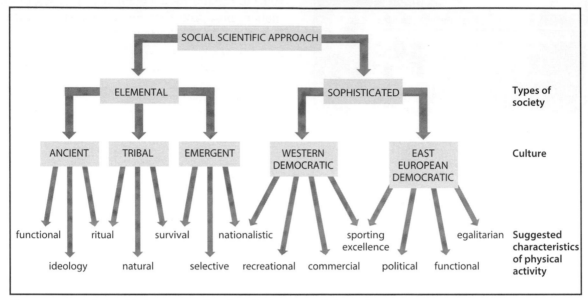

Figure 17.15 Relationship between cultural sophistication and physical activity.

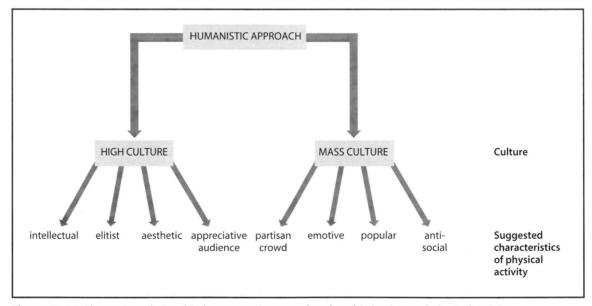

Figure 17.16 Alternative relationship between Western cultural sophistication and physical activity.

 **Summary**

Sport & Culture:

1. **Social scientific** components: **elemental**—ancient, tribal and emergent; **sophisticated**—Western and Eastern industrialized societies.

2. **Humanistic: mass culture**—emotive crowd experiences with anti-social tendencies; **high culture**—aesthetic and elitist attitudes.

17.3 Group Dynamics in Sporting Situations

Now that we have examined the **interaction** between sporting groups and the social setting in which they exist, we need to look inside a sports group to see how it works. This may enable us to overcome problems which might arise from something going wrong at the **intrapersonal** level. You've probably all played in a team which has 'cracked up'.

The term 'group dynamics' suggests simply that within a group there are constantly changing relationships which influence the outcome of what the group is trying to achieve (Figure 17.17).

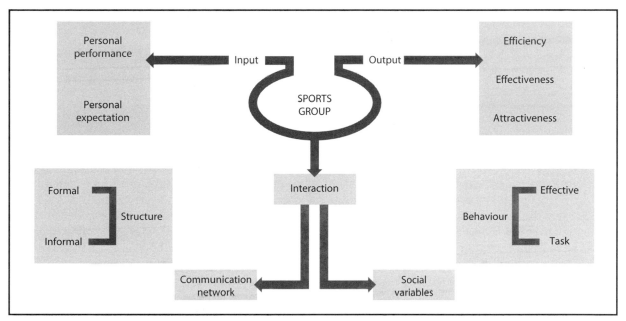

Figure 17.17 The dynamics of a sports group.

 Investigation

17.9: Group dynamics
Get into sets of 4–5 people, decide on a sporting activity and play for a time. Don't just choose a game; include a contest and an individual activity too. Then decide:
1. What did we have to do to make this a group?
2. What are the main objectives of the group?
3. What strategies should we employ to achieve these objectives within the spirit and rules of the activity?
Let's see if you reached similar conclusions to leading theorists in this area. Cratty (1967)

suggested that a group (sports group) is *a collection of people mutually interacting to solve a common problem or general type of problem.*
4. Were you mutually interactive? (That is, everyone contributing!)
5. Did your objectives tease out the problem(s)? Or didn't you even consider what you were playing for?
6. Will your strategies solve the problem(s) by helping you to work together to achieve your objectives? Albeit as a group involved in basketball, fencing, or a cross-country race?

You'll quickly become aware that a group in sport has a **structure**, which allows it to work successfully (Mason, 1966). This could involve fixture arrangements, playing positions, conventions or rules. Similarly, a group involves many **relationships**, which determine how well it works. Here we mean

the sort of roles you might adopt in playing the activity. These may make you a successful group or perhaps merely a contented one. In sport we have this very meaningful word '**team**', which describes group structure, and the expression '**team spirit**', which describes desirable group relationships.

The **input** of a group is all about **personal performance** and **personal expectation**. Here we have a mixture of ability and enthusiasm which will make you a worthwhile member. While the group is operating there is always **interaction** going on (Figure 17.18).

Investigation

17.10: What makes a good team?
1. List what you consider to be the characteristics of a good team and the qualities identifiable with team spirit.
2. Compare your ideas with those of other members of your work group.

Figure 17.18 Things aren't always what they appear on the surface.

When you play a game of football or hockey, for example:

1. Is the structure **formal** or **informal**? (Are you playing in fixed positions or not?)

2. What is the **communication network** like? (Are you using an agreed code?)

3. Are you committed to **effective** or **task** behaviour? (Are you letting the run of the game decide or have you been given a fixed job to do?)

4. What **social variables** are operating on the group? (What are the pressures on winning? What are the rewards? What attitudes are acceptable within the group? Do you have restrictions on membership?)

If we watched an inter-school match, we would soon be able to answer these questions and it would be interesting to compare this interaction with the operation of a professional team. If we are going to understand the **output** of a group we need to look at its **efficiency** (how much does it achieve?); its **effectiveness** (how valuable is it to the group?); and its **attractiveness** (how valuable has it been to each individual?). It should be easy enough to sit down and do this after a match.

A physical performance group is almost invariably held together by the challenges it sets itself. This may be the competitive element in games, the

contest of combat, the perfection-seeking of many individual activities or the adventure of outdoor recreation. Let's call this the **sporting situation**.

It is important to reassert that these challenges are self- or group-inspired and are couched in the experiential medium of play and self-realization. The deliberate infliction of injury, on oneself or others, is not compatible with the desired values of a sporting situation.

The survival of the group is very much dependent on the balanced satisfaction of the four group motives shown in Figure 17.19.

Sporting challenge and competition are contrived situations where cohesion, conflict and expectation are channelled to give a desirable outcome.

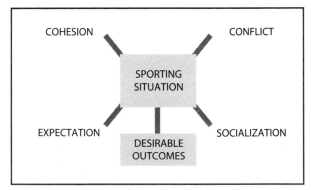

Figure 17.19 Group motives.

Cohesion

Cohesiveness of a group is the result of all the members wanting to remain in the group. It embodies an underlying sense of co-operation (Figure 17.20).

- It can be identified as the essence of team spirit, where there is an **attraction** in belonging to a group with high **morale** and **shared responsibility**.
- It almost always involves the development of friendships, many of which may be long-lasting through mutual interest, e.g. Dr Roger Bannister's famous phrase 'friendships forged in the fire of competition'.
- An individual member tends to follow the collective will of the group in a form of mutual mimicry.

The basic cohesive ingredient of a **match** is the **contract** between two teams to engage in a fixture.

Given that the match always involves **opposition**, the team is drawn together by this outside threat. However, the opposition is required to **conform** to the same rules and this in itself is a cohesive element.

For the winning team there is the **shared reward** of victory and, in a well-orientated losing side, there is a tendency to **close ranks** and work for future success.

When the game ends with the final whistle, opposing sides should be **drawn together**, having put each other to the test. Similarly, the completed expedition, where risk and adventure is shared, results in the cementing of **life-long relationships**.

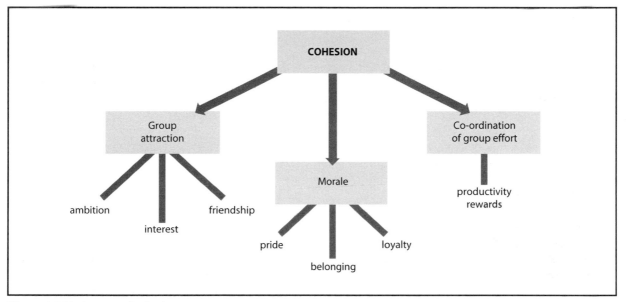

Figure 17.20 Aspects of cohesion.

 Investigation

17.11: Cohesive elements in sport

1. What are the cohesive elements evident in Figure 17.21?
2. Engage in a game of basketball, making a mental note of the cohesive elements and stopping at intervals for discussion; or play a game of volleyball with exaggerated elements of group reinforcement and co-operation, subsequently discussing the advantages of such an approach.
3. Select a sporting activity and explain the cohesive elements within it.

Figure 17.21 A cohesive sport.

Conflict

Testing your mettle, temperamentally and physically, is the essence of physical performance. It is invariably a question of competing **against** self, others and/or nature.

The level of conflict varies in different types of activity and in different specific situations. In games conflict can arise playing against another team, winning a place in your own team or confronting match conditions. Individual activities such as swimming and athletics also include rivalry and conditions, but are concerned mainly with pitting yourself against a previous best performance. In gymnastics, performance also includes subjective assessment and so the contest involves impressing the judges. Finally, the outdoor pursuit situation may involve competition against others and self, but the emphasis is normally on the challenge of the environment.

This is a good point at which to compare functional conflict with instances of outright aggression which lie outside the rules of play. Sport can claim to be culturally valuable only if it can be seen to give individuals and teams an opportunity to discipline themselves in the face of provocation.

This takes us into the conflict which occurs as a result of frustration. Here is a possible cause of instances of outright aggression. Fighting on the field and among spectators may reflect tensions which the game itself has promoted. Some educationists are concerned that sport stimulates aggression in a society which some claim is already excessively competitive.

Man is aggressive; the sporting activity requires commitment and effort; the heat of the moment and the desire to win test temperament control to the maximum. The key, therefore, is **channelled aggression** or **balanced tension**. The coach and athlete work to produce a top performance and this involves lawful strategies to make the most of that particular sporting situation.

If we learn to control aggression through sporting competition, if we satisfy the human need to be aggressive without overstimulation, then educationists may begin to recognize the socialization potential of the sports group.

 Review Questions

1. Discuss the specific conflict elements in: an athletics squad, a hockey team, a judo squad and an expedition party.
2. Look at Figure 17.22 and decide what the headings mean before allocating your different conflict elements to them.
3. Try to relate the following statements to Figure 17.22:
   a. The level of aggression should always be within the spirit and letter of the rules of play, but should also satisfy the needs of the occasion.
   b. The required aggression of a combat sport would be much greater than that needed for an afternoon sail on a lake.
   c. Winning a ball in hockey with the need for commitment against opposition is very different from the personal discipline of refining a gymnastic routine.
   d. Surviving a difficult rapid in a canoe is real and unpredictable, as compared with the tension which exists in the controlled environment of target archery.

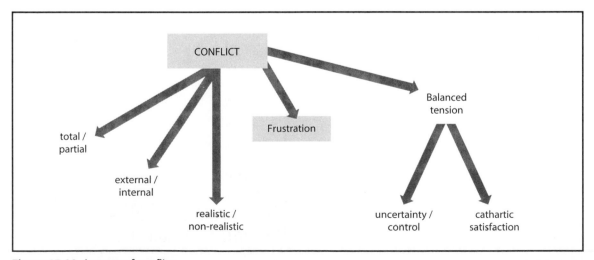

Figure 17.22 Aspects of conflict.

Investigation

17.12: Effects of conflict
Set up some practical conflict role-play situations and monitor the effects, e.g.:
1. An example of gamesmanship.
2. Weak refereeing.
3. Excluding a player from receiving passes.
4. Verbal criticism of team-mates.

Expectation or aspiration

The desire to succeed is fundamental to all sporting groups and to individuals within each group. Problems arise when the aspirations of an individual are not shared by the group.

We can be aware of how good we are and consequently what is feasible; alternatively, we can believe in our potential and speculate on our hopes. In both cases the significant factor is that the expectations should be realizable. Given the challenging motives underlying sport, however, it is important that these expectations should be at the limit of potential achievement in order to challenge the individual and the group (Figure 17.23).

It has been suggested that an individual's aspiration level is related to his perceived standing in the group. If this is not the case, there is likely to be dissension. Frustration exists at an individual and group level when expectations are too high.

It is also important to recognize that an individual who lacks ambition is as counterproductive in a group as someone with unreasonable expectations. Expectation is conditioned by the degree of role freedom in the group. For example, in American football, with the exception perhaps of the quarterback, players have a very **closed** role.

It is necessary for the player to fulfil his/her role to the satisfaction of the coach, other players, supporters and him/herself. Try to tease out expectations **in** this game and then expectations **from** this game.

Netball is another example of individuals accepting specific roles, which may require them to condition their own ambitions.

Saunders and White (1977), in looking at rugby football, suggested that it has a closed structure in terms of rules, but an open system of relationships. In British mini-rugby a wide range of alternatives are open to the young person. He/she is free to explore various alternatives and other members of the group are likely to be extremely permissive.

Remember, a good team player subsumes personal aspirations for the advancement of the team; and a sound coach invariably promotes a variety of objectives along an achievement continuum to stimulate his/her squad with a succession of small victories on the way to a major challenge.

Review Questions

If you want to explore 'expectation' in a practical way:
1. Set up players with unreasonable aspirations.
2. Play people out of position.
3. Introduce a selfish or apathetic player.
Always discuss the intention and outcomes of these role play situations afterwards.

Socialization

At a societal level, socialization (Figure 17.24) is **man's adjustment to his culture.** At a more specific level, it follows that it is also the **sportsman's adjustment to**

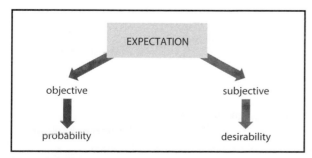

Figure 17.23 Aspects of expectation.

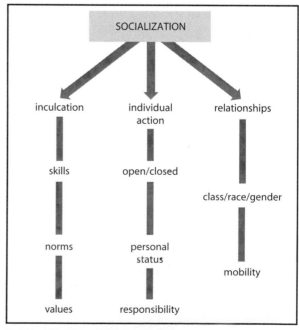

Figure 17.24 Aspects of socialization.

sport as a sub-culture. In relationship terms it would seem that **social adjustments in sport may influence behaviour in society at large**.

It is worth remembering that Lüschen (1968) points out that this might be a **functional** or **dysfunctional** process. We have the potential to produce heroes or villains!

In the field of physical education the teacher uses the sporting experience to inculcate socially desirable skills, norms and values, whereas sport tends to leave the ethics and rules to promote these indirectly.

The degree to which a group is **open** or **closed** decides the extent to which an individual can hope to inculcate social changes. The status of the individual is also significant, e.g. a captain would probably be able to influence the group; a talented player might be able to; but a newcomer would probably not.

At what levels might we presume socialization can take place in a sporting situation? Simply being accepted into a sports group is a social experience. The ethics and rules of the group, team or club require the individual to make a social adjustment.

In the competitive or challenging situation, the individual and the group are required to meet the requirements of the sport in skill and behaviour terms. In playing together with others, the individual learns to submerge his/her own interests in favour of the group. Similarly, he/she has to accept the outcomes regardless of personal disappointments (Figure 17.25).

A sports group may include members from different racial or social class minorities where sport can help in the removal of discriminatory barriers. The sports group which is based on physical performance is a vehicle for social mobility where social constraints still operate in society at large.

Figure 17.25 Why was it so important for the Soviets to beat the Americans at women's basketball?

 # Exam-Style Questions

1. You will have all played in a games team and will realize that this involves not only the players themselves and what they bring to the team, but also the interaction between team members. A flow chart of this experience is shown in Figure 17.17.
a. Selecting a game of your choice, explain what you would expect to offer the team on becoming a member. (2 marks)
b. During a game you would need to communicate effectively with your team. Identify two ways this might be done and the advantages of each. (3 marks)
c. Describe the social relationships which might exist in a team selected solely on ability. (3 marks)
d. Give a number of reasons for wanting to play for the same team the following season. (3 marks)
2. It has been presumed that your team has been selected and run with an emphasis on participation values.
a. What pressures would be applied to your games dynamic if the person in control promoted a 'win-at-all-costs' ethic? (6 marks)
b. Explain the change of focus from cohesion to conflict if a win ethic was adopted. (4 marks)
c. How would the adoption of a win ethic change the structure, formal and informal, and behaviour, task and effective, in a game? (4 marks)
(Total 25 marks.)

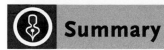

Summary

Group dynamics:
1. **Input** into a group **personal performance** and **aspiration**.
2. **Interaction** in a group—**structure, communication, behaviour** and **social variables**.
3. **Output** from the group—**efficiency, effectiveness** and **attractiveness**.
4. **Dynamics: cohesion**—attraction, morale, shared responsibility; **conflict**—test of temperament and physical **capacity, channelled aggression** and **balanced tension**, problems with **dysfunctional aggression** and **gamesmanship**; socialization—inculcation of values, development of friendships, opportunity for individual action; **aspiration**—objective probability or subjective desirability.

17.4 Roles in Sport and Physical Education

When people find themselves in a social situation they behave in a specific way: in other words, an individual has one or more roles to play in every sports group. There are a number of variables operating which decide what that role is and how it is determined.

Your **status** in the group is probably the most significant single factor; to quote Linton (1936), 'Role represents the dynamic aspect of status.' This means simply that your standing in the group decides how you behave. You might be leader of an expedition, playing your first game in a hockey team or coaching an Olympic athlete. How you act depends on your status in the relationship.

The second variable in role concerns your own **make-up** and, therefore, the way you like to behave with others. How you act depends very much on your personality, and while you can be 'someone else' for a time, this is difficult to maintain and there is usually a 'reversion to type'.

In addition to personal traits, there is the **impact** of the group on the individual or group make-up. How rigidly is your behaviour controlled by others in the group, by the dynamic of the game or by the rules imposed by an authoritative body?

If you want to know more about these dimensions, then you can look into **autonomous** (self-directed) roles and **authoritarian** (imposed) roles (Calhoun, 1987).

If we stay within the spheres of play and games, then you will recall that children's play is very much a set of make-believe experiences, which may involve self-development as well as social development. If you look at games, you will recognize that we artificially restrict our actions to the needs of the team and the game's code: that, as with play, our experiences might lead to personal and social development.

The complexity of the game situation, according to Mead (1967), is that instead of just taking over the role of someone else, for example the striker in a soccer team, you also take on the role of the whole team: that is, you have to maintain your place in the fluid interaction of players and situations for the good of the team. If this is the case, then the value of group role play in a 'serious' sporting situation involves continual judgements, and these experiences may overflow into a more effective life-style.

An extension of this hypothesis takes you into the 'reality' of a role: the view that for roles to be effective they must be internalized. If we only 'play' a role, our commitment lacks the intensity required to fulfil it adequately. An American school for actors uses the technique of 'method acting'. They attempt to internalize the character totally—they become 'them'. In sport we talk about 'intensity of focus'; the performer closes the world down to the immediate objectives of the contest. Incidentally, some opponents use gamesmanship tactics to break down that concentration. When we think of great tennis players like Laver, Ashe and Borg, we realize that when their focus was complete the 'strategies' of Nastase and Connors, although also great players, did not succeed.

Because so much of a person's role is visual, the easiest way to establish it is by observation or by attempting to recreate situations. This is also the best way to understand what can appear to be complicated hypotheses.

Investigation

17.13: Role play in sport

Case Study One

A PE teacher is teaching a group of children soccer. He is very keen to establish the spirit of the game as well as the rules, recognizing that the game, if played with a high moral content, might help to reinforce desirable values. The teacher knows that the game itself tests the self-control of the player; that in games against other schools there is the temptation to retaliate in reaction to fouls and gamesmanship; that the players have the professional game as their model and so may see their heroes practising gamesmanship (Figure 17.26).

1. Set up a role play situation where there is a teacher and a team of young players. The teacher explains why he intends to punish the players severely for any acts of gamesmanship or retaliation during a forthcoming game. Try to establish all the reasons why gamesmanship is counter-productive and anti-social, but encourage the players to voice their reasons for allowing it to take place.

2. Having done this, what would you say if one of the players claimed to have seen you, the PE teacher, playing in a club game on a Saturday afternoon, where you were sent off for a deliberate foul?

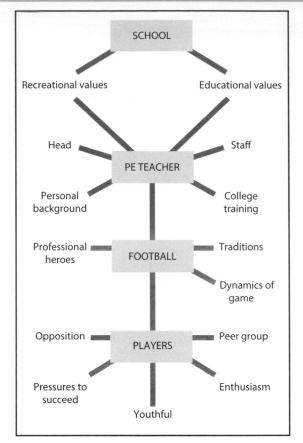

Figure 17.26 A sociogram for Case Study One, Investigation 17.13.

Case Study Two

A party of four are high on an isolated mountain in extreme winter conditions. The group has made camp in a snow hole to decide whether to make a final assault on the summit. The leader is very experienced, but willing to listen to the views of the others. The next most experienced person is a member of the opposite sex, suffering a little from mountain sickness. The third member of the party is young and aggressively headstrong.

Throughout the climb he has been difficult, unwilling to accept group decisions or the authority of the leader. There is a particularly dangerous rivalry between this young person and the second-in-command. The fourth person is the least experienced, and it is her first time ever in such difficult conditions. The leader has had a lot of problems with this person, who is completely lacking in confidence and desperately afraid (Figure 17.27).

Investigation

17.13 continued

1. Set up the four roles and engage the team in a discussion on whether to go for the summit. Before you start, try to establish the individual status of each member; establish their personal feelings and the levels of group responsibility felt by each one.

2. Let's presume the decision was to go for the top. Unfortunately, the experienced climber falls, breaks a leg and has internal bleeding. They manage to get back to the snow hole, but face a 12-hour journey, in white out conditions, to make it down. With only a day's emergency rations they have to decide what to do. The leader listens to the arguments and decides. The alternatives would seem to be: all stay; one or two go for help (but who?); three go, presumably leaving the injured one; or all struggle down with the injured person. Discuss these alternatives and the possible consequences of your decision.

Case Study Three

The coach of a mixed hockey squad is preparing her team for a major championship game. Together with two selectors, the coach watches a practice game and decides that the captain is so out of form that she will have to be dropped for the all-important game. The captain is recovering from injury, but has also suffered the anguish of a relative involved in a car crash. The members of the team have loyalties to their captain and their coach, but also a desire to win this championship game.

1. Set up a role play situation (see Figure 17.28).
2. When you have decided whether the captain should play or not, discuss the degree to which the coach's authority has been compromised if:
a. the game is won, either without the captain or with the captain;
b. the game is lost, either with the captain or without the captain.
Select one of these and act it out.

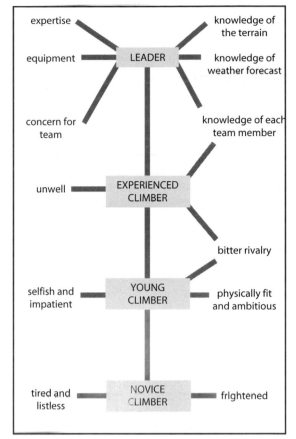

Figure 17.27 A sociogram for Case Study Two, Investigation 17.13.

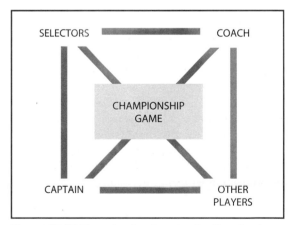

Figure 17.28 The role play situation for Case Study Three, Investigation 17.13.

Investigation

17.13 continued

3. As a result of this study of the coach, are you aware how many different roles she has to play in a situation like this? Each member of the group should take one of the roles shown in Figure 17.29 and explain how he/she would act given this problem with the captain.

The result of the two role play situations will be markedly different, depending on the role(s) the coach decides are most important for each occasion. The lesson to be learnt is that you may have many choices in the way you behave but, by internalizing and thinking through the consequences, your judgement can completely change the process and the product of any given sporting situation.

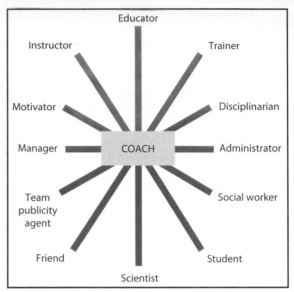

Figure 17.29 Roles of a coach.

The role of the coach

Armstrong (1984) in writing the *Effective Coaching* booklet for the National Coaching Foundation (NCF) Level 2 Programme, produced a series of role play situations which might serve to broaden the understanding of what might be expected of a coach in sport.

Coach and Chairperson of Selectors

The coach feels that she/he has too little say in selection, discussions and decisions, and that selectors do not really know what they are doing. There is a history of poor communication between them.

The Chairperson feels the coach is too autocratic and not sufficiently dispassionate. The Chairperson has years of experience.

Coach and captain

The coach is worried that the strong personality of the captain is undermining his/her authority—the captain is talking of alternative strategies to the players without acknowledging the coach.

The captain feels that the coach's knowledge is inadequate in certain respects and that the players know best because they are the ones facing the challenges.

Coach and physiotherapist

The coach is concerned that a performer is becoming psychologically dependent on the physiotherapist and treatment, and that his/her selection decisions are undermined by this.

The physiotherapist sticks to the point of view that medical assessment comes first to safeguard the future health of the athlete.

Coach and performer

The coach wants a full squad to attend a residential training weekend to help develop team cohesion, even though it is expensive.

The player lives locally and can accommodate a couple of others, all on student grants, and therefore does not see why they need to be resident.

Coach and referee

The coach has been asked by the squad to broach the subject of bias with one of the competition officials.

The official or referee defends his/her position as the objective arbiter of performance.

 Review Questions

1. How does the role of the PE teacher compare with the role of the sports coach?
2. With the professionalization of rugby union, how will the role of the amateur player differ from that of the professional player?
3. Compare the role of a teacher with an outdoor education group with the leader of an outdoor pursuit expedition.

Exam-Style Questions

1. The coach plays an important part in sport at all levels:

a. Use a swimming, athletics or gymnastics situation to explain the need for a coach to adopt the role of an instructor, a trainer and an educator. (6 marks)

b. There are always things to learn in coaching. Explain the roles of scientist and student which the coach might need to adopt in swimming, athletics or gymnastics to achieve effectiveness. (4 marks)

c. When you are coaching children, how would you balance discipline and motivation? (4 marks)

2. Sometimes the coach has to make difficult decisions to achieve short term objectives. How would you explain that your captain should stand down for an important match? (4 marks)

3. You are a PE teacher who expects a high standard of behaviour from the players in your school team.

a. On what grounds would you justify never condoning gamesmanship? (3 marks)

b. How would you explain being sent off in a week-end club game, when confronted with this by the school team on the following Monday. (4 marks) (Total 25 marks.)

Summary

Role play in sport:
1. Alternatives of **role theory** or **action theory**.

2. **Communication skills; sound knowledge skills; range of teaching styles; sensitivity** regarding the many roles required.

Further Reading

Armstrong M. *Effective Coaching*, Pack 13, NCF, 1984.

Baker W.J. *Sports in the Western World*, Rowman & Littlefield, 1982.

Calhoun D.W. *Sport, Culture and Personality*, Human Kinetics, 1987.

Coakley J.J. *Sport and Society: Issues and Controversies*, Mosby, 1982.

Cratty B.J. *Social Dimensions of Physical Activity*, Prentice Hall, 1967.

Dunlap H. Games, sports, dancing and other activities and their function in Samoan culture. In: Loy J. and Kenyon G. (eds) *Sport, Culture and Society*, Macmillan, 1969.

Dunning E. (ed) *Sociology of Sport*, Frank Cass, 1970.

Edwards H. *Sociology of Sport*, Dorsey, 1973.

Fox J.R. Pueblo basketball: a new use for old witchcraft. In: Loy J. and Kenyon G. (eds) *Sport, Culture and Society*, Macmillan, 1969.

Gardiner E.N. *Greek Athletic Sports and Festivals*, Brown, 1970.

Gleeson G. *The Growing Child in Competitive Sport*, Hodder & Stoughton, 1986.

Hendry L.B. The role of the PE teacher. *Education Review*, 1975; 17(2).

Hendry L.B. *School, Sport and Leisure*, Lepus, 1978.

Jones K. Polynesian games. Unpublished MA Thesis, University of Alberta, 1967.

Linton R.M. *The Study of Man*, Appleton-Century-Croft, 1936.

Loy J. and Kenyon G. *Sport, Culture and Society*, Macmillan, 1969.

Lüschen G. *Sociology of Sport*, Mouton, 1968.

Mason N.G. Towards a theory of group action. Research Papers in PE, Carnegie, July 1970.

Mead G.H. *Mind, Self, and Society*, University of Chicago, 1967.

Mills T.M. *The Sociology of Small Groups*, Prentice Hall, 1967.

Rees C.R. and Mirade A.W. (eds) *Sport and Social Theory*, Human Kinetics, 1986.

Riordan J. *Comparative PE and Sport*, vol 5, ISCPES, 1988.

Salter M. Games of the Australian Aborigines. Unpublished MA Thesis, University of Alberta, 1967.

Saunders E. and White G. *Social Investigations in PE & Sport*, Lepus, 1977.

Wohl A. Conception and range of sport sociology. *International Review of Sport Sociology*, 1966; 1.

Chapter 18

Some Contemporary Issues in Physical Education and Sport

The issues approach to the study of physical education and sport allows the student to use a range of disciplines to establish the root of a particular contested area. Having completed a contemporary analysis of any issue in our country, it is valuable to study it from the **historical** perspective, where focus would be on causation, or from the **comparative** perspective, where we might learn from studying other countries.

The suggested order of study is as follows:

- **The Issue**—The group needs to make a serious attempt to identify the different parameters of the problem.
- **Definitive**—Analysis should start by establishing the meaning of the main words being used to describe the problem. In each of the three examples in this chapter, this definitive aspect is covered in some detail, but each group should discuss the accuracy of the definitions being offered.
- **Structural framework**—You need a series of headings to work under, which outline the structural basis of the study area. Only the framework is offered here and so it is necessary for each group to collect and collate data which are specific to the particular problem area. Some of the information has been included in earlier parts of this text, but additional specialized articles and books need to be studied. For this reason a

specialized reading list is given with each topic; students should be encouraged to build files of contemporary articles; and the school should make use of the National Documentation Centre at Birmingham University.

- **Functional**—The data you have collected should also help you to explain *how* the issue operates in this country and you may wish also to consider how it functions in a number of other countries.
- **Cultural analysis**—Regardless of whether you embark on this comparative analysis, it is essential that you put the problem in a social setting. The 'cultural determinant' framework is offered to help you to explain how certain cultural factors might influence the problem.
- **Reformative**—Finally, it is important that you should be able to suggest a series of reform procedures. This may be reorganizing your own country's policy, provision and administration, or may involve the introduction of certain ideas used abroad. The important point here is to recognize the problems which might be associated with the recommended changes.

Issues seem to exist at three main levels: **social**, **institutional** and **subcultural**. A sample issue in each of these has been selected for examination together with a list of alternative topics.

18.1 Societal: Excellence in Sport

The issue

There is a debate on the social ethics of elitism in sport: whether emphasis should be placed on the success of a few over participation by the majority. At an administrative level, the issue is whether a particular society has right balance or whether we can learn from the policies and procedures of other countries.

A structural dynamic of sport is shown in Figure 18.1.

Definitive

For **excellence** to be achieved a high level of **commitment**, **resources** and **expertise** is necessary from each group involved.

Excellence

This is the objective assessment of **quality**. Though in sport the end product is the level of performance in competition, it should not be separated from the support role played by coaches, supporters and administrators.

This can be **elitist** in the sense that certain privileged individuals are given opportunities not available to the majority. If the reward is sufficient, societies may accept this social inequality. If everyone has the opportunity in terms of selection, where the talented are given every opportunity to attain their optimum level of achievement, this is a form of meritocracy which is widely accepted. This justifies rewards given to a few as a result of open selection.

There is an alternative, personalized notion that any enthusiast who achieves his/her optimum level of performance is on an excellence continuum. Where this view is individualized we have a Western cultural analysis; where it is collectivized, as in communist cultures, the society is presumed to reap the reward.

Status

A great deal depends on the status of sport in a society. Where there is a recognition of the cultural

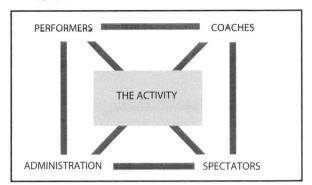

Figure 18.1 Structural dynamic of sport.

importance of sport at national, political and commercial levels, the ideological and financial support will be greater.

The status of the performer is also important. In a country where professionalism exists with high financial rewards, and where the professionals are drawn from the middle class, there is high status. Where there is a strong amateur tradition involving the middle classes, the same may apply, but, in financial terms, the performers may be left to their own resources and prestige may exist only at a personal level (Figure 18.2). However, where amateurism is strongly reinforced by state aid and political significance, the status of the performer will be high.

Figure 18.2 Commitment and pain may be the price of success.

Structure

This is outlined in Figure 18.3.

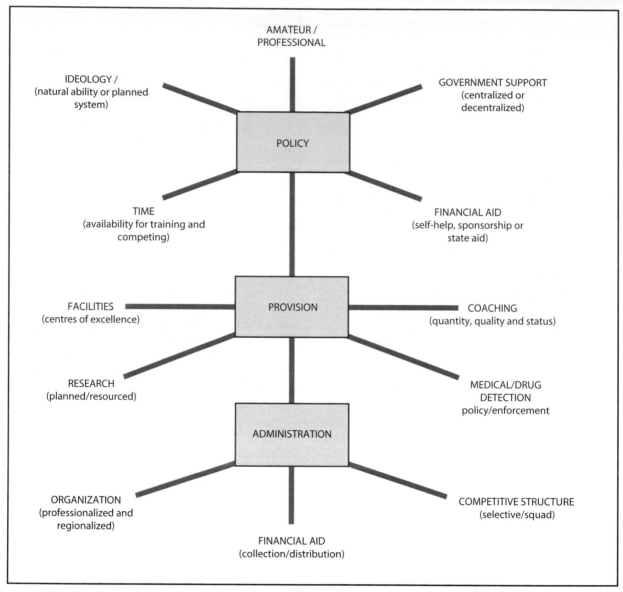

Figure 18.3 Structure of sport.

Function

Policy and practice for children

1. Preparation for excellence in curriculum PE.
2. Extracurricular programmes for excellence.
3. The sports school in operation.

Youth opportunities and the Olympic Reserve

1. Club and/or community facilities for youth excellence.
2. Industrial provision for youth excellence.
3. Higher education and sporting excellence.

Organization and Sporting Excellence

1. Efficiency of the administrative framework for selection.
2. Distribution of financial aid.
3. Equality and use of Centres of Excellence and other facilities.

Status and human factors

1. Effects of status on development.
2. Level of opportunity and esteem for performers. The temptations of drug abuse.
3. Preparation and proliferation of coaches.

Investigation

18.1: Centres of Excellence

Figures 18.4–18.6 reflect excellence: the organization and performance standard of the Tour de France; the Astrodome as an outstanding facility; and a Soviet sports school. What is there in the UK to compare with these?

Figure 18.5 Astrodome in the USA.

Figure 18.6 A sports school in the former Soviet Union.

Figure 18.4 The Tour de France cycle race.

Cultural determinants

Some major determinants are shown in Figure 18.7.

If ONE of these sub-systems is analysed, such as **ranking structure**, it will become clear how much additional knowledge is required to understand links between a problem in sport and the society in which it exists.

Ranking structure

This refers to the status of specific groups of people in a society. Arguably, in the egalitarian Soviet society efforts were made to live up to a socialist philosophy by giving everyone equal opportunity, but history has shown us that the political ideal is not always achieved. In European countries like France and Britain there is a very powerful democratic ideal, but tradition tends to give certain groups an advantage which they try to retain. Thirdly, it is important to recognize that in addition to some people starting off with an advantage, abilities and attitudes vary, and so, in a 'free' society, able people 'get on' better than those who are less able. In economic terms, a capitalist market economy encourages this and so status is fluid,

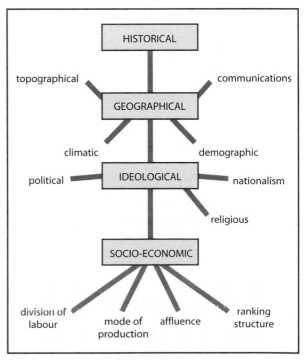

Figure 18.7 Cultural determinants.

reflecting the material success of an individual, which brings them cultural as well as material advantages. American society does have strong 'ranking', explained in the initials WASP (White Anglo-Saxon Protestant) and can be defined as 'hegemony', but allows more opportunities for 'excellence' to be achieved through the ideological support given to opportunism—as they would say 'rags-to-riches'.

Social ranking, therefore, is one of the major factors that determines the opportunity to participate in sport—adequate access to provisions for sport and sufficient self-esteem and social acceptability to enter fully into a high-level sports programme.

The suggestion is that, in an unequal society, certain groups find it difficult to play a full part in sport: that society is **ranked** according to **status**. This may be the consequence of restrictions put on these groups by the dominant groups or reflect a lack of confidence or affluence among the members of that minority group.

In Britain, there is the traditional influence of **social class** which lies at the root of most discrimination, but **gender** bias is also the result of values cemented in Victorian tradition.

Many Afro-Caribbeans and Asians have settled in Britain in the past 45 or so years, and have tended to move into an industrial working class social stratum, which combines the existing class discrimination with the additional problems of occupational rivalry and racism. These negatives are made worse for females, because ethnic minorities tend to retain their own cultural taboos in an adopted social system which already discriminates against females. This is a particularly powerful factor when **religion** also plays a part in gender roles.

Sport, particularly high-level sport, has always been dominated by the dynamic **young** male adult and, consequently, **age**, particularly in the case of the very young and the elderly, has also been a target for discrimination. Young people are often exploited to achieve excellence or are excluded because adults find their presence disruptive. Older people suffer from the accusation of 'being over the top' and there are still only a few sports where 'veteran' events are actively encouraged. 'Lifetime Sport' is a concept which has still to be fully realized in Britain.

Finally, elite sport is normally focused on **physical ability**, resulting in anyone who is not able-bodied being discriminated against. The notion of 'a disabled person being handicapped by society' is one which suggests that discrimination is not limited to sport: in fact sport offers a solution to the problem of people being handicapped by a disability through contests where individuals are able to test themselves against their peers.

Class, gender, age and disability: these are the factors by which our social system classifies and stratifies, ranking individuals and, in so doing, influencing their likelihood of achieving excellence in sport. It is equally important to recognize that the Sports Council's target groups also reflect this social ranking and as a result highlight the constraints operating against the successful implementation of a Sport for All policy.

Reformative
Development potential
1. What might we usefully consider at school level?
2. What youth policies abroad could help in Britain?
3. What organizational and financial improvements might the British adopt?
4. How might we change things at a personal and status level?

Constraints which might operate
1. Cultural resistance to the imposition of foreign methods.
2. Unacceptable influence on the status quo.

Final comments
The model used for this analysis should be adaptable for any national policy or campaign (Figure 18.8).

In addition the framework allows other societal issues to be analysed, such as Sport for All, Recreation and the Countryside, and Health and Exercise.

As a thematic component, it is essential that other parts of this textbook are used to increase understanding and to give supportive information. For example, the issue cannot be understood without clear conceptual understanding; determinants may include physiological variables and so there must be an accurate input from the biological sciences; and it may be advantageous to use your knowledge of other countries to clarify the issue.

Finally, the exposure of a societal issue is bound to take you into more specific issues. These may be institutional or sub-cultural frameworks and an outline of these follows on from this section, but they can also be specific problems which require special analysis. The national lottery and its distribution; professionalism and elite performance; media and sport; advertising and the star performer; and drugs and sport, for example, warrant more than a passing mention and require the knowledge necessary to enable understanding of the more general issue of **excellence**. In order to open some of these doors, a relatively simple outline can frame the issue and enable knowledge to be added as required (Figures 18.9–18.12).

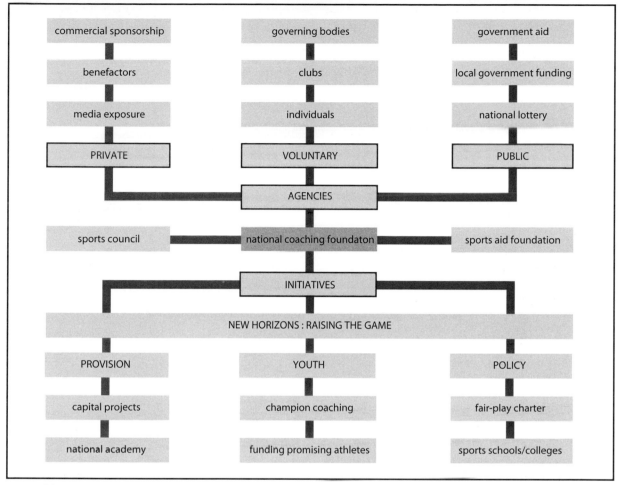

Figure 18.8 Raising the Game: sponsorship, agencies and initiatives.

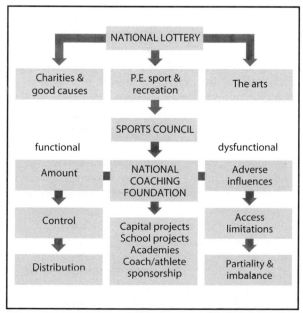

Figure 18.9 National Lottery and its distribution.

Figure 18.10 Professionalism and elite performance.

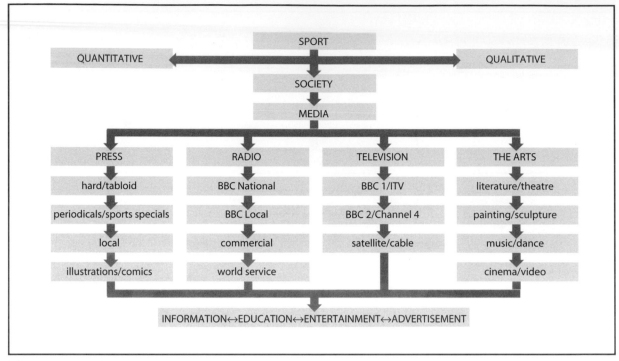

Figure 18.11 Media and sport.

These frameworks can only act as a starting point and it is necessary to produce a more detailed analysis even before supportive information can be added. An example of this second phase is reflected in Figure 18.13, a conceptual map for **drugs and sport**, produced by Glen Cummins in 1993.

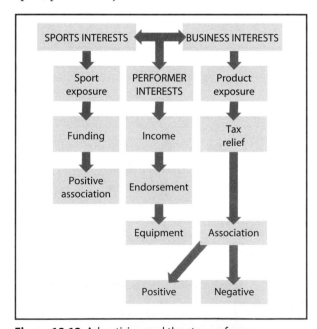

Figure 18.12 Advertising and the star performer.

Review Questions

1. Use a particular sport to show the extent to which excellence is being achieved as a result of elitist ideology, administrative structure and coaching expertise in the UK.

2. Examine the extent to which Sport for All remains a myth in this country given limits in opportunity, provision and esteem.

3. Discuss the use of drugs as a sport issue, which involves the notion of cheating and the risk to health and identity.

4. Advertising can make a star athlete little more than a bill-board, where product association can undermine the performer and the sport. Discuss.

5. The media serves its audience, but not always the interests of the sport. Discuss.

6. Rugby Union is going down a new path to professionalism. Explain the opportunities and pitfalls ahead.

7. Analyse the proposed 1996 initiatives to improve the standard of sport in the UK.

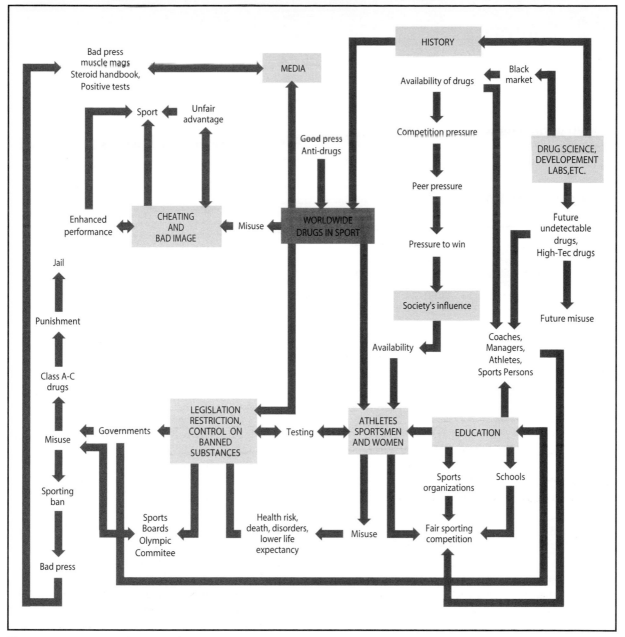

Figure 18.13 Drugs and sport. (*After Cummins, 1993.*)

 Exam-Style Questions

1. To achieve excellence in sport, a high level of commitment, resources and expertise is necessary.
a. Explain these three conditions, using illustrations from your own experience in sport. (6 marks)
b. What is meant when a sport organization is said to be elitist? Explain this in the context of a games club. (4 marks)
2. The National Coaching Foundation and the Sports Aid Foundation are agencies designed to improve standards in British sport. Explain how they attempt to achieve this and the constraints they face. (8 marks)
3. Even in the UK not all games have the same opportunity to achieve excellence. Why is it that badminton appears to attract far less money than tennis in Britain, but neither seem able to produce world champions? (7 marks)
(Total 25 marks.)

Summary

Societal issues:
1. **Structure, function** and **cultural determinants**.
2. **Campaigns** and **policies**; **Excellence** and **sport** or **Sport for All**. Specific issues within these general topics.

3. **Policy**—ideology, government initiatives, public attitude, financial aid, time availability.
4. **Provision**—facilities, coaching, research, medical back-up.
5. **Administration**—organization, financial distribution, competitions, agencies.

Further Reading

Anthony D. *A Strategy for British Sport*, Hurst, 1980.
Calhoun D.W. *Sport, Culture & Personality*, Human Kinetics, 1987.
Cashmore E. *Making Sense of Sport*, Routledge, 1990.
Coakley J.J. *Sport in Society: Issues and Controversies*, Times Mirror/Mosby, 1986.
Coe S. *et al. More than a Game*, BBC, 1992.
Cummins G. *Drugs in Sport Project*, Manchester Metropolitan University, 1993.
Dunning E.G. *et al.* (eds) *The Sports Process*, Human Kinetics, 1993.
Elias N. and Dunning E. *Quest for Excitement*, Blackwell, 1986.
French Information. *125 Sports in France*, French Embassy, 1985.
Hargreaves J. *Sport, Power and Culture*, Polity Press, 1986.
Hemery D. *Sporting Excellence*, Willow, 1986.
Hoolihan B. *The Government and Politics of Sport*, Routledge, 1991.
Hoolihan B. *Sport and International Politics*, Harvester

Wheatsheaf, 1994.
Humphreys J.H.L. French sports hot house. *BJPE*, 1979; 10(1).
Lapchick RE. *Sport in Society*, Sage, 1996.
Lawton J. *The All American War Game*, Basil Blackwell, 1984.
Macfarlane N. *Sport and Politics*, Willow, 1986.
McPherson B.D. *et al. The Social Significance of Sport*, Human Kinetics, 1989.
Nixon H.L. *Sport and the American Dream*, Leisure Press, 1984.
Riordan J. *Sport in Soviet Society*, Cambridge University Press, 1977.
Sage G.H. *Power and Ideology in American Sport*, Human Kinetics, 1990.
Sports Council. *Into the 90s*, Sports Council, 1988.
Sports Council. *New Horizons*, Sports Council, 1995.
Walton G.M. *Beyond Winning*, Leisure Press, 1992.

18.2 Institutional: Outdoor Education

The Issue

There is an accountability argument as to whether the expense and time needed for outdoor education are justified by the experience it offers. It might be suggested that the objectives would be better served through a recreational programme. At an administrative level, the issue is whether a particular society's outdoor education programme can be improved by looking at other systems.

Definitive

Formal education

This is an **institutional** focus. Concern is with what happens in a school or college. It may be part of the curriculum or part of the intramural or extracurricular activity of the institution.

Informal education

A broader concept of education acknowledges that there is a form of social education operating when recreational **institutions** exist to promote a particular

life-style, where the outcome may be a transmission of desirable cultural values.

Outdoor education

This is a means of approaching educational or cultural objectives through direct experiences in the natural environment, using its resources as learning materials.

In all recent school curriculum documents, the term **outdoor adventurous education** has been used. This may be to avoid some outdoor activity being wrongly assigned, but it also identifies the focus of the activities. There are occasions where very young children may go no farther than the playground to taste adventurous activity and in these cases the natural hazardous environment is replaced by contrived challenging situations.

Outdoor pursuits

These are physical activities in the natural environment which place the individual in decision-making adventure situations, and as such are a central part of outdoor education.

Vacation camps

Though recreational, these offer adventure situations in the natural environment and indirectly promote the same values as outdoor education centres.

Escape

There is a strong feeling of escape: from work, from urban existence, as a holiday; as a return to rural simplicity and basic survival; as a return to one's cultural roots; but also as romantic and/or religious awareness of natural beauty, which is an escape to enlightenment.

Desired values

These are outlined in Figure 18.14.

Structural

These are outlined in Figure 18.15.

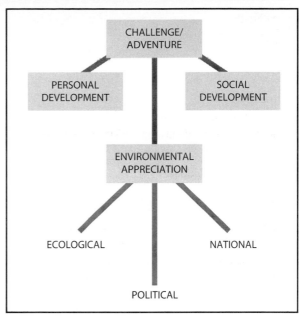

Figure 18.14 Desired values of outdoor education.

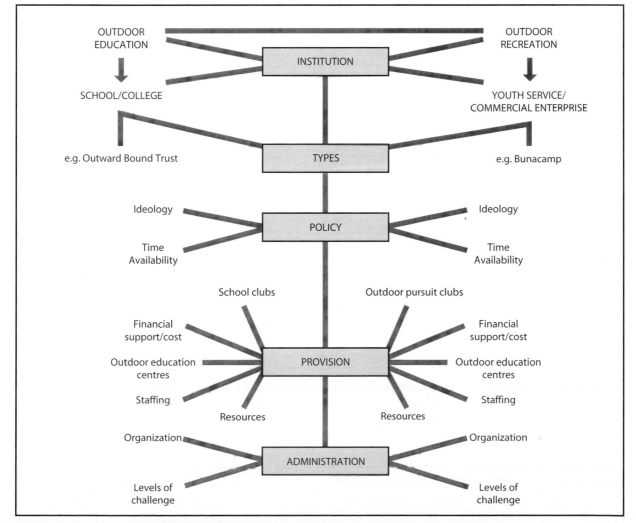

Figure 18.15 Structure of outdoor education.

Function

Policy and practice in the schools

1. Outdoor activity curriculum programmes in primary, secondary and higher education departments.

2. Extracurricular and/or intramural clubs in outdoor activities.

3. Schools and/or colleges with special interests in outdoor activities, e.g. Gordonstoun and Charlotte Mason College (Lancaster University).

Policy and practice in Outdoor Education Centres

1. Outdoor centres belonging to specific schools.

2. Local government outdoor education centres.

3. National Outdoor Education Centres, e.g. Plas y Brenin and Holme Pierrepont.

4. Outward Bound Trust and other adventure schools, e.g. Aberdovey.

Policy and practice of specific associations and schemes

1. Youth associations and their facilities, e.g. Scouts, Pioneers, etc.

2. Adventure youth schemes, e.g. Duke of Edinburgh Award.

Organization of outdoor recreation holiday schemes

1. State-sponsored outdoor facilities, e.g. Pioneer Camps, USSR, and Colonie de Vacance, France.

2. Commercially sponsored facilities, e.g. Manor Adventure, UK, and Bunacamp, USA.

Organization of natural areas of beauty

1. Administration of national and local parks.

2. Promotion of conservation.

Cultural determinants

These are outlined in Figure 18.16.

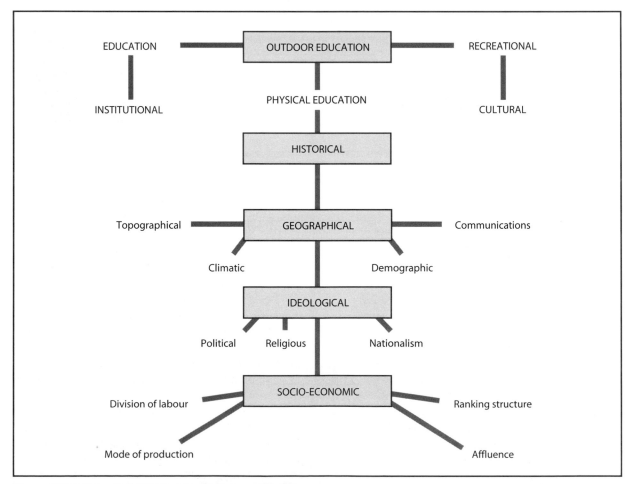

Figure 18.16 Cultural determinants of outdoor education.

Reformative

Developmental potential

1. Can we improve the relationship between physical education and outdoor education?

2. How might we usefully improve outdoor education in and around the school?

3. How might the function of outdoor education centres be improved?

4. How might we extend special schools?

5. How might we broaden opportunities for summer camps and winter holidays for children?

6. How might we communicate the message of conservation more effectively?

 ## Investigation

Figure 18.17 An adventure situation on the Colorado.

18.2: Outdoor education institutions

What are the fundamental differences between a camp school and an Outward Bound School in the USA, and how did these compare with a Soviet pioneer camp (Figures 18.17 and 18.18)?

Figure 18.18 Orlyonok camp on the Black Sea.

Constraints which might operate

1. Limits imposed by our educational and physical educational philosophies and administrations.

2. Cultural resistance to the introduction of foreign methods.

3. Limits imposed by the geographical determinants.

Final comments

There appears to be a serious attempt to educate young people to respect and conserve the natural environment. This education is particularly necessary in a world which is becoming increasingly materialistic and where population expansion puts the natural environment at risk. In a world which is being increasingly urbanized and technological, there is a need for a renaissance of rusticity on the one hand and the opportunity for adventure on the other.

The model used for this analysis should be adaptable to any major institutional issue. It need not be limited to education, but could focus on industry or the armed forces, where one facet of an institution may have to operate alongside others.

There are a number of **educational issues** which are worthy of analysis. Most of these are linked with **sport education**, a term used regularly in Australia and reflecting the place of **sport** on the school curriculum. Champion Coaching, Sports Schools, Olympic Youth Camps, and Raising the Game are UK policies and programmes which have yet to be fully rationalized. Alternatively, there are major areas of education which can be looked at, such as undergraduate programmes, teacher training, play and nursery education, and coach education. Finally, there are other institutions which involve physical education and sports issues, such as sport and the Army, sport and industry, sports' injuries and physiotherapy.

Review Questions

1. Justify the inclusion of Outdoor Adventurous Education on the National Physical Education Curriculum in the UK.

2. What progressions would you expect to see in programmes in Outdoor Adventurous Education from key stage 1 to A-Level Physical Education (OCEAC)?

3. Explain the qualities of the Champion Coaching Project as the first step towards an integrated programme of **sport education**.

4. Discuss the potential and constraints of the John Major Initiative as identified in *Sport: Raising the Game* (DNH, 1995).

5. Discuss the modularization and study of **sport** and **physical education** in Higher Education.

 Exam-Style Questions

1. Many people have classified different sports by identifying certain characteristics which they feel are central components. P.C. McIntosh suggested that there were five key characteristics: competition, combat, conquest, aesthetic and chance.

a. Explain a canoeing or climbing **outdoor pursuit** in the context of conquest. (4 marks)

b. In the context of this outdoor pursuit, explain the potential existence of the other four characteristics. (5 marks)

2. According to the Leeds Study Group (1970) **physical education** is an area of educational activity in which the main concern is with bodily movement:

a. Given that this suggests both physical development and the development of temperament, explain the particular contribution outdoor education can make within the physical education programme. (4 marks)

b. You are leading a group of young people on a canoeing or climbing expedition. Explain the difference between real and perceived risk. (4 marks)

3. The high population density of the UK results in a conflict between different agencies in the countryside. Identify the problems and suggest strategies for:

a. Problems arising in outdoor adventurous activities which have to share limited provision. (3 marks)

b. The potential conflicts between **recreation** and **conservation**. (5 marks)

(Total 25 marks.)

 Summary

Institutional issues:

1. Concepts of outdoor education and physical education; formal and informal education; sport, conservation and escapism.

2. Variables include institutions, systems, policies, provision and administrations.

3. Functional problems include cost and time.

4. Cultural determinants include geographical factors, ideology and socio-economic variables.

Further Reading

Almond L. et al. An Introduction to Implementing the Physical Education Curriculum: A Practical Guide. Loughborough, 17878/159, 1994.

Bacon W. (ed) Leisure and Learning in the 1980s, LSA, 1981.

Bank J. Outdoor development. Leadership & Organization Development Journal, 1983; 4(3).

Department of Education and Science. Learning Out of Doors, HMSO, 1983.

DNH. Sport: Raising the Game, Department of National Heritage, 1995.

DSE. Physical and Sport Education for Victorian Schools, Directorate of School Education, 1993.

Gray D. Access to open country. Sport & Recreation, 1977; 18(3).

Johnson A. School it isn't: education it is. School Sport, 1979; 4(4).

JOHPER (editorials) Intramurals, JOHPER, February 1983; Leisure & tourism, JOHPER, April 1983; Family recreation, JOHPER, October 1984; Leisure today, JOHPER, October 1988.

Lombardo M.S. and Groves D.L. Content and process for outdoor education. JOHPER, March 1978.

Manor Adventure (brochure). The Manor, Craven Arms, Shropshire, 1997.

Mortlock C. The Adventure Alternative, Cicerone, 1984.

NCF. The Story of Champion Coaching, National Coaching Foundation, 1992.

Parker T.M. and Meldrum K.I. Outdoor Education, Dent, 1973.

Rhudy E. An alternative to outward bound programmes. JOHPER, January 1979.

Recommended Periodicals
Jeunesse au Plein Air
JOHPER
Outdoors (PEA.)
Sport in the USSR

18.3 Subcultural: Women in Sport

The Issue
In many societies women do not have an equal opportunity to participate in sport. It is necessary to tease out the desired differences in role from culturally induced discrimination and to look at other countries to see if we can learn from them.

Definitive
It is important to recognize that this is not fundamentally a sport issue, but a case of social inequality which also manifests itself in sport.

The physiological differences between males and females are the source of sexual stereotyping, but cultural traditions and trends distort and exaggerate the male and female roles in society to the extent that basic freedoms are denied.

Where social inequality exists, the forces of a democratic society can press for reform. However, an additional problem exists when social inequality is justified on biological grounds and a policy is enacted which presumes women's predisposition for certain sports.

In Britain for example, the resistance to women's soccer is based on traditional stereotyping and the conservatism of the Football Association (FA). This does not appear to be the case in the USA, where the game is played by both sexes largely because it is a recent innovation and does not rival the prestigious male preserve of grid iron football. In the former Soviet Union, the 'official' view was that women's soccer was physiologically harmful and morally degrading, and every effort is made to discourage it. The view that certain sports undermine femininity is the most difficult to overcome, because it often has the support of many women.

The differentiation of sex roles in society stems from the traditional notion of family life. This tradition recognizes the role of the woman as a wife and mother, where her leisure time is committed to home and family. Though it was, originally, very much a middle-class concept, it became a feature of the respectable working class family, replacing the survival role of the wife as a bread-winner. The development of this stereotype coincided with the emergence of modern sport and this resulted in a dominance by men. However, career women now render the stereotype outmoded.

It is easy to see this as a female problem, but when sex discrimination operates it can result in constraints on males as well as females, as certain sports are considered feminine and so unsuitable for men.

It is this feminine stereotype in sport and society at large which prevents freedom of the individual to operate and so 'Women in Sport' will remain an issue until every person is free to participate in a full range of sports with equal support from the community.

There are a number of routes which may be taken to increase female opportunity in sport. The right to participate could include the right to remain separate from mixed sport, but the choice must be available to the individual. The American Title IX legislation (1972) presumed that for children to have an equal opportunity in an unequal culture, physical education had to be co-educational. The problem with a categorical decision like this is that it stimulates a counteraction from male teachers, who see sports standards slipping. The fact that Title IX applies only to federally aided institutions also presents another anomaly.

There are a large number of myths about the capacity of women to cope in sport. Many of these are being refuted, as illustrated by the successful inclusion of a women's marathon in the 1988 Olympic Games, but it is a slow process of eroding traditional attitudes. In Britain, the Equal Pay Act (1970) and the Sex Discrimination Act (1975) now allow women in sport to go to court if their rights are abused, but it is important to recognize that sex discrimination in itself is not unlawful, only instances where discrimination creates financial consequences. In addition, Section 44 makes concessions in cases:

> *Where the physical strength, stamina or physique of the average woman puts her at a disadvantage to the average man ... as a competitor ...*

This clause may have been designed to protect the female, but can be used to exclude her (Figure 18.19). Similarly, Rule 29 of the Olympic Charter (1983) states that female competitors must be registered female. These so-called sex tests may have been designed to protect genuine female competitors, but feminists might want to know why males should not also be tested.

Figure 18.19 Don't get carried away by all this. Women can use a hammer, but they are still not allowed to throw it!

Structure
This is outlined in Figure 18.20.

Function
It is worthwhile to consider function in terms of the UK, France, the USA, Australia and the former Soviet Union.

Policy and practice in school PE programmes
1. Inequalities in the PE curriculum.
2. Inequalities in extracurricular sport.
3. Inequalities in outdoor education.

Policy and practice in Sport for All programmes
1. Differences in proportional involvement.
2. Differences in the availability of facilities.
3. Differences in the variety of activities.

Policy and practice in sports excellence programmes
1. Variations in selection and coaching.
2. Variations in the distribution of financial aid and income.
3. Variations in career possibilities in sport.

Organizational inequalities
1. Sporting activities not open to females.
2. Sporting activities where sexes are not mixed.
3. Sporting activities where female involvement is taboo.

Cultural determinants
These are outlined in Figure 18.21.

Reformative
Developmental potential
1. What might we usefully change at school level?
2. What organizational and financial improvements might we adopt?
3. How might we change things at a personal and status level?

Reformative?

It takes a great deal of courage and independence to decide to design your own image instead of the one that society rewards, but it gets easier as you go along.

Germaine Greer, *The Female Eunuch*, 1971.

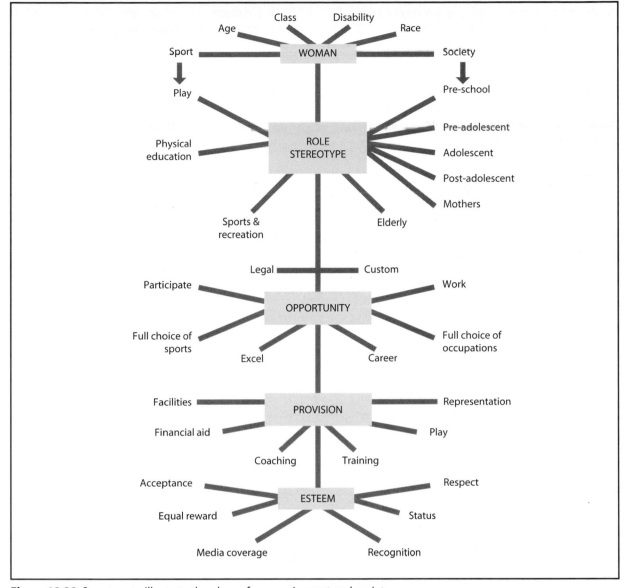

Figure 18.20 Structure to illustrate the place of women in sport and society.

Constraints which might operate

1. Cultural resistance to the imposition of foreign methods.
2. Unacceptable influence on the status quo.

Final comments

The right of the individual to a free choice of legitimate activities or life-styles is a cornerstone of a free society. As yet these rights are not being observed in the context of women in sport. Even if social attitudes are slow to change, there can be no excuse for administrative and financial discrimination to operate. The different contribution that men and women bring to sport enriches the total experience. What is at fault is the singular stereotype of what it is to be a sportsperson.

The model used for this analysis should be adaptable to any major area of discrimination in physical education, sport or outdoor recreation. Other recommended issues for study in this category are ethnic minorities, people with special needs, opportunities for the unemployed, social class discrimination, opportunities for the elderly, potential abuse of young people and regional discrimination. It is essential to acknowledge, however, that these exist on an opportunity ladder, sometimes called cultural stacking, whereby multiples of problems arise—for example, an elderly woman with special needs meets problems from three sources at least (see Further Reading).

Finally, although these are contemporary problems in our society, the source of the issue lies in the past and the solution may lie in other countries, so you must use knowledge from historical and comparative sources to help produce reformative strategies.

There are a number of theoretical principles which need to be explored in the context of sub-cultures and sub-systems in the context of inequality:

1. No **culture** is homogeneous and even within egalitarian societies inequalities are either caused by unfair **systems** or by advantaged attitudes of certain individuals and **sub-cultures**; this is normally reflected in **sport**. This social phenomena is called **hegemony**.

2. The British upper class is traditionally so privileged that they do not enter the public arena in society or sport.

3. The **advantaged** public group in society and sport is the 23–30-year-old **white, able-bodied, middle-class male**.

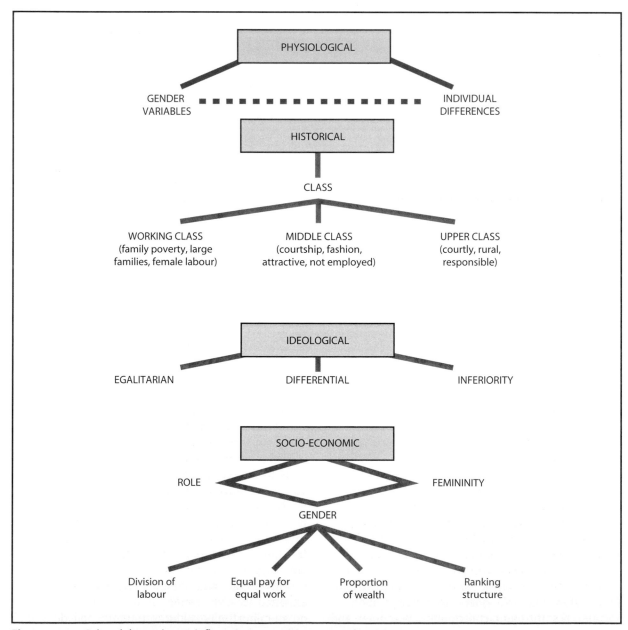

Figure 18.21 Cultural determinants influencing women in sport and society.

4. This gives us a number of disadvantaged sub-cultures: young and elderly, women. disabled, a variety of ethnic minorities and individuals and families caught in a poverty trap as members of the so-called working classes and/or unemployed.

5. To investigate these disadvantaged sub-cultures the three main dimensions are constraints on **opportunity**, **provision** and **esteem**.

6. Recognize the two-way process of society imposing sanctions on certain people, but also on certain people acquiescing in an acceptance of inferiority **or** claiming to be different **or** claiming disinterest.

7. The **radical** group within a disadvantaged sub-culture is often quite small because of the risk of ridicule and isolation.

8. There will always be resistance from a **conservative** elite who will lose advantage by accepting equality. Radicals suggest that this may arise from feelings of inferiority if the traditional advantages are removed.

9. Though not mentioned, **cultural tradition** and **religion** can also play a major part as illustrated by the limited number of **Moslem women** who participate in **sport** in this country.

10. Recognize that discrimination seldom comes singly: **women** in **sport** are disadvantaged, but don't forget the **young girl** or **elderly woman**; or the **woman** from a poor family; the **black woman**; or the **disabled woman**; and perhaps worst of all the **battered woman**. Each constraining feature reduces opportunity and self-esteem.

 ## Review Questions

These have been directed towards physical education, but could be adjusted to review subcultural influences on sport and recreation in society.

1. **Girls and physical education in schools.**
a. What are the links between self-esteem and girls' reluctance to participate in school sport?
b. What is the place of rugby football for girls in the PE curriculum?
c. Can girls throw or not?
d. Is there a possibility that girls are threatening the notion that sport makes boys into men in school PE?
e. Is separatism the answer for girls' PE?

2. **Ethnic minorities and physical education in schools.**
a. What do you say to the young Afro-Caribbean child during the swimming lesson?
b. How do you rationalize the problem of teaching Moslem girls to swim?
c. Can you separate society from culture and explain the case of a Pakistani child supporting the Pakistan cricket team when they are on tour in this country?
d. What effect does Linford Christie have on the aspirations of black schoolboys?
e. How is physical education countering the resistance to the production of male Asian footballers and female Asian hockey players?

3. **Young children and sporting excellence.**
a. What are the problems of early specialization in tennis and why do we do it?
b. What are the dangers of training methods used by some gymnastic coaches and some PE teachers?

c. Can we be physical educators and teach gamesmanship in our extra-curricular sessions?
d. What are the risks we are taking when we treat children like little adults?
e. What are the advantages of integrating recreative notions of play with educative notions of personal development?

4. **Disability and adaptive physical education.**
a. Integration or separation in physical education: what are the pros and cons?
b. Explain the reasons for allowing an able-bodied tennis player to play a wheelchair player.
c. What are your experiences of limitations of **access** for an impaired person in a PE, school or sport situation?
d. What are your views on the encouragement of wheelchair basketball for the able-bodied in any club you run?
e. To what extent does a child with impairments suffer from 'a cycle of oppression' in his/her experience of sport in school?

Some problems occur because disadvantaged sub-cultures do not easily adjust into society, so some groups are not directly involved in formal schooling and thus some additional questions arise.

5. **The elderly and sport.**
a. Should we attempt to integrate **or** separate elderly people who wish to be physically active?
b. How can we separate the elderly from the stereotype often held in sport?
c. How might the notion of **veteran** in sport enhance the club scene?
d. Examine the presumptions that to be elderly is to be senile.

Review Questions

continued

e. What strategies can we adopt to establish a lifetime sport concept for all citizens?

6. Some mixed 'smart' questions in sport.

a. Young at heart is not a question of chronological age in sport. Discuss.

b. 'Let's not patronize people by watering down able-bodied sports, but allow an alternative focus to evolve.' Discuss.

c. What are the genuine links between the athletic and the cosmetic in female sport?

d. 'Let's escape from the constraints of centrality and stacking and allow people to follow their inclinations and talents in sport.' Discuss.

  Some of the answers may lie in looking at the privileged group in our society, i.e. wealthy young white males and their masculine identity in sport.

7. a. To what extent is **sport** a social construction of **masculinity**?

b. Can it be true that **sport** turns boys into men?

c. Muscles and morality: does the achievement of manhood involve physical prowess combined with moral integrity?

d. Masculine or **effeminate**? Does **sport** empower young men to demonstrate force and physical skill (manliness from experiencing their bodies in action) as against sensitivity and appearance which dictates femininity (leading to the demeaning and objectifying of women)?

e. Is it really a question of male vulnerability and is there a basic case of women threatening men's traditional roles in our society in the name of sporting equality?

 Exam-Style Questions

1. The Sports Council released figures in 1982 which suggested that the relative popularity of sport varied within different socio-economic groups. Suggest reasons why the middle-class professional group has participated in sport more than members of the unskilled group. (4 marks)

2. The Sports Council uses the term **target group** in encouraging Sport for All.

a. What is the meaning of the term **target group** and identify sections of the community who fit into it. (4 marks)

b. What are the strategies recommended by the Sports Council? (4 marks)

3. The concept of excellence in sport is often accused of being elitist—it can mean that certain groups of people are disadvantaged.

a. Select one such group and explain how their access is limited in terms of reaching the top in sport. (4 marks)

b. Explain the part played by self-esteem and role modelling in influencing participation at the top level by your chosen group. Use a sporting example to illustrate your answer. (4 marks)

4. Discuss the cultural factors which are responsible for such inequalities still existing in sport in the UK. Refer to any disadvantaged group in your answer. (5 marks)

(Total 25 marks.)

Summary

Sub-cultural issues:
1. **Race, class, gender, special needs, age**, etc. may cause problems because of **discrimination**.
2. **Role stereotypes and variations in** **opportunity, provision and esteem** may cause inequality.
3. **Positive discrimination** might be a short-term possibility.

Further Reading

Age
Gleeson G. *The Growing Child in Competitive Sport,* Hodder & Stoughton, 1986.
Grisogono V. *Children and Sport*, John Murray, 1991.
Sports Council. *Young People and Sport,* Policy Document, 1993.

Disability
Butterfield S.A. PE and sport for the deaf. *Adapted Physical Activity Quarterly*, 1991; 8.
Department of the Environment. *Sport for People with Disabilities*, HMSO, 1989.
National Coaching Foundation. *Coaching People with a Disability*, NCF, 1990.

Race
Allison L. (ed) *The Politics of Sport*, Manchester University Press, 1986.
Cashmore E. *Black Sportsmen*, Routledge & Kegan Paul, 1982.
Sports Council N.W. *Sport and Racial Equality*, Sports Council, 1991.

Women
Blue A. *Grace under Pressure*, Sidgwick & Jackson, 1987.
Fletcher S. *Women First: The Female Tradition in English Physical Education, 1890–1990*, Athlone Press, 1984.
Geadelmann P.L. *Equality in Sport for Women*, American Association of Health, Physical Education and Recreation, 1977.

Gerber E.W. *et al. The American Woman in Sport*, Addison Wesley, 1974.
JOHPER (editorial) The role of women in sports. *JOHPER*, March 1986.
Lenskiyj H. *Out of Bounds. Women, Sport and Sexuality*, Toronto, The Women's Press, 1986.
Mangan J.A. and Park R.J. *From 'Fair Sex' to Feminism*, Frank Cass, 1987.
Oglesby C.A. *Women and Sport*, Lea & Febiger, 1978.
Pannick D. *Sex Discrimination in Sport*, Equal Opportunities Commission, 1983.
Perchenok Y. *Women in the USSR*, Novosti Press, 1985.
Riordan J. *Sport in Soviet Society*, Cambridge University Press, 1977.
Sport & Leisure Supplement. *Women in Sport, People with Disabilities, Young People and Sport (Policy and Frameworks for Action)*, Sports Council, 1994.
Talbot M. *Women and Leisure*, Sports Council, 1982.
Twin S.L. *Out of the Bleachers*, McGraw Hill, 1979.
Women in Sport Booklets, Women's Sports Foundation, 1980–1996.

General
Cashmore E. *Making Sense of Sport*, Routledge, 1990.
McPherson B.D. *et al. Social Significance of Sport*, Human Kinetics, 1989.
Sage G. *Power and Ideology in American Sport*, Human Kinetics, 1990.

Chapter 19

Historical Perspectives and Popular Recreation

19.1 Historical Perspectives

Figure 19.1 Looking at the past helps us to understand the **present** and to do something about the future.

Henry Ford suggested that all history is bunk, but then cars devalue more quickly than culture!

An approach to historical study

The study of sports' history can stand on its own as it increases the knowledge and understanding of people and situations in the past. It can be based on different sports or socially based on different sectors of society at a particular time. In each case the intention is to establish what happened as objectively as possible, attempting not to allow our present situation to affect our judgement.

We would like to suggest that history comes to life when we attempt to interpret the intentions and attitudes of people, as well as their recorded actions. However, we must be careful not to find **what we are looking for** rather than **what really happened**. Remember, we want to **understand** history, not **change** it. For example, it is thrilling to think that Webb Ellis picked up the ball and in so doing invented the game of rugby football ... but it wasn't quite as simple as that!

The focus of this book is on **contemporary physical education and sport**, but we need to look at the past as part of a **continuum of change**, where understanding how things have developed may give us the **keys to the present**.

So how can I become a historian?

The basic approach is to establish a **descriptive record** of events. Look through *Wisden* or some contemporary narrative accounts. The value of this knowledge lies entirely in its accuracy, but be careful—we know from modern reports that they can be biased.

The second level takes us into the **interpretation of relationships**.

You might want to know the links between games in the 19th-century public school and the authority of the headmaster; or between football in a community and the local factory. In this situation, the historian tries to build as complete a picture as possible, providing a greater understanding of the human experience in a social setting

The objective work of Joseph Strutt in *Sports and Pastimes of the People of England* (1801) helps us to understand what popular recreations were like before the 19th century.

Sometimes, even fiction can be helpful in this context. Thomas Hughes, in *Tom Brown's School Days* (1857), may have exaggerated reality, but his romantic style has given us a valuable insight into public school life through a fictional adventure.

The historian is interested not only in one time and place, but in the influence of one situation or experience on another. Thomas Hughes's book may have been inaccurate, but it was believed by generations of schoolboys and almost certainly was the single greatest influence on trends in public school athleticism.

Thirdly, some historians think they can identify causation factors. I suppose I've just done it in the case of *Tom Brown's School Days*. They try to recognize patterns of development and identify the cultural determinants which influenced sport and reflected society. Bailey (1978) looked at sport and the middle classes; Cunningham (1980) studied the industrial working classes in the context of leisure; and

538

Newsome (1961) attempted the even more difficult task of linking sport, education and religion. It is useful for you to read extracts from books like these.

How do I know certain things really happened?

Some historians put up hypotheses just like scientists, but the majority **ask questions** and **look for answers in the evidence** available. This leads to the tricky point that if you don't ask the right questions, you won't find out what really happened.

Equally important, if your evidence is inaccurate, your conclusions are worthless. Still, let's not give up but rather look at types of **evidence**.

Primary evidence is taken to be information reported by a person who was a witness to the event as a direct experience, and could be presented in written or oral form. Written material is more permanent, but changes every time it is rewritten, and oral evidence changes every time it is recalled or retold. For this reason maps, pictures, authentic documents and supported testimonies are most valuable on accuracy grounds, and oral evidence tends to be suspect without support.

Once that evidence is copied or retold, it becomes secondary evidence and that much less reliable.

Try to go to a County Record Office or Local History Study Centre and look at some primary evidence. Most libraries have documents and photographs; they keep old papers and periodicals; and they have books written at the time of the event. Then you can re-approach your contemporary histories to confirm their level of accuracy. A good historian always looks for cross-references.

Finally, take your tape recorder to the oldest people you know and ask them to recall 'the old days'. They'll probably love to talk to you and what they get wrong will, in many cases, be more than compensated for by the insights they will give you into events which would otherwise never be recorded.

Investigation

19.1: Let's test out some evidence

1. The painting in Figure 19.2 was exhibited at the Royal Academy in 1839:

a. Is this a primary or secondary source?

b. How would you justify the claim that this is a valid piece of evidence on the development of football?

c. Interpret the structure of the game from this painting.

d. How does the painting reflect the society of the day?

2. The following extract is from a booklet at the Black Country Museum on the Tipton Slasher.

Figure 19.2 Section of the painting *Football* by Thomas Webster, exhibited at the Royal Academy in 1839.

Sayers was a small man, a middleweight, about 11 stone in weight and five feet eight inches tall. Perry announced that this fight was to be his last and the experts all agreed with him that Sayers would be slashed to ribbons within a few rounds.

Noah Hingley, who had been born a nailmaker, and in 1857 was a thriving industrialist with chain and cable works already established at Netherton, warned the Slasher not to risk his all on the fight.

'Yoh bay gettin' no younger,' he said. 'You're a fighter and yoh con lose—I'm a skamer [schemer] and I con win. Why doh you invest some money with me for a rainy day.'

The Slasher was a stubborn man and he thought he could not lose. Noah Hingley's advice was unheeded. His all was spread amongst the bookmakers at 2 to 1 on. £400 was deposited as stake money.

On the 16th June, 1857, the ring was pitched on the Isle of Grain. Tass Parker and Jack MacDonald, a hideously disfigured old pug who had been a chopping block for many better men, were the Slasher's seconds. Sayers' seconds were Bill Hayes and Nat Langham. Langham was a recently retired fighter, now publican, who had defeated Sayers some years earlier. Tom had been forced to retire blinded in this fight, but there had been no permanent damage to his sight.

This was indeed the Slasher's last fight. He entered the ring at the apparent peak of fitness for he had trained hard, and he

Investigation

19.1 continued

left it a broken, half blind and mentally impaired man. Early in the fight Sayers struck the Slasher a violent blow on the temple.

The Slasher went down like a load of wet cement and his seconds had to work very hard on him to bring him to the scratch.

I believe that the Slasher had a brain injury when he entered the ring and this chance blow activated it, for after this he fought a brainless battle. His skill and ring craft had gone and from the way in which he struck and missed he could not have been focussing properly. The contest lasted for one hour and forty-two minutes, and one of the rounds lasted fifty minutes, a record never likely to be surpassed.

Owen Swift, the Slasher's principal backer, was sickened by the slaughter and stopped the fight in favour of Sayers. The blinded Slasher, who would not surrender, was held down by the four seconds whilst the sponge was thrown in.

Twice during the contest his black eyes had been nicked and the blood sucked from them by Parker and MacDonald. This is an eye witness description of the Slasher at the end of the fight.

'Perry's face had long since lost its humanity. A hideous gash stretched from his lip to beneath his right eye. His right ear was hanging in ribbons and the blood fell copiously on to his chest. He was as mad as a baited bull. Striking the thin air where Sayers was not. For his eyes no longer saw. Where they should have been were two black swellings oozing blood.'

a. i. Is this fact or fiction?
ii. What is the level of objectivity?
iii. Is it primary or secondary evidence?
b. What phrases give you an insight into the prize ring?
c. What does it tell us about the attitudes and opinion of the people involved?
d. To what extent is this a commentary on Black Country life?
e. Where might you go from here, if you were a social historian interested in this topic?

19.2 Factors Underlying the Origins of Sport

We need to know only a little about the origin of some of our older sports and the cultures they grew up in to set the scene.

Tribal
We have been invaded by numerous races in the distant past and each one has brought its own cultural activities with it. Some of our sports can be traced back to the Celts, Romans and, particularly, the Normans.

Ritual
Most sports and pastimes had religious and ceremonial associations, both pagan and Christian. These were joyful festival occasions held on special days. We only need to look at events associated with Shrove Tuesday and May Day to recognize this.

Survival
Many ancient sports have their origin in fitness to survive in dangerous surroundings; the ability to obtain food; and military efficiency with a weapon. Often there has been an interesting transition from functional to recreative in activities linked with survival.

Recreative
In all societies children copy adults in their play. Similarly, all civilizations seem to reach a point where the level of maturity is measured in the recreative pursuits of their leading citizens and the violent activities of the lower orders.

 Review Questions

Without presuming that an activity necessarily belongs in only one category, explain the placement of the following activities:
• stag hunting,
• mob football,
• archery,
• pancake races,
• real tennis.

19.3 The Pattern of Popular Recreation in Great Britain

The term **popular recreation** is used to describe natural, often violent, sports and pastimes (Figure 19.3), which were part of an ancient feudal right to recreation, claimed by all branches of the rural community.

Figure 19.3 Popular recreation: the right to participate regardless of personal risk.

Some landmarks you ought to know about

You should be aware of the Tailteann Games. Watman (1968) tells us they originated around 2000 BC in County Meath, Eire, and continued until 1168 AD with the Norman Conquest of Ireland. It is probable that similar Celtic games existed in Britain at least until the Roman Conquest.

Now to the Romans. Read this extract to form a picture of Roman Britain:

It is unlikely that these sports ever included athletics meetings on the Greek pattern. The nearest point to Britain at which such meetings are known to have been held is Vienne, in the Rhône valley near Lyons. The athletics festivals in this city, established by a bequest in the will of a citizen, were abolished about AD 100 by a magistrate, and on appeal to the Emperor his decision was upheld. The reason for the abolition was that the meetings constituted a danger to the morals of the citizens; such was the reputation of Greek professional athletes in the Roman world at this time. If Greek sport was on the retreat in this way in a part of Gaul where, owing to the influence of the Greek cities of Marseilles, Nice and Antibes, it had earlier been strong, it is highly improbable that it would have crossed the Channel into Britain.

On the other hand, it is certain that the exhibitions of the arena were available in Britain. A dozen amphitheatres have been identified in the province. Two of them are well known, Maumbury Rings at Dorchester in Wessex and the arena of the legionary fortress at Caerleon. These do not compare in size with the vast structures on the Continent. The oval arena of each is roughly half the size of a soccer pitch; the amphitheatre of the small fort at Tomen-y-Mûr, beautifully situated among the hills of Merioneth, would hardly accommodate a tennis court. There is little direct evidence of the entertainment provided in these places, but there is no reason to suppose that in this respect Britain differed from other parts of the Empire. A vase in Colchester Museum depicts gladiators and bear-baiting; it was almost certainly made in East Anglia, and this suggests a familiarity with these subjects in the province. The smaller arenas may well have exhibited cock-fighting, a popular pursuit among the Romans.

The same degree of uncertainty hovers over the question whether the provincials of Roman Britain were able to enjoy chariot racing. A mosaic found in a Roman villa at Horkstow in Lincolnshire and now in the British Museum depicts a chariot race. This of course merely shows that the owner of the villa was interested in racing; it does not prove that the racing took place in Britain.

(Source: Harris, 1975.)

Compare this with the following extract which refers to the contribution made by the Saxons in sporting terms:

Indeed, it is not by any means surprising, under the Saxon government, when the times were generally very turbulent, and the existence of peace exceedingly precarious, and when the personal exertions of the opulent were so often necessary for the preservation of their lives and property, that such exercises as inured the body to fatigue, and biased the mind to military pursuits, should have constituted the chief part of a young nobleman's education: accordingly, we find that hunting, hawking, leaping, running, wrestling, casting of darts, and other pastimes which necessarily required great exertions of bodily strength, were taught them in their adolescence. These amusements engrossed the whole of their attention, every one striving to excel his fellow; for hardiness, strength, and valour, out-balanced, in the public estimation, the accomplishments of the mind; and therefore literature, which flourishes best in tranquillity and retirement, was considered as a pursuit unworthy the notice of a soldier, and only requisite in the gloomy recesses of the cloister.

Among the vices of the Anglo-Saxons may be reckoned their propensity to gaming, and especially with the dice, which they derived from their ancestors.

(Source: Strutt, 1801.)

Investigation

19.2: Popular recreation precepts

1. Try to explain the following **popular recreation** precepts [this may require you to read extracts from Brailsford (1969), Ford (1977) or Malcolmson (1973)]:

a. Feudal basis of the **courtly** and the **popular: courtly** with courtesy and high culture; **popular** with peasant vulgarity and low culture.

b. Both an inherent part of the **Merrie England** concept.

c. **Conservatism** of the **rural gentry** not wishing to change the natural order of country life, with the **escapism** of the **peasant class**.

d. Attacked by the **clergy** as decadent and irreligious; by the **middle classes** because it offended their sense of decency; and by the **industrialists** because they needed a disciplined **work force**.

e. **Popular recreation** against the **Protestant work ethic**.

2. The second step is to link these **precepts** with the **social groups** and **activities** shown in Figure 19.4; and explain why certain **reforms** took place.

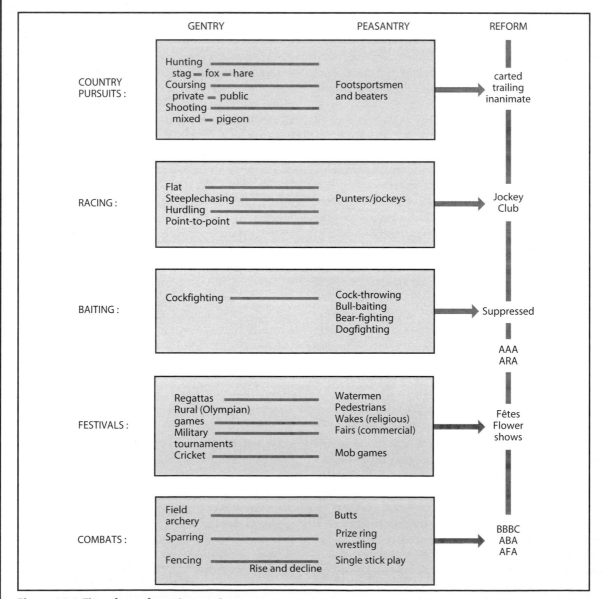

Figure 19.4 The reform of sporting pastimes.

By the 15th century, pagan and Christian recreations were hopelessly intertwined within the concept of **Merrie England**. Another extract from Strutt (1801) should set the scene:

May Day festivals

This custom, no doubt, is a relic of one more ancient, practised by the Heathens, who observed the last four days in April, and the first of May, in honour of the goddess Flora. An old Romish calendar, cited by Mr. Brand, says, on the 30th of April the boys go out to seek May-trees, 'Maii arbores a pueris exquirunter.' Some consider the May-pole as a relic of Druidism; but I cannot find any solid foundation for such an opinion.

It should be observed, that the May-games were not always celebrated upon the first day of the month; and to this we may add the following extract from Stow: 'In the month of May the citizens of London of all estates, generally in every parish, and in some instances two or three parishes joining together, had their several mayings, and did fetch their may-poles with divers warlike shows; with good archers, morrice-dancers, and other devices for pastime, all day long; and towards evening they had stageplays and bonfires in the streets. These great mayings and may-games were made by the governors and masters of the city, together with the triumphant setting up of the great shaft or principal may-pole in Cornhill.

(Source: Strutt, 1801.)

This is the first of a number of pictures which are useful for interpretation purposes; they serve to stimulate discussion; and they help to develop analysis techniques; however, there is not the space to explain more than a selection of these illustrations in the text.

Figure 19.5 is an excellent picture to clarify the development of sport in this country. There are three combative situations which need to be rationalized. The central one is the serious, noble pursuit of **jousting**. It involves two knights and it is not clear whether this is a battle scene or a tournament event. Either way, it is training for war by an elite, who presumed the existence of physical components necessary for a successful combat, but also a code of chivalry which eventually emerged into fair play in a sporting situation. It seems, therefore, that the source of this activity is military and limited to the ruling class and associated with their survival and status.

If we look at the top combat, it seems that this represents children at play, copying the ruling class. They are making do with sticks to represent horses and lances, but are nevertheless 'mastering reality' in the relative safety of a pretend game. This suggests that combats did not have their origin in play, but in serious survival situations, where playing at

the activity came later. This is another useful generalization: that the origin of most sports was serious and functional. As an observed copy, however, it is questionable whether the children's play included an awareness of the chivalric code as they would have been 'playing out' their own values through the observable features of the activity. However, children's fantasies tend to clearly define 'goodies' and 'baddies' and as such values are identified and even polarized.

The bottom combat is on the water in boats. It involves the notion of team, because the rowers are part of the combat, but the seriousness of the situation is reduced because the approach speed of the antagonists is much slower and the consequence of a good strike is a ducking for the other person. Here we have an example of a quintain. The corruption of the noble activity of jousting into a frivolous festival activity, where the crowd has a good laugh and the winners get a prize. The extent to which fair play operated would probably depend on festival regulations. This is still a high-risk activity, where the rigour of life was acted out in the ritual of the folk festival.

This debasement of serious activities was common in Medieval England, where the peasantry 'took a rise' out of the ruling class in their rural festivals. However, the message is that non-serious merry-making often arose out of serious forms of activity and even these frivolous events had serious cathartic and community-building functions.

Figure 19.5 Jousting.

Further extracts from Malcolmson (1973) and Brailsford (1969) also illustrate the idea:

Bull-running in Stamford

Bull-running was a prominent diversion in Tutbury, Staffordshire, Stamford, Lincolnshire, and perhaps one or two other towns. The bull-running in Stamford, held on the 13th of November, was a major festive occasion for the town and its surrounding countryside which attracted each year hundreds of spectators and participants. The sport was essentially a free-for-all bull-fight without weapons, or at best with only sticks and heavy staffs; it seems to have been much like some of the bull-runnings recently (or still) found in parts of France and Spain, and it was characterized by a similar sort of carnival atmosphere. On the morning of the 13th the entrances to the main streets were barricaded, shops were shut up, and at eleven o'clock, with the bells of St Mary's tolling his arrival, a bull was released from a stable to the swarms of onlookers and participants (called 'bullards') who packed the street. The excitement was provided by the ensuing confusion and disorder, and by displays of daring in tormenting the bull—by throwing irritants at him, perhaps, or by baiting him with a red effigy and then manoeuvring out of his way. A talented bullard might pack himself in an open-ended barrel and roll it at the bull: the objective here was to provoke him to toss the barrel, and yet at the same time to avoid getting dislodged or mauled. 'If he be tame,' wrote a hostile observer in 1819, 'he is soon surrounded by the *canaille*, and *loaded*, as the bullards express it; that is, some have hold of his horns, and others his ears, some are beating his sides with bludgeons, and others are hanging at his tail.' A man in trouble would be aided by diversionary antics from his friends. Sometimes the bull was stormed by groups, and often he was simply chased through the streets. After an intermission for lunch the bull was again let loose, but this time he was driven towards the main bridge spanning the Welland River. The bullards surrounded him on the bridge and together lifted him over the parapet and into the water: this was known as 'brigging' the bull. He would shortly make his way to the adjacent meadow where a few dogs might be set upon him (though he was not tied down), and where bullards would give chase for a while around the muddy lowland. In late afternoon he was escorted back to town, frustrated and fatigued no doubt, but not usually mutilated. He was then slaughtered and sometimes the meat was sold cheaply to the poor or served up in the public houses. The odd bull which had refused to be 'brigged' was spared his life.

(Source: Malcolmson, 1973.)

Festival wakes

The inhabitants of Stone, Staffordshire, where the church was dedicated to St. Michael and All Angels, celebrated their patronal festival with bull-baiting, bear-baiting, dog-fighting and cock-fighting.

(Source: Brailsford, 1969.)

Investigation

19.3: Past sporting events

1. Can you now describe the atmosphere at Stamford on 13th November 1819?
2. Can you explain what is meant by a Wake?
3. Do you understand the ritual associated with Medieval festivals?
4. We know that the Norman Conquest led to the establishment of our present nobility. It also led to the development of the **tournament** and the clear division of sports into **courtly** and **popular**. Use Figure 19.5 to describe this class divide through an explanation of the **joust** as against the **quintain**.

You need to know something about the Tudor Dynasty and athleticism. Henry VIII was a champion of most sports, but he also restricted certain activities to the nobility. Figure 19.6 shows Henry throwing the hammer, but he was also a great horseman and a champion real tennis player.

The blackest time for sports in English history was during and after the Civil War (1649). The country was divided into two complex groups. The Royalists tended to be gentry, rural and High Church, while the Parliamentarians or Roundheads were largely merchant class, urban and Low Church. The success of Cromwell led to an imposition of a Puritan lifestyle which continued as an ethic for the lower classes for many years after the Restoration.

Figure 19.6 Henry VIII hammer throwing.

Popular recreation was criticized on religious grounds as well as being identified with the King's Book of Sports.

Some of the cruellest popular recreations were not revived. Cock-throwing, which involved throwing sticks or stones at a tethered cockerel, was banned, but cockfighting continued; and bear-baiting became less popular, even though bull-baiting continued.

 Investigation

19.4: Popular recreation before the Civil War
Read the following:

And as for Our good people's lawfull Recreation, Our pleasure likewise is, That, after the end of Divine Service, Our good people be not disturbed, letted, or discouraged from any lawful recreation, Such as dancing, either of men or women, Archery for men, leaping, vaulting, or any other such harmless Recreation, nor from having of May Games, Whitson Ales, and Morris-dances, and the setting up of Maypoles, and other sports therewith used, so as the same be had in due and convenient time, without impediment or neglect of Divine Service: And that women shall have leave to carry rushes to the Church for the decoring of it, according to their old custom. But withal we doe here account still as prohibited all unlawful games to bee used upon Sundayes onely, as Beare and Bullbaitings, Interludes, and at all times, in the meaner sort of people, by law prohibited. Bowling: And likewise we barre from this benefit and liberty, all such knowne recusants, either men or women, as will abstaine from comming to Church or Divine Service, that will not first come to the Church and serve God: Prohibiting, in like sort, the said Recreations to any that, though conform in Religion, are not present in the Church at the Service of God, before their going to the said Recreations.
(Source: Govett, 1890.)

 Investigation

19.5: The Dover Games
1. In Figure 19.7, how many activities can you name?
2. To what extent were the old 'courtly' and 'popular' concepts also revived?

Figure 19.7 The Dover Games were revived after the restoration of Charles II. Shown are the types of activities that were re-introduced. (*Whitfield, 1962.*)

A country in transition

The Puritan Ethic of the 17th century gave way to the Protestant Ethic in the 1700s, marking the birth of Britain as an industrial nation, as a world power, and as a centre of Evangelism. If these three forces were not enough, the conservatism of rural England was shaken by the emergence of a Regency clientele, with high living in fashionable spa surroundings, architectural genius and the Fancy dominating upper-class life. The Fancy was a mixed group of 'sportsmen' who were preoccupied with horse-racing, cockfighting and the prize ring: totally consumed by the blood, sweat and wager of the contest.

The date which is often used to identify these seeds of change is 1760. Let's look in a little more detail at the three major 'revolutions'.

The **industrial revolution** began with the increased use of coal in smelting and led to factories and industrialists taking over from the ancient cottage industry controlled by independent craftsmen.

This machine age came to the countryside, reducing labour intensity at the same time that enclosure marked a reduction in common land. This was an

agrarian revolution which forced countless farm labourers to take their families to the towns in search of work. It is also important to recognize that the prospect of industrial wages attracted the more ambitious farm workers to the towns.

With machine-operated factories, an expanding capitalist economy and abundant cheap labour, the industrial towns grew at a tremendous rate, a phenomenon which has been called an **urban revolution**. Though this is often identified as a working-class population expansion, it also marked the emergence of a powerful, respectable, urban middle class.

In older towns, this led to many of the old slums being cleared and fashionable shopping centres being built. Each major town became a corporation and built its own town hall, free library, cottage hospital and public swimming baths.

In the heavily industrialized towns, factories and smoke replaced green fields, and tightly packed, back-to-back, terraced houses were built as near to the factory as possible. From 6 a.m. to 6 p.m. for six days a week, men, women and children worked in the 'satanic mills'.

Country life

We now need to consider the impact of these changes on popular recreation. Let's look at **country pursuits** first. Despite the growth of towns, country life continued much as before, particularly as it concerned the **landed gentry**.

 Investigation

19.6: Country sports

1. Figure 19.8 shows the older sport of **otter hunting**. Today, the otter is protected and most people regard it as a loveable creature. In the 19th century, it was hunted and killed mercilessly. Try to explain the Victorian attitude to otter hunting and why we feel differently today.

2. Fox hunting (Figure 19.9), on the other hand, is still very popular in many parts of the country, although there is an increasingly vociferous lobby against it—manifested most vividly by the activities of the hunt saboteurs. Can you identify the attractions of fox hunting to the landed gentry in the 19th century— taking, for example, the athleticism required?

Figure 19.8 Otter hunting.

Figure 19.9. Fox hunting.

Investigation

19.6 continued

3. This ancient sport (Figure 19.10) was very popular in rural England throughout the 19th century. Hares were 'flushed' out of 'cover' and two greyhounds were 'unleashed' by the 'slipper', and the dog which made the 'pussy' deviate the most times won the 'course'. Can you interpret this statement and also establish the attractions of such an event at that time?

Figure 19.10 Coursing.

Rural villages and market towns

Figure 19.11 is an excellent general interpretative medium, reflecting life in a rural village or market town.

It is possible to draw questions from the placement of a settlement at a river crossing, but also as a secure site in a meander. As such, the river acted as a defence, as a source of sanitation, as a communication route and as a recreational facility. In terms of communication, it is important to recognize commerce along the river as well as access across it, as a ford or bridging point.

Our focus is on recreation and so it is important to see the river as a washing and bathing place, where competitions could develop, but also as a river-bank facility, where flooding prevented houses being built on the water meadows. The function-based origins of many sports can also be established from the illustration, where commercial boating and sailing may have given rise to canoeing, rowing and sailing for pleasure; fishing might have been an occupation or a means of supplementing diet, but became a regular pastime; and the same applied to shooting. The ownership of a gun or rod, was one of the ambitions of all young males, including labourers, the only restriction being the game laws.

From this notion of a river town, with the festival occasion in the form of a regatta, it is easy to progress to the notion of market towns and the links between markets, fairs and sportive festivals. This leads on to the more sophisticated developments which occurred in the county towns, which became the focus of such major events as horse racing, county cricket and prizefighting, where major venues were normally on the water meadows.

Finally, it is also important to register the significance of the seasons, more particularly the summer months, with the attraction of bathing, and the cold spells, when the frozen surfaces provided popular skating venues as well as ice fairs.

Figure 19.11 Fishing and fowling in a village.

Investigation

19.7: The reflective and sporting pastime of angling

Izaak Walton identified a sport for every man, but 19th century work patterns and pollution resulted in a class divide for 'game' and 'coarse' fishing. Explain this statement in the context of the 'revolutions' we discussed earlier.

Investigation

19.8: Shooting

1. You may have seen the film *Kes*. It was about the relationship between a boy and a kestrel. Can you examine this and other elements in the sport of **falconry** (Figure 19.12)?

2. **Mixed shooting** also had a similar attachment, this time between a man and his gun-dog (Figure 19.13). Though falconry as a sport is no longer acceptable, pheasant and grouse shooting still are. How do you account for this? Is it due to social privilege, marksmanship, food for the table or something else?

3. **Pigeon shooting** (Figure 19.14) was equally popular, with birds sprung from traps for marksmen to shoot at, but now society has changed this to **clay pigeon shooting**. Why was pigeon shooting curtailed while mixed shooting survived?

Figure 19.12 Falconry.

Figure 19.13 Mixed shooting.

Figure 19.14 Pigeon shooting.

Horse racing and blood sports: the traditional festival occasions

Horse racing (Figure 19.15) is as old as horse riding. The nature of man is to make a contest in any unpredictable situation which allows him to wager his competence against another. Horse racing had two distinct phases of development. The first took place in the reign of Queen Anne when three Arabian stallions were used to start bloodstock breeding in Britain. The second came when the railways allowed horses and crowds access to different racing centres, resulting in a well organized **racing calendar**.

The development of the hunt and horse racing is an important chapter in the development of 19th century gentry life-style. The hunt with its athleticism and ritual reflected the significance of physical endeavour among male and female members of the upper class. The horse was at once a symbol of wealth, a vehicle which increased spatial freedom, a possession which brought pleasure and challenge and reinforced the gentry's affinity with the countryside.

The athleticism of a day in the hunting field should not be underestimated. Riding over rough country for distances of over 60 miles held tremendous risks for the riders and required great courage and skill. The challenge element was enhanced by the decision to hunt the most able adversary in its natural environment, resulting in a personal test in a sporting environment, where the quarry had every chance to escape from ineffective riders and hounds. Here is a re-emergence of the tournament duality of physical endeavour and chivalrous conduct, which has become the essence of rational sport.

Such was the momentum of this athleticism that, after a day's hunting and feasting, the gentry often saddled up in the evening to engage in a friendly, but often wagered, steeplechase as shown in Figure 19.16. The eventual professionalization of the steeplechase as a result of the improvement of bloodstock, the love of the wager and the development of horse racing as a major festival occasion led to regular race meetings and professional jockeys controlled by the Jockey Club, a governing body which was copied by all later sports bodies.

This evolution led to lower-class jockeys being employed, as a servant class, but the athletic commitment of the gentry continued through amateur point-to-point racing organized by individual hunt clubs.

Figure 19.15 The Epsom Races.

Figure 19.16 Steeplechasing.

Investigation

19.9: Horse racing and steeplechasing
1. Use Figure 19.15 to explain the level of organization in flat racing after 1870.

2. Figure 19.16 gives clues as to the development of steeplechasing. Use this visual evidence to explain what might have happened.

Blood sports were relics of an earlier period. They were extremely cruel, but arguably reflected a cruel society, where the function of animals was either to work or entertain. **Cockfighting** went hand-in-glove with the **races**. **Bull-baiting** could always be guaranteed to attract a crowd.

 Investigation

19.10: Blood sports

1. Figure 19.17 shows two fighting cocks, with an apparently respectable crowd. The birds will fight to the death, there will be blood and feathers everywhere and money will change hands—but not until the cock has crowed. Can you appreciate the attraction at a time when a person was hanged for stealing a sheep?

2. Can you apply the attractions of the cockfight to bull-baiting (Figure 19.18), thus explaining its popularity at that time?

3. Can you link this with refrigeration and beating a steak before cooking it?

4. Can you explain why in the UK bulls are no longer baited and yet bullfighting is still acceptable in some countries?

5. Can you link this analysis with shooting, where the gun-dog has been replaced by the bull terrier, but the man/woman has a similar chance to test his/her training and breeding skills, and put money on them?

Figure 19.17 Cockfighting.

Figure 19.18 Bull-baiting.

Popular sporting festivals and pedestrianism

The term **pedestrian** referred to a group of lower class individuals who earned part of their living by competing in certain sports for money. It was a fore-runner of the term **professional**. One of the earliest examples of this was in sculling. Thames watermen competed for the Doggett Coat and Badge on the 1st August annually from 1715 (Figure 19.19). It arose from the idea of wager boats. Small boats ferried passengers across the Thames and wagers were struck to see who could get across first.

A similar situation existed on the roads, in that the upper class employed footmen on their coaches, who took part in wager foot races. These developed

Figure 19.19 The Doggett race.

into challenge events over long distances with wagers being made on the result or on the 'walker' completing his self-imposed task. One of the most famous occasions of this type occurred in 1800 when Captain Barclay completed 1000 miles in 1000 hours for 1000 guineas.

These events became very popular, attracting huge crowds on the major horse-race courses. The best-known competitors were the two Americans,

Deerfoot who toured Britain in the 1860s, accepting challenges at all distances; and Weston, who walked 2000 miles in 2000 hours around Britain in the 1870s and gave a lecture on 'abstinence' each evening.

Early **cricket professionals** fitted much the same mould. They were paid wages to keep the ground in order, coach gentlemen players and play when wager matches were arranged.

Investigation

19.11: The development of cricket

1. What aspects of Figure 19.20 lead you to think it is an 18th-century example of cricket?
2. Figure 19.21 shows a women's county cricket match in 1811. Can you recognize similar characteristics to the men's game, and note the freedom of female opportunity prior to Victorian constraints?

Figure 19.20 Marylebone Fields in 1748.

Figure 19.21 Hampshire v. Surrey.

Having written in depth about the gentry and their values, the illustration of pedestrianism can help us to interpret the popular and courtly cultures. The lower class pedestrian, competing for money, is using his talents to earn a living in a more pleasant environment and with the likelihood of making much more money if he is good enough and is able to use his winnings shrewdly. The question of athleticism is not in doubt, but the need to win may jeopardize any values of looking for a challenge; being able to afford and, therefore, prepared to lose; and being willing to cheat.

If we identify the other competitor as a gentleman amateur who represents courtly values, the suggestion is that his athleticism is based on the testing of self against others and the elements as a personal challenge and that the behaviour code which arises from this is that the challenge is a test of temperament and to cheat is to cheat yourself.

The notion of cheating may be an ethical principle as in the case of the gentleman performer and

adjudged the act of a blackguard and unacceptable, but the notion of cheating by a pedestrian is more likely to hinge on the expedient possibility of being caught and barred from competition. It is too simplistic to presume that principle and expediency is culturally exclusive, but it is easy to see that a pedestrian who competes for money to feed himself and his family may not have the advantage of adopting 'high-culture' ethics when those around him 'play the game'.

It is this apparent stigma of the professional which is at the basis of amateur–professional antagonism. At its most exaggerated in the mid-19th century, even the notion of training was seen to be a debased practice by amateurs as it did not help them to achieve their goal to be able to accept the challenge of any eventuality as a natural consequence of their physicality and temperament. Part of this was rooted in the separateness of feudal society, but also in the amateur notion of the all-rounder as against the specialist or gladiator.

Investigation

19.12: Pedestrian and gentleman amateur
Figure 19.22 shows a 'ped' and a 'gent'. Can you list their motives for competing?

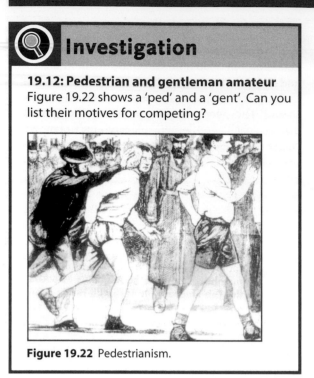

Figure 19.22 Pedestrianism.

Figure 19.23 Town mob football.

The survival of folk games

Folk games were occasional contests between different groups in a community and often involved considerable violence (Figures 19.23 and 19.24). By the 19th century many of them had been suppressed, but some survived as an annual event in more isolated towns. You may have heard of the **Ashbourne Football**, the **Haxey Hood Game**, **Lutterworth Mob Hockey**, the **Hallaton Bottle Game**, and mob football at **Atherstone** and **Derby**.

Figure 19.24 Rural mob football.

Dunning and Sheard (1979) produced a framework to show the structural properties of these folk games (Figure 19.25).

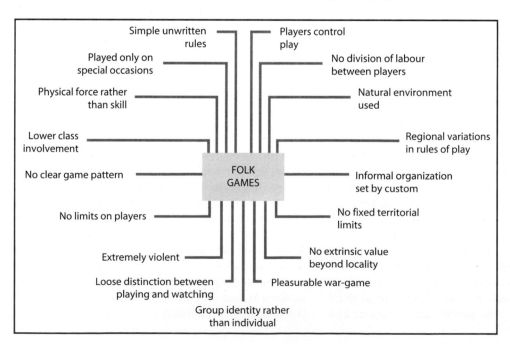

Simple unwritten rules
Played only on special occasions
Physical force rather than skill
Lower class involvement
No clear game pattern
No limits on players
Extremely violent
Loose distinction between playing and watching
Group identity rather than individual

Players control play
No division of labour between players
Natural environment used
Regional variations in rules of play
Informal organization set by custom
No fixed territorial limits
No extrinsic value beyond locality
Pleasurable war-game

FOLK GAMES

Figure 19.25 Structural properties of folk games.

Investigation

19.13: Mob games

1. Can you set up a mob game situation, such as mat-ball, and compare it with a modern game such as volleyball, using a simplified version of the Dunning and Sheard framework (Figure 19.25)?

2. The following is the account of the Derby game given by Glover in his *History of Derbyshire*, published in 1829. How does this description match up with the folk game framework?

The contest lies between the parishes of St. Peter's and All Saints, and the goals to which the ball is taken are 'Nun's Mill' for the latter and the Gallows balk on the Normanton Road for the former. None of the other parishes in the borough take any direct part in the contest, but the inhabitants of all join in the sport, together with persons from all parts of the adjacent country. The players are young men from eighteen to thirty or upwards, married as well as single, and many veterans who retain a relish for the sport are occasionally seen in the very heat of the conflict. The game commences in the market-place, where the partisans of each parish are drawn up on each side, and about noon a large ball is tossed up in the midst of them. This is seized upon by some of the strongest and most active men of each party. The rest of the players immediately close in upon them and a solid mass is formed. It then becomes the object of each party to impel the course of the crowd towards their particular goal. The struggle to obtain the ball, which is carried in the arms of those who have possessed themselves of it, is then violent, and the motion of the human tide heaving to and fro without the least regard to consequences is tremendous. Broken shins, broken heads, torn coats, and lost hats are amongst the minor accidents of this fearful contest, and it frequently happens that persons fall owing to the intensity of the pressure, fainting and bleeding beneath the feet of the surrounding mob. But it would be difficult to give an adequate idea of this ruthless sport. A Frenchman passing through Derby remarked, that if Englishmen called this playing, it would be impossible to say what they would call fighting. Still the crowd is encouraged by respectable persons attached to each party, who take a surprising interest in the result of the day's sport, urging on the players with shouts, and even handing to those who are exhausted oranges and other refreshment. The object of the St. Peter's party is to get the ball into the water down the Morledge brook into the Derwent as soon as they can, while the All Saints party endeavour to prevent this and to urge the ball westward. The St. Peter players are considered to be equal to the best water spaniels, and it is certainly curious to see two or three hundred men up to their chins in the Derwent continually ducking each other. The numbers engaged on both sides exceed a thousand, and the streets are crowded with lookers-on. The shops are closed, and the town presents the aspect of a place suddenly taken by storm.

(Source: Shearman M. *Athletics and Football.*)

Here is a modern description of the Haxey Hood Game:

There is, for instance the Haxey Hood Game in Leicestershire, in which tightly rolled lengths of sacking are used. There is, perhaps, something sinister about the ritualistic method of play, which it has been suggested could be symbolic of the struggle between winter and summer. However, the legend behind the game does not support this theory of the struggle between the seasons. It is said that sometime in the 13th century, while riding on the Isle of Axeholme, Lady Mowbray lost her hood. It was found and returned by 12 peasants from the village of Haxey. As a reward she gave to the village a piece of land, thence called the Hoodland, the rent from which had to be used to buy hoods each year to be played for by 12 villagers. The game is also thought to have been played at Epworth on the Isle of Axeholme.

On the Eve of St. John (23 June) each year at Haxey a committee is elected consisting of 12 *Boggons*—sometimes called *Boggans* or *Boggins*—one *King Boggon* and a Fool.

On the following day at 2 p.m., to the pealing of the church bells, the committee meet dressed in scarlet jerkins and tall hats, except for the Fool who wears a grotesque costume; he has his face blacked and smeared with red ochre and is dressed in trousers of sackcloth with coloured patches and a red shirt. On his head he wears a tall hat with a goose's wing and red flowers adorning it. He carries a short-stocked whip on the end of which is a sock filled with bran.

The boggons then go up to the top of Haxey Hill. There, on the village boundary, they form a circle with the King Boggon in the centre holding 13 hoods. The King Boggon throws a hood and if someone other than a Boggon catches it he tries to run to a nearby public house while the Boggons attempt to stop him. If he succeeds in reaching the pub he demands a shilling. If, on the other hand, he is caught by a Boggon, the hood is returned, to be thrown up again. On the 13th hood throwing, a part of the game known as the *sway* begins. Hundreds of people join in and attempt to force the hood into a public house. If successful, drinks on the house are called for and the hood is kept on the premises for the following year.

(Source: Jewell, 1977.)

The Haxey Game doesn't involve a ball and the Hallaton Game starts with a scramble for hare pies and concludes with a 'bottle' kicking game. Yes, and they are still being played today! Little wonder every attempt was made to stop these activities. In the Middle Ages various kings pronounced edicts; and later, local corporations established by-laws banning street football. We should also recognize the changing times which produced more effective policing, a breakdown of the old rural traditions and the growth of middle-class respectability.

There were as many alternatives involving the use of a small ball and often a stick, each culture seeming to have its own version. The Scots played 'shinty', the Irish 'hurley', the Cornish 'hurling' and the English 'bandy', a game normally played on ice.

Investigation

19.14: Mob stick games

1. Can you pick out the characteristics of this game of shinty (Figure 19.26) and find out why it was being played at Blackheath in London?
2. How many of the mob characteristics are evident in Figure 19.27?

3. Find out if your own local area had a mob game. It would be a worthwhile school or college project to produce a picture of it. For example, if you find yourself in Gloucester Cathedral, look at the mob game carving on one of the misericords and a stainglass window of a 'golfer'.

Figure 19.26 Shinty at Blackheath.

Figure 19.27 One of the most famous mob hockey games was held annually at Lutterworth in Leicestershire.

'Courtly' games

The **sophisticated exclusivity** of **real tennis** was the exact opposite to the **rustic simplicity** of **folk games**. Here was a 'courtly' game borrowed from France and developed as a reflection of high culture in Tudor England. By the 18th and 19th centuries, the game had become the exclusive property of the nobility, supported by a servant class of professionals in the cricket mould.

If we use the Dunning and Sheard (1979) framework we now have a completely different set of characteristics (Figure 19.28).

With the rise in popularity of rackets and lawn tennis, an exclusive clientele continued to regard real tennis as the ultimate game (Figures 19.29 and 19.30). The courts at Lord's, Queen's Club, Hampton Court and Royal Leamington Spa served simply to reflect its 'Royal' status.

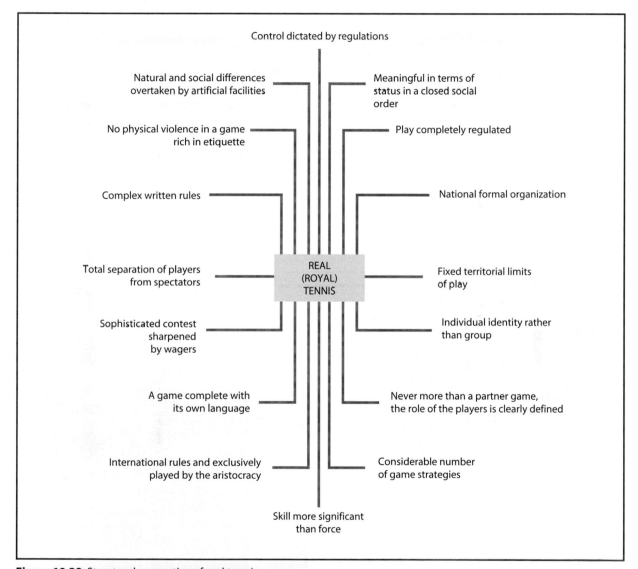

Figure 19.28 Structural properties of real tennis.

Figure 19.29 Even from this early picture of real tennis, you should be able to establish why it was so exclusive, but it is important to recognize what is happening outside the court of play.

Figure 19.30 This picture of the Honourable Arthur Lyttleton playing real tennis is another key to the status of the game. A member of the nobility and a famous diplomat, he was one of England's greatest 'Corinthians'. He was an amateur tennis champion; played cricket for England; was an outstanding soccer player, athlete and golfer; and was also a leading yachtsman.

The rise and decline of contests

Archery and **fencing** share a similar history. They both involved weapons of war and so had great importance, until gunpowder made them obsolete. They would have completely disappeared but for a dedicated band of followers who first of all valued the ceremonial role of both activities and then built each into a sophisticated sport in its own right.

 Investigation

19.15: Archery

1. Can you think of reasons why a churchyard (Figure 19.31) might have been used for this occasion?

2. To what extent does Figure 19.31 tell you whether this is military training or a sport?

3. How does Figure 19.32 express the social elitism of archery?

4. Why was it acceptable for these women to take part?

5. Use Figure 19.33 to explain the transition of an activity from a military training exercise to a sport?

Figure 19.31 An early picture of archery in an English churchyard.

Investigation

19.15 continued

Figure 19.32 When archery was revived in the late 18th century it was part of the Regency movement, an expression of the most exclusive members of society.

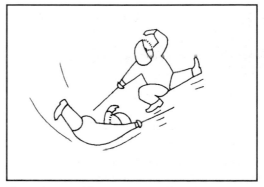

Figure 19.33 Military sports—when does the idea of training for war change to training for sports?

Unlike archery, swordplay cut across society. There was a lower class version of backswords or single sticks, and a 'courtly' version of fencing which owed its status to the duel.

Single stick play (Figure 19.34) was very much part of the rural festival and the intention was to hold contests, where the winner was the first to draw blood.

Fencing (Figure 19.35), on the other hand, was retained after the sword had lost its military function, with the rapier being carried as a ceremonial weapon and used for duelling if a gentleman's honour was questioned.

Figure 19.34 Single sticks.

Figure 19.35 Fencing practice at Angelo's Academy in London. Once duelling was banned, fencing declined, only to re-emerge at the end of the 19th century as part of physical training (alongside gymnastics).

Prizefighting dates back to the 13th century when there were 'gladiatorial' schools preparing individuals to defend themselves and compete if they wished in 'sword and buckle' contests. In Henry VIII's time these so-called professors of defence had formed a company entitled Masters of Defence. This was the cradle of the Noble Art of Self Defence which came to prominence in the 18th century, led by James Figg (Figure 19.36) who opened the Academy of Boxing in London in 1718.

Figure 19.37 shows Figg being beaten by his pupil Jack Broughton. Broughton had already won the Doggett Coat and Badge and went on to become famous by changing the rules of the prize ring and establishing the birth of **pugilism**. He excluded weaponry and wrestling, limiting the contest to bare-knuckle punching and throws. The tradition of teaching the gentry to defend themselves continued, and it was as a result of 'sparring' that 'mufflers' were used—yes, boxing gloves!

Unfortunately, when Broughton unexpectedly lost to Jack Slack in 1750, the Duke of Cumberland, his patron, took it badly (largely because he lost a wager of £10 000), and used his influence to drive the prize ring underground. From this time the Fancy had to run the gauntlet of the police and magistrates, but when good champions came along they still attracted the crowds and huge sums of money changed hands.

When grappling was removed from the prize ring, **wrestling** lost much of its popularity. For many

Figure 19.36 Figg on the 'stage' ready to accept any challenger. As a Master of Defence he had to be able to defend himself against all-comers at swordplay, cudgels, quarterstaff and grappling. He was also employed as a tutor to 'fashionable dandies' who wished to test their skill and this occasionally included ladies.

years it only survived in isolated areas, such as Cumberland (Figure 19.38) and Devon, where individual styles were retained. This pattern changed when professional wrestling became part of the music hall, and when amateur wrestling was included in the revival of the Olympic Games in 1896.

Figure 19.37 Figg and Broughton.

Figure 19.38 Cumberland wrestling.

Exam-Style Questions

1. Outline some aspects of early festivals in Britain, considering their links with Wakes and Fairs. (5 marks)

2. Use Figure 19.22 to discuss the background and aspirations in a 19th century walking race of:
a. A **gentleman amateur**; and
b. A **pedestrian**. (5 marks)

3. The Prize Ring consists of the fighters and their patrons. Explain the status and the function of both groups. (5 marks)

4. It has been suggested that a game has many of the characteristics of the cultural group who play it. Figures 19.27 and 19.29 show examples of real tennis and mob hockey. Describe the characteristics of each game and discuss the extent to which this reflected the class of people who played them. (10 marks)
(Total 25 marks.)

 Summary

Popular Recreation:

1. Historical objectivity, causation and keys to the present.

2. Traditional activities of the common people—by right and by law.

3. Constraints by respectable citizens, church and law.

4. Natural, occasional—holy days, violent and riotous sports and pastimes.

5. Romantic links with rural Merrie England.

 Further Reading

Aberdare Lord. *The Story of Tennis*, Stanley Paul, 1959.
Bailey P. *Leisure and Class in Victorian England*, RKP, 1978.
Baker W.J. *Sports in the Western World*, Rowman & Littlefield, 1982.
Brailsford D. *Sport in Society*, RKP, 1969.
Brailsford D. *British Sport: A Social History*, Lutterworth, 1992.
Cunningham H. *Leisure in the Industrial Society*, Croom Helm, 1980.
Dunning E. and Sheard K. B*arbarians, Gentlemen and Players*, NYUP, 1979.
Ford J. *Prizefighting*, David & Charles, 1977.
Govett L.A. *King's Book of Sports*, Elliot Stock, 1890.
Harris H.A. *Sport in Britain*, Stanley Paul, 1975.
Heath E.G. *A History of Target Archery*, David & Charles, 1973.
Holt R. *Sport and the British*, Clarendon, 1989.

Jewell B. *Sports and Games*, Midas, 1977.
Kent G. *A Pictorial History of Wrestling*, Spring Books, 1968.
Lovesey P. *Kings of Distance*, Eyre & Spottiswoode, 1968.
Malcolmson R.W. *Popular Recreations in English Society*, Cambridge University Press, 1973.
Newsome D. *Godliness and Good Learning*, Murray, 1961.
Shearman M. Athletics and Football, Badminton Library Series, Longmans, Green & Co, 1887.
Strutt J. *Sports and Pastimes of the People of England*, Tegg, 1801.
Vamplew W. *The Turf*, Allen Lane, 1976.
Watman M.F. *History of British Athletics*, Hale, 1968.
Whitfield C. *Robert Dover and the Cotswold Games*, Evesham Journal, 1962.
Wymer N. *Sport in England*, Harrap, 1949.
Young P.M. *History of British Football*, Stanley Paul, 1968.

Chapter 20

Athleticism in 19th-Century English Public Schools

20.1 Background to Public School Development

In looking at popular recreation we have mentioned the European Renaissance, which marked the rebirth of Greek 'idealism' (see Chapter 19). Our main interest lies in the re-emergence of Olympianism and the associated importance of 'Man of Action' and the oft quoted phrase *'mens sana in corpore sano'* (a healthy mind in a healthy body). It is important to recognize that these values came to England at the time of the great Tudor Dynasty and so had all the more impact because Henry VIII championed athleticism as well as nationalism and intellectualism.

The education of the ruling class at this time was through tutors who imparted knowledge, but also leadership qualities as part of the education of an elite. The influence of Roger Ascham on the education of Queen Elizabeth I was considerable, particularly as it concerned his belief that archery reflected a model life-style. It was at this time that the Age of Chivalry was changing to the Age of Courtesy, where men like Elyot suggested that sporting pastimes made man stronger and more valiant, without the need for life to be endangered.

Monastic Schools had existed prior to the Tudors, but the Reformation led to the dissolution of monastic churches, leaving an educational void, which was filled by the endowment of 'free' grammar schools by various monarchs (free in this context means free from church control). It was around this time that Mulcaster became Master of Merchant Taylors School and recognized the value of healthy exercise for boys at the school. Unfortunately, these endowed grammar schools were very small, seldom having more than 30 boys; they were mainly local day schools; and most of the boys left school at 16 years of age. With such small schools, controlled by one 'Master' and consisting of only a schoolroom, there was little likelihood of anything more than mob games being played and even this was frowned upon by 'Masters' committed to the Puritan ethic.

If you want to know more about the roots of our education system, Brailsford (1969) is a very good source of information.

20.2 The Structural Basis of the English Public School System

Definitions

An endowed place of education of old standing to which the sons of gentlemen resort in considerable numbers and where they reside from eight or nine to eighteen years of age.

(Sydney Smith, 1810.)

The only important addition to this is the factor that the children tended to be 'non-local'. It is a useful exercise for readers to find out what they can about one public school and then test their knowledge against the key definitive words identified in Figure 20.1.

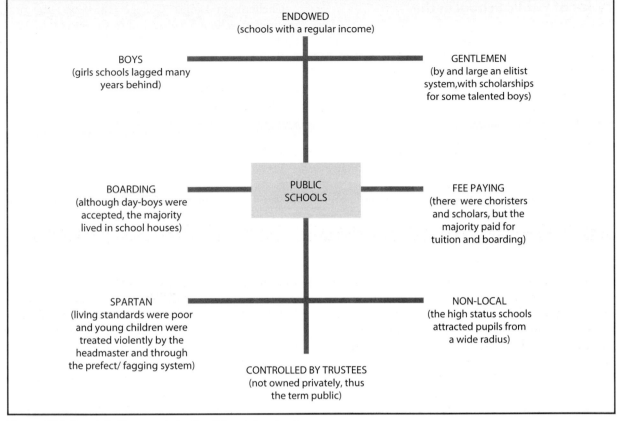

Figure 20.1 Key definitive words for English public schools.

The word **athleticism** (Figure 20.2) is less straightforward to define, because it was a developmental word and the full expression of public school athleticism was not achieved until the 1850s. It had fundamental links with the:

Muscular Christian view of manliness
reflecting:
Physical endeavour and moral integrity.

It is important that you should be able to explain these values in the context of your favourite sport a 100 years ago and today.

If you feel you need to know more about the meaning of these terms in a 19th-century context, read some of Newsome (1961) or Percival (1973).

From around 1860, many changes occurred which led to an exploitation of the English gentleman's love of sport. In modern phraseology, there was almost a 'sports school' situation. This led Smith (1974) to suggest that **athleticism** became 'the exaltation and disproportionate regard for games, which often resulted in the denigration of academic work and in anti-intellectualism.'

With so many old and new schools involved, the problem lies in deciding whether this '**cult of athleticism**' actually led to a lowering of academic standards. To assure yourselves, the group needs to study a number of different public schools to assess the extent to which this might have been the case.

Figure 20.2 Athleticism—playing according to the letter and spirit of the game.

Types of Public School in the 19th Century

If you have managed to look at athletic developments in a number of public schools, you can categorize your examples using the following list and then look around for a local example of each type of school.

Clarendon schools

Examined in the 1864 Clarendon Report, these were nine exclusive boys' schools. They were Eton, Harrow, Rugby, Shrewsbury, Charterhouse, Westminster, Winchester, St Paul's and Merchant Taylors. Each had expanded to take over 300 pupils at the end of the 18th century and the first seven were predominantly non-local and boarding. Matthew Arnold called them 'Barbarian' schools because they maintained the gentry tradition.

Ladies' academies

Finishing schools for the daughters of the gentry, these were normally small and more concerned with elegance and etiquette than with academic learning.

Proprietary colleges

These were middle class copies of the gentry schools. They were built with outstanding facilities to attract wealthy clients and eventually broke the monopoly held by the few elite schools. Cheltenham College (1841) was the first to be opened, with other famous colleges at Clifton, Marlborough and Malvern (Figure 20.3). Matthew Arnold called these proprietary schools 'Philistines' because he claimed they were simply materialistic copies of the traditional gentry schools.

Cheltenham Ladies' College (1854) was the first proprietary school for girls, but by the end of the 19th century almost every major town had a middle-class girls' high school.

Denominational schools

Cathedral Schools at such county towns as Canterbury, York and Worcester were ancient foundations which became Kings Schools after the Reformation, but they remained small until the 1870s.

Towards the end of the 19th century, the Church of England built some new boarding schools to educate the **sons** and **daughters** of the clergy. Lancing college is the best known of these 'Woodard Schools'.

Endowed Grammar Schools

Almost every town in England had its own 'free' grammar school for boys, named after the king or queen who endowed it. Some of these schools built up a reputation in the mid-19th century and became major public schools. The most famous of these are Uppingham, Repton and King Edward's, Birmingham. However, the majority remained small until the 1880s, when there was an expansion of secondary education for boys from the commercial classes.

In general, girls' grammar schools did not appear until the 20th century.

Private schools

These were owned by individuals or families. The quality of education varied considerably, but some of them, for example Malvern Girls' College, eventually became exclusive public schools. Many of these better schools had excellent sporting facilities to attract an upper-class clientele (Figure 20.4).

Figure 20.3 This view of Malvern College shows the impressive school buildings facing the playing fields.

Figure 20.4 Although this picture is called *The Ladies' Cricket Club*, it looks as if the club could be operating from within a private girls' school or ladies' academy.

20.3 The Technical Development of Sports in the Public Schools

Though this was a gradual development over a period of 50 years, it is easier to review it in three stages and limit comment to gentry schools for boys, middle-class schools for boys and middle-class girls' schools.

Stage one: schoolboys and popular recreation

The traditional gentry schools expanded at the end of the 18th century, resulting in a considerable increase in income, which led to improved facilities and staffing. This started a spiral which in turn led to a small number of schools becoming exclusive and being able to charge higher fees.

Boarding gave the boys a great deal of time together outside the classroom, and in their free time they played the games they had learnt at home. These were entirely organized by the boys and ranged from the relative sedateness of cricket to the violence of mob football; from illegal poaching to organized hare and hounds; from casual boating to rackets in the 'quad'.

In *Tom Brown's School Days,* Thomas Hughes writes about the sports Tom experienced at home.

The great times for back-swording came round once a year in each village, at the feast. The Vale 'veasts' were not the common statute feasts, but much more ancient business. They are literally, so far as one can ascertain, feasts of the dedication, i.e. they were first established in the churchyard on the day on which the village church was opened for public worship, which was on the wake or festival of the patron Saint, and have been held on the same day in every year since that time.

In fact the only reason why this is not the case still, is that gentlefolk and farmers have taken to other amusements, and have, as usual, forgotten the poor. They don't attend the feasts themselves, and call them disreputable, whereupon the steadiest of the poor leave them also, and they become what they are called. Class amusements, be they for dukes or plough-boys, always become nuisances and curses to a country. The true charm of cricket and hunting is, that they are still more or less sociable and universal; there's a place for every man who will come and take his part.

Investigation

20.1: Popular sports in schools
1. Upper class boys took various popular sports to the schools. How does Hughes, in *Tom Brown's School Days,* offset the values of rural sports against the intolerance of authorities?
2. Take any example of a primitive game in a public school and explain why it developed its unique qualities.

Some headmasters did their best to stop the more violent activities taking place in school. You will probably know the famous phrase by Butler of Shrewsbury "Football is only suitable for butchers' boys", but at the same time he condoned cricket and was only critical of rowing because of the danger of drowning. Meanwhile, there seems to have been support for cricket and rowing at Eton and Westminster before the 19th century, and the Harrow authorities did not attempt to curtail archery or rackets (Figure 20.5).

In reality, the early headmasters were powerless to stop any of these activities, particularly when they took place away from the school. Flogging was the normal punishment for any kind of disobedience, but, occasionally, there were cases of rioting in the schools and then it was necessary for the militia to be brought in.

Most of the problems arose when boys went into the town or travelled to other schools. There was invariably a great deal of drunkenness and riotous behaviour. Some of the rural sports carried with them a tradition of drinking and gambling, which the boys were only too keen to include in their school life.

A number of key features are associated with this initial phase of school sport. The boys brought the games into the schools and were responsible for their organization. They had the opportunity to play them regularly and so the occasional popular recreations became part of a continuous season of play, and this had a major impact on the regularization of rules. Some sports were already socially acceptable and these were encouraged by the school authorities and, with regular play possible, standards of performance improved dramatically.

Figure 20.5 Racket ball being played in the cloisters at Harrow School.

Where the sports lacked existing rules, the facilities available at the school determined the developmental form of the activity. For example: the 'Close' at Rugby with its soft turf; the 'Quad' at Charterhouse, where the 'dribbling' game emerged; and the unique version of mob football found at Eton, where the 'wall game' was instituted (Figure 20.6).

Figure 20.6 The Eton wall game.

Figure 20.7 Rugby at Rugby School. Dr Arnold was watching this game with a Royal visitor, something he would hardly have done if he had been against the game.

Stage two: Arnoldian influence and the role of a Christian gentleman

In 1828, Dr Thomas Arnold was appointed head of Rugby School; he died in office 14 years later. For well over a century he has been regarded as the father of public school athleticism, largely as a result of the impact of *Tom Brown's School Days* in 1857 (Figure 20.7).

Many modern writers, including McIntosh (1952), Ogilvie (1957), Bamford (1967) and Percival (1973), recognized that Arnold was one of a number of progressive headmasters who established an environment which eventually stimulated athleticism. It is important that you recognize the modern change of emphasis. For example, McIntosh suggested that:

> *While it is probable that Arnold's reforms at Rugby indirectly encouraged the growth of athleticism, both there and in other schools, it is improbable that he was immediately responsible for the change of attitude or that he himself approved of athleticism.*

Also, it was Dr Thomas James (1778–1794), who initially expanded Rugby School and it is now felt that many of Arnold's ideas came from the reforms he had seen operating at Winchester School under Dr W.S. Goodall. It has been successfully argued that Arnold was much more concerned with moral reform—a desire to produce **Christian gentlemen**—than to promote a **muscular Christian** tradition. He believed in a form of 'manly piety' which was moral, intellectual and social rather than physical.

The safest analysis is to recognize that the athletic momentum came from the boys, and Arnold was astute enough to use this enthusiasm to achieve a range of moral reforms which hinged on the boys being given responsibility. Even this level of intention was questioned by Bamford (1967) when he suggested that Arnold's reputation was the consequence of nostalgic staff loyalty, the enthusiasm of some Old Rugbeians and a 'train of fortuitous circumstances' of which the emergence of rugby football as a national game had particular relevance.

Having identified the supposed 'accident' of events, it is important to mention Wymer (1953), who had access to Arnold's family records. He suggests that Thomas Arnold loved cricket to the degree of having his children tutored in the game; that his life-long friendship with the Wordsworths reflected his love of the Lake District and mountain walking; and that his enjoyment of swimming, shooting, sailing and riding suggested that he had a high regard for healthy physical activity.

However, there was a direct conflict between Arnold's moral stance and some of the field sports pursued in the school. He was not prepared to allow poaching, fishing or any activity which involved trespass, on the grounds that it caused friction between the school and the community. On the other hand, he made no attempt to interfere with cricket or football.

 Investigation

20.2: Sporting incidents

Tom Brown's School Days may be romantic recollections of someone's childhood, but there is much to be learnt from reading some of the sporting incidents.

1. Read this extract on a cricket match and see if you can identify the values that the game is presumed to have.

'Come, none of your irony, Brown,' answers the master. 'I'm beginning to understand the game scientifically. What a noble game it is, too!'

'Isn't it? But it's more than a game. It's an institution,' said Tom.

'Yes' said Arthur, 'the birthright of British boys old and young, as habeas corpus and trial by jury are of British men.'

'The discipline and reliance on one another which it teaches is so valuable, I think,' went on the master, 'it ought to be such an unselfish game. It merges the individual in the eleven; he doesn't play that he may win, but that his side may.'

'That's very true,' said Tom, 'and that's why football and cricket, now one comes to think of it, are such much better games than fives' or hare-and-hounds, or any others where the object is to come in first or to win for oneself, and not that one's side may win.'

'And then the Captain of the eleven!' said the master, 'what a post is his in our School-world! Almost as hard as the Doctor's; requiring skill and gentleness and firmness, and I know not what other rare qualities.' ...

'I am surprised to see Arthur in the eleven,' said the master, as they stood together in front of the dense crowd, which was now closing in round the ground.

'Well, I'm not quite sure that he ought to be in for his play,' said Tom, 'but I couldn't help putting him in. It will do him so much good, and you can't think what I owe him.' ...

'I think I shall make a hand of him though,' said Tom, smiling, 'say what you will. There's something about him, every now and then, which shows me he's got pluck somewhere in him. That's the only thing after all that'll wash, ain't it ...'

Finally, if Thomas Hughes is to be believed, there is a lot to be learnt about the Doctor and the role of the Sixth Form in the following extract about a fight (Figure 20.8).

2. What do you gather from this extract and what is to be gained from letting the fight continue?

Meantime East is freshing up Tom with the sponges for the next round and has set two other boys to rub his hands.

'Tom, old boy,' whispers he, 'this may be fun for you, but it's death to me. He'll hit all the fight out of you in another five minutes, and then I shall go and drown myself in the island ditch. Feint him—use your legs! Draw him about! He'll lose his wind then in no time, and you can go into him. Hit at his body too; we'll take care of his frontispiece by and by.' ...

Investigation

20.2 continued

'Ha! Brooke. I am surprised to see you here. Don't you know that I expect the sixth to stop fighting?'

Brooke felt much more uncomfortable than he had expected, but he was rather a favourite with the Doctor for his openness and plainness of speech; so blurted out, as he walked by the Doctor's side, who had already turned back—

'Yes, sir, generally. But I thought you wished us to exercise a discretion in the matter too—not to interfere too soon.'

'But they have been fighting this half-hour and more,' said the Doctor.

'Yes, sir; but neither was hurt. And they're the sort of boys who'll be all the better friends now, which they wouldn't have been if they had been stopped any earlier—before it was so equal.'

Figure 20.8 The fight from *Tom Brown's School Days*.

In addition to the two extracts about the cricket match against the MCC and Tom's playground fight against Slogger (Investigation 20.2), you should also try to read about Tom's adventures with the gamekeeper, when he goes fishing; the problems met by Tom, East and Arthur when they try to enter the Hare and Hounds; and the famous description of the football match, where Tom decides that his help is needed to save the game (Figure 20.9).

Figure 20.9 Tom's exploits at football.

In all five extracts, it is valuable to identify the technical changes which have occurred; to establish the different social relationships which exist; and to recognize the ethics which Thomas Hughes is promoting in this romantic portrait of public school life.

It would be wrong to assume that Thomas Arnold was alone in this process of educational reform. Kennedy of Shrewsbury, Moberly of Winchester, Wordsworth of Harrow, and Hawtry of Eton were all 'new brooms' sweeping away a decadent system of thrashings and classics for a new wave of moral and social education, where athleticism was becoming an instrument for the promotion of a new set of values (Figure 20.10). In sporting terms, the technical changes which occurred between 1830 and 1850 hinged on the regularity of play and the responsibility of the Sixth Form to organize fixtures. In the later schools, the boarding house became an important social feature and one of the roles of the house master was to see that the boys were usefully organized, and this was often achieved through sporting competitions. The desire to get rid of antisocial elements such as gambling, blood sports and poaching was commonplace, and this was achieved by attempting to limit activities to the playing fields.

Figure 20.10 This picture of Cheltenham College and its 'Playground' was typical of the second phase of sports development, in which governors and trustees were prepared to recognize the importance of sport in the life of the public-school boy.

Stage three: athleticism and the Corinthian spirit

The influence of the first generation of progressive headmasters on the pupils was so great that these young disciples carried their interpretation forward to Oxford and Cambridge. It was in the '**melting pot**' of these universities that athleticism became the all-important catalyst and the Oxford–Cambridge competitions in a wide range of sports served to identify the most talented performers. Many of these '**blues**' became assistant masters and not only coached the boys, but played for the school team when required.

It was in the 20 years following Arnold that most of the new proprietary colleges were opened and the headships were awarded to assistant masters from the gentry schools. Men like Cotton of Marlborough, Percival of Clifton and Jex-Blake of Cheltenham were typical of a new breed of headmasters who were enthusiastically in favour of athleticism as an educative medium. In human terms, therefore, the staff were now actively supporting sport in school rather than condoning it.

It was this second generation of teachers who carried athleticism into the 'muscular Christian' era. Expansion in the size, significance and number of schools led to a massive building programme which invariably included a gymnasium and extensive playing fields. The school day included morning academic studies, afternoon games and evenings involved in prep (homework) and House activities. The time spent on playing a particular game could be up to five hours a day, with **professional coaches** and 'blues' producing a standard of play which raised the quality of amateur performance throughout the country.

It was in the public schools that the first football rules were written and it was the fixtures between these schools, and matches with gentlemen's clubs, that started regular organized **rational recreation**. Nor was it simply a technical development. The term rational recreation implies a moral component.

With some additional reading you should now be able to describe the technical changes which occurred in public school sport from 1800–1870. The Clarendon Report (1864) gave considerable recognition to the development of athleticism in the nine elite gentry schools, and the Taunton Commission Report was published in 1868, having gathered information on 782 other public schools and colleges.

Cheltenham Ladies College was included in the Taunton Commission Report and by 1868 they had afternoon games and a wide programme, which included callisthenics, swimming and horse riding. Miss Beale, the headmistress, was not too keen on 'aggressive games' on the grounds that they were not lady-like, but she allowed tennis and rackets, and the School Council eventually persuaded her that a hockey field was also a necessity. A study of specific school histories will help you to see that despite initial opposition, all the girls' high schools had an extensive athletics programme by the turn of the 19th century and were largely responsible for the growth of female athleticism in society at large.

Social control through physical activity in the Public Schools

In looking at technical development, we have been concerned with **recreative and sporting** changes. A second level of analysis lies in the way various authorities used athleticism as a vehicle to control themselves and others.

Investigation

20.3: The moral component of rational recreation

1. What moral elements might be promoted as a result of this rowing fixture (Figure 20.11) between Eton and Westminster?

2. Explain the changing role of people in Figure 20.12, as school sport evolved. Comment on such things as individual and group status, discipline and leadership opportunities.

Figure 20.11 Interschool rowing.

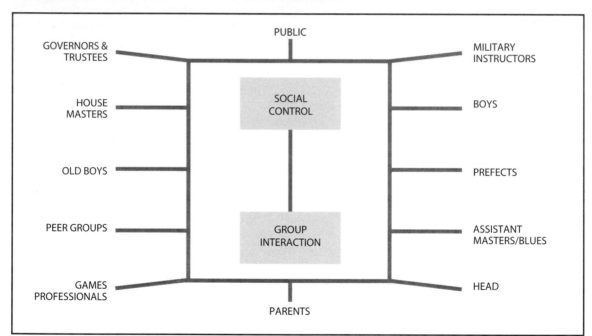

Figure 20.12 People involved in the development of school sport.

20.4 Athleticism and Character Development

Probably the most significant feature of public school athleticism was the belief that school sport was not only a vehicle for personal development, but also was the essence of education, representing a model life-style. It consisted of a fundamental link being made between **manliness** and **godliness** in what has been called **muscular Christianity**—an educational experience involving **physical endeavour** and **moral integrity**.

You may have read Henry Newbolt's poem:
> *There's a breathless hush in the Close tonight*
> *Ten to make and the match to win—*
> *A bumping pitch and a blinding light,*
> *An hour to play and the last man in.*

The verse ends with the well known line (Figure 20.13):
Play up! Play up! and play the game.

It is easy for us to link this with a game we've played with all the tensions of a close finish, but the poet is writing about more than cricket here. He goes on to say:
> *The river of death has brimmed its banks*
> *And England's far and Honour a name,*
> *But the voice of a schoolboy rallies the ranks:*
> *Play up! Play up! and play the game.*

Can you see the importance of the game and the way you play it, if it is preparing you for life and the battlefield? In such a game, to win gracefully and to lose with honour is so much more meaningful; and to do your best could mean being willing to give your life. Honour, bravery, brotherhood, leadership—these are the values the public school saw in the games they played, and they believed that through them these qualities became a permanent part of the player, and also of the person.

Figure 20.13 Play up! Play up! And play the game!

Investigation

20.4: The relevance of athleticism
Figure 20.14 shows an outline of the main values which the public schools linked with athleticism. Comment on the relevance of each of these today:

1. In the context of physical education.
2. In the extent to which they exist in professional sport.

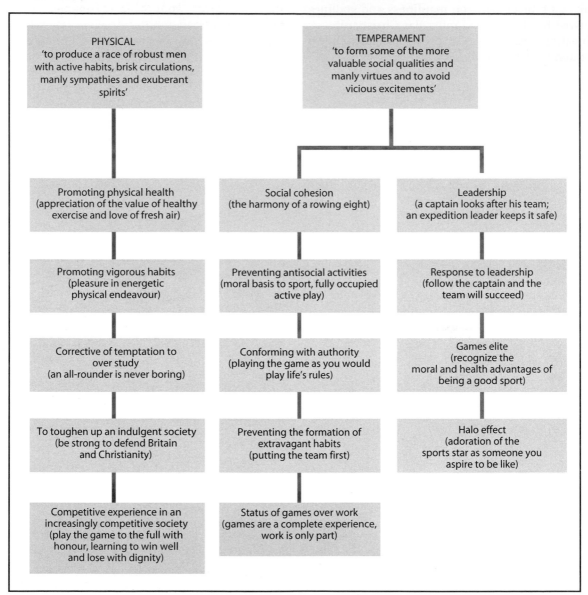

Figure 20.14 Main values linked with athleticism.

20.5 The Influence of Public School Athleticism on Sport in Society

Popular recreation was in decline in the last quarter of the 19th century and was being replaced by **rational recreation**. It is probable that the development of athleticism in public schools had more influence on this trend than any other social factor. Figures 20.15 and 20.16 show the various ways this happened. It is important that you compare these with the present links between physical education in school and sport in society.

It would also be worth your while to obtain a detailed knowledge of one particular public school (there are history texts written on most of them); and also be able to take one of the major sets of activities—cricket, rowing, football, racket games, etc—through the technical changes.

Finally, though not a great deal of reference has been made to girls' public schools, it is important that you should read some of Mangan and Park (1987) and/or Fletcher (1984).

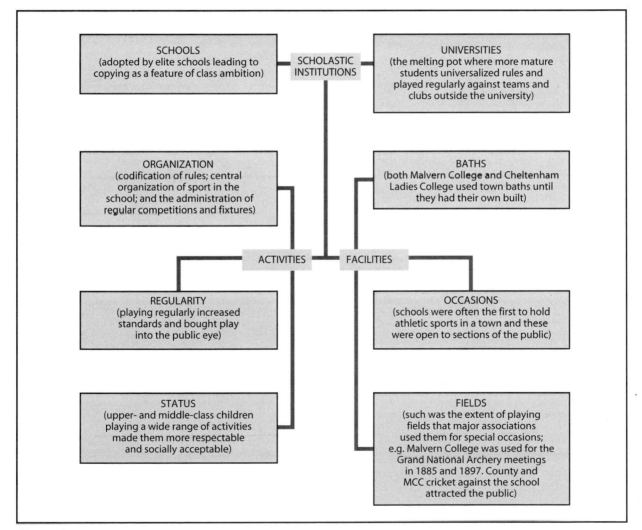

Figure 20.15 Provision.

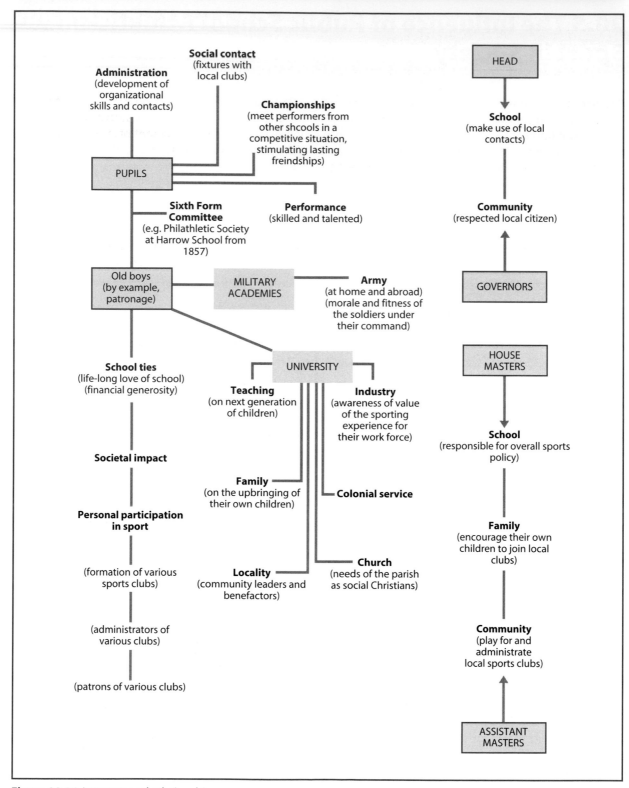

Figure 20.16 Interpersonal relationships.

Review Questions

1. What were the technical developments that occurred in public school sport during the 19th century?
2. How did social control vary in relation to athleticism?
3. What were the main values that the sporting experience was supposed to be giving young people?
4. What was the impact of certain headmasters and other staff on the development of athleticism?
5. Why did the Old Boys have such a large influence on the development of athleticism in their own schools and in society at large?

 ## Exam-Style Questions

1. Explain the initial changes that occurred when boys took popular recreations into the gentry public schools at the beginning of the 19th century. (5 marks)
2. In *Tom Brown's School Days*, Tom fights Slogger because he bullied 'Little Arthur' (Figure 20.8). Explain the attitudes shown by the different people involved in that episode. (5 marks)

3. What were the major influences of the universities on the expansion of athleticism in the public schools and society at large. (5 marks)
4. Discuss the technical developments that had occurred in public schools by the 1870s and the extent to which these demonstrate links between athleticism and character building. (10 marks) (Total 25 marks.)

 ## Summary

Public Schools:
1. Sons of gentlemen, boarding, fee paying, endowed, spartan, non-local, controlled by trustees.
2. Clarendon, gentry schools; middle-class proprietary colleges, denominational schools; grammar schools.
3. **Athleticism:** physical endeavour and moral integrity.
4. Sport and character development in education.
5. Sport as an Instrument for social control.
6. Educational reform and Arnold of Rugby.
7. Impact of public school athleticism on the development of rational recreation in British society.
8. Play up! Play up! And play the game!

 ## Further Reading

N.B. Many of these books are out of print, but are obtainable through lending libraries. Similarly, old schools and local archival centres have copies of school magazines which give some tremendous insights into the place of sport as far as the boys of the school were concerned.

Bamford T.W. *The Rise of the Public Schools*, Nelson, 1967.
Brailsford D. *Sport and Society*, RKP, 1969.
Clarke A.K. *A History of the Cheltenham Ladies College*, Faber & Faber, 1953.
Craze M. *King's School, Worcester 1541–1971*, Baylis, 1971.
Dunning E. and Sheard K. *Barbarians, Gentlemen and Players*, NYUP, 1979.
Fletcher S. *Women First: The Female Tradition in English Physical Education*, Athlone Press, 1984.
Hughes T. *Tom Brown's School Days* (various since 1857).
McIntosh P.C. *Physical Education in England Since 1800*, Bell, 1952.
Mangan J.A. and Park R.J. *From 'Fair Sex' to Feminism*, Frank Cass, 1987.

Morgan M.C. *Cheltenham College*, Sadler, 1968.
Newsome D. *Godliness and Good Learning*, Murray, 1961.
Noake V. *The History of Alice Ottley School*, Baylis, 1952.
Ogilvie V. *The English Public School*, Batsford, 1957.
Percival A.C. *Very Superior Men*, Knight, 1973.
Simon B. and Bradley I. *The Victorian Public School*, Gill & Macmillan.
Smith W.D. *Stretching their Bodies*, David & Charles, 1974.
Smith S. Edinburgh review. In: McIntosh P.C. (ed) *Physical Education in England Since 1800*, Bell, 1952.
The Public Schools Royal Commission Report. Clarendon Commission, 1864.
The Schools Inquiry Commission Report, Taunton Commission, 1868–1970.
Walvin J. *Leisure and Society*, Longman, 1978.
Webster F.A.M. *Our Great Public Schools*, Ward Lock, 1937.
Wymer N. *Dr Arnold of Rugby*, Hale, 1953.

Chapter 21

The Pattern of Rational Recreation in 19th-Century Britain

A new form of physical recreation began to emerge in Britain around the 1850s. It consisted of a formal, morally based presentation of contests, individual activities, games and outdoor pursuits, by respectable members of the community, in a form which no longer contained the excesses evident in popular recreation. It stemmed from the gentry and gentry schools and was enthusiastically taken up by the middle classes and their schools. As a product of social Christianity and liberalism, these sporting opportunities were gradually made available to the working classes, together with a respectable form of professional sport to accommodate a new form of spectatorism.

Elias (1986) called this process the 'genesis of sport', suggesting that primitive sports associated with popular recreation had little or nothing in common with this **rational recreation** (Figure 21.1) as a sophisticated reflection of an industrialized society: that sport as we know it was born in the mid-19th century. This is an interesting theory, but it has loop-holes, some of which are explored by Cunningham (1980).

Figure 21.1 Rational recreation—the test of temperament and physical competence.

21.1 Social Factors Influencing the Development of Rational Recreation in Britain

Urbanization and population expansion

The size of town determined the recreative needs of a community. Old towns had medieval slums which were gradually cleared to make shopping and commercial centres. The larger the town, the greater the distance to the countryside and natural recreative provision. The rate of growth, particularly of the lower class, meant that population outstripped recreative provision. There was a gradual improvement in facilities towards the end of the 19th century with public parks being opened and public baths being built.

Communications and travel

The distance an individual could travel was dependent on the free time available and the cost. An increase in the speed of transport allowed people to travel further in the same time (Figure 21.2). Travel had two basic links with sport:

- as a means of getting to a sporting venue, in the transport sense,
- the process itself was recreative or sporting.

It is possible to link river communications with angling, bathing, fowling and boating. With roads, there was the growth of pedestrianism, and walking race horses, followed later by the impact of the cycle. Finally, the railways opened up the countryside and the seaside resorts. They allowed fixtures to be made in different towns and stimulated spectatorism.

Figure 21.2 An excursion to Epsom Downs.

Communication and literacy

The printed word was a positive influence on sport. The evolution of the free press, the promotion of literacy, the mechanization of the printing industry, cheaper production of weekly newspapers and the publication of pocket editions led to an informed public. This permanent record was also achieved by artists who recorded major sporting events, and in the 1890s photography played a considerable part in promoting and reflecting sport, particularly once pictorial supplements were published by the weekly press.

Religious and secular institutions

You have already read about the negative influences of religion on popular recreation. The picture changed completely when **muscular Christianity** and **rational recreation** came together. Young curates, fresh from public school and university, joined parishes and promoted athleticism for their parishioners. The YMCA, in particular, became an athletic as well as a religious centre, and it encouraged young clerks to engage in a variety of rational sports (Figure 21.3).

Similarly, there were mechanics institutes and working men's clubs which tried to wean the lower-class male away from drink and popular recreation by offering social amenities, literary classes and rational recreations.

The working classes and industrial provision

While cottage industries existed, the workers were able to select their own time for recreation, but factories changed this. Machines determined working hours and pay reflected profits and sales. It was commonplace for men to be working for 72 hours a week for one pound.

A major break-through came with the **Saturday half-day**. Clerks and skilled workers achieved this by the 1870s, semi-skilled worked in the 1880s and most labourers by the 1890s, resulting in most working-class males doing a 56-hour week by the end of the 19th century.

Working-class opportunities for sport must be seen in the context of the squalor of the industrial slums, the poverty of those out of work (Figure 21.4) and low wages, which caused a family-man to work overtime.

The sons of industrialists brought athleticism to the factories and started sports clubs. Initially, this only involved the salaried staff, but gradually facilities were built for shop-floor workers in the belief that it would improve morale and loyalty. An older form of patronage continued to exist where an annual feast or excursion was paid for by the owners. With larger firms this often involved a day trip to the seaside, with all expenses paid (see Figure 21.2).

Figure 21.3
Source: Burton-on-Trent YMCA, 1884–1885.

Figure 21.4 Poverty on the streets.

21.2 The Rational Development of Activities and Games

Swimming, athletics and gymnastics
Swimming and bathing
Recreational bathing

When it was hot, the natural thing to do in river towns was to go bathing. The trouble was it was dangerous, and the sight of naked urchins upset respectable citizens. As a result, bathing stations were built on the river bank.

Spa and sea bathing

'Taking the waters' became a Regency fashion and led to spa towns being built with extensive bathing facilities. The fashion switched to the seaside and led to seaside bathing.

Public baths

The Wash-house Acts (1846) led to many industrial towns building public baths to clean up the labouring classes. They were called 'penny baths' because there was a fixed limit on charges for the second-class facilities.

Competitive swimming

Most of the middle-class swimming clubs were formed in the private Turkish baths. The first national championships were held in 1874 with the formation of the Swimming Association of Great Britain (SAGB), and the Amateur Swimming Association (ASA) was formed in 1884. Water polo mainly developed in the public baths and was codified in 1885. The Amateur Diving Association was not formed until 1901.

Athletics and cross-country
University athletics

Public schools had sports days which formalized the old rural sports. The Old Boys took this idea to Oxford and Cambridge, with the Exeter College Autumn Meeting (1850) being the first amateur athletics meeting. It was run like a horse-race meeting.

The Wenlock Olympian Games

Meanwhile, Dr Penny Brookes re-established an old rural sports at Much Wenlock in a rational form. In 1865 the National Olympian Association (NOA) was formed as a governing body and they defined amateurism.

Amateur athletics

The Amateur Athletic Club (AAC) was formed in 1866 by ex-Oxbridge gentlemen athletes. They also defined amateurism but excluded the working class. They were rivals of the NOA and set up their own National Championships in 1866. In 1880, the Amateur Athletics Association (AAA) was formed; the 'exclusive' clause was removed and 'no financial gain' became the central amateur criterion.

Cross-country running

Almost like the poor man's hunting, many Harrier Athletic Clubs were formed in the 1880s with 'hare and hound races' and 'paper chases'. These clubs also held summer sports meetings, which led to the British tradition of middle-distance running.

Gymnastics

Archibald Maclaren, an intellectual friend of Ruskin and Morris, was a versatile sportsman. An outstanding oarsman, he built a gymnasium at Oxford (1850) and one at Aldershot for the Army (1861). He published texts on gymnastics, and the public schools and urban clubs used his approach rather than Continental methods.

Muscular Christianity and the YMCA

Gymnastics was recognized as a non-competitive instrument for increasing respect for the human body. Liverpool and Manchester YMCAs had a great influence on developments.

Investigation

21.1: The development of rational recreation

1. What does Figure 21.5 tell you about bathing and Victorian morality?

2. Use Figure 21.6 as a basis to explain the development of amateur athletic sports meetings.

3. Describe English gymnastics from Figure 21.7.

Figure 21.5 Bathing huts at the seaside.

Figure 21.6 Athletic sports meeting.

Figure 21.7 Maclaren's gymnasium at Aldershot.

Invasion games

The classification of an **invasion game** in modern times is: a territorially fluid team game with goal targets and involving free play of the ball with variations of body contact.

In rational recreation terms, they were rule-based with a 'spirit' and 'letter' of play; they were highly organized, with governing bodies and affiliated clubs, and played regularly with fixtures, officials and club colours in fixed seasons.

Association football

The public schools changed the mob games into respectable, regular games. Eton, Harrow and Charterhouse promoted a 'dribbling' game which was played under the Cambridge Rules from 1856. Old Boys Teams helped form the Football Association (FA) in 1863. There were ten clubs in 1867 rising to 50 by 1871. By 1905 there were 10 000 clubs with 272 in the FA Cup.

Professionalism was legalized in 1885 and the Football League was formed in 1888. At the opposite end of the scale the Corinthian Club had gentlemen as members and only played friendly games. The game spread to all sections of society with leading clubs being formed from:

- **Old Boys' teams**, e.g. Leicester City from the Old Wyggestonians,
- **Street teams**, e.g. Rotherham (1884) was formed under a street lamp,
- **Employees' teams**, e.g. Manchester City from the Lancs & Yorks Railway Club (1885),
- **Church teams**, e.g. Everton (1878) was a Sunday School team,
- and various other sources, e.g. Sheffield Wednesday was an Early Closers' team.

Rugby football

This code was initially limited to Old Rugbeians. They founded Guys Hospital Club (1843) and Blackheath (1862). In 1871, Blackheath and 20 other clubs formed the Rugby Football Union (RFU), and in 1877 the game was restricted to 15-a-side.

The 'broken time' debate led to a split between southern and northern clubs in 1895 on the subject of professionalism, and this led to 22 clubs breaking away to form the Northern Union, which eventually became the Rugby League.

Hockey

There were initially two separate lines of development. Blackheath and Bristol rationalized the old mob game in a form which lasted until 1895.

Meanwhile, a number of cricket clubs in the Home Counties were experimenting with winter hockey. In 1871 there were clubs at Richmond, Teddington and Sutton. A Hockey Union was set up in 1876 to join the two codes, but they could not agree. In 1886 the Hockey Association was formed, based on the Teddington model, and the Blackheath game slowly disappeared.

Women's club hockey can be traced to an East Molesey Club in the 1880s. The Irish Ladies' Hockey Union was formed in 1894, and a year later the All-England Women's Hockey Association (AEWHA) was established to coincide with the first international fixture between Alexandra College, Dublin, and Newnham and Girton Colleges, Cambridge.

Investigation

21.2: The invasion games

1. Use Figure 21.8 to show how the rational game of Association football differs from mob football.

2. Use Figure 21.9 to show how the rational game of rugby football differs from mob football.

3. What qualities were the girls' trying to promote through hockey (Figure 21.10)?

Figure 21.8 Association football.

Figure 21.9. Rugby football.

Figure 21.10 Hockey.

Target games

The classification of a target game is: it involves a team or pair in a game which has targets such as wickets, skittles or holes. There is alternate play, which restricts body contact, and in team versions each team has a separate role to play, e.g. batting or fielding.

Many of the rational elements of these games developed much earlier because they were less violent. Strict rules of play, spirit and letter were observed and controlled by governing bodies. Though games tended to be on a friendly basis, championships involving amateurs and professionals had early developments.

Cricket

The tour of the All-England XI in the 1840s led to a growth of gentlemen's county cricket clubs. The old village clubs continued alongside these, while there was a massive growth in the number of urban middle-class clubs. (Croquet, rounders and baseball function within the same general classification.)

Regular fixtures at all levels led to increased competition at county level and so more artisan professionals were employed and middle-class amateurs started to play county cricket. Such was the belief in the value of cricket that church leaders, teachers and employers started to encourage the urban working class to play the game.

Women's cricket was limited by Victorian attitudes, but in the 1880s there was a revival of the 'ladies' game as the result of increased athleticism in the middle-class girls' schools.

Golf

This was always the Scottish equivalent of cricket. It suited a smaller population, uneven terrain and an inclement climate. It was also close to the other Scottish game of shinty.

Golf was normally played on 'links' (seaside), and St Andrews has always been the 'home' of the game. In Scotland, golf was a 'popular' game, but in England wealthy Scots introduced it to the upper class and it remained an elite game throughout the 19th century. There was always a lower-class version of the game, even in England, where an artisan club had use of the course in return for keeping it in good condition. Ladies used the men's courses until their numbers grew sufficiently to open their own.

Bowls

Skittles, bowls and quoits belonged to a group of games which were associated with taverns. This delayed their acceptability in respectable circles until middle-class clubs started to be formed and public parks started to provide greens for the lower classes. The Yorks & Lancs Crown Green Association (1888) and the Flat Green Association (1895) were the two governing bodies which co-ordinated fixtures and championships.

Quoiting was very popular in rural areas in the last quarter of the 19th century, but has almost disappeared today.

 Investigation

21.3: The target games

1. Identify the changes in cricket from the 18th century game (Figure 21.11).

2. Use your knowledge of female sport to establish why golf was acceptable for 'ladies' (Figure 21.12).

Figure 21.11 Cricket.

Figure 21.12 Golf.

Investigation

21.3 continued

3. Can you account for the advantages and disadvantages of skittles being associated with taverns (Figure 21.13)?

Figure 21.13
Skittles.

Court games

The classification of these games is based on a court being used for play. There should be no body contact, with alternate play over a net or against a wall and points scored; singles or pairs can play.

The rational game goes back to real tennis, which, because of its exclusivity, was sophisticatedly codified from the 16th century. This game evolved into a variety of forms to suit different situations and conditions.

Rackets

Initially the poor man's version of real tennis, its popularity in public schools, alongside fives, led to clubs being set up throughout the country. The rational stage was achieved when 'open' courts with one wall were changed to indoor 'closed' courts. Prince's Club, and then Queen's from 1886, controlled the codification of the game. The 1880s also saw the introduction of a junior 'squashy' ball, which has led to the modern game of squash.

Badminton

This game had slightly different roots, because there was an ancient pastime called shuttlecock and battledore. This activity was still being played in gardens in the 19th century and legend has it that, on a wet day,

the family at Badminton House (Duke of Beaufort) took the game indoors.

The first rules were written in 1877 by members of the British Army and Diplomatic Corps in India. The Badminton Association was formed in 1893 and the championships were held at Wimbledon, alongside lawn tennis and croquet.

Lawn tennis

The modern game has three main roots. Major Gem introduced a game at Leamington in 1866 and the Leamington Club had written rules by 1870; J.H. Hales introduced Germain Tennis in 1873; and Major Wingfield patented a game called 'Sphairistike' in the same year. The modern rules of lawn tennis were codified by the MCC in 1875, with the All-England Croquet and Lawn Tennis Club being established at Wimbledon in 1876.

One reason why lawn tennis became so popular was the changing role of the middle-class female. In the privacy of their own gardens, it became acceptable for females to play this social game.

Initially exclusive, early tournaments were associated with county cricket. These tended to be played behind closed doors and it wasn't until 1884 that public championships were held for 'ladies' at Wimbledon.

Investigation

21.4: The court games

Figure 21.14 Rackets.

Figure 21.15 Badminton.

1. Can you find some explanations for rackets being played in Fleet Prison (Figure 21.14)?
2. Why do you think badminton did not have a governing body until the 1890s (Figure 21.15)?
3. Discuss the links between lawn tennis, athleticism and female participation in sport (Figure 21.16).

Figure 21.16 Lawn tennis.

Aquatic activities

Rowing

So-called amateur regattas appeared around 1870. They tended to exclude the lower classes as they were run by clubs consisting of public school oarsmen.

The Amateur Rowing Association (ARA) controlled rowing on the Thames from 1879 and by 1885 became the national governing body. The 'exclusion clause' limited competitive rowing to public-school boys. The National Amateur Rowing Association (NARA, 1890) was a rival body which permitted broader participation.

Canoe touring was popular in the last half of the 19th century, largely due to the exploits of John MacGregor and his book A *Thousand Miles by Rob Roy Canoe*.

Sailing

Yachting was a sport of the aristocracy and the Royal Navy. The Duke of Cumberland Cup (1781) was the premier schooner race. Several clubs on the Isle of Wight were patronized by William IV and Queen Victoria.

The America's Cup was first held in 1851 as a challenge between British and American yachts. The winner chose the next venue and until recent times the Americans won every contest.

Dinghy sailing started with the Solent Classes in 1870. Middle-class clubs were formed at Southampton and Portsmouth and promoted races for 21-, 25- and 30-foot craft.

Skating

There were three main lines of development on ice. The oldest were the ice fairs, which were very similar to rural fairs.

Speed skating came from Holland and developed on the Fens. The National Skating Association (1879) controlled the amateur championships and there were also professional championships.

Figure skating developed with improved skates. The world centre was the Serpentine in London. Difficulties were met when attempts were made to develop 'glacariums' and so roller skating rinks developed in the 1870s as an alternative.

 ## Investigation

21.5: Aquatic activities

1. Can you explain the main characteristics of Henley (Figure 21.17)?
2. How many reasons can you find to explain why Britain has never won the America's Cup (Figure 21.18)?
3. Use Figure 21.19 to explain the many attractions of ice and roller skating.

Figure 21.17 Rowing.

Figure 21.18 Sailing.

Figure 21.19 Skating.

Climbing and cycling

Climbing

Life in the mountains initially hinged on shepherds and local people acting as guides. The Romantic Movement brought the gentry to the mountains, but it was the scenery rather than climbing which appealed to most of them. This love of mountain scenery extended to the Alps and snow climbing developed through the Alpine Club (1857). This led to the development of mountaineering—the art of reaching the summit.

Scientists looking for alpine plants opened up the Lake District and North Wales. W.P. Haskett-Smith at Wasdale Head and O.G. Jones at Pen-y-Gwryd were the most famous climbers. This led to rock climbing—the practice of finding the most difficult route up a crag. While mountaineering was very much an upper-class pursuit, rock climbing was taken up by the middle and working classes.

Cycling

An excellent sport to show social variables, it reflected the urban and industrial revolutions in that a machine was used as an urban substitute for a horse. It became the most common vehicle whereby people in towns managed to escape to the countryside. It was very much an urban, middle-class male preserve to begin with. The gentry despised it and the working class could not afford it. It started as a novelty fashion with the hobby horse and progressed, via France, to the boneshaker or velocipede. The inventiveness of English industrialists led to the Ordinary or Penny Farthing. The large wheel allowed increased speed and kept the person above the mud, but it was dangerous. A safer version, the tricycle, was developed, and this was largely used by females and the elderly until the Rover safety and pneumatic tyres were invented.

There were three main branches of cycling. Track racing (British Cycling Union, BCU) was part of the athletic sports meeting; touring (Cycle Touring Club, CTC) became highly organized with consuls, guide books, repair shops and hotels; and, finally, there was the development of road racing. The problem with the latter, was that mass starts were banned and so pursuit racing took its place in England. Mass starts were allowed on the Isle of Man and the Continent, which led to the Tour de France becoming the premier road racing event.

In terms of social class development, the gentry, particularly ladies, took up cycle touring, following the lead of Queen Victoria's daughters. At the same time the second-hand cycle trade allowed poorer people to buy bicycles. Middle-class females followed the lead of the upper class and fashion became an important feature, first with 'bloomers' and later the 'rational dress' (divided skirt).

 Investigation

21.6: Climbing and cycling

1. Why were there very few limits on women climbers (Figure 21.20)?

2. Explain the influence of cycling on female sporting opportunities (Figure 21.21).

Figure 21.20 Mountaineering.

Figure 21.21 Penny Farthing riders.

Exam-Style Questions

1. a. Explain the characteristics of **rational recreation** as shown in Figure 21.8. (5 marks)
b. Describe the main influences on the development of bathing and swimming in the 19th century. (5 marks)
c. Explain why cricket was more immediately acceptable as a respectable game. (5 marks)
e. Use Figure 21.16 to explain the idea that lawn tennis was invented by the middle class and comment on the influence of the game on female participation in sport. (10 marks)
(Total 25 marks.)
2. a. If Public Schools initiated the development of respectable sport in Britain, it was the railway network which allowed it to

spread so rapidly.
i. How did transport limit the spread of sport before the railways were built? (4 marks)
ii. How did the railways influence holiday patterns and the spread of games? (5 marks)
b. Describe the changing relationship between **sport** and **religion** in the UK. (6 marks)
c. The Industrial Revolution took the control of work from the craftsman and gave it to the machine. How did the constraints on free time and wages influence working class sport and how were conditions improved towards the end of the 19th century? (10 marks)
(Total 25 marks.)

Summary

Rational Recreation:
1. **Respectable** sports promoted by the **gentry** and the **urban middle classes**. Instruments of **social reform** for the **lower classes**.
2. **Regular, codified, stringently organized,** **letter** and **spirit of play** emphasized.
3. **Clubs, governing bodies** and **championships** based on the concept of **amateurism**.
4. **Stringently controlled** forms of **professional games**.

Further Reading

Altham H.S. *A History of Cricket,* vol I, Allen & Unwin, 1962.
Bailey P. *Leisure and Class in Victorian England*, RKP, 1978.
Baker W.J. *Sports in the Western World*, University of Illinois, 1988.
Brailsford D. *British Sport: A Social History*, Lutterworth, 1992.
Clark R. *Victorian Mountaineers*, Batsford, 1953.
Cleaver H. *A History of Rowing*, Herbert Jenkins, 1957.
Cunningham H. *Leisure in the Industrial Society*, Croom Helm, 1980.
Dunning E. and Sheard K. *Barbarians, Gentlemen and Players*, NYUP, 1979.
Elias N. and Dunning E. *Quest forExcitement*, Blackwell, 1996.
Ford J. *This Sporting Land*, New English Library, 1977.
Holt R. *Sport and the British*, Clarendon, 1989.
Lovesey P. *Centenary History of the AAA*, Guinness Sup., 1979.

Marples M. *Shank's Pony*, Dent, 1959.
Mason T. *Association Football and English Society*, Harvester, 1980.
Mason T. *Sport in Britain: A Social History*, Cambridge, 1989.
Medleycott J. *100 Years of the Wimbledon Tennis Championships*, Hamlyn, 1977.
Meller H.E. *Leisure and the Changing City*, RKP, 1976.
Richie A. *King of the Road*, Wildwood House Ltd, 1975.
Titley U.A. and McWhirter A.R. *Centenary History of the RFU*, RFU, 1970.
Walvin J. *The People's Game*, Allen Lane, 1975.
Walvin J. *Leisure and Society*, Longman, 1978.
Watman M. *A History of British Athletics*, Robert Hale, 1968.
Wymer N. *Sport in England*, Harrap, 1949.
Young P.M. *A History of British Football*, Stanley Paul, 1968.

Chapter 22

Transitions in English Elementary Schools

22.1 19th-Century Drill and Gymnastics

J.C.F. Guts Muths (1749–1839) was the 'Father of European Gymnastics'. He published *Gymnastics for the Young* and this was a source of subsequent developments in Sweden (P.H. Ling, 1776–1839), in Germany (F.L. Jahn, 1778–1852), in Denmark (F. Nachtegall, 1777–1847) and in Britain (A. Maclaren, 1820–1884).

Maclaren used continental developments, but felt that many features were unsuitable in England. He preferred apparatus work and a mixture of other activities, such as walking and riding, swimming and country pursuits.

Dr Mathias Roth was the leading supporter of the Swedish System in England and was a rival of Maclaren. He supported 'rational gymnastics' for medical and military reasons.

Elementary schooling prior to 1870 was dominated by two major organizations, the National Schools Society (1811), a Church of England association, and the British and Foreign Schools Society (1808), which was linked with non-conformism. Some of these schools had playgrounds and even playing fields, but many in the industrial towns had no playing facilities and could not cope with the massive population explosion, despite a great deal of absenteeism.

The 1870 Forster Education Act was an attempt to 'plug the gaps' in elementary schooling, and led to the establishment of Board Schools. The Act ignored Roth's efforts and the 1871 Code of Regulations only introduced 'permissive' legislation:

Drill for boys only, if given under a competent instructor, for not more than two hours a week, and twenty weeks in the year, could be counted as school attendance.

This consisted of marching, posture exercises and dummy arms drill and was taught by Army NCOs for sixpence a day and a penny a mile for marching, using the *Army Field Exercise Book* (1870). Girls were included in 1873, but the content remained 'free standing' military drill.

Gymnastic apparatus was available in public schools and some open spaces, but the intention of the drill in these working-class schools was to improve the fitness of Army recruits and to instil discipline.

In the 1890s the Education Department recommended the inclusion of some Swedish drill, largely as a result of Swedish-trained inspectors being appointed in London. There was also a trend for qualified teachers to take over the drill from the military instructors.

The Prize Day Programme for the Worcester Board Schools in 1894 (Figure 22.1) reflects this broader approach. Changing attitudes were also evident in a speech by the Rev. C.E. Hopton in Worcester in 1899:

> *I hope that when the Transvaal War (Boer War) is over people will be able to say that those victories had been won on the playgrounds of the elementary schools of England. To teach boys to be brave, noble, honest and self-sacrificing, so that when they went out into the world, those characteristics would stick by them, and would fit them to be worthy citizens of this great country.*

It would seem that at least one **muscular Christian** felt that the same qualities were achievable by poor children as well as by the rich.

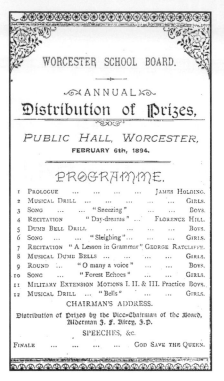

Figure 22.1
Prize Day Programme at the Worcester Board Schools.

22.2 The 1902 Model Course

The Boer War (1899–1902) was fought between the might of the British Empire and the Boers, South Africans of Dutch extraction. Great Britain lost a great deal of prestige because their large, but ponderous, army found it very difficult to defeat a small force of mobile guerrilla fighters.

Back in England, accusations were mainly that the working classes were unhealthy and ill-prepared to fight and, as a scapegoat, politicians blamed the Swedish drill being taught by teachers in the elementary schools. As a result the Model Course was imposed in 1902 in all these schools. It was produced by the War Office and controlled by Colonel Fox of the Army Physical Training Corps (APTC). He was instructed to achieve two main objectives:

- To increase fitness for military service through acquaintance with the discipline of military drill.
- To train children to, 'withstand the hardships of combat and have familiarity with weapons'.

There was a directive that these lessons should replace Swedish drill and military instructors should be used. Boys and girls were involved in this programme up to the age of 12 years, but they were instructed as little soldiers, not children.

 Investigation

22.1: The 1902 Course
It is important that you should have some idea of the content of this syllabus and the method of instruction, and this is a very good opportunity for you to use role-play methods by going through a model lesson. Young people today are not used to the command–response of military drill and so you should find it an interesting experience.

Enact the following lesson (also see Figures 22.2–22.5), where teachers or students can take it in turns to act as instructors.

Note: —— is a long cautionary word;
and ∪ is a short, sharp executive command.

Investigation

22.1 continued

Lesson

1. ̅ ͝   ͝ ͝   ͝   ̅ ͝   ̅   ͝
   Right marker; in two ranks, fall in; right form.

(This means falling in on the marker's left, an arm's distance apart.)

2. ̅   ͝   ̅   ͝
   Stand at ease; atten-tion.

(Repeat this, looking for exact positions and moving together.)

3. ̅   ͝ ͝ ͝   ̅   ̅
   Right turn, one; two; by the left, quick
   ͝ ͝ ͝ ͝ ͝   ̅ ͝
   march; left, right, left, right, (etc). Squad halt;
   ̅ ͝   ̅   ͝   ̅ ͝
   about turn; quick march; squad halt; right turn;
   ̅   ͝
   stand at ease.

4. ̅   ͝ ̅   ̅   ͝ ̅
   Atten-tion; arms bending and stretching,
   ̅ ͝ ͝ ͝ ͝ ͝   ͝
   arms bend; out; bend; up; bend; down; (repeat);
   ̅   ͝
   stand at ease.

Figure 22.2a and b Standing positions.

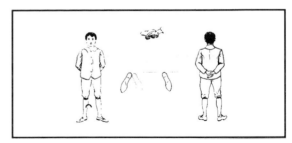

a Stand at ease.

b Attention.

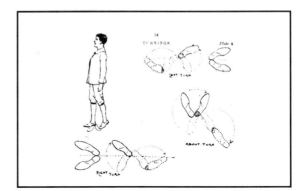

Figure 22.3 Turning.

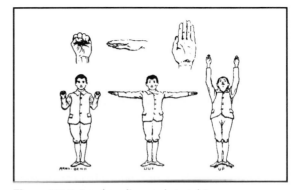

Figure 22.4 Arm bending and stretching.

Investigation

22.1 continued

5. Exercise with staves (corner poles):

⎯ ⌣ ⎯ ⎯ ⌣ ⎯ ⎯ ⎯ ⌣ ⌣
Atten-tion; ready; astride with cross stave ready;

⌣ ⌣ ⌣ ⌣ ⎯ ⎯ ⌣ ⎯ ⌣ ⌣ ⌣
one; two; three; and up; and forward; one; two;

⌣ ⎯ ⌣ ⎯ ⌣ ⎯ ⌣
three; and up; and forward; stave ready;

⎯ ⌣ ⎯ ⌣
atten-tion; stand at ease.

⎯ ⎯ ⎯ ⎯ ⎯ ⌣ ⌣ ⌣ ⎯ ⌣
6. *Deep breathing by numbers; in; out; in; and out.*

⎯ ⎯ ⎯ ⎯ ⎯ ⎯ ⌣ ⌣ ⌣
7. *Marching back to class, left turn; one; two;*

⎯ ⌣ ⎯ ⌣ ⎯ ⌣
quick march; squad halt; fall out (right turn).

Figure 22.5 Exercise with staves.

If you insist on this being done accurately and seriously, you will soon realize the difficulties of synchronized movement and you will be able to judge the degree of exercise you are achieving. You should also question the level of activity, skill and individuality.

• •

22.3 Early Syllabuses of Physical Training

The Model Course came under constant attack from inspectors and teachers and in 1904, the Board of Education set up two **Interdepartmental Committees**.

One committee examined the Model Course and criticized it on the grounds that there was no apparent intent to equate physical exercise with general education, it had a specific military function, it failed to recognize the need to cater for different ages and sexes, and it caused a reduction of subject status through the use of military personnel rather than qualified teachers. The formal recommendation was that a new syllabus be produced which recognized different ages and sexes.

The second committee looked specifically at the 'physical deterioration among the working classes' and recommended that the male adolescent population should undergo training that would 'befit them to bear arms'.

By separating elementary school physical training from military training (Figure 22.6), the cause had been won to re-instate Swedish 'therapeutic' exercises.

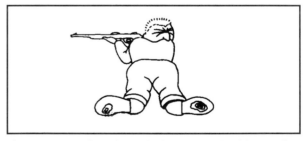

Figure 22.6 Drill or physical education? A healthy mind in a healthy body means keeping your eyes on the target.

The 1904 Syllabus

This was the first Board of Education Syllabus and it set out to satisfy the recommendations of the relevant Interdepartmental Committee.

How the Syllabus covered these intentions

At a **conceptual** level, it identified the **physical effect**—that is the intention to improve health and physique, and the **educational effect**—that is to develop qualities of alertness, decision-making and the control of the mind over the body. This was 1904, but a modern PE lesson quite probably has similar intentions.

Now **how** did the Committees expect to put these into practice? Their view of our subject started from a medical (physiological) base. They wanted to present a system of physical exercises which would improve respiration and circulation, and stimulate nutrition. They envisaged things like play activities: the development of vital capacity through breathing exercises, corrective exercises to improve posture, exercises against resistance and control exercises involving skill learning. Once again you might be surprised at the knowledge and 'vision'.

The problem lay in putting these theories into practice. They produced 109 tables, where each consisted of a series of activities designed to systematically exercise the whole body. The structure of each **table** consisted of such exercises as: arms, balance, shoulders, head and trunk, marching, jumping and deep breathing.

A study of the Syllabus shows that not all the military features were removed; for example, the students were still taught in lines with marching, commands were still formal and 'attention' was still 'pigeon-chested'.

The authorities suggested that the class teacher should give two or three 20-minute lessons a week, but that there should also be daily 'recreative sessions to refresh the child for further study'.

Some of the **content** of the 1904 Syllabus is shown in Figure 22.7 and you should be able to compare this with the exercises in the defunct Model Course.

What may not have become apparent is that in recognizing age variations, the Syllabus separated **infants** into a different category and, for children less than seven years old, play became an accepted part of the lesson. There was also considerable stress on the **open air** and the importance of having suitable clothing.

I PLAY RUNNING OR MARCHING

Play or Running about. The children should, for a minute or two, be allowed to move about as they please.

II PRELIMINARY POSITIONS AND MOVEMENTS

Attention.
Standing at Ease.
Hips Firm.
Feet Close.
Neck Rest.
Feet Astride.
Foot Outward Place.
Foot Forward Place.
Stepping Sideways.
Heels Raising.
Right Turn and Right Half Turn.
Left Turn and Left Half Turn.

III ARM FLEXIONS AND EXTENSIONS

Arms Downward Stretching.
Arms Forward Stretching.
Arms Sideways Stretching.
Arms Upward Stretching.

IV BALANCE EXERCISES

Heels Raising.
Knees Bending and Stretching.
Preparation for Jumping.
Heels Raising (Neck Rest).
Heels Raising (Astride, Hips Firm).
Heels Raising (Astride, Neck Rest).
Head Turning in Knees Bend
  Position.
Knees Bending and Stretching
  (Astride).
Leg Sideways Raising with Arms
  Sideways Raising.
Knee Raising.

V SHOULDER EXERCISES AND LUNGES

Arms Forward Raising.
Arms Sideways Raising.
Hands Turning.
Arms Flinging.
Arms Forward and Upward Raising.
Arms Sideways and Upward
  Raising.

VI TRUNK FORWARD AND BACKWARD BENDING

Head Backward Bending.
Trunk Forward Bending.
Trunk Backward Bending.
Trunk Forward Bending (Astride).
Trunk Backward Bending (Astride).

Note Exercises bracketed should be taken in succession

VII TRUNK TURNING AND SIDEWAYS BENDING

Head Turning.
Trunk Turning.
Trunk Turning (Astride, Neck Rest).
Trunk Turning (Feet Close, Neck
  Rest).
Trunk Sideways Bending.
Trunk Sideways Bending (Feet
  Close, Hips Firm).
Trunk Sideways Bending (Feet
  Close, Neck Rest).

VIII MARCHING

Marking Time (From the Halt).
Turnings while Marking Time.
Quick March.
Marking Time (From the March).
Changing Direction.

IX JUMPING

Preparation for Jumping.

Note Work from this Column should be omitted until the above exercise has been taught under IV.

X BREATHING EXERCISES

Breathing Exercises
  without Arm Movements.
With Deep Breathing, Arms
  Sideways Raising.

Figure 22.7 1904 Syllabus, HMSO.

Investigation

22.2: The 1904 Syllabus

Explain the meaning and intentions underlying the following recommendations:

1. **a.** 'exercises from many well-known systems',
    b. 'suitable for children of school age',
    c. 'without need of apparatus',
    d. 'no exercises likely to prove injurious',
    e. 'to be purposeful',
    f. 'as a minimum of exercises'.

2. You may like to repeat the role-play exercise of Investigation 22.1, emphasizing the changes. Remember, you are now looking at teachers with children, rather than NCOs with little soldiers; there should be a more varied lesson, but still taught through action–response commands.

Major political and administrative changes occurred over the next few years. In 1906 the Education Act was particularly concerned with the welfare of working-class children, and the Open Spaces Act improved urban leisure provision with the development of more public parks. The following year, under the radical Liberal Government of Lloyd George, physical training was directly linked with the Medical Department of the Board of Education, with the appointment of Dr George Newman. An immediate administrative development was the appointment of Miss Rendal and Lt Commander Grenfell as staff inspectors, both with backgrounds in Swedish drill. Meanwhile, Colonel Malcolm Fox was sent to Sweden to learn more about their approach. These events led to a revised and expanded syllabus being published in 1909.

The 1909 Syllabus

In 1909 two new emphases arose. The first was an increase in therapeutic elements, probably directly due to Dr George Newman:

> *The purpose of physical training is not to produce gymnasts, but to promote and encourage the health and development of the body.*

The second reflected a change in social attitude:

> *The value of organized games as an adjunct to physical training is very great, though they should not take the place of the regular lessons of physical exercise.*

Three of the male associations linked with gymnastics objected to the first purpose and the Ling Association, largely representing female teachers, objected to the second, reflecting the gulf between men and women in the PE profession.

In terms of **content** the 1909 Syllabus had 71 tables instead of 109, suggesting that there was a tightening up of alternatives. The work remained 'free standing' with unison response to commands, but Danish rhythmic swinging exercises were also included.

The 1919 Syllabus

This followed the First World War (1914–1918). It is important to recognize the tragedy of this war with so much loss of life, particularly as it virtually wiped out a generation of public school boys. Less well known was the huge number of additional deaths which occurred in a 'flu' epidemic immediately after the war.

If there was a positive outcome it was the improved status of women as a result of their contribution in schools and factories during the war. Blame for the low level of fitness among the working classes was once again levelled at school physical training, but Dr George Newman cleverly deflected this, claiming that remedial exercises and morale boosting recreational activities in convalescent camps had helped to prepare the wounded for a full return to civilian life.

It was Newman's recognition of the 'recreational' which represented the most significant innovation in the 1919 Syllabus.

the formal nature of the lesson has been reduced to a minimum and every effort has been made to render them enjoyable and recreative.

It was suggested that half of every lesson should be devoted to 'active free movements, including games and dancing' and the tables were remodelled to:

place increased responsibility upon the class teacher and to allow scope for personal initiative, freedom and enterprise.

However, particularly in the case of lessons for older children, the tables allowed the old-fashioned teacher to continue to use the old restrictive exercises. The theory that there was a need to:

consider happiness and enjoyment while accustoming the body and mind to external suggestions and stimuli

was made possible for infant children by a complete restructuring of lessons for the under seven year olds. The more serious intention of therapeutic exercise remained central for the older children. The whole class was still expected to work in unison in response to direct commands.

If we look outside the classroom at society, this obedience training and therapeutic focus reflected the rigid social class demarcation before the Second World War, where those in power were anxious to retain a clean, disciplined working class, who worked hard and accepted their 'place' in society.

The 1933 Syllabus

We have now reached a period in history which is within living memory of relatives and friends and so your first task should be to find out from them what life was like in the inter-war years and what they did in PE. They may remember the giddy years of the 1920s when the upper class 'flappers' had their last fling; they might recall the business influence of the urban middle class, which was literally taking over our society; or they might remember the harsh reality of post-war Britain, where soldiers and sailors were demobilized, many of them with injuries, without any planning, little financial support or prospect of work. Never was the social class system more clearly defined, but the compulsory school leaving age had risen to 14 and many secondary schools were being built for working-class children. All these new 'senior' and 'central' schools had playing fields and a gymnasium.

The industrial depression in the 1930s left the working class without jobs, but the crash of the stock exchange and the stagnation of industry also affected the middle classes. It was in the middle of this depression that the last Board of Education syllabus was produced, but it was a highly respected publication and 'has been recognized as the watershed between the best of the past and revolutionary developments yet to come'.

The concept of therapeutic exercise to produce a sound physique remained, but the recognition of gymnastic and games skills was a major step forward, reflecting both the Reference Books published in 1927 for secondary schools. Children were still taught by direct method, but elements of play were carried through into the lessons for older children.

Probably the most revolutionary change was the introduction of group work. All the other syllabuses had been class activities with everyone doing the same thing at the same time. The 1933 Syllabus included a final phase in each lesson in which the class was divided into four or more sets or corners, where different activities were set for each group. This was the first vital step towards the decentralized lesson.

Figure 22.8 shows a table from the 1933 Syllabus. The teacher would select items from each of the six sections, but Part I and Part II would be of about equal length. Where other pages are listed, the Syllabus gave additional information on these pages. Look out for a copy of this Syllabus in second-hand bookshops—there are still plenty around.

PART ONE

1

Introductory Activity

1. Free running, at signal, children run to 'homes' in teams.
(Four or more marked homes in corners of playground.)
All race round, passing outside all the homes, back to places and skip in team rings.
2. Free running, at signal all jump as high as possible and continue running. Brisk walking, finishing in open files, marking time with high knee raising.
3. Aeroplanes. (Following the leaders in teams.)

Rhythmic Jump

1. Skip jump on the spot, three low, three high (continuously)
(Low, 2, 3, high, 2, 3, etc.)
2. Astride jump. *Astride jumping—begin! 1, 2, 1, 2, etc. stop!*
3. Skip jump, four on the spot, four turning round about
(8 counts) and repeat turning the opposite way (8 counts)

2

a. (Astride [Long sitting].) Trunk bending downward to grasp ankles. Unroll. *(With a jump, feet astride—place! [with straight legs—sit!]) Grasp the ankles—down! With unrolling, trunk upward—stretch! With a jump, feet together—place!*
b. (Astride [Astride long sitting].) Trunk bending downward to touch one foot with opposite hand.
c. (Feet close [Cross-legged sitting].) Head dropping forward and stretching upward.
(Feet—close!) Head forward—drop! Head upward—stretch!
(Crouch.) Knee stretching and bending. ('Angry Cats')
(Crouch position—down!) Knees— stretch! bend! up! down! etc. stand—up!

3

a. As small as possible, as tall as possible.
[(Crook sitting, Back to wall) Single arm swinging forward–upward to touch wall.]
[(Crook sitting) Drumming with the feet, loud and soft.]
b. Single arm circling at a wall. (Run and stand with side to wall, nearest hand supported against wall about shoulder height. Circling with free arm. Turn about and repeat.)

4

a. Free running like a wooden man. Finish in open files in chain grasp.
(One foot forward, heel level with the other toe.) Knee full bending and stretching with knees forward. (Several times. Move the back foot forward and repeat.)
(Lean standing.) Hug the knee.
[(Crook lying.) Hug the knees. (Lower the feet quietly.)]
b. Running in twos, change to skipping, finish in a double ring facing partner holding hands. Knees full bend. Knee springing. Hands on ground and jump up.
Knees full bend ! Knee springing—begin! 1, 2, 1, 2, etc. Stop! Placing the hands on the ground, with a jump stand—up!
c. Form a ring. Gallop step left and right, at signal, run and stand with side to wall, nearest hand supported against wall (the other arm sideways). Kick the hand. (Turn about, or run to opposite wall and repeat several times with each leg.)

5

a. Brisk walking anywhere, change to walking on heels or toes, at signal run to open files facing partners.
(Feet-close, Arms forward, Fists touching.) Trunk turning with single elbow bending. (Elbow raised and pulled back. 'Drawing the bow.')
(Feet—close! With fists touching, arms forward—raise!) With the right arm, draw the bow—pull! Let go! With the left arm—pull! Let go! etc. Arms—lower!
b. Race to a wall and back to centre line and join right hand across with partner.
Tug of war with one hand.
c. (Informal lunge with hand support.) Head and trunk turning with arm raising to point upward.
[Left (right) foot forward with knee bent and left (right) hand on knee (informal lunge)—ready!] With arm raising to point upward, head and trunk to the right, (left)—turn! With arm lowering, forward—turn. (Repeat several times.) With a jump, feet change!

PART TWO

6

Class Activity

1. Running, jumping over a series of low ropes.
(In ranks of six or eight in stream.)
2. Frog jump anywhere.
3. Free running or skipping, tossing up a ball and catching it.
(A ball each. Who can make the greatest number of catches without missing?)

Group Practices

1. Running or galloping with a skipping rope. (A rope each.)
2. Running Circle Catch, with a player in the centre, throwing, or bouncing and catching a ball.
3. Sideways jumping over a low rope, partner helping. (Partner astride rope, performer holding partner's hands does several preparatory skip jumps on the spot and then a high jump over the rope landing with knees bent and standing up again.)
4. In twos, crawling or crouch jump through a hoop, held by partner.

Game

Odd Man.
Free Touch with 6 or 7 'He's'. ('He's' carry a coloured braid or bean bag as distinguishing mark.)
Tom Tiddler.

7

Free walking, practising good position, lead into school.

Figure 22.8 A table from the 1933 Syllabus.

22.4 The Effects of the Second World War (1939–1945)

The majority of male PE teachers were enlisted and many were engaged in training military personnel. This was an entirely different war from the previous one, in that there was a mobile rather than a static battle ground, civilians were much more at risk through bombing, and training strategies were concerned with individual initiative and survival rather than the stoic obedience training of old. Large numbers of soldiers were taken prisoner and it was realized that recreative activity helped to maintain morale in the prisoner-of-war camps.

Finally, the threat of air-raids led to the mass evacuation of children from industrial towns to the countryside, giving them a taste of rural life. The bombing itself, with the inevitable tragic loss of life, at least levelled many of the 19th-century slums and resulted in a massive rebuilding programme.

The 1944 Education Act was a progressive piece of legislation, which ensured every child a free education. The tripartite system of grammar, technical and modern schools tended to reflect the class system, but it was soon to be overtaken by a move towards comprehensive education.

These post-war years marked the emergence of a full expression of physical education. The theory behind the inter-war syllabuses had educative intentions, but the 'practical' was predominantly physical training. There were probably four major areas of influence from within the subject:

1. F.J.C. Marshall and E. Major lectured at Carnegie College, Leeds, before the war, publishing several books. Though they continued to accept the 'tables' approach, they were part of a move to increase the importance of skill learning and the use of small apparatus. They were in the Services during the war, but wrote a number of progressive articles for the *Journal of PE* suggesting changes towards contests, self-testing and initiative programmes. Perhaps the most important transitional phrase used was the suggestion that, 'the child was more important than the system'.

2. Leading female physical educationists were also going into print. An article by Veronica Tyndale-Biscoe (1945) described the modern dance extension of Rudolf Laban's work, using phrases like 'the body as a medium of expression'. Similarly, Ruth Clark (1946) wrote about Austrian Gymnastics, referring to movement in an educational medium and suggesting that, 'working on apparatus at his own pace has particular value to the timid child, who gains courage through the discovery for himself of his own capabilities'.

3. **New apparatus**: C.E. Cooke, an organizer in Bristol, visited the Northern Command Physical Training School and saw commandos using scrambling nets and assault course equipment. She felt that young children would 'enjoy the skill and adventure provided by this apparatus' and published her adaptations. With the flush of post-war building, many local authorities introduced their own versions of frame and tubular apparatus in their primary schools, and even old schools were given 'apparatus stations' (Figure 22.9).

4. **The Halifax Experiment**: Miss Dudgeon was working in a children's rehabilitation clinic during the war. The corner-stone of physical training had always been that all children should respond to a set task. At Halifax the individual disabilities of handicapped children led Miss Dudgeon to encourage individual interpretation of open tasks, where children were left to decide rhythm, timing and work at their own level. After the war, this novel approach attracted most of the progressive physical educationists in the country; they noticed that the levels of child involvement, enjoyment and personal skill achievement were unequalled elsewhere in the country.

Figure 22.9 Climbing apparatus in school.

The outcome of these progressive developments was the publication of *Moving and Growing* (Ministry of Education, 1952) and *Planning the Programme* (Ministry of Education, 1953). These 'revolutionary' books replaced the formal training syllabuses by introducing a child-centred approach to primary physical education. Both these publications are still to be found in bookshops. A small sample of the activities is shown in Figure 22.10, and it would be an excellent role-play experience to use these or others from *Planning the Programme* to show how free and individualized physical education had become, compared with the initial Model Course.

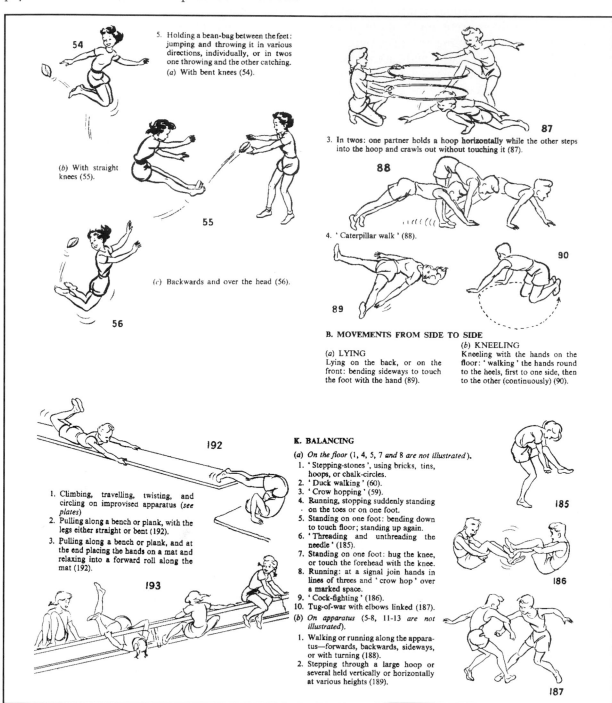

Figure 22.10 PE exercises from *Planning the Programme*. (*Ministry of Education, 1953.*)

R2 Review Questions

1. Use Figure 22.11 to explain the major changes which occurred in junior schools between 1902 and 1954.
2. Compare the physical education envisaged for primary children in *Moving and Growing* with what is done in a secondary school today.
3. Use Figures 22.12 and 22.13 to explain the differences between drill and physical education.

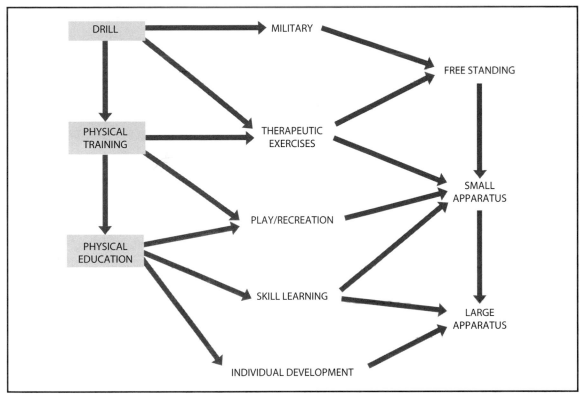

Figure 22.11 Changes in PE in schools between 1902 and 1954.

Figure 22.12 Drill and PT from *Moving and Growing*. (*Ministry of Education, 1952.*)

Figure 22.13 Physical education from *Moving and Growing*. (*Ministry of Education, 1952.*)

Exam-Style Questions

Between 1902 and 1954 Elementary School Military Drill changed to Primary School Physical Education:

1. Describe the 1902 Model Course and explain why it was implemented. (5 marks)

2. Explain the transition to Physical Training and the form it took between 1904 and 1933. (5 marks)

3. How did the teacher and the teaching method change during this time? (5 marks)

4. Discuss the effects of the 1939–1945 War on Physical Education in the Primary Schools of Britain and the emergence of a broad Physical Education Curriculum. (10 marks)

(Total 25 marks.)

Summary

Drill, PT, PE:

1. Founded on **Continental Gymnastics** and **Military Drill**.

2. Need for lower classes to be **Fit to Fight**.

3. **Model Course** followed by **Syllabuses**.

4. Trend from **Military Drill** to **Therapeutic Drill**.

5. **Physical Training**—a system of exercises to improve the health and posture of lower class children at elementary schools.

6. Introduction of **skills** and **group work** in 1933 led to birth of PE with **educational** and **physical values** being recognized.

7. *Moving and Growing* marked the post-Second World War progression in terms of **personal development** and **heuristic teaching method**.

Further Reading

Some articles from *Journal of PE*:
Clark R., Nov. 1946.
Cooke C.E., March 1946.
Major E., Nov. 1943, Nov. 1947, March 1948.
Marshall F.J.C., March 1942, March 1944, Nov. 1945.
'Somerset Cage and Bars', Nov. 1947.
'Southampton Apparatus', Nov. 1947.
Tyndale-Biscoe V., March 1945.

Board of Education. *1902 Model Course*, HMSO.
Board of Education. 1904,1909,1919,1933 Syllabuses, HMSO.
Ministry of Education. *Moving and Growing*, HMSO, 1952.
Ministry of Education. *Planning the Programme,* HMSO, 1953.
McIntosh P.C. *Physical Education in England Since 1800*, Bell, 1952.
Munden I. *Suggestions for Small Apparatus in PE*, Ling, 1947.
Smith W.D. *Stretching their Bodies*, David & Charles, 1974.

Index